# COCHISE

## Chiricahua Apache Chief

THE CIVILIZATION OF THE AMERICAN INDIAN SERIES

9702
SWE

..................................................

..................................................

**DONCASTER**
Doncaster Metropolitan Borough Council

## DONCASTER LIBRARY AND INFORMATION SERVICES

Please return/renew this item by the last date shown.

Thank you for using your library.

# COCHISE

Chiricahua Apache Chief

by Edwin R. Sweeney

University of Oklahoma Press : Norman and London

Library of Congress Cataloging-in-Publication Data

Sweeney, Edwin R. (Edwin Russell), 1950–
    Cochise, Chiricahua Apache chief / by Edwin R. Sweeney. —
1st ed.
       p.   cm. — (The Civilization of the American Indian series ;
v. 204
    Includes bibliographical references (p.    ).
    ISBN 0-8061-2337-0
    1. Cochise, Apache chief, d. 1874.   2. Apache Indians—
Biography.   3. Apache Indians—Wars, 1872–1873.
4. Apache Indians—History—19th century.   I. Title.
II. Series.
E99.A6C577   1991
973'.04972—dc20                           90-50699
                                                     CIP

*Cochise: Chiricahua Apache Chief* is volume 204 in The Civilization of the American Indian Series.

2   3   4   5   6   7   8   9   10   11   12   13   14   15   16   17   18

To my wife Joanne and my three daughters, Tiffani, Caitlin, and Courtney, with love, and Dan Thrapp for paving the way.

# CONTENTS

# ILLUSTRATIONS

## Figures

## Maps

# ACKNOWLEDGMENTS

I am indebted to many persons who have helped me during my research. I would like to take this opportunity to give them my sincere thanks.

Thanks to the Arizona Historical Society, where much of my early research was performed, and to Mrs. Lori Davisson, research historian, who has been particularly helpful with information; to Joe Park, former microforms librarian at the University of Arizona library, who directed me to the Apache material contained in the Sonora State Archives at the Arizona Historical Society; to Simeon "Bud" Newman of the Special Collections Library at the University of Texas at El Paso for his assistance with the Janos material in their holdings; and special thanks to Cynthia Radding of Hermosillo, Sonora, who helped me gain access to important documents in Sonora's state archives.

Allan Radbourne of the English Westerners' Society gave important help, sharing his vast knowledge of the Chiricahua and Western Apaches. I would also like to thank my good friend Dan Aranda of Las Cruces, New Mexico, for accompanying me to several sites, and to his wife, Joyce, for hospitality extended to me and my family.

Several field trips were made more enjoyable in the company of my brother, Kevin Sweeney, of Stoughton, Mass.; Rick Collins of Tucson; Ron and Rebecca (Becky) Orozco, formerly of Cochise, Arizona; Alicia Delgadillo, my tour guide for Cochise County, who is the director of the Fort Sill Chiricahua–Warm Springs Apache Research/Resource Center located in Cochise's stronghold; and one of the nicest persons I have met, Bill Hoy, former ranger in charge at the Fort Bowie National Historic Site, now of Bowie, Arizona, whose door was always open.

I am grateful to Susie Sato of the Arizona Historical Foundation at Arizona State University in Tempe; Susan Ravdin of Bowdoin College, who helped with the General Oliver Otis Howard Papers; Vivian Fisher of the Bancroft Library at the University of California at Berkeley; and Robert B. Matchette, Dale E. Floyd, and Michael E. Pilgrim of the Military Archives Division of the National Archives.

Others who have made contributions for which I am grateful are Bill and Joyce Griffen of Flagstaff; Leland Sonnichsen of Tucson; Harwood Hinton of the University of Arizona in Tucson; Lynda Sanchez of Lincoln, New Mexico; and Morris Opler of Norman, Oklahoma. Thanks are due to Herb Hyde, my editor; to Sarah Nestor, Managing Editor, University of Oklahoma Press; to Don Bufkin, for preparing the maps; and to Karen Hayes of Portal, Arizona, for providing photographs.

I am also grateful for the help and support of Bill Schaefer of Saint Charles, Missouri; Ruth McGarry of Malden, Massachusetts; and my mother, Mary L. Sweeney, of Stoughton, Massachusetts.

Two writers were inspirational in my decision to research Cochise, and I don't hesitate to say that I feel blessed to have met both of them. The late Eve Ball, the Chiricahuas' oral historian, provided encouragement, information, and suggestions. I am eternally grateful to Dan L. Thrapp, the authority on Apache–U.S. military affairs, for his advice and endless encouragement. His constructive comments greatly improved the manuscript.

Finally, thanks to my wife Joanne for never doubting my purpose.

EDWIN R. SWEENEY

*Saint Charles, Missouri*

# INTRODUCTION

As the most powerful chief of the Chiricahua Apaches in recorded times, Cochise was a significant figure in nineteenth-century south-western history. One of the greatest of all American Indian leaders, he was a much-feared yet in many ways admirable man who dominated Indian-white relations on an expansive frontier. He was a chieftain who lived and prospered by war and died in peace after a sometimes pivotal role in a turbulent border region where he was frequently at odds with powerful forces of two nations. Therefore it is somewhat perplexing that until now there has been no thoroughly researched and objective study of him, his career, and his influence.

Cochise was a complex and interesting man with a fine mind, an impressive physique, and unusual talents. He was an accomplished orator in the manner of his people, and an individual of character and honor (the latter by his own standards, which were not those of contemporary American society). His considerable natural abilities, honed to the keenest edge, enabled him to deal on equal terms with governors and generals as with all others. Most whites who met him in peace or truce seemed as impressed with his quiet dignity and supple intelligence as they were with his thoroughly autocratic sway over his people—in itself a most singular phenomenon in Apache culture and tradition.

During the course of a century, information about Cochise's life, deeds, and times has become so distorted and romanticized through legend and myth that sometimes it bears scant resemblance to the truth. By today's somewhat gentler standards, even the basic facts often appear stark and harsh until it is understood that Cochise must be judged not by our precepts, but by those of a barbaric, violent, often cruel, and frequently merciless world. Through his understanding and the rules he fashioned to guide his conduct, he emerges from his milieu as a man of recognizable integrity and principle, a wholly worthy leader of a warrior people.

Certainly Cochise was no saint by white standards (no fighting Apache was), and be it conceded that there were precious few white saints in the Apachería of Cochise's day. This Indian was the paradigm of the Chiricahua fighting leader: an efficient raider and war chief who was bold enough and sufficiently influential to attract plenty of followers on both the band and tribal levels. He won and held continentwide fame in his own times. Only Geronimo's name is more recognizable today, and Geronimo, a far lesser man, did not compare with Cochise by any logical measurement, either in his own day or in history.

Among Cochise's contemporaries were other great Apaches, of course. Cochise did not establish political alliances like those conceived and molded by Mangas Coloradas, his father-in-law, who was the dominant Eastern Chiricahua leader for some twenty years before his death (or execution) at the hands of white soldiers in 1863. Nor did Cochise evince Victorio's skills in the art of guerrilla warfare. His fame was not based on a single whirlwind raid as was that of Nana, Victorio's lieutenant, and he did not possess the military genius of Juh. Yet each of these men was Cochise's ally at one time or another, and although they were not of the same band, each willingly fought under Cochise or at his side. All respected his leadership ability; his fierce, uncompromising hatred toward his legion of enemies; and, above all, his courage in battle and his wisdom in counsel.

Some whites who met Cochise employed the James Fenimore Cooper image of the noble red man in describing him. He was tall for an Apache, built much like his youngest son, Naiche, and resembling him in appearance. No photograph of Cochise has turned up, although at least one reportedly was taken, but from the many accounts of people who spoke with him or engaged him in battle we have some idea of his appearance. He stood about five feet, ten inches tall, one officer remarking that he "looked more than his height on account of his somewhat slender build, and his straight physique."[1] Another found him as "straight as an arrow, built, from the ground up, as perfect as any man could be."[2] Still others described him as "powerful and exceedingly well built"[3] or "of manly and martial appearance, not unlike our conception of the Roman soldier."[4] He weighed about 175 or 180 pounds, according to one estimate,[5] making him a man of heavyweight proportions by nineteenth-century standards. His hair was jet black, although laced with gray in his later years; it was worn, in the traditional Apache style, to his shoulders. He had well-proportioned features, a high forehead, a strong Roman nose, and prominent cheekbones. A white who sat in on a New Mexico council with Cochise reported that his "countenance displayed great force of character," although it seemed rather sad or perhaps meditative in aspect.[6] Alexander Duncan ("Al") Williamson, a sutler at Fort Bowie in 1873–74 and whose customer the chief was, said that "Cochise never smiled. He was severe and grave of aspect."[7] Another observer said Cochise seemed "anything but the most dreaded, warlike, and barbarous savage,"[8] and Brigadier General Oliver Otis Howard, who conferred with Cochise and finally brought him to a lasting peace, echoed this view, writing that Cochise's "countenance was pleasant, and made me feel how strange it is that such a man could be a notorious robber and cold-blooded murderer."[9]

Although Cochise was recognized for the weight he placed on truth and openness, still there were times when his word, given to an enemy, seemed disingenuous, especially when he felt wronged or had been treated treacherously. He often mentioned his respect for truth, telling an Indian agent in 1870: "I want the truth told. A man has only one mouth and if he won't tell the truth he [should be] put out of the way."[10] Cochise once told an army officer: "I want to talk straight. . . . I have no split tongue."[11] In a conversation with his friend Thomas J. Jeffords, first and only agent of the Chiricahua Reservation in southeastern Arizona, he said that "a man should never lie. . . . If a man asks you or I a question we do not wish to answer, we could simply say, I don't want to talk about that."[12] In fact, Cochise used this strategem in several conferences with Americans to avoid answering questions or to change the subject. He was particularly reticent about discussing certain activities about which whites showed curiosity and about which he did not wish to talk.

Cochise's insistence on integrity was demonstrated when the Chiricahuas were in council with Anglos at Cañada Alamosa. Victorio and Loco were questioned about a southern New Mexico stock raid they knew all about but were reluctant to discuss. They appeared ready to deny all until Cochise abruptly "told them to tell the truth. I can say that they appeared to be much relieved" to learn how he thought they should respond, reported an army officer who was present.[13]

Other whites reflected their appreciation of the manner in which Cochise handled the truth as it appeared to him. Fred Hughes, who assisted Jeffords on the reservation, said Cochise "kept his word till the day of his death."[14] First Lieutenant Joseph Alton Sladen, who as Howard's aide accompanied the general on his peace mission to the chief, wrote that not only Cochise but all his people seemed infused with honesty. After spending ten days in the Apache camp he remarked that "in their relations with us they were thoroughly honest. . . . During the [period] I spent in their camp not a single article . . . was lost or stolen."[15]

On occasion, Cochise also could exhibit fair-mindedness. An incident illustrating this occurred in 1860 when an American named John Wilson killed in a duel a warrior who was said to have been a protégé of Cochise. The outcome caused excitement among the Indians until Cochise intervened. "It was a fair fight [and] no blame could be attached to anyone," he ruled.[16] That settled the matter.

Toward his immediate family and the extended family group Cochise "was more affectionate than the average white man. He showed nothing of the brutish nature generally attributed to him," a close observer reported.[17] Just as Victorio's most trusted advisers included his sister, Lozen, so did Cochise respect the advice of his own sister, a woman fifteen years his junior and "in whom he seemed to have great confidence and [she] from her independence and force seemed to justify this faith." The fact that life in his Dragoon Mountains Apache camp was ordinarily a warm and friendly place surprised the few whites who were fortunate enough to visit it. Sladen remembered that the Indians there were "always cheerful, demonstratively happy, and talkative . . . brim full of fun and joking, and ready to laugh heartily over the most trivial matters. They were especially fond of playing practical jokes of a harmless nature upon each other." [18]

No Indian ever went hungry if there was food in camp. Generosity was a marked trait of the Apaches, particularly of a leader among them, and Cochise strongly exhibited it, for he was a good hunter and provider. Sladen related an incident in which a young warrior returned empty-handed from a hunt. The chief called for his own horse, picked up his rifle, and rode away. Hours later he returned with an antelope, which was immediately "divided up and distributed amongst the people present." [19]

Nor was compassion completely foreign to him, although he usually did not display it, as white survivors of battles with him would attest. Amelia Naiche, his granddaughter, told me about a massacre in which a little white boy survived. Most of the Apaches, including Geronimo, favored killing the child, but Cochise lifted him onto his horse and protected him. According to legend, he raised the boy and later gave him his freedom. [20]

The chief was not without blemishes, of course; he was as normal as anyone else in that regard. By nature he was kind and considerate among his people, but he also was subject to abrupt mood changes, a trait most clearly evident when wrongs against Indians were discussed. His own people, too, could incur his wrath; they knew it and were wary of doing so. At times they treated him with fear, though ever with the utmost respect. Asa ("Ace") Daklugie, son of Juh, remembered that as a child he was warned against even looking at Cochise's wickiup lest it be interpreted as disrespect. [21] Like many Apaches, Cochise was not averse to a good drunk, and when under the influence he sometimes became violent, even beating his wives and sister, and abusive to others who crossed his path. Sladen mentioned a time when he "heard screams from Cochise's wife and sister. I saw them fleeing in terror from his bivouac. He was striking and scolding them." During this affair "the Indians showed very plainly that they were alarmed, and soon all got out of sight if not out of the sound of his voice." It may have been during such a binge that his spunky younger wife twice bit him severely. [22]

Despite such lapses, Cochise won devotion from his followers;

they regarded his word as law. His seemingly absolute rule amazed Fred Hughes:

> It was astonishing also to see what power he had over this brutal tribe, for while they idolized him and also worshipped him no man was ever held in greater fear, his glances being enough to squelch the more obstreperous Chiricahua of the tribe.[23]

Sladen, too, was amazed by the chief's practically unheard-of influence among his followers. Anthropologists who have studied Apache culture believe that the "leaders," or chiefs, had "no absolute control" over their followers, that the "authority of the leader is far from absolute,"[24] but with the greatest of chiefs—Mangas Coloradas, Victorio, and, above all, Cochise—control came very close to being absolute. Sladen described the arrival of the captains, or subchiefs, from a raid. They would report to Cochise and the "chief would occasionally ask a question or grunt an approval." On one such occasion Cochise became visibly upset about a warrior's report and his voice "grew louder until he worked himself into a violent passion. He rose to his feet . . . and as the returned warrior [also] rose . . . the chief dealt him a violent blow upon his head."[25] Another observer said Cochise possessed what no other chief was able to boast of: supreme control over his bands. "A private soldier would as soon think of disobeying a direct order of the President as would a Chiricahua Apache a command of Cochise."[26]

Like that of Mangas Coloradas, Cochise's influence extended to various Apache bands besides his own.[27] For example, an army officer reported the following incident on the Cañada Alamosa Reservation of New Mexico. Some Chihennes under Victorio and Loco came in to receive their rations and a few of the Apaches found or traded for whiskey and became drunk. Loco and Victorio cooled the initial crisis, but a drunken warrior returned, gun in hand, apparently eager to make further trouble. At this juncture Cochise appeared, took in the situation, and "gave a yell so quick and shrill . . . its effect was instantly apparent. Some sixty or eighty of his own immediate band rushed upon . . . the offending Indian . . . and seized him and escorted him out." Cochise, in name chief of only the Chokonen band, ordered Victorio and Loco of the Chihennes to leave until everyone sobered up, and they did so.[28] Captain Frederick W. Coleman, an experienced officer who was thoroughly acquainted with the Apaches, said that other Chiricahua chiefs were "mortally afraid of Cochise [and] when he is around they are exceedingly small fry." [29] An army surgeon affirmed that Cochise "was the only Indian chief that I ever knew that could enforce instant obedience to a given command." [30]

Fred Hughes also discussed Cochise's influence among Chiricahua bands. "Although the Indians of the Tularosa [Chihenne] were of a different [band] from that of Cochise," he said, "there is no doubt that he could call upon them and control them whenever he saw fit." Hughes felt that the Nednhis, too, "were afraid of Cochise," as well they might be. In November 1872 after hearing a report (later proved false) that the Nednhis had harmed his friend Tom Jeffords, Cochise told Arizona Governor Anson Safford that if the rumor proved true, he "intended to kill every one" of them. [31]

Cochise's influence among non-Chiricahua Apaches was less pervasive, of course, yet because he was an able and successful war leader, members of Western Apache bands until the mid-1860s joined in some of his forays, and he had close ties with the White Mountain (Coyotero) band, particularly its eastern group. Although he seems to have had little if any contact with the Mescalero Apaches east of the Río Grande, many of the smaller bands west of the river provided plenty of recruits for his enterprises. Cremony said other Apaches thought him "invincible and [so] flock[ed] to his support," [32] and Dr. John White, who in 1874 studied the Western Apaches, considered him to be the only chief "who really exercised control over any of the Apaches" except those in his own band. [33]

It was Cochise's reputation as a war chief that clearly placed him above other Apache leaders. Born about 1810, he had matured during a relatively peaceful period of Apache-Mexican affairs. While he was in his early twenties, however, relations deteriorated and treachery and war replaced tranquility and peace. The Johnson and Kirker massacres (1837 and 1846) left indelible impressions on Cochise, who may have lost family members in them.

Asa Daklugie thought Cochise became chief "when he was a very young man. That meant that his ability as a fighting man was well established and that he was respected by his people." [34] This was essentially the case in that Cochise was a war leader at an early age.

He was, however, overshadowed by more influential and important men until he assumed leadership of his group about 1856–57. He became the leader of the Chokonen band about one year later, which coincided with Anglo arrival in southeastern Arizona. Although apprehensive about the newcomers, he perceived a golden opportunity to receive American rations and gifts while still being able to raid into Mexico. The precarious relationship became strained in late 1859 and early 1860 before it gradually degenerated and hit rock bottom when he was mistreated by an American officer, Lieutenant George N. Bascom, at Apache Pass in February 1861.

After the Bascom affair, with Mangas Coloradas aging, Cochise emerged as the dominant Chiricahua chief on a tribal basis and the most celebrated Apache of the next decade. Two years later, Mangas Coloradas was treacherously murdered. All of this resulted in a fierce and abiding hatred and an ingrained distrust of Americans which lasted for well over a decade. Cochise remained committed to his war until he determined that life as a free Apache was no longer possible. Perhaps in a bit of an oversimplification, he said of Bascom's act: "I was at peace with the whites, until they tried to kill me for what other Indians did; I now live and die at war with them." [35] And fight he did. From 1861 through 1872, except for a few brief stays on the reservation in the early 1870s, Cochise fought the whites like no other Apache. Apache antipathy toward Mexicans was legendary, but Cochise's hatred of Americans exceeded his hatred of Mexicans during the 1860s. For almost a decade he spurned peaceful contact.

The Cochise wars of the 1860s differed significantly from the more celebrated Victorio and Geronimo wars of the 1870s and 1880s. For the first five years (or essentially until the Civil War ended), Cochise remained the aggressor, taking the fight to the few remaining whites in Arizona and boldly attacking ranches and travelers. Throughout this period his people were able to camp and range as his ancestors had. Although forts were established and ranches were worked, the Chiricahua Apaches retained control of most of southeastern Arizona. Cochise's people frequently lived in the Chiricahua Mountains, within a day's ride of Fort Bowie, or in his strongholds in the Dragoons, some fifty miles east of Tucson. The few times he felt pressure from U.S. troops, his access to Mexico was usually open. There were some years when he lived south of the border as much as he did north. By the late 1860s, his war inevitably had become a defensive conflict. Mexican and American counterstrikes led him to retaliate as hard as he could, for he knew no other way.

A powerful warrior, Cochise was renowned for his ability with weapons. James Tevis did not think "Cochise ever met his equal with a lance," while John C. Cremony claimed that "no Apache warrior can draw an arrow to the head, and send it farther, with more ease than he." [36] In his prime, Cochise embodied the essence of Apache warfare. Except when he was surprised or when his family was endangered, an Apache fought only on his terms when success seemed certain. There were a few exceptions, however. When fighting for revenge, he threw caution to the wind and took chances that he normally would not take. Most war parties were organized with this intent.

To all this Cochise brought his own audacious and warlike presence. Although he was never a "red Napoleon" or a military genius, in his day there was no better fighting Apache. He was not a leader who stood in the background while his men fought. In fact, few Apache chiefs were cast from that mold. He led by example. In every single action in which he participated and of which an eyewitness account has been left behind, there is one striking similarity: Cochise led his warriors into battle. This constant leads me to conclude that he, like Geronimo, had a vision telling him that he would not be killed in battle, a feeling shared by at least one American who met him during the 1870s. [37]

Yet this bravery should not be interpreted as foolhardiness. The traditional Hollywood assault against circled wagon trains or enclosed forts (in fact, none of Arizona's territorial posts was completely walled) rarely, if ever, occurred; it was too dangerous and too risky. An Apache valued his life just as much as any white man. He wasn't recklessly brave; in this he differed from the Plains Indian, whose society encouraged the counting of coup on live enemies. An Apache admired stealth: he wanted to dispatch of his foes as quickly as possible without risk to himself. Of course there was some hard skirmishing at times but usually little loss of life, which is easily explained when one understands the nature of an Apache fight. General George Crook pointed out that in most Apache fights a hostile was rarely seen. All you saw were puffs of smoke from the rocks; you rarely saw an enemy. This was the case in many of Cochise's fights, but in other ways he was an atypical Apache, especially in the early years of his war when he was the aggressor and fought for revenge. He showed no mercy to his enemies, who, if captured, were tortured to death in a slow, painful, and inhumane way.

Cochise's survival skills were legendary. For twelve years he successfully eluded troops and volunteers from four states and two countries. His allies were his ancestral mountains and the territorial boundary line, which he used adroitly, leapfrogging back and forth when heavily pressured. His rancherías were almost impossible to surprise, although it was done from time to time. His camps were strategically located in areas which could be defended easily and which offered a haven for safe retreat. His camp overlooking the San Pedro Valley on the slopes of the West Dragoons was a fine example, for if they were threatened, the Indians could easily move higher into the mountains. Sladen marveled at its location:

> Troops must have come up in plain view for some miles and they could easily have been repulsed in any attempt to climb the steep face of the mountains below us, while the scattered rocks and boulders gave ready shelter to the Indians above
>
> The path above us would have afforded a passage to . . . shelter to the women and children, on the other side of the mountain, or if necessary, our entire party could have safely retreated over the ridge onto the other slope of the mountain.[38]

Cochise continued such precautions even after he made his final treaty, thereby revealing that he never completely trusted Americans because of the Bascom affair.

To Cochise's survival skills must be added one more factor: luck. Perhaps it was the element the Apaches called power, of which Cochise had his share. Asa Daklugie referred to it, but the way in which it related to Cochise is somewhat ambiguous. Not being Apache, I would be the first to admit that I do not fully comprehend its concept and significance. To me, the extraordinary thing about Cochise's life was the fact that he was at war with either Mexico or the United States for much of forty years; was involved in countless raids, skirmishes, and fights; was surprised and attacked in his camp on occasion; was wounded several times; and allegedly was killed on a dozen occasions, give or take a few. Yet he survived, which was a testament to his stubborn persistence in the face of white subjugation. Finally, he accepted the hard reality that peace was his only option and succeeded in obtaining a reservation in his country, where he died a natural death. Was it fate, luck, or power? Who knows?

There was little middle ground among southwesterners regarding the Apaches during the last half of the nineteenth century. Many had lost family members or friends to an Apache arrow or bullet. Typical of this dichotomy in perception was a government survey conducted by two Arizona pioneers, both very familiar with Cochise's people. Sidney Delong, post sutler at Fort Bowie and an Anglo who subscribed to the extermination policy as the panacea for the Apache problem, described the Chiricahuas as "savages, with all their vices; intractable; treacherous; not truthful; dishonest; not hospitable; cowards." Chiricahua Apache agent Tom Jeffords, who had a unique friendship with Cochise, described the Indians as "gentle, docile, truthful, honest, hospitable, chaste, courageous." [39] By Apache standards, Jeffords's views were on the mark. Most whites, however, were not familiar with Cochise's people and would have endorsed Delong's opinion.

I have tried to portray Cochise as a leader of unusual ability and influence who played a leading role in the tumultuous period of Chiricahua Apache history between 1830 and 1874. On the whole, he seems to have performed better than any other Apache.

# COCHISE

## Chiricahua Apache Chief

Legend

Spanish & Mexican Presidios
Boundaries
Rivers
Other Places of Interest
Military Posts

location map

Arizona | New Mexico

Scale in Miles

0    40    80

Fort Stanton

SAN ANDRES MTNS.

New Mexico
Texas

Río Grande

Fort McRae

Fort Selden

ORGAN MTNS.

Fort Fillmore

Fort Bliss

Camp Ojo Caliente

Cañada Alamosa

BLACK RANGE

Río Grande

Mesilla

GUAJOQUILLA
(San Eleazario)

Carrizal

PASO DEL NORTE

Chihuahua, Mexico

Ascención

Galeana

Río Santa María

Fort Webster

Santa Rita del Cobre

Fort Thorn

Cook's Canyon

Fort Cummings

MOGOLLON MTNS.

Pinos Altos

Fort Bayard

Mimbres River

FLORIDA MTNS.

Laguna de Guzman

Sierra Boca Grande

Corralitos

San Francisco River

Fort West

Camp Tularosa

Fort Tularosa

Doubtful Canyon
Steins Peak

BURRO MTNS.

Carrizalillo Springs

Río Casas Grandes

JANOS

Road between Bavispe
and Carretas

Fort Apache

Blue River

White River

Black River

Arizona
New Mexico

Fords of the Gila

Gila River

GILA MTNS.

Butterfield Overland Mail Route
(1858–1861)

Animas Mountains

Chihuahua
Sonora

SIERRA MADRE

NATANES PLATEAU

San Simon River

PINALENO MTNS.

Sarampion

SAN BERNARDINO

Río Bavispe

BAVISPE

Fort Apache

Camp Pinal

Camp Picket Post

Fort Goodwin

Aravaipa Creek

Fort Grant

DOS CABEZAS MTNS.

Fort Bowie

Apache Pass

Bonita Canyon

CHIRICAHUA MTNS.

East Stronghold

Western Dragoons

Tex Canyon

Sonora, Mexico
Arizona

FRONTERAS

Cuchuta

BACOACHI

Nácozari

Poza Hediondo

SIERRA ANCHAS

Camp Reno

SUPERSTITION MTNS.

Camp San Carlos

Fort Breckinridge
(Old Camp Grant)

San Pedro River

Dragoon Springs

MULE MTNS.

Camp Wallen

SANTA CRUZ

Chinapa

Arispe

Río Sonora

Fort McDowell

Verde River

Salt River

Gila River

SANTA CATALINA MTNS.

Fort Lowell

SANTA RITA MTNS.

Camp Crittenden

Fort Buchanan

Moury Mines

Camp Mason

TUBAC

Imuris

Magdalena

Río Magdalena

Tonto Creek

Santa Cruz River

TUCSON

Fort Mason

International Boundary

ALTAR

Río Altar

N

Drawn by Don Bufkin

Chapter 1

# THE EARLY YEARS

The Apaches were a warlike and nomadic people who roamed the Southwest, preferring to live in rugged, inaccessible mountains but equally at home in the harsh desert. There are two schools of thought on derivation of the word *Apache*. The first holds it may be from the Yuman word *e-patch*, loosely interpreted to mean "man." The second and more likely possibility has it originating from the Zuñi word *apachu*, which means "enemy." The Apaches called themselves *tinneh*, *dine*, *tinde*, or *inde*, which translates to "man" or "people."[1] These migrants to the Southwest from the Mackenzie River Valley of western Canada were members of the Athapaskan linguistic family, which is divided into three geographic divisions: Northern, Pacific Coast, and Southern. The Apaches belonged to the Southern. Anthropologists and historians disagree about the date of their appearance in the Southwest, some believing they had arrived by the late sixteenth century and others, notably Jack D. Forbes, arguing they were living in New Mexico and Arizona in the 1400s.[2]

The Southern Athapaskans known as Apaches are divided into seven major groupings. The Jicarilla, Lipan, and Kiowa-Apache tribes form the eastern division, and the Navajo, Mescalero, Western Apache, and Chiricahua tribes comprise the western division. The word *Chiricahua* probably was derived from the Opata Indian word *chiguicagui,* meaning "mountain of the wild turkeys." The Chiricahuas are the focus of this study.[3]

The Chiricahuas consisted of four bands. The easternmost, labeled by Morris E. Opler the Eastern Chiricahuas, were known to Mexicans and Americans as the Mimbres, Copper mines, Warm Springs, Mogollons, and the all-encompassing Gilas, names describing geographic locations where they lived. Their territory was west of the Río Grande in New Mexico, and they lived in the Cuchillo, Black, Mimbres, Mogollon, Pinos Altos, Victoria, and Florida mountain ranges.[4] Their leaders from the 1820s through the 1870s were Mano Mocha, Fuerte, Cuchillo Negro, Itán, Mangas Coloradas, Delgadito, Victorio, Nana, and Loco. To the Apaches, they were the Chihennes, or Red Paint People.

The second band, called by Opler the Southern Chiricahuas, was known to Mexicans and Americans as the Janeros, Carrizaleños, and Pinery Apaches, each in reference to specific areas they inhabited. The mountains along the U.S.-Mexican border served as their homeland, although they also roamed deep into the vast Sierra Madre in the Mexican states of Chihuahua and Sonora.[5] Occasionally they wandered across the border into present-day southeastern Arizona and southwestern New Mexico. The Janeros people were so named for their friendly relations at Janos, a small town in northwestern Chihuahua. Their leaders from 1820 through the 1870s were Juan Diego Compá, Juan José Compá, followed by Coleto Amarillo, Arvizu, Láceris, Galindo, Natiza, and Juh. The Carrizaleños lived south of the Janeros people near Carrizal, Chihuahua. Their most prominent leaders in the 1820s and 1830s were Jasquedegá and Cristóbal. In the 1840s, Francisquillo, Francisco, and Cigarrito assumed leadership, followed by Cojinillín and Felipe in the 1850s. Both groups were hit hard by Mexican campaigns from the 1830s through the early 1860s, when the Carrizaleños were virtually wiped out as a distinct unit. To the Apaches, they were the Nednhis, or Enemy People.

Opler named the third band, the one of which Cochise was a member, the Central Chiricahuas. Their homeland was southeastern Arizona, particularly the Dragoon, Dos Cabezas, and Chiricahua mountains.[6] They also ranged north to the Gila River, east into southwestern New Mexico, and south into the Sierra Madre. The

mountains along the U.S.-Mexican border gave them sanctuary
from Mexican and American troops. From the 1820s through the
1870s their leaders were Pisago Cabezón, Relles, Matías, Tapilá,
Yrigóllen, Miguel Narbona, Carro, Posito Moraga, Esquinaline, and
Cochise, who rose rapidly in the mid-1850s to become the leading
chief of his band. To Anglos of the nineteenth century and to the
Apaches of today, this was the band first referred to as Chiricahuas,
known to the Indians as the Chokonens.

The Chiricahuas* recognized one other band, the Bedonkohes,
during historical times. Their territory was northeast of the Chokonens and northwest of the Chihennes in the vicinity of the Gila River
and Mogollon Mountains. The notorious Geronimo was born into
this branch. The smallest of the Chiricahua divisions, the Bedonkohes were assimilated into one of the other bands in the early
1860s, the majority opting to follow Cochise after the death of Mangas Coloradas.[7]

The bands identified one another as related, having "linguistic
and cultural bonds which identify them as one people." The tribal
relationship was expressed in many ways: the three peoples were
usually at peace with one another, visiting was frequent, and social
dances, puberty rites, and marriages were reasons for assembling.
The band served as the political unit of the tribe, and an individual
remained a member of the one into which he or she was born, except when a man married outside his band. In this case, it was Chiricahua custom for the man to live with his wife's people, and his off-
spring were known by the affiliation of her band.[8]

Each band consisted of three to five local groups, each made up of
several families who camped together near a geographic site from
which they usually took their name. For example, during Cochise's
life, camps, or rancherías, were scattered throughout Chokonen
country, perhaps in the Dragoon, Chiricahua, and Peloncillo mountains. Unlike the band, the local group was not a stable unit. The
relationship between members was based primarily on residence
and could be severed because of food scarcity, epidemics, internal
conflicts, or the death of a leader.[9]

Cochise towered over other leaders because in historic times he
commanded allegiance from every Chokonen local group. In contrast, during the same period of the 1860s, the Chihennes recog-

nized at least three local group leaders—Loco, Victorio, and Nana—
and the Nednhis recognized at least two, Natiza and Juh. Chiricahua
local groups often consisted of one or more rancherías, usually separated by some distance and scattered up and down high mountain
valleys. These clusters, called extended family groups, were related
through the maternal chain. A Chiricahua informant described the
extended family as "a group of homes occupied by relatives. At the
very least an extended family is a father and mother, their unmarried
children, and the families of their married daughters." The sub-
groups were known by the names of the family leader.[10]

Into one of the Chokonen local groups Cochise was born. When
and where are not definitely known, although writer Frank C. Lockwood believed that Cochise was born in the Chiricahua Mountains
about 1815.[11] Samuel Woodworth Cozzens, a Mesilla lawyer, and
army surgeon Bernard John Dowling Irwin, both of whom apparently met Cochise about 1860, had different estimates of his age.
Cozzens thought the chief to be about forty-seven,[12] and Irwin
guessed about thirty.[13] The latter estimate is clearly too low when
one considers that an Apache identified as Chis, or Chees, almost
certainly Cochise, was mentioned in 1835 as the leader of a party
that was raiding in Mexico. Furthermore, Cochise was on the Janos
ration lists in 1842 and 1843, at which time he had a wife and possibly a child. For what it is worth, during the 1860s, when he avoided
American contact, sometimes he was referred to as Old Cochise,
perhaps a term used more to show respect than to indicate age. In
the late 1860s and early 1870s there were numerous estimates of his
height, build, and age. In February 1869 an eyewitness thought Cochise to be about fifty.[14] In another interview recorded by an army
surgeon (they were usually good observers), he was thought to be
fifty-eight in 1871,[15] while still another credible report, this one
from Arizona Governor Anson P. Safford, who visited Cochise in
November 1872, put his age about sixty.[16]

Apache accounts are sparse but in agreement. Asa Daklugie believed Cochise about seventy at the time of his death in 1874.[17]
Gillet Griswold's study of the Chiricahua Apaches supports Daklugie's statements, estimating Cochise's birth date at about 1800.[18] I
do not feel that the evidence supports such an early date; my best
guess would place Cochise's birth about 1810, probably in northern

Mexico or southeastern Arizona. It is quite conceivable that he was born in the Chiricahua Mountains as asserted by Robert Humphrey Forbes on the basis of information furnished by Thomas J. Jeffords, Cochise's best-remembered white friend.[19]

Cochise's parents were Central Chiricahuas, or Chokonens, and his father was a leading man at the band level. A common legend, developed by Anglos because Apache oral history seldom recalled individuals or events beyond one generation, has Cochise descended from a long line of leaders. Whether this is true is another matter;[20] again, Apache sources are lacking. Cochise himself claimed that his grandfather had been the leader of all Apaches, probably meaning the Chiricahuas.[21] But this may have been translated or recorded in error; he probably meant his father. Asa Daklugie believed that Cochise was related in some manner to Juan José Compá, a Chiricahua leader of the 1830s. His opinion cannot be dismissed lightly; however, Juan José Compá was not a Chokonen and any relation was probably through marriage instead of blood.[22]

The best contemporary information about Cochise's father was provided by James Henry Tevis,[23] a station keeper at Apache Pass who became well acquainted with Cochise in the late 1850s. Tevis wrote that Cochise's father was the head chief of the Apaches (referring to the Chokonen band) who perished at the hands of duplicitous Mexicans. "The Mexicans invited Cochise's father and some of his noted warriors to a feast," he wrote, "and, by treachery, got him and his warriors drunk and killed them." It was a scene repeated several times in Chiricahua-Mexican relations.[24] In 1875 the *Arizona Citizen* published a biographical article on Cochise, giving a version similar to Tevis's.[25] An incident like the one Tevis described did take place in the summer of 1846 when notorious scalp hunter James Kirker[26] and other mercenaries slaughtered 148 Chiricahuas near Galeana, Chihuahua. Among the dead was the Chokonen leader Relles[27] and perhaps Pisago Cabezón,[28] the most prominent Chiricahua in the first forty years of the nineteenth century. The none-too-reliable James Hobbs, who was a member of Kirker's party, described the incident years later and identified Cochise as one of the leaders of the band butchered by Kirker.[29]

At this date it is extremely unlikely that these discrepancies ever will be reconciled.[30] His father may have been Relles but more probably was Pisago Cabezón. In any event we know that Cochise's father was a leading man at the band level and that as his son Cochise was expected to assume a leadership role, although leadership was not inherited. It was earned, through one's actions and accomplishments; if these were combined with wisdom in counsel, the individual might become a chief. The son of a great chief, however, had an advantage in that he no doubt had received excellent training as a young man and normally would be more prepared than most to follow in the footsteps of his father.[31]

Cochise was born in a peaceful period as far as relations between the Chiricahua Apaches and Mexico were concerned, yet this had not always been the case. For much of the eighteenth century, there had been war between most Apache bands and the Spaniards, who had adopted one policy after another, ranging from extermination to colonization, in an attempt to pacify the incorrigible Apaches.[32] The conflict continued into the 1780s, with, according to Spanish estimates, six hundred Apaches (including some Chiricahuas) attacking Tucson on May 1, 1782, and occupying areas beyond its walled presidio before the garrison drove them off, claiming about thirty enemy killed. Two years later a Spanish force surprised a band of Chokonens at Dos Cabezas, killing nine men, three women, and four children and recapturing a Pima woman taken in the attack at Tucson.[33] Finally, in 1786, recognizing the failure of its diverse policies, the royal crown issued yet another order, called the *Instrucción*.

The new order was based on Spanish experience of the previous quarter-century, which now accepted that extermination alone was impracticable; victory might be achieved by persuading the hostiles to live in peace near Spanish presidios, or forts. The *Instrucción* recognized that the Indian's economy consisted of gathering, hunting, and raiding, with the last also an important part of his society. Perhaps the way to pacify him was to turn him away from his culture, but first he must be subdued through unremitting war. After all, "a bad peace was better than a good war." The *Instrucción* addressed the fundamental issue of attempting to understand Apaches and proved to be the beginning of a forty-year period of generally peaceful but tenuous relations between the two races. It succeeded because it took a realistic, pragmatic approach in addressing the Indian problem.[34]

By the early 1790s most of the Chiricahuas had been compelled to sue for peace, which was granted under the condition that they live quietly in designated areas. This they did, settling at the presidio of Janos[35] in Chihuahua and eventually at other locations along the frontier. Almost at once the Spaniards introduced a systematic policy that was intended to disrupt and destroy the Apache social system. On the one hand, they issued rations of corn or wheat, meat, brown sugar, salt, and tobacco to a reported six thousand Apaches at an annual expense of twenty-three thousand pesos. On the other, they furnished gifts of guns, liquor, clothing, and other items with the duplicitous intention of making the Apaches totally subservient to and dependent on the Spaniards. The guns were inferior and prone to break down, necessitating the services of a Spanish gunsmith to repair them. Furthermore, it was hoped that the Apaches would neglect their bows and arrows, which they used more effectively than firearms. Intoxicating liquors were dispensed freely so that the Indians would acquire a taste for them. "It was at once a highly sophisticated, brutal and deceptive policy of divide and conquer, of peace by purchase, of studied debilitation of those who accepted peace and of extermination of those who rejected it," writes Max L. Moorhead. However cruel and immoral, he concludes, "it was . . . a practical policy and one which offered both races the opportunity for survival."[36]

At first the conditions were confining to the Apaches, who were accustomed to coming and going as they pleased. Eventually they were allowed to leave their peace establishments, provided that permission had been granted. Most historians agree that peaceful relations continued for the remainder of the Spanish period, that is, until 1821, and there is evidence to conclude that it prevailed until 1830. William B. Griffen estimates that perhaps two-thirds of the Chiricahua Apaches were involved with this system. He concludes that the presidio system was essentially a success because the cost in controlling the Apaches was far less than the damage hostiles would have caused and the tremendous expense that punitive military campaigns would have incurred.[37] Consequently, Cochise's people had been at peace for fifteen to twenty years by the time of his birth. Frank C. Lockwood characterizes the period as a "nearer approximation to peace [between Apaches and Spaniards] than at any previous time. . . . It was during these years of respite that mines were opened and successfully operated, churches built and beautified, and ranches prosperously conducted."[38]

Cochise was born during this season of amity. His immediate family eventually included at least two younger brothers, Juan and Coyuntura (Kin-o-Tera), and at least one younger sister. He probably had other brothers and sisters whose names were not remembered. One or two months after birth, when his parents were sure he would live, he received a name suggested either by the midwife or by an unusual event that distinguished his birth; the name bestowed upon him at that time is not known. It was probably as a young adult that he received the Apache name *Goci,* literally translated as "his nose," because of his prominent Roman nose.[39] This information, provided by Morris E. Opler, seems more plausible than the accepted historical statement that Cochise's name meant "wood" or "a quality or strength in wood." Another explanation has the name bestowed upon him because he once supplied firewood to the Apache Pass stage station. This, too, seems improbable because there are references to Cochise in Mexican records dated some twenty years before the station was established.

Apache society was ritualistic; there were ceremonies and supernatural help to explain virtually all aspects of everyday life.[40] There were strong emotional ties to one's birthplace, and upon returning to the site, a child or even an adult might roll on the ground to the four directions. When a child was a few weeks old, his mother or maternal grandmother pierced earlobes so that he would "hear things sooner" and obey quicker. Ever present in Chiricahua parent-child relations was discipline, and obeying one's parents was always emphasized early in life.

A baby spent the first six or seven months of his or her life in a specially constructed cradle; a shaman performing the cradle ceremony, usually the fourth day after birth. The cradle was constructed of oak, ash, or walnut, with sotol or yucca stalk used for the supporting back pieces and buckskin covering the frame. In each phase of construction the shaman prayed that the child would have a long, good life. In addition, he attached amulets, such as bags of pollen or turquoise, to the cradle to protect it. The mother added her own good-luck charms, perhaps the right paw of a badger or the claws of a hummingbird, to protect the baby from malevolent forces. In the cradle ceremony, which was held early in the morning with the members of the local group attending, the cradle was held to the four directions, beginning with the east and proceeding clockwise to the beginning, at which time the baby was put inside. Then a feast or social dance was held.

As a child grew, several rituals were performed to ensure that the individual followed the same steps in life as the mythical Apache culture heroes. The moccasin ceremony usually was held when the child was about seven months old, although it could take place as late as the age of two. As in all Chiricahua ceremonies, a shaman or individual who knew the rules directed the celebration, and, like the cradle ceremony, it also served as a social gathering. After the infant, called Child of the Water, took four ceremonial steps, the shaman saying a prayer after each, a great feast was held.

The next ritual was the spring hair cutting, usually held the spring after the moccasin ceremony. Pollen was applied to the child's cheek and head and "then his hair, with the exception of one or more locks, is closely cropped." The hair was allowed to grow back soon after. Most Chiricahuas paid very close attention to the grooming of their hair, a particular Cochise observed throughout his life.

As a young child, Cochise learned about Chiricahua religion, which focused on the supernatural and "emphasizes the virtues of humility and gratitude." When a child is "old enough to understand his parents, they begin to teach him to be religious, to use religious words and to know Life Giver, Child of the Water, and White Painted Woman." The Chiricahua youth also acquired knowledge about other cultural heroes: the Mountain People, supernaturals living in the interior of sacred mountains, who protected the tribe and were "potential sources of supernatural power." He heard the familiar coyote stories, about the adventures of the wily coyote, an inveterate trickster, which had a moral or a lesson to be learned. All of this was intended to prepare the boy for adulthood.

Parents instructed their children about appropriate behavior. As a leader's son, Cochise received better training than most youths. In

the words of a Chiricahua: "More pains are taken with such children; they are kept out of mischief more. They should not resent
things easily. They are supposed to be better bred. Quarreling
should be beneath them. But, above all, the child is taught respect.
He was told, Don't steal from your own friends. Don't be unkind to
your playmates. If you are kind now, when you become a man you
will love your fellow men." To correct improper behavior, a child
was brought into line with threats; and if this didn't work, the parent
could whip the child, although this was an extremely infrequent occurrence. So it was that Cochise acquired the traits and characteristics of a good leader, for good training usually meant a boy would
turn out to be a good man. Yet supernaturalism dominated each step
in the child's development, the parents constantly striving to protect
their children with ceremonies, rituals, and good-luck charms.

When he was about six or seven years old, Cochise probably took
his first step in training. A male relative, possibly his father, grandfather, or paternal uncle, gave him a bow and arrows so that he
could join other boys in hunting small birds and animals. Boys separated from girls at this age and began playing games, such as hide-
and-seek, foot racing, tug-of-war, and wrestling, all emphasizing
speed, agility, and strength. Horsemanship was also practiced.
"Children from seven years of age and on would go and learn by
themselves when the older people didn't even know about it. There
were always some gentle horses for the boy to ride." Ubiquitous in
all stages of Chiricahua life were ceremonies, shamans, prayers,
songs, and sacred objects.

Physical fitness, self-discipline, and independence dominated the
next stage of preadolescence. The elders encouraged a boy to take
care of his body, for "no one will help you in this world. . . . Your
legs are your friends." The boy began to hunt more, primarily birds
and squirrels, and by these experiences acquired important skills,
such as stealth, patience, and perseverance, to secure his prey. To
guarantee continued success in hunting, he was advised "to swallow
whole the raw heart of the first kill." A boy this age also became
experienced with horses; he learned how to care for them and how
to ride expertly. In his early teens, more responsible scout and guard
duties were assigned. Physical endurance and stamina also were important, and we can presume that Cochise learned well because a

"leader's son never fails to make good, for he is trained and advised from boyhood to manhood."

About the age of fourteen, a boy was ready to begin training as a warrior, becoming a *dikohe,* or novice. When a boy was old and mature enough, he volunteered, his family cautioning him that dangers and hardships lay ahead. Training now assumed a more intense and formal tone. Whereas up to this juncture the extended family group was responsible for the boy's training, now the local group assumed responsibility. Frequently, many young men of the same age were assigned to a shaman who knew about war. The training became more vigorous than before: physical events, such as wrestling, slingshot fights, small bow-and-arrow contests, and races dominated, and discipline and obedience were stressed constantly.

Chiricahua boys developed in many ways. They were assigned tasks to teach them obedience and prepare them for the physical hardships of a warrior. For example, in the late fall or early winter when ice had formed on lakes, they were told to disrobe and jump in. But perhaps the skill that was emphasized most was running. Boys were ordered to run up hills and return just as quickly; races and games were organized to sharpen competitive instincts. During these contests, future warriors and leaders were conspicuous by their actions. From these Cochise emerged, disciplined and physically tuned, ready to participate in the four raids required to become a man.

The youth was now ready for the final phase of the *dikohe* period; when he heard that a raid or war party was being organized, he volunteered for duty and a shaman prepared him for it. The primary concern was the individual's behavior during the raid and his obedience to his leaders. If the *dikohe* acted in an undesirable manner or exhibited signs of dishonesty, cowardice, or gluttony, or was unrestrained and had sexual intercourse during one of the first four journeys, he would be labeled for the rest of his life as unreliable. The *dikohe* accompanied the warriors to learn from them; to do menial camp chores, such as cooking and preparing the warriors' beds; and to stand guard. The novices were protected from danger, for injury to them would reflect on the party's leaders.

During the four raids, the warriors called the *dikohe* Child of the Water. He wore a ceremonial hat for protection and learned special words that were taught him for the occasion.[41] In addition, he had other restrictions: he must drink through a tube and eat all food cold. After the fourth raid, unless there was sharp criticism of his performance, the youth joined the ranks of the warriors. Certainly this was Cochise's status by the time he reached his midteens, and he must have performed exceptionally well during the four raids. Now he could smoke, marry, and have all the privileges of a warrior. And he would have many opportunities to gain recognition as a warrior because the long period of peace between the Chiricahua Apaches and Mexico was ending.

# Chapter 2

# LITTLE WARS

As Cochise matured, relations between the Chiricahua Apaches and Mexico changed significantly. The Mexican Revolution, which began in 1810, forced Spain to divert troops, resources, and funds from the northern presidios to the interior to quell the rebellion. As a result, frontier garrisons were reduced to skeleton strength and soldiers went unclothed, unfed, and unpaid. Affairs worsened after Mexico won her independence in 1821. The revolution had drained public treasuries and depleted the funds required to maintain the presidios and the Apaches.[1] This situation did not happen all at once. Some rations were furnished to Chiricahua bands living near Janos, Fronteras[2] in northeastern Sonora, and Santa Rita del Cobre[3] in southwestern New Mexico.

The federal government in Mexico City permitted the presidio system to decline during the early 1820s. Troop discipline continued to deteriorate, salaries were slashed again, and hard currency was unavailable.[4] Consequently, the Apaches received even less assistance, and some minor raiding occurred. Citizens were called upon to donate cattle and grain to appease the discontented Indians, which served to increase animosity between the two races.[5] At this time, Juan Diego Compá[6] and Pisago Cabezón combined to lead their groups at Janos; Fuerte[7] and Mano Mocha[8] led the Chihennes at the copper mines. In December 1821, 1,423 Apaches received rations in Chihuahua: 442 at Janos (Chokonens and Nednhis), 210 at San Buenaventura (Nednhis), 347 at Carrizal (Nednhis), and 424 at San Elizario (Mescaleros). Although some 1,000 cattle were allocated to feed these bands, the number proved inadequate and some of the Indians went hungry.[9]

Finally, in 1824, the Chiricahuas bolted from their peace establishments—certainly because of the dwindling rations—and sporadic raiding began. Chokonen and Nednhi groups fled Janos, as did the Chokonens living at Fronteras under Matías[10] and Teboca.[11] Although we cannot be sure that Cochise was a member of this group, we can say that most of the Chokonens resumed hostilities.

That summer, a band that had left Fronteras was reported living in the Dos Cabezas Mountains a few miles north of Apache Pass, a favorite camping area of Cochise's local group. That fall, Chiricahua leaders planned several raids against the frontier, apparently unsure of raiding the more prosperous and populous interior districts. Raiding parties struck near Fronteras, Bavispe, and Tubac with relatively slight success: some stock was taken and a few Mexicans were killed. Their raids, however, evoked memories of what Apache terror once was.

Authorities at Fronteras conceded that the depredations were committed by Chiricahuas who had been living at peace. The situation could easily have erupted into a full-scale war, which seemed to Mexicans the Indians' intention. A peaceful Apache at Janos revealed that Teboca's Chokonens had joined Fuerte's and Mano Mocha's Chihennes in southwestern New Mexico and planned an incursion into Mexico. Furthermore, hostile Chiricahuas were lurking in the Enmedio Mountains to ambush travelers between Janos and Fronteras.[12]

Sonora attempted to quell the uprising, planning an offensive composed of troops from Fronteras and militia from Santa Cruz, Bavispe, and Bacoachi. From Arispe, reinforcements were dispatched to Fronteras, but lack of arms, ammunition, and mounts grounded the campaign before it got under way.[13] Yet in November Sonoran soldiers defeated a Chiricahua party; this, combined with the onset of winter, caused the Indians' enthusiasm for combat to wane. On November 12 near Agua Prieta, a small force from Fronteras managed to overtake hostiles and wound several Indians who had raided Cuquiarachi.[14] The next month, Juan José Compá and three other leaders requested an armistice at Santa Rita del Cobre and most of the fighting was over.[15] During 1825, Chiricahua bands returned to their establishments at Santa Rita del Cobre, Janos, and Fronteras, but there is no way of knowing what role Cochise played, if any. Possibly, he could have served as a *dikohe*.

There was a precarious truce for the next few years. Rations were slashed again in early 1828, forcing the Indians to move into the Chiricahua, Enmedio, and Animas mountains to plant, prepare mescal, and hunt for subsistence. Pisago Cabezón raised a few crops at Alamo Hueco, but many of the Indians again had become disaffected about the lack of rations. Nonetheless, through 1829 groups of Apaches remained at Janos under Pisago and Juan Diego Compá, Fuerte and his band remained at Santa Rita del Cobre, and a group of Chokonens under Matías and Teboca remained encamped near Fronteras.[16]

Yet Mexican officials ignored this festering Apache discontent. In early January 1830, Pisago Cabezón, Juan Diego, and other leaders met with the military commander of Janos and made several requests. First they wanted their rations, now reduced to corn alone, to include a portion of meat; they also requested an interpreter and farming tools. Their appeal was forwarded to Chihuahua City, and the response was to the point: although some farming implements were issued and an interpreter hired, rations could not be increased; Mexican troops would receive first priority.[17] This insensitivity can best be explained if one considers that these public officials, living in safety at Chihuahua City, may well have discounted the Apaches as a force to be feared. Yet in reality the Indians had prospered and become more dangerous during their years at peace: many leaders understood Mexican tactics, many Indians could read and write Spanish, many of them had become adept in the use of Mexican weapons. Although statistics are not available, their number must have increased because few warriors were lost to war.

In any event, Apache raiders quickly dispelled the notion. Without food, some Chiricahuas began raiding, for no Apache willingly went hungry. The more militant bands, perhaps including Cochise, had begun depredating in Sonora during the winter of 1830, hitting hardest the districts of Altar, Arispe, and San Ignacio.[18] In late February a great trail of Apaches, with stolen stock from Sonora, was reported at Alamo Hueco, a rendezvous site for the three Chiricahua bands. Sensing widespread hostilities, the commander at Janos was directed "to severely punish any Indians absent without permission." [19]

Unbeknownst to whites and Indians, the forty-year period of controlling the Chiricahua Apaches with the presidio system was ending. In late 1830, Apaches living at San Buenaventura (either a Nednhi or Chokonen group) bolted their establishment for the Sierra Madre. There was little food and an epidemic swept through the area, sickening the entire garrison at San Buenaventura with a fever.[20] Hostiles swept into the interior of Sonora and Chihuahua, raided ranches, and ambushed unsuspecting travelers. Their success no doubt inspired and incited those factions which had been reluctant to sever relations with Mexico. Still, in early 1831, Pisago Cabezón's and Juan Diego's bands were still at peace and on January 31 received their last issue of Mexican rations. Shortly thereafter they fled, perhaps to avoid contracting smallpox, now prevalent at Janos. West at Fronteras, Chokonen bands under Teboca and Matías deserted in late June, citing lack of rations. Cochise remembered this period: "After many years the Spanish soldiers were driven away and the Mexicans ruled the land. With these little wars came, but we were now a strong people and did not fear them." [21]

Hostilities in the spring of 1831 were extensive in that, unlike past uprisings, almost every Apache band under Mexican influence participated. Mexico quickly learned that the hungry Apaches, better armed than those in the revolt of 1824, were still a formidable force. Presidio life had destroyed neither their social organization nor their warlike society. Cochise, now a young warrior of about twenty-one, had developed into a tall, well-built man. Physically, he had a more commanding presence than most of his peers: at five feet ten inches, he was some five inches taller than the average Chiricahua. He usually was associated with the more bellicose groups throughout his life, so we can speculate that he was at the forefront of the 1831 raiding and getting his first taste of victory and loot.

As the Chiricahuas had expected, Sonora and Chihuahua took

countermeasures. In late June 1831 the former organized a force of four hundred men to wage war against the hostiles. However, equipment and other problems pushed the expected departure date from September to October or November and the expedition, if indeed it ever got under way, made no inroads in punishing the hostiles.[22] By October 16, 1831, Apache devastation had become so widespread that José Joaquín Calvo, the hard-line commanding general of Chihuahua, declared war on the hostiles and began preparing for an offensive into Apachería like those of the 1780s.[23]

Raids continued during the first five months of 1832, ostensibly with the severity of the previous summer. Chihuahua was hit hard and forced to request one hundred Opata Indians from Sonora because it lacked "sufficient forces in order to contain the rebellion of the Indian Apaches who were at peace and who every day commit more murders." The Chihuahuans planned to employ the Opatas at Janos in conjunction with quick-striking troops under the command of Captain Mariano Ponce de León. Ramón Morales, the hawkish military commander of Sonora, recommended that the request be denied because of the "critical circumstances which the frontier of this state [Sonora] finds itself." Furthermore, he caustically pointed out, his small force of presidio troops was inadequate to protect Sonora and the one hundred Opatas could not be spared. The governor rejected Morales's arguments and ordered him to dispatch the reinforcements, reasoning that "this objective is beneficial, not only to that state but to this."[24]

Meanwhile, the Chiricahuas were active in the triangular area of Fronteras, Bavispe, and Janos. On March 26, 1832, they attacked the horse herd at Fronteras, forcing Morales to send reinforcements. A week later they captured the mail between Bavispe and Janos, thereby collecting important military information because many Apaches, including Juan José Compá,[25] were literate. About a month later they raided Turicachi and killed a man. These events prompted Ramón Morales to press the governor for four hundred men for a drive into Apachería: one hundred would establish a base camp at San Simon in present-day southeastern Arizona, and the rest would continue north, particularly into the Mogollons of New Mexico, where, it was believed, the hostiles were based.[26]

Chihuahua acted before Sonora did and on May 23, 1832, scored a decisive victory over the allied Chiricahuas near the Gila River a few miles south of the Mogollon Mountains in New Mexico.[27] The hostiles, estimated at three hundred warriors led by Pisago Cabezón, Fuerte, and Mano Mocha, were whipped soundly in an eight-hour battle by 138 men under Captain José Ignacio Ronquillo. The fighting was characterized by alternating charges back and forth until the Mexican troops routed the Indians. According to Ronquillo's windy report, between May 21 and May 23 his troops killed twenty-two Chiricahuas and wounded fifty, some in hand-to-hand combat. The Mexicans lost three men killed and twelve wounded.[28] Again Cochise's involvement is uncertain, but the presence of many Chokonen and Chihenne leaders and his close relationship with Pisago Cabezón make it quite possible that he took part in the fight, which proved to be an intimidating lesson for the Apaches.

This defeat and Sonora's victory against Western Apaches at Arivaipa Canyon (where seventy-one warriors reportedly were slain)[29] compelled the humbled Indians to sue for peace in the summer of 1832. Believing the Indians conquered, Calvo accepted their proposals and on July 28 dictated preliminary surrender terms to Colonel Cayetano Justiniani, an experienced and Apache-wise officer. An obstinate Calvo, however, advocated conditions which had been functional and successful during another era. Essentially, the treaty of 1832 paralleled that of 1810, in which peace had been granted to defeated Mescalero Apaches with no Mexican assistance; the Indians were assigned specific areas where they were to subsist by hunting and planting. Calvo's treaty of 1832 assigned the Mescaleros and Chiricahuas three zones: the Mescaleros from San Elizario to the Sacramento Mountains; the Chihennes from Santa Rita del Cobre to the Negrita Mountains, with the Mogollons included; the Chokonens and Nednhis from Janos north to the Peloncillo and Burro mountains.[30]

Calvo arrived at Santa Rita del Cobre in mid-August. Present were the Chiricahuas (Chokonens), Mogollons and Mimbres (Chihennes), Janeros and Carrizaleños (Nednhis). The treaty, signed on August 21 by twenty-nine leaders, demanded that the Apaches relinquish all stolen stock; this of course was impracticable and few if any animals were returned. Yet they did accept Calvo's concept of three zones with a chief, or general, responsible for the activities in each. The generals were Juan José Compá for the Janos area, Fuerte for the Copper Mines, and Aquién[31] for the Sonoran frontier. The truce did restore order to the frontier, but it was flawed in some respects. First, Calvo maintained his penurious and hard-line policy that the Apaches somehow should subsist without raiding because rations were not part of the agreement. Second, he erred in not having representatives from Sonora present. His provincial plan had small chance for ultimate success, although the immediate situation improved in some ways.[32]

The treaty of 1832 shifted Chiricahua headquarters from Janos to Santa Rita del Cobre, the isolation of which encouraged clandestine commerce. Robert McKnight,[33] a naturalized Mexican who owned the mines, had been present during the negotiations, along with some Americans, among them James Kirker. Their pernicious influence paved the way for a flourishing but illicit trade, with Kirker and McKnight serving as middlemen. Quite simply, the Apaches raided into Sonora and Chihuahua and returned to Santa Rita with their loot, which they traded for food, guns, and whiskey. "The Americans trade guns and ammunition to the Apaches at Santa Rita del Cobre" was a charge heard often.[34] Wrote one historian of the treaty of 1832: "The stage was set to trigger the largest boom in the history of *cambalache* [illegal trade] along the far southwestern frontier."[35]

The truce was destined to fail from the beginning. Lack of subsistence forced most of the Indians to live in the mountains, free from Mexican control, and during the winter of 1833 they resumed their marauding in earnest. Some of Pisago's young men (of whom Cochise was one) raided Janos in February 1833 and in the spring full-scale hostilities erupted at Bavispe, Santa Rita del Cobre, Carrizal, and Janos.[36] For Cochise's people, a three-year war ensued, and it took an enormous toll in lives and property in Mexico.[37]

The first few months after the outbreak, the Chiricahuas, better armed than ever before (primarily because of the illicit trade), swarmed over northern Sonora with impunity. Ranches, towns, and even large cities, such as Arispe and Ures, were raided. From the beginning of hostilities through October 1833, some two hundred citizens were killed.[38]

The new year dawned with similar prospects. On January 8,

1834, a large Chokonen war party surrounded Fronteras and ran off some fifty horses. Cochise may have been present because the two dominant band leaders, Pisago Cabezón and Relles, led the raid. Furthermore, the Apaches struck with audacity, a characteristic of the Chokonens. Two of the other leaders who were recognized were Félix and Tutije, a fast-rising war leader. Captain Bernardo Martínez and a force of presidio troops pursued, confident of routing the Indians if they could overtake them, but a half-mile east of Fronteras the Chiricahuas swarmed from the hills and almost surrounded the command, killing Martínez and three others within sight of the presidio. Afterward they continued south, cleaning out the ranch of Narivo Montoya and then murdering two citizens en route to Bacoachi, where they wiped out another party of six men. Not satisfied with their plunder, they continued southeast to Chinapa, a favorite Chokonen target, which they boldly occupied, running off every head of stock before retiring northward.[39] Fights like these allowed a young warrior to make a name for himself, and Cochise did not squander such opportunities.

The Chokonens returned north to their rancherías in the Chiricahua and Mule mountains, their subsequent movements uncertain. A Tucson rumor had it that Apaches from the Janos and Fronteras regions had joined the Coyoteros (Western Apaches) who were planning to attack Tucson, but no one knew for sure. It was also rumored that the hostiles had firearms, which of course was impossible, and that they numbered six hundred warriors, which was equally absurd. But there were scattered hostilities. On March 30 near the Babocomari ranch they ambushed and killed Captain Leónardo León of Tubac and routed a small force; it was learned that Matías's Chokonens were responsible. The next month, Montiju, a warrior from Matías's group, appeared at Fronteras with startling information: some four hundred Apaches had rendezvoused at Batepito, eighteen miles northeast of Fronteras, where two of the principal leaders, Matías and Tutije, argued about the target. The latter wanted to attack Fronteras, but Matías, who once had lived in peace near Fronteras, demurred, advocating a strike in the interior.[40]

The threatened attack on Fronteras did not materialize, and it was not until three months later that anyone realized what had happened.

In early July a woman who had been captured in the raid at Babo-comari ranch escaped from Matías's camp in the Chiricahuas and somehow made her way to Tucson. According to her, after the argument at Batepito, the bands divided, half under Pisago Cabezón and Tutije heading for the Mogollons and the others, under Relles and Matías, remaining in the Chiricahuas to make mescal. Although she denied that the Coyotero or Pinal Apaches had joined the Chiricahuas, she did confirm that the hostiles were conducting a brisk trade at Santa Rita del Cobre and warned that their next targets would be Tubac and Santa Cruz. Messengers were dispatched to the two places immediately, warning them to prepare for the Apaches. This disturbed Tubac's residents, for the town had no walls or artillery and not many armed citizens, and its water supplies were so scant that the prospect of an Indian siege was unnerving.[41]

That summer Sonora planned an offensive which the Chokonens probably got wind of because in mid-July several leaders appeared at the deserted Opata mission of Cuchuta, twelve miles south of Fronteras, and requested peace. According to Relles, some fourteen leaders would come into Fronteras at the end of July 1834. For some reason the Indians reneged, perhaps because the band was divided and the militant faction saw no benefit to negotiating; they had been at war for eighteen months, and neither Mexican state had mustered an offensive.[42]

Sonora also opposed peace despite the philosophy of Ignacio Mora, who had become commanding general in September. Mexican officials denounced his plans of sending emissaries to the hostiles, who had gone unpunished. Sonora required vengeance, so a campaign was planned and drastic measures adopted. Salaries of public officials were slashed and the savings were used to raise troops. As an added incentive, the volunteers would be allowed to keep plunder. These proposals were delayed, however, when frustrated presidio troops rebelled against Mora. Finally Manuel Escalante y Arvizu, the restless governor described "as a bold man who enjoyed adventure," turned his administrative duties over to Vice-Governor Ignacio Bustamente temporarily and took command for a climactic strike into Apachería.[43]

In late September 1834, Escalante y Arvizu put a force of 442

Apache Pass. Favorite camping site of Cochise's band prior to Anglo arrival in the Southwest. View from Overlook Ridge looking north. (*Photo by Karen Hayes*)

men in the field. Guided by several Opata Indians and seven tame Apaches enlisted from Tucson, the detachment, plagued by hunger and desertions, reached Puerto del Dado (Apache Pass) on October 15. Here the Opatas refused to continue and promptly deserted despite Escalante y Arvizu's threats of execution. To this point the command had found thirteen rancherías, abandoned since the previous summer. Three were discovered in the Chiricahua Mountains and two at Apache Pass, one near the springs and the other in the canyon, two of Cochise's favorite campsites. The Chokonens were believed to have moved north to the Mogollons and the Gila River.[44]

From Apache Pass the command followed an Indian trail north. On October 24 in the foothills of the Mogollons they surprised hostiles returning from a foray into Chihuahua. The Chiricahuas were led by Tutije and Vivora.[45] After a brief but hard fight, Escalante y Arvizu somehow succeeded in capturing "the wicked chief" Tutije and killing two other warriors. The next day the Mexicans withdrew with their important prize, since Tutije was considered to be an important war leader among the Chiricahuas. Escalante y Arvizu, evidently a man who believed in swift retribution, intended to make a point with the other militant leaders. Taking Tutije to Arispe, he paraded him through the streets. Furthermore, instead of using him as a hostage to secure peace, the governor decided to make an example of him, publicly hanging him in the streets of Arispe.[46]

The execution was intended to deter future raids and to teach the Chiricahuas a lesson, but it did neither. In fact, in late 1834 some Chihenne and Chokonen chieftains, including Pisago Cabezón, had sent word to Chihuahua that they wanted peace,[47] but news of Tutije's execution incensed several leaders and they decided to continue hostilities, for revenge must be had. Among those who remained at war were Pisago Cabezón and a young Chokonen daredevil who was beginning to make a name for himself, one who had attracted a small following of young Chokonens: Chis. Only the Nednhis and some of the Chihennes were seeking peace.

Accordingly, on February 12, 1835, Juan José Compá and several other leaders appeared at Santa Rita del Cobre to discuss conditions. They left after a lengthy conference with the sagacious Colonel Cayetano Justiniani, who reported the results to Calvo. Justiniani's account reflected his pragmatic understanding of Apaches, who had agreed to terms and even pledged to join Chihuahuan troops in their defense against the Comanches, an inveterate foe of the Mexicans. The only obstacle was the article which required the return of all stolen stock. Unable to enforce this condition, Justiniani prudently recommended its elimination, reasoning that "the Indians claim that they have very little left," which he discredited, but "in order to compel its return it would take a force of 800 men well mounted and provisioned for four months."[48]

During the conference, the Mexican officer pressed Juan José as to the disposition of the hostiles who had boycotted the talks. Juan José refused to speak for the absentees and said he did not know whether they would make or even wanted peace. Justiniani asked whether the peaceful Apaches would make war on those who remained hostile, one of Calvo's treaty conditions, emphasizing that there would be no armistice unless the Chiricahuas agreed to this article. The Indians held a lengthy conference and agreed "to make war on any of their fathers, sons or brothers who should refuse to accept the good that was offered them." At this point a reference to Cochise appears. Juan José revealed that the hostiles were raiding in Sonora and that one party, led by Chees, or Chis, had left the San Francisco River on a raid into Mexico. This undoubtedly was Cochise and indicates that he had been successful in war since the outbreak in 1831. For a young warrior to attract a following, he must have proved himself an able leader in raids and war. Other raiding parties under Pisago also were out, and Juan José mentioned them because he felt that they should have one last opportunity to accept the treaty. If they refused, he declared, his followers would attack the hostiles, which, of course, was purely lip service.[49]

The agreement was signed on March 31, 1835, by sixteen leaders who represented the moderate faction of the three Chiricahua bands. Because only half the Chiricahuas were represented, the judicious Justiniani was less than sanguine about the prospects for a stable or enduring peace without first gaining the consent of Pisago Cabezón and Fuerte. They were unquestionably the leaders of the hostiles, and both were said to be adamantly opposed to any agreement until they had avenged Tutije's death. Recognizing this, Justiniani cautioned his superiors that the treaty "cannot be considered complete because the Mescaleros and twelve other capitancillos were absent." Those not present included Pisago, Fuerte, Mano Mocha, Teboca, and Vivora.[50] Chees is conspicuously absent, indicating that Cochise probably was in Pisago Cabezón's following.

The other important issue was to gain the participation of Sonora; consequently, Justiniani dispatched Matías to Ures. Sonora, however, was in no mood to negotiate and refused to recognize the treaty. José María Elías González[51] and Bustamente scoffed at the idea of making peace: "A thousand times they have asked for peace and frequently have abused the indulgences which we have granted them, because their requests have had no basis in a true desire for peace, but only to lull us into thinking that the end of the war has come."[52]

Throughout the spring and summer of 1835, Juan José Compá tried to induce Pisago Cabezón and the hostiles to come in, but to no avail. Chokonen groups believed camped near San Simon raided

Bavispe, Janos, and Galeana in April and May. According to Juan José, Pisago had organized two war parties, one against Sonora and the other against the Navajos in New Mexico. Justiniani passed this information on to his superiors, who forwarded it to Elías González at Arispe.[53]

Elías González had been planning an offensive, which departed Fronteras on June 12, 1835, under the direction of his cousin, Captain Antonio Comadurán, a capable field officer familiar with the Western Apaches because of his service at Tucson. His force, consisting of 402 men and two small howitzers, established a base camp at San Simon, from which his troops scoured the territory to the north, yet little was accomplished. The Chiricahuas had detected and easily eluded the intruders. Pisago had moved his people north into the rugged San Francisco Mountains and Gila River country. As a result, Comadurán's command returned to Sonora without achieving anything and the hostiles grew even more confident.[54]

A few months later the Sonoran legislature adopted harsh measures in an attempt to check the onslaught. Recognizing the ineffectiveness of their military establishment, the lawmakers declared war on the Apaches and called on each village and town to take the offensive. Citizens were required to donate funds and supplies to provision these parties. The legislature provided another incentive by authorizing a bounty of one hundred pesos for the scalp of each Apache male over the age of fourteen. Only force would compel the Chiricahuas to return to peace; if not, the alternative was extermination.[55]

A month after the September decree, the hostiles suffered a severe blow when a Sonoran detachment under Elías González found them in force in eastern Arizona. On October 27, 1835, the Mexicans surprised a ranchería and killed ten warriors, including a son of Pisago Cabezón. The Sonorans recognized many warriors who had once lived at Fronteras and Bavispe. Elías González was surprised at the discipline and tactics employed by the Chiricahuas during the fight and attributed it to the influence of Anglo-American traders, who he believed directed the Indians; two Apaches in Tucson corroborated his report. Probably he was referring to James Kirker, who, it was rumored, had joined the hostiles at this time.[56]

By late 1835, Chokonen groups had returned to the Chiricahuas.

News of their activities can be discerned from the statements of a fifteen-year-old captive who escaped from Matías's group. He testified that Matías had eight more captives and a large amount of stolen stock in his possession and confirmed reports of the clandestine trade being conducted at Santa Rita del Cobre, even naming Juan José Compá, whose ephemeral truce had ended abruptly in September, as one of the ringleaders. The Americans bartered powder and guns for stolen stock, according to the boy. Finally, alluding to the sentiment of the Chokonens, he reported that all Apaches wanted war and talked about more raids along the frontier.[57]

Events in late 1835 and early 1836 supported the lad's testimony. On December 18 hostiles killed a man at Cuchuta. The next week they raided Galeana and in early January wiped out a party of five vaqueros at Hacienda de San Pedro, which probably forced its abandonment.[58] Depredations continued in the spring of 1836. A large Chiricahua war party struck near Fronteras in April and killed four citizens before continuing into the interior for more raids.[59]

That spring, Elías González received information which appalled him. According to reports, an enormous force of Navajos, Utes, and Apaches was planning an expedition into Sonora, in particular against Bavispe and Santa Cruz. As with most Chiricahua war parties, revenge again was the motive, this time to avenge the death of Pisago Cabezón's son and the execution of Tutije. Although this force did not materialize—the three tribes were not allies—the report apparently was taken seriously.[60]

The deteriorating condition of the frontier forced Elías González to reappraise Sonora's position. In an abrupt policy reversal, he rationalized that a peace plan was his only option. After all, Sonora had received no aid from Mexico City and the two campaigns of 1835 had accomplished little. His state had neither the money nor the manpower to defeat or even curtail the hostiles. The militaristic policy had failed.[61]

Like Sonora, the Chokonens looked favorably on an armistice. They had been at war for some four years; stock had been accumulated, honors won, and they had proved themselves capable foes of the Mexicans. Pisago Cabezón sounded out the military commander at Santa Rita del Cobre in May and June of 1836 but nothing of substance was resolved. Consequently, Cochise's people turned to Sonora. On August 30, five Chokonen leaders—Relles, Matías, Marcelo, Eugenio, and Miguel[62] (probably Miguel Narbona)—met at Elías González's home at Arispe and agreed to fifteen articles of peace. Both parties promised to reconvene at Fronteras in October to consummate the arrangement.[63]

Elías González had considerable experience, knowledge, and ability in dealing with the Chiricahuas. He became cautiously optimistic about the Chokonen peace solicitations, primarily because Pisago Cabezón had also expressed such desires. He recognized that Sonora must provide subsistence to obviate Chiricahua raiding, so on September 27 he wrote the governor, explained his plan of issuing rations, and asked for advice. The governor's response failed to address the problem but did endorse what Elías González was trying to accomplish; however, the source of funds to finance the operation was largely ignored.[64]

Undaunted, Elias González reached Fronteras in late October and, surprisingly, met Pisago Cabezón. He had just arrived from Santa Rita del Cobre, where, a few weeks earlier, citizens had turned on some peaceful Chiricahuas, killing one woman and two men. The deaths were especially brutal; one man was killed in cold blood and the other two Indians were "beaten, stabbed, speared and shot to death." The two warriors were said to have married into Pisago's family. Incensed, Pisago decided to open talks with Sonora. The entire Chokonen band was present or camped nearby, including Cochise, though it seems doubtful that he participated in the talks. To his surprise, Elías González discovered that Chihenne chiefs Boca Matada (Thick Lips) and Caballo Ligero (Fast Horse) were present and had consented to the articles. The Sonoran leader assigned the Chokonens to live at Cuchuverachi, some ten miles south of San Bernardino, and appointed Marcelo general. He gave the Chihennes the territory from Santa Lucía to the Gila River and named Boca Matada general. Yet neither party could have expected the peace to endure; rations were not a part of the agreement, and the Chiricahuas had not made peace with Chihuahua. More ominous, most of the Chihennes and Nednhis were still hostile.[65]

To remedy this, Elías González sent Pisago Cabezón to Santa

Rita del Cobre on a dual mission. First, he would try to negotiate a
truce with Chihuahua; second, he would try to persuade the hostile
Chihennes and Nednhis to make peace. Pisago and Caballo Ligero
did meet with Robert McKnight and Captain José María Arze, who
informed Calvo of the proceedings. Calvo instructed Arze to make a
tentative peace until formal talks could be held, but by the time Arze
arrived at the mines, the impatient Apaches had left. On January 26,
1837, the captain reported that the Chiricahuas had resumed hostilities, raiding Santa Rita del Cobre and fleeing west. Therefore, he
wrote, "I have inferred that they do not wish peace." [66]

Actually, most of the Chokonens and some of the Chihennes had
decided to live in the area stipulated by the treaty. Fuerte was the
one exception, chooisng to remain aloof in the Mogollons. The
Chokonens encamped near the present Arizona-Sonora line; Marcelo was camped at Embudos Canyon, [67] a few miles southeast of
Cuchuverachi; and other groups, under Relles and Matías, were
living at Sarampion, which was in the lower Peloncillos due east of
the southern Chiricahua Mountains.

After a few months of peace it became clear that Chihuahua's inability to consummate an agreement would cause trouble. In February a Chokonen war party raided that state and returned to Sonora
with some five hundred head of stock. Immediately after that,
buoyed by success, thirty warriors left for a foray into Chihuahua.
Marcelo could not control his young warriors; within days the
Sonoran frontier was hit. [68]

On February 18, 1837, Teboca, a first-class hostile, with a few of
his young men and two incorrigibles from Sayo Siza's group (San
Juan and Rapado) surrounded several men about seven miles from
Fronteras, stripped them, and stole five horses and two hundred
cattle. The citizens' testimony clearly identified the Indians involved in the shakedown. Luiso Romero declared: "I know the chief
Teboca very well. . . . I have seen him at this presidio several times
when he has come here for peace." José Escalante informed the prefect of Arispe, who immediately requested additional information,
implying that he hoped the Indians had not been abused. [69]

Escalante assured the prefect that the Apaches had been treated
well, but they have "laughed at our friendship." At the same time,

the military commander at Fronteras wrote Elías González supporting Escalante's version. After weighing these statements, Elías
González summarily declared that all Chiricahuas not at Fronteras
by March 19 "would immediately thereafter be considered declared
enemies." His decision was not an impulsive one, for he had received several reports about Apache raiding parties. Apaches had
continued to harass the San Bernardino ranch, stealing much stock.
Thus, he concluded, "there is no longer any doubt that the previously mentioned Apaches have broken the peace treaties." He suggested joint punitive action with Chihuahua against the hostiles.[70]

Elías González's intuition proved correct. Most of the Chokonens
fled, especially those who had been raiding in Chihuahua. Relles
and Matías brought their followers to Fronteras but remained in
touch with relatives who left. Marcelo and Vivora ignored the order
and joined the hostiles under Juan José Compá. Cochise's whereabouts were not positively known. He probably left with the hostiles
and may have been in the vicinity for the Johnson massacre, which a
Chiricahua described as the first in "a series of treacherous attacks
made upon us by whites or Mexicans."[71]

The Chiricahuas had begun raiding in March 1837 when they
killed two men escorting a wagon train from Janos to Santa Rita del
Cobre and struck in the Janos–Casas Grandes region, where their
depredations "were preventing agriculture."[72] In Sonora "the frontier towns were helpless" to take action. Governor Escalante y Arvizu issued another timeworn proclamation, declaring: "These ferocious indigents . . . have multiplied their incursions committing all
the atrocities to which they are inclined by their natural bloodthirsty
character." The government was "destitute of resources" and required assistance in food, arms, and money. "War to the death to
the enemy" was the proclamation.[73]

A few weeks after this declaration, Apaches raided the Noria
ranch, which was some thirty miles north of Moctezuma, killing
several people and capturing some women and children. It was
about this time that Charles Ames and a group of Missouri mule
buyers arrived at Moctezuma in the hope of purchasing mules, but
there were none because the hostiles had cleaned out the area, Ames
conferred with John Johnson,[74] an Anglo living in Sonora, and they

decided to pursue the Apaches. Governor Escalante y Arvizu had granted Johnson permission to track down hostiles; whether it was oral, in writing, or just a tacit approval based on the governor's proclamation of early March mattered little. Johnson's compensation would be half of all stolen stock recovered, which satisfied the American's requirements. So the scenario was set: Johnson, seventeen Anglos, and five Mexicans left Moctezuma on April 3. At this point there was no evidence to indicate that Escalante y Arvizu sent Johnson out specifically to get Juan José Compá, as some reports asserted. It was purely happenstance that Johnson eventually came across Juan José's band and not another. Either way, the results would probably have been the same.

Johnson's party followed an Apache trail to Fronteras, where he arrived on April 12 and conferred with the commanding officer, Antonio Narbona.[75] Narbona attempted to dissuade him from continuing by pointing out that the Apaches far outnumbered his small party. Nonetheless, Johnson opted to go on, and Narbona gave him a small cannon or swivel gun. His decision was not as reckless as it seemed. Anglo-Americans were generally on good terms with the Chiricahuas. With a pack train of loaded mules, Johnson hoped the Apaches would perceive him as another Anglo trader, and common sense dictates that this was the case, given the ease by which he made contact with the Indians.

On April 20, Johnson arrived at Agua Fría Springs, located somewhere in the Animas Mountains in southwestern New Mexico, a range that bordered the territory of the three Chiricahua bands. Several rancherías were in the vicinity. Juan José Compá's and Juan Diego Compá's Nednhis were present, as were Chokonens under Marcelo and Vivora. The Apaches should have been somewhat suspicious, for most of the clandestine commerce had taken place along the Mimbres or at Santa Rita del Cobre. Nonetheless, the two groups talked, Johnson claiming they were going to Santa Rita, and agreed to trade, although the Anglos and perhaps the Apaches had treachery in mind. Either that day or the next, the Apaches sold Lautura García,[76] who had been a captive for an undetermined amount of time. According to Johnson, she told him the Indians planned to ambush his party en route to Santa Rita del Cobre.

Friday, April 21, passed without any problems. A profitable trade

ensued, with the Apaches receiving whiskey and other sundries in
return for their stolen mules. Juan José conceded that he would continue hostilities, but in the months to come he claimed that he would
attempt a truce with Sonora; he also boasted that Relles, the Chokonen leader living near Fronteras, reported to him on troop strength
and movements. According to Johnson, Lautora García had warned
him that Juan José was scheming to lead the Americans into an ambush, yet in her testimony at Moctezuma she failed to mention any
Apache double-dealing. In fact, she declared that in the short time
she was a captive she could not understand "their language or their
customs." She characterized relations of the first two days as having
"passed with much friendship." April 22 would be different, although the Chiricahuas seemingly had no reason to suspect the
contrary.[77]

That evening and early on the morning of April 22, Johnson and
his party plotted their treachery; the five Mexicans refused to partake and left during the night. Early the next morning, the Chiricahuas returned to trade and Johnson sprang his surprise. Lautora
García testified that while trading "pañocha and piñole, and when
the Apaches were all mounted, the Americans fired the cannon
charged with metallic scraps" and made an enormous carnage in human bodies. Lautora García was uncertain about the number of casualties, saying only that many were wounded. The fact that the Indians were mounted indicates that they were either just arriving or
just leaving. Regardless, the attack caught them by surprise. After
the first blast, the seventeen Anglo marksmen finished off the deed.
When the slaughter was over, twenty Apaches lay scattered on the
field, including Juan José Compá, Juan Diego Compá, and Marcelo;
certainly many more were wounded and, more important, indelible
psychological scars were left, which deepened the chasm of distrust
between Chiricahuas and all white men.[78]

After the butchery, Johnson quickly retreated to Janos. On April 24
he wrote the governor of Chihuahua and furnished details of his
"battle" with eighty Apaches:

> As I recognized their superior numbers, I delayed my attack from
> the 20th until 10 o'clock in the morning of the 22nd, not feeling it
> possible to wait for a longer time on account of the acts of mistrust

and treachery that I observed from their preparations . . . despite the dangers and obstacles that stood in its way . . . as a result there were left on the field of battle twenty dead Indian renegades, including the three chiefs, Marcelo, Juan José and Juan Diego, whose scalps I have presented to the commander of this presidio [Janos].[79]

Johnson's report was noteworthy for what it did not contain. For example, he failed to mention anything about the cannon, nor did he explain how he killed twenty Apaches without loss to his party.

From Janos, Johnson returned to Moctezuma via Bavispe, where, according to one report, he left the scalps of the three Chiricahua chiefs. At Moctezuma his official report was submitted to authorities; at the same time, Lautora García gave her version. This account was forwarded to Sonora's commanding general, who shuffled it to the governor of Sonora, who passed it along to the minister of war and navy in Mexico City. The deed done, Johnson was compensated with one hundred pesos, seemingly closing the incident.[80]

Many accounts of the Johnson affair, as it became known, were published in the nineteenth century, and each progressively added its own unsubstantiated details. Rex Strickland's article in *Arizona and the West,* based largely on Johnson's official report, sheds immense light on a previously ambiguous incident. It clears up the conjecture as to where the massacre took place, the number of Apache casualties, and some of the circumstances surrounding the attack, yet Strickland's assessment that this new information "reduces the event to its relative trivial dimensions" would have been passionately disputed by Apaches who knew of the event in the nineteenth century.[81]

The perfidious massacre would not be forgotten; to the Apaches, its ramifications were both immediate and enduring. As for Cochise, he probably was not present but might have been in the vicinity. He certainly became aware of the tragedy and joined other Chiricahuas to avenge Johnson's deed. Fifteen years later his father-in-law, Mangas Coloradas, bitterly recalled the incident:

> At another [time] a trader was sent among us from Chihuahua. While innocently engaged in trading, often leading to words of anger, a cannon concealed behind the goods was fired upon my people and quite a number killed.[82]

Mrs. Eve Ball and Jason Betzinez mention the incident. From their accounts it is clear that the Apaches perceived the Johnson affair as one of the worst things ever perpetrated on them, at least until James Kirker got into the act a few years later.[83]

Not all parties in Mexico applauded Johnson's deed. From Mexico City came concerns about the incident, although they were not focused on the inhumanity of it. The minister of war and navy asked Elías González to explain why Sonora permitted an armed party of foreigners to make war against the Apaches. By foreigners he obviously was referring to Americans, with whom Mexico now had uneasy relations over the Texas question. Elías González was ordered to make a "positive and official report" and was admonished that "armed men who are not in your command cannot operate in the territory of this Republic." Governor Escalante y Arvizu responded, and his answer, politically motivated, deliberately distorted the facts. On July 20, 1837, he wrote Sonora's commanding general:

> Your lordship knows very well that it was not a company of armed adventurers that carried out this campaign, as has been falsely reported at the highest level of the government. It was rather several Americans, many of them intermarried and living as neighbors.

Up to this point Escalante y Arvizu was stretching things, but his next statements border on the absurdity:

> However they [Americans] were not going to pursue the Apaches alone, but rather as support troops for a party of Sonoran patriots who had offered to do it at their own expense. Only through mischance and error were the latter prevented from participating in the fighting done by these foreigners together with five Mexicans.

The reply was clearly intended to close the investigation and appease authorities in Mexico City, who Sonora justifiably felt were too far removed to understand the realities of the situation. The governor concluded his report by assuring them that he "would never allow in [Sonora] a gathering of armed adventurers . . . this is especially true considering the current state of the relationship existing between the Republic and the nation to which belong the individuals who have performed this service."[84]

Apache reaction to Johnson's deed was predictable, as it was after Kirker's slaughter at Galeana in 1846, Carrasco's clandestine attack at Janos in 1851, Lieutenant George N. Bascom's egregious handling of the incident at Apache Pass in 1861, and the California Volunteers' cold-blooded killing of Mangas Coloradas in 1863. In all occasions the natural and only Chiricahua response was revenge, hopefully on the parties responsible, but, as one individual expressed it, "they go after anything, a troop of cavalry, a town. They are angry. They fight anyone to get even." [85]

# Chapter 3

# TURBULENT TIMES

The Chiricahua sword of justice materialized immediately after the Johnson affair. Near the Gila the Indians reportedly wiped out a group of twenty-two trappers known as the Kemp party and soon after that massacred a wagon train of twelve men en route to El Paso from Santa Fe.[1] That fall they struck northwest Chihuahua. On September 25, 1837, they captured a young boy named Felipe de Jesús Fuente from Galeana; three days later they attacked a party near Casas Grandes, killing two citizens and wounding four others. On October 1 they stole eighty cattle and eleven horses from Ramos, a hacienda some fifteen miles south of Janos, then raided Janos itself, perhaps because Johnson had retreated there after the carnage. On October 26 the Chiricahuas ambushed two men and two women harvesting crops, and six weeks later a large war party killed a judge and eight other people at Ramos, which forced its abandonment.[2]

These raids convinced Mexico that the Chiricahuas must be stopped. That fall Chihuahua Governor Simon Elías wrote Sonora Governor Manuel Escalante y Arvizu and proposed a joint campaign specifically to punish the Chiricahuas. His plan called for a four-hundred-man force to campaign for six months, using Santa Rita del Cobre as a base. This constant pressure would compel the Chiricahuas to sue for peace, or so the two governors believed. Like so many others, the plan never got off the ground; lack of money and political instability forced postponement.[3]

As 1838 dawned, Simon Elías continued to press for a large army to penetrate Apachería and subjugate the hostiles, but conflicts between rival political factions forced these plans to be scaled down. In Sonora, new Governor José Urrea, a veteran of the Alamo and other historic battles of the Texas revolt against Mexico in 1836, recognizing that the northern presidios must forsake their defensive posture, put two experienced and competent officers in charge of the northern command. Lieutenant Colonel José María Martínez was given command of the presidios of Tubac, Santa Cruz, and Tucson, which in turn was reinforced with troops from Altar, and Captain Ignacio López was placed in charge of the presidios of Bacoachi, Bavispe, and Fronteras. These two commanders, in conjunction with national troops under the intrepid José Ignacio Terán y Tato,[4] were ordered to carry the war into Apachería and keep scouting detachments in the field at all times.[5]

The commands were soon in action. Toward the end of January 1838, Apaches burned the Bacanuchi hacienda near Bacoachi. Immediately Captain Francisco Narbona pursued, killing two hostiles before they vanished into the mountains. About the same time at Santa Cruz, Apaches stole six hundred cattle and were pursued, although unsuccessfully. In February, Urrea ordered his new commanders to scout Apachería. Martínez's command reconnoitered Western Apache territory but was impeded by heavy snows in the mountains; nonetheless, he managed to destroy one ranchería. Meanwhile, in Chokonen country, one hundred warriors ambushed López's detachment, but the Mexicans drove them to the mountains and out of Sonora, or so they reported, before returning to Fronteras.[6]

As it turned out, many of the Chokonens had moved east into Chihenne territory, though not as a consequence of Sonora's efforts. Early that spring Pisago Cabezón called a tribal council, with the leaders concluding to send two war parties against Mexico. The first group of two hundred warriors would be commanded by Tapilá,[7] an up-and-coming Chokonen war leader. Armed with rifles and ammunition purchased from Anglo traders, this band, said to have been accompanied by James Kirker, roared into Sonora and swept down the western slopes of the Sierra Madre. The second group, under Pisago, planned to waylay the wagon train which brought provisions to Santa Rita del Cobre.[8]

In recent years the mines had become unprofitable to operate. Moreover, since the Johnson attack, small Apache raiding parties had annoyed the diggings. No full-scale attack had taken place because Apache war parties found other targets more profitable, and more vulnerable, in Sonora and Chihuahua. Pisago's objective, as with most war parties, was revenge and plunder, in this case the supply train's livestock and provisions.

On March 26 the Chiricahuas moved south by way of the Florida Mountains to Carrizalillo Springs, where Pisago prepared to ambush the whites before they reached the springs. On March 30, Ambrosio Tachan's wagons were moving unsuspectingly through the pass when, about 3 P.M., the Indians swept down on the cattle herd, which was ahead of the main party. The escort and several Americans pushed forward but were unable to do much; the Indians reportedly numbered four hundred—three hundred mounted and one hundred on foot—although this estimate seems too high. The whites halted abruptly and the confident Apaches fell back to the springs, daring their adversaries to attack. There was sporadic gunfire the rest of the day and throughout the moonlit night, but there were no casualties.

Early the next morning, Chato Pisago, son of Pisago, approached the whites, stating that he wished to parley. Pascual Mora ventured out and talked with Chato, who declared that Pisago wished to speak with a citizen from Janos. After a few tense moments, Gabriel Zapata, trusting the Indians, left the wagons and met Pisago Cabezón.

A few years later George W. Kendall met a Chiricahua chief who might have been Pisago. He described the Indian as "middle height, strong and well built, some sixty-five or seventy years of age, and with hair as white as snow." Zapata recalled that

> Pisago came down and the two Indians [Chato and Pisago] together greeted and embraced me. After speaking about several things in a friendly manner Pisago said, "I want peace, I don't want to fight." I answered saying that although I was only a servant of the hacienda I would risk my life and that should they let the wagons and the people pass, I would remain with their band until he should receive a guarantee of protection from either Don Roberto [Robert McKnight] or from the Governor. Pisago agreed to this.

The agreement was short lived and somewhat questionable, for this was a major war party intent on revenge and loot. In any event, Bernavé, a renegade Mexican who once lived at Santa Rita del Cobre, reminded Pisago of the recent atrocities inflicted by whites on the Apaches. First he cited those Indians killed in the Johnson massacre and others who had been "beaten to death with sticks" at Santa Rita del Cobre. Furthermore, since the wagons belonged to Robert McKnight, "the greatest rascal there is," they "should not pass, nor the Americans," insisted Bernavé. Pisago took this under advisement and conferred with his leaders. A short time later he returned with other chiefs, including Manuel Chirimni, who wanted to kill Zapata, but this Pisago would not permit. He allowed Zapata to return with the Indians' demand to "abandon everything and they would not be attacked." Either that day or the next (April 2), the whites abandoned the entire train of ten wagons and its supplies and returned to Janos, arriving there with only twenty-two horses.[9]

Shortly after Pisago seized its provisions, the Chiricahuas attacked Santa Rita del Cobre, killing several citizens and wounding a few others. With the miners desperate for supplies, another train with a seventy-man escort was dispatched from Galeana on May 6. A few Apaches were seen, but no trouble occurred. It was the last supply train to the mines; sometime in late June the diggings were deserted and the public property was transferred to Janos.[10]

No evidence has been found to support John C. Cremony's account that "every man, woman and child" who left the mines was cut off and killed "except for four or five."[11] Two contemporary accounts, one by Frederick A. Wislizenus, who journeyed through northern Mexico in 1846–47, and the other by John Russell Bartlett, an associate of Cremony, left behind reliable versions obtained from citizens. Neither mentioned anything about a wholesale slaughter. Wislizenus wrote that the mines "had to be abandoned on account of hostile Indians, who killed some of the workmen, and attacked the trains."[12] Bartlett was more specific, obviously referring to Pisago's fight at Carrizalillo Springs. He described the ambush in which the Indians took the wagons, mules, and horses, "first giving each who accompanied the train a mule to carry him away. At the same time they sent word to the inhabitants of the Copper Mines that they would allow no further supplies to reach them and, furthermore, would destroy them whenever an opportunity offered, [therefore] the people determined to abandon the place." [13]

In Sonora the situation was just as perilous in the late 1830s. Its presidios, poorly equipped and sparsely garrisoned, were incapable of preventing raids or of mounting offensives, and political instability continued to disrupt affairs. The two rival groups, Gándara's and Urrea's, continued their fight for control of the state rather than focusing their energies on the Apaches. [14] Despite some insignificant Mexican successes (in the summer of 1838 troops killed four warriors near Santa Cruz and a chief and two warriors near Fronteras), the Apaches controlled the frontier, with little resistance from Sonora. [15]

The summer of 1839 was no better. The Indians' audacity increased to the point where they murdered a man inside a house at Santa Cruz and in August ambushed and killed two soldiers outside the corral at Bavispe. [16] Finally, in November 1839, Gándara's and Urrea's forces stopped fighting each other long enough for Manuel María Gándara to lead a campaign to the Mimbres River in southern New Mexico. Gándara's troops killed seventeen warriors, including, he believed, Pisago Cabezón (which proved to be untrue), and confiscated nineteen American rifles. [17] The expedition had little effect and in 1840 the Chiricahuas continued their depredations in Sonora. Authorities continued to blame Sonora's impotence on the turmoil caused by internal conflict. "Since the beginning of the Revolution of 1838, the troops of this department have been occupied in defeating it, leaving few troops to fight the Apaches." [18]

In the late 1830s, Chihuahua suffered heavily from renewed Chiricahua raiding. Affairs were at a low ebb: mines were abandoned, haciendas deserted, and public roads had become increasingly unsafe. Recognizing that presidio troops were no match for the mobile, quick-striking Apaches, its government, influenced by businessmen, opted for a course of action differing from that of its neighbor to the east. Stephen Courcier, once Robert McKnight's partner at Santa Rita, had become one of the wealthiest and most influential men in Chihuahua. He urged the governor to organize a private army of mercenaries to kill as many Apaches as possible—hopefully every hostile living. On April 9, 1839, Courcier called a meeting of the "Society to Make War," appointed the ubiquitous James Kirker to organize the group, and called for public donations of one hundred thousand pesos to support it. Kirker, described as a "blue eyed, gray haired and gray whiskered man . . . short and stout," accepted the position without reservation.[19]

He was a logical choice; he knew the Apaches and was thoroughly acquainted with their territory and their favorite camping areas. Equally important, he was an opportunist usually prepared to take the side most profitable to him; this time it meant Chihuahuan pesos. He was an efficient and unscrupulous businessman who understood the equation that scalps plus confiscated plunder equaled cash. When Apaches were not available, it was alleged that he scalped Mexican peasants and turned their hair in for the bounty. After all, to distinguish between Apache and Mexican hair was virtually impossible. During the 1830s he had played both sides: Anglo against Apache and most recently Apache against Mexican. Now he would reverse the latter role and join the Mexicans against the Apaches. In early April, Amado de La Vega wrote to each prefect, announcing the program and requesting contributions.[20] Although the scheme was considered somewhat extreme, pubic support was enthusiastic and unanimous. On June 14, Angel Trias, president of the municipal council of Chihuahua City, issued an ordinance levying a tax on merchants to support Kirker's outfit.[21]

Kirker's force consisted mainly of American trappers, traders, and Delaware and Shawnee Indians. Over the next year he did succeed in garnering many scalps, some Mexican and some Apache, in addition to having several brushes with Cochise's people. In early 1840 he surprised Pisago's camp, reportedly killing ten warriors and capturing twenty individuals.[22] That spring, Francisco García Conde, Chihuahua's new governor, described as "a portly, handsome man," promptly canceled Kirker's contract on humanitarian grounds. He allegedly ignored Kirker's claim for thirty thousand pesos in unpaid bounty, infuriating Kirker, who exacted compensation by stealing six hundred of Conde's horses and selling them in Santa Fe, or so the story goes.[23]

Kirker's first stint in the scalp-hunting business had caused few casualties as far as the Chiricahuas were concerned. What was more significant, at least in the Apaches' perception, was the organization of a well-armed, well-provisioned, and fearless mercenary group which campaigned in Apache country. This was the only effective way of fighting Apaches, who, it should be pointed out, spent very little time making war. The Chiricahuas put little stock in planting because group campsites varied from season to season. In spring the Indians gathered fruits, vegetables, and mescal and in autumn they harvested nuts and berries. Therefore, the presence of a significant enemy force scouting their country had the potential to disrupt this element of their fragile economy.

The Chiricahuas continued at war throughout 1840 and 1841 as Apache dominance reached its highest point since the 1780s. The Indians were better armed and mounted than ever before. On top of this, their war parties frequently consisted of one hundred or more men, a far cry from their earlier hit-and-run guerrilla tactics. Chihuahua could not stop them, and in Sonora, the Chokonens' primary raiding area, conditions were even worse.

The frontier towns pleaded for additional troops, guns, and ammunition to protect themselves. The alternative, they warned, was abandonment of crops and homes. The continual Apache raids led to poor harvests in both 1840 and 1841 because most citizens were afraid to work their crops. On September 10, 1840, a raiding party stole some stock near Bacoachi. Twelve men, led by Justice of the Peace José Narbona, marched in pursuit. The Apaches were waiting and it was a rout, not a retreat. Narbona and five others were killed. Two weeks later at Cuquiarachi, some twenty-five miles northeast of Bacoachi, Apaches, probably Chokonens, slaughtered six citizens as they worked in their fields. These tragedies compelled many citizens to desert their homes for new lives, some as distant as California.[24]

In the spring of 1841, Captain Antonio Narbona, a capable officer well known to the Chiricahuas, was named commander of the frontier presidios. He had only seventy troops to cover the area from Altar to Fronteras, a distance of some two hundred miles, so of course he could do little. Raiding parties hit Bacoachi more than once that spring; no citizen dared to leave the town's security to work his crops. Narbona did his best, but scant resources meant infrequent success. His requests to superiors produced ambivalent responses from staff officers, who made weak promises of future aid and imaginary campaigns.[25] As 1841 ended the Chiricahuas definitely held the upper hand. They had retaliated with vigor and in

Cuchillo Negro. This important Chihenne chief was painted by John Mix Stanley in 1846. (*Courtesy National Museum of American Art, Smithsonian Institution, gift of the Misses Henry, 1908*)

force since the Johnson massacre, all three bands uniting in a common cause to seek revenge. It was during this period that a powerfully built Chihenne leader came to the fore. His name was Mangas Coloradas.

Mangas, who was born in the early 1790s, was literally a giant among his people, standing six feet four inches tall and weighing two hundred and fifty pounds. As with Cochise, little is known of his early life, although stories and legends abound. He first appeared in documents in 1842, when he was identified as the leader of the hostile Mogollons, probably the branch of the tribe the Chiricahuas called Bedonkohes. Since his status was not achieved overnight, he was undoubtedly known by another name prior to this time. His Spanish name, meaning "red sleeves" or "roan shirt" (either because he wore shirts with red sleeves or because the blood of his victims splattered his shirt), may have been acquired during the tumultuous period after the Juan José Compá massacre. What name he went by before this is not known, but it is possible that he was related to or known as Fuerte, the dominant Chihenne leader from 1815 through the 1830s. Fuerte, whose name implied a strong physique, lived near the Mimbres and Santa Rita del Cobre before disappearing about 1840, when Mangas Coloradas came to the fore. It is possible that Mangas was in the shadow of such Chihenne leaders as Fuerte and Mano Mocha and succeeded them as their influence waned. By 1840 these chiefs were aging and Chihenne leaders like Mangas, Cuchillo Negro, Itán, and Delgadito began to attract followings on the local-group level. In late 1842 a report from Janos noted that Mangas had relatives among the Apaches who were at Fronteras and those living in the Chiricahua Mountains. Cochise certainly would have been in one of these groups.[26]

Cochise must have accompanied Mangas Coloradas on many of the latter's incursions. In the late 1830s or early 1840s he married a daughter of Mangas and Tu-es-seh named Dos-teh-seh ("something at the campfire already cooked"), who was his principal wife throughout his life.[27] Chiricahua custom required a man to live with the local group or band to which his wife belonged; in Cochise's case, perhaps following a brief six- to eight-month trial period, he returned to live with his Chokonens because his status among his people made him too valuable to be gone very long. According to one anthropologist, "the sons of prominent men were obliged to stay close at home."[28] In any event, the relationship between Cochise and Mangas Coloradas developed and was nurtured in the years that followed.

For reasons not altogether clear, in early 1842 many Chiricahua leaders decided to make peace with Mexico. The venerable Pisago Cabezón and the aged Mano Mocha were the leading proponents of an armistice; Mangas Coloradas led the dissenting minority. Many Chiricahuas simply had grown tired of war and peace offered a respite from the five-year conflict: they could mend fences and forestall Mexican campaigns. Consequently, in early April 1842, Mano Mocha appeared at Janos and requested an end to hostilities. After a short council, Captain Pedro Madrigal issued him a pass for safe conduct to Chihuahua City to speak with the governor.[29] Some sort of preliminary agreement was reached, for by the end of April other groups arrived at Janos to discuss terms. On May 11, Chihuahua's commanding general appointed a peace commissioner to consummate a treaty.[30]

As a result, on May 23, Pisago Cabezón sent Vicente, two warriors, and seven women to Janos. The next day, however, they departed abruptly, fearing "they would be betrayed, just as happened at El Paso."[31] This excited Janos's citizens and soldiers and they braced for hostilities. Captain Madrigal must have heaved a sigh of relief when the Chokonen chief Manuel returned to Janos in early June and again emphasized his desire for an armistice.[32] Prospects looked so favorable that *La Luna,* the official state newspaper, editorialized: "It is probable, it is necessary, it is useful, and it is urgent." Accordingly, in late June, Governor García Conde left the capital to conclude the agreement, arriving at Janos on June 27.[33]

The treaty was signed on July 4, 1842, with Pisago Cabezón, Ponce,[34] and other leaders representing the Indians, who consented to cease hostilities, to deliver all captives and stolen horses, to establish their rancherías near Janos, and to make war on the hostile Mescaleros. In return, García Conde, recognizing that the peace treaties of 1832 and 1835 had failed because of Mexico's refusal to issue rations, agreed to feed the Indians. He authorized weekly rations, which consisted of three *almudes* of corn (about two and one-half liters), tobacco, sugar, and meat. Afterward, García Conde went south to San Buenaventura, where Torres and Cristóbal were waiting; they agreed to the same conditions. Significantly, Sonora was not mentioned, possibly because groups of Chokonens had been negotiating at Fronteras.[35]

In mid-July a few Indians filtered into Janos, and in early August other Chokonens arrived, including Pisago. A force commanded by Colonel Elías González had forged into northeastern Sonora on a search-and-destroy mission directed at hostiles under Mangas Coloradas, and its presence concerned Pisago, who asked Madrigal at Janos for protection. Madrigal promptly dispatched four soldiers to warn González to stay out of Chihuahua. Satisfied with these actions, Pisago brought thirty warriors, fifty-five women, and eighty-six children to Janos in August. Cochise did not come in, apparently remaining with Mangas Coloradas at Alamo Hueco.[36]

In all likelihood Cochise had spent part of 1842 in the neighborhood of Fronteras. Many Chokonens under Esquinaline,[37] Teboca,
and Yrigóllen[38] had been encamped near there since early 1842,
waiting to hear whether Sonora would grant them peace and assistance. Their patience had waned by late summer. Sonora's campaign, coupled with the prospect of rations at Janos, persuaded
Teboca and Esquinaline to join Mangas Coloradas at Alamo Hueco;
Yrigóllen moved southeast to San Buenaventura. Cochise and about
ten warriors eventually split from Mangas Coloradas and joined
Pisago's followers at Janos. Cochise first drew rations on October 17,
1842, with his wife joining him on October 24 and October 31. In all
probability, this was Dos-teh-seh, daughter of Mangas Coloradas,
who may have sent his son-in-law to ascertain Mexican treatment of
the Indians. Cochise remained at Janos until early November, and
his name was absent from the ration rolls until the following July.

Janos, Chihuahua. Ruins of the presidio where Cochise received rations in
1842–44 and 1857. (*Photo by Dan Thrapp*)

In light of subsequent events it would seem likely that he returned to his father-in-law and reported favorably on affairs at Janos, for Mangas, who had steadfastly opposed peace, did an abrupt about-face and decided to negotiate.[39]

The great Chihenne sent word in late 1842 that he wished to talk. Chihuahua resonded quickly, inviting him in for a parley. At Janos the peace commissioner, Vicente Sanchez Vergara, succeeded in gathering an authoritative representation of chiefs and held talks with Mangas Coloradas, Itán, Cuchillo Negro, and Teboca in late January or early February. If Cochise was present, he was in the background. The Chiricahua leaders promised to bring in their people that March to conclude the armistice.[40] As a result, Chihuahua's commanding general, Mariano Monterde, left Chihuahua City and reached Janos on March 25 or 26. Mangas arrived on the twenty-eighth and conferred with Monterde for the next four days. Monterde recognized that the Indians were extremely apprehensive because of past Mexican treachery, alluding to the Johnson affair, Kirker's scalp-hunting expedition, and the unprovoked attack at Paso del Norte. Yet as the proceedings developed, Monterde became impressed with the Indians' punctuality, their sincerity, and the importance with which they viewed peace.

Mangas agreed to the same conditions Pisago Cabezón had accepted some nine months before and before departing agreed to send Apache emissaries to Sonora to meet with Governor Urrea. Accordingly, Negrito, the venerable Matías, and Marcelo (another of Pisago's sons), accompanied by Captain Vergara, went to Ures in mid-May and then on to Guaymas, which they reached on June 2. Here they conferred with Urrea, who agreed to peace as long as the Apaches refrained from depredations in his state. In essence, if the Apaches left the Sonorans alone, Sonora would reciprocate.[41]

This ephemeral period of good relations was not destined to continue. Ironically, the truce was already doomed by the time the agreement was made. While the Mexican-Apache peace party was negotiating with Urrea, troops at Fronteras murdered six Chokonen men for no apparent reason. The incident was indicative of the volatility of relations between the two races. In late May, Western Apaches (referred to as Coyoteros to distinguish them from Cochise's Chiricahuas) stole some stock at Fronteras. At the time of the raid, seven Chiricahua men were at the presidio. They volunteered to help the soldiers and after a short pursuit succeeded in recovering most of the stock. At this point, for some inexplicable reason, the Sonoran troops turned their weapons on the Apaches; only one escaped. These cold-blooded murders demanded an Apache response, so Mangas and Pisago retaliated by attacking Fronteras and killing two citizens and wounding one. The militant Chiricahuas were once again at war with Sonora.[42]

Notwithstanding the renewed hostilities with Sonora, many Chiricahuas continued to live in peace at Janos, but the hostiles continued to find refuge and a market for their spoils. Although Janos's authorities knew where the stock and loot came from, they apparently made no attempt to stop it, even rationing those Apaches who returned with the blood and spoils of their victims. Though many of the Chiricahuas had kept their agreements at Janos, the hostiles gave the whole group a bad reputation, at least in the eyes of Sonora.

Cochise was active during this time, stopping in at Janos (his name spelled *Chuchese,* as it would be by Arizonans twenty-five years later) for rations on July 24, 1843. The next week he was not present, but an Indian woman named D-Tosa, perhaps a corruption of Dos-teh-seh, with a child (perhaps his eldest son, Taza, born about 1842) did receive rations. Also present was a woman named María de Chis with two sons. Whether she was another wife of Cochise will probably never be known. He was a polygamous man, so it was possible that they were his relations who were killed before Anglo contact. He disappeared for the next four months, probably joining Mangas and Pisago in southwestern New Mexico. If so, he had a hand in the bloody events of 1843, when Chiricahuas began raiding ruthlessly into Sonora and retreating to Janos to dispose of their booty.[43]

In Sonora, the energetic Elías González would not stand still. On July 20 he wrote Monterde to advise him that he was planning an expedition against the hostiles. An apprehensive Monterde admonished Elías González to punish only those hostiles found in Sonora. Furthermore, he warned, he would consider it a serious crime if any Sonoran troops trespassed into Chihuahua. Monterde at once instructed Captain Madrigal to inform the Janos Apaches of Sonora's campaign, at the same time emphasizing that Chihuahua intended to live up to its end of the treaty.[44]

Savage raids continued throughout 1843, and many appeared to be the work of Apaches drawing rations at Janos. In late September, Sonora's governor complained to Mexico City about the raids, but there was no response. A few months later a Fronteras citizen wrote the prefect of Arispe a despairing letter, which the prefect forwarded to the minister of war in Mexico City. The letter charged that prior to Chihuahua's peace treaty in June 1842 the Apaches

> used to steal both in that Department and in this one in order to sell in New Mexico, with which they were not at war. Since then it is only Sonora that bears the burden of their depredations. . . . Since the towns of Chihuahua are so close by, in a very short space of time the barbarians come over to our towns and commit murders and robberies. Evading the vigilance of our troops, with the quickness of lightning they go back to their camps, where they are protected and defended from punishment by the Commander of Janos.[45]

Federal officials demanded a response from Chihuahua. On January 13, 1844, Monterde, who seemed preoccupied with justifying every move he made, vehemently denied the allegations. In fact, he asserted, his administration had stopped the bloodshed and had effectively destroyed the age-long practice of Apaches raiding into one state and seeking refuge in another. He also pointed out that in the spring of 1843 he had sent Apache leaders to Sonora, where they had made peace. He tersely remarked that Sonora's problems began shortly after soldiers at Fronteras treacherously murdered several Chiricahuas near that presidio. Since then, those Apaches, not the ones living in peace at Janos, had retaliated against Sonora. He closed by citing examples of Apache cooperation in returning stolen stock and assisting troops against the hostiles. It was true that many of the Chiricahuas living at Janos under Manuelito, Chinaca, and Láceris had not been raiding in Sonora; unfortunately for them, beginning in the summer of 1843, they became guilty by association when many of the hostile Chokonens, including Cochise, arrived with Sonoran loot and irregularly received rations.[46]

Conditions intensified in the fall when many Chiricahuas relocated to Janos from Galeana, where smallpox had broken out. Yrigóllen arrived the first week of October, and a month later Coleto Amarillo, a prominent Nednhi leader, began drawing rations. That fall, rations were issued to perhaps eight hundred Chiricahuas. Cochise was at Corralitos from November 27 through December 25 with a group under Relles and Ponce, who was said to have been a good friend of Cochise. Also present were two men named Collotura (Coyuntura) and Juan, both married, both probably brothers of Cochise.[47]

Compounding the lethal arrival of smallpox was another long-standing problem: inadequate rations. The previous spring, Madrigal had reported that his supply of rations was nearly depleted. This forced him to request assistance from residents, which increased tensions between the two parties; any incident could lead to war. In November 1843, Madrigal told his superiors the Indians had become surly and had abused several citizens. This, he wrote, could be attributed to the "lack of military personnel and insufficient rations." By early 1844, affairs had quickly got out of hand once more. Some 600 to 700 Indians were present throughout December, but only 200 remained on January 15, 1844, the number falling to 120 the following week. Most had left because of the smallpox epidemic; a few had contracted the disease and in February several men died, including two minor leaders, Chinaca and Chato Pisago.[48]

By February most of the Indians still healthy had returned to the mountains in northeastern Sonora. From here Mangas Coloradas and Pisago Cabezón led several campaigns against Sonora during the first seven months of 1844. Mangas's first strike occurred on February 7 when a large Chiricahua war party attacked the horse herd at Fronteras, wounded three soldiers, and carried off more than two hundred head of stock. The next month, Mangas Coloradas and Yrigóllen assaulted the vulnerable presidio at daybreak, killing one man and wounding another before withdrawing into the hills. Captain Teodoro de Aros led a force of twenty-nine men, all on foot, after the Indians. About a mile from the fort the overeager Apaches attacked, setting off a skirmish which lasted some five hours before the Indians broke off the fight. The Mexicans lost one man dead and three wounded, including the captain. Several Indians were wounded, among them Yrigóllen and Posito. Mangas's plan failed because several overzealous warriors revealed themselves before the Mexicans had become entrapped; a few minutes more and the entire command might have been annihilated.[49] The Chiricahuas, however, apparently learned a lesson.

After the fight at Fronteras, the hostiles continued into the interior for more raids. In late April another sanguinary encounter occurred in the Oputo Mountains. While retiring north, some Chiricahuas unexpectedly encountered eleven Sonorans and in a sharp clash killed eight and wounded the other three. The Indians later conceded that six warriors were killed, although a rumor that Cuchillo Negro was one of the dead proved false. They returned to the Fronteras vicinity and on April 28 at 8 A.M. surprised Cuquiarachi, riding brazenly through its streets and surrounding the town. By eleven o'clock they had killed several men and had captured three children and one man. At that point the typical parley ensued and the captives were ransomed. Among the Apache representatives were Mangas Coloradas, Relles, Pisago Cabezón, Yrigóllen, Chepillo,[50] and Miguel Narbona. All except Mangas were Chokonens. His presence and that of Pisago Cabezón are strong evidence for Cochise's involvement. The Indians, loaded with plunder, headed for Janos, killing seven more Sonorans along the way.[51]

The next incident convinced Elías González, who believed in swift retribution, that he had to act. Sometime in July 1844 a large Chiricahua war party massacred Ensign Manuel Villa and twenty-eight men near Santa Cruz. Mangas apparently led the Apaches, who successfully implemented the time-worn decoy tactic, a strategy which rarely worked because it required discipline and coordination unusual in Apache warfare. That it did succeed was a tribute to Mangas's status in the Chiricahua Tribe; no other leader could have pulled it off. The war party succeeded in decoying the Santa Cruz force away from the presidio and into the trap. The Mexicans, surrounded before they knew what hit them, were wiped out. Elías González soon determined to take matters into his own hands and snuff out the illicit trade at Janos.

To achieve this, he decided on a campaign against the Janos Apaches. In August he attacked Chiricahua rancherías near Corralitos and Janos, butchering some eighty Indians, most of them women and children. Many innocent Chiricahuas (although some of the men in these rancherías had been raiding) perished in Elías González's attack; many innocent Mexicans would be killed in retaliation.[52] The attack stunned the Chiricahuas; most bolted into southern New Mexico and Arizona, where they regrouped and planned their revenge. Naturally it was war, and Cochise must have been in the middle of it all.

In December 1844, Mangas Coloradas called a council and local groups gathered in the Chiricahua and lower Peloncillo mountains to plan a campaign against Sonora. The goal was captives, perhaps to trade for those held by Sonora.[53] Reports in early 1845 revealed that Apache bands raided deep into Mexico. *Revista Oficial,* the state newspaper of Chihuahua, reported that "peace was enjoyed for thirty-one months, war now exists." [54]

In May 1845, Chihuahua scored an important triumph against the Chokonens living in northeastern Sonora. On May 8 a small raiding party pilfered 117 cattle from Corralitos; fifteen days later, Apaches ran off some oxen there. On May 28 they audaciously entered the corral at the Barranco mines and drove away twenty-three horses. Ensign José Baltazar Padilla, an experienced Indian fighter, with twenty-seven troops and fifty-two citizens, left in pursuit. Padilla followed the trail northwest to the Espuelas Mountains in extreme northeastern Sonora, where he found a large Chokonen ranchería estimated to have a hundred warriors. On June 1 he surprised the Indians and after three days of hard fighting finally withdrew, having suffered four soldiers killed and nine people, five of them citizens, wounded. His force killed fourteen Indians and captured a woman and a child. Whether Cochise was present is not known, but in view of events that followed, there is little doubt that he was in the area.[55]

The Indians moved north into the Chiricahuas and decided to solicit peace with Chihuahua. Accordingly, on June 30, 1845, there appeared at Janos three Chokonens sent by Yrigóllen. Manuelito, Naque, and Matías (the sons of Yrigóllen and Matías were leaders in Cochise's band in the 1860s). Nothing definitive came of the talks at the time, but six months later the Chiricahuas resumed negotiations with Chihuahua, which seemed anxious to explore their proposals.[56]

The pattern of peace, uprisings, and war countered by Mexican campaigns and Chiricahua submissiveness seems difficult to comprehend, yet an examination of previous relations reveals that the Indians had lived peacefully and somewhat prosperously under the presidio system. A whole generation of Chiricahuas matured in it, and many of their leaders (Relles, Matías, Teboca, Yrigóllen) recognized the benefits of living at peace. The Chiricahuas were not an agricultural people, and their many years of close Mexican contact had left them somewhat dependent on the border towns and northern presidios for trade, whether for arms, ammunition, liquor, or food. In addition, they may have heard rumors of Chihuahua's intent to recall Kirker, which was done in early 1846.

The Chokonens and Nednhis feared Kirker, recalling all too vividly his activities in the late 1830s and early 1840s. Therefore, in the spring of 1846, further peace gestures were made, with the entire Chokonen band apparently involved. According to one account, Cochise probably had a hand in these events, which would irrevocably alienate the Chokonen band for many years to come. Discussions began on May 25 with a meeting between Relles and the commander of the San Buenaventura presidio, Ensign Carlos Cásares, a sincere, sensitive, and idealistic officer sympathetic to the Apaches' plight. Cásares, who saw it as an extraordinarily challenging assignment, held initial talks with Relles, Vicente, and Francisquillo. They claimed that Chato, Maturán, and Láceris[57] (a Nednhi leader coming into prominence) shared the same feelings but were apprehensive about coming in, probably because of Kirker's recent activities.[58]

More Chiricahuas came to San Buenaventura on June 12, led by Láceris and Carro,[59] an emerging leader in Cochise's local group. They acknowledged that Janos had been their former establishment but now they wished to settle at Casas Grandes. Two days later José Chato and his band of fifteen warriors made peace, even though Cásares noted that "it is well known that they have committed serious depredations in Namiquipa." Yet Cásares wished to forget the past and was willing to give peace another try. His sincerity and understanding imbued the Chiricahuas with trust, and they placed confidence in what he said. He adamantly refused to issue any rations until the Chiricahuas released every one of their captives. On

June 22, Vicente brought in a captive from Namiquipa; Aceves and Esquiriba had other prisoners they agreed to bring in. Cásares's uncompromising policy had paid dividends.[60]

On June 24 he wrote the commanding general of Chihuahua about the Chiricahuas:

> It is necessary to treat the Indians with gentleness and prudence, never lacking in both. It is also necessary to sustain them and that they comply religiously with the rules, at the same time punishing vigorously those who continue hostilities.

He was much concerned about an issue which was ever present in Apache-Mexican relations but usually not addressed: Apaches trading stock and rations to citizens for liquor and arms. Unlike other commanders, who tacitly condoned and ignored this practice (and reaped some of its rewards), Cásares wrote that he planned to "cut off this pernicious abuse and to establish laws necessary for the public welfare." Unfortunately for both him and the Apaches, his honorable intentions remained unfulfilled.[61]

On June 26, 1846, two days after Cásares wrote the commanding general, James Kirker and twenty-five men left Chihuahua City with the permission of Governor José María Irigoyen, whose instructions, or lack of them, virtually gave Kirker a free hand when operating against hostile Apaches. Irigoyen diplomatically wrote the commanding general at Coyame to solicit his approval; animosity between Kirker and the military had resurfaced, and Irigoyen wished to avoid problems. The commanding general, who was receiving reports from Ensign Cásares about the prospects for peace, concurred with the governor's actions but prudently attached important conditions concerning Kirker's mission:

> [This] operation should be left to the free will of those conducting them. However, I do require that these [parties] do not trample on the law nor kill pacified Indians nor accept foreigners in their ranks.

On July 6 the governor's secretary forwarded a copy to Kirker, but by the time Kirker received it (if indeed he did) irreparable harm had been done.[62]

Kirker hustled up his own fighting force as he moved north. His march began innocuously enough, covering fifty miles northwest to Encinillas, where he picked up forty-nine volunteers. On June 29 he found sixteen dead cattle butchered by Apaches whose trail, according to him, led to Galeana. The next day, thirty-three volunteers deserted because Kirker could not pay them.

On July 1, instead of heading for Galeana, Kirker continued due north to Carrizal. Two days later he moved east, following a hostile trail (or so he claimed) which led to Apache rancherías near Galeana. On July 5 the clandestine plan began to come together. Kirker sent messengers to Juan Ortiz at Galeana and subprefect Manuel de La Riva, who told Kirker the people of his district and those from Janos had decided to attack the Indians living at Galeana because of recent depredations and murders. Early on the morning of July 6, José Ponce arrived at Riva's home and declared that he had killed eighteen Indians at San Buenaventura, thus breaking the truce. This news was music to Kirker's ears. He asserted that they would all "perish at the hands of the ten chiefs with their hordes of warriors" unless the allied Mexicans took action. In an obvious exaggeration, he said "it was kill or be killed . . . more than one hundred times had the Indians been treasonous to us." These statements were pure rationalization, fabricated to justify his own conduct. Consequently, Kirker's forty-four men joined José Morales and some citizens from Janos under José María Zuloaga and set out to kill as many Indians as possible.[63]

It was a double-cross as far as the Chiricahuas were concerned, one of the most egregious deeds ever carried out against them—far worse than Johnson's slaying of Juan José Compá some nine years earlier. Kirker's dispassionate report on the affair lacked details, as did Cásares's emotional account of July 7, but George Frederick Ruxton visited Chihuahua City a few months later and saw Apache scalps on display. He left behind an account which corroborated the Apache recollections of Jason Betzinez and Mangas Coloradas. All three versions agree that the Apaches were invited to a feast and came, under the protection of a treaty, to Galeana. Mescal or whiskey flowed freely that night, Ruxton writing that Kirker was the supplier (though this seems unlikely), so that by the early morning "nearly everyone was lying in a drunken stupor," according to

Apache accounts. That morning Kirker and his compatriots, in cahoots with the citizens of Galeana, killed the inebriated Chiricahuas in their sleep. Virtually all were slaughtered, and their scalps were mounted on poles. In referring to the incident, Mangas Coloradas said that "my people drank and became intoxicated, and were lying asleep, when a party of Mexicans came in and beat out their brains with clubs." Reportedly, 130 Chiricahuas, consisting of Chokonens and Nednhis, were murdered by Kirker's party.[64]

On July 7 a distraught Cásares wrote a letter stating that Kirker, together with citizens from Galeana, Casas Grandes, and San Buenaventura, had surprised and attacked the Apaches, killing 130 without regard for sex or age. He disputed Kirker's claim that the Chiricahuas had committed a robbery at Encinillas which the Apaches claimed was committed by another band. Cásares predicted correctly that the affair would have "far reaching ramifications. . . . All hope for peace is gone." The Apaches, he warned, would take revenge.[65]

Kirker's deed influenced Chiricahua-Mexican relations for several years. Most of the Indians killed seem to have been Chokonens from the bands of Yrigóllen, who lost family members; Carro; and Relles, who was a victim of the slaughter. The Nednhi band, made up of Láceris's Janeros and Francisquillo's Carrizalleños, also suffered losses but not as severe as those of Cochise's people. James Hobbs, who was present, wrote that Cochise was involved and he may have been, given the circumstances.[66]

The double-cross at Galeana, as the Chokonens remembered it, left indelible impressions on Cochise. He may have lost family members, perhaps even his father, who reportedly perished in the same manner as those at Galeana. Undoubtedly it intensified his hatred of Mexicans, and after this he became increasingly aloof to whites, taking his cue from the militant Chiricahuas under Miguel Narbona and Mangas Coloradas.

The Chiricahuas remembered the affair as perhaps the most revolting attack in the annals of Apache-Mexican relations. More than a hundred years later Jason Betzinez referred to it as the "ghastly butchering of our families" and one of the "bloodiest conflicts in which Apaches were ever involved."[67] It would be remembered forever, and its aftermath was predictable. Kirker had in fact laid the foundation for war because all of those Apache losses had to be avenged.

The Chiricahuas took their revenge that fall. According to Betzinez,

> the chiefs considered for a long time the action which they should take to pay back the Mexicans . . . the desire for vengeance burned more fiercely as the days and weeks passed. Finally Baishan [Cuchillo Negro] . . . called a council of the chiefs of several bands. Among those who responded were Cochise, Chief of the Chiricahuas [and] Mangas Coloradas . . . and others whose names I do not recall.

The war party, which consisted of 175 warriors and several novices, started out in late fall 1846. Although there is no corroborating evidence, Betzinez says the Chiricahuas attacked Galeana (he confused Galeana with Ramos, a deserted hacienda near Janos), occupied the town, and killed many of its occupants. "Those who increased their reputations in the battle," he writes, "were Cochise, Mangas Coloradas, Benito and Geronimo."[68] Cochise undoubtedly would have participated in an expedition of this nature, although not as leader of his band; he would have followed Yrigóllen, Tapilá, and Miguel Narbona. By now, though, he had become a leader in his local group.

# Chapter 4

# GALEANA AVENGED

Besides having to confront the Chiricahuas, who were "all stirred up" by the Kirker massacre, in late 1846, Mexico was forced to focus on another enemy: the expansionist Yankees from the north. Fighting between the two countries had erupted on April 25, and the following month Congress declared war on Mexico.

It was not until Brigadier General Stephen Watts Kearny[1] and his Army of the West occupied Santa Fe on August 18 that Sonoran and Chihuahuan officials became cognizant of the American threat. In September, after establishing a government at Santa Fe, Kearny and three hundred men set out to take California. Guided by the consummate scout and mountain man Kit Carson, Kearny cut his route through Apache country. By October his force had been reduced to one hundred men because he sent two-thirds of his command back to Santa Fe when he was informed that California had been taken by John Charles Frémont. He met Mangas Coloradas and other Chiricahua leaders when he arrived at Santa Rita del Cobre, where one of the chiefs went so far as to offer his services against the contemptible Mexicans. Kearny's mission, however, was to reach California, so he continued on the Gila Trail, ignored Tucson and its detachment of Mexican troops, and proceeded to California.[2]

Kearny's expedition was soon followed by the fastidious Captain Philip St. George Cooke[3] and his Mormon Battalion of 340 men, which had left Santa Fe on September 19. Guided by two experi-

enced scouts, Pauline Weaver[4] and Antoine Leroux,[5] Cooke's men
forged a new route, one which would be followed by many overland
travelers in the 1840s and early 1850s until the more direct route via
Apache Pass became known. His force, which actually trespassed
into northern Mexico, greatly alarmed Sonora's leaders, especially
when irrefutable evidence indicated that the Americans and Chiricahuas had made peaceful contact. Rumors of a potential Apache-
Anglo alliance left Sonorans aghast, although this was a remote possibility. Not only did the Chiricahuas distrust the Americans, but the
latter were intent on reaching California and had no interest in ally-
ing themselves with the wild Apaches, whom they viewed with
contempt.

Cooke's command encamped at the deserted San Bernardino
ranch on December 2. The Chokonens were wary and had to be persuaded to come in. A few days earlier, he had assured the Chokonen
chief Manuelito[6] that "the men he called Americans, and who led
the Mexicans to war against the Apache, were men who had run off
from their own country and become Mexicans," an obvious reference to Kirker and Johnson. With these consolations, Manuelito
brought "a superior chief and several others" in from the mountains
to meet Cooke. The superior chief was probably either Yrigóllen or
Miguel Narbona. For many, perhaps Cochise, this was their first
look at American soldiers. Cooke explained his intentions and
offered to trade for mules. Noted for his discipline and organization,
the officer was unimpressed with the Chokonens:

> They are poor, dirty Indians, but are generally dressed in cotton
> shirts and many in trousers. They have fine moccasins, which have
> boot tops. They ride fine horses, which they prefer to mules, and are
> armed with very formidable-looking lances [and] with guns and
> bows. They are ugly and squalid, [and] wear their hair generally long
> and in various fashions. They wear a kind of leather skullcap, now
> and then ornamented with feathers and chinpieces. They seem to
> understand Spanish.[7]

A few days later the Americans continued west toward Tucson and
occupied the town on December 17 (the Mexican troops had temporarily withdrawn). After a short stay Cooke marched to California,
having left a letter at Tucson for Governor Gándara suggesting that
the two countries join forces to fight Apaches.[8]

With the war going on, the Apaches focused their attention on Mexico and, according to Hubert Howe Bancroft, "caused great distress. More settlements were destroyed and even the suburbs of Ures were assailed."[9] Reports from the frontier bespoke a deteriorating military situation, one which would continue for the remainder of the decade. For the most part, Chiricahua raiders enjoyed a wide selection of targets with relative impunity. Cochise, following the lead of his local-group leader, the warlike Miguel Narbona, was certainly in the middle of it all.

Little is known of Miguel Narbona's early life. In fact, Chiricahua informants of Mrs. Eve Ball knew nothing about him; in addition, the sparse oral history available from the Apache perspective does not mention him. The reason seems twofold. First, Miguel Narbona died about 1856, before Anglo entrenchment in southern Arizona, so he was virtually unknown to Americans. Second, and just as important, was the fact that Apache death taboos prohibited mention of the deceased by name.

Fortunately, Merejildo Grijalva, a captive of Miguel Narbona, has shed some light on this intriguing chief with whom Cochise was so closely associated. According to Merejildo, Miguel was captured as a young boy by Mexican troops under Captain Antonio Narbona, Senior, from whom he took his surname. Miguel remained with the Narbona family for almost a decade, becoming educated and Christianized. At the age of eighteen he escaped and rejoined his people. By this time, for some inexplicable reason, he had developed a fierce, lifelong hatred of Mexicans. According to Merejildo, his "daring and prowess won him high position in his band." His insatiable desire for Mexican blood apparently was the result of his years in captivity and subsequent Mexican acts of betrayal upon his people. He was the one Chiricahua leader not involved in any peace discussions after the Kirker massacre. Yrigóllen was the principal Chokonen leader of the late 1840s and early 1850s; the war leader, however, was Miguel Narbona, whose bellicose, intractable personality dominated the militant Chokonens. Wherever Yrigóllen was, Miguel Narbona usually could be found; likewise, wherever Miguel Narbona was, Cochise usually could be found.[10]

In early March 1847 a large Chokonen-Nednhi war party under Miguel Narbona, Yrigóllen, Teboca, Esquinaline, and Láceris surprised twenty Mexicans some four miles southwest of Fronteras. Within minutes the attackers had killed fourteen men and captured two others, including Corporal Juan Chacon. Relief parties from Fronteras and Cuquiarachi were dispatched, with Antonio Narbona riding at the head of the latter group. An interesting confrontation must have occurred when Narbona parleyed with an Indian who told him that the Chokonens might attack Fronteras.[11] The Indians continued into the interior for further depredations. Upon their return north, near Bacoachi, they happened across eleven persons, five men and six boys, whom they waylaid, killing ten of them. Once again they had avenged the Galeana double-cross.[12]

In early April the Chokonens reappeared at Fronteras. On April 5 several Indians led by Yrigóllen, some carrying white flags, appeared suddenly in the hills east of the presidio. Deciderio Escalante, Antonio Narbona, and Captain Mateo Calvo y Muro cautiously went out and parleyed with Yrigóllen, who claimed that every Chokonen leader favored peace. In the light of recent raids, this statement puzzled Escalante. Nonetheless, he communicated their wishes to the governor, but in reality he favored military action, not amelioration of relations. Nevertheless, Elías González was ordered to open negotiations.[13]

The Apache-wise officer arrived at Fronteras in late April. After several councils he finally deduced why the Indians had requested peace: from their contact with the whites, several Chokonens had contracted measles and the disease had infested the band. The prospects of Sonoran retaliation at this time disturbed the Indians. Elías González had no qualms about killing Apaches (witness the eighty men, women, and children killed at Janos and Corralitos in August 1844), but in his words, "considering the present difficulties and the circumstances in which we find ourselves, it seems prudent to me to concede it." Like all Mexicans, he dreaded the prospects of an Apache-American alliance.[14]

The truce was short lived. Apparently some of the Chokonens became healthy because they soon resumed hostilities. First they raided Fronteras, then Cuquiarachi, where they seriously wounded one person and captured a young boy.[15] From there they vanished into the Chiricahuas, where they camped during the summer of 1847, safe from a Sonora still occupied by the American threat. In fact, for the rest of 1847, Chiricahua bands do not seem to have caused much mischief. The Chokonens were relatively quiet, perhaps recuperating from the measle epidemic and deliberately avoiding northern Sonora, where troops had been concentrated in anticipation of an American invasion.[16]

That fall Sonora mounted two expeditions against the Chiricahuas. Although the results were less than spectacular, they stirred up the hornets again just the same. In September, Antonio Narbona swung out of Fronteras at the head of a mixed force of 120 cavalry and infantry. Six days later, on September 13, his force camped at Apache Pass and the following day discovered and ransacked a deserted ranchería, probably in what is known today as Goodwin Canyon. The next day, scouts found another ranchería and four freshly butchered cattle, indicating that the Chokonens were near. Narbona's suspicions were confirmed when his men discovered an Indian woman hidden in the rocks. Frustrated that their prey had eluded them, the Mexicans dispassionately murdered her. Given the Chokonens' actions of the previous spring, where they had showed no mercy, it was a decision that Narbona could justify, yet he himself would eventually pay the price.

Later that same day, several Chokonen chiefs, including Miguel Narbona, shouted at Antonio Narbona from the mountains that they wanted peace and would meet the Mexicans early that evening at San Jacinto Springs, evidently somewhere in the Chiricahuas. Needless to say, the Chokonens reneged on their promise, and Narbona's party returned to Cuquiarachi on September 22. Although Narbona conceded that the results of his scout were disappointing, he commended his men for a good performance. The senseless killing of the Indian woman, however, was a blunder and could have been avoided. Shortly after Narbona's campaign, another Sonoran expedition from Moctezuma captured several members of Yrigóllen's family. These two scouts provided the incentive for a Chokonen response.[17]

In December 1847 the Chokonens had their revenge and their plan worked exactly as designed. Their objective was to wipe out Cuquiarachi and get even with their longtime adversary Antonio Narbona. Cuquiarachi, founded in 1654, was a small village a few miles southwest of Fronteras. Bartlett passed through it a few years later and wrote that the fields "skirted the roads, the rows of pomegranate trees in full bloom, and the orchards of peach, pear and mulberry, all betokened a high state of cultivation." For days the Chiricahuas harassed the town, brazenly threatening Narbona's life. Finally, on December 23, they stormed the village and overwhelmed its residents. Narbona fought gamely but was slain on the porch of his house. Before the assault ended, seven more men and six women had perished and six children had been captured. All of Sonora mourned Narbona's death, but the surviving citizens of Cuquiarachi were especially devastated. Their spirits drained and their will gone, six weeks later they took what possessions they could carry and left Cuquiarachi to the Apaches and the snakes.[18]

About the time Cuquiarachi was being abandoned, a large war party composed of Chokonens, Chihennes, and possibly some White Mountain Western Apaches united for an expedition into Sonora. Their target was the small town of Chinapa, like Cuquiarachi a mission settlement established in 1648. Apaches had raided frequently in recent years, but this time they intended to clean it out, according to the testimony of Manuel Bernal, who was captured during the raid but escaped shortly thereafter. On February 18, 1848, the Apaches surprised Chinapa and burned it to the ground, killing twelve Mexicans, wounding six, and capturing an astonishing forty-two people, mainly women and children.

Miguel Narbona led the Chokonen faction and boasted of recent raids into Chihuahua, indicating that he and most likely Cochise were active there. According to Bernal, the Indians were "all stirred up" by the massacre at Galeana and "would find a way to get revenge." Furthermore, the Apaches were angry because of Sonora's campaign the previous fall (the attack on Yrigóllen's camp). Yrigóllen, whose ranchería was tucked away in the Chiricahuas, planned to exchange the Chinapa captives for his relatives. Initially, Bacoachi officials were uncertain about Bernal's testimony, primarily because Apaches normally did not take adult male prisoners; usually, torture or death was their fate.[19]

In June 1848 there occurred an incident that had lifelong ramifications for Cochise. On June 20 some Mexicans were herding cattle near Turicachi, some fifteen miles south of Fronteras, when they espied a band of Apaches driving a large herd of horses and cattle.

Miguel Narbona and Cochise were returning from a raid when the Sonorans turned the tables and ambushed the unsuspecting Indians, killing two and wounding several others. Three Mexicans were wounded slightly. Next morning the Chokonens, under Cochise and Miguel Narbona, appeared in force at Fronteras; they surrounded and captured five citizens at the *ciénaga* near the presidio. The sentinel at the top of the church saw a cloud of dust and sounded the alarm. Two parties were dispatched, the first consisting of eight citizens and the second, under Eusebio Gil Samaniego,[20] numbering fifteen. When the whites reached the scene, the Chokonens defiantly stood their ground. Soon after, the two old adversaries parleyed. Miguel Narbona, Cochise, and a few other warriors represented the Chiricahuas; Samaniego, with an equal number of citizens, represented the whites. The Apaches ransomed their five captives, although what Samaniego gave in return was not mentioned. Next the

Fronteras, Sonora. Ruins of the presidio where Cochise was imprisoned in 1848. (*Photo by Dan Thrapp*)

inevitable skirmish occurred, probably initiated by the Chiricahuas, seeking to avenge their fatalities of the previous day. In any event, an Indian identified as Negrito Cucchisle (Cochise) was somehow captured and "put in irons and shackled." A blast from the presidio's cannon wounded Miguel Narbona, killed his horse, and put the rest of the Indians to flight.[21]

The evidence points to Cochise as the individual who was captured. First of all, Fronteras, located within the lower limits of Chokonen territory, was a place he frequented regularly throughout his life. Further support comes from the identification of Miguel Narbona, whom Cochise succeeded as chief of the Central Chiricahuas, or Chokonens. In addition, the captive's immense status within his band was revealed when the Indians subsequently exchanged eleven Mexicans to obtain his release. Finally, the definite reference to a *capitancillo,* meaning "little chief" or "subchief," Cochise's position at this time, plus the specific reference to Cucchisle, leaves me to conclude that the captured Chokonen was indeed Cochise. He remained a prisoner for some six weeks, during which time his feelings toward Mexicans became more acrimonious.

The next six weeks were tense for Fronteras residents. Shortly after the skirmish with Miguel Narbona, Captain Calvo y Muro wrote Gándara about the lamentable state of affairs there. The Chokonens, cognizant of the small garrison, had established their rancherías within five miles of the presidio. Their intent, Calvo y Muro thought, "was to watch over everything and every person who passes from here" in order to take captives to exchange for Cochise. Furthermore, his men, inadequately fed and scantily clothed, were constantly on the alert. As a result, morale had deteriorated to a dangerously low level. Of his fifty-six men, eight were on detached duty at Ures, two were mail carriers between Fronteras and Bavispe, eight were sick, and seven were in the guardhouse. This left but thirty-one men for scout duty and other necessary tasks. For this reason, twenty-five troops from Bacoachi were ordered to reinforce Fronteras and a load of provisions and fifty firearms were sent, probably from Bavispe.[22]

The Chokonen siege of Fronteras continued throughout July 1848. Citizens feared to work their fields, and small parties dared not venture from the safety of the fort. In late July, Miguel Narbona, looking for a chance to take prisoners, turned the screws even tighter, moving his camp to within one mile of Fronteras. No supplies were coming to or leaving the fort, and by August 7 the inhabitants had been reduced to eating tortillas, the only food available. Finally Calvo y Muro allowed a party of twenty-three soldiers and citizens to leave the presidio to obtain provisions. Miguel Narbona and Posito Moraga were ready. They allowed the whites to reach Cuchuta before surrounding them and killing or capturing everyone except Jesús Escalante, who was wounded and escaped to Fronteras.

In response, Captain Calvo y Muro reluctantly dispatched a relief party to Cuchuta, where they spotted the Apaches. José Yescas, a soldier who was trusted by the Chiricahuas, conversed with Chino, who said Posito Moraga would bring Corporal Serapio Olguin, four soldiers, and six civilians to exchange for Cochise. The deal was done on August 11. Never again would Cochise allow himself to be taken.[23]

While the ransom negotiations were taking place, a force of troops under Ensign Saturniño Limon[24] entered Fronteras under cover of darkness, hoping to surprise the Indian rancherías in the vicinity. He departed August 13 and was beset with trouble immediately. For almost a week his force scouted the Embudos and other mountain ranges, but the slow-moving troops were no match for the nimble Chiricahuas. Running short of provisions, Limon returned to his supply train at Batepito, planning to provision his force before sweeping north into the Chiricahuas, where the Indians were thought to have gone.

Again he seemed hampered at every turn. At Batepito, hungry national troops had plundered the supply train. Next they decided to mutiny and refused to continue, and if that wasn't enough, Limon received more startling news: the inhabitants of Fronteras had abandoned the presidio for Bacoachi. Completely frustrated, he blamed the fiasco on the people of Fronteras, charging that they had warned the Apaches of his campaign, but this, of course, was an oversimplification. In reality, the constant Chokonen presence during the summer of 1848 compelled the citizens to conclude that prospects at Bacoachi had to be better than their precarious existence at

Fronteras.[25] So it was that the Chiricahua siege, implemented primarily because of Cochise's imprisonment, forced the shutdown of Sonora's oldest presidio.

West of Fronteras at the presidio of Santa Cruz, conditions had reached a similar and equally critical stage. Summer Indian raids had terrorized the neighborhood, and on September 8, Apaches assailed the town, stole seventy cattle, and killed ten horses and three mules. The military commander warned that his presidio would suffer the same fate as Fronteras unless more troops and provisions arrived. Indeed, several men had deserted because of the deplorable conditions.[26]

Governor Gándara did not recognize the plight of the northern frontier until Fronteras was abandoned. Two months earlier, the minister of war and navy in Mexico City had requested information about the Apache problem. Ignoring the realities of the situation, Gándara responded with idealistic optimism, which the situation certainly did not warrant. He contended that if Sonora's six presidios were adequately equipped, fully garrisoned, and led by competent officers, the Apaches would be subjugated within three months. Just in case this was not accomplished, he diplomatically added that victory could be achieved only if the Apaches "don't find protection on the other side of the Gila," territory ceded to the victorious United States in 1848. In truth, Gándara neglected the fact that, for the most part, the Chokonens had remained south of the Gila and within his jurisdiction throughout the 1840s.[27] Yet the governor's viewpoint found unexpected support in Mexico City. Mariano Arista, secretary of war and navy, shared Gándara's beliefs. He proposed a string of forts and settlements across the northern frontier; however, when drawing up his plans, he failed to consider the Apaches' complete domination of northern Sonora and Chihuahua.[28]

Gándara's report evidently evoked a response from Mexico City because the November 3, 1848, issue of *El Sonorense* announced that the indefatigable and incomparable José Mária Elías González had been named the military inspector of Sonora. "This is proof that the Supreme Government has not viewed with indifference the horror in Sonora", editorialized *El Sonorense*.[29]

The Chiricahuas scored another important victory only a few

weeks after Elías González assumed command. In mid-November, Chino appeared at Bacoachi and said a contingent of warriors would come in to make peace. The Chokonens had no intention of returning (they distrusted Captain Calvo y Muro), and Chino's visit was simply to gather military intelligence and trade for whiskey. A few weeks later, Calvo y Muro did scout Turicachi, but the Indians were believed to have moved into the Peloncillos or Chiricahuas.[30]

As Calvo y Muro had surmised, the Chokonens had moved north, hiding their families in the Chiricahuas before heading west against their next target, the presidio of Tubac, which at this time consisted "of a collection of dilapidated buildings and huts."[31] Apparently the presidio was not garrisoned, the townspeople relying on Santa Cruz and Tucson for protection. On December 9 the war party struck, killed nine citizens, and created so much terror that the remaining occupants abandoned the town. The majority relocated to San Xavier, others to Tucson, some to El Soni, while the remainder marched to California with some of Tucson's citizens.[32] Elías González was furious when he heard the news and on January 23 ordered Captain Antonio Comadurán to send twenty soldiers to reoccupy Tubac. Comadurán cautiously demurred, informing his relative that Tubac's population had scattered and that those who had remained in the vicinity were too frightened to return. Furthermore, when news of the orders leaked to his soldiers stationed at Tucson, eight men deserted rather than regarrison the abandoned presidio. Comadurán concluded his argument by depicting Tucson's current state: it lacked food, morale had hit rock bottom, and everyone was afraid the Indians might attack Tucson itself.[33]

By the end of 1848 the Chiricahua Apaches had made the residents of northern Sonora their tenants, extracting rent in subsidies of horses and cattle. When these began to diminish, they convinced their residents that voluntary eviction was better than starvation and death. Meanwhile, optimistic Mexican officials believed that Apache incursions had reached their highest level. They hoped that Elías González's experience and leadership, combined with more federal assistance, would enable Sonora to recapture some of its lost pride and territory.

Besides the Chiricahuas, Elías González had another problem: the lure of gold in California was draining the state of troops and men. The adventurers absconded with many of the government weapons intended for use against the hostiles, and many left their dependents behind; now they were more exposed to Apache raids than ever before.[34] From Tucson in January 1849, Captain Comadurán speculated that the fear of Apaches and the lure of gold in California could cause the total collapse of the frontier settlements.[35]

The spring of 1849 was active for Cochise's people. Although he was not specifically mentioned, his band leader, Miguel Narbona, and Mangas Coloradas were prominent in the region, and almost certainly Cochise enhanced his reputation as an up-and-coming war leader. In March 1849, Miguel Narbona led a Chiricahua war party against the small mining town of Banamichi, situated on the Sonora River some five miles north of Huepac. On March 9 shortly before the noon siesta, an estimated one hundred warriors assaulted the Feliz ranch, which was about a mile from Banamichi. The men were spread out and going about their normal duties when the Indians attacked the ranch, which was populated "by honest and hard working families." Within minutes, in the words of an eyewitness, "all of the people of the ranch were killed," captured, or wounded. It was Chinapa revisited. The Apaches killed seven men and two women and wounded five men. The remaining ten women and four men were captured, along with several small children, including Marijenia Figueira, who was liberated by American troops fifteen years later.[36] The Chiricahuas set fire to the ranch and the surrounding houses.

One mile away the justice of the peace at Banamichi helplessly surmised that "there were some casualties because the savages had burned the houses." Nonetheless, he was unable to send out a scouting party because a few weeks earlier most of the men, some thirty in all, had rushed to the California gold fields, and those who remained were aghast at the thought of encountering Indians. Therefore he sent a frantic note to the prefect of Ures, who in turn dispatched National Guard troops under Rafael Buelna to investigate. By the time Buelna arrived, the Chiricahuas had rounded up their captives and were headed north along the Sonora River, killing two more people and capturing two others at Motopori, five miles north of Banamichi. Later the same day the war party passed near Sinoquipe, but authorities there were helpless; their people lacked arms, provisions, and the heart to go out after "*los Apaches barbaros.*"[37]

Miguel was not finished. His captivity had left him with deep antipathy toward Sonorans; he was the most belligerent, the most incorrigible, and the cruelest among a people noted for ruthlessness toward their enemies. He killed to supply his seemingly insatiable desire for Mexican blood; perhaps he actually believed that the Chiricahuas could drive the Mexicans from northern Sonora. He became obsessed with this thought as the victories, beginning with Cuquiarachi in December 1847 and continuing with Chinapa in February 1848, Fronteras in August 1848, and Tubac in December 1848, continued to accumulate. Without a doubt, he was the most feared Chokonen war leader during the 1840s and early 1850s.

As for Sonora, never was vigorous remedy more urgent, but the ailing government lacked that capacity. In April the Chiricahuas made plans to attack two of Sonora's remaining northern presidios. On April 8 one hundred mounted warriors surprised Bavispe, killing four adults, capturing four children, and burning the surrounding fields.[38] Three weeks later Miguel Narbona, Yrigóllen, Posito Moraga, and Teboquita raided Santa Cruz, whose population of two or three hundred individuals scarcely ventured outside the presidio's walls except in large numbers. A large body of hostiles suddenly appeared north of the town early on Sunday, April 29. The Indians nearly surrounded one family, but prompt response from the congregated citizens drove them away. The next day, two parties of brave citizens left the presidio to work their fields, each a few miles away, one to the north and the other to the south. The Chiricahuas lay waiting and within minutes seven hard-working men lay dead. Saturniño Limon immediately dispatched two parties of ten men, one under Corporal Dionicio Aldecoa and the other under Juan Abad Telles,[39] with instructions to march to the river and aid their neighbors. With the relief party at the scene, the Chokonens withdrew, having carried away most of the town's stock. Afterward, Limon wrote that "more than eighteen men with their families have prepared to emigrate for the interior and the rest of them are searching for their stock. For your consideration I must say to you that circumstances are critical with respect to this garrison."[40]

As the Chokonens returned to their rancherías in northeast Sonora, José Terán y Tato, whose brother had recently been killed by Apaches, left Moctezuma with a force of 118 men and one piece of artillery. Marching north, his command was augmented by 70 men from the towns along the way. On May 10 he arrived at Bavispe and three days later departed for the Pitaicache Mountains, about twenty-five miles east of Fronteras. Near here, at Rusballo, he surprised a small encampment (actually an extended family camp) and killed or captured the entire group. Eusebio Gil Samaniego, who had participated in the capture of Cochise, lanced to death San Juan, a notorious warrior, and another man and captured nine Indians. The prisoners revealed that they were part of Yrigóllen's band and were en route to Janos to trade. They also disclosed that other rancherías were in the Enmedio Mountains and that Mangas Coloradas was thought to be either in the Chiricahua or Florida ranges. Yrigóllen and Miguel Narbona were camped along the San Bernardino River. Cochise, we can assume, was with Mangas or Miguel Narbona.[41]

The Chokonens retaliated quickly. Six days later Yrigóllen, Miguel Narbona, and Tapilá raided Bacoachi, wounded two people, and captured four children. Captain Teodoro de Aros with thirty troops and citizens pursued them west for a few miles, and then the Indians counterattacked, killing two soldiers and two citizens and capturing one soldier (Julian Romero) and one citizen (Félix Montoya). After the fight the Apaches raised a white bandanna. Captain de Aros and three men parleyed with Yrigóllen, Casimiro, and a few others. He tried to persuade the Indians to release their six prisoners, but they refused, instead promising to return within three weeks to exchange captives. The Mexicans returned to Bacoachi, and the Chiricahuas marched victoriously north toward Bavispe, planning to exchange captives.[42]

Ten days later the Indians appeared at Bavispe, where they presumed that their relatives captured by Terán y Tato were held. The Chokonen leaders announced that they had prisoners to exchange, but because only one Indian was held at Bavispe the Apaches relinquished only one captive named Francisco Duran. The commander, probably Captain Reyes Cruz, may have made some promises because the Chiricahuas said they would return within twenty days to exchange more prisoners, the same yarn given Captain de Aros at Bacoachi. This time they appeared as promised but in a fighting mood. At sunrise on June 22 one hundred mounted warriors stormed the presidio, killing one old man, severely wounding another, and carrying off a young boy. They fled north and then broke east into Chihuahua. Despite the few casualties, the Chokonens achieved their objective. With Tubac and Fronteras deserted and morale at Santa Cruz deteriorating, the residents of Bavispe may also have considered abandonment. According to Bavispe's commander, the Apaches' presence had forced the people "to live in constant fear."[43]

Meanwhile, throughout the winter and spring of 1849, Elías González was occupied with drawing up plans to counteract the Apaches' victories. He envisioned a grand Sonoran offensive that would march into Apachería and take war to the hostiles. He certainly had the support of most Sonorans as they rallied behind their popular leader. Local prefects, judges, and ministers pledged money, mounts, supplies, and volunteers for the campaign, which was scheduled to begin in September.[44]

Before those plans could be put in motion, Elías González concentrated on regaining a foothold in northern Sonora. In May he announced his intent to regarrison Fronteras and after that Tubac; if possible, he hoped to coordinate the offensive with Chihuahua. That summer he transferred a troop from Altar to Tucson, sent 50 infantry from the Fronteras company (stationed at Bacoachi) to Tucson, and placed the troops at Santa Cruz under Captain Comadurán. Elías González explained clearly to Comadurán that his primary objective, besides killing Apaches, was to regarrison Tubac. Comadurán's campaign was to occur about the same time Captain de Aros and 118 troops scouted the mountains near Fronteras.[45]

Elías González's much-talked-about offensive was launched from Bacoachi on September 23, 1849. Dividing his force into three divisions, he took one force, which would enter present-day southwest Cochise County, Arizona, and scouted the ranges in that area; Captain Agustín Moreno with 80 troops and the supply train would journey northeast and establish a base camp at Sarampion in the Peloncillos; José Terán y Tato took the third branch of 130 national troops, which would reconnoiter the mountains in northeast Sonora before going to Sarampion at the end of September.

None of these forces enjoyed a particularly auspicious beginning. Elías González's command was plagued with problems. Twelve soldiers deserted within the first four days, and fourteen were left behind at Santa Cruz because of sickness. From the hacienda de San Pedro, his troops marched northeast toward the Chiricahua Mountains, arriving there on September 27 in a driving rainstorm. The next day, twenty-seven men came down with a fever, although one has to suspect that some of these illnesses may have been induced by the prospect of meeting Apaches. On September 29 they reached Apache Pass and found a deserted ranchería, which they thought had been abandoned since the previous July. Still no Apaches were seen; consequently, Elías González decided to suspend operations and join the supply train. He cut through Apache Pass and proceeded south along the eastern face of the Chiricahuas, arriving at Sarampion on October 1.

The pack train was nowhere in sight. The commander waited for a day, then broke camp, taking the route by which the supply train should have come. At San Bernardino he met an American wagon train en route to California via Cooke's route. The Americans told the officer they had seen Apaches along the Mimbres but none since that time. Finally, on October 5, Elías González's command crossed the present-day boundary and stumbled onto Captain Moreno's supply train near the Caguillona Mountains, a small group of hills with a dependable spring some fifteen miles north of Fronteras.

Moreno had remained there because several members of his command were sick. The next day, last rites were administered to eight men who were seriously ill. After two weeks the Sonoran offensive had met with disastrous results: sickness and desertions had hindered the command and the severe weather, and rough terrain had exhausted the stock. The Chiricahuas had avoided the campaign by moving north to the Gila River and Burro Mountains.[46]

Despite these setbacks, Elías González was not ready to give up the hunt. The dogmatic commander desperately needed a victory of any kind; he needed to give the hostiles a show of force. On October 6 he resumed the march, heading north toward the Chiricahuas.

He must have heaved a sigh of relief the second day out when his scouts captured a Chokonen warrior near San Bernardino. The prisoner furnished Elías González with definite information regarding the Chiricahuas' movements. All of the hostiles except Triqueno's group had retired north toward the Burro Mountains because of an epidemic within the bands.[47]

Based on this information, Elías González headed for the Burros, where he arrived October 13. Here he encountered John Coffee Hays,[48] who was in Chiricahua country hoping to make a peace treaty with the Indians. Yet the Apaches were too suspicious of the Americans and eluded them, Hays believed on account of "Americans employed by the Gov. of Chihuahua expressly to fight Indians."[49] After leaving Hays, Elías González finally caught his prey. Guided by Negrito, a Nednhi unjustly imprisoned at Janos the previous June, Elías González found at least two rancherías and succeeded in killing the Nednhi leader Cochi and ten other warriors. In addition, the Mexicans captured five persons and recovered some stock. The Sonoran leader was surprised at the light resistance until the Apache prisoners disclosed that the warriors were absent on a campaign against Janos. With this intelligence, Elías González decided to terminate the campaign in southern New Mexico and move toward Janos, hoping he could surprise the hostiles as they returned to their base camp.

The Apaches had left Janos by the time the Sonoran army reached it. Accordingly, Elías González decided to return to Sonora, thus officially ending his grand offensive. On the surface the results seemed less than spectacular. Although he had failed to strike an important blow against the Chiricahuas, he had forced the hostiles once again to consider Sonora as an enemy to be reckoned with.[50]

The Chiricahua war party against Janos had been organized to avenge Chihuahua's new extermination policy. Cochise's people had more or less avoided Chihuahua throughout 1849, although several had continued trading at Janos. These peaceful contacts had convinced Captain Baltazar Padilla that a truce might be made if Yrigóllen, Posito Moraga, and Carro could be induced to come in.[51] He realized that the militant Chokonens under Miguel Narbona, Teboca, and Cochise entertained no such thoughts. Padilla's hopes vanished on May 25, 1849, when Chihuahua adopted the so-called

Fifth Law, which essentially declared war against all hostiles and encouraged the slaughter of Apaches by bounty hunters. Any individual, regardless of nationality, could enter into a contract with the state to exterminate Apaches. Scalp bounties were fixed at 200 pesos for each warrior killed, 250 pesos for each warrior captured, and 150 pesos for each female or any male Indians under fourteen captured. Eager mercenaries materialized overnight, all hoping to capitalize on Chihuahua's new law.[52]

The scalp hunters enjoyed success until the hostiles withdrew from reach. Then, late that summer, the Apaches retaliated. Their raids extended to the suburbs of Chihuahua City and forced the closing of mines and the evacuation of ranches. An American businessman living in Chihuahua City attributed the depredations to revenge for the scalp hunters' deeds.[53]

In September 1849, Padilla closed the door on peace, at least for the short term, by destroying the ranchería of the Nednhi chief Soquilla[54] in the Florida Mountains a few miles southeast of Deming, New Mexico. Padilla's force killed Soquilla and eleven others and captured nineteen, who were subsequently imprisoned at Corralitos.[55] The Chiricahuas were naturally concerned about the fate of their relatives; accordingly, on October 11 a war party estimated at 150 warriors attacked the horse herd at Janos and ran off every head. A short time later the aggressors withdrew and hoisted a white flag. Padilla went out to parley with Chokonen leaders Yrigóllen, Manuelito, and Posito; Nednhi leaders Coleto Amarillo,[56] Láceris, and Arvizu;[57] and Itán, a Chihenne leader. All of the Indians were well armed and some were drunk, which produced a volatile atmosphere. Padilla convinced Arvizu and Manuelito to come in and talk; the others were too apprehensive. The Indians offered to exchange captives plus the stolen stock for their people; Padilla decided to write his superiors for instructions.

At this crucial moment, twenty-six whites, primarily Americans, freshly arrived from Santa Rita del Cobre, changed the odds. They were within half a mile of Janos when a large group of Apaches— four hundred according to the Americans, two hundred according to Padilla—suddenly appeared. With the presidio's proximity, the whites were not unduly alarmed, which proved to be a fatal mistake for several of its members. A Mr. Thompson recalled:

This was at a place where danger was least expected. A few who were in advance dismounted and prepared to defend themselves, but the Indians gave them to understand that they were friendly that the Apaches and Americans were amigos—that they did not want to fight. They then allowed them to approach, when they commenced shaking hands in the most friendly manner, and even going as far as to take several in their arms and hug them affectionately. After separating them as much as possible they suddenly seized the bridles of the horses and told them they were all prisoners, and then immediately marched them off towards the mountains. The little party finding itself deceived, tried to get together to make resistance, but the Indians took good care to prevent that by surrounding each man with seven or eight warriors.

When they reached the mountains, the Apaches proceeded to strip the Americans, cut open their packs, and steal their horses.[58]

About 5 P.M. Arvizu arrived at Janos and offered to exchange the American captives for the Indians held at Corralitos. After he left, however, the Apaches received news of Elías González's attack in the Burro Mountains. At this point a quarrel arose, with one faction demanding revenge on the captured Americans. Coleto Amarillo counseled against killing the prisoners, noting their importance in obtaining the release of their people. Through his intervention, "the mercy of God and darkness of night," most of the American party, naked and bruised, escaped to Janos. Seven men were not so fortunate; the next day, they were found lanced to death.[59]

Cochise's involvement in this incident is not known. With Miguel Narbona and Mangas Coloradas evidently not present, it would be difficult to speculate what role, if any, he played. Both leaders were in Chihenne country in late 1849, however, attempting to ascertain the disposition of the recently arrived Americans. Cochise was most likely with them.

# Chapter 5

# CHOKONEN ACTIVITIES 1849–56

The end of the United States–Mexican War in 1848 brought something new to the Chiricahua world: American troops in New Mexico, now a territory of the United States. In 1848 the newcomers had several clashes with Indians; most of the fighting, however, occurred in the north against the Jicarillas and Utes.[1] That summer, troops were garrisoned on the outskirts of Chiricahua territory. Captain Enoch Steen[2] and a company of First Dragoons were stationed at Doña Ana, five miles north of Las Cruces, and Steen had a few minor brushes with raiding Chiricahuas in 1849 and again in 1850.[3] These incidents helped to convince the suspicious Chiricahuas to avoid the unknown (Americans) and resume dealing with the known (Mexicans).

Although Chiricahua bands may have wanted good relations with Americans, small raiding parties occasionally harassed southern New Mexico. On December 27, 1849, a band of Chihennes under Josecito captured two boys, named Teofilo and Mateo Savanillo, from Doña Ana. Immediately the party returned to its home base near Santa Rita del Cobre and dispatched Itán to negotiate. En route, Americans reportedly attacked the party, killing and wounding several. Itán and the others limped back to camp, where the incensed Apaches organized a war party to avenge their losses.[4]

The honor of leading the group went to Miguel Narbona. Early on the morning of February 2, 1850, fifty-six Chiricahuas raided Doña

Ana and drove off every head of stock, killed one man, and wounded three others. The Apaches' audacity surprised the American troops, for the Indians had come so close that the troops saw them from their quarters. Captain Steen pursued with a force of dragoons and infantry, but the raiders were already six miles ahead when he started. Steen anticipated that the hostiles would head for the Gila; they struck toward San Diego Crossing. He divided his force. He took a detachment and crossed the Jornado del Muerto,[5] and Lieutenant Laurence W. O'Bannon with twenty-five men marched northwest to cut off the Indians before they reached the Mimbres Mountains. North of San Diego Crossing, O'Bannon's party overtook the Apaches and in a brisk fight wounded at least three warriors and possibly more. One soldier was wounded. After a hard march, in which most of his mounts broke down, Steen's party encountered thirty to forty warriors, "all mounted and dashing about on their horses and cursing us in bad Spanish, calling us to come over and fight them." Even though his force had dwindled to seven men, the Apaches, respecting the Americans' firepower, rode away and avoided a senseless encounter.[6]

These skirmishes, perhaps the first Chiricahua encounters with American troops, left the Indians with a healthy respect for the newcomers. Unscrupulous Mexican traders contributed to the Indians' apprehensions about Americans by spreading rumors that the latter intended to kill all Apaches. As a result, the Chiricahuas again turned to northern Mexico. They also had concluded that an armistice would be beneficial, especially because both Mexican states continued to hold Chiricahua prisoners. The distressed Chokonens and Chihennes had hoped to secure the release of their relatives through negotiations and most groups favored this strategy but not all; Miguel Narbona and Mangas Coloradas characteristically opposed peace at all costs.

Indian peace overtures began in February 1850 when a Chokonen named Antonio came into Bacoachi to request a truce. Because of recent raids, Captain Manuel Martínez promptly imprisoned Antonio but released a woman to return to the Chiricahua leaders. On February 27, Chino, four warriors, and several women arrived, bringing a letter from Posito Moraga[7] offering to exchange their captives for those taken by Terán y Tato the previous May. Martínez forwarded the missive to Elías González, who in turn sent it to the governor, the pragmatic commander recognizing that it would be the first serious Chokonen discussions with Sonora since the treaty of August 1836.[8]

Elías González at once marched to Bacoachi to deal with this important subject. On March 5, 1850, a suspicious and sullen Posito Moraga came in and agreed to return in four days with all of his prisoners, yet he failed to fulfill his promise because he distrusted Sonora and feared a repeat of the Kirker massacre of 1846. Elías González, however, held the trump cards, offering to release his Apache prisoners if the Chokonens would do the same. Finally on March 19 the big catch, Yrigóllen, came in with his captives and the deadlock was broken. Yrigóllen had realistically concluded that acommodation was a necessary alternative to war and agreed to five conditions of peace. Despite this, Elías González was not overly sanguine, admonishing the governor that the Chokonens required time before they "got over the fear that our people are lying in wait to double cross them, as happened at Galeana in the state of Chihuahua and as in fact happened elsewhere." Furthermore, the conditions of the treaty were totally impracticable because they required the Apaches to sustain themselves by hunting and gathering. Elías González knew it was ludicrous to expect the Apaches to remain at peace for any significant length of time without rations.[9]

The Chokonens under Miguel Narbona, Teboca, and probably Cochise were in New Mexico with Mangas Coloradas when Chino first proposed peace. Within a few weeks, they too left Chihenne country for northern Sonora and cast offers of peace. Whether they had any serious intention of ceasing hostilities, however, was another matter.

Teboca himself came into Santa Cruz on March 16 and discussed a truce. After a two-hour conference he left, ostensibly to bring in Mangas Coloradas, who was reported to be in the vicinity. Elías González became cautiously optimistic, characterizing Teboca as "one of the Indians who most resists pacification, although very trustworthy when it comes to any agreement he makes."[10]

He soon received another report that the Chiricahuas, recalling the Kirker massacre, would not reestablish themselves near presidios but would prefer to live peacefully in the Chiricahua Mountains. Unfortunately for both Sonora and those Chokonens peacefully inclined, the Indians were divided into factions: Posito Moraga and Yrigóllen apparently wanted a truce; Teboca and Esquinaline appeared to be leaning toward it; Mangas Coloradas and Miguel Narbona were staunchly opposed. In all likelihood Cochise followed Mangas's lead and had a hand in the bloody raids of 1850–51.[11]

While Yrigóllen and Posito Moraga refrained from raiding, Elías González was overwhelmed with reports of Apache depredations. In early April, Indians killed one man and two women and captured two children from Granados, east of Moctezuma. Near Moctezuma they ran off the horses of Captain Sebastian Reyes. At San Ignacio and Magdalena, Chiricahuas murdered several men and women and captured a young girl. Mangas's band boasted of these killings to an American party they had met and probably traded with.[12] Elías González received other ominous messages. The prefect of Moctezuma echoed the thoughts of most Sonorans, writing that he was "never persuaded that the Apaches' solicitations were in good faith."[13] At Bacoachi, Captain Martínez was unnerved by the testimony of a former captive, José María Mejias, who declared that the Apaches' objective was "to continually wear out this town [Bacoachi] until they can force its depopulation," almost certainly a threat from the tongue of Miguel Narbona.[14]

These events notwithstanding, on April 22, 1850, Elías González concluded a treaty with the moderate Chokonens with rations the key element, which he agreed to issue beginning July 1. Collecting these Indians, many of them hostile and many of them suspicious, was no easy task and he had misgivings, realizing that they had two months to kill before rations were issued. His years of dealing with the Indians had left him cynical: "The outcome cannot be foreseen with complete certainty due to the audacity, double crossing and unreliability of the Indians."[15] Of course the Chiricahuas had the same thoughts toward the Mexicans.

Although Yrigóllen and Posito seemed to favor a cease-fire, the militant faction remained opposed. In early May 1850 a large Chokonen and Bedonkohe war party killed and plundered its way south. The final target was the small village of Soyopa on the Yaqui River about thirty miles southwest of Sahuaripa, which they assaulted on May 25, 1850, killing twelve, wounding seven, and capturing nine before finally returning north. Yrigóllen, who had remained quiet, sent word that Mangas Coloradas and the Chokonen chiefs Teboca, Esquinaline, and Triqueno led the war party.[16]

Meanwhile, at Ures, with the resurgence of hostilities, Governor José de Aguilar wrote Mexico City on June 22 and again on June 28 to plead for federal assistance. On July 25 he reiterated his concerns about the Apache problem, hoping that officials in Mexico City would take some action. "The frontier is deserted," he wrote, "the prosperity lost, and the lands which had been cultivated reflect only the shadow of what they had been and the graves of many victims sacrificed to the fury of the savages."[17] As the Indian war intensified, Sonoran officials accused, indicted, and convicted Apaches living in peace near the presidio of Janos under a treaty consummated on June 24, 1850.

In the spring of 1850, at the time the Chokonens were negotiating with Sonora, Chihenne and Nednhi bands had completed an armistice at Janos. In June Chihenne leaders Delgadito, Itán, Ponce, and Pluma and Nednhi leaders Coleto Amarillo, Láceris, and Arvizu met with Chihuahuan representatives Antonio Guaspe and Alejo García Conde. Conde believed that the Indians were "disarmed and whipped" and were compelled to sue for peace because their New Mexico market had been negated by the American presence. Conde wisely realized that rations were vital to any successful treaty; without them, he feared a repeat of past uprisings.[18] Significantly, Mangas Coloradas and most of the Chokonens remained aloof, although he did authorize the Chokonen Aguirre, a brother of Yrigóllen, to speak for him.[19] In late August, Yrigóllen, the only major Chokonen leader who had expressed interest in accepting Chihuahua's proposal, disillusioned with events in Sonora, finally brought his group to Janos. The remainder of Cochise's band continued depredations against Sonora, skirmishing with troops near Turicachi on August 26.[20]

In September, Miguel Narbona and Mangas Coloradas led another war party against Sonora. First they struck the Santa Cruz–San Ignacio area, cleaning out ranches of their stock. Near Imuris they butchered at least eight citizens before fleeing to Arizona. Believing that peaceful Apaches at Janos were responsible, Elías González wrote Juan José Zozaya at Janos, warning him that his troops would pursue to wherever the trail led—even Janos itself.

One force under Terán y Tato followed hostiles north to the Chiricahuas, Apache Pass, and then on to the Gila. He believed he was pursuing Miguel Narbona and Teboca's followers. Beyond the Gila lay American territory, so Terán y Tato returned to Sonora and on October 30 at Cuchuta jumped Posito Moraga and Triqueno's ranchería, killing two warriors, five women, and one child and taking two prisoners, both members of Triqueno's family.[21]

As 1850 ended, a year in which Apaches reportedly murdered 111 Sonorans, the federal government in Mexico City tried to remedy Sonora's Apache problem and appointed as commanding general and inspector of the military colonies an energetic, capable, but controversial individual who thought himself omniscient: Colonel José María Carrasco.[22] Carrasco replaced the popular Elías González, who had dealt as effectively as possible with the Chiricahuas. The latter had reinvigorated and reinforced the frontier presidios and had carried out coordinated offensives, but the lack of money, resources and the usual chaos in politics had hampered his efforts.

Before Carrasco arrived, a Chiricahua war party invaded Sonora. According to official reports, the Indians divided into two groups, each with at least 200 warriors, and ravaged the state. Mangas led one and Yrigóllen and Posito Moraga the other. In mid-January the Apaches retired north, driving some thirteen hundred cattle and horses before them. Captain Ignacio Pesqueira[23] gathered a force of 100 nationals from Bacoachi and Arispe and headed for Pozo Hediondo, some twenty-four miles southeast of Bacoachi, where he arrived on January 19. At 8 A.M. the next day, Pesqueira detected a cloud of dust and took up pursuit. Three hours later he overtook the Indians, who had taken a defensive position on high ground. What he lacked in judgment he made up in valor as his soldiers charged up the slopes and dislodged the enemy, who fled with Pesqueira's force on their heels. Shortly after, an estimated 250 warriors under Mangas Coloradas counterattacked Pesquiera's party, for whom the fleeing Apaches had been a decoy. The Indians swarmed around the

Merejildo Grijalva. Captured by Chiricahuas in 1849, he escaped in 1859 and became a scout and a thorn in Cochise's side. (*Courtesy Arizona Historical Society, Tucson*)

Ignacio Pesqueira. Future governor of Sonora, he led the troops annihilated at Pozo Hediondo in January 1851 by Mangas Coloradas. (*Courtesy Arizona Historical Society, Tucson*)

Mexicans and in a three-hour battle killed or wounded almost half
the Mexicans, including every officer. The survivors retreated to a
hill and dug in.

At 4 P.M. another party of two hundred warriors under Yrigóllen
and Posito Moraga arrived, augmenting the Apache force to a reported four hundred warriors, although this seems too high. The
Apaches repeatedly assaulted the Sonorans. At 6:30, Pesqueira
withdrew to another hill, relieved that night had finally arrived and
with it a lull in the fighting. The fight was a classic, full of excitement and heroism on both sides and with all the color and drama
of a battle between whites and Indians. Total Mexican casualties:
twenty-six killed and forty-six wounded,[24] perhaps the most successful Chiricahua victory of the nineteenth century. The Apache casualties are not known, as no account from their perspective exists, but
according to a Mexican eyewitness the Sonorans killed or wounded
seventy Apaches—probably an exaggeration.[25]

As to Cochise's involvement, the circumstantial evidence normally would be sufficient to conclude that he was probably there. In
this case, however, there may be other reasons to support his presence. Merejildo Grijalva may have been referring to the Pozo Hediondo fight when he said one of Cochise's earliest successes came
in the early 1850s during a raid that extended as far south as Hermosillo, as did the war party that fought Pesquiera. Cochise returned at the head of his warriors, driving 150 horses and mules.
He kept none for himself, instead distributing them among his
followers.[26]

Geronimo remembered a big "revenge fight" in Sonora. He mentioned that Cochise, Mangas Coloradas, and Juh united to fight
Sonoran troops near Arispe. There are striking similarities between
Geronimo's account and Sonoran reports of the battle. The fight occurred east of Arispe with troops from there and Bacoachi involved.
Geronimo recalled that the troops were from Arispe. Hard fighting
and heavy casualties were reported in both versions, and both accounts say Mangas Coloradas led the Indians. Furthermore, I know
of no other engagement like this in the early 1850s, which was when
Geronimo's fight occurred. Because he dictated his memoirs some
fifty years after the fact, it was perhaps only natural that he made
Cochise leader of the Chokonens when in reality Miguel Narbona

and Yrigóllen were the band leaders in this battle. But if Geronimo's recollections can be trusted, Cochise was there and, like Geronimo and others, enhanced his reputation during the fierce battle.[27]

The Chiricahua victory at Pozo Hediondo incensed Carrasco, who arrived shortly after the defeat. He immediately criticized Elías González and Terán y Tato and a running feud developed, which did little to alleviate the burdens of all concerned. Carrasco at once announced plans to avenge the defeat. By mid-February he had come to a decision: the Apaches at Janos must be punished and he would do it. Accordingly, he led a Sonoran army into Chihuahua and in the early morning of March 5, 1851, surprised several rancherías in the neighborhood of Janos, killing twenty-one Apaches (sixteen men and five women) and capturing sixty-two, among them six warriors. Among the slain was the principal Chokonen chief Yrigóllen and the Nednhi leader Arvizu.[28]

We can only speculate on Cochise's role at this time. Yrigóllen's local group was the only Chokonen unit to make peace at Janos; the remainder of the band and Mangas Coloradas's Bedonkohes continued at war. Undoubtedly Cochise remained with the hostile faction. In fact, just as Carrasco was entering Chihuahua, Miguel Narbona and some fifty Chokonens were striking along the Sonora River at Sinoquipe and Bamori, where they killed several people. One of the victims, before dying, claimed that Miguel Narbona was wounded in the fight. After this, learning that Carrasco was planning a second campaign, the Chokonens retired into present-day Arizona and New Mexico.[29]

Carrasco's second expedition failed to accomplish much, although he did surprise a Nednhi ranchería. Soon afterward he parleyed with three Chokonens near Fronteras (reoccupied in September 1850) and agreed to make peace, providing the Indians obeyed some twenty-eight articles. The Apaches accepted immediately; their sole interest was to obtain the release of the sixty-two prisoners captured at Janos. Unfortunately, Carrasco came down with cholera and died, leaving relations up in the air. Despite this, by late July some four hundred Chokonens had complied with his terms and were camped near Fronteras. In August, Chepillo and Chagaray (both subordinates of Yrigóllen) traveled to Ures to visit their imprisoned relatives, among whom was Chagaray's wife. When nothing was resolved, the two leaders returned to Fronteras, gathered up their followers, and returned to the Chiricahua and Animas mountains; the Chokonens were again at war. No doubt they had a hand in the depredations of August, when Apaches killed fifty-nine Sonorans, bringing the total to more than two hundred in 1851. Sonora announced it would retaliate.[30]

José María Flores succeeded Carrasco as commanding general. He concluded that a major campaign, Sonora's third of 1851, was warranted and necessary, so he made plans for simultaneous operations both north and south of the Chiricahua Mountains, hoping to deprive the Indians of using that area as sanctuary. By late September he had gathered more than 300 men, which he divided into two units. He commanded the first, consisting of 172 presidio troops and two pieces of artillery; the capable José Téran y Tato headed the second division of 150 national troops. A base camp was to be established at San Simon,[31] some fifteen miles northeast of Apache Pass.[32]

In October 1851 the entire command began marching for San Simon. En route Terán y Tato sent out a patrol under the Apache-wise officer Captain Eusebio Gil Samaniego. On October 13, Samaniego's force discovered a ranchería (which proved to be Posito Moraga's and Triqueno's) at Carretas and killed four warriors, two women, and one boy and captured six women and three children. Posito Moraga's wife and relatives of Triqueno were among the captives. Samaniego rejoined Terán y Tato's command south of the Chiricahua Mountains, which they scouted before reaching San Simon on October 21.[33]

Here Flores split his force. He continued north and scouted the Gila country before proceeding into Western Apache territory, where he encountered Indians, killing five warriors and capturing four others. The second division, consisting of Terán y Tato's nationals, scouted east to the Burro Mountains in New Mexico, then southwest along the eastern slopes of the Chiricahuas to the Pitaicache Mountains in Sonora. In the Pilares Mountains in late October, they discovered the Chokonen ranchería of Tapilá, "a most terrible Apache" and killed eight warriors, captured five, and recovered thirty-seven animals.[34] So it was that Sonora's third campaign against the Chiricahuas was brought to a close. With Apache prisoners, Terán y Tato predicted that the Indians would soon solicit peace in order to exchange their prisoners for those held by Sonora. The Chiricahuas did not disappoint him.

In late October, Tapilá, Chepillo, and Chagaray showed up at Bavispe, wishing to exchange prisoners. Details were sparse. According to Mexican accounts, the Sonorans became wary when the Indians arrived, already drunk and obnoxious. In self-defense the Mexicans were forced to kill Tapilá, Ponesino (a brother of Chepillo), and a brother of Chagaray; undoubtedly there was more to this than was reported. These were devastating losses for the Chokonens. Tapilá was a leading war chief, so his death would have to be avenged. Cochise's people moved into the Chiricahua Mountains, where in early 1852 the Chihennes, Bedonkohes, and Chokonens convened for talks to avenge their losses of 1851.[35]

Sonora again took the offensive in 1852. The first campaign got under way in March when Terán y Tato and Captain Miguel Escalante left Santa Cruz for a march into Chokonen territory. On March 18 at the Perilla Mountains in extreme southeastern Arizona they were joined by thirty dragoons under Captain Teodoro de Aros. Late the next afternoon a group of Indians arrived from the Chiricahuas, making signs that they wished to parley. Two Apaches, Delgadito (Chihenne) and Casimiro (Chokonen) conversed with Ensign Manuel Gallegos[36] and agreed to bring in other leaders to talk.

The next morning a party of Chiricahuas estimated at 180 warriors arrived, making signs to parley. Gallegos met them with proposals from Captain de Aros. A blanket was placed between the two lifelong adversaries, with de Aros joining Gallegos and the Chokonens represented by Casimiro, Esquinaline, Miguel Narbona, and at least two of Teboca's sons. Delgadito and a son of Mangas Coloradas (probably Cascos) were also present, as were other Apaches, possibly Cochise and his brother Coyuntura. The meeting took place somewhere north of the Swisshelm Mountains and a few miles west of the southern Chiricahuas. Here "a truce was made with the Apaches, in respect of their superior numbers."

While the two parties were in parley, another large group of Apaches was seen coming from the Chiricahuas. Suspecting treachery, the Mexicans terminated the talks and returned to their camp. Shortly thereafter, Delgadito reappeared and again talked with Gallegos. Earlier that month Mexican troops had attacked his ranchería in the Caguillona Mountains and had captured several of his band. He wanted to make an arrangement for his people who were being held in confinement at Fronteras, but Gallegos had no authority to promise anything; instead, he told Delgadito that they had to leave to find water and grass. The next morning, the Mexicans moved along the foothills on the western side of the Chiricahua Mountains, took a short siesta, and continued on to Bonita Canyon[37] in the Chiricahua Mountains, where they camped.

That evening they noticed Indian fires above the canyon. Consequently, Escalante sent out a small scouting force, who reported that the slopes were crawling with Apaches. At dawn the next morning, March 22, 1852, three hundred to four hundred Chiricahua warriors attacked the Mexican force at Bonita Canyon. They came from all directions, most of them mounted, and wounded Captain de Aros in their first charge. Escalante and de Aros rallied their men, who poured an effective fire on the rampaging Indians. With the element of surprise gone, the Apaches withdrew, maintaining a brisk but ineffective fire for the next two hours. The fight lasted two hours and thirty-six minutes. The Chiricahuas had killed three men and wounded ten, six seriously. De Aros estimated the Indians' loss at twelve dead and thirty wounded. After the fight he moved his force to Apache Pass before he returned to Sonora without any more encounters.[38]

This fight was soon followed by an important triumph over the Nednhis. A 230-man Sonoran force under Captain Miguel Lozada and Captain Eusebio Gil Samaniego found Coleto Amarillo's ranchería in the vicinity of the Florida Mountains, where Padilla had killed the Nednhi leader Soquilla two and one-half years earlier. On March 27 the Sonorans surprised the camp and killed 7 warriors and 21 women and children, captured 16 Apaches, and took 39 mules and horses and 24 head of cattle. Among the dead were Coleto Amarillo and El Chinito, "known for their atrocities in Sonora and Chihuahua."[39] It was a devastating blow to the Janeros local group of the Nednhis; the loss of two important leaders compelled the Indians to move from Mexico's grasp and effect an agreement with the Americans in New Mexico. The remainder of the 1850s was characterized by this behavior: when the Chihenne and Nednhis wore out their welcome with the Americans, they leapfrogged the border into Chihuahua. For the most part, Cochise's people remained in southern Arizona beyond the reach of Mexican troops.

The early 1850s was a time of dramatic change in the leadership of the Chokonens. In 1851 they lost three of their principal leaders; Yrigóllen and Tapilá at the hands of Sonorans and Teboca probably in the same manner. No one leader emerged to dominate the Chokonen band as Pisago Cabezón had in the 1830s and, to a lesser degree, Yrigóllen had in the 1840s.

During the early 1850s, the Chokonen local groups were broken down as follows: the one headed by Posito Moraga, Triqueno, and Teboquita normally lived in the area bounded by Arizona, New Mexico, Sonora, and Chihuahua, with the Pitaicache Mountains their favorite camping area; another, under the leadership of Chepillo, Esquinaline, Yrinco, Aguirre, and Parte, lived in the southern Chiricahua, Animas, and Peloncillo mountains (this was Yrigóllen's old band, and philosophically it was more moderate than the other two); Miguel Narbona, Carro, and Cochise continued to lead the third group of Chiricahuas, whose favorite camping areas remained Apache Pass and the Chiricahua and Dragoon mountains.

As Miguel Narbona and Carro aged and their influence waned, Cochise emerged as leader. One Chiricahua explained: "Ability in war and wisdom make the leader. It's easier to get to the front if you are a good fighter. . . . The leader is not chosen, he is just recognized." [40] This described Cochise's position as he approached his prime in the early to mid-1850s. There were no pacifists among Chiricahua leaders; for a warrior to emerge as chief, he had to combine great fighting skill with wisdom and a deep sensitivity to the less-fortunate members of his group.

From 1852 through 1856, Cochise's Chokonens continued to war on Mexico. Although not specifically mentioned in any of the Mexican reports, Cochise definitely participated in many of the war parties which ravaged Mexico at this time. Even the notorious Miguel Narbona, well known in Sonora, was mentioned but sparingly after 1852. Cochise's war parties left few survivors to identify their assailants. Each winter he joined Mangas Coloradas on expeditions against Mexico, and each year his reputation within the band grew when his warriors returned with large amounts of booty and livestock.

In early 1853, Chokonen groups migrated south to the Chiricahuas and northern Sonora. That March, Mangas Coloradas organized the annual winter expedition against Sonora. After raiding deep into the interior, the Apaches made their ritualistic last stop at Fronteras. On April 11 the war party came across five boys tending their sheep south of the presidio; they dispassionately killed each, then swept through Fronteras and galloped away with most of its stock toward the San Bernardino Valley.

Captain Mendoza rounded up a force of twenty-five men and later that day unexpectedly encountered Mangas's rear guard. A hard fight ensued, with both sides taking casualties before the Sonorans limped back to Fronteras. All told, the Mexicans lost four soldiers killed and two soldiers wounded. The Apaches lost eight dead and several wounded, according to Mendoza's report. Mangas Coloradas acknowledged that he lost three warriors in this encounter.[41]

Two Chokonen war parties invaded Sonora in the summer of 1853. They overwhelmed everything in their path, slaughtering women and children indiscriminately. One party was led by Posito Moraga and Triqueno, the other by Carro, Casimiro, and Yaque. The first raided along the Sonora River; the second hit the small town of Granados. One June morning forty citizens of Granados left their homes to work their crops; the Chiricahuas were waiting and sprang upon them from every direction, killing nine (five men and four children) and capturing one woman and two children. Next they continued south to Tepache, where they ran off several mules and oxen. For the next three weeks they terrorized settlements along the western slopes of the Sierra Madre. The two war parties finally united at Tecoripa, eighty miles southeast of Ures, and routed a party of twenty nationals, killing a captain and three others. The next day, three miles north of Cumuripa, about two hundred Indians destroyed Hacienda de Cieneguita and killed twelve people, wounded two, and captured one.[42] José Vega was seriously wounded but lived to tell his story to Captain Pascual Cota of Cumuripa's National Guard. Cota led a reluctant and jittery group of nationals to the scene of the disaster. His men, however, appalled at the devastation, refused to follow the Apaches. A disgusted Cota vowed that he "would never again lead citizens against the enemy."[43]

The following winter, the Chiricahuas sent another war party against Mexico. Mangas Coloradas, Delgadito, and Miguel Narbona led this incursion into Sonora from the Chiricahuas. Although the foray had been in the planning stages for some time, the Chokonens had only recently become incensed because of an encounter in Sonora. In late January 1854, three prominent men, including Casimiro, were murdered at Bavispe under conditions which suggested foul play.[44] The Chiricahuas avenged these killings and more. Throughout February they pillaged their way south, hitting the districts of Sahuaripa and Alamos. The governor notified towns to mobilize against the hostiles as they returned north, but the Indians easily eluded pursuit.[45]

A few months later another war party was organized, this time under the Chihenne chiefs Delgadito and Costales[46] in conjunction with Miguel Narbona. This band penetrated south to Alamos, where an estimated 200 Apaches attacked the outskirts of the city. By late May, Delgadito and Costales had retired to the Oputo Mountains, and Miguel Narbona was reported at Turicachi. On June 1, Miguel and 50 Chokonens harassed citizens at the *cienaga* near Fronteras. They stole sixteen mules and horses and carried off a boy before heading for the Teras Mountains. Miguel had chosen an advantageous time for this raid: only hours earlier, 135 men had left the presidio to scout the Chiricahua Mountains, where the Indians were finding refuge because of the recent Gadsden Treaty between Mexico and the United States.[47]

The Gadsden Treaty was negotiated in the last days of 1853 when Mexico sold a large tract of land to the United States, pushing the Sonora and Chihuahua borders south to the present boundary.[48] The United States Senate ratified an amended version of the treaty on April 25, 1854. At the time of the sale, according to Hubert Howe Bancroft, there was little concern in either Sonora or Chihuahua because the land sold was essentially Apache country and generally uninhabited,[49] yet the agreement had significant ramifications in the ongoing Chokonen-Sonora conflict. Mexican forces were not supposed to penetrate north of San Bernardino and the present border. Eventually Cochise's people became aware of this and continued to find sanctuary in the Chiricahua Mountains, along the Gila River, and in the Mogollon Mountains.

Initially, most Mexicans viewed the Gadsden Treaty with ambivalence, but implicit threats of Yankee expansionism and explicit threats from American filibusters, coupled with the incessant Apache raids from north of the line, gave Sonorans an increasingly apprehensive feeling toward most North Americans. After the treaty, the Chiricahua Tribe continued to raid into Mexico at will. This exasperated Mexican officials, who accused American settlers and government officials of trading arms and ammunition to Apaches in return for stolen Mexican stock, a charge that undoubtedly had some validity and was repeated countless times during the next decade.[50]

During the mid-1850s there emerged a casual pattern of Chiricahua raids into Mexico followed by retreats to U.S. territory and security. An example of this occurred in the spring of 1855 when a large party of Chokonens and Chihennes joined forces for a raid into Mexico. The Chihennes, living near Santa Rita del Cobre, went west to Apache Pass, where they enlisted a large group of Chokonens, probably under the leadership of Cochise. On their way south, they picked up another group in the lower Peloncillos, probably at Sarampion. Once in Mexico, they split into smaller parties, the Chokonens concentrating on Sonora and the Chihennes under Josecito, Costales, and Itán raiding into Chihuahua.[51]

The Chokonens hit their favorite target, Sonora, before they slipped from Terán y Tato's grasp back into Arizona. The Chihennes returned to their camps along the Mimbres River, where they found that the Americans were ready to make another treaty—the third in the past four years. The major difference in this agreement was that the Americans, for the first time, convinced the Apaches to cede large tracts of land. Many of the Chihenne leaders signed, but Mangas Coloradas demurred.[52]

The mid-1850s was undoubtedly a prosperous time for Cochise and his people. Although living primarily in U.S. territory, they had little contact with Americans, mainly because of the scarcity of traffic and lack of settlements in their country. Cochise's people were not a party to the treaties made in 1852, 1853, and 1855 in New Mexico by the Chihenne and Nednhi bands. This leads to a question: Did the Anglos know of the Chokonens, and if so they recognize them as a distinct band?

The Chokonens, who were to become known to Americans as the Chiricahuas in the late 1850s, were living in southern Arizona, yet references to any band identified as Chiricahuas before 1850 are scarce. The Mexicans generally lumped southern Apache bands, basically the Chiricahua Tribe, into one generic group and called them Gilenos. Historian Ralph Smith, who has done extensive research on Apache activities in Mexico prior to 1858, wrote that he had not "encountered a single mention of the term Chiricahua to identify an Apache tribe or band in . . . the [eighteen] thirties or forties."[53] Mexican archives do contain scattered references to the "Chiricahua" Apaches from 1830 through 1850, but on the whole these references are vague, sparse, and immaterial.

According to Merejildo Grijalva, who lived with Cochise at the time, during the 1850s the Chokonens ranged over an enormous territory: from the Gila River and Mogollon Mountains in Arizona south to the Sierra Madre in Mexico. He recalled that he first met Americans at Stein's Peak, probably in the fall of 1858 or perhaps earlier. The point to be made is that during the 1850s the Chokonen band was living in Arizona within its historic local-group territory. Although some of its leaders were known to Americans, the Indians were not known or referred to as Chiricahuas. Two reports identified Chokonen chiefs as Mogollon Apaches. The first mention was by Captain Joseph Horace Eaton in a report dated December 23, 1855, from Fort Thorn, New Mexico, and the second was by Dr. Michael Steck,[54] agent for the Chihennes, whose sincerity and honesty were unique in a government bureau noted for corruption.

In late 1855 the Chiricahuas raided Mesilla. Eaton pursued the hostiles but could not overtake them before they disappeared into the Burro Mountains. At San Vicente he met with José Mangas, brother of Mangas Coloradas, and Casco, a son of Mangas Coloradas. These two individuals, with whom Cochise was well acquainted, informed Eaton that Chaynee, a Mogollon, had led the hostile party, which was camped near the Gila. In the same report, Eaton shed some light on the Chokonen band, probably having obtained the details from either Steck or José Mangas. The Mogollon chiefs, Eaton wrote, are "Miguel, El Carro, Juan Apache, El Fresco and Capitan Chaynee, fighting men number some say 300, Dr. Steck says not over 150." [55]

Eaton had unwittingly identified the leaders of the Chokonens, who at this time were living in the northern limits of their range. These chiefs were well known to Mexicans: Miguel was Miguel Narbona, El Carro was Carro and El Fresco was probably Francisco, a close associate of Cochise who actually was a leader among the Eastern White Mountain Apaches, a non-Chiricahua band. The identities of Juan Apache [56] and Chaynee are not known.

Further evidence that the Chokonens were sometimes misidentified as Mogollons may be discerned from Dr. Steck's report of September 19, 1856, in which he named Esquinaldine (Esquinaline) as the "principal chief of the Coyoteros" and said two of the subordinate chiefs were "Chagari [and] Cochil." [57] Chagaray was a prominent Chokonen leader and Cochil might well have been Cochise, who may have been a subordinate of Esquinaline at this time.

In any event, few Americans understood the breakdown of Apache bands in the 1850s and 1860s. On several occasions Cochise was referred to as a Coyotero or Pinal, which to twentieth-century students would indicate Western Apache, a distinct tribe from the Chiricahua. As far as Anglo references to Apaches as Chiricahuas, it came into vogue in the late 1850s when Americans established a stage station at Apache Pass. In fact, Steck identified Esquinaline, the same Indian he called a Coyotero two years earlier, as a Chiricahua (or Chokonen) when he first met Cochise's people in late 1858.

With the identity of the Chokonens solved, it must be assumed that they raided New Mexico periodically. Steck recognized this and on the last day of 1855 recommended that the army mount an expedition against the Apaches living near the headwaters of the Gila, who he supposed were the culprits. In early January 1856, depredations in the vicinity of Mesilla were attributed to Apaches living in the Mogollons. Mangas Coloradas admitted that some of his people had participated and that he was unable to restrain them. Steck feared his Chihennes would be unfairly charged for some of these raids; consequently, the military began preparations for an expedition into the inaccessible and almost impregnable Mogollon country. [58]

The campaign, commanded by Captain Daniel T. Chandler, consisted of troops from Fort Craig and Fort Thorn. Steck accompanied the expedition, which struck a large trail of stolen sheep and followed it northwest into the Mogollon Mountains. Here they surprised a ranchería, recapturing 250 sheep and 21 horses and mules. The attack stunned the hostiles, who had not expected pursuit. The soldiers killed one Apache and wounded three or four others, two of whom later died from their wounds according to Refugio Corrales, an Apache captive who was at the fight. This was the camp of El Cautivo, Bedonkohe or Chokonen leader with whom Cochise was closely associated.[59]

In late April 1856 the Chihennes left their homes in New Mexico and joined Cochise's Chokonens for a series of sanguinary raids into Sonora and Chihuahua. According to a Mexican captive, the war party was led by Mangas Coloradas, Delgadito, and one who would strike terror in the hearts of southwesterners for nearly a quarter-century: Victorio. One group under Delgadito and Victorio concentrated on Chihuahua. The second consisted of Chokonens and Bedonkohes under Mangas Coloradas, his son Cascos, and most likely Cochise, who had evolved into a Chokonen war leader by this time. They left Sonora in a state of frenzy most of May. Their goal was horses and captives, for which there was a ready market along the Mimbres and Río Grande, where the Apaches could trade them for guns, ammunition, and whiskey.

Casco's party caused much damage. During the first three weeks of May, the Chiricahuas besieged Baccrac, stealing stock and preventing farmers from working their fields. Fifteen miles north lay Bavispe, whose troops were hunting for Apaches along the border, leaving it virtually defenseless. On May 24 the Indians surrounded it, killed one man, and captured his son. The Apache scourge was worse than anyone had ever seen, reported Bavispe officials.[60]

Meanwhile at Chinapa, some seventy-five miles west of Bavispe, another war party (probably the Chokonen element) virtually decimated the town. Chinapa had a pathetic history of being hit by Chiricahua war parties; in early 1848, Chiricahuas under Miguel Narbona had killed, wounded, or captured most of the town. On May 27, 1856, Apaches burned and destroyed most of the town and killed several of its citizens. The prefect of Arispe informed the governor of the gory attack: "Today the town of Chinapa does not exist. Yesterday at 3:00 P.M. a citizen of that town presented himself to me and expressed in these terms: The Apaches have finished, they have captured Chinapa."

The prefect immediately gathered a force of eighty-five men and marched to Chinapa, arriving there at 11 P.M. and discovering "a most dreadful silence, everything burning in flames and blood splattered everywhere." The party cautiously examined the area and stumbled over three bodies. Not a sound was heard until a barking dog drew the rescuing parties attention to a stone house where many of the women and children, with ten men, had taken refuge. The exit was smoldering, but only the door was burned. The survivors furnished details of the bloody disaster. The Apaches had arrived about eight o'clock, taking one woman prisoner and killing her husband. For the next five hours they went door to door and burned each house. They finally left about one o'clock.[61] The Chokonens withdrew to their rancherías in the Chiricahua Mountains.

Despite their successes in the summer of 1856, some Chiricahua groups were willing to make peace with Chihuahua. Many had become disenchanted and apprehensive about living in U.S. territory. First, members of the Nednhi band arrived at Janos, followed by some Chokonens under Chepillo and Esquinaline, then some Chihennes under Itán and Delgadito. During the spring and summer of 1856, Cochise's following remained camped in the Chiricahua Mountains, making mescal and organizing raiding parties into Mexico.[62] It was about this time that Miguel Narbona died (details are vague) and only Carro and Esquinaline of the old-line Chokonen leaders remained. In the prime of life physically and intellectually, Cochise was recognized as the war leader within his band. Soon he would be the dominant Chokonen chief.

# Chapter 6

# DOUBLE TREACHERY IN MEXICO

During the mid-1850s Americans began to make their presence felt in Arizona. In 1856 American soldiers replaced Mexican troops at Tucson, and ambitious American capitalists rejuvenated the mining region of Tubac. Cochise scarcely noticed their arrival as the Chokonens remained undisturbed by these groups to the west. East of them, however, was a different story. In 1857 American troops, responding to Apache depredations in New Mexico, launched a large-scale offensive known as the Bonneville campaign. It struck Apaches, including some Chiricahuas, but most of the Indians had heard of the expedition and slipped into Mexico, where they hoped to remain until affairs calmed down and American troops returned to their posts. Once below the border, they planned to resume friendly relations at either Fronteras or Janos. Initially Cochise remained aloof, awaiting the results of these meetings. Finally, in the summer of 1857, he cautiously brought his followers into Janos and then Fronteras.

Several Chokonens had been negotiating off and on at Janos for the past two years, although Cochise apparently was not involved. In the summer of 1855, Yrigóllen's old group under Yrinco,[1] Aguirre,[2] and Parte[3] sent emissaries to Janos, but no treaty was consummated.[4] The following summer Yrinco again solicited peace at Janos and to prove his sincerity joined Mexican troops in pursuit of hostiles under the venerable Babosa.[5] They overtook the raiders in

the mountains west of Janos and recovered the stock.[6] Soon thereafter Esquinaline and Chepillo left the Chiricahuas for Janos, also
hopeful of making a truce.[7] Only those Chokonens under Cochise
and Carro remained in Arizona, opposing an armistice for the time
being.

Soon after the Chokonen request for a cease-fire, a few Chihennes, dissatisfied with American treatment in New Mexico, arrived at Janos. Their discontent had festered because of the paucity
of rations and assistance provided by the Americans. Relations
became further strained when an American officer attacked Delgadito's ranchería in April 1856, killing one woman and wounding
several women and children. Steck protested, but his report was discredited by Colonel John Garland, who claimed the Indians were
appeased when compensation was provided. After all, they were
only Apaches.[8]

The Chihennes had another motive: they hoped to obtain the release of Nalze, a son of Monteras who was captured by Padilla's
troops in May 1855. Accordingly, on July 30, 1856, Itán, Láceris,
and Monteras requested a truce at Janos and turned over Prudencio
Aralos, whom they had captured some three months before. Captain
Padilla requested instructions from José María Zuloaga,[9] recently
appointed Chihuahua's peace commissioner. Zuloaga sanctioned the
release of Nalze in the "best interests of humanity," obviously
hoping that the Chihennes would make peace. Soon after, however,
to show his appreciation, Monteras and a small band ambushed
three men on the road from Barranco, killing one and wounding the
other two. Then his band murdered another man near Casas Grandes
before returning to Steck's agency in New Mexico.[10]

Surprisingly, Monteras's actions did not impede negotiations.
Some Chokonens continued to press for an armistice, joined by a
few Chihennes and Nednhis who had decided against returning to
New Mexico. On August 15, 1856, Steck explained to Governor
David Meriwether of New Mexico that some of the Chihennes had
made a treaty with the towns of Janos and Corralitos. "Their reason," wrote Steck, "was that a year ago the people of Janos had
captured an Apache [Nalze] and about three months ago the Apaches
captured a Mexican; a treaty was then concluded in order to exchange captives." [11] On August 19 the official newspaper of Chihua-

hua, *El Eco de la Frontera,* reported the possibility of a peace "as thirty-six of them are now living near Corralitos and will accompany Commissioner Zuloaga to Chihuahua City to make a formal peace with the Governor." [12]

The Indian commission that was to confer with the governor encountered an unexpected delay; two incidents upset the conciliation. In late August, Luis García pursued into Chihuahua a band of Apaches who had been raiding in Sonora. Only through the intervention of the people at Janos were hostilities averted. This incident excited the Indians, who recalled Elías González's and Carrasco's attack, and disturbed Chihuahuan authorities, who found García's actions "criminal and against the dignity and interests of this state." [13] The second event occurred lightning quick and without warning and temporarily stalled negotiations. On September 2 at the siesta hour, Mangas Coloradas and thirty to forty warriors boldly raided Janos, galloping away with more than one hundred head of stock. Padilla recognized several hostiles, including El Cautivo and other Chokonens. Cochise is not mentioned but may have participated in that Mangas led the raid and Cochise was closely associated with El Cautivo. [14]

In all likelihood Mangas was cognizant that a small party of Chiricahuas under Esquiriba was bargaining at Janos but was disinterested in the results; he and Cochise opposed any talk of peace. Yet the raid infuriated and embarrassed Padilla, who imprisoned Esquiriba's party (thirteen individuals, including four men). Employing a strategy which had worked in 1850, Padilla and Zuloaga decided to use the captives as ransom to force Mangas to return the stock and to lure other hostiles into Janos. [15]

Padilla and Zuloaga knew the imprisonment of Esquiriba's group was unjustified because he did not belong to the same band of Chiricahuas that carried out the raid. Moreover, neither Esquiriba nor any members of his band could compel Mangas's party to return the stolen stock, which was the condition set by Padilla for the prisoners' release. Both Padilla and Zuloaga knew better; they had more experience and more contact with the Chiricahuas than any other whites on the North American continent, either Anglo or Mexican. They understood that there was no one supreme chief among the Chiricahuas, no one man whose word was promptly accepted and obeyed by the autonomous bands. This is precisely why, at every peace conference, the Mexicans designated one leader to act as general and another to serve as his second in command. They hoped the white man's political organization would serve to control and influence the independent Apache bands and local groups. History had proved this impracticable, but the Mexicans could not conceive of handling the Chiricahuas in any other way.

Padilla's and Zuloaga's plan worked in one respect. After a few months of parleying, the Indians, who were assisted by a concerned Dr. Steck, came into Janos. On December 31, 1856, the Nednhi leaders Láceris and Felipe, with a party of eleven warriors and fourteen women, arrived at Janos to reopen negotiations.[16] Láceris was from the Janeros local group of Nednhis, who for the past few years had been living along the Mimbres River in New Mexico. Felipe was a Carrizaleño Apache, a local group of Nednhis which lived almost exclusively in Chihuahua; the Carrizaleños had been at war with Mexico since the summer of 1855. For the past eighteen months, Chihuahuan campaigns had proved somewhat effective; one in September 1855 and another in March 1856 had succeeded in scattering the local groups of Felipe and Cojinillín.[17]

The Indians remained at Janos for three days before agreement was reached. Láceris (probably Esquiriba's brother) traveled to Chihuahua City, arriving there about January 19, 1857, and conferring with commanding general José Merino. The general was impressed with Láceris's sincerity and concluded the treaty. The conditions were neither as complicated nor as unrealistic as past treaties, the main points being that the Apaches would release their captives and that the Mexicans would issue rations. When convinced of the Indians' good intentions, Merino would authorize Padilla to free Esquiriba's party.[18]

Láceris brought his Nednhi band of 184 individuals into Janos. In February 1857, Padilla began issuing rations to the Chiricahuas and afterward wrote Merino about the auspicious beginning. The armistice soon attracted more Chiricahuas. In March, Felipe brought in his Carrizaleño group of 98, increasing the number of peaceful Apaches to 282, and events in New Mexico and Sonora soon drove the Chokonens and Chihennes into Janos.[19]

Having heard rumors of the Bonneville campaign, the Chihennes were the next group of Chiricahuas to forsake U.S. territory for Janos. In mid-March, Steck reported that the Chihenne chiefs "and most of their people had gone to Janos to make a treaty." [20] In reality, American treatment of the Apaches had left much to be desired, although the sincere and competent Steck had done all in his power to keep them content. The Indians were unhappy about their rations; Mangas Coloradas had complained to Steck more than once about the lack of them. Almost as important was the cavalier American treatment of Apaches, which caused the Chihennes to wonder whether the grass might be greener in Mexico. Beginning with Chandler's wanton attack in April 1856 and continuing through the winter of 1857, the Chihennes had several encounters with Mexicans and Americans in southwestern New Mexico.

Not all of the incidents were unprovoked. During the first three months of 1857, nine Chihennes were killed in engagements with Americans, making their decision to move into Mexico a little easier. By the spring of 1857, Delgadito and fifty members of his group joined in the peace at Janos; Mangas and the other Chihennes would wait and see. [21]

Cochise's Chokonens had been camped in the Chiricahuas since early 1857, undecided about their next course of action. In February 1857 a local group had attempted to make peace at Janos, but the overture was rejected. Yaque, [22] an inveterate raider and killer, had arrived with several hundred sheep stolen in New Mexico, perhaps implicating him in the cold-blooded murder of Zuñi agent Henry Linn Dodge [23] the previous November. In any event Padilla was uncertain about feeding Yaque's band and wrote Zuloaga for instructions. Zuloaga officially replied that any Indians who had raided in either New Mexico or Sonora must not be rationed. [24] Yet this response apparently did not prevent Yaque from trading his sheep. In March, two citizens from Janos told Steck the Apaches were "carrying on a brisk trade of mules and horses and [had] sold 600 sheep." [25]

The large number of hostiles along the border produced a volatile atmosphere, and Zuloaga and Padilla realized that they had to persuade the Indians to join in the precarious truce. In the spring of 1857 several events occurred, any one of which could have forced the skittish Apaches to bolt. In April a force of 150 Chihuahuan volunteers reached Casas Grandes, planning to attack the Indians, who they claimed had been raiding in the interior. It was of little concern to these volunteers that Láceris's people were innocent; they wanted Apache blood or scalps. Fortunately for all concerned, Padilla had received word of their arrival and immediately dispatched a terse note to Esmeregildo Quintana, who was leading the volunteers, admonishing him that any attack would be "treasonous and disgraceful and should be suspended." Padilla's decisive actions averted a potential crisis.[26] After this, Zuloaga and Padilla redoubled their efforts to bring in all the hostiles living at Alamo Hueco, but to no avail. Mangas Coloradas and Cochise were still taking a wait-and-see approach.

In late May another incident led to more turmoil, which Sonora erroneously blamed on the Janos Apaches. Details are vague, but apparently a few Chokonens had gone into Janos, perhaps to visit relatives or to trade booty. Padilla ordered them seized and placed in the guardhouse, hoping to coerce the hostiles in. Instead this enraged the Indians, who at once raided the ranches of Miguel Samaniego and Agustín Acuña near Bavispe, running off twelve mules and a horse and capturing two children. From Bavispe, Captain Cruz wrote Zuloaga and blamed the raid on the Indians at Janos. Zuloaga insisted that the hostilities were likely the work of those bands living at Alamo Hueco under Mangas Coloradas, Carro, Esquinaline, and Cochise. "These bands," added Zuloaga, "have not agreed to peace and I am doing all in my power to convince them to make peace." Zuloaga also believed that the two captives would be used to trade for his prisoners at Janos.[27]

By late June the hostiles had reached a decision; with the Bonneville campaign scouring the heart of their territory, the Chiricahuas again turned toward Mexico. Mangas's followers opted for Janos and Cochise's Chokonens sent emissaries to Fronteras for the second time in four months. The previous February, Pablo, a son of the old-time Chokonen chief Matías, had come in requesting peace for the entire Chokonen band and Sonora had named a peace commissioner, but nothing of note occurred.[28] By March the Chokonens had retired to the Chiricahuas, where they were reported to be harvesting mescal.[29] In July, Pablo again entered Fronteras and parleyed with Captain Gabriel García. The Apache claimed to speak for

several groups, which, we can infer, included those of Cochise, Esquinaline, Chepillo, and Colchon, and pledged to return in mid-July
with the entire Chokonen band to consummate a truce.[30] García's
plan, which included rations, was endorsed by both the state and
federal governments, but again the Chokonens failed to come in, ostensibly having had second thoughts about trusting Sonora. Some
joined their Chihenne and Nednhi relatives at Janos, while others
raided Sonora before eventually joining Mangas at Janos.[31]

The raids began in mid-July and the state government offered
empty rhetoric to appease local authorities. The prefect of Arispe
declared that the Apaches' peace proposals were a smoke screen: "It
was their cunning and accustomed slyness so that they could harvest
their acorns and commit their accustomed robberies."[32] The *Alta
California* quoted Sonoran Acting Governor José de Aguilar relative
to the Chokonen overtures made by "some of their principal warriors, now on the frontier between Fronteras and Janos . . . desiring
a cessation of hostilities, and anxious to form a treaty of peace; but
no confidence . . . [can] be placed in these savages and robbers;
they had so frequently made treaties and as often violated them, that
they were no longer to be trusted." De Aguilar recommended a war
of extermination against the Apaches, even though Sonora was in no
position to take any offensive.[33]

In the meantime, more and more Chiricahuas visited Janos to receive rations and whiskey and to dispose of their stolen stock. Sometime in July, Mangas Coloradas, Victorio, Sargento, and Riñon
brought in their Bedonkohe and Chihenne followers.[34] Their groups
numbered more than three hundred and according to one report
swelled the Indian population to more than one thousand, although
official Janos records indicated there were about six hundred.[35]

Cochise and his followers showed up in August, probably to dispose of stolen stock and plunder.[36] These wilder Chiricahuas, or
broncos, were a destabilizing influence. Zuloaga and Padilla might
have decided to take this opportunity to do away with as many Chiricahuas as possible. Again details are sparse, but it seems likely that
Mexican officials deliberately issued poisoned rations to .the
Apaches. Cochise, fearful of contaminated rations and aware of a
rumor that troops would be sent to exterminate the friendly
Apaches, returned to the Chiricahuas and security.[37]

After a band council in early September, the Chokonen leaders decided to reopen negotiations at Fronteras, hoping at least to postpone a Sonoran offensive. As proof of their good faith, they returned a captive taken in one of their raids near Matape.[38] By late September, Cochise and most of the Chokonen band of 680 individuals showed up at Fronteras wanting rations. This created enormous problems for the Fronteras commander, Captain Gabriel García. To begin with, he had received no instructions from his superiors; second, he barely had adequate provisions to feed his small garrison, notwithstanding 680 Indians. He sent urgent appeals to the governor imploring him to provide rations for the Apaches until the arrival of the peace commissioner.[39]

More than anything, García wished to take steps before the Americans struck an alliance with the Chiricahuas. The Sonoran government was acutely sensitive to American expansionism, although the arrival of American troops in southern Arizona in 1856 had brought about an ephemeral period of improved relations. It was first hoped that the Americans would prove to be a barrier between Mexico and the Apaches, who had driven out most of the Mexican settlers along the border by 1857. Knowledgeable Mexicans thought they were better off to have the Apaches under their care rather than across the border in the United States, where they could find refuge after their raids into Sonora.[40]

Sonora's new governor, Ignacio Pesqueira, was far from prepared to deal with the Chiricahuas' proposal. Internally, chaos prevailed as skirmishes between rival political parties (Pesqueira's and Gándara's) continued; externally, the federal government in Mexico City was providing less and less assistance. While it once had provided six hundred thousand pesos a year for the state (collected within Sonora for customs duty, paper, and tobacco taxes) to fight Apaches and Yaquis, by 1857 it had diverted most of this money to finance its own needs. These problems were further compounded when Pesqueira was forced to shift troops south of Ures to suppress a Yaqui rebellion. Therefore, at the time of Pesqueira's inauguration, the state was in deplorable condition socially, economically, and militarily.[41]

Pesqueira was absent when García's urgent letter explaining the peace proposals arrived. When informed, the governor promptly named Rafael Angel Corella, a battle-hardened officer who had been wounded in the Pozo Hediondo fight, peace commissioner. Pesqueira's selection of Corella was puzzling in that the latter despised Apaches, having buried the victims of their raids on more than one occasion. The year before, he had led the relief party to Chinapa, finding, in his words, "corpses of men, women and children who were completely nude, and the ground saturated with blood." He preferred fighting instead of feeding Apaches and subscribed to the old frontier axiom that the only good Indian was a dead Indian.[42]

Pesqueira instructed Corella to impose fifteen articles on the Apaches before ratifying an armistice, so as usual, the treaty was full of fallacies, with the Sonorans aiming to domesticate and civilize the Chokonens. The articles covered all aspects of Apache life, and the last decreed that if the Apaches failed to live up to any of the fourteen previous articles, the treaty would be voided and the Indians "severely chastised." Any man who thought the Indians would settle down to farming was simply unacquainted with their background and culture. If Corella had had the opportunity to present these demands to Cochise's people, they would have had a good laugh around the campfire. Although the Indians may have agreed to the terms in principle, they never would have put them into practice.[43]

Before meeting the Apaches, Corella reported to Pesqueira:

> When the savages solicit peace at Fronteras the people believe this is the end of their suffering; but quickly they realize that they have been deceived; that this belief is an illusion . . . these same Indians continue committing their accustomed depredations.
>
> Our experience of many years, your excellency, has made us aware of this astute enemy, experience that we have bought with the lives of our many sacrificed victims; these savages have no good will.[44]

Meanwhile, at Fronteras, Cochise, weary of waiting, left the area in early October. Captain García wrote that the Apaches had left without his knowledge and that Esquinaline had sent his sister to advise him that they had retired only to gather acorns, berries, and other food staples. García pessimistically wrote that the Apaches had either resumed raiding or had gone to Bavispe, where an Apache woman named Lucía had solicited peace. The officer was dubious about the Chokonens' intentions, although Esquinaline's sister "assured me with her life that the Apaches will return."[45]

At 10 A.M. on October 9, 1857, an Apache warrior, his wife, and his two children approached Fronteras. The man might have been Cochise's brother Coyuntura and the woman Coyuntura's wife, Yones. Cochise frequently used his sister-in-law as a messenger because she was probably somewhat conversant in Spanish. The warrior willingly furnished details about the recent activities of the Chokonens, revealing that Cochise was camped with El Cautivo and had sent him to inform García that the Chokonens had retired to Guadalupe Canyon near the San Bernardino River. Many families were infected with a fever, he said, and several Indians already had perished in the epidemic, probably the result of contaminated rations from Janos. Cochise had sent him not only to reiterate his desire for peace but also to deter a potential Sonoran offensive, although none was planned at the time. An incredulous García asked, "If all the Apaches were so sick, who were committing the depredations in the interior?" To this the warrior responded that "they had not lost their passes given to them at Janos and that those committing these depredations must be from the bands living at Janos. This was the information given to them by Colchon, whom they had left a few days before." He also revealed that while "at Janos they were always very sick. Several women and children had died and at least ten men. The survivors had moved to gather acorns that had been previously stored. Also that Nabecilla [a Chokonen man] had gone to gather some gold hidden in the Chiricahua Mountains, which he would take and trade to Captain Padilla at Janos."[46]

Steck corroborated the Chiricahuas' belief that they had been poisoned at Janos. On November 21, 1857, he wrote his superiors that Mangas Coloradas had sent him word offering to return from Janos and live in peace:

[These Apaches] . . . have suffered much from disease and many of them have died from their own story the mortality has been very great scarcely a family returns but has their hair cropped short, the badge of mourning for some near relative. They believe they have been poisoned and I have but little doubt that many of them have as reports have reached here from the citizens of Janos that many of them have been poisoned and the symptoms as described by the Indians resemble those of poisoning by arsenic—probably administered in their rations—whiskey as that formed a part of them.[47]

Steck reported later that more than sixty Chihennes had fallen victim. Cochise's Chokonens had suffered a similar fate.[48]

Meanwhile the Chiricahuas awaited Corella's peace commission, which arrived at Fronteras on November 5. Soon thereafter, Colchon's wife appeared at Fronteras as a representative of three local groups (Colchon's, Cochise's, and Esquinaline's) that were living in the Pitaicachi, Enmedio, and Animas mountains. She acknowledged that several Apaches were still very sick and that ten Chokonen men had died (probably forty to fifty individuals in all), including the prominent Carro and a minor leader named Tinaja. Furthermore, she claimed, Esquinaline planned to honor the peace agreement and settle at Cuchuverachi, a deserted ranch twenty miles northeast of Fronteras. She also said the Americans had communicated with the Chokonens—probably a reference to messages Steck had sent the Chihennes asking them to return to New Mexico, which may have included an invitation to the Chokonens.[49]

Corella's conference with Colchon's wife was ostensibly unsatisfactory. Wary of Corella and his "peace" contingent of seventy troops, the Chokonens remained in the hills. Their actions delighted Corella, who was itching for a fight. He enthusiastically reported that the Apaches had resumed raiding in earnest, though he cited no specific incidents. He therefore requested new orders to pursue those who have "taken up arms against the state." Not all agreed with Corella, however. In mid-November the perspicacious José María Elías González again urged that the state provide rations before the Chiricahuas made peace in Arizona. Captain García endorsed this thought the following month, but no government assistance was in sight.[50]

Mangas Coloradas and Delgadito had returned to Steck's agency by early December. Only the groups under Victorio, Láceris, and a few other minor leaders remained at Janos until early January 1858. They, too, finally returned to New Mexico, their ranks decimated because of the poisoned rations at Janos.[51]

Cochise apparently spent the winter of 1857–58 in southeastern Arizona, away from Mexican control. From here his people resumed their old raiding patterns into Mexico, encountering only token resistance. As long as they depredated below the border, they were left alone by American troops, who were too few and too scattered to give the Apaches any trouble. At Fort Buchanan an American officer allegedly remarked that he would make an agreement to sell arms and ammunition to the Apaches to help them in their raids below the border. When they returned to American soil, they would find a ready market for all of their stolen stock.[52]

The next news of Cochise's people arrived in late April 1858. On the evening of April 28 a small party of two women and two warriors appeared at Fronteras soliciting peace for the ranchería of Lucas, who, with Colchon, had succeeded Posito Moraga as leader of a local group. Lucas was camped near Batepito with some forty warriors. Two days later at 8 A.M., the influential Chepillo surprised the garrison at Fronteras and spoke for his ranchería of fifty warriors in the Chiricahuas. There was no mention of Cochise's whereabouts, but his local group was probably living in the Apache Pass and Stein's Peak vicinity, where Apaches were seen by overland parties.[53]

In May 1858, Cochise was probably raiding in Sonora, having been summoned by Mangas Coloradas. A few months earlier, a company of Sonoran nationals from Cucurpe had clashed with some raiding Chiricahuas and had killed two sons of Mangas, possibly including Cascos.[54] As a result, Mangas organized an avenging war party and Cochise, with his wife Dos-teh-seh losing two brothers, probably joined him and led the Chokonen contigent. They again found Sonora virtually defenseless as prefects of several districts begged the governor for assistance. According to Sonoran reports, more than five hundred Apaches plundered the state "under the pretext of avenging the deaths of Mangas Coloradas' sons." This same account reported that Mangas had declared he would continue killing until three hundred victims were sacrificed, although one would question the anonymous source of this statement. The districts of Moctezuma and Sahuaripa were among the hardest hit. On their return north the Indians raided the ranch of the peace commissioner, Rafael Corella, before running off the horse herd at Fronteras.[55] The Chihennes returned to New Mexico and the Chokonens to the Chiricahua Mountains, where an overland party supposedly met Cochise, who was again considering relations with Fronteras.[56]

Why Cochise was a party to the several peace negotiations at Fronteras in 1857 and 1858 is difficult to comprehend. The most important reason seems to have been his apprehension of Americans, in particular American troops, but one thing is clear: the Chiricahua Apaches were not constantly at war with all groups. For their own self-preservation, they maintained friendly relations with some Indians (for example, the Zuñis in northwestern New Mexico, with whom they traded for guns and ammunition, and the Navajos in the same region, with whom they occasionally traded for blankets) and with some Mexican towns in northern Sonora and Chihuahua.

This balance of power shifted with the arrival of Americans in the Southwest, particularly when ranches, settlements, and forts were established, making the Anglos a force to reckon with. Moreover, as with any society, there were leaders within it who were more peaceably disposed (Esquinaline and Delgadito) and others who were more belligerent (Cochise and Mangas Coloradas). Yet even these war chiefs realized that it was not practical to fight everyone, that they needed a place to dispose of stolen plunder, that their number had decreased because of continued war with Mexico, and finally that American troops had proved themselves to be more than able adversaries. Unprovoked American attacks on the Chihennes had left an impression on the wilder and more suspicious Chokonens, leaving them disinclined to confront the Americans. Stated simply, the message is this: the Chiricahuas, although fierce warriors and highly efficient raiders, did not kill every Mexican or American they happened to come across. These Apaches valued their property, family relations, and lives as much as any other people might. Therefore, they continued to solicit peace at Fronteras because they wished to avoid contact with the uncertainty to the north (Americans) and to a lesser degree the Chihuahuans to the east.

As in the previous fall, the entire Chokonen band was involved, with Cochise's group the last one agreeing to participate in negotiations. In early July 1858 an Indian woman showed up at Fronteras and requested peace for the entire band. She returned on July 11 with five warriors and five women. At this meeting she revealed that she had talked with Cochise, who also favored an end to hostilities.[57] The Apaches left the next day, promising to return within four days to conclude the agreement. Sonora's state newspaper, *La Voz de Sonora,* declared that the Apaches' motives were simple: "They know that within a few days a campaign against them is to begin and for this reason they asked for peace." Furthermore, "the governor knows very well the treacherous manner of this tribe and will not be deceived." Its prophecy was correct; this time the Chokonens would be the ones deceived.[58]

On July 14, 1858, the stage was set for the Indians' appearance at Fronteras. Frustrated by previous overtures which never came to fruition and exposed to Apache hostilities, the Fronteras officials came up with an ingenious plan to slaughter the Apaches, one which had been successful in the past and which the Apaches should have suspected. Although there is no doubt that the Apaches suffered losses (both Mexican and Indian accounts place the number of Apache men killed at substantially the same), there are the inevitable discrepancies between white and Indian accounts of the affair. According to Captain García, the Mexicans were compelled to protect themselves because the Chiricahuas entered the presidio looking for trouble. He claimed that when the Chokonens arrived, many were already drunk, although this seems to defy explanation and is somewhat dubious, given the Apache version. The Apaches contradicted Escalante's report, claiming that the Mexicans liberally furnished them with mescal and then turned their weapons on the unsuspecting Indians. He asserted that the conflict was initiated by a drunken Chokonen who had wounded a soldier, at which time he "gave orders that all Apaches who were drunk, and especially the one who wounded the soldier, be conducted to the guard house until they sobered up."

The Chokonens refused to go, and a general melee erupted in the streets of Fronteras. Colchon attacked and killed one soldier and wounded another before he was cut down by the troops. The soldiers eventually gained control of the fight as the Chiricahuas fled. At once García "marched to their ranchería, carrying as guide one of the Apache prisoners." The troops overtook some of the inebriated warriors and succeeded in surprising the Apache camp near Cuchuta. All told, twenty-six Apache men and ten women were

killed. Besides Colchon, two other chiefs were killed. The Mexicans captured "ten carbines, twenty lances, seven horses, three
mules and two burros." Escalante closed his report by asking for
reinforcements because the Indians "will avenge this and attack me
in great numbers within six or eight days."[59]

This report was obviously biased on several points. As has been
said, the Chiricahuas certainly did not arrive at the peace conference
already drunk. The Mexicans had probably prepared an elaborate
feast and supplied the Indians with all the liquor they wanted. Only
in this drunken stupor could the Chokonens have been so easily entrapped and slaughtered. In fact, a Chiricahua may have referred to
this incident to Morris E. Opler: "The Chiricahua would make
peace with the Mexicans. Then the Mexicans would give them liquor, get them drunk, take them in their houses and cut off their
heads. Then the war would start again."[60] Two months later the
Apaches told Americans at Stein's Peak that they "had been intoxicated and then killed," admitting to twenty-five fatalities.[61]

Why the Chiricahuas lay prone to Mexican treachery is best sum-
marized by Dan L. Thrapp, authority on Apache-military relations:

> Stories of such slaughters of drunken Apaches occur so frequently
> during the frontier years that one must accept them as basically true,
> but one can only speculate how they were engineered so often as the
> Apaches report, and why the Indians fell into the same old trap with
> such regularity. Perhaps peaceful relations between Mexicans and
> Apaches were as common as war, and for purposes of trade and per-
> haps other reasons a tenuous relationship always existed; the occa-
> sional massacres were abuses of this relationship, rather than chance
> incidents in a long period of generally hostile dealings between the
> peoples.[62]

The massacre at Fronteras was a severe blow to the Chokonens. The
loss of three leaders, twenty-three warriors, and ten women wiped
out more than half of a local group. The remaining warriors eventually acknowledged Cochise as their leader at the band level.

Ironically for the Mexicans, the massacre forced the Chiricahuas
into the hands of Americans, the one thing Sonorans most feared.
After the slaughter, the Chokonen groups returned to southern Arizona, from whence runners were dispatched to Mangas Coloradas,

inviting him to join the Chokonens for a foray against Fronteras. A Chiricahua war party was usually organized to avenge deaths. Its objective and scope differed from those of a raiding party in one element: the revenge factor. The objectives of the raiding party were both economic and political, with the stolen stock and plunder serving as a necessary part of their subsistence and giving the warrior an opportunity to enhance his prestige. In contrast, the organization and objectives of a war party revolved around vengeance. Stock and plunder were desired, of course, but they were secondary to revenge. A war party set out to punish a specific ranch, town, district, or state. While a raiding party could have as few as five warriors and usually no more than twenty, the number in a war party could range from thirty or forty to two or three hundred.

Late that summer, warriors gathered at Stein's Peak to prepare for their retaliatory attack against Fronteras. Led by Cochise and Mangas, the party totaled some two hundred warriors. In early September, Sylvester Mowry reported that he met at Stein's Peak with José Mangas, a brother of Mangas Coloradas, who boasted that the warriors were going on an excursion to Fronteras "to wipe out the town." Mowry added that "all of the men had collected at Steins Peak when I passed."[63]

Before departing, the Chiricahuas probably had a war dance, held "only when they go out for revenge and fighting." The dance, in which only the warriors participated, was known as fierce dancing and started at least four nights before the expedition was to begin. It was repeated each night. The overtone of the war dance was serious. Warriors danced and prayed for good fortune. They wished to meet their enemy and kill him; they hoped to capture food and plunder. The war dance allowed the warrior to prepare himself for battle, to work himself into a fighting pitch. Social dances followed the war dance, and at daybreak the participants would retire to sleep. The same ritual continued for three more days, and the war party left on the fifth or sixth day.[64]

The Indians left Stein's Peak about September 12, with Cochise and Mangas Coloradas leading. The entire camp gathered to see them off, with the women calling out encouragement. Scouts were sent out to the front, flanks, and rear. During the march, the men of each cluster, or extended family group, followed their own local group leader. By the evening of September 15 the Chiricahuas, safely in the mountains east of Fronteras, prepared for the attack, which would take place the next morning.

Whether by design or not, the Chiricahua war party had chosen an opportune time to attack. Of the seventy men stationed at the presidio, thirty dragoons were out with Captain Eraclio Escalante on a scout to the Magallanes Mountains, thirty miles northwest of the presidio, and twenty infantrymen had gone to Bacoachi for supplies. Therefore, on the morning of September 16, 1858, only twenty soldiers remained at the fort and several of them were protecting the citizens working their fields. The Apaches attacked at 9 A.M., but the move was ill advised and poorly coordinated. All of the Mexicans were able to reach the safety of the presidio except one, Sergeant Simon, who was killed. The Chiricahuas fought until the citizens and troops "fought them off with rifles and spades and fired three cannon balls to disperse them." Cochise and Mangas retreated into the hills. The element of surprise gone, the Apaches called off the fight, content to wait for another time. Their losses are not known. Why they had made such a poor showing is difficult to comprehend except for their well-grounded fear of cannon fire. Cochise himself had reason to be wary: the cannon may have contributed to his capture at Fronteras ten years before.[65]

After being repulsed at Fronteras, the Apache war party divided. Mangas Coloradas and his Chihennes returned to Stein's Peak in a foul mood; they demanded and received twenty sacks of corn from Butterfield Overland Mail Company stage station personnel. Cochise and his Chokonens, intent on revenge, proceeded into Sonora, raiding, plundering, and killing before returning to the Chiricahuas.[66]

By October, Cochise had returned to Apache Pass, secure from the reinforcements stationed along Sonora's northern border. Intending to discourage American expansionism and impede Apache incursions, Lieutenant Colonel José Juan Elías announced plans to regarrison the frontier with a force of 500 men distributed as follows: 150 to Fronteras, 100 to Bavispe, 100 to a temporary fort on the San Pedro, 75 to Santa Cruz, 50 to Imuris, and 25 to serve as scouts. To gain public support, another Apache campaign was planned and donations were requested. Unlike the previous fall's drive, citizens from Ures and Hermosillo responded by dipping into their pockets for some three thousand pesos, proving that people would pay for exterminating Apaches but not for pacifying them.[67]

In late October, Elías received a report from Fronteras that the Apaches were organizing another war party from Santa Rita del Cobre, where the Americans were providing them with arms and ammunition. Their target was Fronteras, no doubt, because of the July massacre. As a result, Elías left Ures with forty-six men and one piece of artillery bound for Fronteras. He stopped at towns and ranches to receive contributions and recruit volunteers. His march provided him with a vivid picture of the deplorable state of the frontier north of Arispe. He passed Chinapa, which Apaches had burned to the ground twice in the past eleven years and was now deserted. Bacoachi was almost a ghost town, for many families had left to seek refuge in the center of the state. Elías promised that the government would provide security and protection to all; in addition, the prefect of Arispe pledged seed, tools, and stock as an incentive to any hardy citizens who wished to repopulate Chinapa.[68]

Elías arrived at Fronteras about November 10. He strengthened the garrison to 150 men and appointed Captain Cayetano Silva Escalante, a dogmatic campaigner, commander of the National Guard. He also adopted an aggressive policy of keeping patrols in the field, which soon paid off. On December 13, Escalante's command attacked a ranchería in the Otates Mountains, killing 18 Indians and taking 4 prisoners. The Indians confessed that they had come to Sonora on a campaign, although Apache war parties normally did not bring their women and children. Probably they had migrated south for the winter and Escalante had attacked the base camp while the warriors were out raiding. This report, in addition to Steck's information, makes it appear likely that the Chihennes or Bedonkohes were the victims of this attack, in which 16 of the 18 killed were women and children, suggesting indiscriminate killing—not an unusual practice for this time or the "civilized" twentieth century.[69]

Escalante ordered several other expeditions to scout the mountains usually inhabited by the Chiricahuas. By early December he concluded that the Apaches had moved north of the border to U.S. territory. Here the Indians discovered that small parties of Americans had built square adobe stage stations at their usual haunts at Stein's Peak in the Peloncillo Mountains and Apache Pass between the Chiricahua and Dos Cabezas mountains. At one of these places, the first recorded meeting between Cochise and Americans occurred. He was ready to deal with the Anglos.

# Chapter 7

# APACHE PASS

By 1858, Cochise had emerged as the principal leader of the Chokonen band. Other headmen, such as Esquinaline and Chepillo, continued to lead local groups, though smaller than Cochise's. The band, however, lacked centralistic leadership. The venerable Mangas Coloradas still retained ample influence, on a tribal basis, to mobilize large war parties into Mexico, but during the next three years he relinquished this position to Cochise, now the ablest of the militant Chiricahua leaders.

When the Anglos began to make their presence felt in southeastern Arizona, in particular the chaparral-covered hills and ravines of Apache Pass, it was Cochise with whom they dealt. They found a chief who desired peace, not so much because he feared their military might at this time, but because relations with Mexico had broken down. He could not afford to have enemies on both sides of the border.

Those who met Cochise in the late 1850s recognized him as the principal Chokonen chief and were impressed with his stature.[1] Samuel Woodworth Cozzens, who claimed to have met him at Apache Pass in 1859, described him as a "tall, dignified-looking Indian."[2] James H. Tevis, who may have had more contact with Cochise than any other American before 1861, depicted him as "fine a looking Indian as one ever saw. He was about six feet tall and as straight as an arrow, built, from the ground up, as perfect as any man could be. He only had one peer in physique, Francisco, chief of the Coyoteros. I don't suppose that Cochise ever met his equal with a lance."[3]

Cochise's first reported Anglo contact occurred in the fall of 1858 at either Apache Pass or Stein's Peak, and he attended his first official meeting in December 1858 when he conferred with Indian agent Dr. Michael Steck at Apache Pass. These peaceful encounters were significant because they signaled the beginning of a new Chokonen attitude: a willingness to interact with Americans. The willingness was a product of two related events. First there was the growing American presence in southern Arizona, which was manifested by the development of mining activities in the Tubac area, the construction of Fort Buchanan some forty-five miles southeast of Tucson, and the emergence of the Butterfield Overland Mail Company, whose route cut through Cochise's country. Second, Sonora strengthened its northern presidios in the late summer and early fall of 1858, partly to protect itself from American expansion and partly to forestall Apache raiding. Finally, the souring of Chiricahua-Mexican relations, beginning with the Carrasco affair in March 1851 and culminating with the massacre at Fronteras in June 1858, forced Cochise to consider friendly relations above the border.

The Americans' arrival in southern Arizona had not gone unnoticed by Cochise. In fact, there had been a few minor skirmishes between his people and the whites. In June 1857, Captain Richard Stoddert Ewell,[4] a seasoned veteran of the Southwest, jumped a ranchería in the Chiricahua Mountains and captured twenty horses. The next night, the dispossessed Apaches retaliated, recapturing their stock and stealing two cavalry horses.[5] Although Ewell failed to mention Apache casualties, in all likelihood Indian blood was spilled. One month later, on July 20, 1857, Apaches (probably Chokonens) ambushed a small wagon train at Apache Pass and killed two men named Short and Irving, wounded two women, and stole twenty head of cattle. The hostiles were supposed to have suffered the loss of four or five warriors. When news reached Fort Buchanan, Captain Edward H. Fitzgerald, twenty soldiers, and twenty citizens left in pursuit but found no trace of the hostiles, who apparently had slipped across the border into Mexico.[6]

For the next year the overland route through Chokonen country was noticeably free from depredations. Between June 1857 and September 1858, James E. Birch's Jackass Mail Route made some forty trips through Chokonen country without a single hostile encounter, primarily because most of the Chiricahuas were living in northern Mexico at this time.[7] By the fall of 1858, for reasons previously discussed, Cochise had become resigned to establishing relations with the Americans, and if William Hudson Kirkland's reminiscences are correct, in October 1858, Cochise showed that he wished peace.

Kirkland was one of Arizona's earliest pioneers, having settled in the Sonoita Valley in the mid-1850s. On October 24, 1858 (although Kirkland later remembered the incident as having occurred in the early 1860s), he was hauling wood from the Santa Rita Mountains when Cochise and twenty-five Apaches surrounded him and two of his men. Cochise punched him in the back with the blunt end of his lance and ordered the white men to prepare a meal for them. Kirkland recalled that "I didn't know I could cook, but, by God, I found I could cook pretty well." After eating, Cochise let the whites go.[8] A short time after this incident, Cochise established a relationship with the whites at the Stein's Peak or Apache Pass stage stations, which had been constructed as part of the Butterfield Overland Mail Route. The Butterfield Overland Mail Company, which succeeded James E. Birch's Jackass Mail Route, was the culmination of an expanding nation's need for a transcontinental mail system.

By late summer 1858, 141 stage stations were strung between St. Louis and San Francisco along a 2,800-mile route. They were about 20 miles apart, although sometimes the interval was only 9 miles but could be as much as 60. By 1859 there were 200 stage stations. Normally, two to four employees manned each station, although some had as many as eight. The mail company, which employed two thousand men at the peak of its operation, instructed its employees to keep their distance from the Indians and to avoid trouble as much as possible. At the same time, it admonished them to be prepared for Indian attacks and treachery. Consequently, each of the stage stations had a small arsenal of Sharps rifles, plus experienced men who knew how to use them. In September 1858, one year after the company received the contract, the Butterfield Overland Mail Route was operational.[9]

One of the more dangerous sections along the route lay between

James H. Tevis. A station keeper at Apache Pass in 1858–59, he knew
Cochise well and his comments were less than flattering. (*Courtesy Ari-*
*zona Historical Society, Tucson*)

Mesilla and Tucson in the heart of Chiricahua territory. Nine stage
stations threaded this isolated stretch, giving employment to one
hundred men and costing about one hundred thousand dollars a year
to operate, with Giles Hawley providing competent direction of activities.[10] Three stage stations (later expanded to five) were situated
in Chokonen country about equidistant from one another, and each

was to play an important role in future events. The Stein's Peak station was on a bold uplift at the eastern mouth of Doubtful Canyon in the Peloncillo Mountains. Thirty miles to the southwest was the Apache Pass establishment, deep in the defile separating Dos Cabezas and the Chiricahua Mountains. The third station was forty miles to the west at Dragoon Springs, just north of the Dragoon Mountains. All were completed by early September under the direction of William S. Buckley, although the Dragoon Springs station was finished under tragic circumstances. All of the Arizona and New Mexico stage stations had large square enclosures with adobe or rock walls, and each had a dependable water supply.[11]

Evidently some of Cochise's first contacts with stage personnel at the Stein's Peak and Apache Pass stage stations were less than cordial. Anthony Elder, in charge of the Apache Pass station, whipped and chastised a Chokonen warrior after Cochise allegedly raided the stock of the Santa Rita Mining Company. According to James H. Tevis, who succeeded Elder, Cochise threatened revenge, forcing Elder's superiors to transfer him to a position in charge of overland supply. Tevis's reminiscences contain obvious mistakes in chronology and facts and an exaggerated account of his own exploits, but they cannot be disregarded. He knew Cochise well, and his letters to the *Weekly Arizonian* in the spring and summer of 1859 are some of the best source material about Cochise at this time.[12]

During 1859 and 1860, Cochise's local group could usually be found camped at Cochise Canyon (later called Goodwin Canyon), about one mile north of the stage station at Apache Pass. From here his warriors continued raiding, usually in Mexico but occasionally some overzealous young men stole stock from ranches north of the border, apparently against his orders. In early December 1858 he joined Mangas Coloradas for an incursion into Sonora. By mid-month "only the sick and disabled" warriors and the women and children remained at Apache Pass. By the twenty-sixth he was back in the pass and probably was instrumental in returning some mules stolen from the stage station by a few Chokonens. In fact, one chief (perhaps Cochise) declared that the Indians "would not molest the whites" as long as they did "not interfere with their incursions into Sonora."[13]

In New Mexico, Apache agent Steck was informed that the

William H. Kirkland. This early Arizona pioneer unexpectedly met Cochise in October 1858 in the Santa Rita Mountains in southern Arizona. (*Courtesy Arizona Historical Society, Tucson*)

Chokonens had established their rancherías at Apache Pass. Possibly Mangas Coloradas told him about their presence; if not, the stage station personnel at Apache Pass may have done so. The previous summer, New Mexico's superintendent of Indian affairs, James L. Collins, had written Steck requesting information about the Indians living in Arizona. In his reply, the good doctor separated the Mogollon band from Cochise's Chokonens, the first time, to my knowledge, that this was done by Americans. Wrote Steck: "The Mogollon band of Apaches range in the Mogollon Mountains, the

Buras [Burro] Mts, the Head waters of the Gila and the country between Gila and Mimbres and as far south as the Republic of Mexico.
This band has about 125 warriors and five hundred women and children [this was probably the Bedonkohe band]." Furthermore, he
pointed out, "to this band should be added the Band who live on the
Cierra Larga [Peloncillo], Chilihuihui [Chiricahua] Mountains and
the country between these mountains and the Gila. They will number about 150 warriors and five hundred women and children [this
was the Chokonen band or Cochise's Central Chiricahuas]." The
two bands "are identically the same people are intermarried and
make common cause of any difficulty and in their expeditions for
plunder, go together."[14] Steck understood that Cochise's people
were distinct from the Mogollons.

On December 23, 1858, Steck left Fort Thorn for his first visit to
Arizona. He had written Tevis asking him to notify the Chokonens
of his plans. En route he rationed the Chihennes at Santa Rita del
Cobre, finding them quiet and satisfied. From there he followed the
mail route west for 170 miles and arrived at Apache Pass on December 30. Here he "found a Band of Apaches called Jeneros or
Chilicagua [Chiricahua] Mountain Apaches with their chiefs Chees
[Cochise], Es-ken-el-a-ne [Esquinaline] and Fresco [Francisco?],
fifty men 120 women and about four hundred children, totalling six
hundred." Steck believed that "this band of Apaches . . . have
committed no depredations upon the route [to California] for near
two years." To encourage their continued "good behavior," he
issued them rations. Among the presents distributed were several
head of cattle, 20 *fanegas* of corn, 211 blankets, 100 yards of
*manta,* and 200 brass kettles. Cochise no doubt was pleased with
the gifts and perceived this as a golden opportunity: he could raid
into Mexico at will and live in safety at Apache Pass; he would receive rations from Americans occasionally as long as he caused no
trouble.[15]

Next the indefatigable Steck continued west to Fort Buchanan,
hoping to meet Western Apache bands. He conferred with Captain
Ewell, who told him that on January 4 the Apaches had stolen some
horses from the vicinity of the Sonoita and Santa Cruz rivers. As a
result, they decided to visit the Chokonens at Apache Pass, but before doing so they had more pressing matters: they met and rationed

the powerful Pinal and White Mountains Apache bands before journeying east into Chiricahua territory and arriving at Apache Pass on January 25, 1859.

In the presence of Ewell's dragoons, Cochise was conciliatory and returned the stolen stock. He also released a Mexican captive recently taken from San Ignacio, Sonora. Steck reminded Cochise and the other chiefs of the serious consequences if they continued to raid and concluded that "the chiefs seem well disposed and promise to exert themselves to maintain peace." [16]

Steck and Ewell had done their job well, providing the right mixture of gift giving and saber rattling. As long as the Indians kept the peace in Arizona and New Mexico, citizens, military officers, and government agents were content. This attitude, reciprocated by Mexicans when the Apaches lived in Sonora and Chihuahua, was not as hypocritical as appears. To begin with, the Americans were not yet formidable enough to prevent Apache raids into Mexico; in addition, many southwesterners looked condescendingly at the Mexicans, whom they viewed with much antipathy and contempt as tensions between the two countries remained high. Although humane individuals such as Steck did not condone such actions, in reality he was powerless, as was the military, to prevent Apache raids into Mexico.

The agent returned to New Mexico in early February, having promised Cochise that he would return in a few months with more presents. Collins congratulated him and urged him to visit Arizona frequently. Accordingly, in mid-March 1859, Steck again went there and parleyed with the western Apache bands at Cañon del Oro, twenty-five miles northwest of Tucson. Here, in the presence of Ewell and John D. Walker, the brilliant and eccentric agent for the Papagos, Pimas, and Maricopas, a treaty was negotiated. The Apaches agreed not to molest Americans or their property, and Steck promised to distribute rations in return.

Steck's plan did not sit well with some citizens. *The Arizonian,* the first newspaper published in Arizona, disagreed with a policy in which the army and Indian agents went into Apache country to make peace. Instead, it advocated that "when troops go into an Indian country, they should go to fight. If Indians want peace, let them come after it!" Magnanimously, the *Arizonian* did agree that if the

Pinals kept their word, occasionally the government should furnish them with a supply of corn and beef.[17]

With the conclusion of the Pinal treaty, Steck retraced his steps to Apache Pass and on April 1 met with Cochise. Assisted by Tevis and the latter's personnel, he distributed rations to the local groups of Cochise, Esquinaline, and Old Jack,[18] estimating the strength of the three groups at one hundred warriors. Tevis described the scene:

> [The Indians] were formed in a circle in front of the station. . . . First, Cochise, Old Jack, Esconolea and the medicine men; in the next row, warriors; in the third row, young boys under the warrior age; in the fourth row, the chiefs' families: and in the back, the families of the warriors.[19]

After receiving presents, Cochise made plans for another campaign against Fronteras. First his people consumed the corn ration, processing it into tiswin, a weak alcholic beverage which, when consumed after fasting, quickly put the drinker in a state of intoxication. An observer noted that "one drink of tis-win . . . would make a jack-rabbit slap a wildcat in the face." [20]

On April 6, Cochise called a council, which all the warriors attended, drinking tiswin and discussing their next move: an attack on Fronteras to avenge the massacre of the previous July. A scouting party of ten warriors had just returned and reported in favor of an attack. Cochise had invited Francisco,[21] a powerful Eastern White Mountain ally whose one hundred men would bring the total of the expedition to three or four hundred warriors, although Tevis doubted the Indians could raise that many. The attack was delayed until Francisco and his followers arrived and the tiswin had been consumed.

For the next two weeks the Chokonens were exceedingly perverse and continually drunk. They constantly annoyed Tevis, who wrote that "there has not been a day . . . that we have not had trouble with them," primarily because they were not allowed in the station. Without Steck's or Ewell's presence, Cochise was in an obnoxious mood and tried to intimidate the few whites, rationalizing that the station was on Apache land and the government owed him compensation. He soon learned that strategies employed against Americans

were more difficult to implement than those normally carried out
with ease against Mexicans. Tevis summed up the relationship between the isolated Americans and the wild Chokonens: "When any
government train is here they are as gentle as lambs, but as soon as
the train leaves, the devil seems to let loose among them." Fortunately for Tevis, Francisco arrived and on April 24 the war party
departed for Sonora. Only two warriors and the noncombatants remained at Apache Pass.[22]

On April 27 at 8 A.M. Cochise, Elías,[23] and sixty warriors surrounded several citizens working their crops near Fronteras. The
Apaches assaulted the first man they came across, shooting and
lancing him to death. Once the alarm sounded, most of the workers
escaped to the presidio and their surrounding homes, but a few were
not so fortunate. José Nicolas Lillas was irrigating his land when he
found himself trapped; he submitted and was bound immediately.
The Indians also captured two boys, the first a son of Rafael Villa,
a soldier at Fronteras, and the other a son of the town blacksmith.
There was only one reason they were not killed immediately: Cochise had bigger fish to fry. After the initial assault, he and his warriors withdrew to the mountains east of the town.[24]

Cochise's next tactic showed that the Apaches were just as treacherous as the Mexicans, no matter who started it all. To draw his adversary away from the presidio, Cochise displayed a white flag and
placed his prisoners in a position where they could easily be seen.
The captive Mexicans' pleas could be heard by their rescuers, who
must have been apprehensive about meeting the same Indians they
had trapped and whipped only nine months before. Nonetheless the
two parties held a parley, with Cochise offering to release his hostages in exchange for whiskey, pinole, and tobacco. As he was negotiating, his warriors moved into position for an ambush. The
Mexicans sensed this and, "realizing the parley was a fraud," fled
toward the presidio, the Apaches on their heels. The move proved
fatal to Lillas; he was killed instantly. The Indians rounded up the
loose stock and returned to the hills, from whence a wounded warrior took the two boys to Apache Pass. Tevis paid ten sacks of corn
as ransom to obtain their release.[25]

The war party followed an old Indian trail to Moctezuma, which
they planned to take by surprise. En route they ambushed and killed

three men bound for Arispe. Their Moctezuma plans were upended and in the ensuing skirmish the Mexicans mortally wounded Cochise's "favorite warrior," who was not identified but probably was a close relative. Believing he had fallen into a trap, Cochise picked up the injured warrior and retreated to a secure position in the mountains. After conferring with Francisco, he decided to return to Apache Pass; Francisco elected to continue the campaign. The wounded warrior died on the return trip, canceling the great feast Cochise had confidently given orders to prepare. To avenge the fatality, Cochise declared that he would kill twenty Mexicans, which he undoubtedly meant.[26]

By the early summer of 1859, Cochise realized that peace with Americans was precarious. Conflicts between the newcomer whites and the native Apaches were inevitable, of course, because their beliefs, values, lifestyles, and cultures differed so profoundly that clashes could not be avoided. From the time the Chokonens first met Steck in December 1858, there prevailed a tenuous truce, interrupted from time to time by Chiricahua stock raids, which the Indians did not ordinarily consider an act of war.

Cochise must have wanted peace, if only nominally, but it held a different meaning for Americans. The Apaches were accustomed to agreements like those they established with Sonora and Chihuahua, where their raids were condoned and even tacitly encouraged as long as they occurred in another district. So Cochise no doubt saw advantages in making peace with the Americans. First there was the matter of presents, or rations, which, unbeknown to him, would arrive semiannually instead of weekly, as the Mexicans distributed them. Second, the Apaches might be able continue their forays into Mexico and perhaps find a ready market for their plunder at Apache Pass. American nonintervention was dictated by the fact that the nearest U.S. military post was a hundred miles away and the American agent who would supervise the Indians was two hundred miles away. Consequently, Cochise virtually had a free hand, so that an occasional stock raid in Arizona might go undetected.

Important was Cochise's relationship with those Americans with whom he came into contact: Agent Steck, Captain Ewell, and station keeper Tevis. The Chiricahuas wanted the gifts Steck distributed, and they probably feared and respected Ewell's dragoons.

At any rate, Cochise's people behaved when in Steck's or Ewell's presence, although they showed less deference to Tevis and his employees. Tevis himself never trusted Cochise, whom he described in a less than flattering manner:

> [Cochise was] a very deceptive Indian. At first appearance a man would think he was inclined to be peaceable to Americans but he is far from it. For eight months I have watched him, and have come to the conclusion that he is the biggest liar in the territory! and would kill an American for any trifle, provided he thought it wouldn't be found out.[27]

Tevis, who had a tendency to exaggerate, did not think much of Cochise's character, but Apaches scorned a liar and Cochise's integrity within his tribe was beyond reproach. At this stage in Cochise's life, Americans had not yet gained his total respect, so to them his deportment was honesty when it suited him.

What, then, was the relationship between Cochise and the Anglo-Americans? The legends and myths established in these early years must be discussed and analyzed. It has been written, for example, that Cochise "allowed" the mail line to operate through Chiricahua country. Be it noted that the Butterfield Overland Mail Company established its route without asking Chiricahua permission. Although Cochise could have attacked and perhaps wiped out the stage stations at any time, he undoubtedly was aware of the advantages of peace and may even have considered the possibility of troop retaliation. He often seemed to hold the station personnel at Apache Pass in contempt, sometimes blustering against their operations. More than once Apaches piled rocks across the route to impede movement of the stagecoaches, although whether Cochise himself had anything to do with it is not known; the matter has generally been ignored by historians and writers. Two oft-repeated stories would seem to support Cochise's early friendliness toward the white interlopers: that he supplied the stage station with wood and hay, perhaps under contract, and that he prevented attacks on the stagecoaches, in the spring of 1859 even killing four Apaches who dared violate this forbearance.

Both stories lack documentary evidence to support them, which is not unexpected of course. The station had to obtain hay and wood somewhere, and it would be routine for Cochise's women to bring it in—as was done in similar circumstances elsewhere—with no record of such an agreement being preserved. Cremony does not mention the practice, nor does Tevis. John G. Bourke wrote in 1891, however, that "old-timers have often told me that the great chief, Cocheis, had the wood contract for supplying the 'station' . . . with fuel."[28] In his 1915 *History of Arizona,* Thomas E. Farish wrote that Cochise "had a contract . . . for supplying [the Apache Pass station] with wood," although he fails to cite his source.[29] This information, which might be factual, has been accepted by Woodworth Clum, Paul I. Wellman, Ralph Hedrick Ogle, and other writers down to the present day.[30] As far as Cochise's purportedly killing four Apaches who had caused trouble along the mail route, there is absolutely no shred of evidence to support this tale, which apparently was fabricated by John P. Clum. Although Cochise and Esquinaline both offered to overlook the mail route, there is no record of their fighting other Apaches to protect the Butterfield operation.[31]

Cochise seemed friendly, on the surface at least. He reportedly told his warriors that if the mail were left alone, the white soldiers would adopt a laissez-faire attitude toward other things,[32] a sort of Anglo adaptation of the Mexican viewpoint. In addition, on more than one occasion, Cochise returned stolen stock; a chief becoming aware that this had been done might, if he were sufficiently forceful and respected, demand the animals from the thieves and do what he wished with them. In Cochise's case, it was to return them to their proper owners.

One such incident occurred early in the summer of 1859. Cochise had just returned from Sonora and learned that a few weeks earlier there had been a raid for which he doubtless would be blamed. Consequently, he decided to visit Fort Buchanan, or so Tevis reported.[33] Shortly afterward a band of about twenty Indians stole eighty to ninety horses and mules from the Sonora Exploring and Mining Company near Patagonia, the raid being reported to Captain Isaac Van Duzer Reeve at the fort. Reeve blamed the Chokonens and ordered Ewell to follow their trail. It was wiped out by a heavy rain, but Ewell too concluded that the thieves were Cochise's people—as indeed they were. The leader of the party was Parte.[34]

Probably a few men from Cochise's group were implicated. When they returned with their loot, he insisted that it be returned; some may have resisted. Merejildo Grijalva, who was with the Chokonens at the time, said Cochise became so incensed that he not only seized the livestock but killed a warrior who defied his doing so.[35] He sent two of his men to Fort Buchanan with eleven of the animals. On July 21, Captain Isaac Van Duzer Reeve wrote his superiors:

> This morning two Chiricahui Indians of Chees' [band] came in & brough [sic] (11) eleven of the stolen animals.
> This band was encamped on the San Pedro & Chees, having heard of the robbery sent and took these animals & sent them in.
> He sent word that he would try and get all that had been stolen. He says they were stolen by a band of Chiricahuis headed by a chief named "Parte" that they supposed when they took them that they were in Sonora and that the animals belonged to Mexicans!

Reeve added that "Chees appears to be acting in good faith, prompted somewhat, I doubt not, by my visit to the Chiricahua Mountains in search of a site for a post."[36]

Reeve may have assessed correctly Cochise's respect for his troops, but then too the chief may have thought Ewell could trace the animals to his band, hence his prudent decision to return them. Cochise's desire to avoid Anglo conflict seems to have been confirmed in a conversation between Grijalva and Fred Hughes, an assistant to Tom Jeffords and later clerk of the Chiricahua Reservation. Grijalva said that in the late 1850s the Chiricahuas, although continuing their raids into Mexico, "had strict orders from Cochise never to lay hands on anybody or anything within the boundary of the United States."[37] This philosophy seems evident in an 1865 report in which Cochise conceded that during this period he was unable to keep his warriors from raiding but it was not his desire to be at war with Americans.[38]

Throughout the summer of 1859, Cochise maintained friendly relations with Americans. After restoring the stolen stock, he and most of the Chokonens headed straight for the upper Chiricahuas to gather acorns and piñon nuts for winter. These staples were almost as important as mescal in the Chiricahua economy, and it was common for a family to gather five hundred pounds for future use. Only Esquinaline's following remained at Apache Pass, where in mid-

August he met Samuel Cozzens, a lawyer from Mesilla. In his youth Esquinaline had been a bold warrior who had led his tribesmen on many raids against Mexico; now, in his mature years, he had learned moderation and wisdom. Cozzens described him as "rather a good looking specimen of an Apache, about 60 years old and speaks Spanish, very imperfectly, however."

Cozzens had more to tell. He said Esquinaline's local group and "that of Jack, one of the Coyotero Apaches, are now at war. An engagement took place near here a few days ago in which several on both sides were killed and wounded." It was later ascertained that eight to ten warriors were killed in the fight. Cozzens ended his letter with the revealing statement, if true, that "the Chiricahua Indians declare themselves friendly to whites, and willing to protect the mail company." This statement was repeated by Cochise three months later.[39]

By October 1859, Cochise had returned to Apache Pass, intending to spend the winter in the vicinity of Cochise Canyon. On November 6, Steck arrived with rations, which were distributed to some four hundred Indians. He found the Chokonens "very friendly and were gratified for their presents." Cochise returned three stolen animals to Steck and "promised to watch over the interest of the Overland Mail and travellers upon the great thoroughfare to California that passes directly through his country." Perhaps he was sincere in his offer, but the turn of events made it meaningless.[40]

Steck returned to his agency in late November. The harmonious relations he had established with Cochise were beginning to deteriorate, mainly because of Chokonen stock raids north of the border. Captain Reeve, in command of the temporary camp on the San Pedro, was ordered to mount a campaign against Cochise's people, but he was concerned about the mixed signals given to the Indians:

> Department special orders Number 121 suggests a scout against the Chiricahua Indians. Since the publication of that order the Indian agent, Dr. Steck, has visited these Indians, has distributed presents to them, met with and treated them in all respects as faithful friends. It is well known that they have often stolen during the past half-year. . . . They are responsible for about 24 animals stolen in July last from the Arivaca Mine, belonging to the Sonora Exploring and Mining Co.—also 5 animals stolen from Patagonia mine. I cannot

make an expedition against these Indians with the means left in my
possession after another scout against the Pinals; and shall therefore
await further instructions.[41]

A report from Tucson told of increasing raids below the border,
some of which originated from Apache Pass: "These Indians
[Chokonens] are almost continually on the warpath, they are better
armed than the Pinals, having a great many firearms which have
been given to them in exchange for their spoils steeped in the blood
of Sonora."[42] Apparently, Cochise's people had found a market at
Apache Pass to dispose of stock and booty from Mexico.

In late 1859 and early 1860, several events militated against a
continuation of the precarious armistice between Chiricahuas and
Anglos. First, in late 1859, Merejildo Grijalva, with Tevis's assistance, escaped to Mesilla and found employment with Dr. Steck.[43]
The causes of Merejildo's disenchantment with the Chiricahuas have
been widely discussed, focusing on two theories: that the Apaches
killed five of his brothers and that he fell in love with and married an
Apache girl who was killed by her tribesmen.[44] Neither yarn seems
plausible. More than likely, Merejildo had simply become weary of
life with the Indians and wanted a change of scene.

Even more serious were three other incidents that occurred in late
1859 and early 1860; these marked the beginning of Chokonen-
Anglo hostilities. On three occasions Americans were compelled to
kill Chokonen men, two of them in the act of stealing livestock.

In late November 1859, Chiricahuas ran off some mules from the
ranch of Thomas Smith of Sonora, thirty miles below the border.
Smith pursued the raiders with some of his men, overtook them near
Santa Cruz, and in a running fight killed three and recovered his
stock.[45] After he returned to Apache Pass, the leader of the raid, an
"old chief," confessed that he had thought it was Mexicans in pursuit of him or "he would not have stopped to fight." The old chief
may have been Cochise, who at the time was sometimes referred to
that way, but more than likely it was Plume.[46]

Pressure was felt most immediately by the Apache Pass stage
people. From Tubac it was reported on January 14, 1860, that the
"friendly Indians at Apache Pass had given intimations of extensive
preparations for a total extermination of the Overland Mail line

through their country, to be followed by a descent upon the settlements," a gloomy prediction frequently echoed in the frontier press, although an Indian attack on a white settlement north of the border was rare indeed. The writer, lawyer Thompson Turner, a sometime newsman, continued that "if they decide upon this step, they can with ease massacre the men at the stations and seize the exchange horses." Even if Turner had never seen a wild Apache—and there is no evidence he had done so—his passing along this Wild West gossip probably seemed valid to his middle western readership.[47]

Tevis described a similar attempt. Cochise had craved revenge, he said, after Americans on the Sonoita River near Patagonia killed a Chokonen in the act of horse stealing. Cochise, Tevis added, was so incensed that he ordered his Indians to kill anyone who went for water at Apache Springs, but Tevis may well have been exaggerating because no one was killed for doing that and Tevis himself, through his own intrepidity, defied Cochise's order and obtained water from the springs when it was needed.[48]

In any event, Cochise's smoldering animosity toward Anglos burst forth again in early 1860. On January 18, less than a week after the Apaches had threatened the Apache Pass station again, Chokonen raiders seized forty head of stock from Mexicans between San Simon and Apache Pass, although none of the Mexicans was hurt, it was reported.[49] Ten days later a station keeper named John Wilson killed one of Cochise's Mexican captives, a boy named José, in self-defense. Tevis recalled that Cochise "growled considerably" about the outcome, but the former explained that "Wilson was in the right so that was the end of it."[50] Nonetheless, the Chokonens "assembled in large numbers" and threatened to attack the station before Charles Hayden's freight train arrived, which diverted their attention. The Indians surrounded it, killed one yoke of oxen and lanced three other animals. Hayden's men refused to depart for Patagonia unless they got protection, so Ewell was prevailed upon to send them an escort.[51]

Even other Indians began pointing at Cochise's people. The Pinal Apaches, talking peace with the Americans, asserted that the Chokonens, with some help from the Coyoteros, had done nearly all of the stealing thereabouts, and even if they were dissembling, in part, some credence must be given their words. By mid-March relations

between Apaches and Anglos were so impaired that Ewell reported
the Indians to be depredating everywhere and "no tribe that I know
of Apaches is guiltless." [52]

Cochise had plenty of outlets for his growing belligerence, if that
is what it was. In the late winter of 1860 he led a war party into
Sonora, striking terror as he went. He was not alone. During a one-
month period, Apaches slaughtered more than fifty Sonoran men,
women, and children, and no doubt many of the killings could be
laid at his wickiup door. The hostiles' efforts were concentrated
southeast of Ures at Soyopa, Tonichi, Sahuaripa, and Alamos. At
Tonichi and Soyopa, Indians killed thirteen Mexicans before vanish-
ing into the inaccessible Sierra Madre. A particular sanguinary
combat between the two longstanding foes took place toward the
end of March. Cochise, with about one hundred warriors, was returning from Sonora and was about seventy miles below the Arizona
border when the Indians ambushed and killed four travelers on the
road between Cucurpe and San Ignacio. The next day a party of fifty
nationals under Angel Elías pursued the Chiricahuas to the summit
of a hill, up which the courageous troops, at Elías's urging, charged.
The Chiricahuas swarmed out like angry hornets, killing eleven men
at close range; almost all were lanced to death. A wounded man was
left on the battlefield to a fate of certain death, perhaps by torture.
Cochise added seven more victims later that day. [53]

A week later, on April 7, the Chokonens returned to Arizona and
stole some stock from the Dragoon Springs stage station. According
to Samuel Cozzens, who was there at the time of the raid, the Americans suspected Cochise. The next day, Cozzens inquired of Cochise
about the incident and the chief's ambiguous reply caused him to
conclude that Cochise had led the raid, which he probably had. [54]

Meanwhile, back in Arizona, the Chokonens were raiding Tubac
again and threatening a major outbreak. In mid-May a "friendly
Apache" reminded the station keeper at Apache Pass that "it was
the intention of the Indians to clean out the station." [55] Two weeks
later, Cochise's Chokonens ran off the entire herd of the Santa Rita
Mining Company near Tubac. Captain Ewell trailed the thieves to
the Chiricahua Mountains and in early June parleyed with the
leader, in all likelihood Cochise, and compelled him to return some
of the stolen stock, the Apaches claiming to have eaten the re-

Richard Stoddert Ewell. Pictured here as a Confederate general, Ewell was a popular and efficient officer who met Cochise on more than one occasion before the Civil War. (*Courtesy Arizona Historical Society, Tucson*)

mainder. They proposed, however, to provide compensation and asked the officer to return in late June to receive the balance.

On June 25, Ewell and a detachment of seventy-five men, including assistant surgeon Bernard John Dowling Irwin, left Fort Buchanan for Apache Pass. Five days later they met the Chokonens, who returned some of the required stock but the agent of the Santa Rita Mining Company refused to receive five animals as "not being of sufficiently good quality." At the time of Ewell's first visit, Apaches had stolen mules at Tubac, although the chief, probably Cochise, "disclaimed all knowledge of it" and may have been correct. The Apache leader did concede that a robbery had been committed by the Chihennes and that the Chokonens overtook this party and seized two of the mules in order to hand them all over to Ewell. The remainder of the animals had been traded to Mexicans or had died along the route, he said. The two mules indeed proved to be among those stolen from Tubac and Ewell restored them to their owners. In Ewell's opinion, "the perpetrators of this Tubac robbery . . . were strongly in favor of its having been done by these same Indians [Chokonens]." [56]

Cochise insisted that the mules were the best he could offer. An incredulous Ewell decided to examine the Chiricahua Mountains in search of Apache stock because "it is generally supposed that these Indians have large herds of fine stock." After eight days of fruitless searching, the officer concluded that the Indians possessed little or no stock and that he "was satisfied that they had done all in their power to meet the demand." Chokonen raiding inevitably led to Anglo distrust of Cochise's people and the gradual acceptance that if stock were stolen, the Chokonens were guilty. [57]

Ewell's report to headquarters was unusually long for him. Apparently there were some "amateurs" at Apache Pass who disagreed vehemently with his handling of the affair, and Ewell felt they would misrepresent it. Letters written to the *Alta California* and *Missouri Republican* were scathingly critical of "Old Baldy" for holding a parley instead of attacking the Chiricahuas. [58] In his report Ewell defended his policy of negotiating. After all, he had received some of the stolen stock, and any attack would have been in violation of a truce. He concluded by pledging that in the event of another theft he would not ask for restitution but would leave the fort "at night, and attack them when unprepared and try to make an effective blow." He did not get another chance to meet the Chiricahuas. He was ordered to Fort Bliss, Texas, to appear as a judge at a court-martial, after which he went to Virginia on sick leave. On May 7, 1861, he resigned his commission and joined the Confederacy with the rank of lieutenant general.[59]

Ewell's visits merely intensified the growing animosity between the two races. Immediately after his first visit on June 17, 1860, a large number of Chokonens appeared at the Apache Pass station, well armed and ominously painted, to tell the Anglos to quit under the timeworn threat of being cleaned out.[60] Yet portentous from Ewell's second meeting was the report that only 150 Chokonens remained at the pass. Many had cleared out to Janos and Corralitos in northern Chihuahua, where, it was reported, 10 Chiricahua leaders had solicited peace on June 12.[61] This report was the first indication that some of the Apaches again were ready to deal with Mexico, although the Chihennes remained in New Mexico and the more militant Chokonens under Cochise stayed in Arizona to await the results of their relatives' efforts in Mexico.

In June one Chokonen local group had begun discussions with Chino (who had been at Apache Pass), representing Yaque's local group. Their main complaint with the Americans was the infrequent amount and distribution of rations and presents; hence they looked for greener pastures in Mexico. At Janos they resumed negotiations with their sometime adversary and sometime friend José María Zuloaga, who was virtually the economic and political czar of northwestern Chihuahua.[62]

Zuloaga was a pragmatic man who adapted to circumstances. He owned the Corralitos mines and so had a vested but precarious interest in Apache relations as long as the Indians left his area alone. He tacitly encouraged depredations in the United States, Sonora, and even the interior of Chihuahua. Stolen stock and plunder seemed to find their way with suspicious frequency into his possession. Sonoran and American officials accused him of trading arms and ammunition for stolen livestock, yet he was unyielding when he had the upper hand and negotiated from a position of strength (Esquiriba's imprisonment in September 1857 is a case in point). A resourceful man, he understood that his existence depended on com-

ing to terms with the Chiricahuas, furnishing rations when necessary, and providing a market for stolen stock. Where the animals
came from, or how they were obtained, was of little concern to him.

Notwithstanding his growing reputation, the governor of Chihuahua authorized Zuloaga to make peace. The latter triumphantly announced: "It is our good fortune that we did not request peace, they
[Apaches] have solicited the peace and they must abide to the conditions." He also wrote Pesqueira in Sonora that Apaches living in
security across the border continued to raid and murder in Mexico
and suggested that the only way to control these bands was to keep
them under close scrutiny; and the only way to protect the people on
the frontier, he said, was to declare an armistice. Zuloaga obviously
sensed an opportunity to remove the Apaches from American influence and back to Mexico, a tug of war which existed from the end of
the Mexican War in 1848 through the Geronimo wars of the 1880s.
Furthermore, he hoped, Pesqueira would join him and eventually
create in Sonora establishments where the Apaches could receive
rations. He believed that fifteen hundred Chiricahuas eventually
would come in for rations.[63]

Cochise remained at Apache Pass throughout the summer and fall
of 1860. He too was growing disenchanted with Americans, particularly with the trivial amount of assistance provided by the government. The semiannual rations had arrived on March 31 and were
quickly consumed. There would be no more until November, a lapse
of almost eight months. By August even the pacific Esquinaline had
deserted Apache Pass for Fronteras, where on the last day of the
month a woman from his camp requested a truce, saying the Chokonens were dissatisfied with the Americans at Apache Pass. She also
had been sent by several other leaders, among them Parte (at the
time living near Janos) and Delgadito, who had fled New Mexico
because of white encroachment.[64]

Sonora eagerly accepted the Chiricahua offer. Captain Gabriel
García requested instructions from Pesqueira, who replied favorably: "Fronteras is a satisfactory place to administer the peace . . .
treat the Apaches, who have asked for peace, well."[65] As a consequence, by early October a small band of forty-six Indians under
Esquinaline and Delgadito had settled near Fronteras to test the
waters. To prove their sincerity, they turned their weapons over to

García, although these undoubtedly were only their unserviceable or obsolete firearms.[66] Both sides had learned from experience not to trust the other completely.

While all this was happening, Steck completed his arrangements for an Apache reservation to congregate the Mescalero and Chiricahua tribes at Santa Lucía Springs, in the heart of Mangas Coloradas's country in southwestern New Mexico. He had first considered the idea the previous November. Complaints from Apache Pass about Chokonen disturbances probably affected his decision to put the Mescaleros and Chokonens with the Chihennes, in whose territory mining activity was increasing. The previous March, Steck had gone East for personal reasons and while there had conferred with the commissioner of Indian affairs about his plan. The reservation would be fifteen miles square and would include a rich and fertile valley large enough to accommodate several Chiricahua groups, who Steck estimated at 300 men and sixteen hundred women and children, plus the Mescaleros, who Steck counted as 120 men and 600 women and children.[67] Subsequent developments forced Steck to change his plans and the Santa Lucía Springs reservation never became a reality.

Cochise probably would have objected to relocating in Chihenne territory. By the fall of 1860 many Chiricahua groups had become increasingly hostile, and some had relocated to northern Mexico. Even Steck felt the brunt of Apache raids. In mid-October 1860, Apaches reportedly drove off his mules while he was en route to Santa Lucía. Other reports from Tubac and Fort Buchanan suggested that the Apaches depredated because they were starving. More ominously, however, their activities had become more than just the occasional stock raids; they had killed a few Americans. Lieutenant Colonel Pitcairn Morrison, Fort Buchanan's new commander, wrote to his superiors and complained about the depredations; his want for troops, especially cavalry; and his lack of a good guide. He concluded: "I cannot see any other course to pursue than to feed [the Indians] or exterminate them."[68] Conditions deteriorated further in late 1860 when Steck was elected delegate of the Territory of Arizona, as Mowry had been before him, but pending formal organization of the territory, neither man was seated.

Before leaving for Washington, Steck probably met Cochise on

November 10 at Apache Pass, where the Chiricahuas reportedly received their semiannual supplies. Little is known of Cochise's activities at this time, but growing Apache resentment of Americans was evident in the number of Indians appearing at Janos and Fronteras to make peace, among whom were many of Cochise's associates. A month after receiving Steck's rations, Cochise sent a clear signal that he also wished relations with Fronteras. On December 9, Chiquito Teboca, his family (two women, four children, and two men), a Chiricahua woman named Yones and the woman's nine-year-old son arrived at Fronteras seeking peace and rations for Cochise's following.[69] Yones was the wife of Coyuntura, whose reputation was high among the Chiricahuas: "[He] was never known to go out on an expedition with his command of 18 Indians without bringing back stock. . . . He was more dreaded in Sonora than the captains of any other band of Apaches."[70] García received an affirmative reply from Pesqueira; if Cochise could prove his sincerity, he would be rationed.[71]

Ironically, if Pesqueira's reply had come sooner, a whole era of American-Apache conflict and Apache vengeance raids might never have occurred and Cochise's Chokonens might have remained in northern Sonora. This is not to suggest that the Apaches' already strained relations with the Americans might not have resulted in eventual conflict. Raiding probably would have continued under any circumstance, but it might not have been as severe as the devastation that hit Arizona in the spring and summer of 1861. In any event, Cochise did not wait for the governor's reply. By January 1861 he was back at Apache Pass, destined to be involved in one of the most significant and controversial incidents in Apache-Anglo relations, the Bascom affair.

# Chapter 8

# CUT THE TENT: THE BASCOM AFFAIR AT APACHE PASS

As 1861 dawned, Cochise had already spent more than three-quarters of his life in relative obscurity, as far as the non-Chiricahua world was concerned. He was approaching fifty and had two wives (he took a third some years later). According to Chiricahua accounts, his first and principal wife, Dos-teh-seh, bore him two sons: Taza, born in the early 1840s, and Naiche, born about 1856. By his second wife, who was of Chokonen blood but whose name was not recalled, he had two daughters: Dash-den-zhoos and Naithlotonz, both born in the late 1850s or early 1860s. A report from the San Carlos Reservation in 1886 does not concur with twentieth-century Apache recollections; it said Cochise had two widows at that time. By one he had had two children, who died; by the other he had had Taza, Naiche, and two daughters.[1]

Cochise made sure that his sons received a proper education. The older of the two, Taza, nearly twenty, had completed his novice training and was much like his grandfather, Mangas Coloradas, in build. At maturity he carried two hundred pounds on a five-foot ten-inch frame.[2] As the first-born son, he received particular attention. According to Asa Daklugie, Cochise "groomed him for the position" of Chokonen chief. Consequently, Cochise taught Taza "every trail, every source of water, and every secret cache known."[3] A Chiricahua informant explained the development of a leader to Morris E. Opler: "Most of the leaders I knew were sons of leaders. The chief's children get special advice and act in a different way. Because he is trained in a good way right from the start, the leader's son usually turns out to be a real man."[4]

In addition, Cochise passed his medicine power (a resource which took many forms, from having the ability to cure sickness to finding the enemy) along to Taza. During the 1860s and the early 1870s, Taza evolved into a good fighting man and succeeded his father as chief in June 1874. Pneumonia struck him down two years later in, of all places, Washington, D.C.[5]

In contrast to Taza, Naiche was much like his father in appearance. At maturity he stood five feet eleven inches and was considered to be the best-looking man in the tribe.[6] After his father's death he supported his brother's decisions, and when Taza died, he assumed leadership of the Chokonens who remained on the reservation. In September 1881 he fled from the San Carlos Reservation and, allied with Geronimo, led the last of the incorrigible Chiricahuas, who finally surrendered in 1886.

The Bascom affair, which spawned open hostilities between Cochise's people and the Americans, is difficult to reconstruct for several reasons. To begin with, several of the participants' accounts were recorded many years after the event: William Sanders Oury's in 1877, policeman Oberly's in 1886, assistant surgeon Bernard John Dowling Irwin's in 1887, and Captain Daniel Robinson's in 1896. Inevitably, chronology and facts were sometimes distorted, especially in the accounts of Oury and Irwin, both of whom missed the first week's activities. Oury, who reached Apache Pass eleven days after the initial hostilities, left behind a most unreliable account. Irwin's recollections were also lacking in some areas, but his memory was better than Oury's. Fortunately, we have the narratives of two eyewitnesses, policeman Oberly and Captain (then Sergeant) Daniel Robinson, both of whom were present from beginning to end. Oberly's account, often discarded as worthless, is upon close examination sometimes in accord with Robinson's, which was a contrast to every other version. Robinson was not only an eyewitness but a participant in much of the affair. His recollections contain excellent descriptions of the first Bascom-Cochise meeting, Cochise's subsequent escape, the Cochise-Bascom parley of February 5, and the fight at Apache Springs on February 8.[7]

Next, the contemporary accounts furnished by driver A. B. Culver and William Buckley provide but a brief synopsis of what took place before they arrived on February 6 and February 7, respectively. Their reports are reliable but limited because they were not present for the important events of February 4–6. Another concurrent account was written in November 1861 by a soldier, stationed in Arizona, who may have been present for part of the affair. This trustworthy account, which was published in the *Missouri Republican* nine months after the event, contained a vivid description of Cochise's escape and a harsh condemnation of Bascom's actions and judgment (considering it was written by a soldier).[8]

We also have Lieutenant George Nicholas Bascom's official reports of February 14 and February 25. Neither is entirely satisfactory because he attempts to justify his actions. Each contained errors in chronology, and both were ambiguous and perhaps duplistic in some respects, obviously to cover up his egregious mishandling of the incident.[9]

Finally, we have the Apache perspective as articulated by Geronimo, Jason Betzinez, and the published writings of Mrs. Eve Ball, whose version was based on accounts provided her by Chiricahuas. Cochise gave what was perhaps his most detailed version to William F. Arny in October 1870.[10] The Apaches knew the incident as "cut the tent," a reference to Cochise's means of escape. Although Geronimo's version placed Mangas Coloradas in the tent (an obvious error in translation), the remainder of his account is surprisingly accurate. Unlike Betzinez and the Apaches who conferred with Mrs. Ball, Geronimo recalled correctly that Cochise killed his prisoners first. Cochise himself spoke very little of the events at Apache Pass because Apaches normally did not dwell on the past because of death taboos, yet for the remainder of his life he steadfastly maintained that Bascom's mistreatment was responsible for the conflict.

The Bascom affair began rather innocuously. On January 27, 1861, two parties of Apaches raided the ranch of John Ward[11] eleven miles south of Fort Buchanan. One group stole twenty head of cattle, while the other seized a twelve-year-old boy named Félix[12] within three hundred yards of the house. The timely arrival of two Americans thwarted further hostilities. They sent a message to Fort

Mickey Free. Captured by Western Apaches, he was the youth whom Bascom demanded from Cochise. Free was a scout and interpreter during the Geronimo Wars of the 1880s. (*Courtesy Arizona Historical Society, Tucson*)

Buchanan and the next morning First Lieutenant George Nicholas Bascom,[13] a brave young officer with no Indian experience, and a detachment of infantry and dragoons (who had just arrived from Fort Breckenridge) examined the trail but found nothing. Later that day they returned to the fort, ostensibly satisfied that the tracks led toward the San Pedro River and then into Chokonen country; hence Cochise's people were suspected.[14]

Public opinion supported this belief. Evidently John Ward thought the raiders were Cochise's people. Reporting from Tucson, Thompson Turner summed up the matter succinctly: "It is generally believed that his captors are the Apache Pass Indians."[15] As it turned out, the Chiricahuas had nothing to do with the raid, which, according to one historian, was probably the work of Western White Mountain Apaches.[16] Here, in chronological order, is what happened.

*Tuesday, January 29, 1861*

Department headquarters in Santa Fe had furnished instructions regarding the action that the commanding officer at Fort Buchanan should take in the event of Indian hostilities. This morning, Lieutenant Colonel Morrison adopted these orders, which said he was "to pursue and if possible chastise such marauding parties . . . you are authorized to do whatever you think is proper."[17] Furthermore, he was undoubtedly aware of Captain Ewell's pledge, made some six months before, that if Cochise's band raided again he would not ask for restitution but would instead "strike a blow."[18]

With these circumstances in mind, Morrison issued Order No. 4, Headquarters Fort Buchanan, instructing Lieutenant Bascom to "pursue the Indians and recover a boy made captive by them." Assistant surgeon Irwin recalled that Bascom was to "follow the trail until the cattle were found and recovered." If the trail led to Cochise, Bascom was to "demand the immediate restoration of the stolen property." If the chief refused, the young lieutenant "was authorized and instructed to use the force under his orders in recovering it." These orders reveal that Morrison authorized Bascom to use whatever means he deemed necessary to punish those responsible and to recover the boy.[19]

Unfortunately for all concerned, public opinion had indicted and

Lieutenant George N. Bascom. Although he was commended by his superiors for his decisions at Apache Pass, Bascom's actions began the Cochise War. (*Courtesy National Archives*)

convicted Cochise's people because of previous Chokonen raids in the Tubac area. But the Chokonens had never taken captives, only stock. If Morrison had gone by recent history, he would have dispatched troops into Western Apache country, for these were the Indians who were known to have taken white prisoners. Instead, perhaps based on information provided by the same individuals whom Ewell had contemptuously called amateurs, Morrison sent soldiers into Chiricahua country. Bascom and fifty-four men of the Seventh Infantry, mounted on mules, were accompanied by John Ward, who, quite naturally, was "directly interested in the results." The detachment moved east toward Apache Pass.

*Wednesday, January 30, to Saturday, February 2*

Bascom's command marched slowly into Chokonen territory toward Apache Pass. According to one account, he followed the hostiles' trail,[20] but this seems dubious in that the Ward boy was later reported to have been taken to the Black Mountains in Western Apache territory. Nonetheless, Bascom continued across Sulphur Springs Valley, heading for the narrow defile between the Dos Cabezas and Chiricahua mountains. He probably spent the evening of February 2 at the Ewell Springs stage station, some fifteen miles west of Apache Pass.

Cochise, camped in his winter headquarters at Cochise Canyon, probably was informed by one of his scouts that troops were approaching. Their presence was neither unusual nor alarming. Ewell's command had been there twice in the past six months, and troops from Buchanan and Breckenridge regularly escorted wagons through the pass.

*Sunday, February 3*

The column reached Apache Pass near midday. A few miles west of the stage station, Bascom met thirteen troopers under the command of Sergeant Daniel Robinson, a sandy-haired man of medium build,[21] who was returning west after escorting a wagon train to Fort McLane. He furnished Bascom with information about the Indians and the location of their rancherías. Robinson's command joined Bascom's and together they continued toward the stage station,[22]

Bascom campsite. View from the west slope of Siphon Canyon looking northeast across drainage into the probable site of Bascom's first camp, which lies in the center of the picture on the far side of the drainage. (*Photo by Karen Hayes*)

where they met Butterfield Overland Mail employees James F. Wallace[23] and Charles W. Culver, both said to be on good terms with the Indians.

While Bascom conversed with them, Robinson and John Ward questioned two women, "one old and the other young and comely [Juanita]," both apparently part or full-blooded Mexicans. They said they knew nothing of the Ward boy and were told to go to Cochise's camp and tell him that the soldiers wished to parley. About midday, Bascom continued up Siphon Canyon and pitched his tents about one mile from the stage station.[24]

Cochise received the message but did not come in immediately; he may have been awaiting the return of his own runners, whom he had dispatched to the Western Apaches to obtain information on the Ward boy.[25]

*Monday, February 4*

Early that afternoon, Cochise still had not come in and Bascom was growing impatient. About midafternoon he retraced his steps to the stage station and asked Wallace to go to Cochise's camp to reiterate the lieutenant's desire for a meeting. Wallace hesitated, then went reluctantly. In his absence a freighter wagon train passed eastward and camped near Bear Springs, some two miles beyond the stage station. This was the Ortiz train under Romualdo Torres, en route to Las Cruces.[26]

At the dinner hour Cochise arrived. That he did not anticipate any problem was borne out by whom he brought along: his brother Coyuntura; two or three warriors, believed to be nephews; his wife; and two of his children (according to Apache history, one of them was Naiche). "After the customary greeting of How, How," Cochise, Coyuntura, and another warrior went into Bascom's tent to talk; Ward acted as interpreter.[27] During or after eating, Bascom began questioning Cochise about the raid. Cochise denied Chokonen involvement and said the Coyoteros had the boy in the Black Mountains. If Bascom would wait ten days, he would do all in his power to restore him. Bascom agreed to this proposition, according to his report, but in view of subsequent actions, one would have to question whether he actually assented to this or whether he fabricated a story to save himself embarrassment.[28]

Cochise's pledge was obviated by Bascom's next move. Through Ward he told Cochise that his people would be detained as prisoners until the boy was returned. What happened next is the subject of controversy even today. According to Bascom, he released Cochise, who had promised to obtain the boy,[29] yet every other Anglo version, whether it be an eyewitness (Oberly, Robinson), someone involved in the event who arrived later (Culver, Irwin, Oury), or a letter written to the *Missouri Republican* nine months later by a soldier who may have been present, agrees on one point: Cochise escaped. None of these independent reports even hints that Bascom allowed Cochise free passage. In fact, five of the six Anglo accounts state that Cochise escaped by cutting his way out of the tent, and two of these men were present at the time. Culver's account is the only exception. He arrived two days after the incident, and he said Cochise "effected his escape, after a desperate rush through the guard." [30] A military report made two months later also seems to contradict Bascom. Captain Gurden Chapin wrote that Cochise "was wounded by troops from this post at Apache Pass in February," which must have occurred at the time of his escape unless it happened during the subsequent fighting. [31]

The Apaches' story rebuts Bascom's version. Mrs. Eve Ball's informants told her that "Cochise offered to investigate, determine the offenders, and help restore the child. When he was told he was to be a prisoner, he cut a slit in the tent and escaped." Geronimo recalled that Cochise escaped by "cutting through the tent." Cochise told William F. M. Arny in October 1870 that "he cut his way through the tent was fired at by the soldiers and escaped." In 1872 he told an army officer that "with his knife he slashed the back of the tent, and . . . fled up the hill and escaped." [32]

Most accounts agree that Cochise bolted after he learned that he was to be held prisoner. Sergeant Robinson, who was a short distance from the tent, had this to say:

> Finally it was suggested that the sub-chief [Coyuntura] should go and find him [Ward boy] and that Cochise must remain as a hostage. This ended the talk. As quick as lightning both drew forth concealed knives, cut open the tent and darted out, Cochise to the front—at whom the interpreter fired. The sub chief (escaping through the rear) tripped and fell and was captured. [33]

Cochise had reacted instinctively, slitting the tent and scrambling through the astonished soldiers, who, according to some accounts, had surrounded the tent in compliance with Bascom's orders. "Shoot them down," shouted Bascom, to which John Ward responded, quickly snapping off a few shots at Cochise. These were the first of some fifty rounds fired at the Chiricahua chief, who apparently was wounded in the leg or thigh before he reached the top of the hill with his coffee cup still in his hand, he later told an American. [34] Cochise's relatives were not so fortunate; all were captured, and according to Robinson and Buckley, at least one warrior was killed. [35]

An hour later Cochise reappeared on the top of a nearby hill and asked to see Coyuntura. Bascom responded with a volley and Cochise "raised his hand and swore to be revenged." Cochise reminded the whites that "Indian blood was as good as white mans blood; that he and his tribe had been falsely accused; that for the injuries inflicted on him . . . he would have revenge." After making these threats, Cochise disappeared behind the hills.[36]

That evening Bascom broke camp and retraced his steps up Siphon Canyon to the stage station, mainly because its building and corral offered protection for his men and stock. At dusk Apache signal fires could be seen from the surrounding peaks. Despite this, the Americans were not too concerned; they had "twenty days' rations on hand, some forage and a fair supply of ammunition."[37] Yet the odds of restoring order were poor, especially if one Chokonen had indeed been killed. Of more significance, Bascom continued to insist upon the return of the Ward boy, who was in the possession of Western Apaches, a different tribe over whom Cochise had neither authority nor control.

*Tuesday, February 5*

Early this morning the Chokonens "assembled in force on a hill 600 yards south of the station." After a short time the Indians began to disperse, leaving a white flag, which was soon acknowledged by Bascom. A lone warrior approached, saying Cochise wished to parley midway between a ravine and the station, and Bascom agreed. Each party consisted of four individuals: Bascom, Sergeants Smith and Robinson, and John Ward comprised the American party; Cochise, Francisco, and two other warriors represented the Apaches. The two groups met in Siphon Canyon some 100 to 150 yards from the station, yet nothing of consequence could be settled despite Cochise's efforts to convince Bascom that he did not have the boy. According to Robinson's account, Cochise pleaded for the release of his captive friends. Bascom replied that they "would be set free just so soon as the boy was restored." Again Cochise denied having the boy.[38]

At this juncture the Butterfield employees (Wallace, Culver, and a man named Welch or Walsh), who were thoroughly acquainted with the Chokonens, left the stage station, hoping to take matters into their own hands and appease the Indians. Bascom immediately ordered them back, although he had no jurisdiction over civilians, declaring that he would not exchange his Apache prisoners for them if they were captured.[39] Nonetheless, the three courageous but naïve Americans continued, but they made the mistake of going into a ravine and were seized. Seeing this, Cochise and Francisco broke for cover and the Apaches opened fire on Bascom's unarmed party, slightly wounding Sergeant Smith, who had been carrying the white flag. Meanwhile, in the ravine, Welch and Culver managed to knock down their captors and flee towards the station. Culver was shot in the back but was picked up and brought to safety. Welch made it to the corral, where he was killed, in all likelihood by soldiers who mistook him in the excitement for an Indian.[40] The remainder of the Apaches, generously estimated by Bascom at five hundred, including Mangas Coloradas, kept up an intermittent fire. Robinson believed that several Apaches were killed or wounded. That evening the whites could see the Indians' "signal fires blazing from the peaks" and could hear "a war dance . . . in one direction and in another the weird cries of the squaws were distinctly heard wailing over their dead."[41]

The few casualties on both sides plus the fact that each were holding prisoners, who could be exchanged for each other, gave rise to hopes that more hostilities could be averted. In one respect, however, the capturing of Cochise's family would have left him with an indelible distrust of Americans. Even if his relations were eventually exchanged, it would have been a pretty sure bet that open hostilities would have followed.

*Wednesday, February 6, Noon*

Although the morning passed quietly without any sign of Indians, Cochise was watching from the hills. He allowed Sergeant Robinson to lead a party of soldiers and their stock to the springs, some six hundred yards from the station. The Americans anticipated a fight because the trail to the springs led through a winding ravine, an ideal place for an ambush. However, Cochise had no such plans; he was hoping to avoid trouble and perhaps settle things without more bloodshed.[42]

About midday Cochise appeared on a hill overlooking the station (probably Overlook Ridge), leading Wallace, who had "his arms

bound behind his back, and a rope around his neck."[43] The chief
again asked that his family be freed and offered to exchange Wallace
and sixteen government mules. Again Bascom refused and became
even angrier when Cochise explained that the mules had been stolen
"from a government train, of course."[44] Furthermore, he may have
been indignant at Wallace because the civilian had defiantly dis-
obeyed his orders the day before. Bascom clung adamantly to his
position that he would release Cochise's family only when the Ward
boy was restored. According to some accounts, Sergeant Reuben F.
Bernard briefly intervened and tried to dissuade Bascom from his
course, urging him to trade the Indians for Wallace. His suggestions, if indeed he was present, fell flat.[45]

Two legends about this meeting should be addressed because they
have become so steeped in Arizona history that they are accepted as
fact. The first is that Bascom refused to trade because Cochise was
holding four prisoners and offered to exchange only Wallace. In
fact, Bascom knew nothing of the other three prisoners because Cochise did not have them at this time. If he had had other captives, he
would have included them in his proposal to liberate his family.
Four whites would have been more enticing to Bascom than one.[46]
The second legend, frequently told but not mentioned by any of the
eyewitnesses, says Cochise was so infuriated by Bascom's refusal to
trade that he or one of his warriors dragged Wallace behind his horse
"at full length by the neck" to his death. This did not occur because
Wallace later returned.[47]

### Wednesday, February 6, Afternoon

Shortly after three o'clock the stagecoach from the east arrived at
the western mouth of Apache Pass; it was some eight hours ahead of
schedule. It had left the San Simon station before noon, and its occupants were unaware of any danger. At a narrow part of the canyon, perhaps at a place that is today called Tevis Rocks, Cochise's
warriors had barricaded the road with hay and rocks, intending to
set the hay on fire when the stage got there. Its early arrival foiled
the plan.[48] Instead, while the westbound stage approached the station, Cochise had his eyes on Sulphur Springs Valley, from whence
five wagons were approaching the mouth of Apache Pass.

*Wednesday, February 6, Early Evening*

Cochise had been following the progress of José Antonio Montoya's wagon train, loaded with flour for Las Cruces. Montoya had no reason to suspect danger as he and his men began the ascent from Sulphur Springs Valley to the summit of Apache Pass. He had probably made this trip on several occasions, and his only concern was what to give the Apaches in the event they asked for handouts. No one knows for sure the sequence of events, but this is probably what happened: Cochise and a large party of Apaches appeared in a ravine a few hundred yards east of the summit. The Indians may have approached the whites making signs of friendship. Then, at a signal from Cochise, they suddenly surrounded the train, capturing nine Mexicans and three Americans named Sam Whitfield, William Sanders, and Frank Brunner. All of the mules were taken. Having no use for the Mexicans, Cochise had them tied by their wrists to the

Wagon-train massacre site. This gently rolling terrain afforded a good campground for the Mexican wagon train captured by Cochise after Bascom seized his relatives. (*Photo by Karen Hayes*)

wheel spokes and tortured. Next the Indians burned the wagons and killed the Mexicans, but the Americans were taken to his camp in the hope that he could trade them for his family.[49]

That evening he instructed Wallace to write this message: "Treat my people well and I will do the same by yours, of whom I have three [four]." Cochise obviously wished to exchange the four whites for his family. The note, left on the hill and "fastened to the brush," was not retrieved until at least two days later, according to one account. In his report, Bascom implied that he received the note that evening. If he had, his couriers, who left the following day, would have included the information in their reports at Tucson and Fort Buchanan. Instead, the note was not obtained, either because Bascom feared a trap or did not know of its existence. Thus he was unaware that Cochise held four whites until it was too late.[50]

*Thursday, February 7*

Cochise evidently felt that his four prisoners were not enough. He therefore prepared to ambush the eastbound stage, which had left Tucson the morning of February 5 and would reach Apache Pass early this morning. The whites were not cognizant of the recent hostilities and the last thing they expected was an Apache attack, considering the darkness and the proximity of the stage station.

As they reached the summit of Apache Pass they were stunned by a volley of shots which broke the silence of the night, wounding the stage driver, King Lyons, killing one mule, and wounding another. At once William Buckley, the superintendent of the route, jumped from the stage to aid Lyons. The first thing he saw was the burned Mexican train and the charred bodies. After putting Lyons in the stage, Buckley took the reins and forged on toward the stage station, still almost three miles away. About a half-mile away, the Chokonens had torn away part of a small stone bridge, probably thinking that if the first attack failed, the coach would almost certainly capsize. A determined Buckley whipped the mules and forced them to jump the bridge; the stage's momentum carried it across. The rest of the route was just as perilous because the Indians had put rocks in the road and the passengers were compelled to push the stage over the incline as the Chokonens maintained sporadic fire from the hills.

Bridge abutments. Cochise's men tore away part of the stone bridge hoping the stage would capsize. (*Photo by Karen Hayes*)

The coach finally arrived at the stage station about 2 A.M., thereby frustrating Cochise's attempt to take more prisoners.[51]

To everyone's surprise, not an Apache was seen. Robinson recalled that "everything around us was as still as a graveyard."[52] That morning the mules were watered, and the day passed uneventfully, which must have been a blessing for Bascom's command. Why Cochise did not appear to exchange prisoners is not known. He may have felt that Bascom's obstinacy would make any conference fruitless, and it is possible that, in the words of Geronimo, because Bascom did not reply to Cochise's note, the latter interpreted this as a refusal to trade, "so we killed our prisoners, disbanded, and went into hiding in the mountains."[53]

It is possible, though unlikely, that the four Americans already had been tortured to death. The action of the past few days undoubtedly had resulted in Chokonen fatalities. If so, they may have been avenged by female relatives who vented rage on the prisoners. This was the Chiricahua way, and it is possible, though unlikely, that the torture had been carried out without Cochise's consent.

### Thursday, February 7, Evening

No Apaches were seen all day. Cochise had broken camp, removing his noncombatants south into the Chiricahuas. Nonetheless he had decided to take his relative by force if possible. That day he and his warriors prepared for the next day's fight: first a war dance, then the preparation of protective garments and amulets, special prayers asking for success, and finally preparing the bows, arrows, and guns for war.

During the day it was clear to all at the stage station that help was required. Bascom needed a doctor for the men who had been wounded during the previous day's skirmish, and Buckley required additional men to escort the stage. Therefore, shortly after dark, a small party of soldiers and A. B. Culver, who had arrived with the stage from the east and was the brother of the wounded Charles Culver, left to obtain reinforcements. The mules' shoes were wrapped with blankets to dampen sound and prevent detection. Surprisingly, the party had no trouble and gained Sulphur Springs Valley without incident. The soldiers arrived at Fort Buchanan late the following evening; Culver reached Tucson about the same time, having made the 125-mile trip in twenty-four hours.[54]

*Friday, February 8, Morning*

By now everyone had begun "to think they [Apaches] had left the country."[55] Indeed many had, at least the women and children, but Cochise, now allied with Francisco's and Mangas Coloradas's groups, had returned, intent on making one last effort to free his people. Geronimo, who was present, furnished a simple but honest account of Chokonen activities after Cochise cut his way out of Bascom's tent:

> In a few days after the attack at Apache Pass we organized in the mountains and returned to fight the soldiers. There were two tribes [bands]—the Bedonkohe and the Chokonen Apaches, both commanded by Cochise.[56]

Cochise's attack was well planned. The first assault would take place at Apache Springs after the soldiers had finished watering their stock. He hoped Bascom would weaken his defenses at the stage station and send reinforcements to repulse the diversionary first strike. If Bascom took the bait, a large body of warriors would storm the station from the east and free his family. The scheme was sound and bold.

Sergeants James Huber and Daniel Robinson drove the stock through the ravine to the springs. The advance party was led by Robinson, who felt confident that no Apaches were in the vicinity because it had snowed the night before and "no marks or signs" were observed. He "stood on a knoll above the spring" and "the signal was given to send up the animals." On the previous two mornings, the stock had been watered in two shifts; this time, to Robinson's consternation (he called it a misunderstanding), every animal was sent, a grave mistake by Bascom. Still, as the last animal had its fill, no signs of Indians had been seen.

This changed quickly. Just as the return trip was begun, Robinson observed "a large party of Apaches [two hundred, according to Bascom] moving at a swinging gait" from upper Siphon Canyon and threatening to cut the herd and its escort off from the station. Wrote Robinson:

> They were in war dress . . . naked and painted . . . and they were
> singing a war song. . . . They were coming so open and boldly that
> they no doubt expected to sweep all before them without much
> trouble. . . . We opened fire at once . . . [and] forced them to change
> their course so as to leave the way open to the station.

The soldiers responded quickly, directing several well-placed vol-
leys, wounding several wariors, and repulsing the Indians, who retired in the same direction they had come. The respite was brief. A
few minutes later the Chiricahuas swung to the soldiers' right flank
and gained the heights overlooking the springs.[57]

At the first volley, Bascom sent out a small relief party under the
capable command of Lieutenant John Rogers Cooke, who had arrived with the eastbound stage. Cooke rendezvoused with the soldiers at the springs and took command. By this time every animal
had been driven off into the mountains, and the soldiers, now afoot,
were unable to pursue. During the attack a large group of Apaches,
probably under Cochise, appeared opposite the station, looking for
a chance to take it by surprise. Bascom reacted quickly, however,
and diverted his men to the front to repel the attack, which seemed
imminent. To his credit, his decisive response definitely saved many
lives, both red and white. An assault at this time would have been
costly and uncharacteristic of Apaches, who, it should be remembered, very rarely fought unless they were supremely confident of
success. The Chiricahuas fell back out of range.[58]

The fight was over. Bascom lost forty-two mules and the mail
company fourteen. Mail employee King Lyon was killed and Sergeant Robinson was wounded. Bascom estimated the Indian casualties "with certainty but five Indians killed, but think there were
twelve to fifteen more killed or badly wounded. This includes all
since my arrival at the Pass." The Chiricahuas later acknowledged
at Fronteras that three warriors were killed, and Geronimo remembered that several men were killed. Although the whites scarcely
could have known it, they would see no more Apaches. With reinforcements streaming in from the west, the bands split up, with
Francisco and Mangas Coloradas heading for the Gila and Cochise
and his Chokonens for Sonora, but not before they tortured to death
the four American prisoners, leaving their mutilated remains where

they could be found by the whites. This decision effectively slammed the door on negotiations and eventually led to the death of several Chokonens, including Cochise's brother and two nephews.[59]

*Saturday, February 9*

Unbeknown to the whites, the siege was over. This morning, in a blinding snowstorm, assistant surgeon Irwin left Fort Buchanan with fourteen soldiers and one civilian, James Graydon, taking with him medical supplies for the wounded. They would camp that evening at Dragoon Springs.[60] Also on this day at Tucson, William Sanders Oury dispatched a messenger to Fort Breckenridge, informing the troops there of Bascom's plight.[61]

Cochise's Chokonens were also on the move. A few stragglers arrived at Fronteras with news of the outbreak, specifically mentioning that a few Indians had been bayoneted and alluding to the hostilities of February 4. In the days that followed, many more Chiricahuas took refuge in the mountains north and east of Fronteras, from whence they descended on the isolated presidio and began drawing rations.[62]

*Sunday, February 10*

Irwin's reinforcements left Dragoon Springs early this morning, traveling the Overland Mail route. At Playa de los Pimos, which was located south of present-day Willcox, Arizona, Irwin espied some Apaches driving a herd of cattle stolen from Mexico. He pursued and "succeeded in capturing the party consisting of a Coyotero Chief and two warriors" and several head of stock, although one might question how Irwin's party could capture the Apaches, who knew nothing of the difficulties at Apache Pass, unless by ruse. It is generally believed that these Indians were Coyoteros, unrelated to Cochise's Chokonens. Yet it is possible that they were Chokonens or at least Chiricahuas. Irwin, like most Americans, could not differentiate one band from another.[63]

Some two days earlier, some Chiricahuas had conversed with a few citizens outside Fronteras. The Indians said they belonged to the bands of Cochise and Mangas Coloradas and were heading south for a raid into the interior.[64] One might question their veracity, however, for they might have just returned from an incursion. Irwin may have jumped this group. Cochise said repeatedly that the war began when Bascom hanged six warriors (Irwin's three and Bascom's three), thereby implying that the three captured by Irwin were Chiricahuas.

Late in the afternoon Irwin's relief party reached Apache Pass and marched to the station without incident. Although Irwin wrote that the Apaches were off chasing other troops, in reality no Indians were present except for a few scouts.[65]

*Monday, February 11, to Monday, February 18*

For the first three days, Bascom's command had remained at Apache Pass, totally inactive and ostensibly believing they were bottled up. In reality, the only Indians present were scouts, who certainly would not have sought a fight. Yet, inexplicably, Bascom had not sent out any scouting parties, electing instead to await reinforcements from Fort Breckenridge. They arrived on February 14: sev-

Oak tree at the western edge of Apache Pass near the location where Cochise's relatives were hanged. The actual tree was cut down about 1930. (*Photo by Karen Hayes*)

enty soldiers of Companies D and G, First Dragoons, commanded
by Lieutenant Isaiah N. Moore. In all likelihood, Sergeant Reuben F.
Bernard arrived with this detachment.

On February 16 and 17, Moore and Bascom led a command of
110 men and scouted the mountains in search of Apaches. None
were found.[66]

On February 18, Irwin found the bodies of the four Americans—
Wallace, Whitfield, Sanders, and Brunner—all horribly mutilated
and "riddled with lance holes." Oury recognized Wallace's body by
the gold fillings in the teeth. The corpses were buried some three
hundred yards from the charred Mexican wagon train near four large
oak trees.[67] Why Cochise left the bodies where they would be found
is a question only he could answer, but leaving them there sealed the
fate of his relatives. Most of the civilians, soldiers, and officers advocated execution of the six Apache men. According to some accounts, Bascom demurred but was overruled by Lieutenant Moore,
who told Bascom that he would assume full responsibility.[68]

*Tuesday, February 19*

The commands of Bascom and Moore left Apache Pass for their
home forts, the former leaving Sergeant Patrick Murray and thirteen
men to guard the mail station. As they made their way west through
the pass, Bascom had the interpreter explain his intentions to the
Indians.[69] Oberly said the Indians asked to be shot instead of hanged
and requested whiskey.[70] Both requests were denied. The Indians
then accepted their fate and "sang their death songs,"[71] although
one man "begged piteously for his life." Another warrior, probably
Coyuntura, "went to the gallows dancing and singing, saying that
he was satisfied as he had killed two Mexicans in the last month."[72]
Robinson recalled that "the dragoons furnished the lariats; one end
was thrown over the boughs of the trees, while the Indians placed
under them were hoisted so high by the infantry that even the wolves
could not touch them." The hanging took place on four oak trees
under which Wallace and the other whites were buried.[73] The women
and children were released, although Cochise always believed that a
card game had decided their fate—a little-known story also mentioned by Oberly.[74] Bascom's and Moore's commands reached Fort
Buchanan and Fort Breckenridge on February 23.

*Monday, February 25, 1861*

On this day both Moore and Bascom wrote their official reports of the outbreak. Moore's, written from Fort Breckenridge, was brief and factual;[75] Bascom's, drawn up at Fort Buchanan, was longer, ambiguous, and duplistic.[76] He omitted several things which would have been a source of embarrassment. It is also conceivable that his report was written with Lieutenant Colonel Morrison's blessing, although we will probably never know for sure. Morrison, then sixty-five years old, was awaiting departmental approval of his request for a leave of absence and may not have wanted any controversy to hinder it. Bascom, after all, had followed orders, but the results were not what they had hoped for.

An analysis of Bascom's report reveals several errors of omision, obviously an attempt to cover up the blunders that resulted from his poor judgment. No other officers were present during the first four days, so his report is the only one dealing with this crucial period, at least from the contemporary military perspective. If Morrison heard post scuttlebutt critical of Bascom's actions, he must have ignored it. It is also possible, however remote, that he accepted Bascom's report implicitly. To begin with, Bascom failed to mention Cochise's escape and his subsequent wounding, which was common knowledge at the post. He also neglected to mention that his own soldiers probably killed Welch at the stage station; he said only that one of the station keepers was killed (implying the Apaches did it), but other accounts indicate that his own soldiers were the marksmen. Next, he implied that he received Wallace's note on the evening of February 6. In truth, the note was not recovered until at least the eighth and perhaps later. Finally, he did not mention that the loss of the mules at Apache Springs was the result of his poor judgment.

The Bascom affair was a prodigious Anglo blunder, but Cochise must bear some responsibility for not controlling his rage or that of his people in the torturing of his four white prisoners, his only bargaining chips. His decision has caused much discussion among historians, perhaps more than anything else he ever did. Why indeed? There is no simple answer, and in his later years he was reluctant to discuss the matter. Perhaps he had already written them off, believing his people would be killed regardless of his actions. It is also possible (although remotely, in my opinion) that the prisoners were killed without his approval. To Cochise, the hanging of Coyuntura and his two nephews meant war.

But what of Bascom? He was commended by department headquarters. And what of the troops? Referring to the Bascom-Cochise incident, a soldier wrote nine months later: "Tread on a worm and it will turn—disturb a hornets nest and they will sting you. — So with savage Indians: misuse them and you make them revengeful foes." [77]

# Chapter 9

## THE WAR BEGINS

After his relatives were executed, Cochise hated Americans with an abiding and impenetrable passion, perhaps more fanatically than any other Apache. It mattered little that only a few whites had actually wronged him; he hated them all. The loss of Coyuntura distressed him deeply, for Apache brothers were very close, even inseparable if they were in the same local group. It is conceivable that he married Coyuntura's widow, Yones, because Coyuntura's children were blood kin. One of them might have been Chie, or Chee, who was said to have been raised by Cochise.

Initially, Cochise raided and killed to avenge his brother's death; later, as his rage abated, he continued to wage war, and eventually it evolved into a bloody cycle of revenge and retaliation. Throughout the 1860s, American forces were unable to subjugate him as he demonstrated that he had indeed become an implacable foe. Essentially he believed that his people had not begun the fighting and were undeserved victims of American treachery. In February 1869 he told Captain Frank Perry: "I tried the Americans once and they broke the treaty first, the officers I mean. This was at the Pass." [1]

The following year he visited Camp Mogollon (later renamed Fort Apache) and the Cañada Alamosa Reservation in New Mexico to discuss peace. At Camp Mogollon in August 1870 he told Major John Green that "he did not begin the war . . . and only fought for revenge and self defense." [2] Two months later at Cañada Alamosa he confessed to William F. M. Arny that he "had been guilty of murders and thefts . . . since 1860 [1861] when he was treacherously seized and six of his braves hung and he escaped by cutting his way through his prison."[3]

In 1871 and 1872, Cochise granted interviews in which he steadfastly insisted that the war had begun because of the hangings at Apache Pass. He told Brigadier General Oliver Otis Howard in October 1872: "The worst place of all is Apache Pass. There, five [six] Indians, one my brother were murdered. Their bodies were hung up and kept there till they were skeletons. I have retaliated with all my might."[4]

Arizona accounts of the early 1860s supported Cochise's statements about why the fighting began. In May 1861, Captain Gurden Chapin wrote:

> The Chiricahuas, Coyoteros, Pinals, and Coppermine Indians are all at war with us. They have since the action at Apache Pass in February last stolen upwards of one hundred mules and a large number of cattle. They have killed one soldier, several drivers and others on the overland route . . . [they have] also killed several white men, wagonners and farmers.[5]

Another chronicler who was in Arizona when it occurred wrote in November 1861 that the Apache war began with the Bascom affair. Since that time, he said, Cochise had been "the enemy of the white race."[6] John C. Cremony, who arrived in Arizona in 1862 with the California Volunteers, declared that since the confrontation Cochise "has been one of the most bitter, most active, and unrelenting of foes, losing no opportunity to destroy life and property." Cremony, who had a propensity to exaggerate, did not do so in this case.[7]

Other informed Arizona residents from the mid-1860s through the early 1870s echoed these statements. In 1865, N. S. Higgins, who was researching the Western Apaches, heard of the Bascom affair from an old Arizona pioneer who had known Cochise. After the outbreak, he said, Cochise had been "the dread of this country."[8] In the fall of 1867, Arizona pioneer William Oury told William A. Bell at Fort Bowie that after the Bascom affair Cochise "and his entire band fled back once again to their mountain fastnesses never more to come in contact with the white man, unless in the execution of their unquenchable revenge."[9] One year later, Lieutenant Colonel Thomas C. Devin wrote that the incident "aroused him [Cochise] to make war."[10] Captain Reuben F. Bernard attributed Cochise's war to the tragedy at Apache Pass, as did another writer, who said in 1870 that ever since, Cochise "and his tribe have sought and found vengeance."[11]

Twentieth-century writers also say the Bascom affair ignited Cochise's war. To Paul I. Wellman, "it was war to the knife now between Cochise and the white man."[12] Frank C. Lockwood: "His [Cochise's] fury knew no bounds."[13] Historian Robert M. Utley summed up the situation succinctly. After the Bascom affair he said, Cochise possessed "an implacable hostility toward all Americans and [this] spurred him to wage upon them a bloody warfare that lasted for a decade."[14] Although Cochise vowed vengeance, there is no basis for the version put forth by Woodworth Clum, and accepted by some historians, that "ten Americans must die for each Apache the Americans have killed."[15] The Chiricahuas' version, as recorded in several accounts, all say Cochise's war began in February 1861.[16]

At department headquarters in Santa Fe, civil and military authorities moved to quell a full-scale Apache outbreak. James L. Collins,[17] the superintendent of Indian Affairs in New Mexico, unfairly blamed the uprising on Dr. Michael Steck, claiming that if the agent had been present to issue rations, the Apaches would have been content and "the present difficulty would have been, beyond question, prevented." Collins's view was a classic example of the naïveté with which white officials viewed the Indian problem. Steck's presence would not have prevented the hostilities; furthermore, the Indians were upset about the infrequency and paucity of rations, for which the agent could not be faulted. In late February, Collins insisted that Steck be ordered back to his agency, but at this point conditions had deteriorated so much that even the efforts of the influential agent would have been fruitless.[18]

As the Bascom affair was winding down, department headquarters in Santa Fe opted for punitive operations against the Mescaleros and Chiricahuas. On February 10, 1861, it ordered simultaneous campaigns against the Apaches on both sides of the Río Grande. Lieutenant Colonel George Bibb Crittenden was directed to punish the Mescaleros east of the river, and Major Isaac Lynde was instructed to "actively prosecute war against the Apaches from the vicinity of Fort Floyd." [19] When news of the Apache Pass incident reached Santa Fe, the department commander ordered two additional companies of the Seventh Infantry to Fort McLane, which "with the present garrison of Fort McLane, Buchanan, and Breckenridge it is hoped will be sufficient to enable you to sustain vigorous operations . . . at once against the Apaches." Lynde was given a free hand to organize the campaign as he saw fit and was told that headquarters would furnish the necessary resources. [20]

Major Lynde, however, vacillating as always, seemed unable to decide on anything except to remain where he was. This was a stark contrast to Crittenden's campaign, which was "promptly and energetically conducted" and forced the Mescaleros to sue for peace. [21] In fact, after receiving reports from Fort Breckenridge and Fort Buchanan, Lynde concluded that his troops lacked provisions to conduct a campaign. The only meat on hand at any of the three posts was bacon; furthermore, at Fort Buchanan, the mules were "completely broken down and unfit for the field." Lynde argued that "the present force was barely adequate to provide protection" and concluded that "it would be useless to attempt to operate against these Indians." [22]

Actually, any American offensive probably would have accomplished little, for the Chiricahuas had scattered and were relatively quiet. Mangas had headed north to the Gila, but not before he, perhaps with Cochise, cleaned the San Simon stage station of stock. [23] Geronimo recalled that the Indians "went into hiding in the mountains," and "after this trouble [Bascom] all of the Indians agreed not to be friendly with the white man any more." [24] As for Cochise, he plunged south into Sonora and established camp near Fronteras, where some Chiricahuas under Esquinaline, Teboca Chiquito, and Delgadito were living.

Cochise had been in touch with them. The presence of his "broncos" definitely unnerved the Fronteras authorities, who were uneasy, awaiting an explosion. In early February a few of Cochise's Chokonens spoke with some Mexicans near the abandoned town of Cuquiarachi. The Indians' actions intrigued the commander at Fronteras: "I don't know what the intentions of these Indians was in coming to these residents without harming them but I think it was probably for the purpose of finding out about the peace treaties that the other Indians have." Because most of the troops at Fronteras had been sent south to fight the Yaquis and Mayos, the Indians were not followed. This angered Governor Pesqueira, who responded that "in such cases the residents are called together and they have always shown the greatest willingness to help." [25]

On February 9 a few wounded warriors from the fights of either February 6 or February 8 straggled into Fronteras and told of the conflict at Apache Pass. On March 5 additional details were furnished by Teboca Chiquito and Remigio, who said Cochise's followers were agitated because Coyuntura and a warrior named Garanon had been killed. Allied with Francisco's band, the Chiricahuas had raided a train and had stolen more than 150 head of stock, probably implicating them in the February 16 raid at San Simon. The presence of Cochise's followers alarmed even the so-called peaceful Apaches. Delgadito fled Fronteras by the end of February, although it was not clear whether he joined the hostiles or relocated to a safer area to avoid the trouble Cochise's people usually brought.[26]

Once established in northern Sonora, Cochise planned his retaliation, which, for the Apaches, could hardly have come at a more opportune time. Affairs in Arizona were coming apart at the seams. Just as Sonora was vulnerable to Chiricahua raids in the 1840s, so did Arizona prove to be in 1861. The first big blow to the Anglos fell in March, when financial hardship and the imminent Civil War closed the Butterfield Overland Mail Route in Arizona. Many experienced men lost their jobs and left the territory. Quite naturally, Cochise believed that he had forced the abandonment.

The last Butterfield stage from the west reached Mesilla in mid-March and reported that the Indians "had returned in great numbers to Apache Pass." [27] This was almost certainly Cochise. The Chiricahuas tried the white-flag gambit at the stage station, but its personnel were not fooled. Subsequently the Chiricahuas hoisted a black flag, indicating no quarter asked or received.[28]

Despite the increase in Apache signs, no significant hostilities were reported, yet a portending unrest was felt. Both Morrison and Chapin conceded that Cochise was living below the border at Fronteras, beyond their control.²⁹ Although Sonoran reports failed to mention him, this should not be taken as conclusive evidence that he was not present, inasmuch as some activities were never reported. Cochise or his representatives definitely were at the presidio from time to time. Living near it, he had the option of raiding on either side of the border. Finally, in April, he commanded a Chokonen war party consisting of warriors from all three local groups. With Yaque, Parte, and perhaps Remigio, the Chokonens swept north on a campaign against the Americans.³⁰

The first reprisal, a typical Cochise-led encounter, occurred in late April: an ambush of a party of whites traveling through Doubtful Canyon near a place the Indians called Tsisl-lnoi-bi-yi-tu (Rock White in Water), otherwise known as Stein's Peak. *Mesilla Times* of May 11, 1861, reported what happened:

Nine men are missing, and it is feared have all been massacred although there exists some hope that some of them may be retained as prisoners. The Savages inflicted upon some of their victims a horrible torture, and exhibited a refinement in cruelty unparalleled in the catalogue of Indian barbarities. From the expressman Mr. Price, we gather the following particulars: A provision wagon left Tanks station on April 23, Edward Donnelly and Patrick Donaghue in charge, to put a load of flour at the San Cimone Station. They started on their return but never reached the Tanks. The next day two expressmen, Messrs. Paige and O'Brien left the Tanks westward bound and never reached the San Cimone Station and have not since been heard of. On the 27th a coach left the Tanks for the West, in which were five persons Mr. J. J. Giddings, Superintendent of the San Antonio and San Diego Mail Company, Michael Nies [McNeese], Road Agent and Anthony Elder, Samuel Neely and Mr. Briggs, employees of the Overland Mail Company. Two of the mules which left in the coach returned to the Tanks Station badly bruised, and had evidently been in a severe struggle. This circumstance aroused the suspicion of all and our informant went the next day to Fort McLane and applied for an escort of troops to investigate the matter. A Lieutenant and sixteen men were dispatched who on Monday near Steins Peak, met a train of W. S. Grant, Army Contractor, who gave them information of their having a fight with Cochise and his braves and confirmation of the fears that the coach had been captured by the Indians at or near Doubtful Pass [Grant's train had reached Stein's Peak about dark]. . . .

They found scattered along the ravine, newspapers and other mail matter, pieces of harness, etc. The roof of the station (which was some time since abandoned) had been burned, the corral wall had been thrown down, and the Indians had formed a breastwork around the springs. Near the station the bodies of two men were found, tied by the feet to trees, their heads reaching within eighteen inches of the ground, their arms extended and fastened to pickets, and the evidence of a slow fire under their heads. The bodies had been pierced with arrows and lances. They were so disfigured as to render recognition impossible.[31]

The Apaches killed nine men, with Cochise's fury manifesting itself in the torture reserved for those captured alive. According to Oury's account, Cochise and some sixty warriors, whom he placed in ambush at the springs (located a short distance northwest of the station), ambushed Giddings' party "just at dawn of day, as they were approaching the station at Stein's Peak." The driver (Briggs) and Anthony Elder, who had had a run-in with Cochise in late 1858, evidently were killed in the first fire. The uncontrollable mules "ran for about a mile and a half to the foot of the mountains, where the coach was capsized and everything brought to a standstill." According to a Mexican living with the Chiricahuas, the fight between the surviving whites and the Indians continued for the rest of that day, with the Apaches sustaining heavy losses and Cochise himself being wounded in the hard battle. Neely was killed soon after. By the end of the day, the two survivors, Giddings and McNeese, short of ammunition, may have attempted to parley with Cochise. McNeese had been the agent at Stein's Peak and evidently knew Cochise. His decision was a grave mistake. Like Wallace, he trusted that his earlier friendship with Cochise might mean something; his fate, like Wallace's, was the same. Cochise was in no mood to negotiate, and the two whites, said an eyewitness, were "captured and burned alive, head downward."[32]

Cochise had made a nice haul, if we can believe George H. Giddings's claim against the government for restitution. When Giddings received the news of his brother's death, he recruited twenty-five men and marched to Stein's Peak, where he found the ruins of the station and what remained of two stagecoaches. The Chiricahuas al-

Stein's Peak. Located at the eastern end of Doubtful Canyon, this was the site of Cochise's ambush of Gidding's party in April 1861. (*Photo by Dan Thrapp*)

legedly destroyed or seized property valued at $8,335, including thirteen Colt pistols and thirteen Sharps rifles.[33]

The fight had given the Indians new confidence. Cochise followed it with another hard encounter, but this time the Anglos fought him to a standstill. On April 27, 1861, a freight train departed Fort Buchanan for the Río Grande. A detachment of twenty-one troops served as escort, bringing the total of able-bodied whites to about forty. On May 3 they encamped at the abandoned San Simon station (about eighteen miles northeast of the Apache Pass station) and turned the stock out to graze. Suddenly Cochise and about thirty warriors swept down and stampeded the herd, driving it north toward Stein's Peak. At once Jud Jones took five men in pursuit and almost overtook the hostiles. A running fight ensued for the next four or five miles, some of it hand to hand. A warrior threw his lasso over a Mexican, who immediately tied it "around the horn of his saddle and wrenched it from the Indian."

Cochise was in the forefront as usual, boldly charging the whites, before the fight became "a personal contest, [and] the chief Kachees stepped out and called on Jones, upon whom he dispatched four six-shooters." The shots missed, revealing that Cochise's skill with his native weapons far exceeded that with a six-shooter. Although Jones recaptured some of the stock, the Indians got away with seventeen head. According to Jones's report, the whites killed three Chokonens.[34]

Two weeks later, Cochise planned a strike against the soldiers at Fort Buchanan. On May 16 at Monkey Springs, about two miles south of the fort, a group of Chokonens surprised a small army party, killed one soldier, Private Salliot, and fled with two mules, a rifle, and a revolver. Troops followed the trail for three miles before the Apaches scattered. Antonio, an experienced scout, identified the arrows as Chokonen. A few weeks later, Cochise struck again, this time perhaps in conjunction with Francisco. Charles Mowry and three men left the Patagonia mines for Fort Buchanan. Halfway there, Apaches jumped them, killing a man and wounding the driver. Mowry somehow escaped.[35]

The commanding officer of Fort Buchanan, Captain Gurden Chapin, wanted to launch a campaign against Cochise, but his hands were tied. He informed department headquarters that depredations were being committed by Chiricahuas living under the pernicious influence of Mexicans at Fronteras. Consequently, he said, he had petitioned Governor Pesqueira for permission to enter Sonora "for the purpose of chastising the Indians." Pesqueira diplomatically refused, saying the request required federal approval and an incursion would jeopardize the peace at Fronteras. Pesqueira, who was suppressing a rebellion of the Yaqui and Mayo Indians at the time, probably denied Chapin's request because he distrusted the Americans and because he had no troops to protect the northern frontier.[36]

The commander at Fronteras, Captain Gabriel García, shared Chapin's apprehension; Cochise's presence in northern Sonora was just as alarming to him as it was to Chapin. Just as important, however, was the resurgence of Chihuahuan scalp hunters to the east, which pushed the Chiricahuas in from that frontier. In early May,

Yaque, Parte, and Taces brought their people to the presidio and were rationed even though they had been raiding, almost certainly with Cochise.[37]

On May 10 a Nednhi chief discussed peace conditions, which led to the arrival of a large local group under Galindo,[38] the Janeros headman. Sonoran troops from Bavispe had surprised his band, killing one and capturing another at Embudos Canyon on May 1. As a result, he brought in his band, which consisted of thirty men, fifty-four women, forty boys, and twenty-two girls, and agreed to live at Santa Rosa, some eight miles north of Fronteras. But García continued to fear the presence of the broncos, meaning Cochise's followers, who were bound to create problems and influence younger warriors who were anxious to acquire loot and prestige by raiding.[39]

A week later, clearly referring to Cochise and the recalcitrant Yaque, Captain García reiterated to Pesqueira that the large number of recently arrived Chiricahuas had put the presidio, which numbered but thirty soldiers, in a state of alert. "The peaceful Apaches declare that the broncos are very bad and that they have no confidence in them and fear them." Apparently, some of Cochise's people had tried to incite the peaceful Apaches, brazenly boasting that they intended to kill farmers working their crops. Teboca Chiquito warned citizens to be on their guard.[40]

This time, however, Cochise's quarry was Americans, not Mexicans. In his April and May fights, his strength was thought to be somewhere between thirty and sixty men. In June, that figure doubled, indicating that he may have been joined by the Nednhis or other warriors from Mexico and perhaps by some White Mountain Apaches under Francisco. In June, Cochise returned to Arizona and directed another large war party on a destructive sweep through the Santa Cruz Valley. First the Chokonens cleaned out the stock of the San Pedro station, stealing forty-four mules.[41] Next they proceeded west along the northern Whetstone and Santa Rita mountains before abruptly swinging south to the Santa Cruz River. Here he led his war party of eighty to one hundred on a whirlwind rampage through the valley. At the Canoa Inn, the Chiricahuas murdered four men and virtually destroyed the ranch. When Raphael Pumpelly and Charles Poston reached the scene, they were stunned. Pumpelly described the disaster:

The sides of the house were broken in, and the court was filled with broken tables and doors, while fragments of crockery and ironware lay mixed in heaps with grain and the contents of mattresses. Through the open door of a small house, on one side of the court, we saw a naked body, which proved to be the remains of young Tarbox. . . . As in the case of many of the settlers, the first Apaches he had seen were his murderers. Under a tree, beyond a fence that divided the court, we found the bodies of the other American and a Papago Indian who, probably driven in by the Apaches, had joined in a desperate struggle that had evidently taken place. These bodies were pierced by hundreds of lance wounds.[42]

Arizona pioneer Pete Kitchen lost about four hundred head of cattle in the raid. He later recalled that Juh and Cochise led the Apache force, which he thought numbered five hundred to six hundred men (a gross exaggeration) and said he followed their trail into Mexico.[43]

Cochise continued raiding. On June 20 a band of Indians believed "to have been Chiricahuas" attacked the cattle herd of a Mr. Thompson about fourteen miles south of Fort Buchanan and stole every head. Thompson had a brush with the raiders and thought he had killed two warriors. Two days later at dawn "the bold war chief Cochise" led a force estimated at more than one hundred warriors and ran off a herd grazing about a mile south of the fort. The Chiricahuas killed one soldier and one Mexican, then fled, with "one party driving the mule herd towards Mexico, and the other [headed by Cochise] with the beef herd in an opposite direction towards the Whetstone Mountains."

Bascom, Irwin, and nine troopers, guided by Antonio and James Graydon, were in the saddle by 9 A.M. in pursuit of Cochise's party. After a twenty-mile march, Bascom's presence forced the Indians to kill most of the cattle. Near the Whetstone Mountains a group of warriors on foot reinforced Cochise's raiders. Realizing he was outnumbered, Bascom retired to open ground. In the meantime, Cochise had recognized him and made several whirlwind charges, to no avail. The Chiricahua chieftain "called out . . . in English, taunting, and cursing." The soldiers repulsed each assault and Cochise withdrew, having suffered four killed and three wounded; the troops had but one wounded. Bascom's party returned to Fort Buchanan late that day.[44]

Chapin reiterated to his superiors in Santa Fe that the aggressors were Cochise's Chokonens allied with Francisco's Coyoteros. He praised Lieutenant Bascom's conduct and digressed to say he desperately needed cavalry. Infantry, he said, "cannot be brought efficiently into service."[45] Headquarters sent no reinforcements. With the outbreak of the Civil War and the invasion of New Mexico by Confederate forces, the army decided to abandon southern Arizona's only two posts. Fort Breckenridge was evacuated and burned on July 10; Fort Buchanan was evacuated and burned on July 23.[46]

This decision signaled the end of ranching, mining, and all other economic pursuits around Tubac and the mining area. Once prosperous, it had been hit hard by Apache raids and now had no protection. Mines, ranches, and small settlements were hastily abandoned. The final blow fell on either August 3 or August 4. Tubac, where many of the miners and ranchers had taken refuge, was attacked by about one hundred Apaches, who killed two men and took all of the stock. The citizens finally halted the attack and the Apaches left, reportedly losing seven to ten killed.[47] Some historians think Cochise led the raid, and its characteristics (large party, bold attack) certainly were symptomatic of his kind of action, yet he almost certainly was not there; Western Apaches probably were responsible.

By late summer 1861, southern Arizona was virtually uninhabited except for Tucson and a few isolated mines. The Apaches again ruled, their confidence inflated by the departure of the soldiers. The *Tucson Arizonian* described the abysmal scene in southern Arizona:

> Our prosperity has departed. The mail is withdrawn; the soldiers are gone and their garrisons burned to the ground; the miners murdered and the mines abandoned; the stockraisers and farmers have abandoned their crops and herds to the Indians, and the population generally have fled, panic struck and naked in search of refuge. From end to end of the territory, except alone in Tucson and its immediate vicinity, there is not a human habitation.[48]

Although Cochise had been extremely active from late April through June, his Chiricahuas had taken losses in every engagement. He lost a few and perhaps several warriors in the Stein's Peak fight in April, and in early May he lost at least three more in his fight with citizens near San Simon. Thompson believed he killed at least two Chiricahuas in June, and then Lieutenant Bascom reported at least three dead and others wounded. It should be noted that white accounts tended to inflate the number of Indian dead. Even so, Cochise had not escaped unscathed, a prominent historian asserting that "the operations of Cochise probably would have been checked in an early stage had not the Civil War intervened . . . and the troops withdrawn."[49]

Cochise probably interpreted the white exodus on the basis of his experiences in Sonora, where ranches, mines, towns, and presidios had been abandoned as a direct result of Chiricahua raids. Undoubtedly, then, he concluded the same thing when southern Arizona was deserted. At least we may infer this from a statement he made ten years later: "At last your soldiers did me a very great wrong, and I and my whole people went to war with them. At first we were successful and your soldiers were driven away and your people killed and we again possessed our land."[50]

About this time Mangas Coloradas's Chihennes went to war in New Mexico. Most of the Chihennes initially had refrained from joining Cochise's retaliatory raids, a fact corroborated by Cochise in his later years. They certainly had ample justification to commence hostilities, however. In the spring of 1860, "yellow iron" was discovered at Pinos Altos in the heart of their country, and the predictable gold rush on a small scale ensued.[51] Wrote an observer: "All wild with the fever—everything that can leave has gone out. The Overland stages have lost many of their men."[52] Naturally the Chihennes were disturbed, yet they could do little to deter white men obsessed with getting rich.

Conflicts were inevitable with the Indians pilfering stock, or so the miners charged. Finally the unrest culminated in yet another treacherous action by whites against the Chiricahuas. In December 1860 a party of miners led by an old Cochise acquaintance, James Tevis, attacked some Apaches near old Fort Webster, killed four Chihennes, and captured thirteen others. This wanton assault, described by Dan L. Thrapp in *Victorio and the Mimbres Apaches,* put the majority of the Chihennes on the defensive, at least until the whites freed their people, but it was not forgotten.[53]

Some of the Chihennes lingered along the Mimbres throughout January, hoping their people would be released. Mangas and his

Bedonkohes had moved into Chokonen country, having become disenchanted with affairs in New Mexico. In mid-February, as the Bascom affair was winding down, Victorio, Riñon, and Chabnocito cautiously approached Fort McLane (Fort Floyd having been renamed such on January 18, 1861) and conferred with Major Lynde. The officer was eager to mend relations and avert hostilities because he had been ordered by headquarters to "use every effort to dissuade and prevent the settlers from inflicting unnecessary outrages upon the Indians at the same time keeping the Indians from becoming hostile or aggressive." Convinced of their sincerity, Lynde released the hostages, pointing out that

> three sub chiefs of the Apaches came here and professed to be friendly to the Whites and promised to do all in their power to keep peace and prevent any depredations by the men of their bands, and I think they are sincere. I delivered up to them the captives taken by the men from the mines, who have been in confinement here since that time. Chabnocito promised to send for Mangas Coloradas, the Head Chief of the Apaches, and thought he could induce him to come in and make peace. The three sub chiefs mentioned above are of the Bands residing on the Mimbres and vicinity.[54]

Lynde's actions evidently appeased the Chihennes, who remained at peace during the first four months of 1861. Acting agent Pinckney Randolph Tully[55] rationed them on February 18, March 8, March 28, and April 18, when plans for raising crops were discussed. On March 26, Estevan Ochoa wrote Steck claiming that the Western Apaches, Chokonens, and Mescaleros were the bands doing the depredating. The Chihennes evidently had not yet begun raiding.[56]

Mangas Coloradas squashed Tully's hopes of keeping the Chihennes peaceful. Perhaps because of the alleged whipping at Pinos Altos, perhaps because he realized the whites were steadily poaching his country, or perhaps because he felt bound to join Cochise and drive out the Americans, Mangas went to war. According to one report, he "threatened extermination to all whites within the limits of his range."[57] In May 1861, while Cochise was occupied in Arizona, Mangas began raiding the Pinos Altos–Fort McLane vicinity. His first target was a Mexican train near Pinos Altos, which the Apaches jumped, killing one man and running off the mules.[58] Two weeks later they cleaned out the stock at Fort McLane, prompting Tully to write Collins: "What has led to this outbreak I am at a loss to know. They have had their rations regularly issued to them." [59]

By early June the allied Chiricahuas had all but closed the road between Mesilla and Tucson. Agent Lorenzo Labadie arrived at Mesilla en route to Tucson, where he was to investigate the condition of the Apache *mansos,* or tame Apaches. He discovered that affairs had deteriorated so much that he was unable to procure transportation to Tucson. He notified his superiors that Indian hostilities had forced citizens to abandon their fields and miners to desert their diggings. This was probably the origin of the *Santa Fe New Mexican*'s report that the Pinos Altos mines had been abandoned, a rumor also picked up by the *Missouri Republican.*[60] Pinos Altos was far from deserted. These rugged, gold-crazy individualists provided a good deal of southern New Mexico's protection for the next several months, engaging in several brisk fights with the allied Chiricahuas.

The Chihennes continued raiding. On June 3 at Cook's Peak they ambushed a train belonging to Ellsburg and Ambury, killing two Mexicans and stealing two mules. In mid-June they raided Pinos Altos and on June 18 struck a hay camp some three miles from there, killing John Gillem and wounding another man. A state of war now existed between Americans and the Chiricahua Tribe.[61]

Indian agent and physician Michael Steck returned to New Mexico in mid-July, but the conflict had become general and he reluctantly conceded that "I am unable to do anything. . . . It may be many months before the presence of an agent will be needed here." [62] He was right, except it was years, not months.

The situation deteriorated rapidly as Cochise gained new allies. In early July he moved east to join forces with Mangas Coloradas and drive the remaining whites from Chihenne territory. This was when he emerged as a war leader at the tribal level. Historian James McClintock notes that Cochise now "had the ability to gather together more fighting men than any Apache chieftain of modern times." He proved it again and again during the next year.[63]

In July and August 1861, Cochise and Mangas made their temporary headquarters in the vicinity of Cook's Peak, called by the Apaches Dziltanatal ("Mountain Holds Its Head Up Proudly").

Here they hoped to cut off the Pinos Altos miners from Mesilla. Cook's Springs, about eighteen miles north of present-day Deming, New Mexico, had a dependable water supply, which made it a mandatory stopping spot for troops and travelers. It was thought to be the most dangerous point in southern Arizona and New Mexico except for Apache Pass, wrote Brigadier General James H. Carleton in 1865.[64] In fact, if actual encounters and casualties were tallied, it would have far exceeded those committed at Apache Pass and Stein's Peak. Between 1861 and 1863, Apaches ambushed and killed about one hundred whites here, which, for a change, may not have been too much of an exaggeration.[65] Travelers left behind grim and morbid descriptions of the area. "Passed many human bones along the road,"[66] a soldier wrote in his diary, while another observed: "Place all along is graves, broken wagons . . . piles of rocks denoting a grave . . . a human skull with face."[67]

It was into Cook's Canyon in July 1861 that a party of seven Americans rode. Former employees of the Butterfield Overland Mail Company, they were known as the Free Thomas Party, which consisted of Freeman Thomas, Joe Roescher, Mat Champion, Robert Aveline, Emmett Mills, John Wilson, and John Portell. All were said to have been experienced frontiersmen who were "picked for the dangerous duty they had to perform." Their job was to transport the mail to California. The whites left Mesilla on the morning of July 20; by the next evening they had reached Cook's Canyon, where they were waylaid by a party of Apaches probably numbering between one hundred and two hundred.[68]

All available evidence indicates that Cochise was there, though he may not have been in overall command, given Mangas Coloradas's presence. According to William S. Oury's account, the attack surprised the Americans, but Thomas quickly responded and ordered the driver to leave the road for high ground. This achieved, they stripped the coach of guns, ammunition, water, and other essentials and sent the team down the hill, hoping this would satisfy the Chiricahuas. It did not. Next morning, the Indians renewed the fight, which settled into a sniping duel with the besieged Americans, who had constructed a breastwork of rocks, about two feet high, at the top of a small hill.

At this point it becomes difficult to reconstruct the sequence of events. Various stories reflect the imagination of the writer rather than the facts. What we do know, from accounts of those who arrived on the scene shortly after the fight, is this: the Indians poured a devastating fire on the entrenched Americans. Daguerre and Thabault, who arrived a few days after the fight, described the scene:

> All about this wall the ground was strewn with battered bullets. Every rock and stone within many yards, which could have partially secreted an Indian, had bullets lying near. One small tree, some 150 yards from the wall, had the marks of eleven balls in it.

The Indians eventually killed all seven men; four bodies were found within the breastworks, two some 50 yards in the rear and the other, presumably John Wilson, 150 yards away. According to some accounts, Mangas Coloradas left after the second day, but not before taking heavy losses. Other accounts claim that Cochise was wounded before his men finished off Thomas's party the next day.[69] When Daguerre and Thabault discovered the horrifying scene a few days later, every body had been stripped, the arms of most had been broken, and all had bullet holes through the head. Tevis came across the remains and recalled that "the buzzards had picked the eyes out of the bodies."[70]

Although they had suffered casualties, Cochise and Mangas reportedly bore witness to the courage of the seven Americans. Mangas allegedly admitted to Jack Swilling that the Americans had killed twenty-five warriors and crippled many more; moreover, according to Mangas, if his Apaches had been as brave "as these few white men, he could whip the world."[71] In contrast to Swilling, Oury went to the other extreme and claimed that Cochise confessed he lost 175 warriors, Cochise also paid tribute to the seven Americans, declaring that "with twenty-five such men he would undertake to whip the whole United States."[72] Both accounts overstated Apache losses, and Oury's was perhaps apocryphal. It was inconceivable that Apaches, even fighting for vengeance, would have exposed themselves to a loss of that magnitude.

The Chiricahuas retired to northern Chihuahua after the fight. Oury said Cochise told of his role in the battle at Corralitos. Keith Humphries, a historian in the Las Cruces area, heard a story in the 1930s from Natividad Padilla, who said he was at Janos when the

Chiricahuas ventured in to seek treatment for a wounded son of Cochise, probably Taza, shortly after the Cook's Canyon fight. The
Apaches traded their victims' gold watches for ammunition.[73] A report from Fronteras at this time also confirmed the Chiricahuas'
presence in Chihuahua: "The Apaches have been trading their plunder taken from the Americans at Janos and Corralitos."[74] After a
short rest, the allied Chiricahuas departed, their thirst satisfied, bell-
ies filled, and ammunition restored, thanks to the generosity of their
sometime friend, sometime enemy, José María Zuloaga. Toward the
latter part of August they returned to New Mexico and assumed their
temporary headquarters in the hills around Cook's Peak.

About this same time, a group of Americans comprised of ranchers
from the Tubac, Sonoita Creek, and Tucson area were abandoning
their homes for more civilized parts. The recent attacks by Cochise's
Chokonens and the Western Apaches, plus the abandonment of Fort
Buchanan, had compelled these courageous individuals to leave
while they still had their lives. Known as the Ake party (named for
Felix Grundy Ake, a fifty-year-old farmer), the wagon train consisted of six double wagons, two buggies, and one single wagon
when it reached Tucson. Here it was reinforced by several other
people, including Moses Carson,[75] who was a half-brother of the
celebrated Kit and was himself a brave and experienced Indian
fighter. The caravan left the Sonoran desert on or about August 15,
heading east, and was made up of twenty-four men, sixteen women,
and seven children. They carried many of their possessions and
herded several hundred head of cattle, sheep, goats, and horses.
They were, in effect, an open invitation to Cochise and Mangas.[76]

Ake had hoped to accompany the soldiers who evacuated Fort
Buchanan to the Río Grande, but when they reached the rendezvous
site at the Cienega, about twenty miles east of Tucson, they discovered that the troops had already departed. Nonetheless, Ake opted to
continue, believing that his party was large enough to discourage an
Indian attack. Indeed, Apache ambushes on parties this size were
rare, if not unheard of, in U.S. territory.

The eastbound whites saw no Indians along the route, although at
Apache Pass they observed "ropes and some bones and rags a-hang-
ing" at the Bascom execution site. Forging on to the Mimbres, they
encamped and heard that some two hundred Apaches had wiped out

nine Mexicans at Cook's Canyon, which Ake's party was scheduled to traverse the next day. Ake and his men were dubious of the report, believing it had been fabricated. The next morning, the wagon train left for Mesilla before sunrise, hoping to reach Cook's Canyon before the torrid summer sun took its toll.[77]

That morning, Cochise's scouts espied the small wagon train, which he knew would continue on to Cook's Springs. Eyewitnesses estimated the number of warriors at more than two hundred; all were hidden on both sides of the hills, which ran parallel to the road. The whites trudged into Cook's Canyon with Phillips's wagon in the front, followed by Ake's wagon and then the rest. The ambulance in the rear contained most of the women and children. Despite the warnings about Indians, neither scouts nor skirmishers had been deployed, so the whites were woefully unprepared for an attack.

Cochise and Mangas launched the attack as the last wagon entered the mouth of the canyon, and then, "without no warning at all, the Indians come hellity-larrup, just a-swarming outen the rocks." Mariano Madrid, a teamster, said the hostiles some "dressed like soldiers [and] armed with cap guns." They immediately stampeded the cattle and sheep herds. As the stock fled up the hill, Ake, Wadsworth, and several of the mounted men counterattacked and repulsed the Indians, but not without cost: James May was killed, Wadsworth wounded fatally, Thomas Farrell wounded, and Thomas Redding (or Reden) suffered a broken leg, which, however, did not prevent him from continuing the fight. As the wagons were circling, Redding and the mounted men "charged again and again . . . and held them off from getting right down in the wagons." Finally all of the wagons were circled except two: the lead one, which the Phillipses were forced to abandon, leaving behind everything but their money, and the rear one, carrying most of the women and children, which had reversed direction at the first volley and fled west. Several men, including Sam Houston, a nephew of the noted Texan, escorted it to the Mimbres.[78]

Several Apaches plundered the Phillips wagon while the remainder maintained a withering fire from the hills, finally killing the brave Redding. With the protection of the wagons, the whites responded and inflicted some damage. One woman, a daughter of Ake married to George Davis, courageously "stood behind a wagon and loaded guns all day."[79] Moses Carson fought "like hell, brave as a lion and quick as a cat, with his white head dodging around." The fighting subsided early in the afternoon when Mariano Madrid killed one last Apache. The Indians then disengaged and withdrew with their plunder. According to one report, they had stolen four hundred cattle and nine hundred sheep.[80] The whites retreated to the Mimbres.

Meanwhile, the women and children had reached the settlement along the Mimbres and sent a dispatch to Pinos Altos, where a company of Arizona Guards under elected officers Captain Thomas J. Mastin, Lieutenant Thomas Helm, and Lieutenant Jack Swilling were stationed. Although they had been mustered into Confederate service, their primary duty was to fight Apaches and "to reopen the road between Mesilla and Tucson, [and] especially to rout the savages from Apache Pass."[81] The next day a group of thirty-five men started in pursuit, but instead of going to Cook's Canyon they "made a straight shoot for the Florida Mountains in the hope of catching up with the Indians, and knowing that they could not travel very fast with the sheep, we might have a chance to overtake them."[82]

Mastin's hunch paid dividends. The Guards were secreted in ambush as the Indians approached the foothills of the barren Florida Mountains. The whites immediately charged the Apaches, whom Hank Smith estimated at eighty, and in a running fight retook several pack mules and cattle and routed the Chiricahuas, killing eight according to one report. Mastin pursued them back toward Cook's Canyon, where the Indians made a halfhearted attempt to regroup. A minor brush occurred with no further casualties.[83]

Mangas and Cochise had scored impressive victories in late July and August, but the ambush carried out by the Arizona Guards at Florida Mountains had dampened their celebration. Naturally it would be avenged.

# Chapter 10

# CAPITAN GRANDE

In early September 1861, Cochise and Mangas returned to northern Mexico, where they discovered that relations at Janos had become strained. Joaquin Terrazas, a tireless and inveterate Indian fighter, had led a scout which killed eleven Apaches in late August. This offensive made Janos too hot for the Chiricahuas and this, combined with the lethal arrival of smallpox (which eventually infested the Río Grande Valley), forced Cochise and most of the Chiricahuas back into their mountain sanctuaries along the border.[1] From here they were bound to cause turmoil on both sides of the line. That fall, Cochise was reported in the Animas Mountains, where, according to Apaches at Corralitos, he had organized yet another war party, intending to attack either Fronteras or Janos. Neither was hit because the Americans remained his priority.[2]

Knowing that Mexico offered him refuge, Cochise began cultivating relations at Fronteras. He had been in contact with Remigio, who had succeeded Esquinaline as leader of that small Chokonen local group and who now joined Cochise in mid-September for a campaign in New Mexico. Once again the Chihennes and Bedonkohes were united for an attack on the hated miners at Pinos Altos. It was a tribal venture.[3]

Cochise and Mangas might have achieved their objective had it not been for the arrival of Captain Mastin and fifteen Arizona Guards shortly before the attack. Mastin had been sent to Pinos

Altos by a lean, blue-eyed Indian hater, Confederate Lieutenant
Colonel John Robert Baylor,[4] whose feelings epitomized frontier
thought that the only good Indian ws a dead Indian. In September,
Baylor sent instructions to Mastin, giving him a free hand to deal
with the Apaches. The instructions were tantamount to genocide, if
that was what Mastin wished. Even if the Chiricahuas solicited
peace, Baylor ordered Mastin to "kill them anyway he could; and
did not care whether he made them drunk, poisoned them, or shot
them on sight."[5]

The Chiricahuas were in the vicinity of Cook's Springs on September 26, hidden in ambush for Charles Hayden's wagon train. Yet
the presence of Mastin's command, which escorted the train through
the canyon, probably convinced Cochise, who recalled the success
of the Arizona Guards a month earlier, to call off the attack. Accom-
plishing this, Mastin's group marched toward Pinos Altos and
camped near the site of present-day Hurley.[6] At 10 P.M. the sentinel
heard voices that he thought were Indians. The camp was aroused
immediately and the Guards prepared to defend themselves, but no
attack came. After an hour's wait, Mastin pushed on to Pinos Altos,
arriving there at daybreak and drawing supplies at Roy and Sam
Bean's store. As the Guards split up for their own camps, the Chiricahuas emerged from the hills and attacked.[7]

The initial assault apparently was a surprise, although today residents will say that the Apaches were lined up shoulder to shoulder at
the top of the hills overlooking the town. Hollywood would have
loved that scenario, but Cochise and Mangas failed to take this ostentatious display into account. In reality, the two leaders had a
carefully conceived and coordinated plan. The number of Indians
involved has never been determined with accuracy, although there
may have been nearly two hundred. Early on the morning of September 27, 1861, they struck simultaneously at the mining camps
that spread out from the main town. Many of the miners were cornered in their diggings and were unable or too frightened to venture
out; the remainder fought from their log homes.

Hank Smith and three men rushed to his cabin at Whiskey Gulch
and eventually drove the Indians away. Soon afterward, he retreated
to the main camp and found the Chiricahuas and whites in "hand to
hand combat." Early in the fight the Indians attempted to set fire to

many of the log homes, a tactic employed successfully in Mexico, but these experienced and intrepid miners were well armed and could not be dislodged. Fierce fighting continued through the morning. By noon the battle was concentrated around Bean's and Roman's supply stores in the center of town. It was here that Captain Thomas Mastin was mortally wounded. At Roman's store two other men were killed. Finally, about 12:30 P.M., the Guards fired the cannon at Roy and Sam Bean's store. Nails and buckshot splattered, routing the aggressors, who had a well-grounded fear of this weapon. The miners counterattacked and "never gave them a chance to concentrate again." Thirty minutes later the fight was over.

Both sides had heavy casualties. The Indians left ten bodies on the battleground and were believed to have carried off twenty more killed and wounded. The whites lost five dead (Mastin, Private J. B. Corwin of the Arizona Guards, and three civilians) and seven wounded. Though the numbers suggest a victory for the whites, in the days that followed many of the whites deserted the mines for either Santa Fe or Mesilla.[8]

The encounter at Pinos Altos was but another in a series of hard-fought engagements between the Chiricahua Apaches and the remaining whites in New Mexico. It had been a show of force, a warning to the whites. The Indians had seized the offensive behind the two greatest Chiricahua leaders of the mid-nineteenth century. A Chiricahua war leader "would go before [his men] in battle, and perform great feats to spur them on,"[9] so we may assume that Cochise was one of them and that Mangas Coloradas was the other.

After the Pinos Altos fight the Indians left the area. Mangas and his followers probably moved northwest to the remote Gila country; Cochise and his Chokonens plunged into Mexico, perhaps near Fronteras, where Remigio and many warriors who had joined him in the fighting had made peace. It was a logical decision. To the north he had fought several pitched battles against the Americans and he and his band needed a rest. To the east, Chihuahuan troops were making life miserable for the Apaches. In particular, their efforts temporarily closed the Janos-Corralitos market, where the hostiles usually found refuge to dispose of their plunder for food, liquor, and ammunition. Terrazas's campaign had been followed in late September by a scout from Paso del Norte which jumped a band near Lake

Guzmán, killing seven Apaches and capturing sixteen. In one of
these fights a brother of Mangas Coloradas was killed, perhaps
Phalis Palacio or another relatively unknown man named Chaha.[10]
Hence Fronteras appeared to be a viable alternative; at the least
peace discussions would suspend any campaigns in that state, if any
were planned.

With this in mind, in late October 1861, Cochise sent Yones to
Fronteras to request a truce. The report filed by the commander was
important because it revealed Cochise's status within the Chiricahua
Tribe:

> Today at two in the afternoon an Apache woman, the wife of the
> late chief Coyuntura, came in and asked for peace in the name of the
> chief Chis [Cochise]. She was accompanied by eight women from
> those settled here. This chief has requested peace several times, but it
> has not been granted him because of the people at Janos. . . . But
> today it has been granted to him since they now are united and say
> that he is the big captain. He is at the *head of them all,* according to
> what is said by the Indians when they come to get their rations. More-
> over, they also say that he has all the warriors stationed from Mesilla
> to Sarampion waiting for the enemy [Americans] to come and make a
> campaign against him. This Indian should report within twenty days
> and have a force of only ten men.[11]

Two points merit analysis: first, that the Apaches considered him
the *capitán grande,* or "big captain," and second, that he was the
chief of all the warriors from Mesilla to Sarampion, in the Peloncillo Mountains, indicated that Cochise, with Mangas aging, had
become the dominant leader within the Chiricahua Tribe. At his
father-in-law's request he had brought his Chokonens into Chihenne
territory and together they had proved to be formidable foes of the
remaining whites in southern New Mexico. This leads to the second
point: that Cochise was anticipating an American campaign because
of his actions since the Bascom affair.

The report was forwarded to Governor Pesqueira, who ordered
Cayetano Sanchez, the prefect of Moctezuma, to "make an effort to
overcome all difficulties that may occur to achieve this very important goal."[12] A thankless task it was. While Pesqueira advocated a
peace policy, he failed to address how Sanchez and the garrison

at Fronteras were to support the Chiricahuas. In the end Cochise stayed away.

Cochise kept his base of operations in northern Mexico for the last few months of 1861. In late November it was reported from Corralitos that he had gathered a large force and was planning to attack either Janos or Bavispe. In early December hostiles assaulted a party near Bavispe and killed Sergeant Miguel Enriques and a corporal. Then they invaded Sonora and extended their depredations further into the interior, though Cochise's role, if any, is not clear.[13]

A large contingent of Chiricahuas continued to receive rations at Fronteras in early 1862; for many, this would lead to death. Smallpox spread like wildfire, and many Chiricahuas fell victim. According to *Estrella de Occidente,* the disease decimated Apache bands in both Chihuahua and Sonora. By February 11 at Fronteras alone, thirty-two Chiricahuas had died (seventeen warriors, seven women, and eight children). Among the dead leaders were two of Teboca's sons (Chiquito Teboca and Vicente Teboca), Parte, and Vivora, an old chief who was present at the capture of Tutije in 1834 and the Juan José Compá massacre in 1837. *Estrella de Occidente* smugly editorialized: "We hope that more Indians die to decrease the numbers of this horrible tribe."[14]

Fortunately, Cochise had kept his local group clear of Fronteras. By the end of 1861 he had his eyes set on southern Arizona, where only two settlements of consequence remained: Tucson and the Mowry, or Patagonia, mines. "The whole of Western Arizona is now a scene of desolation" reported the *Missouri Republican,*[15] and another traveler grimly added that "little mounds of stones, with rude wooden crosses over them, were visible all along the roads."[16] In August 1861, Sylvester Mowry, owner of the mines, had implored the secretary of war in Washington to send troops and other assistance. His letter depicted the deteriorating situation in the once prosperous region: "Every farm and rancho is abandoned, the people having taken refuge in Tucson, Tubac or followed the troops. The loss of property is immense. I am holding my place at great expense. In fact it is a garrison. . . . I am constantly prepared for a fight." Furthermore, declared Mowry, hoping to get Washington's attention, the "Arizona Apaches . . . openly boast that they have driven the Americans, soldiers & all, out of the country."[17]

Mowry had good reason to be concerned about Arizona's plight. According to a Mexican captive living with the Chokonens, Cochise "had constant information of everything at the Mowry mines during the year that the troops were withdrawn." The chief was very anxious "to break it up" and force abandonment. Somehow, probably from Mexicans at Fronteras, he had threatened Mowry that "he would wipe it out as he had all other American settlements."[18]

Mowry, who compared Apaches to rattlesnakes and felt they should be treated as such, recalled that "the Apaches made a great combination of all their forces and sent me word through Cachees, their great fighting captain and a man of signal ability, they were going to take my place." As a result, the American capitalist "made a perfect garrison of the mines—surrounded the houses with high walls loopholed for fighting—armed all my men who work with a gun in one hand and tools in the other."[19] This, he believed, would deter Cochise from attempting a direct assault, since the cost in Apache lives would have been prohibitive.

In late 1861, with smallpox rampant in northern Mexico and Chihuahua on another scalp hunt, Cochise shifted his headquarters to Arizona. Chokonen local groups probably camped during the winter of 1861–62 in the Huachuca, Dragoon, and Chiricahua mountains. From these locations his scouts maintained a close watch on the Mowry mines. A large war party drove off 181 cattle, near Tucson, which may have been Fritz Contzen's herd grazing at San Xavier. A few Americans and one hundred Papagos overtook the Indians, killed a few, and wounded several others.[20] Whether Cochise had a hand in this is not known, but he probably had a role in the next incident. In early December, Indians wounded two men near the mines, one of whom may have been early Arizona settler Thomas Gardner. If so, Cochise was definitely involved, and his actions revealed he would resort to any means to kill an enemy, especially an American. The story was evidently first told by Thomas Jeffords, which lends credibility to the incident.

In the early sixties, returning to the mines [Mowry] one day from Santa Cruz, whither he had gone for provisions mounted on a spirited horse with but one companion, he saw two Indians approaching on horseback. He soon recognized Cochise, who made the peace sign

Thomas Gardner. Pictured here in his later years, Gardner was wounded by Cochise about December 1861. *(Courtesy Arizona Historical Society, Tucson)*

and rode up apparently for a parley. He carried his cocked gun across his horse in front of him. Maneuvering for a favorable position, he shot without raising his rifle. Gardner fell shot clear through the body just in front of the spine; Cochise snatched for the rein of the coveted horse, but the animal galloped away pursued by the Indians. Gardner recovered from his wounds.[21]

After this encounter Cochise again tried to assemble a force to put pressure on Mowry's mines, attempting "in every way to make a combination with the other bands to attack the mines." Notwithstanding his reputation as a war leader, he was unsuccessful. The Chokonen and Nednhi groups living in Mexico were incapacitated by smallpox and Mangas's Chihennes were discussing a truce at Pinos Altos in New Mexico. As a result, only Cochise's immediate followers undertook forays against the Americans in southern Arizona.[22]

In the winter and spring of 1862, Cochise and his warriors am-

bushed several parties coming or going to the mines. Toward the
end of February in a canyon halfway between the Mowry mines and
Santa Cruz, Sonora, he waylaid Elliot Titus and a companion known
as Delaware Joe (said to be a Delaware Indian). They were traveling
along the road when the Indians opened fire, killing Delaware Joe in
the first volley. Within seconds Titus's horse was killed, but the im-
perturbable American made for the other end of the canyon, fighting
"very bravely and coolly for several hundred yards, doing much
execution with his shotgun and revolver," according to the Chiricahuas. Titus had almost reached safety when an Indian in his rear
shot him through the thigh. Realizing that escape was impossible,
he put a bullet through his brain, fulfilling a pledge "that he would
kill himself rather than be taken alive." In respect for Titus's bravery, Cochise reportedly ordered his warriors to leave the body
alone. Titus's "beautifully mounted" revolver was taken by Cochise
and became part of his arsenal.[23]

Some five or six weeks later Cochise was again prowling in the
neighborhood of the mines. Consequently, Mowry requested help
from Captain Sherod Hunter,[24] who, with some seventy-five Confederate troops, had occupied Tucson on the last day of February 1862.
The people in Tucson welcomed the command, regardless of affiliation, hoping it would furnish some protection against the Apaches.
Mowry wrote of those dangerous days: "If the Devil would have
helped me fight Apaches, I would have asked his help at any price
except my soul."[25] Hunter's stay was hardly noteworthy, and he did
no Indian fighting. He tactfully refused Mowry's request, declaring
"that the precarious position in which I am placed will not permit
me to take my command immediately to your assistance."[26]

A scout by Hunter's command might have driven the hostiles off.
Instead, toward the middle of April, Cochise's Chokonens annihi-
lated a small party en route to Santa Cruz from Mowry's mines.
Wrote Mowry:

> I had sent seven peons with a cart and yoke of oxen to Santa
> Cruz. . . . Sent also an explorer as escort . . . a few miles from Santa
> Cruz a large body of Indians killed them. A woman and child were
> also killed. Body of the child was hung to the cart wheel. Indians
> stole a yoke of oxen, a colts revolver, rifle, 6 shooter and several hun-
> dred dollars in silver bullion.

With the abundance of Indian sign, only Mowry could explain why he sent such a small and relatively unarmed party with only one man as escort. A larger force might have repulsed the Indians.[27]

Cochise directed this cruel and brutal massacre and rode the chestnut mare he took for the next few years.[28] It would appear that he was waging a war of attrition against Mowry's stronghold, and he might well have succeeded had not volunteer troops from California, sent to drive the Confederates from Arizona and New Mexico, arrived on the scene.

Hunter left Tucson on May 4, 1862, when he heard the California Volunteers were coming. The next day at Dragoon Springs, Cochise and Francisco jumped the rebels, killing four men and running off thirty mules and twenty-five horses. José Mendibles,[29] a captive of the Western Apaches who was present at both this fight and the Bascom affair, declared that Francisco was present, undoubtedly with his ally Cochise. After this encounter, Hunter's force forged ahead to New Mexico and arrived there without further trouble.[30]

During the spring of 1862, Cochise had been in touch with his Chihenne relatives in New Mexico, who had their own problems to deal with, namely Baylor's Confederate troops. In January, Baylor had received reinforcements under the command of Brigadier General Henry Hopkins Sibley,[31] who had moved his troops from Fort Fillmore to Mesilla. About this time, some Chiricahuas ran off one hundred horses belonging to Sibley's troops. Baylor, itching for revenge because Mescalero Apaches had massacred fourteen Texans the previous August, marched out, "accompanied by many native-born citizens of Arizona and New Mexico." The Indians drove the stock into Chihuahua; Baylor's force dogmatically pursued the trail into Janos and then Corralitos, where he trespassed into Zuloaga's home and captured nine Chiricahuas. Then he practiced what he preached. Believing "it justifiable in killing the Indians and recovering the animals," Baylor dispassionately executed the adults (one man and three women) and captured the children. Apparently they were Chokonens from the group of Miguel Yrigóllen, now a captain in Cochise's band.[32]

In late February or early March the Chihennes, probably including Mangas, talked peace at Pinos Altos. According to William Fourr, Mangas was in the area at this time. Baylor issued an infamous order which reeked of duplicity, brutality, and insensitivity and was born of ignorance. From Mesilla on March 20, 1862, he instructed Captain Thomas Helm, commander of the Arizona Guards at Pinos Altos:

> I learn from Lieutenant J. J. Jackson that the Indians have been in to your post [Pinos Altos] for the purpose of making a treaty. The Congress of the Confederate States has passed a law declaring extermination to all hostile Indians. You will therefore use all means to persuade the Apaches or any tribe to come in for the purpose of making peace, and when you get them together kill all the grown Indians and take the children prisoners and sell them to defray the expense of killing the Indians. Buy whiskey and such other goods as may be necessary for the Indians . . . I . . . look to you for success against these cursed pests who have already murdered over 100 men in this Territory.[33]

Fortunately for Mangas, he avoided the mines and a few months later joined Cochise in an attempt to repel the advances of the California Column, which, the Indians believed, had come to punish them.

The California Column was organized to counteract the Confederate invasion of New Mexico. The volunteers, numbering 2,350 troops, were under the command of Brigadier General James Henry Carleton, an experienced and energetic officer who had served in New Mexico. Carleton's objectives were to drive the Confederate forces from Tucson and the Mesilla Valley, to reoccupy the abandoned southwestern forts, and to reestablish federal rule in Arizona and New Mexico. By the time he arrived the rebels had been effectively defeated. Besides guarding against a Confederate invasion, his role for the remainder of the war would be to make Arizona and New Mexico a safe place for travelers, to provide security for miners and ranchers, and to revitalize commerce. The Apaches were the major obstacle to the achievement of these goals and Carleton, like Baylor, felt that most Indians were animals and deserved killing.

On May 20, Colonel Joseph Rodman West,[34] whose giant ego dwarfed his diminutive stature, and the first elements of the California Column occupied Tucson. On May 24, Carleton ordered Fort Breckenridge and Fort Buchanan reoccupied. By June 5, most of the column had reached Tucson. Hoping to restore order, Carleton declared martial law three days later. Furthermore, he arrested "nine of the cutthroats, gamblers and loafers who have infested this town to the great bodily fear of all good citizens." Tucson rapidly became a law-abiding town.[35]

Isolated in Tucson and unaware of the strength of his enemy forces stationed along the Río Grande, Carleton decided to communicate with Brigadier General Edward Richard Sprigg Canby,[36] who had driven Sibley's command out of New Mexico in late March, two previous attempts having proved unsuccessful. Expressman John Jones, Sergeant William Wheeling, and a Mexican guide named Chávez were selected for this dangerous mission.

The trio left Tucson on June 15. Traveling primarily by night and resting by day, they approached Apache Pass in the late afternoon of June 18. A mile or two west of the pass, the whites saw Apache smoke signals and hastened through the canyon. A few miles east of the pass they saw Apaches who "jumped up from their hiding place in the brush." Jones's party dismounted and the Indians "mounted their horses and came on at a gallop." Chávez was wounded in the hip and could not remount. Jones recalled:

> The Mexican begged us not to leave him. We told him we could not save ourselves. We mounted up and started. The sergeant, I think, never got from among the Indians. They followed after me on horseback yelling, saying "now let's have a race. Mucha buena mula, mucho bravo Americano." I shot one in the side, shot another in the shoulder; six pursued until sundown.[37]

Miraculously Jones got through to the Río Grande, where he was captured by Confederate troops. Nonetheless, he somehow sent word to Canby that "the Column from California is really coming."[38]

Two days after Jones's party left Tucson, Carleton ordered Lieutenant Colonel Edward E. Eyre and a force of 140 men of Companies B and C, First California Cavalry, to make a scout of the area between Tucson and Mesilla. Eyre's command reached Apache Pass at 6 A.M. on June 25 and encamped at the abandoned stage station. Fresh Indian signs were seen, "but no attention was paid them as it was thought that the Indians would not dare come near so formidable a force as ours."[39] This imprudence revealed itself in the command's comportment, with one soldier recalling that "horses were scattered everywhere."[40] Shortly before noon, four shots were heard near Apache Springs and Indians were seen on the hill where the first Fort Bowie later was built. Immediately the volunteers prepared for a fight, at least until Lieutenant Colonel Eyre arrived. He had been ordered to avoid engagements with the Indians if possible. Even though he was told that three men were missing, he hoisted a white flag and the so-called Pemmican Treaty ensued.[41]

Cochise was wary and more than an hour passed before he could be induced to come within range to talk. By this time, seventy-five Indians were present, "their lances flashing in the sun and their bows and rifles sticking above the bushes and rocks." Finally, Cochise and a dozen warriors held a parley with Eyre and his interpreter, a man named Newcomb. An eyewitness described Cochise as "a big Indian. He carried a fine rifle and two six shooters and rides as fine a horse as anybody."[42] Cochise, who undoubtedly perceived the volunteers as a threat to his people, must have been amused at Eyre's naïveté. Wrote the latter:

> We wished to be friends of the Apaches; that at present I was only travelling through their country and desired that he [Cochise] would not interfere with my men or animals; that a great Captain was at Tucson with a large number of soldiers; that he wished to have a talk with all the Apache Chiefs and to make peace with them and make them presents.

Cochise assured Eyre that his people were peaceful and agreed to return at sunset. This satisfied the officer, who issued presents of tobacco and pemmican. Cochise must have mocked Eyre's simplicity; his word given to the enemy when at war was disingenous. If Eyre was foolish enough to believe him, all the better for the Indians.[43]

After the conference, soldiers found the bodies of three soldiers: John Maloney, Albert Schmidt, and James Keith. All had been stripped, shot through the chest, and lanced through the neck. Eyre sent out a frenzied but fruitless pursuit of the Indians, who could be seen in the conical peaks overlooking the mesa, probably Helen's Dome and Boroce Peak. Eyre prudently moved his troops two miles east of Apache Pass and made camp. Later that night, Cochise's warriors fired a few rounds into the camp, wounding one man and killing a horse. The next day the command left for New Mexico and on July 4 occupied Fort Thorn.[44]

Thanks to Eyre's candor, Cochise made preparations to ambush the next party of soldiers traveling through Apache Pass. Perhaps it was at this time that he invited Mangas and his Bedonkohes and Chihennes to join him at the pass. He would not be disappointed; with the exception of a small force left behind at Tucson, Carleton had prepared a systematic march of his command to the Río Grande. On July 9, West ordered Captain Thomas L. Roberts, First Infantry, California Volunteers, to take a command of a 126-man detachment made up of 72 men of Company E, First Infrantry; 24 men of Company B, Second Cavalry, under Captain John C. Cremony; 20 men of Company E, First Infantry, under Lieutenant W. A. Thompson (his company manned the two howitzers); and 10 men of Company H, First Infantry, under First Lieutenant Alexander Bartholomew MacGowan. Like Eyre, Roberts was ordered to avoid "a collision with the Indians . . . and caution all of your men to do so until they become the aggressors." The 22 teams and 242 head of stock made an attractive target.

Roberts's command left Tucson at 4:30 A.M. on July 10 and marched twenty miles to the Cienega, arriving there at 6 P.M. The command rested the next day and resumed its trek in the early hours of July 12, halting at the San Pedro River, where horses and men were watered and rested. At this point Roberts, as instructed, left MacGowan's detachment and three cavalrymen to guard the supplies which were to be left for the next group of troops. Roberts further divided his command, taking sixty infantry, the howitzers, and eight troopers to Dragoon Springs. Captain Cremony, with the rest of the command, forty-five infantry and cavalry, remained with the train and cattle. At 8 A.M. on July 13 Roberts's detachment arrived at Dragoon Springs, remaining there until 5 P.M. the next day, July 14, when he and his sixty-eight men began their march to Apache Pass, which lay forty miles to the west.[45] There can be little doubt that Cochise and Mangas watched the command from the time it left Dragoon Springs. The dust kicked up by the whites would have been visible for miles. The two leaders had prepared an ambush with a body of warriors estimated to number between one hundred and a ridiculous eight hundred.[46] In addition to Cochise and Mangas, many of the Chiricahua leaders who became well known in the 1870s and 1880s were said to have been present, including, according to Apache accounts, Juh, Victorio, and Nana. Some of Francisco's Eastern White Mountain Apaches may have participated.[47]

Unfortunately, no detailed account from the Indians' point of view was recorded. In later years Cochise allegedly told a participant that when the Americans came "straggling into the pass" after a march of forty miles in nineteen hours with only a cup of coffee, he was confident "of killing everyone."[48] Asa Daklugie echoed Cochise's sentiments and told Mrs. Eve Ball that the Indians were confident of stopping the soldiers' attempt to reach the water.[49] The Apaches had superior numbers, secure positions, and the element of surprise in their favor, yet the volunteers prevailed, with both sides concurring that Thompson's howitzers, which fired forty shells, proved to be the key in averting a catastrophe.[50]

Most accounts agree that the soldiers reached Apache Pass about noon, although Private John Teal recalled that it was about 10:30 A.M. Cochise and Mangas allowed Roberts's command to reach the abandoned stage station. "Then just as the company halted and broke ranks at the station" the Indians, "well armed with rifles and pistols,"[51] attacked the train from the rear. The first volley, which came within eighty yards of the troops, killed one private and wounded a teamster. The fatigued and thirsty soldiers responded immediately, rushing back to support the rear guard and rescue the train. Here they fought off the Indians with the aid of a few well-placed shots from Thompson's "jackass battery." The Indians were routed and four killed here, according to military reports. The soldiers escorted the train to the stage station.

Yet they were still six or seven hundred yards from the spring and faced the same problems Bascom encountered seventeen months before. About 1 P.M., Captain Roberts deployed his men and proceeded cautiously up the narrow canyon toward water. The Apaches, probably led by Cochise, began firing from the "rocks and ravines on the hills on both sides of the spring [and] kept up a rattling fire." The Indians had constructed breastworks on the two hills which overlooked the springs and were invulnerable to rifle fire. Private Barr was killed and another man wounded. At this critical moment, Roberts acted decisively and it would be difficult to say how he

Battle of Apache Pass. Roberts placed his howitzers slightly to the left of center of this photo and shelled the Apache positions above the springs. (*Photo by Karen Hayes*)

could have done any better. He deployed his command, sent two parties of skirmishers into the hills and ordered Lieutenant Thompson to begin shelling the heights above the springs. Amid this fierce fighting, the howitzer began lobbing shell after shell, forcing the Chiricahuas to scatter "like quail in every direction," carrying their wounded and dead with them. During the fight an unlikely hero emerged: a dog named Butch, "who ran around the brush and chaparral, barking and scouting Indians before losing one toe during the fight, shot off by the Indians."[52]

The fight for the springs ended about 4 P.M. The official casualties for the whites were two killed and two wounded; Roberts estimated that the Indians had suffered a loss of at least nine dead.[53] In contrast, Cremony, who arrived the following day, claimed that he learned from a "prominent Apache who was present in the engagement, that sixty-three warriors were killed outright by the shells, while only three perished from musketry fire."[54] Cremony's propensity to overstatement is evident here. Conversely, Apache versions understate the incident, claiming that few, if any, were killed.[55] In truth, the number of Apache casualties cannot be determined with accuracy any more than the number of Indians engaged in the fighting. Dan L. Thrapp writes: "The Indians no doubt saw it as a happy chance for possible loot . . . and were very sure that they could break it off and get away when they chose; that was the nature of an Apache ambush."[56]

The fighting over, Roberts dispatched Sergeant Mitchell and five troopers to join Cremony, who was en route to Apache Pass with the government train of twenty-one wagons and the remainder of Roberts's command. The horse soldiers succeeded in getting through the pass but a few miles west of it twenty Apaches, reportedly under Mangas Coloradas, attacked Mitchell's party. The Indians killed two horses, wounded one man, and cut off Private John W. Teal, who had been leading his fatigued horse. Mitchell's party escaped, but Teal's fate seemed hopeless until "a lucky shot by me sent the chief off in the arms of his Indians."[57]

According to legend, the chief shot off his horse by Teal was none other than Mangas Coloradas. Legend also says that the wounded leader was taken to Janos, where a doctor saved his life. Both accounts are from the pen of Cremony, which leaves them open to suspicion, but the Apache version given to Mrs. Ball corroborated Cremony's account.[58]

Cochise continued the fight the next day, positioning his warriors behind breastworks on the two hills overlooking the springs. But the troops again dislodged the Chiricahuas, who scattered after a few shells landed in their vicinity. Soon after that, Cremony's cavalry occupied the breastworks, which "were skillfully arranged, being made of large rocks piled on each other, with convenient crennels for musket practice." The command moved on to San Simon the following day.[59]

Although the fight at Apache Pass was a virtual standoff, it had significant ramifications. Captain Roberts wisely recommended that a fort be established near the springs. "Otherwise every command will have to fight for the water, and . . . are almost certain to lose some lives." Carleton, who arrived at the pass about July 27, heeded Roberts's advice, judging it "indispensably necessary to establish a post in what is known as Apache Pass" because of the "hostile attitude of the Chiricahua Indians." Consequently, in General Order No. 12 he decreed that Fort Bowie would be situated at Apache Pass and garrisoned by one hundred men of Companies A and G, Fifth California Infantry, under Major Theodore A. Coult. The fort's main responsibility was to keep communications open on both sides of the Chiricahua Mountains. Apparently, Carleton's extreme Apache views were not yet completely formulated as is attested by his orders "to attack all Apaches" unless they bear flags of truce. In the months that followed he issued orders to reject any such overtures before attacking the Indians.[60]

Construction of the fort began on July 28, and by August 14 a wall surrounded it. Indians were lurking in the neighborhood and in early August ambushed and fatally wounded an unarmed soldier six hundred yards from the post. Cochise had not returned in force, and Coult felt that his camp was "pretty safe from any attack of Indians, unless they should come in overwhelming force and desperately storm the hill," which, he correctly pointed out, was "contrary to their usual mode of warfare." For the next several years Cochise appeared at Fort Bowie with his warriors but refrained from attacking it. It remained a permanent fixture in southern Arizona, much to the chagrin of both the Apaches and the soldiers stationed there. In fact, Major Coult went so far as to suggest the abandonment of the post during the winter because of expected heavy snowfall. Carleton disagreed, which abruptly put an end to the discussions.[61]

In late July, Carleton left Apache Pass for the Río Grande. Two miles east of the pass he found the bodies of nine white men who had left Pinos Altos on July 9 bound for California; on July 13, as they approached the pass, the Chiricahuas had ambushed them.[62] Cremony told how these unfortunate frontiersmen were surprised:

Two miles east of the pass, right in the clear and unobstructed plain, there is a gully . . . six to eight feet deep, a quarter of a mile long, three or four yards wide, and cannot be seen from horseback until the rider is within fifty yards of the spot. With consummate cunning a large body of the Apaches ensconced themselves in this gully, knowing that the travellers would be somewhat off their guard in an open plain. . . . The scheme proved eminently successful . . . the hardy miners rode forward with their rifles resting in the slings across the saddle bows, their pistols in scabbards, and their whole attention absorbed in the pass they were about to enter. When they had arrived within forty yards of the gully or ditch, a terrific and simultaneous fire was opened upon them by the concealed Indians, which killed one-half their number outright, and sent the remainder wounded and panic stricken to seek safety in flight. They were immediately pursued and massacred to a man.

These were the corpses that Carleton had stumbled upon. The Indians had burned one man at the stake, "the charred bones and the burnt ends of the rope" still visible.[63]

This was only the beginning of Carleton's journey through Apachería. The remainder of his march was marked by skeletons, skulls, graves, and charred wagons, all stark testimonials to the audacity and brutality of the Indians. Upon reaching Santa Fe to take command of the Department of New Mexico, he received more reports from the superintendent of Indian affairs, emphasizing the critical condition of the territory because of Apache raids. Furthermore, the Indians had gone unpunished, and this galled the stern officer. These frightening pictorials left Carleton with a vivid glimpse of Apache warfare. Thus he turned his attention, every bit of it, to the Indians because he knew no other way. Where his previous orders had been to avoid conflict with the Indians, in the fall of 1862 he redirected his enormous energy and indefatigable zeal against the Apaches.

Carleton was a disciplinarian, a martinet, and a highly principled man who imposed his morality and devotion to duty on his subordinates. A devout Christian, a good family man, and a gentleman, he was unwavering to those who dissented from his views. His main problem was his focus, his perspective. The view from his lens was too narrow, yet he carried out his duties with a zeal and energy which the Department of New Mexico had never seen. He became the absolute ruler of New Mexico during the Civil War; his decisions, based on his morals and convictions, were, of course, correct. He could not be dissuaded.

Carleton inevitably offended many people. His Apache philosophy can be summed up in one word: extermination. He would give no quarter, and during a time when many southwesterners had lost friends or relatives to Apache raids, where humanitarians were as scarce as supporters of Abraham Lincoln in Richmond, Carleton's rigid, unyielding policies toward Apaches were initially supported

by most southwesterners. A decade later, General George Crook
waged constant war against the Apaches to force their subjugation.
He treated them with firmness combined with compassion and dignity when they capitulated. In contrast, Carleton accepted only unconditional surrender, and when some of the bands were ready to
yield, instead of grasping this opportunity, he tried to stamp it out
by imposing conditions that were totally unacceptable to the Indians. By that time, he had become obsessed with a psychopathic
hatred of Apaches.

In the end it was Mangas Coloradas, not Cochise, who incurred
the wrath of Carleton and his subordinates' antipathy toward the Indians. By October 1862 his extreme and militant Apache policy had
evolved; he ordered his men to reject all flags of truce and to kill all
male Indians capable of bearing arms.[64] Robert M. Utley writes that
Carleton "brought a rare understanding of Indian warfare and a
ruthlessness in applying it."[65] So it was that his extermination policy began. No matter how cruel, inhumane, and immoral it appears
to have been to us armchair judges of the twentieth century, we must
not overlook the fact that Cochise and Mangas practiced the same
policy, yet the whites professed to be civilized and thus more understanding than the Indians and, considering themselves superior,
were much more at fault than the Indians. Added to this was the fact
that Cochise, Mangas, and other noted Apaches never thought of or
practiced extermination or genocide, while that was what many Anglos persuaded themselves was a proper course.

After the fight at Apache Pass, Cochise and Mangas took their
people to Mexico. In late July, Cochise was reported near Fronteras,[66] while Mangas allegedly was taken to Janos, where a doctor,
under threats of death, extracted the ball from John Teal's carbine.[67]
Mangas, now past seventy, soon returned to his beloved Pinos Altos
and requested peace. Unfortunately for the Chihennes, Dr. Steck,
whom they longed to see, was no longer agent and the army ruled
the territory.

The new agent for the Gila Apaches was Fernando Maxwell.
Little is known about his activities and his accomplishments, if any.
He apparently remained in seclusion at Santa Fe until the following
spring. In any event, his absence forced Mangas to deal with the

military, who abruptly dismissed any thoughts of an armistice, Carleton writing, "I have no faith in him." [68]

The story of Mangas's death has been told many times and needs no in-depth analysis here. Suffice it to say that against the better judgment of his own people he went to Pinos Altos for a parley, was seized, and shortly afterward "killed while attempting to escape," a euphemistic way of saying he was executed. [69]

The capture and killing of Mangas, pernicious in every respect, naturally increased the antipathy between whites and the Chiricahuas. If death had come in battle, the Indians would have responded differently, but it had not. Thrapp puts it best: "The greatest tragedy of the affair was less the death of the aging chieftain than the lasting distrust generated on the part of Apaches toward white Americans and soldiers." [70] Mangas had been eager for peace, realizing that he could not defeat the Americans, so Chiricahua suspicion of whites now reached new heights. The Chihennes, led by Victorio, Nana, Loco, and Riñon, and the Bedonkohes, under an obscure chief named Luis, perhaps a son of Mangas, again joined forces with Cochise.

For Cochise, the loss of his father-in-law deeply grieved him. If his hatred of Americans had subsided since Coyuntura's death, Mangas's death reinvigorated it and reminded him that the Americans could not be trusted. To the Chiricahua tribe, the execution of Mangas was indeed "the greatest of wrongs." [71]

Chapter 11

# COCHISE WILL NEVER BE FRIENDLY

After the Apache Pass fight of July 15, 1862, Cochise made straight as an arrow for the mountains southeast of Fronteras. He needed time to lick his wounds and to reflect upon what had happened. At the least his people were safe from American troops, for Cochise had no conception that his Chokonens were not Carleton's first priority. The battle had neither disabled nor taken the fight out of him; he remained bitterly opposed to any talk of peace, especially with Americans, even though his Chihenne allies under Mangas Coloradas felt otherwise.

About July 24, Cochise and "a party of Chiricahua broncos . . . passed by here [Fronteras] and have scattered by distant routes." The presence of over "300 of all sexes and ages" disturbed Fronteras authorities, who feared Cochise's Chokonens. Furthermore, the regular force at Fronteras numbered but thirty men, leaving the citizens "without security for their lives or interests." Captain Gabriel García came to the reluctant conclusion that he could not take any offensive measures; his force was too small and his artillery piece inoperable. Yet this minor crisis dissipated and Cochise caused no reported trouble at this time in Sonora.[1]

Their arrival troubled García, but it was not his only concern. In early July, Miguel Yrigóllen, Elías, and Aguirre led 156 Chokonens, including 28 men, and brought their followers in. They had been living near Janos when a group of Chihuahuan volunteers from

Guerrero destroyed their camp, capturing 11 of their band.[2] They joined the remnants of Remigio's group, whose ranks had been decimated by smallpox. Toward the end of that month Santiago, Delgado, and José Manda brought their people in, bringing the total living near Fronteras to 262 Chiricahuas, including 52 warriors. These leaders were all closely associated with Cochise and several probably participated in the Apache Pass fight.[3]

While Remigio and other chiefs worked hard at stabilizing relations at Fronteras, Cochise remained undisturbed in the Sierra Madre probably in the vicinity of the Teras Mountains. In August, Plume split from Cochise and brought his extended family group to Fronteras, and in late August *Estrella de Occidente* editorialized that the armistice has "produced good results" and succeeded in "reducing them to a social life [in which] their basic needs are satisfied."[4]

This optimistic report was intended to prepare the citizens of Ures for the arrival of a delegation of Chiricahuas under Remigio to discuss a formal treaty with Pesqueira.[5] The governor, embroiled in fighting off the French invasion of Sonora, promised to conclude a treaty as soon as possible.[6] Cochise, wary and suspicious of Sonora, refused to be a party to any agreement, his actions revealing his contempt for both the treaty and those Chokonens who would contemplate peace.

Pesqueira was delayed, and Apache raids inevitably increased in late 1862. He quickly promised to retaliate against the hostiles, who had "left a trail of blood" in their wake.[7] The situation worsened in January 1863 when Apaches, probably Chiricahuas, butchered a party of twelve Sonorans near Huasabas; only one boy escaped.[8] Pesqueira responded angrily and reinstated the scalp bounty, reinforced the garrison at Fronteras, and reestablished a force at Bacoachi. Furthermore, alarmed by reports that the Chiricahuas at Fronteras were raiding, he decided to go there and investigate.[9]

Pesqueira reached the presidio on the hill in late March 1863. His first step was to issue an edict prohibiting trade between Apaches and Mexicans, warning that harsh punitive actions would be taken against any citizen continuing this insidious practice.[10] He recognized that the Indians were depredating in both Mexico and the United States, perhaps responding to a charge that Major David Fergusson had made from Tucson the previous fall.[11] In response, the governor wrote Brigadier General West at Mesilla admitting that the Indians had been raiding across the line into the United States while implying that a similar state of affairs existed at Mesilla.[12]

Undoubtedly there was a semblance of truth about this age-old practice. Cochise had done so for much of 1861, and there was no reason to believe that he had ceased. In later years he conceded that "a great many of us were one time at peace at Fronteras and some of the Mexicans used to tell us to come up here and steal American horses, which are big and worth a great deal of money in Mexico."[13] One such raid occurred at Fort Bowie, only eighty miles north of Fronteras, in the fall of 1862. On October 5, Apaches attacked the herd at the fort. Two parties of troops unsuccessfully pursued the Indians west for ten miles, in all probability Cochise's Chokonens. Captain Hugh Hinds reported that "the Indians are getting hungry and bold but retreat before my scouting parties at all times. They appear to want the stock and care little about fighting for it." This was the essence and character of an Apache raid: minimum risk. No stock was worth a life.[14]

In any event, more than half the Chokonens agreed to a formal truce, the conditions of which were rigid and restrictive. Pesqueira concentrated on controlling the Chiricahuas through close vigilance and by placing responsibility in the hands of the chiefs. He demanded two roll calls per week and insisted that all arms be turned over to the military commander. Of course the Chiricahuas may have assented to this, but in practice it never took place and their best arms were cached for future use. The final demand, one tried unsuccessfully in past treaties and the one which would eventually undo this one, compelled the men to serve as scouts against hostiles, primarily Cochise's Chokonens. In return, Pesqueira agreed to issue rations of corn or wheat, tobacco, whiskey, and some clothing. At this time the Indians numbered 270 and were led by Santiago, Remiqio, Miguel Yrigóllen, and Taces.[15]

Cochise's absence tended to indicate that he was in Arizona, for it had been only a short time since the execution of Mangas Coloradas. Compounding this was the wounding of Mangas's wife, Tues-seh; the killing of one son, probably Seth-mood-a;[16] and the capturing of another. As a result, within a few days, Cochise's wife,

Dos-teh-seh lost her father and a brother killed by troops, a brother captured, and her mother wounded. Naturally revenge must be had.

In the days following Mangas's murder the remaining Bedonkohes joined Cochise, perhaps on a permanent basis.[17] According to Geronimo, they "retreated into the mountains near Apache Pass" although their intentions were not clear;[18] his recollections are corroborated by contemporary military reports. On February 16, 1863, some four weeks after Mangas's death, Indians suddenly appeared in the hills overlooking Fort Bowie. Displaying a flag of truce, six women eventually came into the post and the following day twenty more came in; one hundred warriors were visible in the hills. Unfortunately, no report has been found that would either identify the Indians or explain their motives. Cochise's emissaries may have been scouting the vulnerability of the eighty men garrisoned at the fort, which was too strong for an attack. In any event, troops scouted for Apaches on February 17 and 18 but failed to find any.[19]

Lieutenant John F. Qualey wrote Fergusson concerning the Indians' visit. His report has not been found, but Colonel David Fergusson's reply, as instructed by Brigadier General West, indicated that both officers knew of the Chiricahuas' talk of an armistice. From Tucson on March 12, Fergusson informed Qualey:

> I have been directed by the general commanding the District of Arizona to instruct you to order back all flags of truce presented by Indians. To do this instantly on their being presented and then to attack the party sending them and to endeavor to make their woman and children prisoners and to send your captives to Mesilla whenever an opportunity shall offer . . . also to war on the grown male Indians whenever and wherever found, without hesitation or exception.[20]

There would be clashes when the weather turned warm.

Geronimo's chronology is somewhat confusing, but he clearly recalled that his Bedonkohes joined Cochise shortly after Mangas Coloradas's death. This was probably in March 1863, when Cochise "took command of both divisions." Soon after that, "we were again attacked by another company of United States troops . . . we were repulsed and decided to disband."[21] Geronimo may have been referring to an incident which occurred on March 22, 1863. Apaches "supposed to have been Chiricahua and Gila Apaches" attacked the herd at Fort West[22] and ran off sixty horses. The boldness of the attack surprised the troops, for the horses were less than a mile from camp and were guarded by a sergeant and twelve men. That evening Captain William McCleave, one of the army's best Indian hunters; eighty-one men; and two guides, including Juan Arroyo, left with ten days' rations, vowing "either [to] retake the horses or Apache blood enough to pay for them."[23]

McCleave chased the raiders west for some seventy miles to the Black River, then struck the trail again. Believing a ranchería to be near, on March 27 he stumbled upon a camp situated along the Río Bonita, a tributary of the Gila River, said to have been a favorite camping place of Cochise. The soldiers attacked and routed the Indians, killing twenty-five Apaches in twenty minutes. The troops lost one man dead, Private James Hall. Whom McCleave attacked is not known. Bonita Creek was in White Mountain Apache country, where the Chokonens were to be found from time to time, and a report in early March saying that Chihennes had fled to Coyotero country leads to the possibility that the victims were Chiricahuas; the band, however, remains unknown.[24]

The Bedonkohes and Chokonens scattered, Cochise apparently moving south into the Chiricahuas, bound for Sonora. On April 25 a large band of Indians approached Fort Bowie from the north. Captain Benjamin F. Harrover gathered a force of twenty-five men and encountered the Apaches near the springs. Here a minor brush ensued before the Indians retreated, the whites in pursuit. The Apaches, armed with "many guns of large caliber also several rifle muskets," succeeded in wounding one soldier. Harrover thought several Indians were killed or wounded. From the report and the large body of Indians involved, West concluded that Cochise and his band were involved, and they probably were.[25]

By the second week of May, Cochise had shown up at Fronteras, ready to fight anyone in his way, whether be they citizens, troops, or peaceful Chiricahuas. His appearance had a frightening effect on everyone in the vicinity, where the peace consummated six weeks earlier was on the verge of collapsing.[26]

Problems had surfaced from the beginning because the treaty was a most unpredictable arrangement at best. Pesqueira had ordered two detachments to scout the mountains north and east of Fronteras for those Chokonens and Nednhis who had refused to come in. In compliance with the terms of the treaty, Remigio and four warriors guided a command of forty men led by Captain José Escalante to examine Batepito and Pilares. The Chokonen leader Santiago and five of his men scouted for the second command of seventy men led by Captain Angel Elías, who would reconnoiter the Arizona-Sonora boundary.[27]

Neither force accomplished much, but Elías's troops found a Chokonen ranchería in the Anibacachi Mountains twenty-five miles northwest of Fronteras near the Arizona line. It may have been the camp of Delgado, who had come in with Santiago the previous July, but one of Santiago's warriors, who probably had relatives in this local group, deserted the Sonorans and warned the encampment. Not everyone escaped; one child was captured and a Chokonen warrior named Gándara was killed and scalped. Meanwhile, Escalante's scout was uneventful, he and his men eventually scouting Turicachi before returning to Fronteras after a 360-degree journey.[28]

The desertion of the scout was the first sign that the armistice would be short-lived. Even more serious, Chiricahua raiding parties continued raiding in the interior while living under the pretense of peace. Two warriors returned to Fronteras with stock stolen from Sahuaripa; it was confiscated and two Apaches were imprisoned, which produced a volatile atmosphere. They escaped, and a few days later the small groups of Miguel Yrigóllen, Taces, and Lorenzo bolted in the direction of the Teras Mountains. Lieutenant Colonel Buenaventura led forty-five troopers in an attempt to overtake them but was unsuccessful.[29]

At this crucial stage Cochise arrived at Fronteras on a trading mission, his intent being to exchange loot for food, guns, and ammunition. Currently at war with the United States and with Chihuahuan troops scouting aggressively throughout the Janos area, he probably wished to maintain peaceful relations at Fronteras, yet some kind of difficulty ensued, probably because of Pesqueira's edict banning trade with Apaches. In later years Cochise recalled an incident that occurred at Fronteras in the early 1860s. Evidently it began when the Indians were disposing of American stock. "When [our] people came back there with" the stolen stock, the people of Fronteras "killed them and took the horses and saddles away."[30] This act, or something similar, touched off the explosion. Cochise returned with his men, killed several citizens, and the armistice disintegrated. The Chiricahuas, "incited by Chis," headed for the mountains. Once again Cochise was at war with all whites and Mexicans.[31]

For the remainder of 1863 and 1864, Cochise's activities become somewhat difficult to trace. We get glimpses of his whereabouts from escaped captives and occasionally from the Chiricahuas' actions. He returned to southern Arizona after the incident at Fronteras and his people spent the rest of the spring gathering, baking, and storing mescal. He remained in touch with his Chihenne and Bedonkohe relatives to the east and north and planned a summer campaign in southern New Mexico to avenge Mangas's death.

As it turned out, Cochise was fortunate to have avoided northern Chihuahua, where the scalp-bounty system was in full swing and the Nednhis were being systematically hunted down. Joaquin Terrazas and his volunteers were having a field day against the Carrizaleños, killing Cojinillín, whose scalp was worth five hundred pesos, a considerable sum in these days.[32] Finally, in early 1864, Zuloaga assisted Terrazas in capturing Felipe and forty-six others, which incapacitated the remaining Carrizaleños and virtually destroyed them as a distinct group.[33] Their remnants, under Gorgonio and El Zurdo, probably were absorbed into the Janeros unit of the Nednhi band, by this time led by Juh,[34] a heavy-set but first-rate war chief who fought side by side with Cochise throughout the 1860s.

Meanwhile, in the spring of 1863, West and Carleton began vigorously thumping their war drums. In mid-March, Carleton had reminded West: "I do not look forward to any peace with them, except what we must command. They must have no voice in the matter. Entire subjugation or destruction of all the men are the alternatives."[35] Truly, this policy of unconditional surrender as regards Cochise's people was a fiasco and served to exacerbate already poor relations.

Although Carleton had not mentioned Cochise, West in southern New Mexico recognized his importance. In late May he wrote Colonel David Fergusson, commander of the District of Western Arizona at Tucson, suggesting that he plan a campaign against Cochise and his band, believed to be living in the Chiricahua Mountains.[36] Nevertheless, in the summer of 1863 it was reported that the

"Apaches are quiet" in southern Arizona. Pressure from northern Mexico, plus some unfinished business (avenging Mangas's death) may account for the Chokonens, Bedonkohes, and Chihennes joining in the summer of 1863 to fight the whites; Cook's Peak would be their headquarters. The audacity and brutality of their attacks surprised West, who had discounted the Chiricahuas as too fragmented to take the offensive.[37]

The first of several hard fights took place about June 17 when Chiricahuas killed First Lieutenant L. A. Bargie and two other men opposite San Diego Crossing on the Río Grande. The Indians, "apparently pertaining to the parties of the chief (Mangas Coloradas) who was killed some time ago by the Californians near Pinos Altos," applied the same barbaric treatment to Bargie's body as the troops had to Mangas. The courageous officer was found with "his head cut off, his breast cut open, and his heart taken out."[38]

Captain Emil Fritz pursued the Indians west, thinking they were "Mimbres River Indians" or Mangas's Chihennes. West was incensed by the outcome of the fight and ordered Captain McCleave to put his Fort West command in the field against the Indians. West's fury may be inferred from his terse but explicit instructions to McCleave:

This band of Meimbres [sic] River Indians must be exterminated to a man. At the earliest possible moment that the condition of your command will admit of it, you will undertake this duty. Use every available man. . . . Scour every foot of ground and beat up all their haunts.[39]

Cochise's Chokonens likely did not have a hand in Bargie's death, which was probably the work of Luis's Bedonkohes and Victorio's Chihennes. A few weeks later, however, he apparently joined these two leaders and they set up shop at Cook's Canyon.

On July 11 a small detachment of seven men under Sergeant E. V. Hoyt was escorting a supply train east to Las Cruces. At Cook's Canyon he was attacked by a large body of Indians, which resulted in the abandonment of three wagons and nineteen mules. Four soldiers were wounded and four Indians were killed, but Hoyt's party eventually reached Las Cruces with their lives.[40]

About two weeks later a detachment of California Volunteers

commanded by Second Lieutenant John Lambert left Las Cruces and entered Cook's Canyon at 5 A.M. on July 24. The allied Chiricahuas were ready and opened fire, wounding a sergeant and killing a private. After driving the Indians back, Lambert circled his wagons, which probably saved lives because the Apaches, estimated at between 150 and 250 warriors, were concealed in ambush. After five hours of skirmishing the Indians tried to set fire to the grass, which failed to ignite. Next, in a rare tactic for Apaches, they prepared an assault from three directions. This frightened Lambert. With his options dwindling fast, he abandoned two wagons, supplies, and twelve mules, hoping the Indians would not pursue; they did not. What Lambert did not realize was that Captain Chauncey R. Wellman and his command were approaching Cook's Canyon from the west. Wellman caught a quick glimpse of the retreating Apaches but thought that they were too strong to pursue; he overtook Lambert's command, and both arrived at Las Cruces about noon on July 25.[41]

There is some evidence that Cochise joined Victorio (they were said to be great friends, according to Mrs. Ball) in these hard fights, but there is no direct proof. Only Cochise could have gathered such a body of warriors, and the absence of Apaches in Arizona in the summer of 1863 tends to indicate that he may have been in New Mexico. The locality of Cook's Peak, the characteristics of the fight, and the fact that some of the stolen booty was recovered in the Chiricahua Mountains six weeks later points to his participation. In fact, the hostilities led to the establishment of Fort Cummings in Cook's Canyon on October 2, 1863.[42]

West, always ready to explode when it came to Apache victories, was initially irate over Lambert's actions. Later he grudgingly admitted that Lambert's judgment might have been correct, but "still it is a defeat and . . . has enabled the Indians to provide themselves with subsistance." Consequently, he issued Special Order No. 39, calling for an extensive campaign against the Apaches of southern New Mexico. He reiterated his belief that the Indians must be pursued until exterminated. In fact, he considered the situation so important as to go to Cook's Canyon himself. On August 10 he met Captain McCleave, who had established a base camp on the Mimbres from which he could campaign against the hostiles.[43]

Cochise returned to Arizona after the fight and focused his attention on the Americans living at Apache Pass. In late August a party of seventy-five Apaches stole every horse from Fort Bowie. The Indians had broken into three groups and the raid was efficiently and effectively carried out.[44] But these successes were not destined to continue.

On September 5, Captain James H. Whitlock discovered and destroyed an Indian camp in the Chiricahua Mountains. Three days later he found the Chokonens (likely led by Cochise, who was thought to be in the area) "in force [and] a very spirited fight for about 15 minutes" ensued in which two whites were wounded. Among them were Juan Arroyo, Whitlock's skillful guide, whose competence in the 1860s would have been rivaled only by the incomparable Merejildo Grijalva. More shots were exchanged the next day before the Indians vanished deeper into the mountains. Items taken from the Indian village were "sufficient evidence of the Indians being the same that attacked Lieutenant Lambert's party." Whitlock later said Luis, the Bedonkohe leader, was present.[45]

The Chiricahuas faced aggressive campaigning from below the border. Stung by its fruitless policy of pacification, Sonora declared that "peace with this class of enemy is a Utopia, an unrealistic project."[46] The intermittent Chiricahua-Sonora peace treaties between 1831 and 1863 were now a thing of the past, although Apache distrust and the enmity of Sonorans probably was the primary reason, rather than Sonora's official hard-line rhetoric.

During the summer of 1863, Bavispe and Bacerac had mobilized national troops to hunt Apaches believed to be living in the Animas Mountains, yet nothing of note occurred. In late September, Captain Eraclio Escalante led a scout from Fronteras and attacked Taces's Chokonens in the Pitaicache Mountains. The soldiers killed Taces and a woman and captured two others, one of whom escaped during the night and warned other Chiricahua rancherías, likely including Cochise, who was reported in the vicinity.[47] Eskinya, a Chokonen who figured prominently in events of the 1870s, succeeded Taces as leader of that small local group.

Once again the Chokonens scattered, some heading for the Chiricahuas, others to the Huachucas or Dragoons. Thanks to the testimony of an escaped Mexican captive, we have some insight as to Cochise's situation in the fall of 1863. The American and Mexican offensives had forced the Apaches to keep on the move; as a consequence "they were starving." Furthermore, the Chokonens had "been very unsuccessful in their late raids into Sonora in search of booty and that their arrows had become useless and their ammunition exhausted." This report was corroborated several months later by another former captive. The two posed immediate problems for the Indians, especially if they were willing to act as guides. Accompanied by Mexican and American miners, the escapee led them on a scout which succeeded in surprising a Chokonen ranchería near the San Pedro; five Indians were killed and another captured. Although the location of the Indian camp was not specifically identified, it was probably in either the lower Dragoons or the Huachuca Mountains.[48]

Mexican troops continued to make their presence felt in late 1863 and early 1864. In November 1863 the indefatigable Captain Eraclio Escalante and ninety men from Bavispe wiped out a Nednhi ranchería near Janos, killing twenty-one Indians, including six warriors, and capturing seven others. Their leader, Susopa, was among the dead.[49]

It was the Chokonens' turn in early 1864. Leaving Bacoachi, Captain Cayetano Silva led a force into southern Arizona, scouting the Mule and lower Dragoon mountains before crossing the Sulphur Springs Valley to the Chiricahuas. On February 12 his scouts discovered a ranchería, perhaps at Turkey Canyon, called by the Indians Tsetagolka, or Mound of White Rocks. Silva divided his troops into three groups: Lieutenant Manuel Gallegos, an experienced Apache fighter and 30 infantry to the right; Lieutenant Feliciano Ruiz with a force of nationals to the left; Captain José Escalante with the cavalry to the center. At daybreak the three commands converged on the village, which proved to be Santiago's and routed the unsuspecting Apaches. As in previous fights, no prisoners were wanted, but somehow 3 children survived and were not killed. Men, women, and children were cut down indiscriminately. Six warriors and 15 women and children were reported killed.[50] Five months later a Chokonen warrior named Ka-eet-sah admitted that the Sonorans had killed "about thirty in one day, among them all of his family."[51] By the time the news reached Tucson, the total dead in the fight had increased fivefold to 107 and it had occurred thirty to forty miles south at Fort Bowie.[52]

The surprise was so complete because the Chiricahuas had evidently decided to request peace at Fronteras. Emissaries had already been sent; in fact, these messengers may have actually entered the fort and held discussions before the attack. Captain Silva ordered out Captain José Jesús Escalante and fifteen dragoons to overtake and attack the Indians if possible. Near Fronteras, Escalante completed his mission, killing three Indians and capturing three more children.[53]

With northern Mexico on the offensive, Cochise had probably established his winter camp in the northern region of Chokonen country, trying to avoid white contact. Toward late February, only a few weeks after the annihilation of Santiago's group, the Bedonkohe leader Luis, three warriors from his band, and fifteen Chokonens from Cochise's band left the Gila country for a raid against their old antagonists, the miners at Pinos Altos. The Chokonen chief awaited the outcome, but if Luis had succeeded, "Cochise and his tribe would have come the next time." An Apache scouting party had appeared at Pinos Altos on February 13 and threatened the citizens, declaring they would return about February 25.

The miners sent word to Captain James H. Whitlock, who was in camp along the Mimbres. With twenty-one men he left the night of February 24 and arrived at Pinos Altos the next morning. Luis led the Bedonkohe-Chokonen party into Pinos Altos about noon; at dusk Captain Whitlock's command moved into town and, assisted by citizens, killed thirteen of the eighteen warriors, including Luis, his three Bedonkohes and nine Chokonens. Mexicans scalped the Apaches and brought the hair to Carrizal, Chihuahua, for the bounty.[54] Whitlock also retook a Mexican captive named Marijenia Figueira, who had been captured at Banamichi by Miguel Narbona in 1849.[55] Her testimony revealed the destitute condition of the Chiricahua hostiles:

> All the Indians that came in with this party were living near the mouth of the Black River. We came by Fort West: have been eight days coming. The Navajoes are at war with all the other tribes that I know of. They took all our stock; left us very poor; very poor indeed. We have no stock except 3 ponies, and 1 of these soldiers got last night. We have no dried meat; have nothing to live upon except mescal. . . . Can occasionally kill a deer. Have no powder or guns. Our

guns are nearly all worn out . . . we have no clothing. We have to live
down in the valleys. We cannot live up in the mountains; it is too
cold. Runon [Riñon] and Victoria [Victorio] get powder and lead
from a man named Zuloaga, who lives in Corralitos Mexico. . . .
Zuloaga is always on friendly terms with us even when his government is at war with us.[56]

The Chiricahuas avenged Luis's death on March 22, 1864, running off seventy-two mules from a government train at Camp Mimbres.[57] Whitlock, now a battle-hardened Apache fighter, elected to
wait a few days before pursuing, hoping the raiders would relax
their vigilance. The command of seventy-two officers and men left
on March 27 and followed the trail west toward the mountains north
of Stein's Peak. Whitlock, however, decided to use a circuitous
route, moving north to the Gila River and cutting the trail near Safford or Solomonville, which led to a ranchería in the Graham Mountains. The Indians were woefully unprepared for the attack. The
troops "charged their camp," killed 21 "wretches," and looted the
village. Whitlock believed the ranchería contained 250 individuals
"supposed to be [of] the Chiricahua tribe," which, if true, meant
this was Cochise's camp, for no other Chokonen local group would
have been this size. It was probably Cochise who led the force of
poorly armed warriors who skirmished with the troops but soon
withdrew. The Chiricahuas lost their homes, property, and stock and
possessed but two or three guns.[58]

About one month later Cochise retaliated, apparently having been
joined by some Bedonkohes and Chihennes, for he showed more
strength than to have drawn only from his Chokonens. With a force
estimated at one hundred to two hundred warriors, the Chiricahua
war party lay concealed in ambush in the steep hills of Doubtful
Canyon near Stein's Peak. A detachment of sixty men under Lieutenant Henry Stevens rode into Doubtful Canyon early on May 4.
Although a notorious site for Apache ambush, the men did not anticipate danger and Juan Arroyo had failed to detect the Indians'
presence. Wrote one of the soldiers: "We did not know that there
was an Indian within 20 miles of us."

As the sun was coming up, Stevens's command passed the abandoned stage station near Stein's Peak and the Apaches launched their
surprise. The silence was broken by whoops from the rocks and

Doubtful Canyon. On May 5, 1864, Chiricahuas showered arrows on Stevens's command from both sides of the canyon. (*Photo by Dan Thrapp*)

crevices on both sides on the canyon. The first assault wounded four men as the Chiricahuas, lacking guns and ammunition, "poured arrows into our ranks by the hundred." Undaunted, Stevens, whose horse was killed in the opening assault, rallied his men in a manner which would have made Hollywood proud. Ordering his troopers forward, he "swung his hat around his head and encouraged the men all he could while in the act of swinging, an Apache shot an arrow through [it]." After a forty-five-minute fight the Indians, who "had fought like devils," withdrew to higher positions in the mountains. Lieutenant Stevens reported that ten Apaches were "left dead on the ground"; moreover, he thought, twenty or more were wounded. The troops' losses consisted of one man missing in action, one mortally wounded, one with a broken arm, and three others slightly wounded.[59] Carleton praised Stevens, gleefully passing the report on to Washington and describing the encounter as "a handsome little fight."[60]

Cochise was probably at both Whitlock's and Stevens's fights. From Fronteras it was rumored that he had been killed in one of them, which would tend to support his presence in one or perhaps both engagements.[61]

Stevens's command was proceeding to Fort Bowie to participate in General Carleton's grand Apache campaign. Now that he had subdued the Navajos, Carleton turned his attention to the Apaches, determining to subjugate them. This would be "a serious war; not a little march out and back again." His objective was simple: "to hunt and destroy all but the women and children."[62]

In April he had begun making the necessary administrative and organizational plans, in which he excelled. He planned a pincerslike assault against the Apaches north of the Gila. Troops would be pulled in from everywhere, and Carleton urged ranchers, merchants, miners, and even the Pimas, Maricopas, and Papagos, the Apaches' traditional enemies, to take the field.[63] He envisioned that the Apaches would be defeated and forced to seek refuge in northern Mexico. To ensure their entrapment, he requested that Governors Pesqueira and Terrazas place troops along the border, where the fleeing Apaches could easily be ambushed.[64] He revealed his obsession with defeating the Apaches when he assured Captain Tidball at Fort Bowie that he would "do all that mortals can do to bring this Apache war to a speedy and final end."[65] He would whip them before Christmas, he said confidently.[66]

Public sentiment supported wholeheartedly his policy. A letter from Tucson in Janaury 1864 declared that Arizona was "virtually in the hands of Apaches." The Apache "must be hunted to his own secret strongholds and shot down like a wild beast whenever found."[67] Richard McCormick, secretary of Arizona Territory, concurred believing that popular opinion was in "favor of an utter extermination of the ruthless savages."[68]

Actually it was the Western Apaches, not the Chiricahuas, who absorbed the brunt of Carleton's offensive. U.S. soldiers scouted the White Mountains, where some three hundred warriors were reported, and Major Nelson Henry Davis did succeed in killing forty-nine and capturing sixteen near the confluence of the San Carlos and the Gila. Cochise, said to be on the Gila with Francisco's band, easily eluded the slow-footed troops, who were no match for the mobile Chokonens.[69]

Carleton's troops encountered one local group of Chokonens that summer, but Cochise was not among them. On July 10, Captain Thomas Theodore Tidball left Fort Bowie with fifty-eight men and twenty-two days' rations to scout the Chiricahuas; Merejildo Grijalva served as guide. The command marched southeast along the western slope of the Chiricahuas through country which few, if any Americans, had traveled. The first night, the command camped in the mouth of Bonita Canyon, where the Chiricahuas had fought the Sonorans twelve years before. The next day's march was a few miles southeast, and camp was made at Pino Canyon on the night of July 11. The next day, Tidball continued south along the western foothills, stopping at the mouth of Turkey Canyon. Finally, on July 14, the command penetrated the heart of the Chiricahuas to the summit, bivouacking near Fly's Peak. From here the command marched northeast for six or seven miles before striking an Indian trail, which led some seven miles to Cave Creek Canyon. Merejildo called this Río Ancho (Broad River), which coincided with the Apache name of Tu-n-tel-jin-li ("Water Broad Going").

Tidball immediately sent Sergeant Brown and twenty men to follow the trail. Shortly thereafter he encountered Plume, who stood his ground, perhaps protecting his own small group, which consisted of four or five warriors and about fifteen women and children. First, Plume began shooting arrows, without effect, and then, for devilment, began throwing rocks. This was condoned until he severely bruised a trooper; at this point the soldiers were forced to kill him. But old Plume had not died in vain, for the rest of his group escaped. His camp consisted of five wickiups on the side of a high mountain near the summit, which overlooked the San Simon Valley. It was probably near Portal Peak.[70]

The next day Tidball continued south along the eastern foothills and discovered more Chokonens. The Indians were too suspicious to approach but agreed to come in to Fort Bowie in eight days to make peace, a typical ploy to halt pursuit. Four days later Merejildo conversed with a warrior named Ka-eet-sah,[71] who decalred that his Apaches "belonged partly to Mangas' and partly to Chies'

[Cochise] bands and that they had a treaty and traded with the people of Janas [Janos]." As to Cochise's whereabouts, Ka-eet-sah disclosed that he was still on the Gila with the Coyoteros, probably meaning Francisco's Eastern White Mountain band. With the Apaches aware of his presence, Tidball marched across Sulphur Spring Valley to the Dragoon Mountains before returning to Fort Bowie on July 31.[72]

By this time Carleton believed that many of the Apaches had fled to Mexico and in spite of the inauspicious beginning he continued to believe that his troops could subdue the Indians by December.[73] This illusion was shared by few. He directed Major N. H. Davis to campaign against the hostiles living in northern Chihuahua. Davis moved his command into Chihuahua, scouting Alamo Hueco, Espuelas, and Boca Grande, but found no Apaches. To put to rest the rumors about José María Zuloaga trading with Apaches, Davis marched to Janos and Corralitos and talked with Zuloaga, who convinced the American that the complaints had no foundation. One wonders whether Davis, had he concluded that the charges were correct, would have executed Zuloaga as Carleton had advocated. But Davis, a thoughtful and pragmatic man, felt it best to dismiss the allegations and, fortunately for all concerned, Carleton's undistinguished plan was not implemented.[74]

While Davis was reconnoitering northern Chihuahua, other scouts were busy along the Gila, and a new post, Fort Goodwin, was established in Western Apache country. With such increasing American activity, Cochise may have left Coyotero country for the Chiricahuas or the Dragoons. In early August a war party of some eighty warriors swooped down on Cuquiarachi and stole one hundred head of stock. Their trail led to southern Arizona. In early October, Indians were prowling around Fronteras, their rancherías believed to be either in the Dragoon or Chiricahua mountains.

In November a force of eighty men left Fronteras, scouted the Mule Mountains, and found nothing before moving toward Cochise's stronghold in the Dragoons. They found Indians in the southern foothills, so Captain Manuel Gallegos and thirty men set out in pursuit. Suddenly a party of forty to fifty warriors appeared in the rear. Another force was dispatched but could not overtake the

Apaches—undoubtedly Cochise's for no other Apaches lived in this range. The troops returned to Sonora but left a force at Cuquiarachi because the Indians had threatened another attack.[75]

One month later, troops from Bacoachi, Fronteras, and Bavispe concentrated and took the offensive. In December, they struck a trail of stolen cattle in the Animas Mountains. On December 11 the combined force of 125 men remained in ambush but saw no Indians; the next day they saw smoke. Quickly, three divisions were formed: a force on each flank and one in the middle. The Sonorans surprised the camp, destroyed it, and killed 39 Apaches (9 warriors and 30 women and children). In addition, they captured 28 Apaches, including 3 babies who froze to death on the return march to Bavispe. It is not known which band was hit, but from the location it would appear to have been a Chokonen or Nednhi local group.[76]

In January 1865 came signs that four years of war had worn out the Chihennes, who, under Salvadora, Victorio, and the venerable Nana,[77] expressed a desire for peace. The issue was simple, the solution complex. Should the military commander (Carleton) or the superintendent of Indian affairs (now Dr. Michael Steck, the Chiricahuas' former agent) handle the negotations?[78] Carleton decided the military had sole jurisdiction and he of course could not be dissuaded. He alone would determine whether the Apaches should be considered pacified (sufficiently whipped) or hostile. And he wanted no interference from civil authorites.

Carleton's reservation policy would remain. All Apaches and Navajos who wanted peace would be required to move to Bosque Redondo on the Pecos River, a place hated by everyone concerned except Carleton. If the Indians refused, they faced extermination. Referring to Cochise, Carleton revealed his misconceptions, shared by most Anglos concerning Apache organization: "Cochise continued to hold out, when he falls the Pinal Apaches will succumb."[79] The Pinals were a band of Western Apaches and completely independent of Cochise's Chiricahuas.

The Chihennes fervently wished to see their old agent, Steck, whom they remembered fondly, and Steck wanted to see them. The obstacle was Carleton, who went so far as to deny Steck an escort to Pinos Altos. Thus the Apaches were forced to negotiate with the

Victorio. The great Chihenne chief who in 1865 said that "Cochise will never be friendly" to Americans. (*Courtesy National Archives*)

military; nonetheless, on March 20, Nana and thirty-three individuals (eighteen of them warriors) met Second Lieutenant John K. Houston near old Fort Webster. The talk ostensibly satisfied Nana. Four days later, Victorio arrived at the Mimbres River, claiming that he wanted peace if he were allowed to live on the Gila or the Mimbres; he even offered to fight hostiles and help recover stock. No matter how desperate, however, "he would not go to the Bosque or let his people." Cochise was a different story, admitted Victorio, declaring that he had attempted to convince him to make peace but the Chokonen leader "*does not wish it and will never be friendly more.*"[80] His country was still sparsely settled, and American troops had not yet come close to subjugating him.

Chapter 12

# CATCH THE WILD FOX

The year 1865 was destined to be Cochise's most active since the first year of his outbreak. We can follow his trail easier today than did the army and civilians who were so anxious to put an end to Apache hostilities, Cochise's in particular. Cochise's war continued because hostilities between him and Americans had become normal relations. For the first eighteen months after Coyuntura's death he had taken the offensive, but after the Apache Pass fight, his war had become more of a defensive one. Perhaps even more important, it had become a way of life for Cochise.

There was precedent for his actions. In 1846, Mexicans murdered his father, which touched off a decade of war before friendly relations were reestablished at Janos and Fronteras in 1857 because the Chokonens feared the presence of American troops in their country. Cochise was a pragmatist, yet this side of him emerged only after he came to accept that war was a losing proposition. His people had never been completely subjugated by anyone, Mexican or American, and in the mid 1860s there was no reason to think that U.S. troops would prove otherwise.

In January 1865 there was a large body of Apaches between Fort Buchanan and the San Pedro River. On January 4, thirty Indians attacked the mail express between Fort Bowie and Tubac; the two men escaped to San Pedro Crossing, but the Indians took their horses and mail. Eight days later the Apaches struck again, ambushing a wagon within a mile of Tubac and killing one man and wounding another. Captain John L. Merriam reported the incident, vowing to make a campaign against the hostiles, who deserved "prompt and severe punishment."[1]

A month later Cochise swept into the same area with a war party of seventy to eighty Chokonens. On February 17 they ambushed three people near the Santa Rita mines, killing William Wrightson and Gilbert W. Hopkins and capturing a Mexican boy. Shortly afterward, "Cochise and some 20 of his best and bravest warriors" assaulted the Santa Rita hacienda but were driven back by the sharpshooting of John T. Smith,[2] a former California volunteer, aided by a woman who later became his wife. As the besieged whites fired through loopholes, the "Indians began to drop off" and were driven back to the hills.[3] Swinging east, Cochise crossed the southern foothills of the Santa Ritas before moving north toward abandoned Fort Buchanan, where a vedette station had been established. On the afternoon of February 17 the war party thundered down on the station. Wrote Corporal Buckley:

> No signs of Indians for some time back. On the morning of attack one man went hunting (he is still missing), and in the afternoon two men went, as usual, to cut hay for the horses. I was sitting at the door of the house when an Indian shot me through the thigh. This was the first knowledge we had that the Indians were around. I drew my pistol and shot the Indian at the same time Private Berry shot another. The Indians now closed in large numbers (seventy or eighty) round the house, and soon had it on fire. We kept them off until the roof began to fall in . . . when I saw that the only chance for saving our lives was to force our way through the Indians. We broke from the house amidst a shower of arrows, . . . [we] kept them off till we got to the hills, when they gave up the chase, and we made it safely to Santa Rita.

The raiders made off with six horses, two carbines, 250 cartridges and about 200 rations.

The characteristics of the attack, the number of warriors involved, plus the fact that some of the plunder later was found in Chiricahua camps, leads to the probability of Cochise's presence.[4] Two days later, Apaches raided a ranch near Tubac but were repulsed with one warrior reportedly killed, which was of little consolation to the whites of that region. The Indians had driven everyone out only a few years before, and only within the past year had any semblance of mining and commerce been resumed.

Papago scouts told their agent, Mathias O. Davidson, that the Apaches were organizing a "force to strike a terrible blow in this vicinity." Davidson urged Carleton to send help in the form of arms and men, but by this time the general's responsibility no longer included Arizona and he was involved in a controversy with Dr. Steck, which merely prolonged the Apache war in the Southwest.[5]

After the vedette station raid, Cochise returned to the mountains along the border, and for the next month Chokonen and Nednhi bands invaded northern Mexico. Four raiding parties hit the Janos–Corralitos–Casas Grandes region, causing farmers to lose more than seven hundred total working days, according to José María Zuloaga. A garrison at Janos was sorely needed, he said. Little did he realize that matters would get worse.[6]

Toward the end of March, Cochise made plans for an expedition against Mexico, evidently to avenge relatives killed in the Animas Mountains the previous December. Runners were dispatched to Chokonen and Nednhi local groups, inviting them to join him in the Chiricahuas for a foray into Sonora. Since some of the troops from Bavispe were involved in the massacre at Dzisl-di-jole ("Round Mountain"), Cochise and probably Juh planned the ambush. Juan José Zozaya, an experienced observer on the Apache-Mexican scene, estimated the war party to number between 150 and 200 warriors, about the combined strength of Cochise's and Juh's bands.[7]

Cochise was almost certainly the leader of this war party because Victorio, who had sent a messenger to Cochise, reported the chief was absent "out on a scout."[8] This term could have meant that Cochise was out raiding with a few warriors or out with a major war party. The Chiricahuas designated both terms as "they are scouting about."[9] This time, he was at war.

They selected a site which lay along the road between Bavispe and Janos. The distance between these two towns was about sixty miles by road. The first twenty-five miles east from Bavispe traversed the northern tip of the great Sierra Madre—through innumerable canyons which offered the Indians ideal sites for ambush. In early April a party of eleven men left Bavispe for Janos. They followed the road east for about twelve miles to a place called Ta-

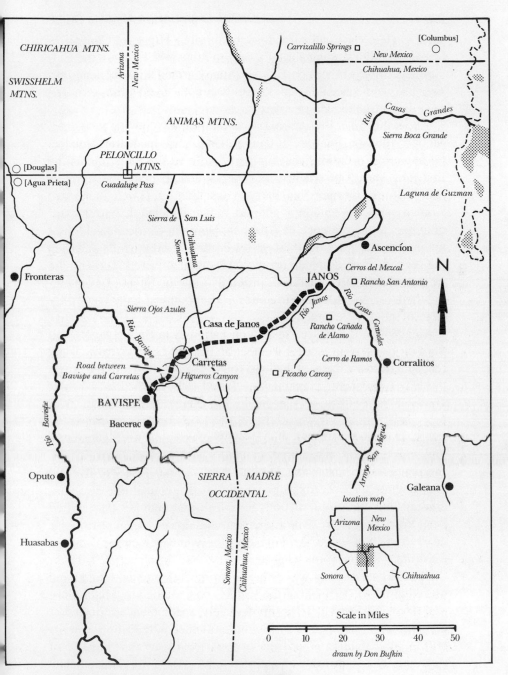

CHIRICAHUA MTNS.

SWISSHELM
MTNS.

Arizona
New Mexico

PELONCILLO
MTNS.

○ [Douglas]

○ [Agua Prieta]

Guadalupe Pass

ANIMAS MTNS.

Carrizalillo Springs  □

[Columbus] ○

New Mexico

Chihuahua, Mexico

Río          Casas          Grandes

Sierra Boca Grande

Laguna de Guzman

Sierra de  San Luis

Chihuahua

Sonora

Ascención ●

● Fronteras

Sierra Ojos Azules

Río Bavispe

Casa de Janos

JANOS

Cerros del Mezcal
□ Rancho San Antonio

Río Janos

Río Casas Grandes

Rancho Cañada
de Alamo

N

Road between
Bavispe and Carretas

Carretas

Higueros Canyon

Picacho Carcay

Cerro de Ramos

Corralitos ●

BAVISPE

Bacerac ●

Río Bavispe

Arroyo San Miguel

Oputo ●

SIERRA    MADRE

OCCIDENTAL

Galeana ●

Huasabas ●

Sonora, Mexico

Chihuahua, Mexico

location map

Arizona    New
Mexico

Sonora         Chihuahua

Scale in Miles

0     10     20     30     40     50

drawn by Don Bufkin

Location of Cochise's ambush, Sierra Madre

savare. Here the road turned north through Higueras Canyon to Carretas before veering abruptly east to Janos. At Tasavare the Chiricahuas, most of them on foot and many armed with rifles and revolvers, were concealed behind rocks on both sides of the pass. Ten men died instantly and one was captured.

About this time, Luis García's wagon train was moving west from Janos to Bavispe, unaware of danger. García had made the same trip on numerous occasions, but his party suffered the same fate as the first. On April 5 he reached the unoccupied Hacienda de Carretas and the next morning his party, consisting of eleven men, two women, and two children entered a place called Lagartos, still oblivious to the presence of Apaches. Here the Chiricahuas had set up another trap, with the first volley coming from the hills and then the second, from a hidden arroyo. All the men were killed and the women and children captured, probably with the intent of exchanging them for Apaches held in Sonora. The train was looted and sixty head of stock were captured.[10]

Meanwhile at Bavispe, seventeen nationals under Sergeant Juan Serraño had left on April 4 to meet and escort García's train. They reached Tasavare the next day and found the corpses from the previous day's massacre. Stunned but alerted, they pushed on to meet García's train but never reached it. At Higueras Canyon the war party attacked, and it was a virtual repetition of the two earlier attacks. Three men escaped, but thirteen lay dead and one wounded in Higueras Canyon. The three survivors fled east to Janos for reinforcements, which came in the form of Juan José Zozaya and twenty-three men. Zozaya's party cautiously scouted the site, concluding that every one of both Serraño's and García's parties had been killed by gunfire. The Indians' trail led north because Cochise crossed the border into Arizona after these engagements.[11]

Military affairs were changing in Arizona. On January 20, 1865, the District of Arizona was removed from Carleton's command and placed in the Department of the Pacific, commanded by Major General Irvin McDowell.[12] He immediately recommended Brigadier General John Sanford Mason,[13] who combined administrative skills with a good fighting record, as commander of the new District of Arizona. This approved, on February 20, McDowell, Mason, and John Noble Goodwin, Arizona's first governor, convened in San

Francisco. One of the items discussed was the Apache situation, and all concurred that Arizona's prosperity hinged on the Indians' subjugation. Whether they discussed Cochise is not known, yet shortly after Mason reached Arizona in May he recognized Cochise's importance by calling him "the very worst Indian on the continent."[14]

The new commander faced almost insurmountable problems. The number of troops was insufficient to conduct campaigns against the hostiles. Moreover, they lacked adequate clothing, supplies, and horses. Communication among the scattered military posts was sporadic and uncoordinated; consequently, few victories had been won. Yet Mason's arrival with reinforcements, plus the federal government's approval in raising volunteer troops, possibly averted another crisis in southern Arizona and may have turned the tide in Apache-Anglo relations, although no one could have realized it at the time.[15]

Mason reached Maricopa Wells on May 30 and confirmed recent reports that "the Indians really have possession of this Territory." He decided to view at first hand the situation in southern Arizona. On June 8 he arrived at Tubac, calling it a "worthless town" and apparently discussing the Apaches with citizens. He reported that the hostiles were living in the mountains north of the Gila, except for a few Indians in the Huachuca and Chiricahua mountains.[16]

By this time Arizona's new commander had formulated his Apache policy, one which reflected an understanding of the Indians and a willingness to provide for those truly subdued. He advocated a reservation policed by the military as the first step in controlling Indians who surrendered. The army would take the responsibility of feeding and clothing those who desired peace; for those who continued to resist, Mason advocated launching campaigns into their territory to destroy their rancherías and compel them to sue for peace.[17] As for Cochise, he continued to resist, moving his base of operations into northern Mexico when pressured to do so. He was not prepared to make peace as long as he could find refuge south of the border.

Mason continued his tour from Tubac, going to Fort Bowie, where "a salute in his honor [was] fired." Here he heard rumors that Cochise was camped north in the Sierra Bonita Range (Mount Graham), near the spot where Whitlock had surprised him the year before. Consequently, on June 26, Mason issued special orders instructing Lieutenant Colonel Clarence E. Bennett to take every available man and attack Cochise. Merejildo Grijalva would act as scout.[18]

Bennett departed that evening with forty-three men, three civilians, and two scouts, Merejildo and Lojinío, a tame Apache. Marching west out of the pass, the command turned north and followed an old Indian trail along the western foothills of the Dos Cabezas Mountains, called Nakibitci (Two Heads or His Two Tails) by the Chiricahuas. On June 29 the troops found a deserted ranchería which was thought to have been Cochise's; it had contained two to three hundred Indians. From here Bennett continued his march to Fort Goodwin, rested for a few days, and on the evening of July 2 set out to return to Bowie. En route, Merejildo discovered two more rancherías, one a Chokonen camp containing articles from the attack at Fort Buchanan five months before and the other belonging to Francisco, who after a skirmish had appeared in the mountains and "abused everybody, declared he would never make peace with the whites, and said the Apaches did not intend to." The command recovered twenty-seven beef cattle from Francisco's camp before arriving at Fort Bowie on July 6. Bennett recommended that "vigorous efforts should be made to annihilate the bands of Cochise and Francisco."[19]

In the meantime Cochise apparently had reached a decision. Sensing an American buildup of citizens, troops, and emigrants, he decided to move south into Sonora. In late June he and Francisco led a large war party of 150 warriors, which included recruits from the Western Apaches. His stay in the northern limits of Chiricahua country in 1863 and 1864 had gained him several allies, including Esh-kel-deh-silah, the influential White Mountain chief whom Cochise gave a Mexican captive.[20]

This war party, which apparently divided into two groups, wreaked much devastation throughout July 1865. On July 7 or 8, it attacked Ochoa's ranch, killing two women, three children, and one man. On July 11 it wiped out a German family named Amelung twenty-two miles east of Tucson at the Cienega and killed the mother, father, youngest child, and several Mexicans while capturing two boys. The booty from these attacks was supposed to be ten thousand dollars in gold plus several wagons and some stock.[21]

Cochise swung east and struck again two days later, this time against six soldiers southwest of present-day Willcox. This group had left Lieutenant Colonel Bennett, then en route to old Fort Breckenridge, to return to Bowie. It had gone but five miles when seventy-five Apaches waylaid them. The first volley killed a private, wounded two soldiers, and killed or wounded five of the six mounts. The soldiers fled, leaving the wagon, stock, and harness behind, and struggled on foot to the post, having suffered severely from thirst, and reached Fort Bowie on July 14. Captain Merriam vowed to avenge the attack, which he believed was committed by the Indians whom Bennett had fought a few weeks before. Yet his command was too dispersed: fourteen men were at Tubac, three at Fort Goodwin, three with the express, ten at San Pedro Crossing, and several were performing daily post duties. His morning report showed only ten privates on duty, and he feared that the Apaches would attack Bennett's command at old Fort Breckenridge.[22]

Bennett discovered a trail of one hundred Apaches on July 15, in all likelihood Cochise's party. Cochise, however, after attacking the troops near Croton Springs, plunged southwest against the ranches in the Santa Cruz county. During the next week he tried twice to run off the herd at the San Rafael ranch, a short distance north of the border, but was unsuccessful on both occasions.[23]

Unbeknownst to Cochise, Mason had ordered a "scout and exploration of the Huachuca Mountains and San Pedro Valley." In compliance, on July 19, 1865, Captain Hiram A. Messenger with thirty men, two citizens (Oscar Hutton and E. K. Brown), and two guides left the Mowry mines. What was to be a simple reconnaissance ended up in an encounter with an Apache war party led by Cochise himself. The first day out, Messenger found an Indian trail near Canelo Hills. On July 22 he followed it into Sonora, camping six miles south of the Arizona border near the deserted adobe presidio of Terrenate, some fifteen miles east of Santa Cruz. Late that day, two soldiers named Compton and Hicks went hunting. When they failed to return, Sergeant Kelly and Private Henry left to search for them. About 4 P.M. Compton and Hicks arrived at camp, reporting that ten Apaches had fired on them.

At once Captain Messenger took 15 men to search for Kelly and Henry. His small force came to a ridge; wisely, he deployed his troops before entering an ominous-looking canyon. At this point the Indians, estimated at between 100 and 150, fired on the troops, who fought a rear-guard action back to the main camp. The Apaches, "whooping like devils and pimping like bull frogs," surrounded the soldiers but respectfully stayed out of rifle range. The Apache leader (believed to be Cochise) was perched on a ridge and commanded by "motion of the hand to advance, retreat, close up or deploy." This continued for several hours until a heavy rain rendered the Apaches' bows ineffective. One soldier was wounded and the Indians suffered no reported casualties.

That night the Apaches moved north into the Huachucas and could be heard whooping and singing, evidently celebrating a victory. The next morning the bodies of Kelly and Henry were found stripped and lanced. Kelly had died instantly; Henry apparently made a good fight, as attested by the pools of blood found near him. For good measure the Indians had smashed his skull with a rock. The guides, Antonio and Marcial,[24] examined the arrows and pronounced them to be from the Chiricahuas (Chokonens), Pinals, Gilenos, Coyoteros, and Sierra Blancas, with the Chokonen arrows "much the greatest," indicating that Cochise had been joined by several Western Apaches in the fight. Marcial and Antonio, both of whom knew Cochise by sight, believed that he had led the war party and personally conducted the fight.[25]

News of Cochise's whereabouts soon was received by Captain Hiram Storrs Washburn,[26] who was in southern Arizona enlisting men for the Arizona Volunteers at the new Fort Mason.[27] Manuel Gallegos, a former Sonoran officer who had joined the volunteers with the rank of lieutenant, had just returned from a recruiting mission at Bacoachi with twenty-six Indian fighters. He probably brought word that Cochise was reported to be in the vicinity of Fronteras.[28]

The Arizona Volunteers were organized to fight Apaches. Although two companies were mustered in at Tubac, they never posed much of a problem to Cochise. Recruiting had begun in earnest about mid-July 1865, with the officers primarily Americans and the soldiers primarily natives of Sonora. Captain Washburn wrote Governor Goodwin and predicted that he would have his company prepared for "Apache hunting" by mid-August. He pointed out that he had enlisted eighty recruits, mainly Mexicans, which he believed would promote "amity and mutual confidence between the two nations." Moreover, he felt that their past experience in Apache campaigning boded well for the success of the volunteers.[29] His was not shared by all Americans. An Anglo who was well acquainted with the volunteers said "it was a mixed command a few white men [and] several of that variously tainted race called Mescican." Furthermore, some whites "looked upon these troops as scum."[30]

Sometime in August, Cochise notified authorities at Fronteras that he and his subordinate chiefs, Miguel Yrigóllen, Delgado, José Manda, Remigio, and Elías, would come in and make peace.[31] Four hundred Chokonens were expected. The Mexicans could not turn to the state government for help because the French had driven Governor Pesqueira and his supporters from Sonora. The invaders' army, situated at Hermosillo, had no intention of fighting Apaches, who, for most of 1865, found northern Sonora an "open, unprotected field . . . for their robberies and murders," according to an American living in Hermosillo.[32] Their options limited, the officials at Fronteras turned to the Arizona Volunteers for help.

Washburn realized that capturing Cochise would be a delicate mission, but the end would justify the means. Thus he had no compunction about using tactics which would have made Baylor or Carleton proud:

> Chicusa [Cochise] now that he is made rich from the robbery at the Cienega, July 11, wants to have a good spree and a few fancy articles of half civilized life. So as usual on occasions of a full treasury he has been in to Fronteras soliciting peace. Fronterans understand well the game, partly from fear, but chiefly from a desire to barter their mescal and other surplus articles for the coin, pistols and various other articles acquired by the Apaches jurisprudence, gave their consent and immediately sent word to me that the celebrated Apache general Choqueese will soon appear before them . . . with 400 Indians. . . . At first these warriors will be very suspicious and will only fall into the snare by the most careful and astute dissimulation, which with liberal portions of mescal will soon gentle them, so that by the most cautious and most careful concert on our part and that of the authori-

ties at Fronteras we may almost safely calculate in getting nearly the whole of these Indians without the loss of a man.[33]

Subsequent developments forced a change in these plans.

Like most Americans, Washburn viewed Cochise as the key and quickly became obsessed with either subduing or capturing him. He became increasingly frustrated after receiving definite information that Cochise was near Fronteras, but he was helpless to take action. Washburn's enthusiasm waned as he became hamstrung by a lack of money, clothing, guns, and supplies. On September 1 he reported that neither arms nor supplies had been furnished and that every man had become ill from "eating crude fruit and sleeping on the wet ground without blankets." In addition, his company had not even been formally mustered because the official documents had not arrived. More than anything, it seemed that the conscientious officer feared that some other command would capture Cochise and deprive him of credit.[34]

Perhaps had Washburn's command been equipped and turned loose against Cochise, as it would be during the winter of 1866 against the Indians of central Arizona, the Chiricahuas could have been routed and forced across the border. Instead, his volunteers remained inactive and Cochise moved farther east to the vicinity of Janos. Here in late August two large bands, probably Cochise's Chokonens and Juh's Nednhis, were encamped, which forced a party of Americans to alter their route to avoid the Indians.[35]

By October, Cochise had returned to the Chiricahuas and Washburn inquired about reward money if he could capture him or any other Apache leader. He claimed that Cochise's whereabouts was "well known and my men can take him if they can get arms." He seemed determined to orchestrate a dramatic success for himself, having concluded that seizing Cochise would give him an excuse to visit Washington, where he had personal business. He wrote Governor Goodwin on October 9, 1865: "I suppose if I will catch your old Wild Fox Kechise, General Mason will give me an order to take him to you in Washington."[36]

That fall several Apache leaders discussed peace, including Cochise, who was in the vicinity of Fort Bowie in late October. With cold weather approaching, perhaps he was prepared to consider a temporary cease-fire with the hope of living unmolested in the Chiricahuas. He was undoubtedly aware that his two dependable allies, Francisco's Coyoteros and Victorio's Chihennes, were also discussing terms at Fort Goodwin and Pinos Altos, respectively.

Cochise's unexpected arrival at Fort Bowie and his talk of a truce puzzled Major James Gorman, who had been ordered to make war, not talk peace. On October 30 many Chokonens were reported in the hills overlooking Fort Bowie; white peace flags and smoke signals were visible everywhere. The next day they reappeared and their leader, perhaps Cochise, "jabbered and howled industriously." Major Gorman, who shared the army's prevailing dislike of Indians, claimed that "he had no authority to make a treaty," actually believing that the Apaches deserved to be shot. Feelings had not changed much in four years.

Shortly after this, an officer and a civilian left the post and met the Chiricahuas, telling them to return in twelve days, at which time Major Gorman would have received orders from his superiors. Over the next two days, several Chokonen women entered the post and were fed and clothed. Unfortunately, no reports have been found to determine what transpired, but they were definitely identified as Cochise's people and he undoubtedly was in the neighborhood.[37]

Regardless of what was said to the Indians, Major Gorman decided to lead an expedition against them. He left on November 1 with thirty-four men for the Pinery, ostensibly to cut wood. Although Gorman failed to mention it in his report, a civilian eyewitness wrote that two large wagons, normally used for gathering wood, were concealed with soldiers so as not to arouse the Indians' suspicion. Evidently the strategy worked. The day after he left, five Apache women entered the post and remained all night.[38]

Meanwhile, Gorman marched through the Chiricahuas, camping by day and moving by night, perhaps trying to vindicate himself from past allegations of inactivity, incompetence, and drunkenness. Early on the morning of November 5, Merejildo Grijalva located a Chokonen ranchería, which he assumed was Cochise's because a sentinel had been posted on a high ridge and Cochise was one of the few Indians known to take this precaution. Preparations made, Gorman left eight men with his horses and took the remainder on foot toward the encampment. They succeeded in slipping past the lookout before he discovered them and warned the village. The Indians quickly scattered up the mountains, while the troops swept down on the ranchería and indulged in target practice against their foes. They found another ranchería about a half-mile away, but Gorman remarked disappointedly that "the Birds had flown leaving everything behind them." Seven Indians were killed and one soldier wounded in the fight, which reportedly took place sixty miles south of Fort Bowie. This is certainly wrong because that would place the engagement almost in Sonora. The fight occurred in the southwestern Chiricahua Mountains probably some thirty-five to forty straight-line map miles, which would be around sixty by trail.

Gorman's command captured many things which implicated Cochise's people in the raids of the previous winter and summer. Included were several items from the attack on the vedette station at Fort Buchanan on February 17; a saddle belonging to Mr. Wrightson, killed the same day; and several articles taken from the German family killed at the Cienega in July. Many native items were found and destroyed, including large quantities of mescal, dried meat, baskets, and cooking utensils. Merejildo believed this was Cochise's camp (and his opinion was rather conclusive evidence), as did Major Gorman, who contended that "Cochise and his band have committed more depredations than any other equal numbers of Indians in this part of the territory."[39]

Whether this was Cochise's local group is not important; the significance is how he might have perceived the attack. The Chokonen had made peace overtures, and admittedly it was highly improbable that anything meaningful could have been concluded. In all likelihood, a peace of any duration could not have been consummated, for Cochise had not been sufficiently whipped and the Americans would not have allowed him to use Arizona as a base to raid into Mexico. Yet an officer from Bowie had told the Indians to wait twelve days for a response to their proposals; instead, Major Gorman had seized this opportunity to make a campaign in which he killed seven Chokonens, some of them probably women and children. Gorman's campaign erased any thoughts that Cochise, if indeed he was sincere, might have harbored about an armistice.

Cochise also shared in the misunderstanding. He had waged a ruthless war against Americans for the previous five years and in the past year had been as hostile as ever, sparing neither women nor children. Now, with winter approaching and no assistance available from a French-controlled Mexico, he opted to give the Americans a try, perhaps hoping to camp in the Chiricahuas as he had done in the past.

Despite Gorman's success, Cochise remained encamped in the Chiricahuas during the winter of 1865–66. Although troops had scouted the mountains twice in the past sixteen months, they had not conducted a winter campaign, so Cochise could not have expected Mason to conclude that a major campaign against the Chiricahuas was warranted and necessary. Mason made plans for simultaneous operations both east and west of the Dragoons, hoping to deprive Cochise of using that area as sanctuary. In mid-December, Colonel Charles W. Lewis left Fort Mason for the Huachuca Mountains, where Cochise "the Chiricahua chief and famous rifleman" was reported to be living.[40] Three detachments scouted along the San Pedro and the Huachucas and Dragoons but found no Indians. Lack of good footwear forced one division to curtail its scout. The second force, under Captain Porfirio Jimeno, ambushed a group of hostiles at Sulphur Springs on December 24, killing one Indian and wounding two. The third command scouted the Dragoons and found a deserted camp in Cochise's west stronghold before returning to Fort Mason in late December. Replenishing their supplies, the troops returned to Sulphur Springs and united with Jimeno, whose force had been bivouacked for several days.

Next, Lewis decided to examine the Chiricahuas. He detoured to Fort Bowie, replaced Marcial Gallegos with Merejildo Grijalva, and on January 6 plunged south. But the Apaches were vigilant. Two days out the Americans found a large ranchería in the southern Chiricahuas, perhaps the vicinity of Rucker Canyon, where Gorman had found them two months before. It had been deserted two days before. Even so, sixty to seventy warriors could be observed in the high mountains; the women and children had fled into northern Mexico, with the men following the next day. Lewis followed the trail of these fleeing Chiricahuas into Sonora, halting at Fronteras, where he found the people destitute because the "Indians had robbed them of everything." He abandoned the pursuit and returned to Fort Mason. The command's disorganization and Captain Jimeno's lack of initiative "deprived us the pleasure of finding the whole Chiricahua tribe of Indians at home," lamented an officer, although Cochise's people probably would have detected the force even if Jimeno's command had been more aggressive. Very few could come up with Cochise when he was on guard. After Gorman's attack, he was not about to be surprised again.[41]

The winter campaign was over, a dismal military failure which did nothing to improve the Indian situation. Yet it was a moral victory in the eyes of General McDowell in San Francisco, who unrealistically claimed triumph because of "driving Cochise's band into Sonora."[42]

Other factors in late 1865 also muddied the waters. These further shaped Cochise's perceptions about Americans and certainly were instrumental in his decision to spend much of the next three years living in Mexico, beyond the reach of U.S. soldiers. He was beginning to lose some of his allies. First, on November 10 troops at Fort Goodwin gunned down Eastern White Mountain leader Francisco, allegedly while trying to escape. Francisco had been imprisoned for his part in the Cienega attack the previous summer. Moreover, a falling out of sorts had come between Cochise's Chokonens and the White Mountain and Pinal bands of the Western Apaches. Both were said to be "bitter against the Co Chise's band of Indians who were undoubtedly the perpetrators of all the emigrant road massacres" in the past few years.[43]

At Pinos Altos in late 1865, Victorio's Chihennes repeated their peace attempts of the previous spring, hoping for an alternative to Bosque Redondo or extermination. What followed became known as the Bean Treaty, either because the Apaches were served a dinner of beans or because of the presence of Sam Bean, an early settler at Pinos Altos. Several Chihennes ventured into Pinos Altos with peaceful intentions, and in a premeditated attack the Americans killed three Apaches while "drinking coffee in a house," with results which may be imagined very easily. According to one account, Victorio himself was "shot in the cheek." About three weeks later he avenged this attack, slaying four soldiers and wounding another near Fort Cummings.[44] Incidents like Gorman's attack, Francisco's execution, and the Bean Treaty convinced Cochise and Victorio that

Americans favored a continuation of the war and that the fighting must go on.

Driven out of Arizona, Cochise moved into northwestern Chihuahua to the vicinity of Janos, which a large number of Apaches had surrounded in mid-January 1866 and cut off communications. Word was somehow transmitted to Lieutenant Colonel Edward Willis at Fort Selden, situated on the east bank of the Río Grande twelve miles north of Doña Ana. Willis obtained permission from Mexico to enter Chihuahua "for the purpose of hunting Apache Indians." Taking forty-five men, he marched east to Fort Cummings and received reinforcements of twenty-five men. From here the command proceeded south to Janos, but the Apaches, whom Willis believed to be Mimbres (Chihennes) and other bands, detected them and fled to the mountains. Since the Chihennes were active in the Pinos Altos region at this time, the bands most likely involved were Cochise's Chokonens, freshly arrived from the Chiricahuas, and Juh's Nednhis, although there is no tangible proof.[45]

Meanwhile, in Arizona, Brigadier General Mason was being assailed from all sides. His lack of success against the Apaches had generated an expected uproar among citizens, the territorial press, and even within the military. All recognized that the Apache situation had not improved during the first year of Mason's stint, although the Arizona Volunteers had accomplished much against the Indians of central Arizona.[46] In the south, however, Cochise's Chokonens continued to raid. The troops were disparaged by remarks that they "cannot protect themselves much less than people. . . . Few or no Arizonians die a natural death."[47]

Everyone had a solution and most continued to advocate extermination. The military lacked resources and a penurious Congress, more concerned about Reconstruction, paid little attention to Arizona. One ingenious individual advocated a plan in which the United States would purchase from Mexico the lower peninsula of California for ten million dollars. The next step would require an expenditure of thirty million dollars to round up and drive all the Indians there. Finally, the government would place a cordon of forts to maintain order, similar to the Spanish presidio system of the 1700s. If the Apaches misbehaved, the government could withhold food and starve them to death. This policy was suggested by a writer in San Francisco, no doubt sensitive to Apache lifestyle and culture. Indeed, perhaps he should have proposed it to Cochise, who, if he could be found, might have jumped at the opportunity![48] Fortunately, this lamebrained scheme was not considered at department headquarters of the Military Division of the Pacific, commanded by Major General Henry Wager Halleck.[49] Yet Halleck conceded that Mason's winter campaign was a failure and "too extensive for his means." The general implied that Mason failed to understand the Apaches' mode of warfare, so he sent Brigadier General McDowell to Arizona to investigate and to recommend a solution.[50]

Other methods of dealing with the hostiles were considered, including using friendly Apaches. In early 1866 the Pinal and Coyotero Western Apaches continued friendly relations with the Americans at Fort Goodwin. In conference with Lieutenant Colonel Robert Pollock, they found it convenient to blame Cochise's followers as the "perpetrators of all the emigrant road massacres" of the past few years. In fact, Pollock believed he could induce these Indians to act as guides against the hostile Chokonens.[51] In Tubac, citizens went a step further, hiring tame Apaches as mercenaries against their incorrigible brethren and also, according to one report, paying them one hundred dollars for each scalp brought in.[52]

In early spring 1866, Cochise laid plans for a foray (originating from either northern Mexico or the Chiricahua Mountains) against the ranches in the Santa Cruz and Sonoita Valley. In April, after making several stock raids, the Chokonen war party besieged the San Rafael ranch, located a few miles southeast of the junction of Sonoita Creek and the Santa Cruz River. The owner of the hacienda, Rafael Saavedra, and his servants retreated to the main house at the first fire. The Apaches burned the smaller structures and captured a young woman who cried out, "For God's sake, save me." Against his family's objections, Saavedra heroically left the hacienda and somehow saved the woman but was killed in the process, or so the story goes. The ranch soon was abandoned. Thomas Yerkes lost sixty-six head of stock in this raid and claimed that Cochise's band was the perpetrator. Juan de López, a servant at the ranch, even identified Cochise, whom he believed was wounded slightly. It was but one more of the countless times Cochise was reported killed or wounded.[53]

Shortly after this raid Esteban Ochoa hired, armed, and equipped tame Apaches to track the hostiles. These Indians felt much antipathy toward their unpacified relatives, claiming their sole purpose in life was to avenge their own dead, killed by the wild Apaches. Accordingly, a party of twenty-five left Tubac in late April and picked up the hostiles' trail, reportedly Cochise's Chokonens. Somewhere in southeastern Arizona or northern Sonora, they found the ranchería of Cochise, "Chief of the Coyoteros de Chiricahuas," and attacked it the first week of May. When the fight broke out, one man, evidently a chief, tried to rally his warriors but was killed and scalped, as were three others. The ears were cut off, although one was left behind "for the devil to take to the dead Apache."[54]

Three weeks later Cochise retaliated. On May 31 he led at least 100 warriors (two other reports put the number at a ridiculous 260 and 300 to 400) and stole Camp Wallen's herd, which was grazing three miles from the garrison. This post, established only three weeks earlier on the north bank of Babocomari Creek, was situated just north of the Huachuca Range and south of the Whetstones. In theory, the post was supposed to "prevent hostile incursions of Sonora Apaches and the band of Cochise." Apaches swooped down from the east, south, and west and made off with fifty-seven horses, ten to twelve mules, and seventy-two head of cattle; only five horses remained at the post. Sergeant Henry I. Yohn and five others, joined later by a civilian, pursued the Apaches. Half a century later, Yohn recalled that the hostiles tried to surround his party but failed to do so. At this point, "Cochise was pointed out to me. He was commanding the Indians and rode a magnificient black horse."[55]

The next day, Captain Isaac Rothermel Dunkelberger, fifty-four troops, and sixteen tame Apaches left Fort Mason and arrived at Wallen on June 3. The scouts worked the trail for some fifty miles along the Arizona-Sonora line before the Indians scattered like quail. The scouts reported that the raiders were Cochise's band and numbered "eighty to one hundred warriors," a far cry from the three to four hundred estimated by Camp Wallen's commander.[56]

The large number of Apaches horrified the commander, Captain

William Harvey Brown, who, thought one soldier, "possessed very few soldierly qualifications."[57] He dreaded an Apache assault on his post, knowing that his men were unequipped to resist. Brown had seventy-two men: sixteen without carbines, sixty without cartridge boxes, and thirty-three without sabers. In a forceful letter to his superiors, he protested that "it is very wrong to expose men thus in an Indian country,"[58] although one wonders whether he would have felt the same way if his troopers had been sufficiently equipped. Brown was also afraid that a large band of Apaches could easily overrun the camp. His sincere concern reflected his lack of understanding of Apache guerrilla warfare, for Cochise had neither the inclination, nor the patience, nor the firepower necessary to put Wallen under a prolonged siege. The camp had a quiet summer and fall.

Cochise had little, if any, contact with American troops for the remainder of 1866. Mason's winter campaign had failed and the Arizona Volunteers had been discharged during the summer. On June 10, Mason was replaced by Lieutenant Colonel Henry Davies Wallen, who relinquished command to Colonel Charles Swain Lovell two months later. Lovell lasted only until November, when McDowell decentralized the District of Arizona into five subdistricts, hoping each would become more effective in fighting Indians.[59]

These administrative changes had little effect on Cochise, who remained in northern Mexico for the rest of the year. Raids into the United States furnished subsistence and trading material at Janos and at Casas Grandes, where it was said that Apaches showed up like clockwork every Saturday to trade plunder and even gold for lead and bullets.[60]

In August, Cochise himself was seen by Francisco Martínez, a Sonoran citizen, who was dumbfounded by the reception the Chiricahuas had received. He said Cochise, "with his entire band and a great deal of stock," showed up at Janos and was treated "very well" by the authorities. In fact, Martínez reported, they said they "were very happy to see him." A friend of Martínez tried to buy his own horse, which had been stolen by the Indians in Sonora, but they refused to trade unless they were given powder or ammunition, both of which reportedly flowed freely at Janos.[61]

Naturally Sonoran citizens became alarmed at the increase in illicit trade at Janos; they recalled the consequences of the treaties of 1842, 1850, and 1857. Just as predictably, raids into Sonora continued, and the Chokonens and Nednhis who were trading at Janos were blamed. A large band of Apaches swept through the streets of Fronteras on August 30, killed a man and a woman, and ran off some stock. Cochise may have been shot in the neck during this fight. On September 10 another raiding party, probably the same one, ambushed and killed two men near Cuquiarachi. Outcries from Sonoran officials followed, blaming the people at Janos for harboring the hostiles and for providing a market for trade. Sonora would suffer "double than what we had previously suffered" forecast an observer from Bavispe. In mid-November, seventy Apaches raided Bavispe, and the stock was believed to have found its way to Janos.[62]

Chihuahua also suffered at the hands of Apaches. In late August a war party said to number two hundred overran the town of Cruces in the district of Namaquipa. More than twenty people were killed, several wounded, and several captured.[63] Raids of this nature, combined with Sonoran complaints about fraudulent activities at Janos, ultimately prompted Chihuahua to act. In December Cayetano Ozeta led a group of volunteers from Guerrero, in southwestern Chihuahua in the foothills of the Sierra Madre. After a tedious scout they succeeded in surprising Cochise's camp on December 22 at the Espia Hill, some seven or eight miles southeast of the Boca Grande Mountains northeast of Janos. They killed five warriors and one woman and captured four others.[64] Even Cochise's sanctuary in northwestern Chihuahua was no longer safe, and his band once again scattered north into the Chiricahua and Animas mountains, hoping to steer clear of both American and Mexican troops. It would not be an easy task.

# Chapter 13

# TOO MANY MEXICANS

Throughout 1867 and 1868, Cochise maintained his pragmatic philosophy of avoiding Americans, living primarily in the mountains of northern Mexico, southeastern Arizona, and southwestern New Mexico. From these safe retreats Chokonen and Nednhi parties continued to raid southern Arizona, Sonora and, to a lesser extent, Chihuahua.

Of Cochise little was known. His encounters with Americans were fought only on his terms, and few lived to identify him, adding to the mystique which surrounded him. Many people wondered whether he was living, while others thought "he had taken up his abode in northern Mexico."[1] This uncertainty notwithstanding, practically every report, whether it originated from the army, the Bureau of Indian Affairs, newspapers or pioneers, concurred on one thing: Cochise was the most able, most intelligent, and most hostile of the Apaches. Subjugate him and only then would peace come to southeastern Arizona.

After the attack at Boca Grande in late 1866, Cochise's people scattered into the Animas and Chiricahua mountains. In January 1867 he organized a war party against Sonora, intending, according to a captive who was with the Apaches, "to make many prisoners in order to exchange for their own people captured by the troops of Chihuahua," obviously a reference to Cayetano Ozeta's triumph.[2]

In early February a large band of Chiricahuas, possibly led by

Cochise, attacked seven men near Cumpas, killing four and capturing two. One, a boy named Priciliano Rivera, inexplicably turned up at Moctezuma six days later; somehow he had escaped or had been turned loose by the Apaches. His story was interesting. He declared that the Apaches numbered fifty-five, were accompanied by a citizen from Janos who helped "plan the campaign," and intended to ambush travelers between Moctezuma and Granados. The unlikely presence of a renegade Mexican was a common occurrence in the late 1860s and perhaps explained why the Indians had increased their attacks on American mail riders. These cutthroats understood the value of the money which the mail usually contained.[3]

With Sonora aware of his presence, Cochise diverted his operations to Arizona. In mid-February it was reported that "he was on the warpath with his entire force and some of his men could be seen daily from Fort Bowie." Undoubtedly they were responsible for the death of mail carrier Charles Fisher on February 19, 1867, seven miles east of Bowie.[4] Cochise's next target was the Mowry mines, which contained a fine cache of weapons (thirty repeating rifles and several Colt revolvers) plus an abundant supply of ammunition stored in the main house. Several eyewitnesses reported that Cochise led the Apaches, who, according to various estimates, numbered between forty and eighty warriors.

On the morning of the fight, five Americans were at the mines: Thomas Yerkes, Robert Reed, Richard Doss, Edward Marcy, and Edward Hunting. Yerkes and Reed were visitors; the others were employees at the mine. Early that morning Yerkes and Doss went outdoors and saw two Indians with rifles aimed at them. They fled toward the house; Yerkes made it safely, but Doss was wounded "severely in the legs." This was the beginning of a brisk fight between the Indians and the five whites.

Within minutes the Chiricahuas surrounded the house, took possession of the corral, and climbed onto the roof. Edward Marcy was "shot dead through a window." Yet the whites "had plenty of arms" and, shooting from loopholes, "kept up a regular fight." Next Cochise tried to set the buildings on fire but failed. About ten o'clock Oscar Buckalew, the mail contractor, arrived. He boldly penetrated the Indians' line and dashed into the fortress, but not before the Apaches killed his horse and shot him in the leg, a wound serious enough to require amputation later. Soon afterward Oscar Hutton and another man approached and observed the fight. They fled for help at once, with the Apaches in hot pursuit for a few miles. Knowing they would bring soldiers, Cochise withdrew to a nearby hill, baffled by the firepower from the few whites in the house. Yerkes and Buckalew both heard the chief, whom they assumed was Cochise, deliberating with his men. Expecting reinforcements, Cochise broke off the engagement.

In the meantime, the two whites dashed into Santa Cruz, gathered a force of thirty-one citizens, and sent messengers to Camp Wallen. At once Captain William Harvey Brown collected forty-four men and launched a rather indifferent pursuit, earning him the disdain of McDowell at department headquarters in San Francisco. Learning the details of the encounter, Brown termed it "an unusual daring Apache fight." He concluded that Cochise undoubtedly was responsible because of the nature of the combat and "the large number of good arms" displayed by the Indians, although an eyewitness claimed that only one-fourth of the Apaches had firearms. Thomas Yerkes said he learned from other Indians that "Cochise himself was there." By the time reinforcements arrived, the main body had crossed the border into Sonora, and soon after that Cochise returned to his base camp in the Chiricahuas.[5]

During the spring of 1867, Mexican and American military leaders were drawing up plans to take the offensive against Cochise. No longer contending with the French, Sonora directed her energies against the Chiricahuas living in northern Mexico, with Pesqueira announcing that his soldiers would pursue and exterminate Apaches. With this in mind, he reestablished garrisons at Bavispe, Bacoachi, and Santa Cruz. Atypically, Chihuahua cooperated and the two states carried their campaigns into southeastern Arizona and southwestern New Mexico, an area which had been unscouted by American patrols and was off limits to Mexican troops.[6]

Concurrent with Mexico's offensive, the new commander at Tucson, Colonel Thomas Leonidas Crittenden,[7] designated Cochise public enemy No. 1 and laid plans to subdue him. His good intentions notwithstanding, he lacked officers and men in his district to keep continual patrols in the field. Those few penetrating Apachería were easily eluded by Cochise. Fort Bowie, the one post from which aggressive scouting might have paid dividends, was inadequately garrisoned throughout the mid-1860s, having an average of only one officer and forty-five men. The garrison was strengthened after a military inspector recommended in early 1866 that "the operations of Cochise and his band are the terror of the Southern country. It is my opinion that the troops here [Fort Bowie] could be employed to advantage in going for him."[8]

Even with the additional manpower, scouts were made typically in response to Apache raids and had only a minute chance of overtaking any hostiles.[9] Nonetheless, Crittenden succeeded in putting several detachments in the field, which, although not injuring Cochise, did force him south along the border, where he was vulnerable to Mexican campaigns.

The first victory over the Chiricahuas came in early April 1867 when Chihuahuan troops under Cayetano Ozeta, one of the most active of Mexico's Indian hunters, followed a trail into the southern Chiricahuas. Here they found a Chokonen or Nednhi local group headed by Tuscas and succeeded in killing or capturing the entire encampment. Ozeta's troops killed twelve (including eight warriors), captured twenty-six, and recovered a captive from Arispe. They also confiscated twelve horses and mules and recovered articles of United States mail, implicating this group in the death of mail carrier Charles Fisher some six weeks earlier a few miles east of Fort Bowie. This was a severe blow to Cochise, who was in the Chiricahuas but arrived too late to give Ozeta a fight.[10]

In late April Sonoran troops captured an Apache who admitted that he was en route to the Chiricahuas to join Cochise on a campaign. Cochise had sent runners to other Chiricahua groups calling for "a great reunion," which attracted not only his Chokonens but some of the Nednhis living in the Teras Mountains in Sonora. Many warriors flocked to his summons and joined him in a foray into Mexico to avenge Ozeta's victory.[11]

While most of the Chiricahuas were raiding in Mexico, the subdistrict commander at Tucson had Cochise on his mind. On May 10, 1867, Captain Brown, always sensitive to the opinion of his superiors, wrote Crittenden suggesting a "large party of troops at some suitable time to visit the Chiricahua or Guadelupe Mountains in search of Cochise and his band."[12] That June, Crittenden grumbled that he had hoped "to drive off or destroy Chiz [Cochise] and his band," yet his forces were incapable of an offensive. His only three company posts were needed to supervise the Western Apaches.[13]

While Crittenden contemplated taking the offensive, Cochise beat him to the punch. Having returned from Mexico, he led a party of seventy warriors on raids near Tubac. On June 13, Chiricahuas attacked a wagon train, killing one man, wounding two others, and running off sixty head of cattle. The next day they ran off the horses of the Papago scouts at Calabasas and raided a ranch in the vicinity.

Lieutenant Colonel Edward McGarry, commanding the Subdistrict of Santa Cruz, which had been created specifically to subjugate Cochise, ordered out detachments from Tubac and Camp Wallen. This unenlightened officer, who had a powerful friend (McDowell) at department headquarters and would soon be relieved of command because of public intoxication, authorized the unnecessarily harsh measure of hanging Indian captives. Fortunately, the scheme was not implemented and his superiors subsequently revoked his orders. In any event, the command from Wallen, guided by Merejildo Grijalva under Lieutenant Edward Johnston Harrington, started in hot pursuit and on June 21 overtook a small group of Indians in the southwestern Chiricahuas, killing three warriors and wounding one.[14]

Harrington's dogmatic scout was interesting because it proved that a U.S. command led by a tenacious officer with a skillful guide could damage Cochise. He reported:

> On the morning of Friday, the 21st . . . as the command was rounding a curve in the Chiricahuas an Indian on horseback was seen riding leisurely along . . . evidently unaware of our presence. The order was given to charge, but simultaneously the Indian discovered us and with a loud yell dashed away at full speed toward the rancheria which came in sight a moment later . . . The majority of our horses being barely able to strike a trot we were unable to catch up with them before they . . . escaped up the side of the mountains, which it was impossible for us to follow with any show of success. . . . [Yet] the chase was kept up with the result of killing three Apaches and wounding it is supposed mortally a fourth. . . .
>
> . . .The command withdrew to the rancheria. Here everything was destroyed. The lodges, twelve in number were found to be filled with the greatest abundance of everything used by an Indian. At least a five

month supply of roasted mescal was burned together with hundreds
of dressed skins and hides. . . . I would state that the force of Indians
that made this attack . . . numbered no less than seventy warriors and
belonged to the band of Cochise. . . . They did not, however, all keep
together but separated into different bands some making their way
into Sonora and the others, numbering about twenty, returning to
their rancherias which we attacked.[15]

Harrington's success led Crittenden to conclude that Cochise
could be found in the Chiricahua Mountains. If so, he believed that
troops could "probably get a fight," although first they had to find
him. With this in mind, in July he planned a pincerslike campaign
"to destroy Chachiz and his band" by converging on the Chiricahua
Mountains. He ordered McGarry to take a force from Tubac and
proceed east into the Chiricahuas; at the same time, he directed Captain Guido Ilges from Camp Grant to scout southeast and "if practicable to go as far as the Chiricahua Mountains." Ideally the two
commands would flush out any hostiles before they eventually
united.[16]

Cochise detected the commands and easily eluded the troops,
probably crossing the border into Sonora. As a frustrated soldier
tersely reported on the essence of Apache hunting: "Chase them and
they sink into the ground or somehow vanish, look behind and they
are peeping over a hill at you."[17] In spite of what Crittenden
thought, Cochise and his Apache guerrillas would fight only on their
terms unless they were cornered and given no alternative.

Once in Mexico the Chiricahuas faced a revitalized Sonoran army
led by the capable and indefatigable Lieutenant Colonel Angel
Elías, who had countered Apache inroads with regular patrols along
the border. On July 2, 25 mounted Indians surprised a small party
near Caguilloña and killed two men before fleeing north toward the
Chiricahuas.[18] A week later Elías headed a mixed force of 137 cavalry and infantry from Fronteras in a sweep for hostiles along the
line. After two weeks of uneventful scouting, the Sonorans cleaned
out a small ranchería north of Agua Prieta, probably in the Perilla
Mountains, killing 3 warriors and 6 women and capturing 6 children. Elías returned to Fronteras and, keeping the pressure on, sent
out another force of 104 men. It departed on July 19 and four days

later discovered Apaches and killed 2 more. Whether these were
from Cochise's local group is unknown; the important consideration
was that Sonora had taken the offensive.[19]

So would the Apaches. On August 2, Apaches "in great numbers" killed two men and three women along the road between
Huepac and Arispe. Nine days later, forty-three Apaches attacked
farmers near Bacoachi and murdered one man and wounded another. Two days later, on August 13, this same band ambushed another man near Bacoachi. On the last day of August a large group
deprived Cumpas of its stock, although national troops recovered
most of the animals. The Sonoran press labeled the hostiles "a
mournful plague" and claimed that the state had been unable to
drive them out or contain their incursions. North of the border, the
*Alta California* in San Francisco, wrote that the Apaches, forced
south by American troops, were overrunning Sonora. The country
around Fronteras and Bacoachi was ravaged, according to an
American observer. By that fall it was reported that Apache hostilities in Sonora were worse than at any other time since 1861.[20]

Typically, Sonora pointed its finger at others for its own inability
to protect its people. A common charge heard along the frontier was
that the Americans armed and provisioned the hostiles. While some
of the Western Apaches probably raided from Fort Goodwin and
some unscrupulous traders continued their clandestine traffic in
guns and ammunition, those complaining should have scrutinized
their own nation, particularly at Janos. Cochise had continued on
good terms there, which was beneficial to him and to the citizens of
Janos, who could travel, plant, and raise stock without fear of attack. That fall, investigators gathered testimony at Bavispe and
Moctezuma from citizens who had observed the trade conducted at
Janos.[21]

The inquiry focused on affairs between Janos citizens and the
Chiricahua bands, an oft-repeated complaint. The commission concluded that an informal peace existed for the sole purpose of
crooked trade, that the Apaches traded stolen Sonora livestock for
guns and ammunition, and that these inhabitants went so far as to
warn the hostiles of Mexican campaigns. Furthermore, a well-
defined distribution network had been established to dispose of

stolen stock, with the booty inevitably finding its way across the U.S. border to El Paso or New Mexico.

These charges echoed the allegations made by Elías González in 1844 and Carrasco in 1851; like those, they were certainly well founded. The investigation's results were forwarded to Chihuahua's government. In early 1868 it responded and regarrisoned Janos, which had not seen permanent troops since their withdrawal in early 1858. This action shut down one of Cochise's last reliable places to trade, at least for the time being.[22]

The importance of this action should not be overlooked or underestimated. The redeployment of troops at Janos abruptly interrupted the Chiricahuas' trafficking in Mexican and American booty in exchange for guns, ammunition, and liquor. This notorious market, characterized by one American officer as a den of thieves, had been accessible to Cochise throughout the 1860s. Its reoccupation was significant in that, combined with Sonora's aggressive campaigns, he would eventually be forced to seek refuge in Arizona.[23]

For part of the winter of 1867–68, Cochise camped at a place the Indians called Dziltilcil, or Black Mountain, otherwise known as Sarampion in the Peloncillo Range, long a favorite Chiricahua retreat. From here he may have had a hand in the parties that harassed Fort Bowie fifty miles to the northwest. On November 5, 1867, the commanding officer at Fort Bowie, Lieutenant John Cuthbert Carroll, and mail rider John Slater were decoyed into an ambush and killed a few miles west of the post. Second Lieutenant Edward Buckley Hubbard initially attributed the outrage to Apaches from Fort Goodwin. Although many warriors undoubtedly slipped away from time to time, some joining the hostile Chiricahuas, this deed probably was the work of Cochise's band. He was known to have been in the vicinity, and it took place in the heart of Chiricahua country. The days following the murders the Indians "were hooting and guying the soldiers from the clifts and boulders on the mountain sides . . . mostly in Spanish," which tends to point to Cochise's Chokonens, for normally they were the only Apaches who operated in that area.[24]

For the next month Indians lurked near Fort Bowie, looking for an opportunity to run off the herd. Lieutenant Robert Pollock re-

Fort Bowie, 1867. (*Courtesy Arizona Historical Society, Tucson*)

ported large numbers in the hills on December 10 and 11. Twelve brave warriors tried to run off the herd but were repulsed. Their presence alarmed Pollock; he feared an attack by the Indians, who were "growing very bold indeed."[25] Yet none came at this time and the Indians retired to their winter camps.

Sonora and Chihuahua continued to pressure the Chiricahuas in 1868. Joaquin Terrazas and Cayetano Ortiz, with a force of 250 volunteers, patrolled Chihuahua's northern frontier, exterminating Apaches whenever found. For the first time in many years the two Mexican states had cooperated to achieve their goal. The Chihuahuan troops crossed into Sonora and Sonoran troops entered Chihuahua without the petty bickering which had characterized past relations. In addition, both states ignored the U.S. boundary and trailed Apaches into southeastern Arizona and southwestern New Mexico.[26]

In early 1868, Cochise remained at Sarampion, no doubt feeling his band secure. Few American troops had scouted that section of the country, and Mexican troops normally did not trespass into American territory. By accident, his whereabouts would become known. Benigno Arvizu and a Chihuahuan force had reconnoitered northern Chihuahua during the first three weeks of February; no Apaches had been encountered. About mid-February a Chiricahua raiding party stole some horses at Casas Grandes; Arvizu seized this opportunity and followed the trail to Sierra Blanca, a small group of hills twelve miles northeast of Fronteras. About February 20 the Mexicans surprised a small camp, killed one Chokonen, and captured another. The prisoner said Cochise was camped at Sarampion, some forty miles northeast.

With a chance to strike Cochise or the *cabecilla* (used to denote a head chief), Arvizu sent forward his best mounted troops, sixteen in all, under Cayetano Ozeta. Crossing into Arizona near the San Bernardino ranch, they continued northeast toward the lower Peloncillos. Cochise apparently had not expected troops from Mexico, which may explain how, on that raw winter day, Arvizu was able to surprise Cochise's camp and wound several warriors. The Chokonens fought a brief rear-guard action before withdrawing. Arvizu's command succeeded in capturing a small boy and some stock. Cochise and a score of warriors from other camps harassed Ozeta's command all the way out of the mountains before the intruders wisely withdrew west into the San Bernardino Valley, having lost but one man wounded.[27]

Nothing more was heard of Cochise until May 13, 1868, when a hundred Apaches attempted to run off the herd at Fort Bowie but were foiled by "the use of the breech loading arms." The Indian trail led south into the mountains.[28] Other Chiricahuas were observed in the Stein's Peak area, where a traveler reported many Indian campfires.[29] Two weeks later they returned and waylaid a Cook and Shaw mail coach.

The ambush took place ten or twelve miles east of Apache Pass, with the Indians killing or capturing the entire party of four men (two soldiers and two citizens). After the first volley wounded the driver, John Brownley, Charles ("Tennessee") Hadsell grabbed the reins and reversed direction toward Fort Bowie. A brisk running fight ensured for six miles before the stage came to a stop. Then, for some reason, the whites apparently surrendered, although they were armed with rifles "and 40 rounds of ammunition and one or two pistols." The Indians took the wounded Brownley and "ripped off his clothes, scalped him and tied a rope to his feet, tied the rope to a saddle and drew him a quarter of a mile." Troops later followed the Indian trail south for fifteen miles into the Chiricahuas, where they discovered the bodies of the two soldiers. They had been "tortured and suffered such a death as only an Apache Indian can invent." Sonoran troops found Hadsell's body after attacking a Chiricahua ranchería a few months later. One of the soldiers lamented that it was "one of the most horrid affairs I have ever heard of."[30]

Meanwhile, in Mexico the Chiricahuas continued to be hounded by the dogmatic Sonorans, who launched successful scouts in the spring of 1868. In March troops attacked a ranchería, killing four and capturing three, in the Teras Mountains, probably a Nednhi unit. In June two more warriors were killed on the border. In July, Cochise, feeling pressure from all sides, resorted to his old ploy of soliciting peace at Janos; that would offer refuge in northern Chihuahua. Yet as six Chiricahuas negotiated with Ozeta, sixty Apaches rampaged through Casas Grandes, wounded a man, and stole more than fifty horses. When Ozeta heard this news, he promptly imprisoned the six peace emissaries.[31]

Troubles mounted for Cochise and the Chiricahuas, who had hoped to reestablish friendly relations with Chihuahua. They were living at Alamo Hueco and the Hatchet Mountains, which were home to a Chokonen local group called the Dzilmora people, although all three bands used the area as a base to raid into Mexico. The shutdown of the Janos trade forced some of the Chiricahuas to turn to a place they called Kegotoi (Dilapadated Houses), otherwise known as Cañada Alamosa and today called Monticello, a small settlement in New Mexico. Several parties of Apaches were reported trading there in mid-August when troops from Fort McRae encountered one hundred Indians south of Cañada Alamosa. The Apaches signaled that they wished to talk but after a short parley fired upon the whites, wounding two men before fleeing south toward Chihuahua.[32]

Cochise probably felt threatened from all directions by the late summer of 1868. Unexpected pressures arose from the north when in late August troops from Fort Cummings attacked a small camp in the Hatchet Mountains, due east of the Animas Mountains, killing two Indians and capturing two children. Two days later another skirmish resulted in another warrior's death and another child's capture. Later accounts reported that these prisoners were from Cochise's band, which had fled toward Janos and Alamo Hueco.[33]

In the summer and fall of 1868, Sonora continued its campaigns against Cochise's people. Governor Pesqueira's loyal commander, General García Morales, directed these, now that he had been able to suppress the Yaqui and Mayo rebellions in the southern part of the state. Beginning in May 1868, Morales directed his attention to the Apaches, who reportedly had killed 116 Sonorans during the past twenty-seven months. Consequently, Sonora declared another war based on extermination, which received the support of the federal government. By late summer Morales had sent a strong force into the field, a force which had the potential to inflict serious casualties on the Chiricahuas. He hoped the Indians would be kept on the run until they became exhausted and were forced to surrender unconditionally.[34]

The Chiricahuas felt the effects of this campaign immediately. In August a force from Bavispe crossed into Chihuahua and discovered a small ranchería in the Carcai Mountains (one of Juh's favorite campsites), where two warriors and two women were killed. In October, Captain Sacramento Monroy, recently appointed commander at Bavispe, struck the Indians, quite possibly Cochise himself. In early October, Indians stole some stock at Bavispe; Monroy and forty-three men picked up the trail and followed it north to the Enmedio Mountains. Three days later, on October 16, his persistence was rewarded. His scouts cut the trail and surprised a ranchería at Alamo Hueco, killing twelve persons (four warriors) and capturing nine others. This was definitely a Chokonen local group.

Chino, who was a brother of Posito Moraga and who had helped free Cochise at Fronteras in 1848, was at Janos soliciting peace at the time. Cochise was thought to have been in the vicinity, but no one knew for sure. After his victory, Monroy marched to Janos and demanded that the Apaches be turned over, but Ozeta refused.

Among Monroy's prisoners were members of Chino's family; he quickly produced two Mexican captives and exchanged them for his wife and child. Monroy returned to Bavispe, irate that Ozeta had not allowed him to attack Chino's group. He promptly fired off a report to General Morales, taking Ozeta to task for refusing to surrender the Apaches. As a result, Morales decided to investigate Ozeta's conduct and lead another scout.[35]

Clearly, for Cochise things were getting out of hand in Mexico. The military pressure was the primary reason he decided to move north to the Gila River and Mogollon Mountains, where he had not been seen for several years. Thus he fortuitously avoided Morales's next campaign, which left Bavispe on October 20 with the intent of striking Chiricahuas at Janos, as Elías González and Carrasco had done in years past. The next day, Morales camped eight miles west of Janos, having secreted himself in ambush. Two days later he detained and interrogated six citizens and on the basis of their statements sent Captain Francisco Toyos and forty men to attack the Indian villages in the neighborhood of Janos.

Again a Sonoran force caught the Apaches napping, several of whom were actually at Janos negotiating with Ozeta. Toyos's soldiers routed the band and killed twelve Chiricahuas, including Aguirre and Elías, two of Cochise's subordinates and longtime companions. Among the dead were two children and eight women; the Mexicans also recovered a captive from Guaymas.[36]

With any hope for peace gone, Ozeta threw his hat into the ring, moving to kill or capture as many Chiricahuas as possible. First, after Toyos's assault, he imprisoned the Chiricahua peace party of twelve individuals who were at Janos discussing terms. The next month he prepared his own offensive and attacked a ranchería north of Janos, killing twelve more Apaches, including José Mangas (brother of Mangas Coloradas), who may have been living with the Chokonens. In December, Ozeta marched triumphantly to Chihuahua City with twelve scalps and ten prisoners. After a short stay he returned to the frontier to continue his campaign.[37]

Although Cochise himself seems to have escaped these attacks, he certainly felt the losses. In February 1869 he admitted having lost more than one hundred of his band within the past year, although his

Dragoon Mountains. View from the ridge looking east into Sulphur Springs Valley. (*Photo by Karen Hayes*)

claim that many of them died of sickness is incomprehensible unless he meant lead poisoning.[38] Lieutenant Colonel Thomas Casimer Devin,[39] Arizona's new district commander, questioned whether Cochise himself had been injured by the Mexican campaigns but correctly added that "his band have just been well thrashed in Mexico."[40]

In November 1868 there surfaced definite information corroborating Cochise's relocation to Arizona. Solomon Barth, a trader with the Western Apaches, recalled that in late 1868 he unexpectedly ran into Cochise, who at the time was visiting the Coyotero chief Pedro near the future site of Fort Apache. According to Barth, Cochise stripped him and his six companions and confiscated their goods, leaving them with only their shoes. It was only through Pedro, who intervened because he knew Barth, that Cochise spared the Americans' lives. Reminiscences are sometimes suspect but on this occasion Solomon Barth's recollection was corroborated by a contemporary newspaper account of the incident. On November 11, 1868, the

*Arizona Miner* published a story about Barth's encounter with Cochise, but the newspaper doubted that the Chiricahua leader had participated because of the place where it had taken place:

> From Messrs. Young and Bryant who recently came through from New Mexico, we learn that while they were in camp at Zuni, Sol Barth [and] George Clinton, formerly of this county, with some Mexicans arrived at the villages from the White Mountains almost naked and in a starving condition. They had left Zuni but a short time previous with a pack train of some 20 head of animals and goods and trinkets specially suited to trade with the Indians. With them was an Indian guide. After crossing the Mogollon range . . . the members of the party were seized, one by one, by Indians, deprived of their arms, stripped of their clothing, and threatened with death and would have been murdered but for the interference of an Indian who knew Sol [Barth]. . . . Sol told Messrs. Bryant and Young that the Indians who robbed him belonged to Ca-Cheis' band, but we doubt this as Cacheis and his band live over 100 miles east of where he had been robbed.
>
> If what we heard of Sol Barth is correct, we do not pity him for his misfortune. It is believed here and in New Mexico that he has been in the habit of trading these Indians, powder, lead and guns.[41]

Albert F. Banta's version, which was obtained from two Mexican captives, agreed with Barth's. Banta also met Barth when he returned to Zuñi.[42]

The *Miner,* which was skeptical of Cochise's presence in White Mountain Apache country, represented what most Arizonians believed. After all, Cochise had been in southern Arizona or Mexico for the past several years and there was no reason to think he would abandon his homeland for Western Apache country. Yet in December there surfaced conclusive evidence that he was in the vicinity of Fort Goodwin and might come in to that post. A few Chokonens did stop in early that month and the commanding officer wrote to Tucson for instructions. Devin ordered him to continue rationing the Indians who remained on the reservation but to carry out expeditions against the "Coyotero, Chiricahuas and Pinal Apaches who have not been permanent dwellers upon the reservation."[43] As for Cochise, wrote Devin, "if he wants to come in he must surrender himself and family or leave them as hostages."[44]

In late December an *Arizona Miner* correspondent writing from

Goodwin reported optimistically that Cochise was still expected in.[45] Nonetheless, for some reason, perhaps because of Devin's unrealistic terms or perhaps because of the prevalence of malaria at Fort Goodwin or perhaps because he felt the Americans would hold him accountable for past deeds (something he was acutely sensitive to), he failed to come in. Instead he headed for the Dragoon Mountains, where he hoped to spend the winter without trouble.

Devin began to have second thoughts about his inflexible conditions, realizing that they had been or would be rejected by Cochise. On January 25, 1869, he wrote:

> Cochise, the boldest and most enterprising Apache in the Territory, and who for the past seven years has been a terror in Southern Arizona, has sent me word that if I will allow him to return to his home (in the Chiricahua Mountains) and remain there, he will not only remain at peace but be responsible for the safety of the Overland road and the stock in its vicinity. All this he used to effect before the attempt to take him prisoner aroused him to make war. I have offered to meet him at Dragoon Springs if he will come in, and hear his proposal. He is undoubtedly the ablest Indian in Arizona, and could be made very useful if it were found that he could be trusted.[46]

Questions remain to be answered as to how Cochise communicated with Devin to make this remarkable offer. If he and Devin could have consummated an agreement at this time, several hundred lives and untold thousands of dollars could have been saved, yet neither party pursued these possibilities. After a brief, inconclusive meeting with Captain Frank Perry, Cochise once again vanished from American contact.

Although Cochise was beginning to feel the squeeze from the military on both sides of the border, he had not yet accepted that the old way of life was ending. That he even considered peace indicated that the reality of his situation had overwhelmed his intense antipathy toward Americans. His rage had subsided, and now it was time to seek a new path for his people, who were dwindling fast. He may have wanted peace, but not peace at the price of freedom. That would come later.

# Chapter 14

# THE AMERICANS ARE EVERYWHERE: WE MUST LIVE IN BAD PLACES TO SHUN THEM

On January 20, 1869, Captain Frank W. Perry ("a gallant and efficient officer," according to Devin)[1] left Fort Goodwin with a detachment of one officer, sixty-two soldiers, two guides, one surgeon, and a Coyotero Indian named Phillippi, "who said he would take them into Cochise's camp." After an unadventurous two-week march, they reached the Dragoons and bivouacked. The next morning, probably February 5, they "captured" two Chokonens. Later that day, Cochise himself met Phillippi and haughtily declared that "but for the fact he meant peace they should never go back." Surprisingly, he agreed to meet Captain Perry the next day, his first sincere face-to-face peace parley with Americans since the Bascom affair almost eight years earlier to the day. An attentive individual provided a good look at the powerful but aging chief: unfortunately, Perry's official report of the conference has not been located.[2]

An account of Perry's remarkable interview with the elusive Chiricahua was published in the *Arizona Miner* on March 20, 1869. The observer described Cochise as "about 6 feet 2 inches, strongly muscled, with mild, prominent features, hooked nose and looks to be a man that means what he says."[3] It would appear that Cochise had indeed accepted the inevitability of peace but still retained a profound distrust of Americans. An extract of the talk follows:

> *Cochise*—What are you doing out here, Captain?
> *Perry*—Come to see you and prospect the country generally.

Colonel Thomas Casimer Devin. A well-liked and much-respected officer in the Southwest, Devin vowed to "kill or capture" Cochise after the Stone massacre at Dragoon Springs. (*Photo from* Third Cavalry)

*Cochise*—You mean you come to kill me or any of my tribe, that is what all your visits mean to me. I tried the Americans once and they broke the treaty first, the officers I mean, this was at the Pass. If I stop in, I must be treated right, but I don't expect they will do all they say for us. I won't stay at Goodwin, it is no place for Indians. They die after being here for a short time. I will go in to Goodwin to talk to you, after I hear how you treat Indians there. I will send in two of my Indians who will let me know (he did send in two squaws). I lost nearly one hundred of my people in the last year, principally from sickness. The Americans killed a good many. I have not one hundred Indians now. Ten years ago I had 1000. The Americans are everywhere, and we must live in bad places to shun them. I can't give you any mescal, as there is another scout on the other side and we can't make any fires to roast it.[4] The Coyoteros are stronger than we are, and steal stock from us; some of them say you came to kill us but some Indians lie. My Indians will do no harm until I come in, which I may do inside of two months.

*Perry*—I heard you were wounded often but you walk all right.

*Cochise*—I was wounded twice. First near Santa Cruz, in the leg twelve years ago. I had a bad leg for some time afterward. Next near Fronteras, two years ago, in the neck. We are known as the Gamo Apaches. I would like some bread and tobacco and a blanket.

Captain Perry filled Cochise's request, "but the soldiers went hungry for about three days."

The detachment continued to Fort Bowie, having received no specific commitment from Cochise. He would not come in at this time, preferring the precarious life as a free Apache to the inherent restraints at Fort Goodwin, where smallpox and other sickness prevailed, or at Cañada Alamosa, where most of the Chihennes submitted to an unofficial truce. He would await further developments before deciding on a course of action.[5]

Meanwhile, having been unsuccessful in his quest to meet Cochise, Devin began active operations against the Apaches. His superiors egged him on, urging active and unrelenting warfare. In March he assembled his subdistrict commanders at Tucson and ordered them to begin campaigning. That spring, summer, and fall, troops scoured southern Arizona.[6] In particular, Captain Reuben Bernard led several successful sorties against the Chiricahuas, keeping them

on the run and providing the troops with invaluable knowledge of
the territory.

Despite a newspaper report that the troops in Arizona were
"having a jolly time in sending Indians to the happy hunting
ground," in reality the army could do very little to prevent depredations and to protect Arizona's nine thousand inhabitants.[7] Its fourteen military posts, garrisoned by twenty-one hundred troops, could
not cover all areas of potential conflict. The army's strategy of subjugation centered on the dispersion-concentration theory. The dis-
persion concept, a defensive policy similar to Mexico's presidio system, provided for forts throughout Indian country. In theory, these
would demoralize the Indians while affording protection to settlers
and travelers. The concentration concept, an offensive policy, put
posts at strategic points from which troops could be rapidly dispatched in response to hostilities.[8]

Neither policy worked, and combining them also failed, especially in Arizona, where the outposts were undermanned and too
scattered to prevent hostilities. Similarly, offensive campaigns usually took too long to assemble and lacked coordination and communication with nearby posts. Rarely were troops from more than one
post employed against Cochise. The few successful movements,
typically in response to Apache depredations, had a common de-
nominator: a successful guide or scout. Without one, the troops
were virtually helpless.

As for Cochise, despite his peaceful expressions, Chokonen raids
continued and actually increased in southern Arizona because the
pressures from Mexico had forced him to establish his rancherías in
the Dragoon and Chiricahua mountains. He led many of the raids
and many of them were concentrated in the Sonoita Valley, one officer writing that the Indian trail usually led "in the direction of the
Chiricahua Mountians . . . [where] a band composed of deserters
from the other tribes live and is led by a chief known as Cochise."[9]

In 1869 and 1870, Cochise spent much of his time in southern
Arizona. It was no coincidence that these years were two of the
bloodiest in southern Arizona history. His people needed "to make
a living" and that, of course, meant more raiding, much of it in Arizona but with an equal amount in Mexico. A pioneer recalled that

"during the years of 1868, 69 and 70 in my opinion we suffered most from the cruelties of the Apaches."[10] The intelligent John Spring wrote that from "1868–1871 Cochise's band killed no less than thirty-four of my friends and acquaintances within a radius of 50 miles of Calabasas."[11] He could not have known for sure who was responsible for all of these depredations and murders, but many certainly could be traced to Cochise's wickiup.

The raiding continued in the spring of 1869. On April 21, Apaches overwhelmed a government train near Camp Crittenden, killing two soldiers and capturing twelve mules. One week later they swept down on John T. Smith's ranch near Tubac and ran off 130 horses. The intrepid Smith and fourteen Mexicans pursued, but the hostiles counterattacked and repulsed the whites.[12] These incidents and similar ones were reported to the superintendent of Indian affairs in Arizona, who wrote that "the conduct of the Indians throughout the Territory during the months of April and May is in no ways improved. From nearly every portion of the interior news of depredations committed by the wild Indians of the territory continue to reach me."[13]

The summer of 1869 was no different. Cochise, as he would do for the next three summers, made his headquarters in the Dragoons. From here small groups raided in all directions. Early that summer Apache raids threatened "to break up the entire settlements" of the Sonoita and Santa Cruz valleys. On June 9 the Indians attacked Yerkes's ranch and killed a man. In June also they killed "old man" Pennington and his son Green. On July 3 hostiles surprised the settlements on the San Pedro, killing three men and running off the stock.[14] And the Chiricahuas directed their attention to the vulnerable mail riders between Tucson and Mesilla. Three mails were captured during an eight-day period, shutting down the line.[15]

These raiding parties often led to more encounters, some of which were brisk engagements. In July a Chokonen party swept down on Imuris, Sonora, and ran off some stock. Fifteen nationals pursued them to Santa Cruz, where they enlisted seven more men and twelve presidio soldiers, all commanded by Lieutenant Florencio Ruiz. On July 16 the command struck the trail, which led north into Arizona and then east to the lower San Pedro. The next day the tenacious Mexicans overtook the Apaches about four miles south of

the Dragoons and succeeded in recapturing the herd and killing two
Indians. But the country was swarming with hostiles, and an hour
later at least thirty Chokonens appeared from the Dragoons. Frightened, Ruiz wisely broke off the engagement and returned to
Sonora.[16]

Throughout the summer of 1869, Mexican troops continued to
threaten Chiricahua bands living in northern Mexico and southern
Arizona. In July, probably while Cochise was skirmishing in the
Dragoons, two Mexican patrols killed several Chiricahuas, including Cochise's old associate Chino, in the mountains of northern
Sonora.[17] In August the indefatigable Cayetano Ozeta launched yet
another offensive from Chihuahua. Finding no Apaches in northern
Mexico, he cautiously decided to encroach into U.S. territory. At
Guadalupe Canyon he encountered two Chiricahuas, one a warrior
training a young boy in the art of making arrows. Ozeta's men
wounded the man in the arm before capturing him and the boy. The
man revealed that about four miles north there was a ranchería
which contained sixteen warriors and one hundred individuals.
Their leaders were "very well known in Janos by their savage
raids," implying that either Cochise or Juh was in the vicinity.[18]

Ozeta, suspecting that the gunfire had alarmed the ranchería, hustled his force to the village but found it hastily abandoned; stock,
saddles, and hides had been left behind. The Mexicans remained
there for the night, observing a flurry of Chiricahua smoke signals,
which alerted other groups to his presence. On September 7, Ozeta
tried to lure the Chiricahuas into the open by retreating south into
Mexico to the Enmedio Mountains, hoping the Indians would pursue. The ploy failed. Although a few Apaches had kept constant
watch, they were much too cautious to attack. The Mexicans
reached Janos on September 17 and Ozeta left for Chihuahua City
on September 26, leaving troops behind to protect Janos.[19]

In September it was rumored in Sonora that the Chiricahuas were
planning "a large campaign against Fronteras" in retaliation for
Sonora's successful scouts of the previous summer.[20] Cochise was
probably instrumental in organizing this war party, which even attracted warriors from the Western Apaches. Luckily for the people of
Fronteras, it did not get below the border. In late September a band of
Pinals led by Bob-chee-a-a set out to join Cochise. The Pinals had a

minor brush with U.S. troops some twenty-five miles northwest of Camp Grant on September 28. From there Bob-chee-a-a's band headed for the San Pedro River and then the Dragoon Mountains, where it apparently joined Cochise.[21]

Evidently the allied Apaches intended to head south, skirting the Dragoons, before striking east to the Chiricahuas to pick up additional Chokonens and Nednhis. During the day on October 5 an eagle-eyed Apache on a high vantage point in the Dragoons saw a mail coach moving across Sulphur Springs Valley. This unexpected and fortuitous prospect of easy plunder was something Cochise could not pass up. Six white men were with the stage: Mr. Kaler (the driver), John Finkle Stone[22] (owner of the Apache Pass mine) and four soldiers of Company D, Twenty-first Infantry, who approached Dragoon Springs at sundown on October 5. They evidently felt secure because the Apaches rarely attacked after dark; furthermore, Kaler and Stone had made this same trip on numerous occasions. The Indians were waiting.

During the day Cochise had prepared an ambush similar to the one east of Apache Pass in July 1862. According to the report of Devin and the recollections of William Sullivan, who was with the relief party, the fight took place "near the forks of the Goodwin and Bowie roads opposite Dragoon Springs."[23] This would place it a few miles east of the Dragoon stage station. All accounts concur as to the circumstances. Cochise had placed his men in a small gully which ran parallel to the road. Covered by grass and soapweed and further obscured by darkness, the Indians lay completely concealed from the unsuspecting Americans. As the stage approached, the Apaches showered arrows and bullets on it and its escort, apparently killing the driver and three soldiers at the first volley. The stage turned from the road and galloped south before encountering mounted Indians, probably under Cochise, who overwhelmed Stone and the other soldier. The fight lasted only a few minutes and the six whites discharged only six rounds.

Cochise struck again at 10 A.M. on October 6 about twelve miles west of Sulphur Springs. Fifty to sixty warriors, accompanied by three white men (all concealed behind boulders), jumped a herd of 250 cattle owned by William Eastwood and George Scott. The American party, consisting of seventeen men, one woman, and two

John Finkle Stone. An Arizona entrepreneur killed at Dragoon Springs on October 5, 1869. (*Courtesy Arizona Historical Society, Tucson*)

children had left San Antonio bound for California. The cattle were strung out for about a mile when the Apaches, some dressed in the clothing of the murdered Stone party, made the first of three charges on the herd. The fight continued for more than three hours, with the Indians mortally lancing one man through the body and forcing five drovers to flee to Bowie. During the clash, Scott and a man named Smith Haile aimed a half-dozen shots at the leader, whom they believed to be Cochise. To their dismay, each missed its mark.[24]

Later that day a government train destined for Bowie found the remains of Stone's party. Again the Apaches attacked; twice they charged, but each time Sergeant Mack and his men of Company E, Twenty-first Infantry, staved off the agressors.[25]

In the meantime, one of the Texas cowboys, named Scott, dashed into Fort Bowie about 8 P.M. on October 6 and reported the details of the attack. With Captains Dunn and Bernard absent on patrol, Lieutenant William Henry Winters, the senior officer at the post, mounted every available man (twenty-five troopers) and, guided by Merejildo Grijalva, sped toward Sulphur Springs. En route, Winters received a messenger informing him of the Stone massacre. "Doubly enraged at the murder of his friend Stone," he forged on to Dragoon Springs, reaching there at 1 A.M. on October 7. He found six corpses and scribbled a message to Devin in Tucson, blaming Cochise and suggesting that troops from Camp Crittenden might head off the Apaches near Mule Pass on the Sonora line. Winters vowed to punish the hostiles: "Nothing can be done for the dead, I now start for the Indians and hope I may come up with them."[26]

After the assault on Mack's detachment, Cochise herded the cattle along the eastern foothills of the Dragoons before crossing the valley toward the lower Chiricahuas. At daybreak on October 7, Merejildo cut the trail, which, as he had predicted, would cross Sulphur Springs Valley to the Chiricahuas and then, he believed, lead into Mexico. Consequently, at nine o'clock, Winters sent another dispatch to Captain Bernard at Fort Bowie: "I am hot upon the trail and hope to be up with the cattle by daylight tomorrow. They are Cochees band and are returning by the Chiricahuas about fifty miles south of the post; if some men could run down the eastern side of the mountain, they may cut them off." It took the courier twenty-seven hours to get this information to Bernard, who was in the saddle

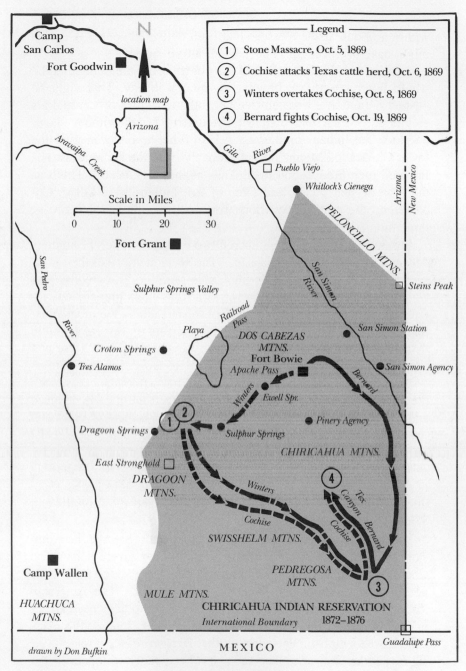

Location map: **Arizona**

Scale in Miles
0  10  20  30

Legend
1  Stone Massacre, Oct. 5, 1869
2  Cochise attacks Texas cattle herd, Oct. 6, 1869
3  Winters overtakes Cochise, Oct. 8, 1869
4  Bernard fights Cochise, Oct. 19, 1869

Camp San Carlos
Fort Goodwin
Aravaipa Creek
Gila River
Pueblo Viejo
Whitlock's Cienega
PELONCILLO MTNS.
Arizona / New Mexico
San Pedro River
Sulphur Springs Valley
Fort Grant
Steins Peak
Railroad Pass
San Simon River
Playa
DOS CABEZAS MTNS.
San Simon Station
Croton Springs
Fort Bowie
Apache Pass
Tres Alamos
Winters
Ewell Spr.
Bernard
San Simon Agency
Dragoon Springs
Sulphur Springs
Pinery Agency
East Stronghold
CHIRICAHUA MTNS.
DRAGOON MTNS.
Winters
4
Tex Canyon
Cochise
Bernard
Camp Wallen
Cochise
SWISSHELM MTNS.
Cochise
PEDREGOSA MTNS.
3
MULE MTNS.
HUACHUCA MTNS.
CHIRICAHUA INDIAN RESERVATION
International Boundary  1872–1876
Guadalupe Pass
drawn by Don Bufkin
MEXICO

Southeastern Arizona, Battle of Chiricahua Pass

within an hour. If the message had been delivered sooner, Cochise might have been caught in the jaws of a trap.[27]

All that day Winters followed the hot trail like a bloodhound; he would not rest until he brought his quarry to bay. That night he pushed on and at 8 A.M. on October 8 the tenacious officer and his command, which had marched twenty-two hours without sleep, overtook the Indians on the east side of what he believed were the lower Chiricahua Mountains but probably were the Pedregosas. His fatigued men fired "upon the Indians as they advanced." This was the Apache rear guard, and three of five Indians were killed; Cochise and the mounted warriors were with the cattle some two or three miles to the east.

Although they were outnumbered two or three to one, the soldiers "rushed forward with enthusiasm." The vivid memory of their massacred friends at Dragoon Springs, plus Merejildo's recognition of Cochise, pushed these brave men forward. Winters immediately attempted to prevent the Indians on foot from reaching the mountains. Sensing this, Cochise led the mounted warriors on several assaults, diverting Winters's attention. Cochise was riding a gray horse and "giving orders as he always is known to do." Wrote Winters: "Many efforts were made to kill Cochise but without success, with his mounted warriors he several times charged the men in advance and although conspicious and special attention directed to him and many shots fired at him, he escaped." Merejildo also paid special attention to Cochise, who exhibited his skill on horseback, "but everytime he got a chance to shoot, Cochise would slip over to the side of the horse, hanging on the horse's neck." The fight lasted about ninety minutes, until the Indians on foot reached the foothills and Winters withdrew.[28]

Winters had scored an impressive victory: he recovered the entire cattle herd and most of the mail while inflicting severe damage on Cochise. He reported that his command killed twelve warriors, even noting which soldier had done the sharpshooting. The American loss was two wounded. Of course the proof would have been an actual body count; this is not to imply that Winters intended to overstate his accomplishments, for, as the *Arizona Miner* wrote, "Cochise, for the first time since 1861, has been badly whipped."[29]

Cochise had little but bitter experience to show for the Winters fight, yet for some reason he kept his band together, rejecting the usual option of scattering or crossing into Mexico, probably because of the ubiquitous Mexican patrols. Instead he moved north into the Chiricahuas, probably not expecting American troops to return; it was a miscalculation that cost him dearly. He had not counted on the determination of either Devin, bound "to kill or capture" him,[30] or Captain Reuben Bernard, a relentless and tireless campaigner from Fort Bowie who correctly believed that his primary responsibility was to disable Cochise and his band.

On October 9, 1869, Lieutenant Colonel Devin issued Order No. 23, in which he directed Bernard to follow Cochise's trail to wherever it might lead. Consequently, on October 16, Bernard began the first of what would be four patrols during the next month. Marching by night, he skirted the eastern face of the Chiricahuas and on October 18 arrived at the scene of Winters' fight. The next day he picked up the trail and followed it to the "top of the highest mountain in the vicinity," where he found a deserted village. A few hours later, Merejildo found the trail, which led west into Tex Canyon for another ten miles before he discovered fresh tracks. After a five-minute gallop, Bernard found another abandoned camp. He took a small force and continued into a canyon; Merejildo took five men and headed for a rocky mesa. About halfway up they were attacked from the heights by an estimated one hundred to two hundred Apaches, who opened fire "from all parts of the rocks above us." The Indians were close enough to use their accurate bows and in the initial attack succeeded in killing two men and wounding one.

For the next thirty minutes a desultory, ineffective fire continued. Bernard collected his force and decided to attempt to outflank and dislodge the Indians. But Cochise had anticipated this, positioning his warriors so that "every point on the mesa was well guarded." He allowed the troops to approach to within one hundred feet before unleashing a withering fire, which drove them back. Unperturbed, Bernard took thirty cavalry to the right; Cochise again responded and rebuffed the troopers.

The battle continued from a distance the rest of the day until near sunset, when Lieutenant John Lafferty was shot as he tried to recover the bodies of the men killed in the initial firing. The Apache bullet fractured and "carried away the greater portion of the lower

Reuben F. Bernard. A veteran of Arizona, Bernard was the most energetic and capable officer stationed at Bowie. (*Courtesy National Archives*)

jawbone." The mesa was carpeted with Indians, and Bernard concluded that the situation was hopeless for assault. He prudently withdrew, declaring that he would have needed twice as many men to dislodge the Apaches. Nonetheless, he believed that his men had punished Cochise severely: he reported eighteen warriors killed and several wounded. Like Winters's numbers, these are suspect and probably overstated; after all, Cochise enjoyed an advantageous position and there is no mention of actual bodies.

The fight took place in the southcentral Chiricahuas on very rough and broken ground covered with rocks, trees, and bushes. Although the exact location has not been determined, the evidence points to Tex Canyon near where Camp Rucker was later situated, both favorite strongholds of Cochise and Juh. The battle was supposed to have occurred twenty-five miles northwest of the Winters fight. This location was much more north than west, but the distance is about correct. It was also supposed to be about forty-five miles from Fort Bowie, which, by trail, is about right. The Apaches moved north after the fight, and Bernard noted that the last leg of his scout was in the northeast section of the Chiricahuas. Despite this, there was positive identification of another site as the battleground in the memoirs of Captain Frederick Elisha Phelps. He had an encounter with Chiricahuas in August 1872 at Horseshoe Canyon, where "some years before a desperate fight between Apaches and Lafferty's troop of our regiment had taken place." In any case, Phelps may have been referring to the Russell fight in October 1871, which definitely took place at Horseshoe Canyon.[31]

Bernard admired the Apaches' fighting skills and courage, respecting Cochise's conduct and strategy in particular. He reported that the Chiricahua warriors "were recklessly brave." As for Cochise, Bernard thought he was "one of the most intelligent hostile Indians on this continent." Even so, he vowed to leave again on October 24 "with every man I can mount."[32]

With definite information about Cochise's position, Devin in Tucson ordered reinforcements to Fort Bowie: one company from Camp Crittenden and two from Fort Goodwin. The fact that they were not sent earlier revealed that no one expected Cochise to remain in the Chiricahuas, at least the more accessible regions. Major Henry R. Putnam at Goodwin pointedly asked Captain Dunn why reinforcements had not previously been requested: "Had you given me definite information on the subject I should have had a sufficient force present with you before this time to have assisted in destroying that scoundrel and his band."[33]

Although the reinforcements had not arrived, Bernard left again on October 24, repeating his march of a week before and halting at the battleground on October 26. Surprisingly Cochise was still around. The next day, as the troops marched through a canyon, the Indians opened fire. There were no casualties, and Cochise withdrew to a spot where Bernard dared not venture. That evening a few Chokonens came down from the hills and conversed with Bernard's scouts, questioning what terms or conditions might be offered. Bernard's terse reply was unsatisfactory, for "if they wanted peace they could come in and accept such terms as would be given them." This was unacceptable to Cochise. The fact that he even considered capitulating indicated how desperately he must have perceived his situation to be.[34]

Reinforcements arrived the next day, Captain Thomas Searle Dunn and 19 infantry from Bowie, but not the cavalry troops from Goodwin that Bernard had requested. Dunn was responding to Bernard's plea that he had located Cochise "where I cannot hurt him. If troops have been sent to Bowie, please send them forward at once." Bernard sent him back to Fort Bowie with a six-man cavalry escort. Finally, on October 29, Captain Harrison Moulton, Lieutenant Albert John Garrett, and 31 men arrived from Crittenden, increasing Bernard's force to 118 men. In the early morning of October 30 the command marched in three columns to the top of the mountain, where the Indians had last been seen. The following day Bernard discovered Apaches and another skirmish occurred, with a couple more warriors reported killed. His troops exhausted, the persistent officer finally abandoned the pursuit. One participant wrote: "It was impossible to drive them from such a place, as they were armed." Bernard returned to Fort Bowie on November 2.[35]

By this time, troops had been pulled in from everywhere. First the reinforcements from Fort Goodwin arrived, swelling Bernard's force to 156 men, which also included detachments from Camp Crittenden and 21 Mexican cavalry from Fronteras. But Cochise had decided to avoid Bernard and led the soldiers "over the worst country [he] possibly could," finally splitting up into small groups to rendezvous at some prearranged point. Totally exasperated, the indefatigable officer gave up the scout, letting Cochise go "to some other mountain." He succeeded in killing a warrior, however, from whom he recovered a Springfield rifle taken during the Stone massacre.[36]

To Cochise the battle of the "rocky mesa" was at best a stalemate. Although he had countered and frustrated Bernard at every turn, compelling him to give up the chase on three occasions and finally to leave him alone, the several engagements were costly lessons; several good men had been killed. In the words of Dan L. Thrapp it was "a remarkable stand against overwhelming odds in opponent numbers and arms, and a sure mark of his skill and ability under pressure."[37]

Cochise had never faced American adversaries like the dogmatic, Apache-wise Bernard and Winters, who, guided by the consummate scout Merejildo Grijalva, were more than capable of following him over the roughest of country. Dr. Levi Dorr, who accompanied the troops from Camp Crittenden, summed up the situation in a letter to a friend: "Heretofore officers have not tried to fight Indians in such impregnable mountain passes but their late doings [Stone massacre] & it being Cachiese was a stimulus." In later years Cochise admitted that he refrained from attacking government mail coaches because he knew "all the soldiers would be ordered out to avenge [any] death[s]," a lesson he learned the hard way after the Stone massacre.[38]

For the remainder of 1869, Devin pushed his subordinates to keep the pressure on Cochise. Some Chokonens were reported to have fled to the Animas and Guadalupe mountains; Cochise and his own local group were believed to have retired north to the Burro Mountains. Devin heard this rumor and, hoping to punish him further, ordered Major Putnam to reconnoiter in the Burro Mountains in hopes of picking up Cochise's trail. Trying to motivate Putnam, Devin delivered a pep talk, declaring that "the officer who succeeds in destroying him [Cochise] will earn not only the highest encomiums from his superior but the gratitude of the people of Arizona as well."[39]

Cochise had indeed moved north, probably following the Peloncillo Mountains to the Gila country. Bernard's persistence compelled him to contemplate peace again. The chief was beginning to realize that peace was vital to prevent the extermination of his people. He had two options: try Coyotero country near Fort Good-win or await the results of Chihenne peace discussions at Cañada Alamosa. Cochise had sent a message to Loco, a Chihenne chief, that he would bring in his band once he was assured of the whites' good intentions. Until then, he recuperated in the extreme northern limits of Chiricahua territory, living near the Eastern White Mountain Coyoteros, with whom several Chokonens had intermarried. Although this band had been close allies of Cochise in the early 1860s, they had "not banded with Cochise . . . for marauding for a number of years, but frequently exchanged corn for the others stock."[40]

In December 1869 and January 1870, Cochise camped along Bonita Creek, a tributary of the Gila. Here he was safe from Mexican troops, and if he were pressured by U.S. troops he could easily slip into the impregnable and relatively unexplored Mogollon Mountains, considered sacred by the Chiricahuas. Authorities at Fort Goodwin were unaware of his presence, or at least did not report that he was near. For his part, Cochise was discrete in his movements. According to a captured Chokonen, he and his family lived near Fort Goodwin and received "supplies from the Indians at that post." The implications are not that startling; what this really meant was that Cochise traded with Apaches who were receiving rations at Goodwin. If he had come in, the officers at the post would certainly have reported it.[41]

Major David Ramsay Clendenin, commander at Fort Goodwin, was not aware that Cochise was in the vicinity, perhaps believing that the hostiles had remained in southern Arizona. This may be inferred from correspondence in early 1870s. In early January at Fort Bowie, Captain Thomas Dunn requested Western Apache scouts from Fort Goodwin to "act in conjunction with the enlisted Indian scouts and troops in scouting after Cochise." Devin concurred, as did Clendenin, yet this concept of using an Apache to catch an Apache was not employed against Cochise at this time.[42]

In mid-January 1870 some of Cochise's band left Coyotero country bound for the Dragoons. As a result, Captain Bernard, Merejildo, and sixty-three men from Fort Bowie marched west toward the Dragoons. Merejildo cut their trail near the entrance of Cochise's east stronghold and followed it south about eight miles along the

Cochise's west stronghold, Dragoon Mountains. Bernard attacked a Chiri-cahua camp a few miles south of here in January 1870. (*Photo by Karen Hayes*)

foothills. Here the trail turned sharply west to the top of a mountain (probably Black Diamond Peak), where they found a deserted ranchería overlooking Sulphur Springs Valley. Merejildo again struck the trail, which led northwest over "the roughest portions of the mountains" for ten miles, leading to the top of another hill, perhaps Dragoon Peak. Finally, on January 28, he found the Chokonen ranchería a few miles southwest of Cochise's west stronghold.

Bernard pushed his men forward, riding "over as rough a country as horses could possibly travel," and attacked the camp, killing thirteen and capturing two before the Indians melted into the rocks and hills, leaving behind all their possessions. The troops found a bar of gold taken from John Stone, plus some mail correspondence. The captives revealed that Cochise was in Coyotero country but had "turned the command over to two subchiefs named respectively Chackone[43] and Schogo."[44]

With the advent of spring in 1870, Cochise returned to his country, perhaps to the Chiricahuas, where Indians were reported in

March. That spring and summer there were more Chiricahua raids, destruction of property, and the inevitable murders on both sides of the border. Indians raided the Sonoita Valley in March, hitting Gardner's ranch once again and fleeing toward the San Pedro River. Troops from Camp Crittenden, accompanied by Gardner, followed the raiders (Cochise's "entire band was on the raid") and saw smoke signals in the Dragoons and Huachucas. Perhaps in the Dragoons, Gardner and the soldiers attacked a ranchería and claimed they killed several Chiricahuas.[45]

The severity of these raids induced the secretary of war to place 125 Spencer and Sharps rifles at Fort Lowell to be distributed to eager citizens.[46] In Mexico, Sonora maintained its two-hundred-peso scalp bounty, and Chihuahua, claiming that American troops had forced the Apaches south, mounted a major offensive of two hundred men under veteran Indian fighter Joaquin Terrazas.[47]

That spring Cochise was reported raiding in Sonora, which seems confirmed by his conspicuous absence in Arizona. In late March small raiding parties were detected near Bavispe and followed to the Arizona border. The Mexicans surprised the ranchería, killing five Indians, capturing three, and recovering two hundred head of cattle. Another Sonoran scout found a village of thirty wickiups in the Teras Mountains, but the Apaches were a step ahead and escaped into the hills. Additional U.S. mail was recovered, probably from the Stone massacre. Whether this was a Chokonen or Nednhi group was not clear; the significance was the relentless Mexican pressure.[48]

In June 1870 two raiding parties left the Dragoons. One killed a man and stole some stock from Thomas Gardner, who claimed that in 1873 and 1874 Cochise admitted he had led the raid. The Indians made a beeline toward the Dragoons.[49] Meanwhile, at Fronteras, a Chokonen raiding party ran off some stock. The presidio commander, Adrian Maldoñado, and a company of troops followed the trail into the lower Dragoons, probably to the vicinity of Bennett Peak, where they discovered a ranchería in the early evening of June 26. Maldoñado dismounted his command, leaving eight men with the horses while he and the remaining fourteen pushed forward to attack. The Chokonen had detected the Mexicans and a vigorous sixty-minute skirmish ensued, after which the Indians fell back out of range. Maldoñado thought he had repulsed them, but the real reason for their withdrawal was the arrival of reinforcements, possibly under Cochise because the fight assumed a different flavor. There was a second Chiricahua assault, this time from the front and both sides; four marksmen were hidden among the rocks and their firing began to take a heavy toll. Decidedly outnumbered now, Maldoñado retreated, having lost two men killed and one wounded. He believed that he had killed five Indians.[50]

That summer, Apache war parties ravaged southern Arizona. Cochise's Chokonens, from their strongholds in the Dragoons, destroyed farms and ranches and ambushed solitary travelers and small parties. On July 17 a large Chokonen war party raided Blanchard's ranch, stealing his stock and burning the ranch to the ground. A week later the same party, it is supposed, attacked Tubac, whose thirty inhabitants watched helplessly as the Indians looted the town and drove away most of the stock. Afterward this band continued into Sonora, where Cochise was reported (erroneously) to have been killed in a skirmish near Dolores. The report delighted the *Arizonian*, which added that "the worst Indian who ever strung a bow or pulled a trigger is defunct."[51]

Raids continued in August and Cochise, guilty or not, was blamed. On August 7, some Apaches, thought to be under Cochise, surrounded two wagons at Davis Springs, about eighteen miles from Camp Crittenden. Two men were killed and one was missing and presumed dead. That evening the mail rider to Tucson discovered the grisly remains and reported the incident to Captain Moulton at the fort. The captain set out with twenty men and followed the Indians' trail northeast for forty miles. The Apaches, generously reported at two hundred, ambushed Moulton from a strong position behind some rocks. Moulton abandoned his chase and the Indians continued on to a ranch at the Cienega, killing two men and forcing its temporary abandonment.[52]

With the accounts of sanguinary Apache raids, destruction of property, and loss of life everywhere, Cochise's next move caught Arizonans by surprise. In early August he sent a messenger, perhaps his wife, Dos-teh-seh, to Camp Mogollon and requested peace. She conferred with Major John Green, saying that Cochise "wanted to make peace with the whites and was tired of war and that he would like to make arrangements to come in and see me himself." A stupefied Green did not know how to handle the possibility of dealing with the elusive Chiricahua chief. He wrote headquarters: "He is such an old offender, I thought it best to ask instructions from the Department Commander in regard to his case."[53]

No response from the new commander, Colonel George Stoneman, has been found, but we can deduce that Green received permission to parley with Cochise because at the end of August, Cochise showed up at Camp Mogollon. With winter approaching, the grass poor, his ponies thin, his sanctuary in the Dragoons invaded by Mexican troops, his country patrolled constantly by U.S. troops, he reluctantly decided to put aside his enormous distrust of Americans. As usual, the facts are in dispute, the Indians saying he came in as the conqueror and the whites claiming he arrived as the conquered.

# Chapter 15

# WE ARE ABOUT EVEN: COCHISE VISITS TWO RESERVATIONS

Cochise came in to Camp Mogollon (soon to be renamed Camp Thomas and then Fort Apache) about August 30, 1870, and met with Major John Green, who had the thankless task of rationing and containing some one thousand Western Apaches, primarily of the two White Mountain bands. That he chose Camp Mogollon to test the waters rather than another post indicated his continued distrust of Americans. No doubt he felt that he could not go to Fort Bowie, for that was where he had been betrayed, as he believed, by the Americans and he would not risk it again. Fort Goodwin was unhealthful and, he may have felt, too dangerous for him to enter, so he chose the next-best place: distant Camp Mogollon, where, he believed, he might get a fair shake. The noteworthy conference took place outside the post; Cochise refused to place himself completely in the hands of the soldiers.

Although Green's report to department headquarters has not been found, at least three versions of the parley exist, each written from Camp Mogollon to newspapers. On September 17 the *Weekly Arizonian* published the first letter, which furnished an eyewitness account of the meeting. The *Alta California* published a letter November 14; it contained Green's version as well as the Apache side, both recorded by Silvester Mowry two weeks after the parley.

The *Arizonian*'s letter presented a good description of Cochise but offered nothing about his motives and little information regarding the parley. Cochise "came in about the 30th of August . . . made peace . . . and said that Colonel [Major] Green was a good man and had treated him well, and that consequently he should return to his own country and put a stop to all hositilities. . . . He claims that he was treated very badly at Camp Bowie some years ago but thinks that he has killed about as many as he has lost and now that he is about even."[1]

In contrast, Mowry's revealing letter provided two accounts, one from Major Green and the second allegedly from the White Mountain Apaches. According to Green, Cochise

> was very respectful; said he had been fighting the Americans for thirteen years, and now was tired and wanted to sleep. The troops had worried him, killed almost all of his band. He thought we were about even, and would like to come on the reservation and be chief of the Bonito River Apaches and that he would protect the road from Camp Bowie to the San Pedro . . .

Furthermore, Cochise provided insight as to his influence among the Western Apaches and his ability to draw from their ranks for his war parties:

> He believed the Pinals would make peace if he did, as he was really the great war chief. . . . Whenever he wanted men for a large war party, he sent to all the tribes for volunteers, and they came. . . . He claimed that he did not begin the war thirteen years ago, and only fought for revenge and self defense.[2]

Mowry's alternate version, which he obtained from the Western Apaches, probably seemed more characteristic of the bloodthirsty Apaches envisioned by most white Americans. Accompanied by twelve well-armed warriors, Cochise arrived wearing "ostentatiously ivory handled revolvers and a gold chain recognized to have been Colonel Stone's." Furthermore, the story goes, he was "insolent to such a degree that the interpreter was afraid to translate." Cochise claimed "the troops were cowards and the Americans were liars. . . . He would go on killing as long as he pleased."[3]

This account, which differed dramatically from the two independent Anglo versions, might have been in character a decade before, but not in 1870. Cochise was no longer the arrogant Chiricahua, nor was he ostentatious. Instead, his tastes were simple, his demeanor dignified. From here on, in every discussion with Americans, he expressed a desire to stop the killing and showed a healthy respect for American troops. Certainly he might have arrived well armed and highly suspicious and might even have worn Stone's gold chain, although that seems dubious. His presence might well have unnerved the interpreter, a normal result considering the power, prestige, and influence Cochise held among the Apache people. The one certainty would seem to have been Cochise's sincere wish to be left alone and to live in peace. Pedro, a White Mountain chief, corroborated this in an interview with Colonel George Stoneman two weeks after the Cochise-Green conference.[4]

Green's actions stirred up the hornets, in particular the territorial press, which was incredulous that he let Cochise out of his grasp. Even worse, the officer had not made any promises that he could not keep, much to its dismay. Green hoped that he had taken the first delicate step in gaining Cochise's confidence, and he had handled an extremely sensitive situation in an admirable way. He had exercised restraint, and it is impossible to say what the eventual outcome might have been had he done otherwise. If he had tried anything duplistic or had he attempted to coerce Cochise to come in against his wishes, irreparable harm might have been done. Nonetheless, the press vilified Green because he had let Cochise out of his grasp. One ridiculous assertion was that Cochise had his warriors surround Green, instructing them "to fire if he [Green] said anything that did not please Cochise."[5] The *Arizona Citizen* espoused the opinion that was prevalent in Arizona, editorializing that the most effective way to control the Apaches "would be greatly facilitated and rendered lasting by prefacing it with a temporary shortage of food, arms, and ammunition and giving them generous doses of cold lead."[6]

For his part, Cochise had not promised to remain at Camp Mogollon because he apparently was uncomfortable in Western Apache country. Relations between the Chiricahuas and Western Apaches evidently had become strained, with Cochise's people uninvited intruders. So he decided to return south to his ancestral home in the Chiricahuas.

About this time, Colonel Stoneman[7] was traveling through southern Arizona on an inspection tour. He had commanded the District of Arizona since August 1869 and had assumed command of the new Department of Arizona the following May. He disliked the climate (he referred to Tucson as a "hot, sickly town"),[8] and his cavalier and condescending manner quickly alienated and antagonized most Arizonans. So did his policies, which showed little thought, no imagination or initiative, and a superficial understanding of the Apache problem.

Symptomatic of this was the issue of the location of department headquarters. Stoneman decided it would be at Prescott during the summer and at Drum Barracks, California, during the winter, where the weather was more benign than that of northern Arizona at that season. It was a grave mistake. Typically, he underestimated the resentment and uproar it would provoke in the press and among civilians. His justification was viewed as a bunch of nonsense. Stoneman believed it would "satisfy the people, prevent clamor, and obviate the embroilment of the civil authorities of Arizona with the Indians."[9] This statement demonstrated that he was as incompetent a forecaster as he was a department commander, for precisely the opposite occurred.

His military policies were just as frightening to Arizonans. Foremost was his position as a cost cutter: he centralized troops in strategic areas to combat the hostiles. To those Indians sincere for peace, the reservation system would continue. In one respect, Stoneman was an atypical military man in that he favored subjugation of the hostiles "by moral or religious influences, the field is open, the harvest is ready and awaiting the laborers," although his motives could perhaps be questioned.[10]

In the end it was his inactivity and his attitude that did him in. When his report for 1870 was published—he proposed that five posts, including Fort Bowie, be closed—Arizonans screamed bloody murder. Said the *Arizona Citizen:* "Never was a man less fit than he for high responsibilities."[11] Edgy from criticism, Stoneman responded by threatening the people of Tucson with a troop withdrawal unless they ceased their complaints.[12]

Stoneman had begun an inspection tour from Fort Whipple on August 30—about the time that Cochise and Green were parleying. Going northeast to the Little Colorado River, he followed it east near present-day Holbrook, then veered south to Camp Mogollon, arriving there on September 11 and meeting several White Mountain chiefs, who told him that Cochise wished to live in peace near Bonita Creek. How Stoneman perceived this offer and whether he understood its significance is not known, yet, according to one correspondent, he opposed giving Cochise sanctuary.[13]

The correspondent was none other than the ubiquitous Sylvester Mowry, who had accompanied the paymaster on his route through southern Arizona. Leaving Tucson on September 2, Mowry wrote several letters to the *Alta California* in San Francisco, published under the title "Arizona Notes by the Way." His first stop was Camp Crittenden, where he found but "two officers and two men fit for duty." The situation was so critical, he asserted, that if Cochise realized its "weakness he could at one blow wipe out everything here."[14] Of course Mowry knew better than to imply that Cochise, or any other Apache, would attack a fort and risk needless fatalities, but a smattering of white lies never hurt a story.

They next went to Fort Bowie and then on to Fort Goodwin. At the latter post he learned that Cochise had requested peace, so he added some color for his San Francisco readers, writing that [Cochise's] hands [were] reeking with the blood of his victims hardly cold in death." From here Mowry's route lay north to Camp Thomas (formerly Camp Mogollon), where he arrived on September 14 and obtained Green's version of the meeting with Cochise. In any event, noted Mowry, Green's plan was "only an experiment and if it failed on a years trial there was nothing left but extermination."[15]

While Mowry expounded on him, Cochise was in the Chiricahuas talking over the possibilities of relocating his band, particularly since cold weather was approaching. In the end his Chokonens rejected the move to White Mountain country, perhaps influenced by a message from Victorio or Loco,[16] whose peace experiment at Cañada Alamosa was beginning to bear fruit. An important council was to be held with a special agent from New Mexico who wished to confer with all the Chiricahua leaders.

Like Cochise, the Chihennes had also been at war since 1861, except for a few unsuccessful cease-fires in the mid-1860s. In May 1869, Loco and Salvadora[17] (a son of Mangas Coloradas) solicited peace at Cañada Alamosa, having determined that this course was vital if their people were to survive. Victorio concurred but was too

suspicious to come in. Shortly thereafter, Loco went to Fort Craig
and talked with Lieutenant Colonel Cuvier Grover, who assured him
that his band would be left alone if it remained quiet.

Meanwhile, William Clinton, New Mexico's superintendent of
Indian affairs at Santa Fe, had no Southern Apache agent and was
uncertain about the next step. He even considered moving the Indians to the Navajo Reservation—if the Navajos would have them.
While these behind-the-scenes negotiations went on, Loco settled  ·
opposite Fort McRae on the Cuchillo Negro, named for the former
Chihenne leader, and received spartan rations. At Santa Fe the district commander, Colonel George Washington Getty, recommended
that "if possible an agent of the Indian Department be sent . . . to
induce them to remove to a permanent reservation."[18] Fortunately
for all parties concerned, on July 20, 1869, First Lieutenant Charles
Edward Drew[19] was appointed agent for the Southern Apaches, who
came to like and respect him.

Drew reached Chihenne territory in late August and found Loco
and his local group (only 17 warriors out of 150 people) camped ten
miles west of Fort McRae. Loco had visited McRae twice early that
month, although his sincerity and motives were questioned by Captain John Curtis Gilmore.[20] Loco told Drew he wanted "a good
peace and no lie," and Drew reported optimisitically that "they
appear willing to make peace and I think that with proper care
and by treating them honestly and justly the whole of the Apache
tribes may be brought in from the warpath."[21] Whether this included
Cochise was not clear; at the time he was occupied with Bernard's
troops in the Chiricahuas.

Drew continued to meet with the Apaches in September and October, performing his duties competently and skillfully and proving
to be in the words of one historian "one of the best [agents] the
Apaches ever had."[22] He earned the confidence and trust of the
Apaches, perhaps the most important ingredients in dealing successfully with recalcitrant Indians who had been at war for almost a decade. What Loco and Victorio really wanted was a reservation in
their own country with the government providing food and clothing,
hardly an inappropriate request. Drew passed their wishes on, but
his requests ran into red tape with his superiors, who failed to ac-
knowledge his efforts and neglected to forward instructions. This

was the precarious state of affairs in December when Cochise sent word to Loco that he would come in if the reservation experiment worked.

Cochise's message to Loco was prompted in part by the several hard fights with Winters and Bernard in the fall of 1869. Loco told Drew about Cochise's proposal. As usual the Chokonen chief was wary, citing past acts of treachery, yet just the hint of his coming in excited Drew. The agent recognized Cochise's importance among the Indians and wrote to Clinton:

> Cochise . . . the most daring robber and bloodthirsty of the Apaches, had said he would come in and join him [Loco] as soon as a treaty was made, but he wished to be satisfied that there is no treachery about it, and that if he comes in he will not be betrayed and killed as his people have been in times past.[23]

But Cochise stayed clear of Cañada Alamosa, mainly because Drew had encountered one obstacle after another and thereby failed to bring stability to the reservation.

Drew had inherited a no-win situation: the army had no faith in the Indians against whom it had waged war, and the Bureau of Indian Affairs had neither the funds nor the manpower to manage the Indians. The Apaches, desperate for peace, had been forced to put their destiny in the hands of whites they distrusted. Drew risked his life to obtain the Indians' confidence, yet the people he called on for support gave him no help. His communications to Santa Fe were not acknowledged; no visible aid, either in terms of emotional encouragement or in money for food and blankets, was forthcoming. Drew, who nowadays would be called a self-starter, managed his Indians in much the same style Tom Jeffords employed a few years later. He took an agency that had been vacant for eight years and appeased a race whose recent experiences with white Americans had been irrevocably hostile. Little by little he gained their confidence, but he still lacked tangible support from the Indian Bureau.

Compounding Drew's problems were other difficulties endemic to the history of the West, especially the Southwest. He encountered obstacles with whites, who were "strongly opposed to any attempt to make peace with the Apaches." "No doubt they have their own reasons," he said, alluding to the contraband trade at Cañada Ala-

Thomas Jeffords. Cochise's best-remembered white friend, Jeffords played a significant role in bringing peace to the Southwest and was the only agent of the Chiricahua reserve. (*Reproduced by permission of the Huntington Library, San Marino, California*)

mosa. Scalp hunters from Chihuahua, who had crossed into New Mexico and vowed to attack Loco's and Victorio's people, were another situation that needed to be addressed. District headquarters in Santa Fe ordered the commanders at Forts McRae, Cummings, Bayard, and Selden to arrest any armed Mexicans entering the United States. This served to deter most mercenaries. But the largest task Drew had was to rebut charges by two experienced frontiersmen turned Indian traders who were attempting to enhance their position with the Indians—a euphemistic way of saying they wanted more independence to turn a dollar. The accusers were none other than Elias Brevoort[24] and Tom Jeffords, who alleged that Drew had been furnishing liquor, among other illicit things, to the Indians.[25]

On Clinton's recommendation, Jeffords and Brevoort had been appointed traders "with the Mimbres and Gila River tribe" on December 20, 1869.[26] Clinton had been acquainted with both men at Santa Fe. In addition, he had received excellent references about them from several of Santa Fe's citizens, who attested to their good character. Jeffords "professed to be well acquainted with these Indians," implying that he had dealt with the Apaches before the fall of 1869. Clinton hoped Jeffords would assist the inexperienced Drew. In fact, the frontiersman may have been involved in Loco's first peace initiative the previous spring. In all probability, however, Jeffords's acquaintance with the Chihennes did not extend to Cochise's Chokonens at this time.

In late January the traders brought a stock of goods from Santa Fe to Cañada Alamosa. Within the next two months they had at least two meetings with Drew, who made sure the pair knew who was boss. When they found they could not intimidate him, Jeffords and Brevoort mounted a smear campaign to discredit him, hoping to get him removed. Jeffords may have been unofficially campaigning for Drew's position, as he would do more than once during the next few years, yet his and Brevoort's power play backfired. The investigation exonerated Drew and laid skepticism to their allegations. Instead the commissioner of Indian affairs in Washington, Ely Samuel Parker, a full-blooded Iroquois Indian, revoked their licenses.[27]

Thomas Jonathan Jeffords, enigmatic and controversial, was a "tall, spare man with reddish hair and whiskers of considerable length."[28] Little is known of his early life. He was born in 1832 on

Chautauqua Lake near Maryville in extreme western New York and came west before the Civil War. In the 1850s he was said to have been a sailor on the Great Lakes. It was at this time that he apparently received the title of captain, which he retained for the rest of his life. In 1858 he was employed in laying out the road between Leavenworth, Kansas, and Denver, Colorado, where he practiced law for a short time. He then drifted south to Taos, New Mexico, and prospected in 1859 and 1860. With the outbreak of the Civil War, he scouted for Brigadier General E. R. S. Canby, bringing dispatches to Tucson in July 1862, and was said to have guided Brigadier General James H. Carleton's California Column east into New Mexico.[29]

Jeffords's activities after the war are more difficult to trace. He did some prospecting and eventually became involved in mail operations. In October 1867, George W. Cook, a former officer in the New Mexico Volunteers who had been involved in peace talks with the Chihennes in early 1865, and John M. Shaw of Socorro, New Mexico, who became the Chihennes' agent in 1874, formed the Southern Overland U.S. Mail and Express Line and operated a line of passenger coaches between Santa Fe and El Paso, connecting at Mesilla for Tucson and Los Angeles. Jeffords became affiliated with this route as a "conductor on the mail line" between Santa Fe and Tucson, as reported in the *Santa Fe New Mexican* of July 28, 1868, although he was referred to as Jeffies. Any doubt about his identity was cleared up three months later with a statement that "George W. Cook and Captain Jeffords of the Southern Overland Mail are stopping at the Exchange Hotel [in Santa Fe]." According to Alice Rollins Crane, who interviewed Jeffords in 1895, his responsibility included the area between Socorro and Tucson.[30] He left this position in early 1869, did some prospecting, and moved into southern New Mexico to the vicinity of the Cañada Alamosa.

Exactly when Jeffords became acquainted with the Chiricahuas is not known with certainty. His first contacts, however, were almost certainly with the Chihennes and not Cochise's Chokonens and perhaps occurred as early as 1865 in the ill-fated peace parley near Pinos Altos. Jeffords was clearly acquainted with Loco and Victorio by the summer of 1869. A few months later, he and Brevoort applied for the position of Indian trader for the Southern Apaches (although one might speculate what materials the Apaches had to barter; the answer, of course, was stolen stock). Clinton recommended approval because Jeffords "professed to be well acquainted with these Indians. I told him . . . to assist the agent in every way he could."[31] Jeffords was clearly familiar with the Chiricahuas by the fall of 1869, and if we follow the traditionally accepted story, he had already gained Cochise's friendship.

Aside from his long life (he died in 1914 at eighty-two), Jeffords's activities are intriguing. Unlike many frontier characters, he was neither a braggart nor ostentatious; on the contrary, he was a reticent man who spoke little of himself and preferred to be left alone. Wrote historian C. L. Sonnichsen:

> Jeffords offered little help to those who wanted to know more about him. He talked with his pioneer friends about the early days but he made little attempt to get his extraordinary story on record and made no effort at all to correct the misstatements and mistakes that got into circulation.

Yet in spite of his reluctance to beat his own drum, he was a jovial and easygoing man who enjoyed good times and good company. S. W. Grant, a soldier stationed at Fort Bowie in the 1870s, recalled that Jeffords "was always jolly, rather witty and hard to confuse. I remember we used to have dances at the post now and then—just the laundry women and the soldiers. Once, one of the women complained that he stepped on her toe. With much apparent concern he asked, 'which toe, madam?'"[32]

Actually it was Jeffords who may have unwittingly created his own legend in his statements to Thomas Farish and Robert Forbes in the last few years of his life. The traditional story has Jeffords, at the time supervisor of the mail route, riding alone to Cochise's camp in 1867 to make a personal compact under which Cochise agreed to refrain from attacking his mail riders. Jeffords told this to Robert Forbes, and it has been reported so much that it is thought to be fact and history.[33]

Farish is the primary source dating Jeffords's first meeting with Cochise in 1867, yet he almost certainly and incorrectly deduced this. He quoted Jeffords as saying that he first met Cochise after "having been an Indian Trader under a commission from Mr.

Parker, Secretary of the Interior."[34] Parker assumed office in April 1869 and granted Jeffords's license on December 20, the latter receiving it in January 1870. This point cannot be overemphasized. Clearly, if we use Jeffords's own recollections, his first meeting with Cochise must have occurred no earlier than 1870. Although this in itself is not conclusive evidence (Jeffords could have a faulty memory), it finds support in other reliable accounts.

Jeffords first acknowledged knowing Cochise in February 1871,[35] which is, of course, not incontrovertible evidence. In November 1872 he told Arizona Governor Anson Safford that he had known Cochise for three years, thereby placing their first meeting in 1869 or 1870.[36] Finally, the reliable Fred Hughes, who should have known the facts, since he was Jeffords's assistant in the early 1870s, declared that the pair first met at Cañada Alamosa, probably in the fall of 1870,[37] which I believe is supported by the scant available evidence.

Farish and Forbes differ concerning Jeffords's motives. Farish stated that Jeffords aspired to gain Cochise's friendship. Shortly before his death in 1914, Jeffords apparently told Farish about his first meeting with Cochise, although he failed to mention anything about a compact to protect his mail riders. Jeffords said Cochise

> had killed twenty-one men to my knowledge, fourteen of whom were in my employ. I made up my mind that I wanted to see him. I located one of his Indians and a camp where he came personally . . . I went into his camp alone, fully armed . . . I spent two or three days with him, discussing affairs, and sizing him up. . . . This was the commencement of my friendship with Cochise and although I was frequently compelled to guide troops against him and his band, it never interfered with our friendship.[38]

In contrast, Jeffords had told Robert H. Forbes in 1913:

> In the early 1860s he had a contract for the carrying of mail between Tucson and a point east, through dangerous Apache country. The delivery was by riders on horseback whom he paid liberally, but he rarely settled with them because they were killed enroute by the Apaches. He stated that he lost twenty men in this way and that he, himself, had the scars of Indian arrows on body.
>
> The situation became so bad that he determined upon a most dangerous contact with Cochise to make arrangements for the pas-

sage of his riders with mail through Indian country. Alone he rode
into Cochise's camp in the Dragoon Mountain Stronghold and dis-
mounting and laying aside his weapons, made his way to Cochise's
wickiup where the astonished chief asked him if he expected to return. Jeffords, speaking the language, stated that he came to talk with
a brave and honorable man about his riders passing through Apache
territory. Cochise, admiring the bravery of a man who would dare to
enter his camp, entered into conversation which resulted in the agreement which Jeffords desired.[39]

The Jeffords legend began here and was then romanticized and pop-
ularized by Elliot Arnold in his book *Blood Brother* and the motion
picture *Broken Arrow*. I have not found any records predating 1913,
either from Jeffords's contemporaries or from Jeffords himself, supporting what Jeffords told Forbes. If this incredible story were true,
it certainly would have been known by some of his associates and
perhaps even by some fo the Chiricahuas.

In contrast, some of Jeffords's contemporaries who knew about
the relationship had other opinions concerning its origin. One Indian agent wrote that it began while "having been a trader with
the Apaches for some length of time."[40] An army officer wrote
that Jeffords met Cochise while "prospecting in the mountains in
Cochise's country and was supposed to have effected friendly relations with Cochise"—virtually the same story related by Governor
Safford in late 1872.[41] Frank C. Lockwood, whose book *The Apache
Indians* stood as the best synthesis of the Apaches until the arrival of
Dan L. Thrapp's works, concurred, writing that Jeffords had quit his
job with the mail company and turned to prospecting. He visited
Cochise to "see if some agreement could not be entered into so that
he might pursue his *work* unmolested." By his work, Lockwood
was referring to prospecting.[42]

There is another argument which substantiates my thesis that no
such pact existed. A review of Apache ambushes on mail riders in
Chiricahua territory reveals that several attacks occurred between
1867, the accepted historic date of the compact, and 1872, when
Cochise finally made peace. In fact, near Apache Pass in May 1868,
Cochise's Chokonens slaughtered a mail rider and tortured to death
another, along with two soldiers. The mail riders were employed by
Jeffords,[43] so any agreement between him and Cochise must have

been consummated after this point and before the time Jeffords left Southern Overland, probably in early 1869. Yet Apache attacks on mail riders continued, with no discernable pattern, until Cochise's final peace in 1872.

The Apache version was told to Mrs. Eve Ball, their oral historian. Jeffords's visit was not a voluntary one but the result of his being captured by Cochise's men. The Apaches also say that Cochise spared his life because Jeffords displayed no fear. According to Asa Daklugie, their relationship began about ten years after the Bascom affair, placing the event about 1870–71.[44] Morris Opler wrote that his "informants had little to say about Jeffords . . . largely because of death taboos" but that his "best guess [was] that Jeffords became acquainted with Cochise in the capacity of a trader."[45]

After examining all the evidence, I believe the Jeffords-Cochise relationship began in the fall of 1870 when Cochise visited the Cañada Alamosa Reservation. As for Jeffords's alleged truce with Cochise to protect mail raiders, the only evidence we have is what Jeffords told Forbes in 1913. This finds no support in any previous statements or correspondence that would corroborate it.

Some contemporaries perceived Jeffords as a disreputable character and an opportunist who would sell anything to anyone in order to turn a profit. A number of army officers viewed him as a troublemaker, perhaps because of his complicity in the Drew controversy, perhaps because he used unconventional procedures to control the Indians, or perhaps because of conjecture that he sold guns and whiskey to the Indians, a charge made more than once. In fact, one officer claimed to have been present during a transaction[46] and another claimed he had witnesses who would testify against Jeffords.[47]

Jeffords was not a saint; if indeed he traded with Cochise when Cochise was considered hostile (and from October 1870 to October 1872, Cochise was on and off the reservation) and if indeed he pursued the job as Indian agent (evidence supports this, although he denied it), it should not overshadow or obscure the immense public service he performed. A historian has described him as "a rough self-reliant man able to cope with the times."[48]

Shortly after the Jeffords-Brevoort shakedown, Lieutenant Argalus Garey Hennisee, described as having "good talents, character and soldierly requirements," succeeded Drew as agent, the likeable officer having died of thirst after becoming lost in the mountains during a scout for hostile Mescaleros. Hennisee had served previously as agent for the Mescaleros, and in time he gained the confidence of Loco and Victorio.[49]

When Hennisee reached Chihenne country, he found 360 Chihennes but only 46 warriors present. This would change as word spread through Apachería that regular rations would be provided. With winter approaching, other bands came in. By late August 1870, some 540 Apaches were present, and Hennisee believed that more liberal rations would entice in more Apaches, perhaps even Cochise. He also requested farming implements, but this suggestion fell flat because Clinton's budget was used up. Hoping that Washington could offer help, Clinton wrote the Bureau of Indian Affairs; still no help came. Acting Commissioner of Indian Affairs William Cady ignored Clinton's plan with the standard bureaucratic response: "You are aware of the amount appropriated . . . [you] can decide how to allocate it." Clinton had other agencies to run, all with strained budgets, and could not accommodate unforeseen expenses.[50]

In October, William F. M. Arny,[51] a zealous religious reformer, arrived in Southern Apache country, eager to find a solution to the conflict which had raged throughout the 1860s. Appointed special agent the previous March, he had visited the Utes, Navajos, Zuñis, Hopis, and Pueblos. At Albuquerque in early October he met Hennisee, who agreed to gather the Indians at Cañada Alamosa for a council about October 22. Arny arrived in Apache country in mid-October. Here he met Victorio's and Loco's people and, to his pleasant surprise, found that Cochise had cautiously come in with thirty-four of his men—ninety-six Chokonens in all. Tom Jeffords was also in the vicinity.[52]

Cochise, committed to peace provided certain conditions were met, arrived on October 20. This excited Arny, who called him "the principal chief" of the White Mountain Apaches, Coyoteros, and Chiricahuas,[53] and Cochise immediately became the focus of attention. Hennisee and Arny, with Richard C. Patterson[54] interpreting, interviewed the reclusive chief.

The physical and emotional toll of a decade of war showed plainly

The canyon between Cañada Alamosa and Ojo Caliente, two active points in Cochise's time. (*Photo by Dan Thrapp*)

on Cochise's face as he spoke that first day. His speech was true to form. As he had with Perry and Green, he blamed the whites for beginning the war, at the same time admitting that his band had killed and robbed since that time; he had lost many men and now had more dependents than he could provide for. He carefully

avoided answering questions about specific past activities and refused to answer any questions which required a commitment of any
type. Arny and Hennisee judiciously failed to press him. Here are
excerpts from the interview as transcribed by Hennisee:

*Arny*—The Great Father wants to know what the Indians want so
as to keep peace.

*Cochise*—I have been to the White Mountains [Camp Thomas] to
learn how they talked and am now here to hear what you have to say
so that I can take the word back to my people at Chili Cowi
[Chiricahua Mountains].

*Arny*—This paper was written by the Great Father and I read what
he says to his children.

*Cochise*—I want to talk first, I have come to hear you talk. If the
government talks straight I want a good peace. My people . . . hide
in the mountains and arroyos and keep out of the way. I want the truth
told. A man has only one mouth and if he won't tell the truth he is put
out of the way.

*Arny*—The Great Father wants a good peace and they must stop
the killings and stealing and go upon a reservation or he will send
soldiers after them again and continue to do so until they are willing
to make peace.

*Cochise*—The Apaches want to run around like a coyote, they
don't want to be put in a corral.

*Arny*—The Great Father didn't want to put them in a corral. He
wants them to eat and dress like a white man, have plenty of everything and be contented, wants to know where they want to receive
their rations. . . . Talk it over among yourselves and tell me early
tomorrow what you want, where you want the rations issued. . . .

*Cochise*—We want it so that the whites and everybody can travel
where they please, build their fires at night, lay down and rest in
peace. . . . [I will] talk to all the tribes and learn what they want so
that I can talk straight. . . . I am going out to talk to the other Indians
and have them leave the roads clear.[55]

The conference ended the next day. Cochise explained that he
could not be held accountable for depredations committed by other
bands, for he was the leader only "in my own country," meaning
Chokonen territory. Yet he agreed to "send out for my people to
keep the roads clear." The Indians believed that their reservation
would be at a place they chose because that is what Arny had said to

them. Arny failed to anticipate the problems that this seemingly innocuous statement would create. He recommended that the government immediately provide food and clothing to the Apaches, whom he characterized as "the most vicious, barbarous and uncivilized" Indians in North America.[56]

Arny reached Albuquerque in early November and prepared a thorough report to Parker, outlining six potential reservations for the Apaches: Camp Thomas, Gila River, Mimbres River, Cañada Alamosa, Fort Stanton (east of the Río Grande in Mescalero country), and Fort Tularosa, situated some fifteen miles north of the town of Reserve above the Apaches' sacred Mogollons. After hearing Hennisee's recommendations, Arny advocated Fort Tularosa as the reservation site. It was a practical decision in that it removed the Apaches from the "vile whiskey sellers" at Cañada Alamosa, had good water and grass, and logistically supplies could be brought in from the Río Grande at reasonable rates. Furthermore, Arny declared, "the Indians themselves, I believe would prefer it to any other location," althought it is a mystery how he arrived at this conclusion. Finally, he recommended that no treaty be made until the reservation had been established and the Indians relocated. Those off the reservation would be considered hostile and the military could deal with them.[57]

Cochise had remained at Cañada Alamosa, but not without notice. After receiving rations on October 21, 1870, he tried to live quietly and renew old friendships with his Chihenne relatives and probably became acquainted with Tom Jeffords, who was the subject of a complaint for trading whiskey to Apaches for a mule.[58] Yet very few people believed that Cochise would stay put, such was his reputation. At Fort Bowie a skeptical Bernard was perturbed that Cochise was on a reservation, believing he would remain only till "spring or as long as he can keep quiet and collect some ammunition."[59] Two days later, on November 25, he wrote the commanding officer at Fort McRae:

> I hear that the chief Cochise and his band of Chiricahua Apaches is now on the reservation near your post. You will confer me a favor by forwarding this to the Indian agent in charge of the Indians. I wish him to let me know whether Cochise is on the reservation or not. I am charged with the duty of keeping him and his band from committing

depredations on the travellers on this road and settlers in this vicinity. If Cochise is now on the reservation, I feel confident that he will remain there only long enough to get us off the alert, when he will make an effort to take in some party. I . . . request that should he (Cochise) leave the reservation for any cause whatsoever, that I be notified of the fact at once so I may be on the look out for him. [When] he [Cochise] leaves to hunt . . . this will probably be his excuse to get away.[60]

Be that as it may, at the time of Bernard's request, Cochise had already left Cañada Alamosa for the Chiricahua Mountains to collect the remainder of his band. Leaving with Hennisee's consent, he took his brother-in-law, Salvadora, and two other men, telling the agent he would return with his people. On December 2, Captain George Shorkley responded to Bernard's letter:

In conversation with the agent yesterday he informed me that Cochise with 3 of his men left the reservation on November 16 with the declared intention of bringing upon the reservation all of his tribe and that this was to be done in five moons. The agent states that the remainder of the men Cochise brought in remain upon the reservation. From the pacific course pursued by Cochise it is believed that he desires a permanent peace.[61]

Hennisee confirmed Cochise's departure in a letter to Nathaniel Pope, who had succeeded Clinton as superintendent of Indian Affairs in New Mexico, and in anticipation of Cochise's return warned that immediate government aid must be sent or the Indians, whose patience was nearly exhausted, would leave at the first sign of spring.[62] Pope immediately fired off a letter to Parker, declaring that

Cachise is the most powerful and the most warlike chief of the Apaches and for a long time has been the terror to the citizens of southern New Mexico. His visit to Canada Alamosa . . . is considered a friendly demonstration and if he can be induced to settle upon the proposed reservation . . . I am sure that depredations . . . will cease in a short time.[63]

Cochise returned to the vicinity of Cañada Alamosa in early December but faced several fresh complications, a situation not conducive to controlling the heretofore hostile Chokonen. Hennisee acknowledged that "it will be several days before I learn whether or not it is true. [If so,] it is one of the most important events that ever happened to this territory."[64] Unfortunately for the suspicious Apaches, Hennisee was replaced by Orlando F. Piper,[65] who could not have come at a worse time. Cochise had met Hennisee and had shown trust in the agent by returning to Cañada Alamosa. Piper, a Presbyterian layman, was miscast as Hennisee's successor. These wild Indians required a strong but delicate hand; and Piper, according to an associate, "may have been a very good preacher but he was entirely out of his place as an agent."[66]

Cochise faced another obstacle upon his return. Washington had decided to move the Apaches from Cañada Alamosa to Fort Stanton in Mescalero country. Although many of the Chihennes maintained close relations with their Mescalero brethren, most did not wish to move east of the Río Grande, claiming they were unfamiliar with that country and unhappy with its cold winters. Cochise would never have considered moving. Piper quickly determined that the Indians would unanimously reject an order to locate at Fort Stanton: "It would be like beginning all over—they would resist, flee to the mountains." Cañada Alamosa offered "wood, water, pasture and good soil," reasoned Piper. "If the reservation is here there is no reason why they can't be satisfied."[67]

The government's inability to feed and clothe a thousand Apaches compounded the problem. Piper desperately needed one thousand blankets; Pope could send only two hundred. These significant shortages, combined with the new agent, plus the fear of removal, convinced Cochise to remain uncommitted. In mid-December someone, probably Tom Jeffords, told Piper that "Cochise is not at Canada Alamosa [but] that he could be brought in at a short time if sent for."[68] On December 23, Piper interviewed Loco, Victorio, and Nana and inquired of Cochise. They responded "he has gone after his people and will be back when the corn is up."[69] Fed up with the uncertainty about the future of the reserve, Cochise had returned to Arizona, probably taking those who had come in with him the previous October.

In Washington orders were issued for the War Department to supply subsistence to the Apaches, but Colonel Getty claimed he had barely enough beef to feed his own troops. Thus Nathaniel Pope, who had succeeded Clinton, was forced to cut funds for other agencies to buy supplies. For his part, Piper worked diligently throughout January 1871, urging the Indians to consider the proposed reservation at Fort Stanton. All attempts failed; "they positively refuse to go."[70] On the last day of January he recommended that the agency be located at Cañada Alamosa in anticipation of Cochise's return, which he believed was imminent. "Cochise would soon be in with his band," Piper said naïvely. In the end, the aging leader would return only if the situation at Cañada Alamosa stabilized.[71]

Chapter 16

# NO REST, NO PEACE

Cochise began the winter of 1871 in southeastern Arizona, awaiting the results of affairs at Cañada Alamosa. Once the situation there settled down, he decided, he would return to the reservation. He was tired of war. Unfortunately, Cochise's plans went awry and he found himself embroiled in one conflict after another as American troops hounded him and his people from one place to another. During the first six months of 1871, he found it impossible to avoid collisions with citizens and troops and said of this period that the Americans allowed him "no rest, no peace."[1]

Agent Piper was also busy in early 1871, hoping that once the government discarded the ill-advised Fort Stanton idea, Cochise would return. Piper's wishes notwithstanding, little had been accomplished to alleviate Cochise's apprehension: rations were irregular and scarce, clothing and blankets had been issued in small quantities, and the question of removal to Mescalero country remained a distinct possibility. To make matters worse, Cochise became involved in a series of hard fights in which Apache blood was spilled. All in all, the first six months of 1871 must have been confusing and troubling for the once powerful chief.

The first three weeks of the year passed uneventfully for Cochise, who was thought to be camped in the Chiricahuas. Troops had examined these mountains in late December but found no signs.[2] In mid-January, small parties of Indians began making for the Chiricahuas. At about the same time, a group of fifteen prospectors left Ralston, New Mexico (near present-day Lordsburg), for the Chiricahuas, where, according to a captured Apache woman, gold could be found. On January 23 some thirty miles south of Apache Pass, Apaches ambushed the party, wounding two men named Robert Schell and Hugh O'Neil.[3] Two others fled to Fort Bowie and reported the incident to Captain Bernard, who dispatched Captain Gerald Russell, a hard-fighting Irishman who had risen through the ranks, and thirty troops to the scene of the attack. Bernard was convinced that the Indians "are without doubt the band of Cochise as no others ever visit this range . . . close watch will have to be kept up to prevent depredations." Russell's scout found no trails, for the Indians had moved deeper into the mountains and some moved north toward the Gila River.[4]

From their winter camps, small Chiricahua raiding parties went out to make a living, their objective primarily stock. Toward the end of January a few warriors pilfered every head of stock from travelers near Fort Bowie. Other raiders ventured toward Silver City and on February 5 stole fourteen mules and horses. Certain of pursuit, they headed west to the Gila before shifting direction to the southwest and their destinations in the Chiricahuas. If they were pursued, the troops would halt at the Gila, or so the raiders thought. It was unusual for New Mexican troops to enter Arizona, which was part of a different military district, although the Apaches may not have realized this.

When news of the raid reached Fort Bayard, Captain William Kelly; fourteen men of Troops C, Eighth Cavalry; one packer; and Juan Arroyo, a skillful guide who was in the same class as Merejildo, left in pursuit. Kelly proceeded first to Silver City, where he was joined by seven citizens under James Bullard, a confirmed Indian hater. They followed the raiders' trail to the Gila, where it abruptly turned south along Mangas Creek, then continued into the Burro Mountains. Here on February 8 a party of seven troops joined Kelly, increasing his force to thirty-one men. The march was resumed as Arroyo cut the trail, which veered southwest through the Peloncillos and then turned west into the Chiricahuas. By February 12, the troops had penetrated the eastern Chiricahuas, following "a well beaten trail to the summit." At 1 P.M. Bullard's citizens found

the Indian camp, in all likelihood a few miles southeast of Chiricahua Peak some thirty miles southeast of Fort Bowie. That the pursuit
from Silver City was unexpected may be discerned by the Indians'
lack of a sentinel, a precaution Cochise usually employed. The
whites quickly made preparations and in a blinding snowstorm
poured a devastating fire on the bewildered Apaches. The fight
ended abruptly as the Indians deserted their camp, leaving behind
all of their possessions. The New Mexicans had achieved a complete
victory: fourteen Apaches dead (the bodies were counted), an estimated twenty wounded, and one captured.

Next the Americans turned to the task of looting and burning the
ranchería, which contained seventeen well-built wickiups. Among
the confiscated property were two thousand five hundred pounds of
beef and mule and horse meat, a priest's cassock, blankets, lead,
two rifles, five revolvers, and American military papers dated May
1868, implicating this group in the attack on the Southern Overland
U.S. Mail Company stagecoach at Apache Pass that month. Some
of the stock stolen from Silver City also was recovered. The next
day Kelly's party returned to the ranchería and found that the Indians had placed skins, manta, and other items around the body of
their leader, which led at least one observer to speculate that Cochise was among the slain. Actually the band was either a local
group of Cochise's Chokonens or quite possibly a Nednhi band win-
tering in the Chiricahuas. In fact, Geronimo may well have been involved because the results of Kelly's fight closely resembled what he
later described in his autobiography. In any event, Cochise was neither present nor involved.[5]

While Kelly was hunting Indians, a Chiricahua raiding party from
Cochise's group stole sixteen horses from Fort Bayard. On February
13 the post commander issued arms and provisions to thirty citizens
so they could follow the Indians. Heading the posse was a noted
Apache fighter, John Bullard (whose brother Jim was with Kelly).
His command followed the trail on a northwesterly course and
skirted the Mogollon Mountains to the San Francisco River country.
About February 24, Cochise's camp was found in the nearby mountains. After dividing his command, Bullard unexpectedly encountered an Apache who was fleeing to raise the alarm. Then, according to the *Las Cruces Borderer,*

[Bullard's] companion fired first, wounded the Apache in the thigh. Bullard shot him through the chest. As he sank to the ground the Apache drew with both hands a revolver from his belt and aimed with deadly precision at the Captain's breast. Bullard was reloading, saw the movement, and spoke to his friend to fire quick, but alas; too late. Almost simultaneously the revolver of the Apache and the rifle of Bullard's companion fired. The top of the Apache's head was blown to atoms and Bullard sank slowly to the ground. As he rested upon the turf Bullard opened his shirt bosom and examined his wound, then sinking backward died without a groan.[6]

By this time, other civilians had taken positions around the ranchería and unleashed a withering fire, forcing the Apaches to fall back. Fourteen were left dead in the village, among them Salvadora, who had left the reservation with Cochise the previous November.[7]

Not long after the battle Piper obtained the Indian version of it, confirming that Bullard had run into Cochise. In his monthly report dated March 31 the agent wrote that

10 or 12 new Indians have come in within a few days. They are said to be from Cochise's band. They are so shy that I thought best not to talk to them at present. They were in the fight with Captain Bullard's party. Three Indians who left here last fall were killed in the same fight. One of them was a son [Salvadora] of the old chief Mangas Coloradas.[8]

That spring Cochise was involved in other skirmishes, forcing his people to move from one place to another. On March 17 a small group of Apaches returning to Arizona from a raid into Chihuahua, ran off two mules from Fort Bowie. Russell, eleven soldiers, and two guides followed the Indians to the mountains north of Stein's Peak. On March 21 they discovered a large Chokonen ranchería of thirty to forty warriors and in a brief skirmish reportedly killed three Apaches. After the fight he returned to Bowie for reinforcements.[9]

Two days later the relentless officer departed again with thirty men and three citizens. Marching by night, they reached Pedrocito Canyon in the Peloncillo Range and discovered a deserted ranchería which contained a "tress of auburn colored woman's hair carefully wrapped in paper, . . . a gentleman's glove and a small book." From the direction of their trail, he concluded that "it is almost certain that a portion of the Indians had just returned from Old Mexico, in which case it would seem that they had been implicated in the perfidious massacre of Mr. Charles Keerle and wife about the [1st of March]."[10]

Russell tenaciously continued the pursuit and on March 28 overtook the Indians near Duncan, Arizona. Dividing his force into three platoons, he easily routed the Chiricahuas, who left their entire camp and possessions in the hands of the soldiers. Debris littered the ground. Russell thought he had killed fifteen Apaches and lamented that he would have killed more except "that two thirds of my command were recruits, while the greater portion of the old soldiers were with the pack-train, as it required the most active and experienced men for packers." In closing his report, he echoed the frustrations of many army officers, declaring "that the number of troops at this Post is entirely inadequate to [perform] their multifarious duties." Russell had defeated a Chokonen group which had been at Cañada Alamosa because ration tickets signed by Lieutenant Hennisee were found in the ranchería.[11]

Kelly's, Bullard's, and Russell's triumphs compelled some Chiricahuas to seek refuge at Cañada Alamosa, where Piper had gradually begun to improve relations via increased rations, additional clothing, and the abandonment of the Fort Stanton option. There were reports that many wounded warriors had limped back to the reservation, but not Cochise. Both Piper and Pope understood that only humane treatment and consistent policies would bring him in. The solution, they agreed, was to offer liberal rations. Piper, who had advocated this policy to Pope, received unsolicited support from New Mexico's Governor William A. Pile. On March 18, 1871, Pope wrote Indian Commissioner Parker in Washington and explained that the hostile Apaches, led by Cochise, were off the reservation. To convince the wary chief to return, they needed to promise him rations, he believed. Yet even with this flurry of activity, the severe losses he had suffered, and the new military leaders in Arizona and New Mexico, who planned extensive campaigns to obliterate him, the chief was not prepared to come in.[12]

The same day Pope was writing Parker, the latter was thinking about Cochise. Perhaps a face-to-face meeting in Washington with

the Great White Father would solve their differences, so Parker
wrote Pope:

> You are instructed to request the Apache Chief Cochise and such
> other chiefs of that tribe as you may deem to be a proper person on
> account of his influence among the tribe to visit this city [to] confer
> with the Department in regard to the condition and welfare of their
> people.[13]

For the next year, well-meaning whites would try to persuade Cochise of the benefits of going East, but before they could do so he
first had to be found.

On March 29, Pope instructed Piper to send out messengers to tell
Cochise that he would meet him at any "such place as he might se-
lect."[14] The logical choice for this important and dangerous task
was Tom Jeffords, who by this time was well known to Cochise. In
February, Piper had informed Pope that

> there is a man by the name of Jeffries [Jeffords] living at Canada Ala-
> mosa that is well acquainted with Cochise having been a trader with
> the Apaches for some length of time. He informs me that he believed
> that he can induce Cochise and his band to come in and settle on a
> reservation and is willing to make the effort provided he can have as-
> surance from the Indian Department that he will be liberally compen-
> sated for his time and trouble in case of success.[15]

Jeffords was either unavailable or Piper was unwilling to meet his
terms for compensation. Instead, the agent enlisted José María Tru-
jlllo,[16] a short, dark-haired, fifty-one-year-old Mexican who was the
justice of the peace at Cañada Alamosa, to head the search party
because the Indians would not go alone, fearful of meeting troops.
They left about April 11 and made for the Gila River and then
Stein's Peak, where Cochise had last been reported, but they found
no fresh signs. They returned to Piper ten days later, convinced that
Cochise had moved south, either "to Chihuahua or Sonora . . . with
most of the hostile Apaches to avoid the numerous scouting parties
of troops from the different posts in Arizona."[17]

Cochise had left the Gila River country but had not yet reached
Sonora. With most of his band, perhaps joined by a few Western
Apaches, he had returned to southeastern Arizona for a raid into

Mexico. They rendezvoused in the Dragoons, where he had camped in relative obscurity the previous two summers. In mid-April he made his presence felt. On the evening of April 13, Indians stole some cattle from a ranch on the San Pedro River. Five cowboys pursued what they thought was a small raiding party. After proceeding about four miles, they were overwhelmed by a reported one hundred Apaches, who killed three of the cowboys and wounded the other two. Early the next morning the Indians jumped the eastern mail rider, Mark Revelin (better known as Brigham), killed him and, as with Keerle's victims, cut his body "into small pieces," obviously to avenge their losses of the previous months.[18]

Late on April 14 a mail driver discovered Indians at Sulphur Springs; he wisely refused to proceed and sent a message to Fort Bowie. Early the next morning Russell, thirty troopers, and Merejildo Grijalva were in the saddle. Marching all day, they arrived at Dragoon Pass that evening and bedded down for the night. They found Revelin's body early the next morning. Russell sent Merejildo

Western Dragoon Mountains. Russell retired to this valley after his fight with Cochise in April 1871. (*Photo by Karen Hayes*)

and six men to follow the trail, which led to one of highest points in the Dragoons. Here he turned back and joined Russell, who had entered the Dragoons from the west. The scout thought the Apaches numbered about one hundred: fifty on foot and an equal number on horseback. He believed the Indians were waiting in ambush in the heights above them. With darkness approaching, he decided to remove his force to the San Pedro Valley and continue the chase the following morning.

Cochise had anticipated Russell's move. The hostiles' trail ostensibly led into the canyon, but Cochise had opted to backtrack and position his warriors in Russell's rear on both sides of the hills. Just as Russell began to retire from the mountains, the war party opened fire. Russell recalled that "the attack was commenced by firing one shot, then a volley, then a yell from every direction." The troops were surrounded and heavily pummeled, although, miraculously, no one was hit. Under Russell's steadying hand, his men refused to panic. After his troopers dismounted and secured their horses, they gave the Indians a hot reception. As the Apaches were "completely entrenched," Russell ordered a retreat toward the valley after a twenty-minute fight. Neither party suffered any known casualties. Russell was sure that Cochise had led the Indians, stating "now this is one of Cochise's tricks for he is positively the only Indian in the country who waits for troops and resorts to this kind of strategy." Furthermore, Merejildo may have recognized either Cochise or his voice because Major Andrew Wallace Evans noted that the Apaches were commanded by "Cochise in person."[19]

Russell decided that "it would be a useless risk to go into the mountains after Cochise with so few men." Consequently, he sent a runner to Evans, requesting reinforcements. Shortly after, his force arrived at the San Pedro settlement, where he learned the details of the April 13 fight. He dispatched another courier to Fort Lowell in Tucson. On April 18 the reinforcements from Bowie reached Russell, swelling his force to sixty-three men. He marched back to the Dragoons and by early morning of April 19 had climbed to the highest point in the range, probably Mount Glenn, which was only a few miles north of Cochise's two strongholds. From here he could discern Chiricahua campfires.

Cochise had left a few scouts to watch Russell's movements. That night he slipped west to the San Pedro and followed the river south into the Huachucas, while others cut west toward the Whetstone Mountains. Russell tenaciously followed the hostiles for two days before he was forced to abandon the chase because of a severe attack of inflammatory rheumatism. He believed that Cochise "with his band can be found without fail" in the Huachuca Mountains.[20]

At Tucson, Captain Alexander Moore, an experienced officer in the Southwest, commanding Fort Lowell, organized a series of patrols against the hostiles south of the Gila. Feeling that Cochise might slip into Sonora, Moore wrote Governor Pesqueira of his intentions to protect the settlements by regular details along the border. Regarding Cochise, Moore pledged that he would "totally annihilate this band," which, he believed, was living in the Dragoons or Chiricahuas. If Pesqueira approved, Moore proposed to follow hot trails into Sonora.[21]

At the time, Pesqueira's troops were making inroads against the Apaches, prompted in part by the scalp bounty. The U.S. reservation policy had restricted the Apaches' ability to come and go as they pleased. Furthermore, attrition was taking its toll as Cochise's war headed into its second decade. Since the Sonoran offensive of 1867–68, the only Apaches who periodically remained in Mexico were Juh's Nednhis, although some Chokonens may have camped in Mexico from time to time. By early 1871 the Mexicans could sense that the tide had turned; no longer could large Apache war parties ravage the state and leave burned ranches and destroyed towns behind them.

Pesqueira probably appreciated Captain Moore's information concerning the Apaches along the border, though it came as no surprise. He had received reports from his subordinates that there were rancherías in the Huachuca and Mule mountains. A mid-April scout forced a Chiricahua group to abandon its village in the Sierra Madre and leave behind everything. Cochise's people were pressured no matter where they went.[22]

Cochise usually did not range as far west as the Whetstone or Huachuca mountains. He had been pushed from the Gila country into southern Arizona as U.S. troops made one patrol after another. By early May he had probably moved his camp back to the Dragoons, living at the very top of the mountains, from which he could observe the valleys on both sides. He soon learned of the Camp Grant massacre, one of Arizona's darkest moments, in which some one hundred Apaches were slain.[23] The details of this well-known affair will not be repeated here; suffice it to say that it rivaled, if it did not surpass in barbarity and savagery, any of the atrocities committed by Indians against whites. These same Tucson citizens, it was rumored, planned a similar action against Cochise in early May.[24]

In the meantime, Captain Moore had dispatched troops to southern Arizona in search of Cochise. One scout was led by Lieutenant Howard Bass Cushing, whose sole objective was to kill Apaches in general and Chiricahuas under Cochise in particular. Cushing stood five feet seven inches and had great determination; he seemingly possessed no fear and had boundless energy. Captain John G. Bourke remarked that Cushing was "the bravest man he ever saw,"[25] which was quite an accolade considering Bourke's long and distinguished service in the West. This flamboyant pair, Bourke and Cushing, had led several successful scouts against the Mescaleros and the Western Apaches, but there is no evidence to indicate that they had ever fought Chiricahuas. Cochise, to Cushing's dismay, had not been totally whipped.

Cushing had become obsessed with subjugating Cochise. The previous September he had discussed with Stoneman and Mowry the possibility of going out after him. According to Mowry, Cushing "was in great hopes and determination of capturing Cochise and his band."[26] With Cochise's whereabouts known, Captain Moore ordered Cushing to scout the Sonoita and Santa Cruz valleys. He scoured southern Arizona for one week before he was decoyed and killed by Chiricahuas near the Whetstone Mountains on May 5, 1871. Two other men died in the fight, and the Indians were believed to have suffered heavy losses.

Contemporary accounts attributed Cushing's death to Cochise, who was blamed for virtually every depredation in southeastern Arizona. Sergeant Mott described the Apache chief as a "thick, heavy set man, who never dismounted from a small brown horse during the fight." This description does not fit Cochise, and historian Dan L. Thrapp argues convincingly that the Apache leader Mott observed was Juh, the prominent Nednhi leader. Mrs. Eve Ball's informants corroborated Thrapp's conclusions that Juh led the Apaches who defeated Cushing.[27]

Cochise was probably in Mexico at the time. In May he led a war party against Sonora in response to several recent Mexican campaigns. On April 24, Colonel Elías had scouted as far north as Apache Pass and after a short stay at Fort Bowie started for home. En route, his scouts located a small ranchería in the southern Chiricahuas. Elías quickly divided his force, surrounded the camp, and easily obliterated the entire encampment of ten individuals (killing four men and four women and capturing two children).[28] Word spread quickly throughout Apache country. It was quite conceivable that Cochise led the Sonora raid to retaliate for Elías's campaign. In any event, his war party wreaked havoc in northern Sonora.

Cochise remained in Sonora for about two weeks before returning to Arizona. From Santa Cruz came a report that one hundred Apaches under him were raiding the state. On May 13 the Chiricahuas attacked a small party near Baviacori and captured Antonio Ochoa. In an unusual ploy, the Apaches (perhaps Cochise) forced Ochoa to write a letter to authorities in which they threatened to kill their captive if they were pursued; if not followed, they offered to sell him at either Santa Cruz or Fronteras. The Apaches felt threatened by the reinforcements of troops in northern Sonora, but whether their proposal was considered by the Sonorans is not known. There is no record that the Apaches returned their captive.[29]

On May 23, Cochise's war party, now estimated at sixty men, ambushed eleven men about a mile south of the border in the vicinity of the Patagonia Mountains; the Indians killed two and wounded two. The following day they attacked the Agua Fria ranch, wounding two men, then hit Calabasas, killing J. B. Blanchard and George K. Saunders. Both fights, which occurred on May 24, were hard fought, with the boldness of the attacks characteristic of a Cochise war party. One white man, John Petty, shot several Apaches, one of whom might have been Cochise, who returned to camp slightly wounded. The Apaches were well armed with "needle guns and Henry Rifles, no arrows were used"—further evidence that this was probably Cochise because his band was the best armed of all

Apaches. After these forays the hostiles fled east toward the San Pedro and then split, Cochise for the Dragoons and another party for the Huachucas and Chiricahuas.[30]

Cochise arrived at the west stronghold about May 24 or 25 and learned that José María Trujillo, with the assistance of a couple of Chihennes, had found his camp about May 15. Pope had sent Trujillo's mixed party of Apaches and Mexicans out on April 26 with orders not to return until they found Cochise. Although they discovered his camp, they could persuade only about a hundred Chokonens, primarily women and children with three leaders, to return to Cañada Alamosa. Cochise's own family and immediate followers refused to go until he returned from his raid in Sonora.[31] Shortly after his return, nine warriors departed to join their relatives at Cañada Alamosa. They arrived on May 31 and revealed that Cochise "has returned from his raid and is now at camp wounded." Thinking this might be an opportune time to bring him in, Pope tried to organize another party to "go to the camp and wait till Cochise returns but [I] find great difficulty in persuading or hiring persons to go for the trip is a very dangerous one."[32]

This time Tom Jeffords agreed to go, with Pope and Piper contracting to pay him one thousand dollars for his service. He left on June 7 with a good idea of where Cochise had last been seen. Besides himself, two Apaches and two Mexicans (Florentino Gonzáles and La Virgin Sánchez) comprised his party. Heading west, Jeffords reached the northeast end of the Chiricahuas on June 15. Here he left Gonzáles with the mules, and Jeffords, Sánchez, and the two Indian guides started for the Dragoons. The next day they found Cochise and delivered Pope's offer of rations, protection, and the invitation to visit Washington.

Yet even the influential Jeffords could not persuade Cochise to leave Arizona. The chief admitted that "he also desired peace and would be glad if his people were at Canada Alamosa but that his country was filled with soldiers and he was afraid to continue with his women and children." He might come in when "the troops were withdrawn" from his country.[33] Even Jeffords's letter of safe conduct guaranteeing him protection could not dissuade Cochise, who remained adamant, probably because of the recent Camp Grant massacre, or so Jeffords believed. Jeffords reluctantly left. He arrived at Cañada Alamosa about June 26 and reported to Pope his conversation with Cochise.

For some reason, both Piper and Pope were somewhat dubious about Jeffords's veracity. In his first report, dated June 28, Pope said he was "disposed to credit" Jeffords's story because the facts were "confirmed by the Indians who were with him." Shortly after that, an impressionable Piper wrote that "it is the general opinion that he did not see Cochise."[34] The whole matter was apparently drummed up by a man named Coffman, who had wanted to accompany Jeffords but was denied unequivocally because the Indians refused to take a stranger along. This ruffled Coffman, who did not have to look far to find others who would discredit Jeffords, always a controversial man. Hoping to clear up any misunderstanding, Jeffords wrote Pope on July 24, sending affidavits of the two Mexicans who accompanied him:

> Enclosed please find evidence complying on my part to the letter with our contract. After your leaving Canada [Alamosa] there must have arrizen a doubt in your mind of good faith on my part. Its cause I do not ask though if it is from anything that Mr. Coffman said to you when he went to Santa Fe I regret it.[35]

In 1872, Brigadier General Howard confirmed Jeffords's visit. "I have indisputable proof that he [Jeffords] visited Cochise in these same mountains . . . at the time you sent him. Ponce and chiefs separately told me where they saw him." By then Jeffords had received half the money promised him.[36]

In the summer of 1871, Cochise tried to avoid troops until the right opportunity to return to the reservation presented itself. He remained in southern Arizona fully two and one-half months after he saw Jeffords and, except for a couple of encounters, successfully avoided white contact. American troops were everywhere, and at no place—not even the Dragoons, Chiricahuas, or Mexico—was he safe from potential catastrophe. Although he tried to live as quietly as possible (with some raiding into Mexico), he steadfastly avoided hostilities in southern Arizona because he knew the military would vigorously follow any of his parties. He was a prisoner in his own country.

In spite of his isolation, Cochise was cognizant of the military buildup in southern Arizona, undoubtedly aware that a large column of troops had left Tucson in July under Lieutenant Colonel George Crook. Crook replaced Stoneman, who had been swept out in a wave of condemnation led by Governor Anson Safford. Once a staunch supporter, Safford turned on Stoneman after reading his recommendations to close five posts. The governor complained to the secretary of war and in April met with President Grant, who promised to find a suitable replacement. Crook was selected.[37]

Military activities were also heating up in New Mexico. The new commander, Colonel Gordon Granger, whose quarry also was Cochise, had drawn up plans for an extensive campaign involving two hundred troops. He intended to cooperate with the Department of Arizona "to scout the Chiricahuas" and effect the "destruction of this notorious Indian [Cochise]."[38] Yet even as these two military commanders made preparations to carry out their responsibilities, government officials in Washington had a change of heart. They were appalled at the Camp Grant massacre, and this influenced government policy regarding the Apaches for the next few years. A new policy was adopted, one based on deeply humanitarian notions.

This philosophical dichotomy prevailed not only in the Southwest but was found on the national level. Two letters published in the *Army and Navy Journal* a week apart represented two diverse solutions to the Apache problem. The first responded to the Camp Grant affair and the second was provoked by the death of the popular and dashing Cushing. The theme of both letters was the government's treatment of Apaches. Samuel Forster Tappen, respected and much admired for his courage and integrity, had been a member of several peace commissions to the Plains Indians. He skeptically pointed out that "speculators and adventurers in Arizona want an army there, and to get it an Indian war must be provoked at all hazards." Without knowing much about the Apaches, he emphatically condoned their mode of warfare, conceding that "if any people in the world were ever justified in making war and for the most excessive casualties upon their enemies, the Apaches were."[39]

Tappan's views were countered a week later by the ubiquitous Sylvester Mowry. Enraged by Cushing's death and disgusted with vacillating federal policy, he attacked the "pseudo philanthropists—

the Senators or members of Congress—who, from a maudlin sympathy, cry out for religion and blankets for the Indians, or vote the troops to put an end to their bloody orgies." Place these benevolent men in Arizona and they would empathize with southwesterners, bellowed Mowry. He advocated a simple solution: Give Crook adequate troops and "perfect freedom of action" and only then would the Apaches be exterminated or finally subjugated.[40]

Tappan and Mowry, both sincere in their convictions, typified the beliefs of two groups. The former spoke for the eastern humanitarians, philanthropists, and religious leaders who were appalled by government mistreatment of the noble red man. On the other side stood Mowry, speaking for most westerners, who had suffered from years of Indian raids, and the army, which was eager to rectify past criticism of inactivity and incompetence. The western press criticized the inconsistent government policies; The concerns of eastern humanitarians would vanish if they lived in Apache country, it said. For the most part, the southwestern press preached military force as the solution. The *Las Cruces Borderer* delightedly announced that the army's "good work was progressing—within one month some fifty Indians had been made 'good Indians.'"[41] A Tucson newspaper added that the Apaches must be "thoroughly subjugated by military power and any attempts to compromise before they are reduced to this condition is accepted by them as an acknowledgement of weakness and cowardice."[42]

At this stage in May 1871 arrived the best Indian fighter in the United States Army, a courageous man and a relentless campaigner who had sympathy and compassion for the Indians, George Crook. His reputation had preceded him, and if the advance notices were true, he would prove to be the very antithesis of the passive Stoneman. "Indian hunting is Crook's specialty," wrote a correspondent. "The fact is Crook is nothing but an Indian anyway . . . his mind, physiognomy and education are all Indian."[43] The *Arizona Citizen* noted that he was "a Lieutenant Colonel who would fight the Indians and know how to do it."[44]

Praise for Crook came from all quarters, while in the next breath came the qualifier: if the government would allow him to implement his policies. Wrote a correspondent from Fort McDowell: "Will the government aid him as he needs or will the Quaker policy still

continue to rule and he go under like his predecessors?"[45] Another
tersely predicted: "He will clean out the Apaches, provided the poli-
ticians leave him alone."[46]

In his autobiography Crook wrote that "he did not want the assignment" because he was "tired of fighting Indians." His feelings
were assuaged because he believed the position was temporary, after
which he could move on to something less challenging.[47] Yet his actions belied an ambivalent or apathetic attitude. After he arrived in
Tucson on June 19 in his characteristically unpretentious, unob-
trusive manner, his first step was to confer with citizens, scouts, and
officers to learn all he could about the Apaches. He quickly assimilated this information and concluded that the hostiles must be defeated in their own terrain. Once this was accomplished, he would
treat them in a fair and humane manner, establishing strict but com-
passionate policies. The consensus of those to whom Crook spoke,
however, was that Cochise had to be defeated. It was therefore
against Cochise that Crook planned his campaign:

> Ranging down into Mexico and New Mexico are what are known
> as Cochise's band. Their numbers being variously estimated at from
> 80 to 300 warriors. This chief has the reputation of being very smart
> and an uncompromising enemy to all civilization and has such an in-
> fluence over the two other tribes [Pinals and Coyoteros] that their
> warriors are only too glad to join him in his numerous raids . . . , it is
> against Cochise' band that I propose concentrating all my energies for
> the present.[48]

On July 11 Crook's column of 204 men left Tucson for Fort
Bowie via the same trail used by Carleton's California Column nine
years before. His avowed objective was to subjugate Cochise and his
band. When his command reached Bowie, it struck north, Crook
believing he was on Cochise's trail. But Cochise was in southern
Arizona. After two weeks of unsuccessful scouting, Crook arrived
at Fort Apache on August 12, 1871. There, to his astonishment,
he discovered Trujillo and Loco, whom Piper had sent out to find
Cochise. Crook was astounded that Trujillo was trying to find the
same Indian he was trying to defeat. Totally exasperated, he ordered
Trujillo to return to New Mexico, even instructing him which route
to take, on the grounds that "two of this party were recognized by

several of my men as being Cochise's worst men and whom they knew to be ringleaders in some of his past outrages." Crook added magnanimously that he did not arrest them (although he believed they were spies) because he did not want to "interfere with the policies of the Indian Department."[49]

By this time, much to Crook's consternation, the government had finally arrived at its Apache policy. On July 17 the War Department had issued orders instructing him to suspend operations until a new peace commissioner had an opportunity to seek a peaceful solution with the hostiles. Crook says he became aware of this order on August 27 when he arrived at Camp Verde. He suspended his campaign, albeit grudgingly, writing Washington that if authorized, "with my present arrangement and knowledge, I have not the slightest doubt of my ability to conquer" and secure "a lasting peace with the Apache race in a comparatively short space of time."[50] He was not boasting.

Crook's reaction was predictable. Despite his admirable qualities, he was at times intolerant of those who disagreed with his views and methods, including his superiors. The arrival of the new peace commissioner, Vincent Colyer, was not well received by Crook, who, with the benefit of hindsight, wrote caustically that he "had been sent out by the 'Indian Ring' to interfere with my operations . . . and was going to make peace by the grace of God."[51] As for Cochise, weary of life on the run, he was ready to bring his people to a reservation.

# Chapter 17

## CAÑADA ALAMOSA

Vincent Colyer, Quaker and humanitarian, had been sent by President Grant partly in response to the Camp Grant massacre and partly to persuade Cochise to visit Washington. As far as most southwesterners were concerned, particularly the partisan press, Colyer's humanitarian ways were egregiously misguided when applied to the Apaches; to them, he was an uninformed easterner who at best possessed a superficial understanding of the situation. To be fair, his mission would accomplish some good. Historian Dan L. Thrapp wrote that he established "a series of reservations which was to form the framework of the system for settling the Indians that is in existence to this day."[1]

Colyer's assignment incensed most southwesterners. First, his appointment as peace commissioner had suspended Crook's offensive; second, Colyer, edgy from scurrilous attacks on his character and motives, became openly critical of white treatment of the Apaches. The *Daily New Mexican* at Santa Fe referred to him disparagingly as an "old philanthropic humbug." The *Arizona Miner* went a step further and slandered his character, calling him a "cold-blooded scoundrel [and] a red-handed assassin." According to its editor, John Marion, Arizonans should "dump the old devil into the shaft of some mine, and pile rocks upon him until he is dead." Governor Anson Safford, whose position required impartiality, tried to give Colyer the benefit of the doubt and advised patience. He felt that

Colyer would eventually recognize the error of his ways and the situation then would be turned back to Crook for resolution.[2]

Colyer and a small escort of troops reached Cañada Alamosa in mid-August 1871. Here he met Piper, who he thought was "a discreet and able officer," yet he found few Apaches. They had stampeded after hearing a rumor that some whites from the Mimbres were planning a repetition of the Camp Grant massacre. A few days later, Piper convinced seventy-five Apaches to return; a few months earlier, he had fed one thousand. Colyer categorically blamed all of the problems on unreasonable citizens: "Is it not a shame that a few lawless white men can thus be allowed to overturn all the good work of the Government . . . [and] risk the bringing about of a costly war?"[3]

His conclusion was a classic example of the naïveté with which white peace commissioners approached the Indian problem. Colyer's analysis was an oversimplification in that he exonerated the government from any responsibility. Yet for the past two years the government had procrastinated in providing help and security for these same Indians. If it had adopted a consistent and humane position, practically every Chiricahua, including Cochise, would have settled on the reservation.

Meanwhile, as Colyer was en route to New Mexico, Pope and Piper continued to do all they could to locate Cochise and persuade him to come in. Although Trujillo's party was turned back by Crook in mid-August, other Apaches may have given Cochise Colyer's message. On August 14, Colyer wrote, "Cochise heard from," although no specifics were given.[4] Finally, on August 19 or 20, some forty Chokonens arrived at Cañada Alamosa, followed by Cochise's brother Juan and another seventeen on the twenty-first. Cochise had sent them, believing "they would find a good piece here" and that "they must come and stay." These Chiricahuas brought the first definite news about Cochise since Jeffords had returned in late June. Whether Cochise was responding to Colyer's invitations was neither known nor important. The bottom line was that he had decided to move back to the reservation. Arizona, he commented later, "was a bad place"; if he had remained, in all probability he eventually would have been captured or killed.[5]

These freshly arrived Chokonens brought news that Papagos had surprised Cochise's camp along the Arizona-Sonora boundary, scattering his band. Needing stock to move his people to New Mexico, Cochise's men had pilfered forty horses from Pagagos living in northern Sonora. The Papagos, led by a chief named Miguel, followed the trail into the coniferous Santa Rita Mountains in southern Arizona. At daybreak, Miguel's party caught the ranchería by surprise. The results, as published in the Sonoran press, were strikingly similar to what the Indians later told Colyer. According to the Papagos, the Apaches offered "little resistance, abandoned their horses and ran up the mountains." Some five or six Chokonens were killed and their ears cut off and turned in for the bounty. The Apache version was similar. They admitted to Colyer that some five or six had been killed before Cochise retired to the inaccessible part of the mountains, having first killed his horses for food. At the time of the attack Cochise was sick, either from a recent wound or from the illness which would claim his life some three years later. This incident took place in mid-August 1871.[6]

The rest in the Santa Ritas had been good for Cochise's people, but morale had to be deteriorating. Troops had hounded them ever since they left Cañada Alamosa; on both sides of the border, soldiers seemed omnipresent. It was time for Cochise and his men to think of the less-dangerous reservation life if they wanted to survive as a people.

While Colyer was conferring with the Chihennes about the site for a reservation, Cochise was making plans to leave Arizona. Yet he still needed mounts, and Camp Crittenden, being within easy striking distance, was a reasonable choice. There was little doubt that Cochise was present because some of the captured horses were later seen in his possession at Cañada Alamosa. In addition, the nature of the raid was characteristic of Cochise. It occurred about midmorning on September 4, 1871, when twenty-five warriors charged the herd at Crittenden, which was guarded by one sergeant and seven privates. The surprise was complete and the Indians' appearance was "so impetuous and unexpected that many of the herders were panic stricken." In a moment, the entire herd of fifty-four horses and seven mules was in the hands of the Apaches. According to an unofficial account—which might explain the ease in which the attack was carried out—Cochise had dressed "six or eight of his

most trusted men in the garb of the Papago hay cutters. They rode
right through the parade grounds and on to the herds . . . when all
of a sudden, the Indians gave the war hoop." Whatever the particulars, pursuit was fruitless. An officer tersely remarked that "infantry
upon foot could accomplish nothing in rescuing a fleeing herd
driven by well mounted Indians."[7]

While the Camp Crittenden raid was taking place, other Chiricahuas duplicated Cochise's feat by running off some eighty head of
stock at Fronteras[8] before crossing into the United States. Cochise
now had sufficient animals to move his people to Cañada Alamosa.
Here the great Chiricahua chief, now past sixty and with his health
deteriorating and his people decreasing in number, hoped to spend
the rest of his days at peace with as little American contact as
possible.

Once in New Mexico, Cochise found that Colyer's entourage had
left, but not before setting aside a reservation northwest of Cañada
Alamosa. On September 23 or 24, the chief turned to the one white
he trusted and sent a runner to Tom Jeffords, then living at Cañada
Alamosa. Cochise offered to "deliver him[self] up to the government in any manner he chose," thereby revealing the faith he placed
in Jeffords and his futility of living as a free Apache. On September
26, Jeffords told Piper that Cochise was in the vicinity, saying it
could take ten days to bring him in; later that evening he qualified
the projection to either "tomorrow or the next day without fail."
Piper at once wrote Pope, asking him to "get here with as little delay as possible" and recommending that Jeffords "be liberally compensated," for the scout had yet to receive any of the thousand dollars he had been promised.[9]

Still the old warrior remained suspicious, as was attested by the
manner in which Jeffords was brought to his camp. W. H. Harrison
was with Jeffords when Cochise's messenger showed up at 11 P.M.
on September 27. Harrison recalled:

We opened the door and our Indian courier came in and told the Captain to come over at once so we mounted and rode about three hours,
came to his outpost, but the guide took us through alright to Cochise's
camp, where, with about two hundred warriors, we drank Tissween
and smoked an hour before we started for Canada Alamosa."[10]

On the morning of September 28, Cochise arrived at the agency and met Orlando F. Piper.

Piper was awestruck to meet the man he had heard so much about during the past ten months. He courteously invited Cochise into his quarters to talk. Cochise demurred, saying "no we talk out here," and his "Indians spread some blankets" while the chief's bodyguards scrutinized every movement. Piper was no match for Cochise, according to an eyewitness.[11] The agent's report was succinct:

> Cochise and his band came in on the 28th. He says that he wants peace, that his people are nearly all killed off. I have had several talks with him and gave him and his party presents and double rations. He expressed himself well pleased with the reception given him and was satisfied that I was acting in good faith. I feel satisfied that he is anxious for peace.[12]

Apparently Cochise was camped on the Cuchillo Negro, about twelve miles south of the agency, with thirty warriors and some two hundred members of his band.

Piper immediately wrote both Pope and Captain George Shorkley about Cochise, asking the latter, "Can't you come up and see the great warrior of the Age?" He felt that Cochise was a man of "great natural talents" who could be "of great advantage" to the agency if his confidence could be obtained.[13]

As expected, Cochise's arrival was greeted with much excitement. Nathaniel Pope rushed down from Santa Fe to meet him and try to persuade him to visit Washington. In early October he and Piper conferred with Cochise. More of Cochise's men had arrived, bringing his following to perhaps 60 men; soon, Chiva[14] (or Cheever) showed up with another 190 individuals. Chiva, a Bedonkohe or Chokonen chief, remained prominent throughout the Geronimo wars of the 1880s. Piper suggested that since Cochise was "very shy of soldiers . . . no troops should be sent here for a short time."

Cochise promised to remain at peace and agreed "to send runners to all roving bands to tell them what he had done and to advise them to go to the reservation at once." Most of the Chokonens would follow him in; nonetheless, there were some who "could not be induced to come in," and Cochise emphasized that he could not be held responsible for their actions. In return, Pope pledged to "feed, clothe and protect him and all his Apaches" and invited him to visit Washington.[15] Yet Cochise still feared treachery. It was reported "that a guard of his own men watch him and those who visit him at all times; his horse is saddled and placed near him nightly and for many nights he slept with the lariat in his hands." The suspicious chief would not consider leaving his country and place himself in the hands of any Americans.[16]

After the meeting, Cochise moved his group farther west along the Cuchillo Negro to the foothills of the Black Mountains, camping at a place later called Chise.[17] He wanted to be left alone, but his arrival had created a great deal of publicity. The press continued to view his presence with uncertainty and became increasingly skeptical when raids continued in southeastern Arizona, Cochise's normal stomping ground. One engagement in particular generated much controversy because it took place near Apache Pass, and the experienced officer involved suspected that he had fought Cochise. Of course he had no idea that Cochise was sitting in his wickiup some two hundred miles northeast at the time of the engagement.

On October 21, 1871, sixty Chiricahuas burned a ranch at San Simon, some twenty-five miles northeast of Fort Bowie. One man was killed and another was slightly wounded but managed to make his way to Bowie, arriving there the next day. The indomitable Gerry Russell took twenty-five men and marched to San Simon, finding the burned ranch and the body of Richard Barnes. Russell struck the trail and ascertained that because it came from the east, it must have originated from Cañada Alamosa, although one must question how he could have come to this absolute conclusion. He followed the trail along the eastern slopes of the Chiricahuas until it veered directly west into Horseshoe Canyon of the Chiricahua Mountains, northeast of the spot where Bernard had fought Cochise two years before. As his men halted to water their stock, the Apaches "from all directions with the most fiendish yells . . . opened a double crossfire." The first volley killed Russell's guide, a popular and athletic civilian named Bob Whitney.[18] The fight raged for four hours before the Apaches withdrew. Besides Whitney, Russell's command had one trooper wounded and two horses killed; the Apache losses were unknown, but as the soldiers had fired two thousand rounds "with great deliberation," Russell believed the Indians had been severely punished.[19]

Based on several factors, Russell honestly felt that Cochise had led the Indians, which naturally provoked another controversy because Cochise was supposed to be peacefully settled on the reservation. The press delightedly disparaged the peace policy, proudly claiming, "I told you so." Russell offered his well-reasoned explanation for identifying Cochise as the leader to the editors of the *Las Cruces Borderer,* who had interviewed Cochise in the Black Mountains on October 27, only three days after Russell's fight in the Chiricahuas. Russell explained:

> To say that Cochise was seen standing on a rock and identified is simply nonsense; I am sure I never said so and if any man of the party said so he was certainly mistaken. . . . But I did say that Cochise was there for the following reasons. The trail which I followed led into Horseshoe Canyon from the northside and left it on the southside; continuing down the valley at the same time the Indians were in the canyon waiting for me. Now this is one of Cochise's tricks. . . . The attack was commenced by firing one shot, then a volley and then a yell from every direction. Now I was attacked by Cochise when there was no doubt as to his presence in the Dragoon Mountains last April in precisely the same manner; . . . besides all this an Indian yelled Yo Cachise in plain English [and] Chivero.[20]

Chivero was a reference to Merejildo Grijalva, whom the Apaches had mistaken for Bob Whitney. Russell's argument was sound, but Cochise was not present. The fight was almost certainly the work of Juh's Nednhis, together with some of Cochise's Chokonens who had not made peace.[21]

Russell's attributing the raid to Cochise agitated the press and stirred up questions about Cochise's peaceful intentions. Word reached Vincent Colyer in Washington, and he immediately telegraphed Pope, asking "Has Cochise left Cañada Alamosa on warpath? When did you last hear from him?" Ten days later, Pope assured Colyer that "Cochise has not left the reservation," a fact that Tom Jeffords corroborated a few months later.[22]

It was this same widespread skepticism of Cochise's presence and his intentions which had prompted the editors of the *Las Cruces Borderer* to visit him. "Knowing the intense interest entertained by the people of southern New Mexico regarding the celebrated Apache Chief Cochise, . . . we determined for the benefit of the public to venture our scalp within reach of his blood stained hands." Accompanying them was Charles Coleman, a former Butterfield Overland Mail employee who had known Cochise at the Apache Pass stage station in 1860.

The editors went west to the agency, where they were joined by Piper, before proceeding to Cochise's ranchería fifteen miles southwest of the agency. Cochise was lying in his wickiup and came out when he recognized Piper's voice. After introductions, Coleman asked, "Do you know me Cochise?" Cochise thought for a moment and abruptly exclaimed, "Yes. Charley—Apache Pass, much time ago, put shoes on mules." Dos-teh-seh also recognized Coleman, as did many of the older warriors. Coleman commented that Cochise "had changed very little since 1860, except that he was not so fleshy and strong as then."[23]

Journalists by trade, the editors of the *Las Cruces Borderer* succeeded in obtaining the most revealing and insightful interview ever granted by Cochise, who may have opened up because they were not government officials. A relaxed Cochise carefully responded to the reporters' questions without the evasiveness which characterized most of his interviews with Anglos. Of course he refused to talk of past actions, undoubtedly fearing white retribution. The editors described him as a "tall and finely formed man . . . little indication of age. His hair is intensely black, his face smooth and slightly ornamented with yellow ochre. His mouth is splendidly formed and flexible, his nose prominent and his eye expresses no ferocity. . . . His countenance is pleasant . . . a sense of melancholy and thoughtfullness is clearly discernible." When asked why he had left Arizona, Cochise replied that he had been "allowed no rest the past year, that the people of Arizona would give him no peace, that the country was bad and everything there pinched him." In keeping with every other interview, Cochise blamed the war on the Americans. Now he wanted his views made public: "Tell the people that I have come here to make peace, a good peace, that I like this country and wish to spend the remainder of my life here at peace with all men."[24]

Cochise expressed two concerns during this talk. The first was that hostile Chokonens remained out in the Chiricahua Mountains (a local group which had not made peace), in southern New Mexico (a small group of Chokonens or Chihennes under Miguel Tuerto), and north and west of Lake Guzmán (Juh's and Geronimo's Nednhis). He thought his own Chokonens living in the Chiricahuas would eventually make peace, but the Nednhis would fight "until the last one was killed." He did not want to be held responsible for their actions.

The second point he emphasized dealt with the impending removal to the new reservation at Tularosa. The editors had quickly realized the importance of this delicate subject because Cochise's reply to every question was "coupled with a request that he might live and die here and not be removed to another reservation and in this expression Loco and Cheever joined with." The Indians' removal seemed to be the uppermost idea in their minds. The editors' last statement referred to the new reservation established by Vincent Colyer two months earlier a hundred miles northwest of Cañada Alamosa. It was a place where the Apaches were disinclined to live, and if they were compelled to go there, "one half to two-thirds will take to the mountains, and become more desperate than ever," warned the editors of the *Borderer*. For once the press was speaking from insight and not unfounded rumors. How right it would be.[25]

No one paid serious attention to these warnings. Colyer had inspected the proposed reservation during his whirlwind visit to the Southwest and had selected it because its mountainous location was remote from white settlements and was surrounded by "arable lands, good water and plenty of wood and game." His white man's logic was correct, but his understanding of the Chiricahuas was shallow. The Indians did not want to move; the area around beautiful and picturesque Cañada Alamosa was their home. They had countless reasons, some valid and others seemingly trivial: the Tularosa location was too close to the Navajos; swamplike conditions prevailed in the summer and it was too cold in the winter; the water was bad; the grass was unhealthy; and on and on. Although these arguments appeared frivolous to whites, they were real to Indians. Another factor in their refusal to move was the government's decision to establish a military post there, which upset the restive Apaches. Finally, perhaps their most significant objection was the remoteness from Cañada Alamosa, which had fast acquired the same reputation as Janos, where open market conditions prevailed and the Indians could unload their stolen stock and rations for whiskey and other sundries. This was perhaps the primary factor for their opposing the move to Tularosa. Some unscrupulous residents at Cañada Alamosa capitalized on these fears and undermined the goverment's policy by spreading rumors and lies about Tularosa.[26]

Loco and Victorio had been steadfastly opposed to Tularosa from the beginning. Cochise seemed indifferent at first and then became antiremoval. A few days after his arrival, Piper wrote that Cochise "does not make the selection of a reservation as a condition of peace," but in his next sentence it was evident that Cochise was against the idea. Piper continued: "I do not think that the objections he makes to going to Tularosa are on his account but on account of the desire of the chiefs that have been here some time." At no time did Cochise absolutely refuse to go to the new reservation, yet by the same token he never promised that he would move.[27]

Piper had at first been optimistic that his wards would move. On September 30, two days after Cochise's arrival, he wrote that he did not anticipate trouble and that the agency would be moved by October 20.[28] The first hint of a potential problem surfaced nine days later when he wrote a private letter to the Presbyterian board in Philadelphia admitting that he feared "trouble in getting the chiefs to consent to remove."[29] Three days later, Granger telegraphed Brigadier General John Pope of the Apaches' refusal and wondered whether he should "delay establishing a post."[30] Finally, on October 17, New Mexico's superintendent of Indian affairs, Nathaniel Pope, unable to delay any longer, informed his superiors in Washington that he had met with Cochise, Victorio, and Loco. They wished to remain at Cañada Alamosa but he felt they would follow the agency, at least "when they get hungry." Reluctantly he admitted that "it may be necessary to humor them until spring."[31]

Piper seemed to vacillate in his position, having the unenviable task of carrying out a policy which neither he nor the Indians desired. Throughout October, Cochise quietly supported Victorio and Loco, emphasizing that while he preferred Cañada Alamosa, he would consider moving if the two Chihenne leaders consented. Piper did all he could to convince Loco and Victorio, even offering

them a horse as a bribe to go to Tularosa. On October 19 he suggested that they should not "delay the removal till spring" unless
another reservation was under consideration. The next day he conferred with Cochise, Victorio, and Loco. Exasperated and ener-
vated, Piper wrote Nathaniel Pope of the Apaches' defiant response
to removal—almost certainly Victorio and Loco speaking with the
tacit support of Cochise:

> I have used every argument in my power and made all the promises I
> could to induce the Indians to go to the new reservation. They posi-
> tively refuse to go; saying that I may take the rations and give them to
> the bears and wolves.

In conclusion, Piper reversed his previous position and recommended that the Tularosa proposal be abandoned. If so, he felt that
"thousands, probably millions of dollars" would be saved. To explain his change in heart, he offered to come to Washington to express the Apache view, a favorite ploy used by some agents to procure a trip to the East.[32]

This uncertainty prompted Brigadier General John Pope,
Granger's superior, who commanded the Department of the Missouri, to dispatch Lieutenant Colonel Nelson Henry Davis from
Leavenworth, Kansas, to New Mexico to "report as accurately as
possible" on the state of affairs at Cañada Alamosa. Davis had
met Victorio and other Chihennes in 1865 and had formed rigid,
Carleton-like perceptions of Apaches. He described Cochise as "the
terror and curse of the people of Arizona and New Mexico" and in a
classic overstatement declared that the Chiricahuas were responsible
for "the murder of more men, women and children and the loss of
more property by theft than probably any score of chiefs." Although
Davis apparently did not meet Cochise, he concluded that Cochise
had come in only because many of his warriors and relatives were
killed. Previously, asserted the inspector, Cochise had "declared
that he would never make peace with the whites," failing to mention
or consider that Cochise had made that statement some six and a
half years earlier, when circumstances were much different.

Davis did recognize that the Indians "objected to going to
Tularosa." Therefore, he suggested, the government should allow
the "Indians to remain for the present at Cañada Alamosa as a mat-

ter of economy." His rationale, however, was not based on humane
convictions but, rather, on his inherent distrust of Apaches. After
all, he conceded, the reservation "is an experiment and I question
whether thay are sincere in their profession of peace and will remain
peacable longer than until spring and warm weather." Davis obviously felt that any effort to move the Indians would be a waste of
time and resources, which, he reported, was also Granger's
opinion.[33]

Meanwhile, as October drew to a close the Indians, perhaps sensing the whites indecisiveness, remained unyielding in their refusal
to move. On the surface, Cochise's role may have appeared subservient to Victorio's and Loco's, but their position would have been
untenable without his support. The day after Davis's report was received, the two arms of government in New Mexico sprang into action. Colonel Granger wrote Piper and inquired about the likelihood
of removal and Piper replied that if coerced "they may flee to the
mountains of Arizona."[34] At the same time, Nathaniel Pope told
Washington that the "Apaches positively refuse to go" and added
that "I don't think it wise or practicable to move them by force but if
the department decides it would be better to do so now than in the
spring." The chiefs had issued an ultimatum: the agency would remain at Cañada Alamosa or they would go to war. The error was in
not moving the Apaches as soon as Cochise came in. If this had
been done, the Indians probably would have gone and the whole
controversy about removal would have been avoided, although the
portended unrest may have occurred anyway.[35]

Pope's communication was passed along to the secretary of the
interior, Charles Delano, who immediately decided to consult with
Colyer, recently returned from "Apache country" and supposedly
familiar "with their wants."[36] Thus on November 6, 1871, Colyer,
Delano, Secretary of War William W. Belknap, and President
Ulysses S. Grant discussed Tularosa. After Colyer briefed them on
the situation, they concluded to allow the Indians to remain at Cañada Alamosa for the present. Colyer telegraphed the verdict to Pope,
cautioning him to tell the Indians that their stay at Cañada Alamosa
was "limited in duration and that they must prepare to move for
Tularosa as soon as possible." Two weeks later, Delano decided
that the transfer would occur as soon as practicable in 1872. Conse-

quently, Lieutenant General Philip Sheridan issued General Order No. 8, ordering the removal to Tularosa and the establishment of a military post to be named Fort Tularosa.[37]

This decision reached Cañada Alamosa in early December. Soon afterward many Chiricahuas left for the mountains and others for Mescalero country east of the Río Grande. Among the latter were Nana and Horache, who were apparently responsible for the attack on Shedd's ranch on Christmas Day 1871 and for the killing of a man near the Organ Mountains.[38] As for Cochise, Piper typically misread his intentions, reporting that he and his Chokonens remained, seemingly content after the announcement postponing the removal.[39]

Granger realized that it would not be practical to relocate the Indians before spring. Besides requiring time to plan and organize the move, he would not contemplate this mission without the presence of Superintendent Pope, who was absent on personal business and would not return until February. Compounding this was the problem of a winter move. Consequently, Granger decided to delay the entire relocation until April 1, 1872, with the actual transfer to take place on May 1. His superior, Brigadier General Pope, concurred and the date was established.[40]

With the removal date fixed, Cochise grew even more unapproachable, although his name swirled around in several more controversies while he remained on the reservation. In December he requested permission to leave the reservation to hunt. Knowing that some of the Apaches had already fled and recalling that when Cochise left a year earlier he had not returned for ten months, Piper wisely refused.[41] On December 31 he completed his quarterly report, noting ominously that "Cochise and most of his band are here. They are very restless and suspicious." Citing the presence of Mexicans at Cañada Alamosa, Piper asserted that "evil disposed persons are continually circulating reports that troops are after them to drive them to Tularosa."[42]

Throughout December the agitators from Cañada Alamosa stirred up trouble. Early that month many Indians traded their rations for whiskey, leaving them "destitute of food" and starving. Fearing more trouble, Piper requested help from Fort McRae, which came in the form of a noncommissioned officer and nine men. On December 12 he issued blankets as the soldiers looked on to prevent any trading. The citizens at Cañada Alamosa, many of them masters of crooked devices, retaliated by arresting Piper later that day. Little wonder that Piper repeatedly commented about the deleterious effect these "evil disposed persons" had on the Apaches, referring to the Chihennes and not Cochise's Chokonens who remained in the mountains. Cochise's appearance at the agency became less and less frequent. He would send his family in for rations; he himself wanted to be left alone.[43]

That was virtually impossible. First, Crook was angry about the continuation of scattered raids in southeastern Arizona, either the work of Western Apaches, some of Cochise's own band who had refused to make peace, or Juh's Nednhis, still as incorrigible as ever. In any event, these activities enraged Crook, who was publicly dubious of Cochise's sincerity and inwardly angry that Cochise had escaped his grasp and deprived him of the satisfaction of subduing the great Chiricahua. He began his sniping in early December, writing to his superior in San Francisco, Major General John McAllister Schofield and suggesting that Cochise be forced to return to Arizona, "where he belongs," and that "he be required to show some sincerity in his professions of peace" by helping troops to subdue other Chiricahuas who had remained hostile. To the pragmatic Crook, Cochise "should control his people for good as effectually as he had heretofore for bad." Schofield forwarded Crook's request to Washington with this comment: "Whether it is practicable or not is another matter."[44]

Soon yet another issue entered the drama and added more fuel to Crook's discontent. In late November 1871, Charles Brown, a Tucson businessman, just in from southern New Mexico, reported to Captain Moore at Tucson that the horses stolen from Camp Crittenden "are now at Cañada Alamosa in the possession of Cochise." Moore immediately sent a note to Crook, inquiring whether he should try to recover the horses.[45] Eventually Nathaniel Pope received Moore's communication, which he forwarded to Piper, asking him to investigate. Piper soothingly replied that when Cochise arrived from Arizona, he "had in his possession three or four horses supposed to belong to the cavalry. Two of them had shoes on their feet. The brands had been so defaced that it was impossible to tell what they had been." Pope reluctantly concluded that the matter should be dropped.[46]

Military headquarters at Santa Fe thought otherwise, ordering Captain George Shorkley at Fort McRae to investigate. Shorkley was an officer with considerable experience, knowledge, and ability in dealing with the Chiricahuas. On April 6, 1872, he logically explained why the mounts could not be recovered:

> Cochise and his men are not now at or near Canada Alamosa . . . any efforts made by me to recover the animals would be futile and were the Indians at Canada Alamosa, no serious efforts could be made by me without alarming or offending the Indians as they were told at the time they came into the agency that all ordinary property there in their possession would be assured to them. It is believed that the animals are not now worth the effort necessary to recover them.

Shorkley's letter closed the matter, although it undoubtedly failed to mollify Crook.[47]

The editors of the *Las Cruces Borderer* added their own two cents' worth after Chiricahuas captured both the eastbound and westbound mail near Fort Bowie on January 25, murdering three men. The Apaches, dressed in army shirts and well armed with needle guns, probably headed south to their ranchería near Batepito, Sonora, which was fifteen to twenty miles below the border. After these atrocities the editors of the *Borderer* called for the mail company to hire Cochise and his warriors "to escort the mail . . . with enough warriors to accomplish the object. Himself and a half dozen warriors I think will be sufficient." How Cochise responded, or whether Piper even made the offer, is not known."[48]

In all likelihood, Cochise would not have been receptive. About this time Piper had written to Vincent Colyer about Cochise, who had become a recluse towards the whites:

> I do not know what to say of Cochise. . . . He does not seem disposed to place confidence in anything said to him. He has not been on to the agency since the order for their removal has been made public; he has regularly sent in for rations.[49]

Cochise was apparently going to bide his time on the reserve through the winter. In early January, Tom Jeffords told Captain Shorkley that Cochise was now camped in the forested San Mateo

Mountains, probably in the lower valleys near Vicks Peak (named for Victorio) twelve miles north of the agency. The chief "would come in for the big talk," according to Jeffords, who was referring to a conference to be held with Colonel Granger and Superintendent Pope. Until then, "fearing that the [agency beef] may be poisoned," he would remain in the mountains and hunt his own meat.[50]

Jeffords told Shorkley that "many of the Indians are dissatisfied with the agent Mr. Piper [including], Cochise and some of the captains." Shockley concurred, writing "that this dissatisfaction exists I have no doubt." With respect to the Tularosa removal, Shorkley believed that Jeffords "wants the Indians to go to Tularosa and took much pains to convince me of this. I am satisfied he thinks it will advance his interest very much if the Indians go peacefully."[51] Shorkley was right on target. Jeffords had made plans to construct a building at Tularosa, probably with the hope of being appointed post sutler, but the idea was vetoed by Colonel Granger. He informed Jeffords "that under existing orders no citizen can be allowed to settle or build on a government reservation without special permission from the Secretary of War."[52]

Throughout February, Cochise remained in the mountains and did not bother to visit the agency. Lieutenant Colonel Thomas Devin stopped briefly at Cañada Alamosa, hoping to see the Indian he had offered to meet three years before; Cochise, however, was "out in the mountains and could not be got in."[53]

Those who wished to see Cochise had to go to his camp. On the last day of February, Piper and Jeffords visited him and invited him to Washington. Again Cochise would not consider leaving, suspecting treachery if he placed "himself in the hands of Americans." Piper also reported dissension between Loco's Chihennes and Cochise's Chokonens, an inevitable occurrence with the camps in close proximity to each other. Recently the bands had "one or two pitched fights"; in all probability, either tiswin or whiskey was involved, which resulted in the death of two or three Apaches and the wounding of several others. This alone may have convinced Cochise that he had overstayed his welcome in Chihenne country.[54]

Finally, in mid-March, the plans for the big talk about Tularosa were made. The government's hope for calming the crisis and relocating the Apaches hinged on convincing the Indians of two things:

Gordon Granger. Commander of the district of New Mexico, Granger met Cochise in March 1872 at Cañada Alamosa and later boasted to Crook that "Cochise will go wherever I send him." (*Courtesy National Archives*)

first, that a trip to Washington to visit the Great White Father would be to their benefit; second, that Tularosa was their only choice. If they refused to move, the troops would be called out. As it turned out, neither option was attractive to Cochise, although Victorio consented to visit Washington, according to Piper. The government would rue the day that it adhered to this stupid, shortsighted policy of placing the Apaches at a place they came to detest. The wonder of it all was that those involved never learned their lesson.

Colonel Granger, who proudly boasted to Crook that Cochise "will go wherever I direct him," arrived in an optimistic mood. His first objective was to "do all I can to induce Cochise, Salvadora, Loco, and Victorio" to visit Washington, although he would have had a miraculous task in convincing Salvadora, considering that he had been killed in the Bullard fight more than a year earlier. Granger's entourage arrived at Cañada Alamosa on March 17. The following day, the Indians began arriving, and on the nineteenth Cochise appeared and the parley began. Granger and Nathaniel Pope tried desperately to persuade the chief to visit Washington, but to no avail, with Cochise declaring that he would rather talk on top of a mountain. Removal to Tularosa was next on the agenda, and May 1 was the assigned date on which it would occur. The Indians objected, which Pope summarily labeled as "unimportant and . . . frivolous," expecting that most of the Indians would follow the agency in need of provisions. He would be dead wrong.[55]

Cochise's responses were typically evasive because the presence of army officers usually inhibited his replies. A transcript of the meeting was published in the *Santa Fe Daily New Mexican* and reprinted by the *Arizona Miner*. Granger and Pope did all in their power to persuade him to visit Washington. His inherent distrust of Americans can be discerned from his remarks. After all, Bascom had arrested him for acts committed by other Apaches. What would happen if he went to Washington and "two or three of his warriors should steal while I am gone. It would make me look like a liar." Cochise's health was deteriorating, but the basic reason he declined to go seemed to be his profound distrust of Americans.

Cochise also was concerned about the Indians still at war, and he assured Granger that "this must look strange to you, but they are not my people. I would like to go to them and tell them of what you have said." Granger replied that "the Great Father will thank you very much if you bring about such a result."[56]

Two other eyewitnesses recorded fascinating descriptions of the aging chief. Assistant surgeon Henry Stuart Turrill wrote that Cochise "impressed me as a wonderfully strong man, of much endurance, accustomed to command and to expect instant and implicit obedience." Turrill felt that Cochise was "the greatest Indian that I have ever met," which was quite a compliment considering that he had been in contact with the Sioux and Cheyennes.[57] Dr. Anderson Nelson Ellis, post surgeon at Fort Craig, described Cochise as "five foot ten inches . . . lithe and wiry every muscle being well developed and firm. A silver thread was now and then visible in his otherwise black hair, which he wore cut straight around his head about on a level with his chin." Ellis also recorded Cochise's speech, which provided a vivid picture of the frustration of a man who realized that his time was passing, that his people were on the verge of extinction, swept over by the whites invading Apachería. Cochise made his feelings clear; he had no wish to leave Cañada Alamosa:

> My blood was on fire, but now I have come into this valley and drunk of these waters and washed myself in them and they have cooled me. . . . I speak straight and do not wish to deceive or be deceived. I want a good, strong and lasting peace.

While his attentive audience listened, Cochise referred to himself, uncertain as to the white's expectations. He continued:

> The white people have looked for me long. I am here! What do they want? . . . Why am I worth so much? . . . I am not God. I am no longer chief of all the Apaches. I am no longer rich; I am but a poor man. . . . I came in here because God told me to do so. He said it was good to be at peace—so I came! . . . God spoke to my thought and told me to come in here and be at peace with all. . . . The Apaches were once a great nation; they are now but few, and because of this they want to die and so carry their lives on their finger nails.

The chief ended his oratory by leaving no doubt about where he wanted to live:

> I want to live in these mountains; I do not want to go to Tularosa. That is a long ways off. The flies on those mountains eat out the eyes of the horses. The bad spirits live there. I have drunk of these waters and they have cooled me, I do not want to leave here.[58]

Cochise had never agreed to removal, yet his objections barely fazed Granger and Pope, who casually dismissed his importance and even granted him permission to leave Cañada Alamosa in order to communicate with the hostile Chiricahuas and "try to persuade [them] to go to Tularosa." The council ended on March 20. Within ten days Cochise left, with the consent of Granger and Pope, with only a slim chance of returning as long as the new reservation was to be at Tularosa.[59]

# Chapter 18

# DRINK THE SAME WATER, EAT THE SAME BREAD: THE COCHISE-HOWARD TREATY

A few days after the Granger talk, Cochise left the reservation with the stated intention of rounding up members of his band who had remained hostile, yet clearly this was not his only reason for leaving. He had no desire to relocate at Tularosa, and he may have been hoping that his departure would convince the Americans to cancel or postpone the removal. According to an informed source, he "could not have been induced to go there [Tularosa] under any consideration."[1]

Even so, the new reservation was established and Cochise looked for alternatives. Casting another glance at northern Mexico, he again courted Janos, remaining near it for some time before pressure from Mexican troops forced him to return to Arizona. During the summer of 1872, his warriors resumed their old way of life: raiding, torturing, and murdering, particularly in southern Arizona. Cochise took no part in these hostilities, ostensibly remaining in camp to protect his people from the seemingly omnipresent U.S. patrols. It was in this setting that a new peace commissioner, General Oliver Otis Howard, with Tom Jeffords's help, found Cochise in the fall of 1872.

Cochise left Cañada Alamosa about March 30 or April 1 in typical Apache fashion: neither the military nor the Indian agent had a definite idea of where he had gone.[2] Devin said he heard that

Cochise had returned to the Chiricahuas but was dubious because "I think he has had enough and only wants to be left alone."[3] In early April, Captain Shorkley at Fort McRae, responding to an inquiry from Crook, informed district headquarters in Santa Fe that neither "Cochise nor his men were at the reservation and are not likely to return."[4] Piper seemed bewildered and was unwilling to hazard a guess as to Cochise's whereabouts.[5]

Whether Cochise would return was a subject of debate among whites who knew him. Before leaving he reportedly told José García, a citizen from Palomas who occasionally supplied the reservation with beef, that he would be absent for about a month to "find members of his band" and bring them to the reservation.[6] Another person close to the scene wrote the *Missouri Republican* that Cochise "has gone off, by permission, to try to induce some more of his band to come in. . . . No doubt is entertained by those who know him of his being back by the time and at the place appointed. All fears in regard to Cochise may be at once dismissed."[7]

Once he was off the reservation and in the mountains he considered home, Cochise's decision was easily made. He had never been a reservation Indian and good weather was approaching; furthermore, he was unable to persuade all of his Chokonens to move to Tularosa. If the reserve had remained at Cañada Alamosa or if the agent had been Steck or Jeffords instead of Piper, Cochise might have returned. To avoid American troops, he made his way back into the mountains and again turned to Janos for refuge and supplies.

By mid-April 1872, some two weeks after leaving, Cochise sent a runner to Tom Jeffords informing him that he was moving farther west. Either for security or protection, he asked Jeffords to accompany him, leaving his options open in case he decided to return to New Mexico. Jeffords had to refuse; he had recently broken some ribs in a fall and was not up to the rigors of travel.[8]

In the meantime, plans were drafted in early April to move the Apaches from Cañada Alamosa to Tularosa. Piper eventually succeeded in relocating 350 Indians from Victorio's, Loco's, and Gordo's bands, to hated Tularosa,[9] assisted by Jeffords and Zebina Nathaniel Streeter.[10] By the end of May, Chiva brought his group of

60 or 70 Bedonkohes and/or Chokonens to Tularosa. Cochise had "told him to take his people to Tularosa, saying that he would follow if they were well treated at the agency."[11]

All involved in the move pronounced it a success despite the absence of a thousand Apaches who had fled Cañada Alamosa and were roaming southern Arizona and New Mexico. The previous October, Piper estimated that 1,900 Apaches were on the reserve, almost certainly an unintentionally inflated number. Of these, only 350 went to Tularosa, leaving more than 1,500 Indians to account for. Cochise's following, perhaps 300 individuals, had left for Arizona and northern Mexico. Another 400 had moved east of the Río Grande to the Mescaleros' reservation at Fort Stanton, where they were unwelcome visitors. The remainder were in southern New Mexico.

Many of the Apaches had gone to join Nana and his son-in-law Horache, both of whom had left Cañada Alamosa the previous December, at Fort Stanton. On May 1, Ponce,[12] a son-in-law of Cochise described as "about 35 years old [with] a stutter in his speech," and Escani took 305 Indians to Fort Stanton, hoping to remain there. Their appearance startled Captain James Franklin Randlett, who informed Devin: "They [Ponce and Escani] stated that the band had left Canada Alamosa about five weeks since . . . that Mr. Piper knew they were coming to visit their relatives here, that they would like to remain here until the rainy season." Randlett refused their request but was dismayed because the Mescaleros' agent, A. J. Curtis, had rationed the Apaches when they arrived.[13]

Once Tularosa was established, Devin had orders to round up all Indians off the reservation and force them in. Although he had enough troops to snap the whip at the laggard Chiricahuas, he had to do so without antagonizing those who were off the agency. The task required great delicacy and the implementation of a firm policy. The Indian Bureau and the military, however, were indecisive in their actions.

Devin faced a series of delays which postponed his military action. Originally he was to treat as hostile any Apaches not at Tularosa by April 29. On May 5 he arrived at Tularosa, where he lingered for a few days before moving to Fort Craig on May 9, where he received a request from Pope "that I commence no operations . . . until the Indians have a little more time—say June 1."[14] It was believed that every Chiricahua who intended to go to the reservation would be there by that time. The rest were spread throughout the territory, and scattered raiding had resumed in southern New Mexico. A correspondent for the *Missouri Republican* conceded that the policy was a failure because of delays in carrying it out. The program should have been implemented "vigorously and at once. It is sheer madness vacillating so long between the policy of Extermination and . . . Reservation."[15]

Throughout May, both Pope and Piper continued to think Cochise would return, but their hopes dissipated with reports of renewed Apache depredations in New Mexico and Arizona and rumors that Cochise had made peace at Janos. On the last day of May, Piper reported that "one of Cochise's men is here and it is thought that he has been sent to see how things were here."[16]

Chokonen raiders made Arizona aware of their presence. On May 1 at Fort Bowie the tracks of about thirty Indians were discovered near the post herd, but they were unable to steal it. Their trail continued south.[17] Three days later at the foot of Stein's Peak, a small group of Chiricahuas ambushed and killed mail rider Henry Abrahams, mutilated his body, and burned his buckboard. Merejildo Grijalva discovered the remains and determined that the Apaches had come from the Burro Mountains.[18] Later that month it was reported from El Paso that Cochise and about three hundred Apaches were at Janos; this was corroborated by eyewitnesses. He had clearly rejected Tularosa.[19]

By mid-May most of the Chokonen and Nednhi bands were in northern Chihuahua; the former had moved there to avoid U.S. troops, the latter to escape persistent Sonoran campaigns into the Pitaicache and Espuellas mountains, which had kept Juh's followers on the run. Eventually they moved into Chihuahua and Janos to elude the aggressors. In late April and early May, three Sonoran detachments scoured the usual Apache strongholds. Lieutenant Manuel Gallegos and forty men patrolled toward the Pitaicaches, Lieutenant Joaquin Samaniego and thirty men traversed the San Pedro along the Sonora-Chihuahua border, and Colonel Cayetano Silva with another force reconnoitered the mountains along the Arizona-Sonora boundary. This offensive compelled the truculent spirits led by Juh and Geronimo to enter Chihuahua and solicit peace at Janos. According to their messenger, they numbered thirty-three men and had been living in the Pitaicache Mountains. One of the warriors admitted that they had "suffered much from misery and hunger a consequence of the repeated Sonora campaigns. They are unable to prepare their mescal, that they are forced to live all their time in the hills; that recently two babies had died from hunger." Moreover, if peace were granted, Juh even consented to join Mexican troops against hostiles, which, considering his reputation, would indeed have been a sight to behold.[20]

Once the Nednhis opened negotiations, Cochise sent in two of his captains, Julian and Collali, and soon after that Remigio and Peñon[21] (probably the notorious Pionsenay). When convinced that no treachery was planned, he himself came in, undoubtedly to do some trading and renew old acquaintances. Since the civil authorities at Janos were not empowered to consummate a treaty, they instructed the Apaches to proceed to Galeana for further talks, but there were too many bad memories there and the Apaches stayed clear. In any event, Cochise was at Janos (at least two individuals told Devin they had seen him there) and remained in the vicinity for perhaps a month. He probably received reports about Tularosa and contemplated his next move.[22]

Devin feared that Cochise would use Janos as a base from which to raid on both sides of the border, and almost certainly this occurred to some extent. In late June, Cochise was again reported near Janos, where he probably remained until early July, when Sonoran troops crossed the border and destroyed Juh's ranchería in the Carcai Mountains. The entire camp was captured and ransacked. After this attack, Cochise crossed the border and returned to Arizona, probably to the southern Chiricahuas, before eventually returning to his beloved Dragoons.[23]

Once in Arizona, Cochise's captains were dispatched in different directions to make a living. He was through raiding and now spent his time planning and coordinating forays; he had groomed his son Taza, now in his late twenties, to succeed him. As his father had been, Taza was well trained for a leadership role. With Cochise's war chief, Nahilzay, Taza led many raids in the Sonoita Valley, which erupted in violence in the summer of 1872. The soldiers could do little to stop or even slow down the raiders. In mid-June a scout from Camp Grant examined the Dragoons but found no Indian sign. Late in the month another scout under Lieutenant Charles Bendire pursued Apaches into the Dragoons and recovered some twenty head of cattle; apparently this was a Chokonen group which subsequently moved northeast to the Stein's Peak area. Although Cochise's whereabouts were unknown, by midsummer 1872 he had returned to the Dragoons, from which he could either move to the Chiricahuas or slip back into Mexico.[24]

In late July, Devin's troops, scouting the Arizona–New Mexico border under Lieutenant William Stephenson, struck a Chokonen band in the upper Sulphur Springs Valley a few miles south of the lofty Graham Mountains. Climbing a steep mountain, the Americans spotted the Indians and charged the ranchería. The Apaches deserted their camp, making "but feeble resistance, firing a few shots." The troops killed one and "captured and burnt sixteen large lodges, together with several hundred pounds of mescal, all their camp equipage." Other confiscated material revealed that these Indians had been at Cañada Alamosa and had also "recently been trading with Mexicans," probably at Janos. This group numbered sixty individuals and was believed to be a "part of Cochise's that sent Colonel Bendire out of Dragoon Pass about a month ago."

Stephenson marched to Fort Bowie and while there met Merejildo Grijalva, who declared that the "bags, moccasins and beadwork captured . . . are the same as those made by the women of Cochise's band." From Bowie, Stephenson's command headed south and on August 6 destroyed a ranchería in the southeast Chiricahuas and succeeded in killing two Apaches, according to one report, before returning to Fort Bayard.[25]

With American troops swarming throughout their territory, some Chokonens (even Cochise himself, according to one report) apparently considered moving to Tularosa. At the end of August a band of White Mountain Apaches ran into some of Cochise's people, perhaps the same group Stephenson hit in Sulphur Springs Valley. They told the Coyoteros they "were going to Tularosa and that Cheis had already started to reach there that moon," which would have meant early September. With winter approaching and Cochise's options fast dwindling, he might have considered Tularosa, but he remained in southern Arizona and Apache raids continued.[26]

Many of these were the work of Cochise's people. On August 27, Lieutenant Reid T. Stewart, a popular young officer, left Camp Crittenden to attend a court-martial in Tucson. A small escort accompanied him but could not travel fast enough for the impetuous officer, so he took the buckboard and his driver, Corporal Joseph P. G. Black, and pushed ahead of the escort. Black, who had carried the mail over this same route for three years, protested but was overruled by Stewart, who had boasted, "I am not afraid of these Apaches. I can lick a whole regiment of them."[27] About 11 A.M. they entered Davidson Canyon, located between the Empire and Santa Rita mountains. The Apaches were waiting. Possibly led by Taza, they killed Stewart quickly with a bullet in the head. Black attempted to escape but the Indians captured him, tied him to a tree, and tortured him to death. The escort arrived too late and, finding itself outnumbered, continued on through the canyon to Tucson. That same day, Apaches murdered seven Mexicans in the Santa Cruz and Sonoita valleys.[28]

These ferocious raids prompted many southwesterners, including Crook, to doubt Cochise's sincerity about peace. Most Americans were skeptical with good reason: Cochise had talked peace with Perry in February 1869 and Green in August 1870 and had stayed at and left Cañada Alamosa in the fall of 1871 and the spring of 1872. Very few cared or understood why he had left and why he continued raiding; what was clear was that his people had reverted to their old way of life.

The situation became so hazardous in the Sonoita Valley that several farmers seriously considered abandoning their homes as soon as they harvested their crops. Thomas Gardner, whom Cochise wounded in the early sixties, declared that he would "willingly make a fast, firm treaty . . . and give them [Apaches] one quarter of all he raised."[29] All in all, Cochise's actions contradicted what he had said the previous fall.

Like his predecessor, Vincent Colyer, Brigadier General Oliver Otis Howard was a humanitarian and a deeply religious man. Born in Leeds, Maine, in 1830, he entered West Point after graduating

General Oliver Otis Howard. He negotiated a final truce with Cochise in October 1872. Although the truce was flawed in some respects, it did bring peace to southeastern Arizona for the first time in over a decade. (*Courtesy National Archives*)

from Bowdoin College in 1850. He finished fourth in a class of forty-six and taught mathematics at West Point until the outbreak of the Civil War. In June 1861 he resigned his commission to become colonel of the Third Maine Regiment. He saw action in several major battles, losing his right arm at the Battle of Fair Oaks on May 31, 1862. By the end of the war, he had been promoted to brigadier general of the army and major general of the volunteers. During the war he became known as the Christian Soldier, which undoubtedly helped him receive an appointment as commissioner of the Freedman's Bureau, an organization charged with supervision of roughly four million liberated slaves; a more concerned man could not have been chosen for a virtually impossible task, for Howard brought honesty, compassion, and humane convictions. At the same time, his lack of administrative skills, his idealistic and simplistic views, and his universal trust in his fellow man set off a round of rampant corruption.[30]

In February 1872, with the threat of renewed Apache hostilities and recognition that Colyer's mission had not solved the Apache problem, Secretary of the Interior Charles Delano concluded to send the scrupulously honest Howard to Arizona and New Mexico to "take such action as, in your judgement, may be deemed best for the purpose of preserving peace with the Indians in these territories." Furthermore, wrote Delano,

> the Department invests you with full powers and a general discretion, to be exercised, as your own good judgement may dictate in carrying into effect its views in relation to these Indians. . . . The great object of the government is: *First* to preserve peace between the U.S. and these as well as all other tribes of Indians. *Second:* To induce them to abandon their present habits of life and go upon permanent reservations.[31]

Howard was acceptable to both church and humanitarian groups and the military. He also would outrank every officer in the Southwest. His main objective, he later recalled, was "to make peace with the warlike Chiricahuas under Cochise."[32]

Crook was displeased about the arrival of another commissioner, which once again forced him to delay military action. The fact that

Howard outranked him seemed to chafe him even more. Howard reached Arizona in April and on the fifteenth met with Crook, whom he thought was "a very fine officer ready to work heavily with me."[33] It was a cautious, correct courtesy call, but rapport did not develop. The pragmatic Crook did not reciprocate the same respect toward Howard. Questioning Howard's incessant piety, which to Crook seemed incongruous in Apache country, he incredulously complained that Howard was "clothed with even greater powers than those given Mr. Colyer."[34]

One of Howard's first requests of Crook was to meet Cochise, then thought to be at Cañada Alamosa. Accordingly, Crook wrote Granger and requested that Cochise be furnished an escort to Fort Apache. By this time, however, Cochise had left the reserve and an interview could not be arranged.[35]

Howard recalled that he heard only the phrase "kill em, kill em" as the solution to the Apache problem. In late May he reached Fort Apache and made several fruitless attempts to communicate with the Chiricahuas. He did succeed in appeasing Western Apache bands and took a delegation of Arizona Indians to Washington, where he arrived on June 20. After a short stay, countless interviews and speeches, and a meeting with President Grant, the delegation left Washington on July 10. Before returning to Arizona, however, they detoured to New York to visit Vincent Colyer and the Dutch Reform Society of New York before resuming the 2,500-mile journey west.[36] Howard's assistant this trip was a young and courageous officer of medium height with black hair and a heavy mustache. His name was Lieutenant Joseph Alton Sladen.[37]

Howard reached Santa Fe in early August and conferred with Nathaniel Pope, asking his advice about the best way to communicate with Cochise. Pope said Jeffords once delivered a message to Cochise and "that he was confident that the man had dealt honestly with him."[38] Howard's next stop was Fort Apache, where he made plans to communicate with Cochise, who was believed to be in southern Arizona. On August 12 he wrote his wife:

> I find by rumors of depredations below here that Cochise and his band are likely to be reached from here as from Tularosa and so I may be delayed at this post longer than I had anticipated, starting from

Lieutenant Joseph A. Sladen. Howard's capable aide, he spent an interesting ten days in Cochise's camp and discovered that the Apaches were human beings after all. (*Carlisle Barracks Photo, Joseph A. Sladen Collection, U.S. Army Military History Institute, Carlisle Barracks, PA*)

here to meet Cochise if possible. I am trying to communicate with Cochise. I find I cannot hurry and may be delayed some time.[39]

Two days later he reiterated these plans to Herman Bendell (superintendent of Indian affairs in Arizona) and dispatched Concepción (a Mexican raised by Aravaipa Apaches) and George Stevens[40] to locate Cochise and procure an interview.

Howard waited for two weeks until Concepción and Stevens returned, unsuccessful in their mission. "Not ready to give up the chase," he decided to make one last attempt to find Cochise through the disenchanted Chihennes living at Tularosa. While at Fort Apache he and Sladen had learned of "a mysterious white man known to the Mescalero [Chihennes] who had visited Cochise frequently and was on friendly terms with him, and who could, if he chose, find Cochise and carry to him any message."[41]

Before leaving Fort Apache, he tactfully wrote Crook and apologized for having interfered in Arizona affairs and "making such radical changes, but . . . I feel assured that you know that my purpose is fixed to help you all I can." Crook was not convinced and the letter only irritated him because he felt that Howard's sanctimonious actions were insincere and unrealistic for the Arizona frontier.[42]

Howard and his party started for Tularosa on August 30. The second day out they met a man named Milligan and quartered at his ranch, "the only dwelling between Camp Apache and Fort Tularosa," some seventy miles southeast of Fort Apache. Milligan corroborated what Howard and Sladen had heard there, stating that Jeffords was the only white man who could communicate with Cochise.[43] On September 4 while approaching Tularosa, Fred Hughes, "the Tularosa interpreter," met the party with a letter from Piper saying that the Chihennes "were fearfully discontented" and that many had left the reservation; only three hundred remained. En route, Hughes and Howard talked about Cochise, the former telling the general that he had heard "from the Indians at Tularosa enough to satisfy me that Cochise was ready to make peace." To accomplish this, he also advised Howard to find "Captain Jeffords to take with him on his mission as Jeffords had already met Cochise and the latter had taken quite a liking to him."[44]

Reaching Tularosa, Howard dispatched Jake May, his Spanish interpreter, to Cañada Alamosa to bring Jeffords in. Next he met Agent Piper, who he thought "had a good heart . . . tried to do his duty and do right, but the Indians for some unknown reason do not like him." Shortly after that he held a council with Victorio, Loco, Nana, and Chiva. Howard was impressed with Victorio, whom he described as "a fine looking man . . . about five feet ten and well formed." But the leader who really caught his eye was Nana, a "very thick set [man] with a large head—much bigger than mine." The general sympathized with the Indians' main complaint: that they were forced from Cañada Alamosa to Tularosa over their objections.[45]

While Howard tried to placate the Chihennes, agreeing to visit Cañada Alamosa and inspect it, Jeffords arrived at Fort Tularosa on September 7. He had been out with troops trying to round up hostiles who had refused to move;[46] he had spent most of the summer in the vicinity of the reservation, renewing his request for permission to build a trading post. He was in Luther's store when General Howard approached and introduced himself. Jeffords later conceded that he had been skeptical of the general "on account of his well known humanitarian ideas, and to my mind, posing as a Christian soldier."[47]

After introductions, Howard asked Jeffords to find Cochise and bring him in for an interview. After "considerable deliberation," Jeffords responded: "General Howard, Cochise won't come. The man that wants to talk to Cochise must go where he is. . . . I'll tell you what I'll do, I will take you to Cochise. Will you go there with me, General, without soldiers?" Howard quickly replied, "Yes, if necessary." The frontiersman may have been testing the general, not believing that the latter would accept his offer, but Howard was determined to complete his mission and bring peace to the Southwest.[48]

For the next week Jeffords made preparations for the journey while Howard, Piper, and Pope met with the Chihennes, who used every argument they could think of to be returned to Cañada Alamosa. During the council the Indians' disrespect for Piper surfaced. Victorio said "the agent is getting old and he had better go home and see his children, and take care of them."[49] It was no coincidence that two days later Piper requested a leave of absence, which Howard granted, evidently believing that the diligent but miscast Piper and the restless Apaches would be better off without each other. On September 16 he issued Piper a thirty-day leave with permission to apply in Washington for an additional thirty days. In effect, this released Piper from his arduous duties. The general promised to use his influence to find Piper other employment with the Indian Bureau.[50]

On September 16, Howard, Jeffords, Loco, and Chie examined Cañada Alamosa, after which Howard acquiesced and decided that the government should scrap the ill-advised Tularosa and return the Apaches to Cañada Alamosa under the assumption that all of the Chiricahuas, including Cochise, would come in. At this time no one had any conception that the venerable chief might have other ideas.

Another important development took place that day. Evidently with Nathaniel Pope's support, Howard appointed Tom Jeffords agent for the proposed Cochise Reservation, which he planned to reestablish at Cañada Alamosa:

> For the special work of gathering the nomadic Apache Indians upon the 'Cachise Reservation' and of being their agent subsequently, subject to the regulations of the Indian Bureau, I hereby appoint Thomas J. Jeffords. He will report to the Supt. of Indian Affairs for New Mexico and be under instructions from here and higher authorities.[51]

This contrasts with the traditional version, as related by Jeffords, that Cochise insisted upon him as agent and that Howard had to persuade him to accept the job. As a matter of fact, Jeffords willingly accepted the position even before the historic pact was agreed to, although his appointment undoubtedly helped the final outcome. The boundaries of the proposed reservation were set:

> The Rio Grande to be the Eastern boundary—the northern line commencing at a point six miles on the Rio Grande north of the mouth of the Rio Canada and running direct to the summit of the south end of the San Mateo Mountains and thence westerly to include the springs known as "Canada de Alamo" . . . to a southerly direction along the summit of the Mimbres Mountains to a point known as "Mule

Springs" or "Oak Grove" a point about 14 miles north of Fort Cummings. South line to run in an easterly direction to the Rio Grande
just including Fort Thorn or as sometimes called "Santa Barbara."
Add to this the Sierra del Caballo.[52]

Who would have thought that Cochise might have other plans?

With affairs settled, Jeffords and Howard focused on the arrangements for locating Cochise. At Tularosa, Jeffords had convinced
Chie[53] to accompany the party, provided they could find Ponce, a
relative by marriage to Cochise, and procure his services. Howard
sent the supply wagon, driven by Albert Bloomfield, to Fort Craig.
Bloomfield, a Frenchman, had come to Arizona in 1861 and was
well known to Victorio's people. He was ordered to replenish supplies before proceeding to Fort Bowie. Jeffords also enlisted the
help of Zebina Streeter, the so-called White Apache, expanding the
party to five white men: Howard, Sladen, Jeffords, May, and
Streeter. Before leaving Cañada Alamosa, Howard bought a horse
for Chie in payment for his services.

They departed on September 18, 1872, to search for Ponce, who
had the "ability to guide us to the old chief's camp." They found
him and his band of fifty-nine, including notorious raiders Ramón
Chico and Sánchez, on the Cuchillo Negro River and persuaded him
to accompany the party. To do so, Howard provided him with a
horse and allowed his group to remain at Cuchillo, where they
would be furnished subsistence until their chief returned.[54]

On September 19, the party complete, Jeffords and his two
Apaches began the task of finding Cochise, who was believed to be
in the Chiricahuas.[55] Leaving the small settlement of Cuchillo, they
struck out southwest, probably rounding the Mimbres Mountains to
the south and reaching Fort Bayard on September 23. Supplies re-
plenished, the next day they resumed their search, continuing west
toward the Gila and halting at Silver City to have a horse shod.
Howard purchased two shirts for his Indian guides and hired a cook
named J. H. Stone. Before leaving, the general gave a speech on the
peace policy (which the hardy miners probably scoffed at) and then
resumed the march. About ten miles west of Silver City, the party
encountered a group of prospectors led by James Bullard, whose
brother John had been killed by Cochise's band in February 1871.

To the general's astonishment, Bullard wanted to kill the Indians, which Howard courageously prevented by stepping in front of Chie and Ponce, saying, "You will kill me first." Bullard left, "cursing the peace policy," although after Howard's success he acknowledged that he had been wrong and that the mission benefited the Southwest.[56]

They struck the Gila near Redrock before sweeping south toward the Peloncillos. In these foothills Chie and Ponce found signs indicating that "Cochise Apaches" had been in the vicinity. They astounded Sladen and Howard by announcing "the number of the party, the band which they belonged, and the time that had elapsed since they were here." Finally, about September 27, at a place Howard called Peracino Springs (several miles north of Stein's Peak), they succeeded in communicating with Nazee, a Chokonen leader, who soon brought his entourage of sixty into camp. This was probably the group Stephenson had struck in late July. One old woman, "wrinkled and haggard," was a wife of Cochise. Nazee revealed that the chief was in the Dragoon Mountains.

Nazee admonished the general to reduce his party if he wished to see Cochise.[57] This alarmed Sladen, but not an impervious Howard. Convinced of divine guidance, he sent Streeter, May, and Stone to Fort Bowie with a note to the commanding officer ordering him to "send out no scouts in this direction or in any, to interfere with the peace I am in a fair way of making." Streeter and company arrived at Bowie on September 29.[58]

Howard, Sladen, Jeffords, Chie, and Ponce entered the Sulphur Springs Valley "aiming for a depression in the Dragoon Mountains, a dozen of fifteen miles south of the Tucson Road called Middlemarch Pass."[59] They spent the evening of the twenty-ninth at the Sulphur Springs station. At midnight they departed, reaching the foothills of the Dragoons early the next morning, where they made a dry camp. At dawn, after only a few hours' sleep, they entered the Dragoons, with Ponce and Chie making smoke signals to indicate that their party had come in peace before going into camp.

Early that afternoon Chie left. A few hours later two young Indian boys appeared to guide them to the Apache camp. Taking a "long steep tiresome ride until the summit was reached," they finally emerged into the west stronghold. Here a few Chokonens under

Middlemarch Pass, Dragoon Mountains. Howard's party entered the mountains through this pass in search of Cochise. (*Photo by Karen Hayes*)

a warrior named Tygee were camped. To everyone's disappointment, Cochise was camped a few miles away and would not meet Howard's party until the next morning. The uncertainty about how he perceived their presence and his making Howard wait another day fostered an air of pessimism. Sladen was dubious of their prospects: "None seemed to know how he would react to them bringing two white men into his camp." Only Howard remained sanguine, believing that the major obstacles had been overcome.

Cochise had been watching their progress for several days. From the high peaks in the Dragoons, it has been said, his eagle-eyed scouts could discern troops as they left Apache Pass. Only through the presence of Jeffords and his two relatives had he allowed Howard access to his camp, which, as it turned out, made Howard a welcome visitor.

Early that morning (October 1), word spread through Tygee's camp that "he is coming." Immediately the Indians formed in a circle and spread blankets to receive their chief. Cochise's brother Juan, "a fierce looking Indian . . . short and thickset" arrived first, armed with a spear and bow and arrows. He dismounted, warmly embraced Jeffords, and was introduced to Howard. Moments later, Cochise arrived with his sister,[60] his youngest wife, and youngest son, Naiche. He "dashed to where we were gathered from his horse, and gave Jeffords the same warm greeting that Juan had accorded him." Next he turned to Howard, and Jeffords introduced him, saying to Howard, "This is the man." Cochise shook hands, responding, "Buenos días, Señor." After affectionately greeting Ponce and Chie, the chief was next introduced to Sladen: he shook Sladen's hand and repeated the welcome he gave Howard.

Before discussing business, Cochise spoke with Jeffords, Chie, and Ponce. He asked Jeffords whether the general would talk honestly and "do as they say they will." Jeffords replied, "Well, I don't know, I think they will but I will see that they don't promise too much." Next Cochise interrogated Ponce and Chie for about ten minutes, wanting to know everything about Howard: his history, status, and objectives.

As Cochise conversed with Ponce and Chie, Sladen carefully studied the chief, describing him as

a remarkably fine looking man fully six feet tall, as straight as an arrow, and well proportioned, the typical Indian face, rather long, high cheek bones, clear keen eyes and a Roman nose. . . . A yellow silk handkerchief bound his hair, which was straight and black, with just a touch of silver.[61]

Satisfied with Ponce's and Chie's report, Cochise turned to Howard and asked the purpose of his visit. The general succinctly replied that "I have come from Washington to meet your people and make peace, and will stay as long as necessary." Cochise responded:

Nobody wants peace more than I do. I have done no mischief since I came from Canada Alamosa, but I am poor, my horses are poor and I have but few, I might have got more by raiding on the Tucson Road, but I did not do it.[62]

Howard proposed to consolidate the Chokonens and the Chihennes and remove the Tularosa agency to Cañada Alamosa. To everyone's surprise, Cochise initially objected, declaring that he himself would go, "but I am sure it would break my band." Then he surprised Howard and Sladen by suddenly asking, "Why not give me Apache Pass? Give me that and I will protect all the roads. I will see that nobody's property is taken by Indians."[63] He refused to make a decision until he talked the matter over with his captains, who were out raiding—or, as Cochise euphemistically termed it, "making a living." Howard agreed to wait until the chief could gather his people.

At once runners were sent out to bring in his men. Fearing that his returning warriors might clash with troops, Cochise insisted that Howard ride to Fort Bowie to notify all troops that a "cease fire was in effect." At first the general demurred, proposing to send Sladen. Cochise objected, saying, "The soldiers may not obey Captain [Lieutenant] Sladen. They will obey you. I want you to go. Jeffords and Captain Sladen can stay here." In a way, the chief was testing Howard's sincerity, wondering whether the general would back his words with action. The general acquiesced and later that same day departed for Bowie with Chie as his guide.[64]

The pair traveled throughout the night, with the most arduous part of the journey spent crossing the Dragoons' "rugged heights and deep gulches." Howard tore his "coat in shreds, pricked my legs with thorns." Through Chie's perseverance and expertise, they finally reached the Sulphur Springs stage station about midnight, where Nick Rogers, the station keeper, took them on to Apache Pass. On October 2, Captain Samuel Storrow Sumner reported to General Crook:

> At 7AM this morning the general accompanied by one Indian reached this place. He had . . . met Cochise yesterday. General Howard left here at 2PM today on his return to the Dragoon Mountains. . . . He requested that no scouting parties be sent out from this point during the present position of affairs.[65]

Howard also telegraphed the commissioner of Indian affairs in Washington and instructed the commanding officer at Fort Lowell to notify "Crittenden and other posts near you and General Crook that they [Indians] may not be fired upon when doing no mischief."[66]

Sumner furnished Howard with supplies: two thousand pounds of corn, a sack of coffee, sugar, and flour plus some cloth purchased from the post trader. Sumner concluded optimistically that "there seems to be some liklihood of getting Cochise to go on a reservation," yet he was perplexed that Howard was considering including the area around Apache Pass.[67]

With provisions and accompanied by his entire party (Bloomfield, May, Streeter, and Stone), Howard started the forty-mile return trip to the Dragoons. They spent the first night (October 2) at the Sulphur Springs station. The next morning they cut through Dragoon Pass to the western side of the mountains, where they were met by Sladen, Jeffords, and several Indians. They learned that Cochise had relocated his camp a few miles northeast of the west stronghold the night before after one of his raiding parties returned and reported they had killed several whites. On September 30, these warriors had ambushed Sergeant George Stewart's party near Thomas Gardner's ranch, killing four of the six soldiers. Cochise said he didn't "think the troops can follow the trail of my Indians but if they do, they will be in here to-night and we will have a fight." No troops were near, but Cochise was not one to take chances, so he moved his camp into the inaccessible heights of the Dragoons, where the "entire band could at a moment easily conceal themselves behind boulders and crags."[68]

The next day, October 4, the ranchería was moved back to the west stronghold, where all awaited the return of Cochise's subchiefs to discuss peace. Howard and Sladen spent the next week in the stronghold, although Sladen apparently made one trip to Bowie. The two officers left behind interesting accounts of life in an Apache camp and furnished a good description of Cochise's character, intelligence, and the autocratic influence he held over his followers. On one of Sladen's first nights among the Chokonens, he witnessed a Chiricahua tiswin drunk: "Suddenly I heard sharp screams from Cochise's wife and sister and I saw them fleeing in terror from his bivouack. He was striking and scolding them and his voice was loud and harsh." Sladen was extremely relieved when Jeffords assumed control of the situation and calmed Cochise down.

Another incident described by Sladen illustrated Cochise's pragmatic ways. A wounded warrior had arrived at camp, probably from the September 30 fight near Gardner's ranch. He "was kept hidden away among the rocks" and the Americans could hear Cochise praying for his recovery "to the Great Father" and "the response of the assembly—for all the Indians had gathered around him." Because

Sladen had a medical background, Howard offered his services. "But Cochise would not consent to this. His reply was most sensible. The man was dangerously ill and might die . . . if he did die my people . . . would think that the Captain [Sladen] had given him bad medicine and they would want to kill him." Sladen agreed.[69]

Each day, one or more of Cochise's captains returned and reported to him. Sladen described the scene:

> Their return was always noticed with some formality. When they rode up they went at once to the stone where Cochise was seated, dismounted and sat down upon the ground, with great deliberation, and without any demonstration of emotion of any kind, they reported to the Chief; a short conversation ensued, in an ordinary tone, as if they had been present all the time, and then they retired to some hiding place to their own immediate family.[70]

As late as October 7, Howard continued to push for Cañada Alamosa as the reservation site.[71] The first captain to return was a thirty-five-year-old warrior named Nahilzay,[72] Cochise's brother-in-law, who strongly favored peace. But as more and more Apaches came in, many "rough and very troublesome," combined with Cochise's feeling that a reservation in Arizona would "cancel all old scores," the general gradually acquiesced to the chief's desires, rationalizing that it was the only way to keep them content.

On October 10 the last captain returned. He was "a short and stout man" who acted as Cochise's interpreter from Apache to Spanish. Sladen wrote that he was "a very important factor in the negotiations and the old chief often deferred to and referred important questions to him before deciding them." He was an obstreperous individual disliked by both Howard and Sladen. He "had been captured by the Mexicans as a child and had been a captive among them for many years." His identity is not definitely known but, given these descriptions, he may have been El Cautivo, the Captive, who was involved in the Dodge murder of 1856 and was with Cochise near Fronteras in October 1858. He was the last of Cochise's captains to return; only Taza and another leader were beyond recall, raiding in Sonora.[73]

The identity of the captains is somewhat in doubt because neither Howard, Sladen, nor Jeffords left behind a list of them. From piec-

ing together all of the available evidence, I believe the following Indians were captains in Cochise's band and possibly attended the
council. Strong cases can be made for Cullah (Collali), Remigio,
Julián, Peñon, Eskinya, Nahilzay, Nazee, Nasakee (Nah-zar-zee),
Tygee (Targash), Chacone, José Manda, and El Cautivo. Besides
these twelve Chokonens, two other warriors were up-and-coming
leaders within the Chokonen band: Chato and Chihuahua.

Cullah, Remigio, Julián, and Peñon had been with Cochise at
Janos in the spring of 1872. Cullah, born about 1825, had succeeded Yaque as chief of one group and survived the smallpox epidemic of 1862. He accompanied Taza to Washington in 1876 and
headed a small Chokonen group at San Carlos in 1877. Remigio
had succeeded Esquinaline in the early 1860s and had fought under
Cochise during the 1860s. Julián had succeeded Cochise's old friend
Elías as leader of a small extended family group in the late 1860s.
Pionsenay, or Peñon, was a first-rate Chokonen incorrigible whose
actions led to the closing of Cochise's reservation in 1876. Pionsenay's brother or half-brother was Eskinya, a member of Elías's and
Tace's group in the early 1860s. He was said to have been Cochise's
head medicine man and one of the more influential leaders within
the Chokonen band. As has been mentioned, Nahilzay was Cochise's war chief and was well known to both Fred Hughes and General Howard. He also appeared on the San Carlos census in 1880 as
a member of Naiche's band. In addition to these six, there were two
other old-time Chokonen leaders who might have been captains.
José Manda had been a subordinate of Cochise throughout the 1860s
and may have been with him at Cañada Alamosa in 1871–72.
Chacone, whose followers were attacked in the Dragoons by Bernard in January 1870, may have been present if he was still living.

The three Americans mentioned three other leaders: Nazee, a
prominent Chokonen man, went to San Carlos with Taza and was a
member of Naiche's band in the 1880 and 1884 censuses. Nasakee
was with Pionsenay in the 1876 outbreak. Tygee passed from the
scene by the mid-1870s.

Chato and Chihuahua, two Chokonen leaders of the 1880s, were
probably on Cochise's reservation, but whether they attended the
historic conference is not definitely known. In later years Chato
spoke openly about his life on Cochise's reservation and may have

Council Rocks. Located on the western slopes of the Dragoon Mountains, this was the probable location where Cochise and Howard met. (*Photo by Karen Hayes*)

accompanied Taza to San Carlos.[74] Fred Hughes recalled that Chihuahua was on Cochise's reservation, a fact corroborated by the informants of Mrs. Eve Ball. He accompanied Taza to San Carlos.[75]

Finally, there is the Indian I have identified as El Cautivo, Cochise's interpreter. In later years Sladen came to the logical conclusion that this man was Geronimo, based on his physical appearance and cruel and vindictive mannerisms. But he was almost certainly wrong. Sladen mentioned that this man had been a captive among the Mexicans, a description that does not apply to Geronimo. However, the evidence is equivocal regarding Geronimo's presence. Neither Howard nor Jeffords made any mention of him, and the reliable Fred Hughes claimed that Geronimo came to the reservation with Juh's Nednhis in November 1872; Charles T. Connell reported the same. Nonetheless, Geronimo claimed he was present and years later Captain Samuel Sumner confirmed this in a letter to Sladen.[76] Sumner should have known because he was at the council and also commanded Fort Bowie in 1872–73. In any event, if the notorious Geronimo was present, he played an inconspicuous role.

The Indians held a council among themselves the next day. Wrote Jeffords:

> General Howard wished to attend this pow-wow but I told him to stay where he was; that they would let us know if they wanted to make peace. After a while I knew by the noise in their camp that it was all right, and that they had decided for peace, and so told the general. Cochise then came up and told the general that they were ready to make terms of peace.[77]

The terms of the treaty were simple. Howard set aside the reservation Cochise wanted, saying later that "it was not the one I preferred but the only one I could get the Indians to agree to." He also "promised that the government would furnish the usual supplies of food and clothing." Finally, he agreed "that they should have Thomas J. Jeffords as their agent." The latter was a moot point, since Howard had appointed him special agent the previous month. In return, "Cochise and his captains promised to abstain from all unlawful acts they commit . . . what they call war," and Cochise pledged to "keep the roads in all that vicinity open."[78]

After these conditions were agreed to, Cochise declared poetically that "hereafter the white man and the Indian are to drink the same water, eat of the same bread, and be at peace."[79] To dispel his fears, Cochise insisted that the officers from Fort Bowie be present at the formal parley to be held the next day. Accordingly, on October 11, Howard sent Stone to Fort Bowie to request Captain Sumner's presence and cautioned Sumner to bring "two officers besides yourself, the doctor and a driver. . . . Do not take more men."[80] That same day he also wrote Crook, advising him that he had decided to give Cochise the Chiricahua Mountains as a reservation and declaring that the Indians would "cease from war and be contented." Consequently, "I have concluded to try them."[81]

Sumner was less than delighted about the prospect of riding all night to meet Cochise in council. Yet at 1 A.M. he, Captain Joseph Theodore Haskell, Lieutenant Charles Bird, and Dr. Edward Orr left Bowie and reached Sulphur Springs at six in the morning. Rest-

Treaty Peak, also known as Knob Hill. This peak had a white flag placed at its summit by Cochise to indicate to all that he had made peace. (*Photo by Karen Hayes*)

ing for two hours, they pushed on to Dragoon Springs and arrived there at 11:45, fifteen minutes before the conference was to begin.[82]

After formal introductions, the council began, with Cochise, his captains, and his warriors, some fifty in all, present. Naturally, Cochise dominated the conversation, reciting past acts of white injustice, treachery, and the unforgettable Bascom affair. He asked what his people had done to deserve such treatment and why the troops from Fort Bowie had been "down on him and his people." The officers listened courteously and explained that the troops' business was to pursue hostiles, but "as soon as he was willing to make peace, we were willing to do all we could to show him we wanted peace." Cochise replied that he was "getting old and would like to live at peace from this time on; but that if the white man would not let him do it, he would go away from here and fight him."[83]

While the council was in progress, Captain Haskell had a good opportunity to size up the chief. As were most other whites, he was impressed with what he saw:

The reports that we have had of Cochise have always given us to understand that he is old, used up, crippled from wounds and exposure, and of no account whatever as a leader or a chief. How mistaken we were! We met Cochise and thirteen of his captains, and Cochise is as different from the others of his tribe, as far as we saw, as black is from white. When standing straight he is said to be exactly six feet tall. I took a good look at him and made up my mind that he was only five feet ten inches. He is powerful, exceedingly well built, bright, intelligent countenance, and as fine an Indian as I ever laid my eyes on. . . . He was clean from head to foot. I looked at his scalp, his hair, face (painted fresh), neck, body, arms, and legs and he was clean. Most of the others were so filthy that you could scrape enough dirt off them to start a potato patch.[84]

After Cochise and one of his captains, probably El Cautivo, spoke for some three hours, the conversation finally turned to the terms of the treaty. The boundaries were confirmed:

Beginning at Dragoon Springs, near Dragoon Pass, and running thence northeasterly, touching the north base of the Chiricahua Mountains to a point on the summit of Peloncillo Mountains or Steins Peak range, thence southeasterly along said range through Steins Peak to the New Mexico boundary; thence due south to Mexican boundary, thence westerly along said boundary fifty-five miles; thence northerly following substantially the western base of the Dragoon Mountains to the place of the beginning.[85]

For his part, Cochise pledged to keep his Indians on the reservation and protect the Tucson road. After the conference concluded at 4 P.M., Howard's party prepared to leave for Tucson, but not before Cochise (whom Howard called "the most manly of all the chiefs") and the general had one brief final meeting, with Cochise saying good-bye in English.

That day, Howard traveled to the San Pedro River. The next day, a Sunday, he rested and caught up on his correspondence, writing Crook about the results and particulars of the reservation. He also wrote Jeffords, authorizing him to hire one clerk, one teamster, and two laborers and advising him that the agency "will be independent till I can see the Indian commissioner." For the time being, Jeffords was to draw whatever supplies he needed from Fort Bowie.[86]

Meanwhile, Sumner's party had returned to Fort Bowie, deeply concerned about the reservation site. On October 15, Sumner wrote that the location "may be unfortunate for both whites and Indians as the temptation to raid from there will be great." Furthermore, he added grimly, "I anticipate trouble in the reservation from Sonora, these Indians can slip across the border at any time . . . and return to their homes with stolen stock." He warned that problems were bound to occur because "the Mexicans will be likely to follow" raiding parties onto the reservation. He was right on target.[87]

The one-armed Christian general had carried out a courageous mission. Jeffords, not one to throw out unearned accolades, wrote: "I doubt if there is any other person that could have been sent here that could have performed the mission as well; certainly none could have performed it better."[88] Howard, with "Divine Help," had succeeded in making peace with Cochise, which Cochise kept faithfully for the remainder of his life. The problem with the treaty, as Sumner pointed out to Crook, was the proximity of the reservation to Sonora, with which Cochise had not made peace. As Cochise put it: "The Mexicans are on one side in this matter and the Americans on another. . . . I made peace with the Americans, but the Mexicans did not come to ask peace from me."[89]

Even if Sonora had requested peace with Cochise, it would not have mattered. Howard certainly did not grant Cochise permission to raid in Mexico. Although Cochise himself would not raid, he still considered his people at war with Mexico; thus he would make no efforts to prevent hostilities below the border. In fact, at this time it is doubtful that he even contemplated such. After all, who would the Chiricahuas raid if not the Mexicans? His Chokonens would find refuge and a market for their booty on the reservation.

Although the Howard-Jeffords-Cochise treaty brought peace and stability to southeastern Arizona for the first time since 1860, the same could not be said for Mexico. The Chiricahua Apaches continued their sanguinary raids below the border, with many originating from Cochise's reservation.

## Chapter 19

## THE CHIRICAHUA RESERVATION

The reservation established for the Chiricahuas was the subject of bitter controversy from the beginning. The press and Crook censured Howard because he seemingly gave in to all of Cochise's demands, in particular a reserve which was fifty-five miles wide, which adjoined Sonora, and which was independent from the military. Crook looked for justification to interfere and soon found plenty: incessant outcries from Sonora about the raiding from the new agency. He reprimanded Howard at every opportunity and even proposed sending troops to take over the reserve.

Cochise made no bones about his Indians raiding into Sonora; "I made peace with the Americans and not the Mexicans" was his standard reply. Although he apparently never left the reservation, during its first year of existence he made few, if any, attempts to restrain his people. By the same token, Jeffords proved somewhat insensitive to these charges, adopting a laissez-faire attitude and rationalizing that the Mexicans deserved whatever they received because of past mistreatment of the Chiricahuas.

Cochise sent out runners to gather the remainder of his people and to inform other Apaches that he had made peace. His Indians placed a pole with a white flag along the Tucson Road, a sign indicating to all travelers that they were at peace. Jeffords next began the task of organizing his agency. The most vital ingredient, rations, was furnished from Fort Bowie, where he received nine thousand pounds of

East stronghold, Dragoon Mountains. Cochise made his camp in this vicinity during the reservation years. (*Photo by Karen Hayes*)

corn, and at Tucson, where General Howard purchased some thirty-six hundred dollars' worth of supplies. On October 16, Jeffords rationed 450 Indians and set about, with Cochise's help, to bring more Indians to the reservation.[1] About October 20 he found the Stein's Peak band, probably with Chie's and Ponce's help, and brought them in. An observer numbered them at 60,[2] but a year later Jeffords reported 150.[3] This was a Chokonen group, quite possibly the local group of Chihuahua, who was said "to have been a very young chief when Cochise was very old," according to Mrs. Eve Ball, and "a leader during the last part of Cochise's life," according to Morris Opler.[4]

This accomplished, Jeffords sent Ponce, Chie, and Streeter to Tularosa. The guides, whom Jeffords compensated with cloth and tobacco, were expected to return to Arizona with their followers, along with Chiva and Gordo, yet for some reason, this did not happen. Streeter, meanwhile, had carried a message from Jeffords to Fred Hughes,[5] offering the latter a job as clerk of the reservation. Hughes consented and arrived on November 2.

He found the agency established at Sulphur Springs in a ten-by-twelve house rented from Nick Rogers for fifty dollars a month. The quarters were woefully inadequate. Jeffords, Hughes, and one worker had to live and work in this confining area. There was no space to store the Indians' rations. As a result, they were left in the open and a good quantity became spoiled. A few days later Hughes met Cochise:

> To show how suspicious the old fellow still was, he came accompanied by about fifty warriors. They made their camp about half a mile from the agency but within sight, they then commenced sauntering up to the agency building in squads of twos and threes until some fifteen or twenty had reached there, then seeing everything was all right they took Jeffords down to where Cochise was and he brought him up . . . [he] took me by the hand with both of his, told me he had heard of me before and that from this day on he was going to be my friend. He kept his word till the day of his death.[6]

In the meantime, Cochise had sent a runner to the Nednhis living near Janos, inviting them to partake of the truce.[7] Led by Juh, Geronimo, Nolgee, and Natiza, they had been on the run since the previous summer, keeping one step ahead of Sonoran scouts, before resuming friendly relations at Janos. They finally came in about November 20 and met Jeffords and Hughes at Pinery Canyon, some fifteen miles south of Apache Pass. Hughes recalled that this band "was under the command of a chief named Natiza and they were in reality Indians belonging to the government of Mexico."[8] The Nednhi population was variously placed at either two, three, or four hundred depending on who made the estimate. Hughes believed that this band of Apaches pretended indecision about peace and "wanted to be mean and were afraid of Cochise." Finally, after some procrastination, they assented to the same stipulations as Cochise's Chokonens.[9]

The Nednhis were a continuous source of trouble. What sort of relations they had had with Americans, if any, was not clear. Besides rations, the main reason they decided to live in Arizona was the security the reservation offered. From here they could easily slip undetected across the border to raid, then retreat to the sanctity of the agency. Cochise may have invited them knowing that raids into Arizona would continue unless he had them under his eye.

As Cochise had promised, Indian raids in southern Arizona ceased. Howard, who had been publicly abused by the press, began to receive the favor from many southwesterners. On November 1, Samuel Orr wrote the general from Fort Bowie that the citizens were "beginning to look upon the peace arrangement in a more favorable light." And the Apaches' apprehension subsided after visits to Sulphur Springs and Fort Bowie, where they had been treated well. Even so, concluded Orr, "the papers have ceased their howling for the present and all well meaning people give you credit for what you have done."[10]

Further evidence of Cochise's sincerity may be discerned from two letters written by men who previously had subscribed to the extermination policy. Thomas Hughes, who had settled on the Sonoita in 1868, had been victimized by several Apache raids. On November 23, 1872, he wrote Howard to express his "heart felt thanks for making peace with Cochise and his band of cut-throats." During the previous eighteen months, he had "lost nearly everything I could call my own except my life." Moreover, during that same period, "12 men have been killed by the Indians on my ranch which is only two miles from the military post of Camp Crittenden." Since the peace had been made, "everything has been going along very nicely . . . not one Indian sign has been seen in these parts since peace was made with Cochise."[11] A few weeks later another Arizona pioneer, Sidney Delong, one of the few whites who had participated in the Camp Grant massacre, wrote Howard and conceded that the armistice was working. "Thus far no cause for complaint has arisen and . . . you are entitled to the thanks of this people."[12] Delong, who operated the trading post at Bowie, had other reasons to be happy: the Indians were trading him the loot from their raids in Mexico.

Regardless of the armistice, the press continued to predict that the peace would not endure; after all, Cochise had come onto reservations before but eventually had left. But this reserve was in his country, and he trusted and respected the agent. On November 16 the *Arizona Miner* prognosticated that Cochise "will keep the peace but not beyond next summer." [13] Two weeks later the *Arizona Citizen* could not resist adding that "Cochise . . . so far has deported himself [well] . . . but, there is something in the genial sunshine of the spring months which usually overcomes his good resolves, and he is not responsible for climatic operations." [14]

Governor Safford visited Cochise in late November and was convinced that the chief wanted peace, yet he warned that "some real or imaginary cause may at any moment may set them again on the warpath." [15] Referring to Jeffords, Safford wrote: "I do not believe any other man living could now manage them, wild as they are." This unanimous skepticism on the part of Arizonans should not be casually dismissed as the sentiments of Indian-hating whites. Cochise had first made peace overtures in late 1868 and since that time his actions had shown he would do what he pleased unless he was content with government treatment. Almost predictably, the rations and supplies Howard had promised were slow in coming, and an exasperated Jeffords wrote letter after letter to obtain them, but without success. [16]

To begin with, Jeffords was disappointed with Washington's decision to put him in the Department of Arizona, reporting to Dr. Herman Bendell, superintendent of Indian affairs in Arizona. He had hoped to be assigned to the jurisdiction of Nathaniel Pope, whom Jeffords opined would "better understand the difficult position which I am placed." [17] Unfortunately, other views prevailed and on November 14, 1872, Jeffords was instructed by telegram to report to Bendell. [18] A communication problem surfaced immediately, with Bendell telling Jeffords how paperwork should be performed and how letters should be folded. On January 2, Bendell asked the agent to provide a list of the supplies that were required, promising that "every effort would be made to furnish them." [19] Jeffords had written Bendell on December 20 requesting "prompt action, for the present in all business pertaining to this agency," but he did not provide specifics. Four days later he again urged that supplies be furnished as "the government promised." Bendell asked for specifics, which failed to mollify Jeffords, who had only beef to issue the Indians and their patience was nearly exhausted.[20]

To be fair, Bendell was caught in a bind: in addition to budgetary problems, he had run into indifferent Washington bureaucrats who expected him to perform miracles without adequate funds. There was no deficit spending in the 1870s. Bendell was not discriminating against the Chiricahua Reservation; he treated the Fort Apache and Camp Grant Indians the same way he treated the Chiricahuas. His major problem was managing a superintendency on a budget which allowed for three agencies but now, after two peace commissioners, had seven. "How am I to contract debts in order to fulfill the promises made to the Indians . . . by the special commissioner? I have no funds on hand applicable for procuring food, shelter or transportation for the Indians."[21] The responsibility for this predicament lay with the Bureau of Indian Affairs and the secretary of the interior; it was their duty to ensure that sufficient funds were allocated to meet the government's commitments.

The situation could have exploded, but it did not. Cochise's health was failing, and he lacked the strength and will even to think of fighting another war. All he wanted was to be left alone. He had plenty of time to indulge in tiswin drunks, which perhaps dulled the pain of the disease which eventually took his life. Just as important, he had an agent he trusted and a reservation in his ancestral country. If rations were slow in coming, his people could sustain themselves by raiding into Mexico and by hunting and gathering, as they had done before the peace.

The indecisiveness perturbed Jeffords more than Cochise, who probably was not surprised that promises were not kept. The situation was exacerbated on January 24 when Bendell told Jeffords, as he had other agents, that his funds were exhausted: "Contract no debt without authorization from this office." Nine days later, Bendell allowed Jeffords to purchase small amounts of corn, but his creditors had to wait until the next fiscal year to be paid.[22] An incredulous Jeffords decided that he had had enough, so he turned to the one person who could get him some answers: General Howard.

Jeffords first complained to Howard about Bendell's "evasive replies" about when supplies would be furnished. He warned that his Indians might become unruly if food was not forthcoming—and quickly. Jeffords wondered what action he could take. The Indians, who now numbered 1,025, had complied with the agreement. "Not a single complaint has been made against them," yet the government's promises had not been carried out. Howard took immediate action, probably sending the letter to Charles Delano, secretary of the interior, who on March 5 telegraphed Bendell: "See that Chiricahua Reservation is furnished with all needful supplies. Don't neglect this duty."[23]

Bendell had recognized that the Chiricahuas "cannot be retained upon the reservation without being fed." Budget restrictions had forced him to provide with the resources on hand, and he had informed his superiors in Washington, who had ignored the problem and left Bendell without support. As frustrated with his superiors as Jeffords was of him, Bendell tendered his resignation on February 28, 1873, and it was accepted on March 24.[24]

In the meantime, he acted on Delano's orders, telegraphing Washington on March 11: "Chiricahua Reservation will be immediately supplied as directed."[25] That same day he also informed the Indian commissioner that the supplies should last until June 30. Three days later he advised Jeffords that he had ordered 23,000 pounds of corn, 1,820 pounds of coffee, 3,640 pounds of sugar, and 910 pounds of soap and salt. Although this problem was solved, Jeffords still had not received any funds to pay his creditors. While this crisis was averted, another one erupted.[26] It had been gathering momentum ever since the reservation was created: raiding into Sonora. The protagonists in this controversy were Crook versus Howard, Cochise versus Mexico, and Jeffords versus practically everyone else. The issue in each case was continued Chiricahuas forays from a U.S. government agency into a neighboring country. Jeffords, inclined to make excuses for his Indians, was criticized severely in some quarters, and with some justification.

As Captain Sumner had predicted, the savage and brutal raids into Sonora had continued, probably no more or no less than in previous years. The problem became magnified because of the reservation's proximity to Sonora's border. There was no doubt that much of the raiding could be attributed to the Chokonens and Nednhis living on the reservation, at times in conjunction with the Chihennes from Tularosa. Also, Western Apache bands from northern reservations made incursions, but these were decreasing each year as the government tightened its control of these bands. Experienced southwesterners understood the consequences of locating the reservation near the border. Perhaps Jeffords should have warned Howard, who failed to comprehend the intense hatred which had evolved from three centuries of Apache-Mexican conflicts. More than any other Apache band, the Chiricahuas had fallen victim to the Mexican machete and musket. Likewise, the Mexicans had fallen victim to the Chiricahua lance and bow.

Cochise himself had not understood the ramifications of raiding into Sonora, despite Howard's stern objection. After all, from 1858 to 1861, while living at Apache Pass, he had led large war parties into Mexico without objections from Americans. And while the Apaches living at Cañada Alamosa, their raiding parties occasionally slipped into Mexico with impunity. Furthermore, Cochise had raided into Arizona while living in Mexico, where the citizens of Fronteras and Janos encouraged the depredations because of the booty the Chiricahuas obtained. This had been a way of life along the border, but it must and would change. Cochise realized this, but he had not calculated that it would have to be so soon.

During the Indians' first four months on the reservation, there was heavy raiding into Sonora. The participants evidently were the younger Chokonen warriors and the turbulent Nednhis under Juh and Geronimo. To Cochise, the raiding was unimportant and he declined to halt it.

Sonora's complaints began a few months after the treaty. Each depredation was charged to Cochise, and article after article assailed Howard's character for allegedly permitting the Indians to cross the border. In mid-December 1872 the Sonoran representative in Mexico City complained bitterly to Porter C. Bliss, the U.S. consul, that Howard had granted Cochise permission to raid into Mexico and that the commander of Fort Bowie had orders to protect those who were blameworthy. On December 20, Bliss asked Washington for a response. Sonora's most prominent newspaper, *Estrella de Occidente,* reported that not only had Howard granted Cochise permis-

George Crook. Cochise eluded his grasp, which upset the commander of the department of Arizona. (*Courtesy Arizona Historical Society, Tucson*)

sion to raid below the border but had also furnished guns, saddles, and mounts. These ridiculous allegations were made repeatedly for the next eighteen months and were quite similar to American complaints against Fronteras and Janos in the 1860s.[27]

These charges were music to Crook's ears. He had only contempt for Howard,[28] whom he considered naïve and peace hungry. Moreover, Howard had unwittingly provoked Crook by innocently recommending that Fort Apache and Fort Bowie be transferred to the Military District of New Mexico—away from Crook's command. General Sherman, who deferred a decision until he heard from Crook and General Pope, noted that it "would much embarrass . . . Lt. Col. Crook."[29] The idea made little sense from a logistical point of view and ultimately was rejected. If anything, Arizona and New Mexico should have been one military department, especially since by this time the only real problems remaining were the Chiricahuas, who roamed over the southern parts of both states. Second, Colyer's and Howard's policies and actions were a joke as far as Crook was concerned. Before the Apaches would submit, they had to be defeated in battle; thus he had no empathy for either Howard or Cochise.

Looking for a legitimate reason to interfere (and the Chiricahua raiding into Sonora was), Crook determined that the "whole peace system had been a fraud" and struck upon a plan that would bring Cochise under his jurisdiction. His solution was a simple compliance with General Order No. 10, which, among other things, called for a daily roll call of all Indians on reservations.[30] If it were enforced, he believed it would accomplish two things: discourage depredations into Sonora and provide the military with some control over Cochise. Jeffords and Hughes both objected, predicting that Cochise would not submit to a daily count. They felt certain that if this policy were enforced it would drive "them to the warpath," something Hughes thought Crook wanted.[31] Their feelings were echoed by Colonel Delos Bennet Sacket (from the inspector general's office), who predicted that if they were forced to muster, Cochise and his whole band "would take to the mountains and we would have a second affair upon our hands."[32]

Crook's plans and strategy revolved around the Chiricahuas' refusal and subsequent outbreak; they would surely bolt for the mountains of Sonora. Consequently, he told Governor Pesqueira on January 9, 1873, that if the Chiricahuas refused the roll call, "I will commence hostilities against them without delay." He urged Pesqueira "to place strong detatchments along the border," to which the latter responded favorably, thanking Crook for his concern. Before Crook carried out these plans, however, he apparently had second thoughts and decided to send a party to confer with Cochise and obtain his preceptions of the treaty.[33]

What Crook really wanted was an excuse, or at least some justification, to intervene and implement his plans. In late January, Captain William Henry Brown, Lieutenant Charles Henry Rockwell, Lieutenant John Gregory Bourke, and a small escort arrived at Sulphur Springs and requested an interview with Cochise on behalf of Crook. From here Brown wrote Jeffords:

> General Crook has instructed me to have an interview with . . . Cochise and I am now here for that purpose. . . . General Crook has directed me not to enter the Indian camp with any armed men lest the presence of troops offend the Indians and tend to disturb the friendly relations which now exists and which General Crook is anxious to preserve in all its integrity. I shall be glad to meet Cochise and yourself at this place or any other place you may select.[34]

Jeffords arranged the meeting and on February 3, Brown's contingent met Cochise in the Dragoons.

The erudite Bourke recorded the interview, which probably occurred in the east stronghold. He described Cochise as "6 ft. in stature, deep chested, roman nosed, black eyes, firm mouth and a kindly and even somewhat melancholy expression. . . . He seemed much more neat than the other wild Indians." Interestingly enough, Cochise's youngest wife may have been the one individual who did not fear the chief. Envious of his oldest wife, she had bitten the chief on both hands and had left two scars, which caught the attention of Bourke. The interview was carried out in a businesslike manner, with Captain Brown directing the questions and Cochise responding:

> *Brown*—The General has sent me to Cochise to find out what he understands these terms [peace treaty] to be and, especially with reference to the movements of troops within the reservation.

John G. Bourke. An ethnologist and army officer, Bourke met Cochise in
February 1873 in the east stronghold of the Dragoon Mountains. *(Courtesy
Arizona Historical Society, Tucson)*

*Cochise*—The troops were to pass and repass by the road on the
reservation the same as ever, according as the emergencies of the service might require but none were to come upon the reservation to
live, nor were citizens to do so.

*Brown*—What stipulations, if any, were made in the treaty with
regard to the people of Mexico?

*Cochise* (After first avoiding the question)—The Mexicans are on one side in this matter and the Americans on another. There are many young people whose parents and relatives have been killed by the Mexicans, and now these young people are liable to go down, from time to time and do a little damage to the Mexicans. I don't want to lie about this thing; they go but I don't send them.[35]

Brown told Crook about the interview and Crook must have been chagrined. It was clear to Bourke and Crook that Cochise did not think he had violated the agreement. This, plus the problem that no written treaty existed, forced Crook to cancel plans for a military takeover of the agency. He was compelled to write Pesqueira and concede that he had "encountered obstacles" and must await "further instructions from my government."[36]

During the first three months of 1873, Apache raiding in Sonora continued, much of it originating from the Chiricahua Reservation. A review seems to indicate they were no more severe than those of the previous two or three years. The Sonoran press blew the situation out of proportion and delightfully criticized U.S. handling of the Apaches. The situation was exacerbated with the printing of letters from Tucson—and even San Francisco—from individuals who were not aware of the facts. This led to slanderous and disparaging statements about Howard. If anyone should have been blamed, it should have been Tom Jeffords.

He maintained a remarkable influence with his wards. Not everyone concurred with his methods, yet all agreed that he was the only white man completely trusted by Cochise. Jeffords, although a public official, displayed a cavalier, unsympathetic, and insensitive attitude toward Mexicans. He had adopted the Apache belief that the Mexicans deserved what they received on the basis of past actions. He revealed his true feelings when he told a Mexican officer that "he did not consider it his duty to name those who had [raided] and when they returned he would ration them."[37] Even worse was his remark to the *Arizona Citizen* that "he did not care how many Mexicans his people killed . . . that for acts of treachery with those Indians, the Mexicans deserved the killings." Jeffords later acknowledged that this was his private belief and not his public stance.[38] Yet it was clear that he and Cochise did little to discourage the raids when they could have.

The depredations proved to be more than stock raids, as Jeffords had asserted. On Christmas Day 1872 a small party raided Imuris, stole some stock, and killed Paulino Armento. One week later, Chiricahua raiders ran off twelve horses and mules from Bacoachi. Soon after that, Apaches, perhaps the same band, ambushed and killed state mineralogist Juan García and a judge, Pablo Valencia, nine miles from Ures. In mid-January a party of twenty Indians murdered three citizens outside Ures; ten days later another citizen was ambushed near Ures. Toward the end of January along the road between Santiago and Ures, Apaches surprised Susano Valenzuela and his wife, killing both. According to *Estrella de Occidente*, seventeen Sonorans were killed between January 1 and February 7, 1873.[39] Although the Chokonens and Nednhis could not have had a hand in every killing, most of the perpetrators could probably be traced to the Chiricahua Reservation. Fatalities continued at this rate for the first six months of 1873, when, according to an informed estimate, Apaches had killed more than one hundred Sonorans.[40]

The Sonoran press lashed out at the government of Sonora and the United States for not protecting defenseless people. The solution, lamented *Estrella de Occidente*, was to make "each town, each village, each hamlet, and each congregation an encampment because the Apaches are everywhere." Reports from Santa Cruz, Magdalena, and Tucson stated that Cochise "the famous savage" had made peace only on the condition that "he be allowed to make war on Sonora" and use the reservation as protection after his forays into Sonora. *Estrella* conceded that it did not know whether Howard had acceded to this demand but it was certain "that the Apaches who are at peace in Arizona are permitted by the American leaders to make war on this state." The reference here was to Captain Sumner's inability to act because the reservation was independent of the military. In the end, doing nothing was almost as serious a violation as abetting the raiders.[41]

When asked about the raiding, Jeffords vacillated, answering in a manner intended to close the issue. On February 20 he admitted that his people did "only a small part" of the raiding.[42] A month later, responding to the commissioner of Indian affairs in Washington, he categorically rebutted the charges, insisting "that neither Cochise nor any of his subchiefs had left the reservation since they made peace." The agent's assertions notwithstanding, one must read be-

tween the lines of Jeffords's statements.[43] Although neither Cochise
nor his subchiefs had left, this did not mean that his younger warriors or the unruly Nednhis had not.

In March an official from Sonora visited Fort Bowie with the dual
purpose of delivering supplies and attempting to perfect a truce with
Cochise. The delegation was headed by Juan Luna[44] and Cayetano
Silva, officers in Sonora's National Guard. While at Apache Pass
they met Jeffords, who helped arrange a conference with Cochise.
The two officers, in the presence of Jeffords and Sidney Randolph
Delong,[45] post trader at Bowie, extended an invitation for a permanent truce, but Cochise declared "he would not think of it." He
staunchly denied having raided below the border, claiming that
these incursions were the work of the Chihennes and the Nednhis.

Juan Luna offered a well-reasoned explanation of why he was
convinced that some of the raiding originated from the Chiricahua
Reservation:

> I was received courteously by Cochise and I am satisfied that he
> has not personally raided in Sonora since the peace . . . but . . . with
> what I did observe, I remain completely convinced that his Indians
> have committed depredations. . . .

Luna then enumerated the evidence he saw while in Cochise's camp
and on the reservation: twelve horses stolen from Bacoachi; the rifle
which belonged to Juan García, killed a few months before; clothing
which belonged to Pablo Valencia, also killed a few months before.
In fact, the truculent Nednhis were less than discreet about their
raiding, one warrior boasting that they killed every Mexican they
encountered and another admitting that a subchief had been killed
along the Sonora River the month before. Luna concluded that prospects for a solution were dim. "The Apaches showed me a profound
hatred" and "were against peace." Cochise even had to restrain a
warrior who wanted to take Luna's horse in payment for his brother
who had been captured by Mexicans.[46]

At this parley Delong invited Cochise to Fort Bowie for a visit. A
few days later he came in, his first peaceful visit to Apache Pass
since the Bascom affair twelve years before. His arrival generated
much excitement. He entered the post on the morning of March 27,
1873, accompanied by his family and twenty warriors. Captain

Joseph Haskell observed his arrival and his encounter with his old captive and nemesis, Merejildo Grijalva, in a letter:

> On his arrival he met our post guide, Mary Hilda [Merejildo Grijalva] who, as you recollect, used to be a captain [captive] with Cochise. Mary Hilda offered him his hand before he dismounted, but Cochise told him he would not shake hands with him until he whipped him; so he got down off from his horse, and struck him two or three times with his whip and then they had a friendly embrace, and commenced to talk over old times.

Cochise met the officers, embraced Captain Sumner, and assured everyone that he was delighted with the peace. That afternoon he and his family (he had brought two wives, as well as his two sons, Taza and Naiche) had lunch at Delong's store before leaving at three o'clock. Captain Haskell concluded his letter by saying that "not a depredation of any kind has been committed by them since our peace agreement last October."[47]

This was the first of several visits by Cochise to Fort Bowie and Delong's store. Delong's clerk, Al Williamson, saw Cochise on several occasions and recalled that he was a stern and taciturn man. Occasionally he would bring in things to trade, such as deer skins, but his primary purpose for visiting was to assure everyone that he was satisfied with peace and to have a few drinks with the officers. As night approached, he would depart, having established strict rules that his people should leave before sundown.[48]

That spring Cochise moved his camp from the Dragoons to the Dos Cabezas Mountains fifteen miles north of Fort Bowie. As the Indians became more familiar with the whites, they began to visit the post more frequently, making Merejildo's "services at the post almost invaluable."[49] They continued to raid in Sonora, however, and Delong's store received additional merchandise and profits. Al Williamson recalled:

> I bought from one Indian, a silver mounted ivory handled pistol that he told me he had killed a Mexican officer, in order to get it. I saw seven Indians ride up to the store one day on seven Mexican ponies with silver mounted bridles and saddles. I asked them where they got them and they said Sonora. I have seen squaws come into the

store with their babies dressed with under garments trimmed with lace, all obtained in their raids.[50]

In mid-May a Nednhi-Chokonen group, reinforced by some Chihennes from Tularosa, organized a war party to Sonora and Chihuahua. Captain Sumner and Al Williamson had been hunting near San Simon when, on their return, they met fifty Indians, "well mounted and well armed . . . their bodies painted" and "naked except for loincloths." Sumner immediately wrote Jeffords that the Indians had told him they were going hunting but he took "this to be a blind" and hoped the agent would "take some action on the matter should the report be true." Jeffords investigated, but the Indains had already left.[51]

For Jeffords, matters could not have been much worse, it seemed, but they soon became so. Another letter from Indian Commissioner Edward P. Smith in Washington had arrived, requesting information on the raiding in Sonora. Jeffords again stated that neither "Cochise nor any of his sub chiefs have been engaged in raiding into Sonora" but conceded that "maybe some of the young people go." He was guilty of telling half-truths because as agent he was responsible for the acts of Juh's and Natiza's Nednhis, yet he had made no attempt to halt or to discourage them.[52]

Some of the Chiricahuas were raiding in northern Mexico and in early July 1873 returned to the reservation with a captive boy from Chihuahua. When informed, Jeffords dutifully proceeded to the ranchería in the Chiricahuas and found the boy, Panteleón Ignacio Rocha, in Geronimo's possession and brought him back to the agency. Rocha had been captured from Concepción, Chihuahua, about June 25. Captain Sumner offered to take responsibility for the boy's safe return, and Jeffords probably turned Rocha over to him.[53]

That summer the agent encountered more problems when the disenchanted Chihennes and Bedonkohes left Tularosa and came to Cochise's reserve. Tension between the Chihennes and whites had increased considerably during the first six months of 1873 and finally reached a climax that summer. The Indians longed for Cañada Alamosa but could not go there. As a result, sporadic raiding had begun in New Mexico that spring and some of the raiders sought refuge on the Chiricahua Reservation. By June, two to three hundred Chihennes had arrived and Jeffords rationed them, reasoning that if he did not, they would raid to subsist. This infuriated Major William Redwood Price, who was assigned the unpleasant duty of rounding up hostiles in New Mexico. He asked Sumner to drive them from the reservation back to New Mexico. Sumner demurred, noting that "I am not authorized to drive them off."[54] The reply incensed an already irate Price, who began a major smear campaign against Jeffords, uncharitably concluding that he was a "creature of Cochise's" who had attained his position through illicit trade.[55]

To be fair, neither Jeffords nor Cochise had encouraged these intrusions, both realizing that trouble would erupt eventually. By this time Cochise had come to understand that the raiding into Sonora had reached a critical stage and that he would have to take some action. The newcomers were led by Chiva, Gordo, and Sánchez; the first two had been close allies and were not the Indians that Cochise's people had quarreled with two winters before. Nonetheless, the prospect of interband conflicts, less distribution of rations, and more raiding into Sonora by a band over whom he had no control led Cochise to conclude that the fugitives should return to New Mexico.

The Chihennes' arrival increased the negative publicity the reservation was receiving. As expected, Price's allegations concerning Jeffords became the subject of an investigation undertaken by the commissioner of Indian affairs in Washington. Predictably, Howard and Crook put in their two cents' worth, with Howard staunchly defending Jeffords, saying that

> common rumor in New Mexico is not a good foundation for an opinion of character. Seldom did I find a man there speak well of another. So I did not reject the services of a brave man like Jeffords who perilled his life to make peace because of slanders not proved . . . even if they came from a commissioned officer.

Furthermore, Howard suggested, if Sonora wanted peace, all it had to do was send a representative to Cochise, who would then grant a truce, or so Howard believed, revealing his naïve perceptions and simple solutions to an age-old and very complex problem.[56]

Crook confidently attacked every one of Howard's points, noting that Sonora had sent a representative, who was treated "with distain." He criticized everything associated with Cochise's reservation. He defended the character of Major Price, pointing out his fine war record, although he equally ignored Howard's distinguished career. Finally, almost as an afterthought, he fired one more shot and denounced the informality of Howard's peace with Cochise and the lack of a signed peace treaty. No other Apache bands had signed agreements, and Howard had not deviated from his orders.[57]

The acting Indian commissioner, H. R. Clum, reviewed the case and concluded that "as far as this office is concerned Cochise has with great fidelity kept his promise to refrain from marauding notwithstanding the promise of rations and assistance made to him by General Howard has been only partly fulfilled by the Government for want of funds." This hardly appeased Crook, who claimed that the special treatment given Cochise was having a demoralizing effect on other Apache bands.[58] According to Bourke, the Chokonens called the Western Apaches squaws because they were not "strong enough to insist on a reservation without soldiers."[59]

On September 16, 1873, Indian Commissioner Smith wrote Sonora's Governor Pesqueira to clear up misapprehensions regarding the Chiricahuas' agency. Smith emphasized that the Howard-Jeffords-Cochise agreement "never took the form of a treaty. No writing was drawn, no paper was signed." He assured Pesqueira that "General Howard did not grant Cochise the privilege of raiding into Sonora . . . [quite] the contrary." Quoting Jeffords, Smith said Cochise had "restrained members of his band who desired to raid into Mexico." Finally, he categorically denied that the government had issued arms, ammunition, horses, or saddles to the Apaches, as had been reported frequently in the Sonoran press.[60]

Unfortunately, Pesqueira did not receive Smith's letter. He became aware of it from John Hittell, editor of the *Alta California* in San Francisco, with whom he had carried on a running correspondence about the Apache problem. By this time Pesqueira had come to accept that Howard had not given Cochise permission to raid into Mexico, yet he asserted that the Apaches continued to show up with American horses, arms, and equipment, although one wonders how many eyewitnesses actually reported this. Pesqueira astutely pointed out that he was not concerned whether the Howard-Jeffords-Cochise treaty was in writing, for he correctly believed that

> the principal point is that the Department in question is responsible for the the acts of Cochise and his tribe, living on the Chiricahua reservation in peace, but who have made systematic incursions into Sonora to raid and murder Mexican citizens. . . . Neither local, civil or military authorities have attempted to impede these [incursions] . . . nor has anyone been authorized to intervene.

He pointedly asked: What if the situation were reversed? Would Americans tolerate it?[61] *Estrella de Occidente,* commenting on Jeffords's denial that Cochise was raiding, editorialized sarcastically: "Oh innocent Apaches! Oh Cruel whites! Oh distinguished officals! Who continues these murders in Sonora with impunity if Cochise tells his people that they should behave?"[62]

Jeffords had begun to feel the squeeze. By late summer 1873 he was being assailed from all sides—the Tucson press, the Sonoran press, military officers—and to top it all off, there was an investigation in Washington. No doubt he contemplated and came close to resigning. Finally, in late September, he admitted to Commissioner Smith that forty or fifty warriors were raiding in Sonora and justified it on grounds that the government had failed to furnish blankets for the coming winter, although raiding parties were usually organized for other reasons besides obtaining blankets.[63]

These pressures forced Jeffords and Cochise to address the consequences of continued raiding; finally, they determined to put a stop to it. In August a few Coyoteros stole some stock from the Patagonia mines. Cochise found them in the southern Dragoons and recovered three horses and a mule.[64] The next month, Jeffords and Cochise restored eight animals to citizens from Santa Cruz, Sonora,[65] and in October, Jeffords turned over some animals taken from Oquitoa, Sonora, which had been tracked to the agency.[66] Cochise understood that the raiding had to stop and, in the words of Jeffords's assistant, Fred Hughes, was "determined it shall be no longer."[67]

By this time, Cochise's health was deteriorating, but he still controlled his own band and was prepared to force the Chihennes and Nednhis to adhere to his wishes. In October 1873 he commented to inspector William Vandever that the whites should order the Chi-

hennes to return to New Mexico. Vandever also reported that fric-
tion existed between Cochise and Natiza, probably because of the
Nednhis' extensive raiding into Mexico.[68] Finally, in November
1873, Cochise decided to make his position clear. Jeffords was
transferring agency headquarters from San Simon (where it had
been since being moved from Sulphur Springs the previous August)
to Pinery Canyon, mainly because San Simon had proved unhealthy: five children had died. Cochise took this opportunity to call
a council of all the warriors and headmen and made it understood
that this was his country and that those who wanted to remain in it
must "refrain from raiding in Sonora [or] leave the reservation."[69]

From this point on, the raiding from the Chiricahua Reservation
diminished significantly. It could not have happened at a better time.
The commissioner of Indian affairs, Smith, had received requests
from the War Department to turn the reservation over to Crook.
After seriously considering this proposal, he refused but admonished Jeffords that he would do so unless the raids stopped. He
wrote Jeffords: "Give Cochise distinctly to understand that unless
the line between his reservation and Mexico can be thus guarded his
reservation will be turned over to the military and he will be obliged
to bring his men to a daily roll call."[70] By the time Jeffords received
this message, he had already decided to resign. He was exhausted
from his arduous duties, disillusioned by the lack of funds, and
weary of the constant criticism.[71]

As 1874 dawned, Cochise clearly understood Smith's threat. He
and Jeffords had "succeeded without trouble . . . in driving off all
the Indians who did not belong to Cochise's band." The agent reas-
sured Smith:

> I am happy to inform the department that it has been now over two
> months since any complaints whatever have been made against these
> Indians either by the citizens of this territory or by the people living
> on the other side of the Mexican line, and I have strong hopes that we
> have heard the end of this raiding in Sonora. . . . The Indians here
> have also appeared more settled and satisfied during the last two
> months than at any other time since peace was made.[72]

About the time Smith received Jeffords's letter, the government
was considering yet another option: moving the Chokonens to New

Taza. Cochise's eldest son, he succeeded his father as chief. (*Courtesy Arizona Historical Society, Tucson*)

Chihuahua. This prominent Chokonen warrior was a group leader at the time of Cochise's death. (*Courtesy Arizona Historical Society, Tucson*)

Mexico. For his part, Cochise believed that he had remained faithful to the terms of the treaty and wondered why the government was so willing to break its word and force him onto a New Mexico reservation which had been closed two years before. Such talk was academic as far as he was concerned, for he knew his end was approaching. It would be Taza's and his headmen's decision.

## Chapter 20

# GOOD FRIENDS WILL MEET AGAIN

A few months after the San Simon council in which Cochise ordered a halt to the raiding into Sonora, Fred Hughes wrote a seemingly innocuous letter to the *Las Cruces Borderer* suggesting that Cochise's people could easily be consolidated with the Chihennes on a reservation in New Mexico. Believing that Vandever had officially advocated this as a solution, Hughes endorsed the idea and declared that it would "settle our Sonora difficulties." Moreover, only "a half dozen warriors" would object, or so he thought.[1]

Vandever had made no such recommendation, although privately he may have proposed it to Hughes or Jeffords. Hughes had not intended that his proposal become government policy. New Mexico's superintendent of Indian affairs, Levi Edwin Dudley, happened to read his letter and promptly forwarded it to Indian Commissioner Smith in Washington. Smith perceived that it might put a stop to the Sonora controversy and on March 19, 1874, ordered Dudley to proceed to the Chiricahua Reservation to ascertain Cochise's feelings about removal.[2] The transfer seemed logical to most Anglos. In the first place, it would consolidate two agencies into one, saving considerable expense. Even more important, it would remove the fighting Chokonens from the Sonoran border, thereby eliminating easy access into Mexico.

Leaving Santa Fe in early May, Dudley interviewed many citizens along the way; all were "universally opposed to removal" because they were apprehensive about disrupting relations. Dudley found that most whites praised Howard for his efforts: if the general returned to the Southwest, "he would find a warm welcome, and receive the thanks of the people." On May 21 he met Jeffords at Pinery Canyon and learned that Cochise, seriously ill, was in the Dragoons and that Juh and some of the Nednhis had left the reservation for Mexico.[3]

Some had gone the previous December, perhaps as a consequence of Cochise's edict. Others, including Juh, who had succeeded Natiza as leader of the Nednhis, had returned to Janos and resumed negotiations with Mexico. Juh claimed that "he never wanted to live in the United States." That spring he sent representatives to make peace at Janos and Galeana, where authorities asked Sonoran officials to suspend military operations for the time being. Although they were skeptical, they granted the request. Soon afterward a woman from Juh's band went to Ures to arrange a truce. The ceasefire had been in effect for only a few weeks before the Nednhis were charged with raiding and once again pushed into Arizona by Sonoran troops in late July. An old leader named Eligio (a relative of Coleto Amarillo) was captured at Janos by Sonoran troops and summarily executed. This terminated negotiations with Mexico.[4]

On May 22, Dudley and Jeffords started for the Dragoons to meet Cochise. Dudley recalled that

> the old Chief was suffering intensely and I at first thought he would not outlive the night. I found a ready welcome as soon as his son [Taza] explained who I was, for I had been expected; and when I gave him a photograph of General Howard and myself taken together my introduction to his favor was complete. The picture was frequently examined by the old chief during my stay and always followed by the warmest expression of feelings of affection for the general.

Dudley had a short conversation about removal, but within an hour Cochise became "much exhausted." Dudley left and returned to Fort Bowie, impressed with both Jeffords and Cochise.[5]

A few days later he returned to the Dragoons for another visit and found Cochise "still alive but failing rapidly." As to removal to New Mexico, Cochise declared he would leave the decision to his son Taza, but he made it clear that he preferred to remain in Ari-

zona. Dudley reported to Washington "that these Indians can be removed at any time. . . . Agent Jeffords said he could give me two
hundred and fifty who would return with me at once." Dudley digressed to express his view concerning Jeffords's unique influence
on the Indians:

> I am convinced that should you decide to remove these Indians
> Agent Jeffords can do so. . . . I have seen no man who has so com-
> plete control over his Indians as Agent Jeffords and I am sure that if
> they removed he would be the best man to make agent at Hot Springs.
> He does not answer all the requirements of an agent; none that I have
> seen do fill the bill in every particular. Jeffords can and does maintain
> discipline and he has the influence to bring Indians to his reservation
> and keep them there, and if they go away he generally knows where
> they have gone.[6]

His conclusion that Cochise's Chokonens might easily be relocated
was disputed by Hughes and Jeffords. Hughes now estimated that
only half would move, while Jeffords reported that any attempt
would result in renewed hostilities. "The government had not
enough troops to move them," claimed the Chokonens. Jeffords's
report convinced Smith to defer the decision on removal.[7]

Cochise's health had been deteriorating for several years. While
at Cañada Alamosa, he ate very little because of a stomach ailment
which was complicated when he made peace and had more time to
indulge in tiswin drunks. Nine months after his treaty, an officer
wrote that "Cochise is growing old and infirm . . . and is constantly
drunk on tiswin."[8] The following April, Lieutenant Colonel Roger
Jones reported that Cochise's death was imminent, "as it is known
he has been very sick for months past."[9] A few weeks later, Fred
Hughes arrived in Tucson and told the *Citizen* the Chiricahua leader
was "very sick" with "little hope of recovery."[10] Finally, on May
30, the *Citizen* reported that Cochise was dying, having been
"troubled by dyspepsia ever since he came on the reserve."[11]

With Cochise's death imminent, attention turned to who would
replace the man who had led the Chokonens for the past eighteen
years. Hughes said there were "three prominent aspirants: Cochise's
son [Taza], the big medicine man [Eskinya][12] and the war captain
[Nahilzay]. Another informed source labeled Cochise's captains

NA-CHISE, -- Son of Cochise,

Naiche. Cochise's youngest known son, he was the last hereditary chief of the fighting Chokonen. *(Courtesy Arizona Historical Society, Tucson)* "unmitigated scamps" (presumably alluding to Pionsenay, Eskinya, and El Cautivo) who "could not live without making mischief and trouble." [13] Hoping to ensure a smooth transition and a continuation of his policies, Cochise named Taza his successor. According to Asa Daklugie, Cochise had groomed Taza to succeed him, and his leading men, including Eskinya and the loyal Nahilzay, agreed to support Taza. Cochise's last instructions to his people were "to forever live at peace" with the whites and to "always do as [Jeffords] tells them." [14]

One of Taza's first acts was to find the Indian who had bewitched his father. If the spell was removed, the Indian would live; if Cochise died, the culprit would be burned at the stake. The alleged witch was found, but nothing could restore Cochise's health. Jeffords convinced Taza to spare the Indian's life. [15]

On the evening of June 7, 1874, Jeffords and Cochise had their final meeting. Cochise, who had been in and out of comas during the past few weeks, knew that death was near. As Jeffords was about to depart, Cochise asked him, "Do you think you will ever see me alive again?" Jeffords replied, "No, I do not think I will. I think that by tomorrow night you will be dead." Cochise agreed, saying, "Yes, I think so, too—about ten o'clock tomorrow morning. Do you think we will ever meet again?" Jeffords, surprised by the question, replied, "I don't know. What is your opinion about it?" Cochise responded that "I have been thinking a good deal about it while I have been sick here, and I believe we will; good friends will meet again—up there [pointing to the sky]." [16]

The next morning in the east stronghold, Cochise died, probably of dyspepsia or some form of stomach cancer. News of his death spread rapidly. There was tremendous sorrow throughout the rancherías. Fred Hughes recalled that "the howl that went up from these people was fearful to listen to [and] was kept up through the night until daylight next morning." [17]

According to custom, a close relative (probably either his wife Dos-teh-seh or his trusted sister) prepared Cochise for burial. This consisted of bathing his body, combing his hair, and dressing him in his best clothes—all done to prepare the deceased for afterlife. The burial probably took place later that day. Usually only close relatives were present: undoubtedly his sons, his three wives, a shaman,

Fort Bowie, 1874. The important post looked like this at the time of Cochise's death. (*Courtesy Arizona Historical Society, Tucson*)

and other members of his extended family group.[18] In this case, however, much of the Chokonen band was there, at least according to Jeffords, who wrote Indian Commissioner Smith:

> It is a custom among these Indians when one of their number dies to burn some clothing, blankets etc. at the grave of the deceased. . . . Upon the death of Cochise, I found that his whole band had stripped themselves of almost their entire clothing and burnt it at his grave for the purpose above described.[19]

A few days later, Jeffords gave an account of the burial to Al Williamson, who repeated it to historian Frank C. Lockwood:

> He was dressed in his best war garments, decorated with war paint and head feathers, and wrapped in a splendid heavy, red, woolen blanket that Colonel H. C. Hooker had given him. He was then placed on his favorite horse . . . [which] was guided to a rough and lonely place among the rocks and chasms in the stronghold, where there was a deep fissure in the cliff. The horse was killed and dropped

into the depths; also, Cochise's favorite dog. His gun and other arms were then thrown in; and, last, Cochise was lowered with lariats into the rocky sepulcher—deep in the gorge.[20]

The location of Cochise's grave was never revealed by his people or by Jeffords, the only white man who knew. It was a secret the frontiersman carried to his grave.

So ended the life of one of the greatest Apache leaders of the nineteenth century, one who had successfully eluded troops of four states and two countries, a man who harbored intense hatred toward the Mexicans who had killed his father and the Americans who had hanged his brother and murdered his father-in-law. He had fought back with all his strength, but in the end he realized his people would have to live in peace or be exterminated. It was ironic that this courageous Apache leader, who could always be found leading his men into battle, died a natural death on a reservation.

Cochise's death created a tremendous void in Apache leadership. No other leader, except perhaps Victorio, had faced the overwhelming onslaught of whites and Mexicans and had resisted until it was no longer safe to be a free Apache. No other leader had succeeded in obtaining a reservation in his country, one which was run by the Indians in conjunction with their agent without military interference. Perhaps no other Apache chief exhibited more wisdom, courage, fighting ability, and control of his followers than had Cochise.

The days, weeks, months, and years following his death were turbulent for his people. Had he lived, some of the problems might well have been avoided. Suffice it to say that the Chiricahua Reservation was broken up almost two years to the day after Cochise's death. Most of his local group followed Taza and Naiche to the hated San Carlos Reservation. Some did not. Allied with their Nednhi and Chihenne brethren, the remainder of the fighting Chiricahuas gave the Southwest a decade of intermittent war which culminated in the surrender of Naiche and Geronimo in September 1886 and the removal of almost every Chiricahua Apache to Florida. It was twenty-eight years before Cochise's people returned to the Southwest. Ironically, those who chose to return settled on the Mescalero Reservation in New Mexico, the very one Cochise rejected in 1870.

# NOTES

*Introduction*

1. United States Army Military History Institute, Joseph Sladen Papers, Sladen to Alice Rollins Crane, October 26, 1896.

2. James Henry Tevis, *Arizona in the 50s,* 149.

3. *Boston Evening Transcript,* November 6, 1872.

4. Smithsonian Institution, J. B. White Manuscript No. 178.

5. Smithsonian Institution, N. S. Higgins Manuscript No. 180.

6. Anderson Nelson Ellis, "Recollections of an Interview with Cochise, Chief of the Apaches," *Kansas State Historical Society Collections,* 13 (1913–14), 391.

7. Frank C. Lockwood, *The Apache Indians,* 125.

8. Higgins Manuscript.

9. Oliver Otis Howard, *My Life and Experiences Among Our Hostile Indians,* 205.

10. National Archives and Records Center, Records of the Bureau of Indian Affairs, Record Group 75 (RG75), Microcopy T21 (T21), Roll 12 (R12), Hennisee to Clinton, October 31, 1870, Appendix A.

11. *Arizona Miner,* April 20, 1872.

12. Thomas Edwin Farish, *History of Arizona,* 229.

13. RG 75, T21, R12, Hennisee to Clinton, October 31, 1870, Appendix B.

14. Arizona Historical Society (cited hereafter as AHS), Fred Hughes Collection.

15. Sladen Papers, manuscript titled, "Making Peace with Cochise, Chief of the Chiricahua Apaches," 51. Copy in AHS.

16. John C. Cremony, "Some Savages," *Overland Monthly,* 8 (March 1872), 203–4.

17. Fred Hughes Collection.

18. Sladen, "Making Peace," 28, 52; Sladen Papers, Sladen to Crane, October 26, 1896.

19. Sladen, "Making Peace," 39–40.

20. Interview with Amelia Naiche, January 17, 1979.

21. Eve Ball with Norah Henn and Lynda Sanchez, *Indeh: An Apache Odyssey* (cited hereafter as Ball, *Indeh*), 23–24.

22. Sladen, "Making Peace," 44; John G. Bourke, *On the Border With Crook,* 235–36.

23. Fred Hughes Collection.

24. Morris E. Opler, *An Apache Lifeway,* 466–69.

25. Sladen, "Making Peace," 44.

26. Edward L. Keyes, "Some Recollections of Arizona and Cochise," *The United Service,* July 1890.

27. The Chiricahua Apaches consisted of four autonomous bands: Chokonens (Cochise's band), Chihennes, Nednhis, and Bedonkohes.

28. Henry Stuart Turrill, "A Vanished Race of Aboriginal Founders," *Publication Number 18 of the New York Society of the Order of the Founders and Patriots of America,* February 14, 1907, 22.

29. RG 75, T21, R17, Coleman to Acting Assistant Adjutant General (AAAG), District of New Mexico, October 18, 1872.

30. Turrill, "A Vanished Race," 21.

31. Fred Hughes Collection; *Arizona Citizen,* November 30, 1872.

32. Cremony, "Some Savages," 205.

33. White Manuscript No. 178.

34. Ball, *Indeh,* 23.

35. Lockwood, *The Apache Indians,* 106.

36. Tevis, *Arizona in the 50s,* 149; Cremony, "Some Savages," 203.

37. Levi E. Dudley, "Cochise, the Apache Chief, and Peace," *The Friend,* August 7, 1891.

38. Sladen, "Making Peace," 42.

39. Jeffords report dated July 20, 1874, Bancroft Library.

*Chapter 1*

1. Ralph Hedrick Ogle, *Federal Control of the Western Apaches 1848–1886,* 5; Frederick Webb Hodge, *Handbook of American Indians North of Mexico,* I, 63.

2. Ibid.; Jack Douglas Forbes, *Apache, Navaho and Spaniard,* xi–xxiii.

3. Grenville Goodwin, *The Social Organization of the Western Apache,* 1; Juan Nentvig, S.J., *Rudo Ensayo: A Description of Sonora and Arizona in 1764,* 21.

4. Opler, *Lifeway,* 1–2.

5. Ibid., 2.

6. Ibid.

7. Stephen M. Barrett, *Geronimo's Story of His Life,* 12–14; Ball, *Indeh,* 22; Angie Debo, *Geronimo: The Man, His Time, His Place,* 71.

8. Opler, *Lifeway,* 462–64.

9. Ibid. Harry W. Basehart, "Chiricahua Apache Subsistence and Socio-Political Organization," unpublished manuscript, University of New Mexico, 8–9.

10. Opler, *Lifeway,* 181.

11. Frank C. Lockwood, *Arizona Characters,* 62; Frank C. Lockwood, "Cochise, the Noble Warrior," *Arizona Highways,* February 1939, 6–7.

12. Samuel Woodworth Cozzens, *The Marvellous Country, or Three Years in Arizona and New Mexico,* 86.

13. Bernard John Dowling Irwin, "The Fight at Apache Pass," *Infantry Journal,* 32 (April 1928), 2.

14. *Arizona Miner,* March 20, 1869.
15. Ellis, "Recollections," 391.
16. *Arizona Citizen,* December 7, 1872.
17. Ball, *Indeh,* 23.
18. Gillet M. Griswold, "The Ft. Sill Apaches: Their Vital Statistics, Tribal Origins, Antecedents," unpublished manuscript, Field Artillery Museum, Fort Sill, Oklahoma, 24.
19. AHS, Robert Humphrey Forbes Collection.
20. John A. Rockfellow, *Log of an Arizona Trail Blazer,* 80.
21. Turrill, "A Vanished Race," 20.
22. Ball, *Indeh,* 22.
23. Tevis was born in Virginia in 1835, came to Arizona in 1857 or 1858, and soon afterward took employment with the Butterfield Overland Mail Company at the Apache Pass stage station. He became well acquainted with Cochise, and his memoirs, *Arizona in the 50s,* plus his letters to the *Weekly Arizonian,* provide information about Cochise during this period. Tevis left Apache Pass in late 1859 and eventually surfaced at Pinos Altos, New Mexico, in late 1860. He died in Tucson in 1905. Tevis, *Arizona in the 50s;* Dan L. Thrapp, *Encyclopedia of Frontier Biography,* 1411–12.
24. Tevis, *Arizona in the 50s,* 114–15.
25. *Arizona Citizen,* May 22, 1875.
26. James Kirker was born in Northern Ireland in 1793 and emigrated to the United States in 1810. He journeyed west in 1817, settling in St. Louis before finally moving to Santa Fe in 1824. In the late 1820s he moved to Santa Rita del Cobre in present-day southwestern New Mexico, where he became associated with the Chiricahuas. In the late 1830s, the governor of Chihuahua hired him to kill Apaches instead of beaver. His contract was canceled in 1840 but renewed in late 1845, and the following July his group slaughtered 148 Chiricahuas at Galeana. For a biography of Kirker, see William Cochran McGaw, *Savage Scene: The Life and Times of James Kirker, Frontier King.* David J. Weber, *The Taos Trappers: The Fur Trade in the Far Southwest, 1540–1846,* 221–25.
27. Relles (Reyes), a moderate Chokonen leader of the 1830s and 1840s, was well known in the Fronteras region. He participated in the August 1836 truce with Sonora and joined Pisago Cabezón in the peace treaty of 1842 at Janos. Hostilities resumed in 1844 and he joined raids into Sonora. He was the prime mover in the May 1846 truce at Galeana before falling victim to Kirker's scalp hunters in June 1846.
28. Pisago Cabezón, 1770(?)–1846(?), probably a Chokonen, succeeded his father when the latter died at the hands of Sonoran troops in the Enmedio Mountains about 1793. Pisago came into Janos about 1795 and remained during the presidio period, although at times he became disillusioned and bolted to the mountains. He had several wives and by the 1820s was the patriarch of an unusually large extended family group and perhaps had as many as thirteen children. Many of the noted Chokonen leaders of the 1840s and 1850s were members of his local group and probably were related to him. These included Tapilá, Carro, and Casimiro. Pisago passed from the scene in 1845 or 1846, possibly a victim of Kirker's massacre. University of Texas at El Paso, Janos Collection Roll 10 (cited hereafter as JA with roll number), de Gavo to Casanova, May 5, 1792.
29. James Hobbs, *Wild Life in the Far West,* 88.

30. Frederick Webb Hodge stated that Cochise succeeded his father, Nachi, as chief. The source for this statement is not known; it would appear, however, that someone confused the facts. George Wratten, interpreter and confidant of the Chiricahuas, read Hodges' statement and wrote the Bureau of American Ethnology, saying that Hodge should have said Nachi, son of Cochise, succeeded his brother Taza as chief of the Chiricahua Apaches. During the 1840s there was a minor leader named Naqui or Naque who lived near Janos and was a member of Pisago Cabezón's band. I think it unlikely that he was directly related to Cochise, given his relatively unimportant place in Chiricahua history. Hodge, *Handbook,* 317; Smithsonian Institution, George Wratten to Bureau of American Ethnology, May 4, 1907, copy in author's files.

31. Opler, *Lifeway,* 464–70, contains a good account of the role of a leader in Chiricahua society.

32. For an excellent summary of Apache-Spanish relations during the latter eighteenth century, see Max L. Moorhead, *The Apache Frontier: Jacobo Ugarte and Spanish-Indian Relations in Northern New Spain, 1769–1791.*

33. Kieran McCarty, *Desert Documentary: The Spanish years, 1767–1821,* 44–46.

34. Moorhead, *The Apache Frontier,* 123–29; Max L. Moorhead, *The Presidio: Bastion of the Spanish Borderlands,* 95–114.

35. Janos was founded as a presidio about 1691 to protect Mexico's northern frontier. It played a significant role in Chiricahua-Mexican relations for most of the eighteenth and nineteenth centuries. Moorhead, *The Presidio,* 21.

36. Moorhead, *The Presidio,* 101, *The Apache Frontier,* 126–28.

37. William B. Griffen, "Apache Indians and the Northern Mexican Peace Establishments," in *Southwestern Culture History: Collected Papers in Honor of Albert H. Schroeder,* 189.

38. Lockwood, *The Apache Indians,* 28–29.

39. Morris E. Opler to author, March 1, 1982. Opler points out that most Chiricahua names "tend to follow some physical or behavioral peculiarity of the individual bearing it or it refers to some well known event in which he was involved." Many Americans commented on Cochise's nose. For example, Al Williamson, who met him in 1873–74, described Cochise as "tall and straight . . . he had a Roman nose." Lockwood, *The Apache Indians,* 125. For an excellent discussion of the derivation of Apache names, see Goodwin, *Social Organization,* 522–35.

40. The source for the rest of this chapter, unless otherwise noted, is Opler, *Lifeway,* 13–18, 25–37, 67–75, 135–44.

41. Morris E. Opler and Harry Hoijer, "The Raid and War-Path Language of the Chiricahua Apache," *American Anthropologist.* 42 (October–December 1940), 617–34. This article contains a list of seventy-eight such words.

*Chapter 2*

1. Joseph F. Park, "The Apaches in Mexican-American Relations, 1848–1861," *Arizona and the West,* 3 (Summer 1961), 133–35; Joseph F. Park, "Spanish Indian Policy in Northern Mexico, 1765–1810," *Arizona and the West,* 4 (Winter 1962), 343–44.

2. Fronteras, about one hundred miles west of Janos and thirty miles south of present-day Douglas, Arizona, was established as a Spanish presidio about 1692 and remained an important frontier outpost for the next two hundred years. It was

an attractive target for Chiricahua raiders, Cochise in particular, from the 1830s through the 1870s. Moorhead, *The Presidio*, 22.

3. Santa Rita del Cobre is in southwestern New Mexico six miles northeast of Bayard. Situated in the heart of Chihenne country, the mines were discovered about 1800 by Apaches, who told Lieutenant Colonel José Manuel Carrasco, an officer at Janos, about them. Lacking funds, Carrasco sold out to Francisco Manuel Elguea, a Chihuahuan banker, who obtained a grant from Spain to establish a settlement and work the mines. By early 1804 they were evidently producing copper because troops were relocated from Casas Grandes to provide protection. The settlement came to depend on Janos for supplies and assistance. The mines were abandoned about June 1838 because of Apache hostilities and unprofitable operations. JA, R15, Salcedor to commander of Janos, February 3, 1804; *Mesilla Times*, October 18, 1860; Dan L. Thrapp, *Victorio and the Mimbres Apaches*, 18. John Russell Bartlett, *Personal Narrative of Explorations and Incidents in Texas, New Mexico, California, Sonora and Chihuahua* I, 227–28; T. M. Pearce, *New Mexico Place Names: A Geographical Dictionary*, 149.

4. Stuart F. Voss, *On the Periphery of Nineteenth Century Mexico: Sonora and Sinaloa, 1810–1877*, 48–49.

5. JA, R13, Barela to Vizcarro, December 23, 1821. William B. Griffen, *Apaches at War and Peace: The Janos Presidio, 1750–1858*, 124–25.

6. Juan Diego Compá (1772–1837), probably a Nednhi, was a brother of the more well-known Juan José Compá. He succeeded his father as chief after his father died of natural causes in 1794. He was generally at peace for the next forty years, although he was overshadowed by his better-known brother. He and his brother were killed in the Johnson massacre of April 1837. For an excellent discussion of the Compá family, see William B. Griffen, "The Compás: A Chiricahua Apache Family," *American Indian Quarterly*, 7 (Spring 1983), 21–49.

7. Fuerte (Spanish for "manly" or "strong") was one of the important Chihenne leaders from 1810 through 1840. The copper mines–Mimbres River area was his home base. One can speculate that he was in some manner related to Mangas Coloradas. It is also possible that since he passed from the scene about 1840 and Mangas Coloradas appeared suddenly about 1842, they were the same individual. William B. Griffen, who has done extensive work in this area, concurs with my conclusion. Griffen to author, December 26, 1986.

8. Mano Mocha was born about 1780 and one of his hands was maimed in a fight with a bear, hence his Spanish name. His Apache name was Tuin, and it is not clear whether he could have been a Bedonkohe leader, since his band territory was mentioned frequently as the Mogollon Mountains, or a leading man of the Chihennes. He dominated a local group for some thirty years and in his early years was reported to have been an important war leader. In the mid-1820s, James Ohio Pattie met him at the copper mines and was treated in a friendly manner. His actions in the 1830s and 1840s paralleled the more moderate faction of the Chiricahuas. He frequently participated in the peace discussions, but when he was dissatisfied he would lead his band to the mountains and war. He passed from the scene in the mid-1840s. James O. Pattie, *The Personal Narrative of James O. Pattie of Kentucky*, 120.

9. JA, R13, document entitled, "List of Apaches at Peace, December 1, 1821."

10. Matías, born about 1790, was a Chokonen leader with generally pacific views. Like Relles, he made his headquarters near Fronteras from the 1820s until

his death in the mid-1840s. On several occasions he became actively involved in peace negotiations, even traveling to Guaymas, Ures, and Chihuahua City to secure peace. After his death in the mid-1840s, his sons Pablo and Elías became group leaders but not on the band level because Cochise had arrived on the scene.

11. Teboca, a contemporary of Matías, was born about 1790 and led a local group of hostile Chokonens through the 1830s and 1840s. He had several sons who were associates of Cochise, among them Tullotte, Naquebre, Guero, Vicente, and Chiquito. Teboca passed from the scene about 1851, possibly killed in the Pozo Hediondo fight.

12. AHS, Film MC-6, Archivo General de Mexico, Roll 150, File 31, Eredia to Urrea, November 15, 1824; Villascueva to Urrea, July 24, 1824.

13. Ibid., File 32, Urrea to Secretary of War and Navy, November 16, 1824.

14. Ibid., Eredia to Urrea November 12, 1824.

15. JA, R16, Military Commander at Santa Rita del Cobre to the Military Commander 1st Sección, December 30, 1824.

16. JA, R21, Simón Elías to Commander at Janos, August 6, 1828; Commander at Janos to Military Commander of Chihuahua, December 28, 1828; various ration lists for 1828; AHS, Sonoran State Archives (cited hereafter as SA with roll number), Roll 12, Bustamente to Urrea, March 29, 1825; Muro to Elías González, April 25, 1831.

17. JA, R23, Melgar to Military Commander of Janos, February 6, 1830. Griffen, *Apaches at War and Peace,* 131–32.

18. Hermosillo, Sonora, Archivo Historico de Sonora, (cited hereafter as AHSH), Prefect of Arispe to Governor, January 13, 1830; Arvizu to Governor, February 17, 1830; Alcalde of San Ignacio to Governor, March 1, 1830.

19. JA, R24, Melgar to Military Commander at Janos, July 5, 1830.

20. JA, R23, Franco to Military Commander at Janos, December 21, 1830.

21. Turrill, "A Vanished Race," 19–20. JA, R4, various ration lists.

22. SA, R12, Simón Elías to Governor, June 28, 1831; AHSH, Commanding General to Governor, June 23, 1831; Governor to Commanding General, July 5, 1831.

23. Francisco R. Almada, *Diccionario de historia, geografía y biografía chihuahuenses,* 38.

24. SA, R12, Morales to Governor, February 23, 1832; Governor to Morales, February 26, 1832.

25. Juan José Compá (1786?–1837), a Nednhi leader, was the brother of Juan Diego Compá and the son of El Compá. In 1794 he attended the presidio school at Janos, which explains his literacy in Spanish. As Juan Diego Compá aged, Juan José assumed leadership of a local group but was never a dominant Chiricahua, as were Pisago Cabezón and Mangas Coloradas. A leading advocate in the peace treaties of 1832 and 1835, Juan José was killed in the Johnson massacre in April 1837. Griffen, "The Compás," 37–40.

26. SA, R12, Morales to Governor, March 27, May 9, 1832.

27. Ibid., Governor of Chihuahua to Governor of Sonora, document entitled, "Triumph over the Apaches," June 7, 1832.

28. Ibid.

29. Ibid., Arvizu to Madeno, June 27, 1832.

30. JA, R5, Conde to Justiniani, August 30, 1832.

31. Aquién was probably a Chokonen, but no other reference to him has been

found. William B. Griffen suggests that he perhaps could have been Matías, given the particular area assigned to him. Griffen to author, December 26, 1986.

32. Almada, *chihuahuenses*, 38. Unfortunately, no list of the twenty-nine leaders who agreed to the treaty has been located, although it probably exists somewhere in the archives of Mexico City.

33. Robert McKnight came to New Mexico in 1812. Soon after, suspected of being an American agent, he was arrested and imprisoned for nine years in Chihuahua and Durango. In 1826 or 1827 he and Stephen Courcier took over the operations of Santa Rita del Cobre, from which he was said to have made a fortune. He was involved in several Apache-Mexican treaties in the 1830s. Charges were brought against him in 1837 for illegal trade with the Indians. He resigned in early 1838, eventually resurfacing at Corralitos in the early 1840s. Bartlett, *Personal Narrative*, I, 228-29; Ross Calvin, ed., *Lieutenant Emory Reports: Notes of a Military Reconnaissance*, 98; Dwight L. Clarke, ed., *The Original Journals of Henry Smith Turner with Stephen Watts Kearny to New Mexico and California, 1846-1847*, 85-86; JA, R28, Zuloaga to Military Commander at Janos, March 7, 1838.

34. SA, R13, Elías González to Governor, July 6, 1834; JA, R6, Calvo to Ponce de León, December 15, 1835; *El Fanal de Chihuahua* (Alcance), November 4, 1834; Weber, *Taos Trappers*, 221-22.

35. Joseph F. Park, "The Assassination of Juan José Compá," unpublished manuscript in author's files, 15.

36. In a letter to Mexican officials, Juan José Compá furnished the Apache version: "The Apaches in Agua Nueva have risen in revolt, saying that one of them was killed and justice has not been done them. These Indians say they have killed several Christians and have stolen horses. Immediately thereafter they sent messengers to the Apaches in all places telling them they wanted to kill all Christians at Agua Nueva. Likewise the Apaches at Janos say they have been told the same by their neighbors at Janos. Moreover the chief Costilla has left Bavispe. He says the commander of the garrison told him they wanted to kill or sieze them." SA, R12, Arregui to Vice-Governor of Sonora, May 15, 1833.

37. Robert C. Stevens, "The Apache Menace in Sonora, 1831-1849" *Arizona and the West*, 6 (Autumn 1964), 215; Ralph A. Smith, "Indians in American-Mexican Relations Before the War of 1846," *Hispanic American Historical Review*, 43 (February 1963), 43.

38. Stevens, "The Apache Menace," 215-16.

39. SA, R13, Bustamente to Governor, January 8, 1834; Bustamente to Governor, January 14, 1834; Narbona to Governor, January 13, 1834.

40. Ibid., Bustamente to Escalente y Arvizu, April 26, 1834; Juan González to Escalante y Arvizu, April 5, 1834. Juan Elías to Governor, April 3, 1834.

41. Ibid., Ramírez to Commander at Tubac, July 3, 1834; Elías González to Governor, July 6, 1834; Elías to Governor, July 4, 1834.

42. Ibid., Villasquez to Governor, July 14, 1834.

43. Park, "The Assassination of Juan José Compá," 15.

44. SA, R13, Escalante y Arvizu to Bustamente, October 21, 1834.

45. Vivora, born in the late 1790s, had a long and fascinating life. His father was an important leader in the 1790s until his death in 1803 or 1804. Vivora's actions usually paralleled those of his close associate and band leader Pisago Cabezón. Like Pisago, he agreed to peace in 1836 at Fronteras and in 1842 at

Janos. He reportedly was present at the Juan José Compá massacre in 1837 but escaped unharmed. He also eluded the Kirker scalp hunters in 1846 but could not evade the white man's lethal disease of smallpox, to which he succumbed at Fronteras in early 1862.

46. SA, R14, Escalante y Arvizu to Bustamente, November 2, 1834; Mora to Bustamente, November 21, 1834; Governor of Chihuahua to Bustamente, November 18, 1834; Hubert Howe Bancroft, *History of the North Mexican States and Texas,* II, 654.

47. In the fall of 1834 several Chiricahua leaders had sent a messenger to Paso del Norte soliciting peace. The list sounds like a who's who of the 1830–40 chiefs; among them were Cuchillo Negro, Itán, Fuerte, Pisago Cabezón, Tapilá, Teboca, and Juan José Compá. *El Fanal de Chihuahua,* November 4, November 25, 1834.

48. JA, R28, Calvo to Justiniani, January 20, 1835; document entitled, "Conditions of the Preliminary Peace with Juan José Compá"; Justiniani to Calvo, February 12, 1835.

49. SA, R13, Rey to Escalante y Arvizu, May 9, 1835; Justiniani to Commanding General, Chihuahua, April 3, 1835.

50. Ibid.

51. Elías González was probably the most important military leader in Sonora during the 1830s and 1840s. He was born into a prominent family at Arispe in 1793, joined the military in 1809, and rose to captain in 1822. In 1827 he was named adjutant inspector for Sonora and Sinaloa. Seven years later he became commanding general of Sonora, succeeding Colonel Francisco Javier Arregui, whose presidio troops were in a mutinous state. In 1836 he negotiated a peace treaty with Chiricahuas at Arispe. In 1844 he led Sonoran troops against Chiricahuas living near Janos, who he thought were raiding into Sonora. In 1851 he retired in controversy. He was a capable leader who understood Apaches. Francisco R. Almada, *Diccionario de historia, geografía y biografía sonorenses,* 239–40; Voss, *On the Periphery,* 69, 85.

52. Stevens, "The Apache Menace," 217.

53. SA, R13, Elías González to Escalante y Arvizu, June 27, 1835; JA, R24, Justiniani to Military Commander at Janos, June 19, 1835.

54. SA, R13, Elías González to Villascuna, June 1, 1835; Elías González to Governor of Sonora, June 17, 1835.

55. Voss, *On the Periphery,* 69–70.

56. *El Noticioso de Chihuahua,* December 4, 1835.

57. JA, R6, Calvo to Ponce de León, December 15, 1835.

58. Ibid., Calvo to Military Commander at Janos, January 15, 1836; AHSH, Folder 74, Elías González to Governor of Sonora, December 19, 1835; Elías González to Governor of Sonora, January 19, 1836.

59. AHSH, Folder 75, Escalante to Governor of Sonora, April 2, 1836.

60. SA, R14 Elías González to Governor, February 10, 1836; *El Noticioso de Chihuahua,* April 22, 1836.

61. Stevens, "The Apache Menace," 220

62. Miguel Narbona, born in the early 1800s, was a Chokonen captured by Sonoran troops about 1812–14. He remained with the Narbona family for some ten years before he returned to the Chiricahuas. His role in the peace of 1836 was a minor one: he probably acted as interpreter in the discussions. In the 1840s and

1850s he became an inveterate raider. Cochise apparently became his second in command in the late 1840s and early 1850s. Miguel Narbona died about 1856.

63. *El Noticioso de Chihuahua*, November 25, 1836; AHSH, Folder 74, Elías González to Commanding General, October 1, 1836. Griffen, *Apaches at War and Peace*, 172.

64. Griffen, *Apaches at War and Peace*, 172.

65. Ibid.

66. JA, R27, Calvo to Ponce de León, October 11, 1836; JA, R27, Arze to Ponce de León, January 26, 1837.

67. Cañon de los Embudos (Canyon of the Funnels) was about fifteen miles south of the present Arizona-Sonora line below the San Bernardino ranch. It was the site of a historic conference involving Brigadier General George Crook and Geronimo in March 1886.

68. SA, R14, Elías González to Governor, February 12, 1837; AHSH, Folder 102, Escalante to Governor, February 26, 1837.

69. SA, R14; Elías González to Governor, February 26, 1837.

70. Ibid.

71. Jason Betzinez with William Sturtevant Nye, *I Fought with Geronimo*, 1.

72. *El Noticioso de Chihuahua*, May 26, 1837.

73. SA, R14, Escalante y Arvizu Proclamation, March 5, 1837; AHSH, Folder 102, García to Governor, March 3, 1837; Escalante to Governor, February 22, 1837.

74. John Johnson, a native of Kentucky and later a resident of Missouri, was a hatter by trade. He probably arrived at Oposura, Sonora, in 1827 and with a partner, José Antonio Aguirre, acquired title to a hacienda. From here, he made trips to Santa Fe and established trading contacts with other Anglos, among them Robert McKnight and James Kirker, and with several Apache leaders, including Juan José Compá. He died in 1852. Rex W. Strickland "The Birth and Death of a Legend: The Johnson Massacre of 1837," *Arizona and the West*, 18 (Autumn 1976), 257–86.

75. Antonio Pascual Narbona was an experienced Indian fighter who commanded Sonora's northern presidios during the early 1840s. It was his father who reportedly captured Miguel Narbona. He was well acquainted with the Chokonens, personally leading several campaigns into the Chiricahua Mountains, which eventually made him a marked man. The Chokonens finally killed him on the porch of his home at Cuquiarachi on December 23, 1847. *El Sonorense*, March 17, 1848.

76. Juan José's band probably captured Lautora García (evidently massacring her family) in early 1837. Her testimony at Moctezuma shows clearly that Johnson misrepresented some of the facts when he made his report at Janos. She later married into the Ramírez family and died at Oputo in 1879. Henry S. Brooks, "A Scrap of Frontier History," *California*, 2 (October 1880).

The Johnson account was pieced together from four primary sources. His official report, written at Janos two days after the massacre, was published May 5, 1837, in *El Noticioso de Chihuahua*. Johnson returned to Oposura on April 30 and again reported to local authorities, who interviewed Lautora García and obtained her important story. The report was sent to the governor, who commended Johnson's actions. AHSH, 102, Johnson's and Lautora García's testimony taken at Moctezuma, May 5, 1837. Henry Brooks's account, cited above, contains relevant material about Lautora García. Benjamin D. Wilson's account, in the Bancroft Library, is somewhat garbled and confused but does contain some important peripheral information.

77. AHSH, Folder 102, Johnson's account; Lautora García's account; *El Noticioso de Chihuahua,* May 5, 1837.

78. *El Noticioso de Chihuahua,* May 5, 1837.

79. Ibid.

80. Ibid.; SA, R14, Elías González to Governor of Sonora, May 10, 1837.

81. Strickland, "The Birth and Death of a Legend," 258.

82. *Condition of the Indian Tribes: Report of the Joint Special Commission,* 328.

83. Ball, *Indeh,* 22; Eve Ball, *In the Days of Victorio: Recollections of a Warm Springs Apache,* 46; Betzinez, *I Fought with Geronimo,* 1.

84. SA, R14, Governor to Ignacio Elías González, July 20, 1837.

85. Opler, *Lifeway,* 335.

*Chapter 3*

1. Park, "The Assassination of Juan José Compá," 27.

2. University of Texas at El Paso, Juárez Collection, Roll 8, Prefect of Galeana to Prefect del Paso, October 9, 1837; Varela to Prefect del Paso, October 26, 1837; *El Noticioso de Chihuahua,* December 11, 1837; July 19, 1838.

3. SA, R14, Elías to Escalante Y Arvizu, October 11, 1837.

4. José Ignacio Terán y Tato, born at Bacoachi in the early 1800s, was undoubtedly one of the wealthiest men in northern Sonora. During the late 1840s and early 1850s he personally financed and directed several campaigns against the Chiricahuas. He died in France in 1868. Almada, *sonorenses,* 784.

5. *El Restaurador,* January 30, 1838.

6. Ibid., February 6, March 10, 1838.

7. Tapilá, born in the late 1790s, probably was related to Pisago Cabezón, since he appears on the Janos ration lists from 1816 through 1819. In the early 1820s he probably married a woman of the Cide (Side) group, for he was included in Cide's camp at various times between 1822 and 1828. Likewise, in 1835 he was mentioned in a census taken at the Copper Mines, again as part of Cide's ranchería. He was mentioned on several occasions in the 1840s to the early 1850s, most of them involving hostile actions. He reportedly played a prominent role in the Pozo Hediondo fight of January 20, 1851. In November 1851 he was killed at Bavispe, where he had gone to discuss a truce and prisoner exchange.

8. *El Noticioso de Chihuahua,* April 12, 1838.

9. Ibid.; George W. Kendall, *Across the Great Southwestern Prairies,* I, 429.

10. *El Noticioso de Chihuahua,* June 21, 1838; JA, R27, Record of Events, July 1837. Griffen, *Apaches at War and Peace,* 176.

11. John C. Cremony, *Life Among the Apaches,* 32. Other writers, including Paul I. Wellman, have used Cremony's account. Wellman says "the three to four hundred souls who left Santa Rita were almost wiped out. Scarcely half a dozen ever reached Janos . . . the bleaching skeletons of all the rest sprawled on the road between." Paul I. Wellman, *The Indian Wars of the West,* 260. J. P. Dunn, *Massacre of the Mountains,* 315–16, cited Cremony's account, as did Stephen Longstreet, *War Cries on Horseback: The Story of the Indian Wars of the Great Plains,* 29–31. Mrs. Eve Ball offers an account from the Apache perspective: "Many set out for the border, but not one reached it. Not one." Again, evidence for this is

lacking, which leads one to speculate that some of her informants read Cremony's book. Ball, *In the Days of Victorio*, 46. There is gross exaggeration in almost every incident described by Cremony relating to Apache-Mexican or Apache-Anglo affairs. On the other hand, Bartlett, who traveled with Cremony and probably heard the same stories told at the same time, faithfully recorded each incident.

12. Frederick A. Wislizenus, *A Tour to Northern Mexico Connected with Col. Doniphan's Expedition in 1846 and 1847*, 57–58.

13. Bartlett, *Personal Narrative*, I, 228–29.

14. Bancroft, *History of the North Mexican States*, II, 656–59.

15. *El Restaurador*, August 28, 1838.

16. AHSH, Folder 96, Elías to Governor, June 19, 1839; Prefect of Bavispe to Governor, August 19, 1839.

17. Ibid., Folder 104, Gándara to Governor, December 3, 1839.

18. Ibid., Folder 110, Governor to Moreno, August 20, 1840.

19. McGaw, *Savage Scene*, 120–21; Hobbs, *Wild Life*, 81. It is ludicrous to suggest that Kirker entered this arrangement to protect the mining interests of his friends at Santa Rita del Cobre, Robert McKnight and Stephen Courcier, although legend says this was justification for his notorious deeds. At the time he was recruited, the mines had been deserted for ten months; moreover, evidence suggests that Kirker had collaborated with the Indians at exactly the time the mines were abandoned. In fact, Chihuahuan authorities accused him of directing the Apaches who attacked the wagon train at the end of March 1838. Perhaps he had advised the attack, but the Apaches told Gabriel Zapata that Kirker had recently traded them new firearms and at that time he was with Tapilá on a raid into Sonora. Not coincidentally, in mid-May, Kirker passed Socorro, New Mexico, en route to U.S. territory with a "large quantity of horses and mules together with his fellow countrymen." He had just left the Chiricahuas, whom, as Kirker later conveniently recalled, had taken him prisoner while trapping and forced him to accompany them. In any event, in July 1838, Chihuahua's governor wanted him arrested for "criminal and pernicious conduct."

20. Juárez Collection, Roll 9, de La Vega to Prefect District del Paso, April 2, 1839.

21. Park, "The Assassination of Juan José Compá," 24.

22. *El Antenor*, January 21, 1840.

23. McGaw, *Savage Scene*, 130–31.

24. AHSH, Folder 108, Morales to Secretary of the Department, September 21, 1840. *La Luna*, October 27, 1840.

25. AHSH, Folder 120, Pareda to Gándara, April 16, 1841; Folder 123, Cuesto to Governor, January 8, 1842.

26. JA, R30, Military Commander at Janos to Governor of Chihuahua, September 1, 1842.

27. Griswold, "Ft. Sill Apaches," 24, 32, 132. Griswold's biography has Dos-teh-seh born about 1838, which is clearly too late by about fifteen years. Taza, Cochise's oldest son, was born in the early 1840s, at which time Dos-teh-seh was in her late teens or early twenties. The name of Mangas Coloradas's wife was Tu-es-seh, according to Mrs. Eve Ball. Ball to author, June 5, 1978.

28. Keith Basso, letter to author, February 22, 1979.

29. Juárez Collection, Roll 11, Varela to Prefect del Paso, April 12, 1842; JA, R28, Ugarte to Madrigal, April 26, 1842. *La Luna*, April 19, 1842.

30. JA, R29, Aguirre to Military Commander at Janos, May 15, 1842.

31. JA, R29, Madrigal to Military Commander, Chihuahua, May 26, 1842. The Indians were referring to an incident in which several Apaches were killed. Josiah Gregg wrote that it occurred in the summer of 1839 when authorities enticed several Apaches into an ambush at Paso del Norte, where some twenty warriors were "treacherously dispatched in cold blood." Josiah Gregg, *Commerce of the Prairies,* 206–7.

32. JA, R29, Conde to Military Commander at Janos, June 9, 1842.

33. *La Luna,* June 28, 1842.

34. Ponce, born about 1810, was a literate Chihenne leader who was said to have been a good friend of Cochise. Like his contemporary Delgadito, he was a moderate leader who participated in the Janos agreements of 1842 and 1851 and signed treaties with Americans in 1852 and 1853. His group was on good terms with the Mescaleros, their neighbors east of the Río Grande. It was probably his son Ponce who guided General Howard to Cochise in 1872. The elder Ponce was killed by one of his own people "in a drunken frolic" in late June or early July 1854. RG 75, T21, R2, Steck to Meriwether, July 8, 1854.

35. *La Luna,* July 15, July 19, 1842.

36. JA, R30, Madrigal to Commander in Chief, September 1, 1842.

37. Esquinaline, a moderate Chiricahua leader born about 1800, headed one of the less-militant Chokonen local groups. A close associate of Cochise in the late 1850s, he was the Indian whom Tevis called Esconolea. During the late 1840s and early 1850s he was closely associated with Mangas, oftentimes uniting with the Chihenne leader for raids into Sonora. He was one of the leaders in the Chiricahua victory at Pozo Hediondo in January 1851. In the mid-1850s he saw his band dwindling and, with pressure from both American and Mexicans, tried to live in peace, first at Janos, then at Fronteras, and finally at Apache Pass with Cochise. In 1859, Samuel Cozzens described him as "a rather good looking specimen of an Apache, about sixty years of age and speaks Spanish, very imperfectly, however." He died in the early 1860s. *Missouri Republican,* August 29, 1859.

38. Yrigóllen was the dominant Chokonen leader from the early 1840s until his death at the hands of Sonoran troops at Janos in March 1851. His son, Miguel Yrigóllen, was a subordinate of Cochise in the early 1860s. Edwin R. Sweeney, "I Had Lost All: Geronimo and the Carrasco Massacre of 1851," *Journal of Arizona History,* 27 (Spring 1986), 35–52.

39. JA, R30, Janos ration lists of October 17, 24, and 31, 1842. AHSH, Folder 127, Elías González to Governor, January 26 and May 14, 1842.

40. *Revista Oficial,* February 7, 1843.

41. Ibid., April 18, 1843.

42. Griffen, *Apaches at War and Peace,* 199. JA, R30, Monterde to Madrigal, June 8, 1843; AHSH, Folder 134, Ignacio Elías to Governor, June 6, 1843.

43. JA, R30, ration lists of July 24 and July 31, 1843.

44. JA, R30, Monterde to Madrigal, August 18, 1843; SA, R14, Bozanigra to Governor of Sonora, December 6, 1843.

45. AHSH, Folder 134, Subprefect of Arispe to Governor, December 18, 1843.

46. SA, R14, Bozanigra to Governor of Sonora, February 8, 1844.

47. JA, R30, various rations lists, November 27, 1843, through January 15, 1844. Griffen, *Apaches at War and Peace,* 205–8.

48. Griffen, *Apaches at War and Peace,* 205–8.

49. Bancroft Library, Louis Alphonse Pinart Collection MM381, Documents 65, 69, and 72.

50. Chepillo drew rations at Janos from October 16, 1843, through December 4, 1843. In 1844 he joined Mangas and other Chokonens on raids into Sonora, later admitting that he killed a citizen near Fronteras. He became the leader of a Chokonen group in the early 1850s after the death of Yrigóllen and Tapilá. He was closely associated with Esquinaline, and both were reported to be living in the Chiricahua Mountains during the summer of 1856. Chepillo was involved in the peace negotiations at Fronteras in the summer of 1858 and probably was killed in the July 1858 massacre near that presidio.

51. Pinart Collection, Document 73; AHSH, Folder 146, Corella to Governor, May 3, 1844.

52. Ibid.; Park, "Apaches in Mexican-American Relations," 135; Alcance al número 35 de la *Revista Oficial,* August 28, 1844. *Revista Oficial,* September 24, 1844. Sonora conducted an investigation in order to justify its actions at Janos and Corralitos. The results can be found in the Pinart Collection at Bancroft Library. The probe focused mainly on the stolen Sonoran livestock and loot which Antonio Narbona and Elías González recovered in their attacks. It implicated, from the names of those involved, many influential civil officials at Janos and Corralitos. At Janos, Narbona confiscated stock, found in the Apache ranchería, which belonged to Sesario Corella, along with about six hundred pesos believed to have been stolen at the same time. He recovered the weapons of Francisco Alday and Arenito Vezinos, both of whom had been killed at Santa Cruz the previous month. Several head of stock were found in the possession of Janos citizens. Narbona found some in the possession of Juan José Zozaya, an influential citizen who served as peace commissioner to the Apaches in 1850; it had been stolen from Agustín Barela in June. Another Sonoran citizen, Seberiano Valencia, testified that he ransomed his own horse, stolen by the Apaches, from Zozaya at Janos for twenty pesos.

Results were similar at Corralitos. The owner of the mines, José María Zuloaga, had in his possession several horses and mules stolen in Sonora. Among them was stock from Sahuaripa, which infuriated Elías González because they had come from a raid led by Cigarrito in which nineteen people were killed. A horse belonging to Fernando Moreno was found in the possession of Angel Aguirre. Stock belonging to Sonoran citizens Bautista Valencia, Francisco Sicara, and Luis García was found, too. To top it off, Robert McKnight, former owner of the Santa Rita mines, now living at Barranco, had Sonoran livestock in his possession. Apache casualties numbered eighty to one hundred dead, with twenty or thirty killed at Janos and the remainder by Elías González's party near Corralitos.

53. Pinart Collection, Document 80, García to Elías González, January 1, 1845.

54. *Revista Oficial,* February 25, 1845.

55. Ibid., July 1, 1845. JA, R31, Ugarte to Janos Commander, June 20, 1845.

56. JA, R31, Conde to Padilla, July 20, 1845. JA, R28, Summary of Disbursements, July 1, 1845.

57. Láceris (Láceres, Pláceris) was a Nednhi leader of the Janeros group. He, too, matured in the presidio system and probably was related in some manner to the Compá family. He was born in the early 1800s and by 1842 had two wives and at least two children. He was at Janos from October 1842 through early 1844. From 1846 through the late 1850s, he was probably the most prominent Janeros leader of

the Nednhi band. A moderate, he generally preferred peace to war, although in the late 1840s he joined the Chokonens for many forays and was one of the ringleaders in the October 1849 capture of an American wagon train near Janos which resulted in the death of several Americans. Closely associated with Candelario, a son of Juan José, he was the leading Nednhi spokesman in the Janos treaties of 1850 and 1857. When affairs became brisk in northern Mexico, he migrated north, joining Delgadito and Mangas Coloradas in the peace with Americans in April 1853. He remained in New Mexico until the summer of 1856, when he returned to Chihuahua and began negotiating at Janos. He probably died in the late 1850s.

58. *El Provisional,* June 9, 1846.

59. Carro, a Chokonen leader of the late 1840s through the mid-1850s, had been, like so many of the Chokonen leaders, a member of Pisago Cabezón's group. He was a moderate leader, not as pacific as Esquinaline or as militant as Miguel Narbona, Tapilá, or Teboca. After the double-cross at Galeana, he, like most of the Chokonens, took to the warpath for the next decade. In July 1850 during a parley at Bacoachi he admitted that the permanent homes of his band were in the Chiricahua Mountains. In the summer of 1857 he made peace at Janos and died that fall, evidently killed by poisoned rations he received at Janos. SA, R16, Martínez to Governor, July 22, 1850.

60. *El Provisional,* July 7, 1846.

61. Ibid., July 14, 1846.

62. AHSH, Folder 160, Governor of Chihuahua to Governor of Sonora, July 6, 1846.

63. *El Provisional,* July 21, 1846.

64. George Frederick Ruxton, *Adventures in Mexico and the Rocky Mountains, 1846–1847,* 153–54; Mangas Coloradas's version was published in *Condition of the Indian Tribes,* 328; Betzinez, *I Fought with Geronimo,* 3. Betzinez put the massacre at a place called Kintal by the Apaches, which he believed was Ramos. He was wrong. Ramos was never more than a hacienda and at no time could it have eight hundred to a thousand inhabitants, as Betzinez asserted. Investigation reveals that the Chiricahua name for Casas Grandes was Kin-n-Teel ("house broad"), and the massacre occurred southeast of there at Galeana—further evidence that it was probably the incident described by Betzinez.

65. *El Provisional,* July 14, 1846.

66. Hobbs, *Wild Life,* 87–88.

67. Betzinez, *I Fought with Geronimo,* 1.

68. Ibid., 4–9.

*Chapter 4*

1. Born in 1794 in New Jersey, Kearny fought in the War of 1812 and several successive Indian campaigns before being named commander of the Army of the West in May 1846. He died in St. Louis in 1848. *Webster's American Military Biographies,* 212–13.

2. One chief told Kearny, "You have taken New Mexico, and will soon take California, go then and take Chihuahua, Durango and Sonora. We will help you. . . . The Mexicans are rascals; we hate and will kill them all." Calvin, *Lieutenant Emory Reports,* 100.

3. Philip St. George Cooke was born in 1809 at Leesburg, Virginia. He graduated from West Point in 1827 and saw action in the Black Hawk War of 1832, after

which he was promoted to first lieutenant. He was promoted to captain in 1835, saw more action in the Mexican War of 1846 and remained loyal to the Union in the Civil War, eventually reaching the rank of brigadier general. He wrote a manual on cavalry tactics and retired in 1873. He died in 1895. *Webster's American Military Biographies*, 79–80.

4. Pauline Weaver was born in Tennessee in 1800 to an American father and a Cherokee mother. He came west as a member of the Hudson's Bay Company and was one of the first whites to explore Arizona. He died in 1867 near Camp Lincoln (later Camp Verde), Arizona. Jay J. Wagoner, *Early Arizona: Prehistory to Civil War*, 254; Thrapp, *Encyclopedia*, 1525.

5. Antoine Leroux was a famous mountain man of the Southwest. Born in St. Louis, he came to New Mexico in the early 1820s and eventually settled at Taos. For the next twenty years he trapped and hunted throughout the Southwest. In 1852 he served as guide for Bartlett's boundary survey on its return from San Diego. He died in New Mexico in 1861. Thrapp, *Encyclopedia*, 848.

6. Manuelito, a Chokonen leader, was born in the 1780s. He received rations at Janos as early as 1810 as a member of Asquienalte's (Asquenitery) band, which had made peace in the 1780s. Manuelito was a leading spokesman during the peace of 1842, and it was his band that bore the brunt of Elías González's attack in August 1844. His influence had declined by the mid-1840s with the rise of Miguel Narbona and Yrigóllen. He died of exposure in the winter of 1849–50. *El Faro*, July 2, 1850; *Revista Oficial*, September 24, 1844; Alcance al número 35 de la *Revista Oficial*, August 24, 1844.

7. Philip St. George Cooke, *Exploring Southwestern Trails, 1846–1854*, 123, 129–30.

8. Ibid., 159–60.

9. Bancroft, *History of the North Mexican States*, II, 670.

10. AHS, Merejildo Grijalva, Hayden File.

11. *El Sonorense*, March 26, 1847; AHSH, Folder 175, Escalante to Governor, March 6, 1847.

12. AHSH, Folder 175, Justice of the Peace at Bacoachi to Governor, March 31, 1847; Folder 176, Cuesta to Governor, April 3, 1847.

13. Ibid., Folder 175, Escalante to Governor, April 6, 1847.

14. Ibid., Elías González to Governor, May 3, 1847.

15. AHSH, Folder 176, Escalante to Governor, May 6, 1847. AHSH, Folder 175, Escalante to Governor, June 14, 1847.

16. In fact, Western Apaches, reportedly Pinals, solicited peace at Tucson in August and October 1847, although no worthwhile agreement apparently was made. *El Sonorense*, October 8, 1847; AHSH, Folder 176, Military Commander at Tucson to Governor, October ?, 1847.

17. AHSH, Folder 175, Narbona to Prefect of Moctezuma, September 22, 1847; *El Sonorense*, October 8, 1847.

18. Bartlett, *Personal Narrative*, I, 273. *El Sonorense*, March 17, 1848; AHSH, Folder 199, Escalante to Governor, December 24, 1847; February 10, 1848.

19. *El Sonorense*, March 17, 1848; AHSH, Folder 199, Arvizu to Governor, March 1, 1848. The fate of these forty-two prisoners is uncertain. The young children probably grew up as Apaches and others may have been returned by the Chiricahuas in compliance with subsequent peace agreements.

20. Eusebio Gil Samaniego, a native of Bavispe, was well known to Cochise

and the Chiricahuas. Called Chato ("flat nose") by the Indians, he was a stern officer who led several campaigns against the Apaches. Evidently he was a man who asked no quarter and gave none.

21. SA, R14, Samaniego to Governor, June 21, 1848. The descendants of Cochise knew nothing of his having been captured at Fronteras. Granddaughter Amelia Naiche told me she had not heard of the incident. Neither had Mrs. Eve Ball, recorder of Chiricahua oral history. This is not surprising when one considers that very little historical information from the Indian perspective existed before 1870. In fact, none of Mrs. Ball's informants ever mentioned prominent Chiricahua leaders, such as Yrigóllen and Miguel Narbona. Interviews with Amelia Naiche, January 17, 1979, and Mrs. Eve Ball, January 17, 1979.

22. SA, R14, Calvo y Muro to Gándara, June 28, 1848.

23. Ibid., Calvo y Muro to Governor, August 19, 1848; Limon to Calvo y Muro, August 12, 1848.

24. Two years later Limon was killed by Apaches at Cocospera Canyon while serving as an escort for the Inez González party. Alan Radbourne, "Ambush at Cocospera Canyon," *English Westerners Tally Sheet,* (July 1979), 63–76.

25. *El Sonorense,* September 6, 1848.

26. Ibid., October 6, 1848.

27. Ibid., October 25, 1848. The Treaty of Guadalupe Hidalgo ended the United States–Mexican War of 1846. The United States agreed to restrain Indians from raiding into Mexico, to rescue any captives, and to extract compensation from the Indians for these raids. With respect to the Apaches, this was hopeless. The United States would have needed to establish forts along the Arizona and New Mexico border, and a penurious Congress was not about to approve additional expenditures. J. Fred Rippy argues convincingly that Mexico used all of her available resources to protect the northern frontier, but to no avail. J. Fred Rippy, "The Indians of the Southwest in the Diplomacy of the United States and Mexico, 1848–1853," *Hispanic American Historical Review,* 2 (August 1919), 363–96; Richard N. Ellis, *New Mexico Historical Documents,* 10–32.

28. Rippy, "Indians of the Southwest," 387–89.

29. *El Sonorense,* November 3, 1848.

30. SA, R14, Tuvera to Prefect of Ures, December 19, 1848.

31. Bartlett, *Personal Narrative,* II, 302.

32. SA, R15, Comadurán to Commanding General, December 14, 1848.

33. SA, R15, Comadurán to Elías González, January 26, 1849.

34. *El Sonorense,* April 15, 1850. This issue contains a summary of the individuals who emigrated to California. In all, 5,664 men departed Sonora, and this total included only five of the nine districts reporting.

35. SA, R15, Comadurán to Elías González, January 26, 1849.

36. Captain James Whitlock defeated a band of Chiricahuas near Piños Altos on March 1, 1864, killing thirteen warriors including Luis, a Bedonkohe chief probably related to Mangas Coloradas, and recapturing Marijenia Figueira. She provided details of the Banamichi raid, in which her mother and father were killed. She had been a servant for Luís and his family since that time. *The War of the Rebellion: A Compilation of the Official Records of the Union and Confederate Armies,* 34, Pt. 1, 122–23.

37. SA, R15, Cordova to the Prefect of Baviacora, March 9, 1849; Miranda to Prefect, March 13, 1849; *El Sonorense,* March 21, March 23, 1849.

NOTES TO PAGES 71–75

38. SA, R15, Samaniego to Terán y Tato, April 24, 1849.

39. Juan Abad Telles, in his late fifties, was the grandfather of Mickey Free, who had a prominent role in Arizona history and the life of Cochise. It is ironic that Cochise, who probably participated in this attack, may have fought the grandfather of the boy who played such a prominent role in the Bascom affair in February 1861. My thanks to English historian Allan Radbourne for bringing this to my attention.

40. SA, R15, Limon to Elías González, May 1, 1849.

41. *El Sonorense,* June 1, 1849; SA, R15, Terán y Tato to Governor, May 29, 1849. The Chokonen prisoners were sent to Ures and Hermosillo for confinement. Among them were the wife and mother-in-law of Demos, a leading Chiricahua warrior who had an instrumental role in peace negotiations during the spring of 1850.

42. SA, R15, de Aros to Governor, May 24, 1849; de Aros to Secretary of War and Navy, July 13, 1849. Montoya was subsequently set free, while Romero was tortured to death over a period of several days. He left behind a wife and two young sons.

43. SA, R15, Terán y Tato to Governor, June 19, 1849; Elías González to Governor, June 22, 1849, *El Sonorense,* July 20, 1849. Duran's testimony was interesting. A war party of two hundred men was planning to raid along the Sonora River in late June. He also confirmed the increasing Apache activity at Janos, which illustrated the peculiar and precarious relationship between the Chiricahuas and Captain Baltazar Padilla, José María Zuloaga, and Juan José Zozaya, the leading military and public officials of the area. Duran confirmed that stolen Sonoran plunder was traded at Janos; furthermore, Zozaya had written a letter to Chief Babosa declaring that the people of Janos were his friends. Duran also revealed the Apaches' close contact with New Mexican traders, including a man named Armijo who supplied the Apaches with American rifles, powder, balls, cloth, and other provisions. According to him, the Chiricahuas feared the Americans and believed the latter were planning a campaign against them.

44. SA, R15, Elías González to Governor, July 12, 1849.

45. *El Sonorense,* June 1, August 3, 1849; SA, R15, Elías González to Minister of War and Navy, July 13, 1849; Elías González to Governor, July 15, 1849.

46. SA, R15, Elías González to Governor, October 30, 1849; document titled "Diary of Operations by Colonel José María Elías González in Pursuit of the Indian savages."

47. Ibid.

48. John Coffee ("Jack") Hays was born in Tennessee in 1817, became a captain in the Texas Rangers at the age of twenty-three, and led several successful scouts against Comanches. On April 11, 1849, he was named subagent for the Río Gila in New Mexico. Hays reached San Francisco in January 1850 and reported on an alternate route to Cooke's, that being through Puerto del Dado (Apache Pass), which saved more than 150 miles of travel. In all likelihood, Elías González told Hays about the more direct route. Thrapp, *Encyclopedia,* 634; *Alta California,* February 1, 1850.

49. Annie Heloise Abel, ed., *The Official Correspondence of James S. Calhoun While Indian Agent at Santa Fe and Superintendent of Indian Affairs in New Mexico,* 34.

50. SA, R15, Elías González to Governor, October 30, 1849.

51. JA, R32, Padilla to Commanding General of Chihuahua, March 22, May 26, 1849.

52. Ralph A. Smith, "The Scalp Hunt in Chihuahua—1849," *New Mexico Historical Review*, 40 (April 1965), 116–40. In the first few months the Carrizaleños were hit hardest. Their old chief, Jasquedegá, and twenty-two others were killed at Carmen on June 6, and in early July a son of Mano Mocha was killed at Corralitos. *El Faro*, June 23, August 14, 1849.

53. Missouri Historical Society, Solomon Sublette Papers.

54. Soquilla, born about 1800, was leader of a small Janeros local group. He had matured in the presidio system of the early 1800s and was a member of Asquienalte's band in 1816 through the mid-1820s. He figured prominently in the Janos peace of 1842, joined the Chiricahuas in the Sonora raids during 1844, and suffered the consequences when Elías González attacked his camp near Corralitos in August 1844. He had one wife and four children in the Janos census of 1843 and 1844.

55. JA, R32, Padilla to Inspector of the Colony, September 12, September 15, 1849.

56. Coleto Amarillo (Yellow Jacket) was, with Láceris, the dominant leader of the Nednhi band in the late 1840s and early 1850s. He was the leading spokesman for the Chiricahua bands in the peace consummated at Janos in June 1850. Sonoran troops killed him in April 1852 north of Lake Guzmán. His son, known by the same name, headed a small group through the early 1860s.

57. Arvizu, born in the late 1790s, probably was related in some manner to Manuel Chirimni. He was at Janos during the 1820s until the outbreak of 1831, participated in the Janos peace treaties of 1842 and 1850, and was killed at Janos by Sonoran troops under Colonel José María Carrasco in March 1851. Sweeney, "I Had Lost All," 52.

58. *Alta California*, May 16, 1850.

59. *Alta California*, May 16, 1850; *El Faro*, November 3, November 20, 1849; January 5, 1850. JA, R32, Padilla to Military Inspector, Chihuahua, November 6, 1849.

*Chapter 5*

1. Robert M. Utley, *Frontiersman in Blue, The United States Army and the Indians, 1848–1865*, 85.

2. Steen was born in Kentucky in 1800. Cited for gallantry in the Mexican War, he was wounded on August 16, 1849, in a fight with Chihennes near San Diego Crossing, which was on the Río Grande about ten miles southeast of present-day Hatch, New Mexico. In the late 1850s he was stationed at Fort Buchanan and might have met Cochise. Historic Stein's Peak was probably named after him. He retired with a rank of lieutenant colonel in 1863 and died in 1880. Thrapp, *Encyclopedia*, 1363; Francis B. Heitman, *Historical Register and Dictionary of the United States Army*, I, 919.

3. Thrapp, *Victorio*, 23.

4. AHSH, Folder 221, Martínez to Elías González, April 23, 1850. *Santa Fe Weekly Gazette*, March 19, 1853.

5. Jornado del Muerto, translated "journey of death," was a waterless stretch of about ninety miles from Rincon to San Marcial in south-central New Mexico. Pearce, *New Mexico Place Names*, 77.

6. AHSH, Folder 221, Martínez to Elías González, April 23, 1850; *Santa Fe Weekly Gazette*, March 19, 1853. According to Teofilo and Mateo Savanillo, Miguel's party suffered heavy losses.

7. Posito Moraga was a prominent Chokonen local group leader of the late 1840s and early 1850s. He probably died in the mid-1850s. His brother, Chino, was a subordinate of Cochise in the 1850s and 1860s.

8. AHSH, Folder 221, Elías González to Governor, February 13, February 28, 1850.

9. AHSH, Folder 221, Elías González to Governor, March 22, 1850.

10. Ibid.; AHSH, Folder 221, Ybarra to Elías González, March 22, 1850.

11. Ibid.,; *El Sonorense*, May 10, 1850.

12. *El Sonorense*, April 15, 1850.

13. SA, R16, Elías González to Governor of Sonora, May 13, 1850.

14. AHSH, Folder 221, Elías González to Governor, April 30, 1850.

15. *El Sonorense*, May 10, 1850; AHSH, Folder 221, Elías González to Governor, April 30, 1850.

16. *El Sonorense*, June 7, 1850. *El Faro*, June 25, 1850. AHSH, Folder 221, Elías González to Governor, June 25, 1850.

17. Rodolfo F. Acuña, *Sonoran Strongman: Ignacio Pesqueira and His Times* (cited hereafter as Acuña, *Pesqueira*), 8.

18. *El Faro*, July 2, August 17, 1850.

19. Ibid.; AHSH, Folder 221, Zozaya to Elías González, June 25, 1850.

20. *El Sonorense*, September 20, November 15, 1850. AHSH, Folder 221, Ramírez to Governor, August 30, 1850.

21. *El Sonorense*, November 15, 1850; AHSH, Folder 221, Terán y Tato to Governor, November 1, 1850; Elías González to Governor, November 11, 1850; SA, R16, Navamuel to Governor, October 5, 1850.

22. *El Sonorense*, January 31, 1851. Carrasco, born in 1813, reached the rank of lieutenant in 1833. He distinguished himself in the U.S.-Mexican War of 1846. He reached Sonora in January 1851 with forty troops and died in July 1851 of cholera. Almada, *sonorenses*, 146.

23. Pesqueira, born December 16, 1820, in Arispe, was educated in Europe. He returned to Sonora in 1839 and joined the local militia, or National Guard. By 1845 he had risen to captain and, as his biographer notes, "was suddenly catapulted from obscurity to statewide prominence" after the Pozo Hediondo fight. In 1857 he became governor of Sonora, a position he held throughout most of the 1860s and into the 1870s. He died on January 4, 1886. Acuña, *Sonora Strongman*.

24. *El Sonorense*, January 31, 1851; *El Correo*, February 11, 1851. In an issue dated May 30, 1851, *El Sonorense* charged that "Anglo scoundrels" had armed and led the Apaches, who were well armed with rifles and six-shooters. The Indians killed fifteen and wounded twenty-five from Bacoachi and killed eleven and wounded twenty-two of the fifty nationals from Arispe. AHSH, Folder 224, Villascusa to Governor, April 28, 1851.

25. Eduardo W. Villa, *Compendia de Historia del Estado de Sonora*, 242-44. Villa errs in dating the fight January 7.

26. AHS, Merejildo Grijalva, Hayden File.

27. Barrett, *Geronimo's Story*, 51-54.

28. For events leading up to Carrasco's campaign, see Sweeney, "I Had Lost All," 35-45.

29. *El Sonorense,* March 28, 1851.

30. AHSH, Folder 230, Flores to Quintana, August 15, 1851; Campo to Governor, July 21, 1851; *La Voz del Pueblo,* July 30, August 6, 1851.

31. San Simon was well known to Mexicans in the 1840s. At this time there was probably a running stream and at places the terrain was very marshy with willow groves, hence the name Cienega de Sauz (Willow Swamp). In 1859 the Butterfield Overland Mail Company established a stage station here, primarily for changing stock. Will C. Barnes, *Arizona Place Names,* 51.

32. *La Voz del Pueblo,* September 10, October 8, 1851.

33. AHSH, Folder 230, Flores to Governor, December 15, 1851.

34. *El Correo,* November 22, 1851.

35. *El Sonorense,* November 7, 1851.

36. Manuel Gallegos served as an officer in the Arizona Volunteers, 1865–66, and directed Sonoran campaigns against the Apaches in the early 1870s.

37. Bonita Canyon is in the Chiricahua Mountains some fifteen miles south of Apache Pass. Today it is under jurisdiction of the National Park Service and is a popular camping area.

38. SA, R16, Terán y Tato to Governor, April 2, 1852; *El Sonorense,* April 20, 1852.

39. SA, R16, Lozada to Blanco, April 12, 1852; *El Sonorense,* April 16, 1852.

40. Opler, *Lifeway,* 466.

41. *El Sonorense,* April 22, 1853; SA, R16, García to Governor, April 14, 1853; Thrapp, *Victorio,* 32–33.

42. SA, R16, Arvizu to the Justice of the Peace, Granadas, June 16, 1853; Lavadi to Commander of the Opatas, July 14, 1853.

43. SA, R17, Cota to Juzgado de Paces, Cumuripa, July 19, 1853.

44. Casimiro's daughter was one of twelve Chiricahuas captured by national troops under Flat Nose Samaniego in January 1854. The Chokonen chief succeeded in exchanging Mexican prisoners for his daughter, but during the ensuing negotiations Sonoran troops opened fire, killing Casimiro and two other warriors; the Indians retaliated by killing two of their hostages. In the following months the Chiricahuas avenged this incident by killing several of Samaniego's relatives and the son of Captain Reyes, the two Mexican leaders involved in the affair. SA, R17, Samaniego to Governor, February 2, 1854; Reyes to Governor, February 3, 1854.

45. SA, R17, Justice of the Peace, Alamos, to Governor, February 19, 1854; Terán y Tato to Governor, March 7, 1854; Samaniego to Governor, March 14, 1854; Padilla to Governor, February 17, 1854; Ballestero to Governor, February 21, 1854.

46. Costales was a subordinate of Delgadito who rose to prominence because of his fighting ability, even though he was not an Apache. Born at El Carmen, Chihuahua, he was captured as a youth by Apaches and was raised by the Chihennes. He was murdered by Mexicans on December 31, 1856, while on a mission for Dr. Michael Steck, agent for the Chihennes. Thrapp, *Victorio,* 5, 8, 52–53.

47. SA, R17, Prefect of Moctezuma to Prefect of Ures, May 24, 1854; SA, R18, García to Governor, June 24, 1854; Gándara to Governor, July 14, 1854.

48. The Gadsden Purchase was the result of the efforts of James Gadsden, minister to Mexico, who conducted the negotiations to purchase land below the Gila River in order to construct a transcontinental railroad along the Thirty-second Parallel. Gadsden agreed to pay Santa Anna fifteen million dollars, but the U.S. Senate

reduced the purchase price to ten million. Ellis, *New Mexico Historical Documents*, 41–46.

49. Bancroft, *History of the North Mexican States*, II, 693.

50. See, for example, SA, R18, Moreno to Governor, June 17, 1856; AHSH, Folder 283, Gomez to Governor, April 7, 1855; Pesquiera to Governor, November 3, 1855.

51. JA, R36, Padilla to Commanding General, Chihuahua, May 28, 1855.

52. Chiricahua bands had made treaties with the Americans in July 1852 and April 1853. Most of the Chihennes and the Janeros local group of the Nednhis participated; apparently, few of the Bedonkohes and none of the Chokonens were present. Under terms of the second treaty, the U.S. government agreed to feed the Apaches and to provide protection as long as the Indians abstained from depredations in Mexico. Neither party fully lived up to its part of the agreement; the Indians continued raiding in Mexico and the federal government furnished little food, seeds, or tools to farm, although the concept of Apaches' farming on a sufficient scale to feed themselves was a gross misconception on the part of well-meaning whites, indicating their lack of understanding of Chiricahua culture. Thrapp, *Victorio*, 27–34, 43–45.

53. Smith, "Indians in American-Mexican Relations," 39.

54. Steck was born in Pennsylvania in 1818 and graduated from Jefferson Medical College in Philadelphia about 1843. He went to New Mexico in 1849 as a contract surgeon with the army and in late 1854 was appointed agent for the Southern Apaches, essentially the Chiricahuas. He was an honest and able agent, trusted by the wild Chiricahuas. He died in 1883. Thrapp, *Encyclopedia*, 1361.

55. National Archives and Records Center, RG 393, Records of United States Army Continental Commands, 1821–1920, Letters Received, Department of New Mexico (cited hereafter as RG393,LR,DNM with citation), Eaton to Nichols, December 23, 1855.

56. Cochise had a brother named Juan, and this could have been him. But little is known of his activities and status, although as the son of a chief he might have been considered a minor leader. He was held in high esteem as a fighter and as a man.

57. Zimmerman Library, University of New Mexico, Michael Steck Papers, Box 2, Folder 2, document dated September 19, 1856.

58. RG393, LR, DNM, E10, 1856, Eaton to Nichols, March 17, 1856; Steck Papers, Box 2, Folder 1, Steck to Davis, February 17, 1856.

59. Thrapp, *Victorio*, 48–52, has a complete account of the events leading up to the Chandler attack and its ramifications; RG393, Entry 3179, Records Relating to Indian Affairs, Department of New Mexico. Testimony of Refugio Corrales to Captain Henry L. Kendrick near Zuñi, New Mexico. Corrales, who had been a prisoner for some sixteen months, supports my theory that the Chokonens and Mogollons (Bedonkohes?) were close allies at this time. In the spring of 1856 he had gone with his captors, whom he identified as Mogollons, to the Chiricahua Mountains to obtain agave, or century plant (mescal), one of the more important food staples in the Chiricahua economy.

60. *La Voz de Sonora*, May 30, 1856; SA, R18, Moreno to Governor, June 17, 1856; JA, R36, Padilla to Steck, November 3, 1856.

61. *La Voz de Sonora*, May 30, 1856; Almada, *sonorenses*, 76.

62. RG393, E3179, Records Relating to Indian Affairs in New Mexico; JA,

R36, Diary of Events, Padilla to Military Commander, August 1, 1856; *El Eco de la Frontera,* August 19, September 16, 1856.

*Chapter 6*

1. Yrinco, a minor Chokonen leader, was born in the early 1800s. A member of Pisago Cabezón's band, he appears on the Janos ration lists in 1842–44. His brother was Manuelito, the Chokonen leader who met Cooke's party at San Bernardino in the fall of 1846. Yrinco was a leading advocate for peace in the Chokonen negotiations with Sonora in 1850. He passed from the scene in the late 1850s.

2. Aguirre, a brother of Yrigóllen, was at Janos in 1842–43. He was an ally and subordinate of Cochise from the late 1850s until he was killed in October 1868 by Sonoran troops in the mountains near Janos.

3. Parte was a hostile Chokonen leader who was at Janos from 1842 to 1844. An associate of Cochise, he died at Fronteras in February 1862 of smallpox.

4. JA, R36, Padilla to Zuloaga, September 22, 1855; Zuloaga to Padilla, September 23, 1855.

5. Babosa, born about 1790, was a literate Chiricahua leader and was said to have been a good friend of Juan José Compá.

6. JA, R36, Diary of Events, June 1856.

7. Ibid., July 1856.

8. Thrapp, *Victorio,* 49–51, has a complete account of this unfortunate affair.

9. JA, R36, Zuloaga to Padilla, July 31, 1856. José María Zuloaga was born in the city of Chihuahua in 1804. He joined the military as *cadete* in 1816 and rose to the rank of captain before retiring in 1839. A controversial man intimately acquainted with the Chiricahuas, he was in the middle of the contraband trade for a quarter of a century. Beginning in 1844 there were countless accusations by Sonoran and American officials regarding his conduct. As late as 1864, James H. Carleton pointed an accusing finger at him. He died on June 31, 1868. Almada, *chihuahuenses,* 576.

10. JA, R36, Padilla to Steck, November 3, 1856; Zuloaga to Padilla, July 31, 1856.

11. National Archives and Records Center, RG75, Records of the Bureau of Indian Affairs, Records of the New Mexico Superintendency of Indian Affairs, 1849–80, T21, Roll 6 (cited hereafter as RG75, T21 with roll number), Steck to Meriwether, August 15, 1856.

12. *El Eco de la Frontera,* August 19, 1856.

13. Ibid., September 16, 1856.

14. JA, R36, Padilla to Steck, November 9, 1856; Padilla to Zuloaga, September 2, 1856.

15. JA, R36, Padilla to Zuloaga, September 3, 1856.

16. University of Texas at Austin, Janos Collection, Padilla to Governor, January 2, 1857.

17. *El Centinela,* September 15, 1855. *El Eco de la Frontera,* April 18, 1856.

18. JA, R37, Merino to Padilla, February 4, 1857; Merino to Padilla, February 25, 1857.

19. Ibid., Padilla to Merino, February 10, 1857; Rancherías at Peace, April 1, 1857; SA, R19, Merino to Governor of Sonora, March 14, 1857.

20. Steck Papers, Box 2, Envelope 4, Steck to Meriwether, March 14, March 15, 1857. The Bonneville campaign was intended to punish hostile Apaches, in

particular the Mogollon Apaches, but the Indians the offensive was intended to strike had slipped away into Mexico. Instead the White Mountain Western Apaches suffered the most: some forty warriors killed or wounded near Mount Graham. The important Chihenne chief Cuchillo Negro was also killed in another minor engagement. Utley, *Frontersmen in Blue*, 156–57.

21. New Mexican citizens followed a band of Apaches into the Florida Mountains in January 1857 and killed Flacon and his two sons. *Santa Fe Weekly Gazette*, February 14, 1857. On March 9, Lieutenant Alfred Gibbs pursued a party of raiding Chihennes to the northern slopes of the Mimbres Mountains, killing six and mortally wounding another. Gibbs himself was wounded. *Santa Fe Gazette*, January 22, 1858; Dale E. Floyd, *Chronological List of Actions etc. with Indians from January 15, 1837, to January, 1891*, 18; Heitman, *Historical Register*, II, 403; Nona Barrick and Mary Taylor, *The Mesilla Guard, 1851–1861*, 26.

22. Yaque, or Yaqui, was a first-rate Chokonen incorrigible. Born about 1820, he was one of the hostiles who, while living at peace at Janos in 1843–44 and 1850–51, led repeated raids into Sonora, even boasting about several murders he committed. He was probably the leader referred to by Tevis and Cozzens at Apache Pass in 1859–60 as Old Jack, probably a corruption of *Yaque*. Old Jack's belligerent personality seems to fit Yaque, who passed from the scene in the early 1860s. Tevis, *Arizona in the 50s*, 95–96; AHSH, Folder 234, Testimony taken by Colonel Carrasco at Janos; Pinart Collection, Documents 74, 79.

23. Henry Linn Dodge was captured in Zuñi country in November 1856 by raiding Chiricahuas and killed shortly thereafter, perhaps in retaliation for the unprovoked Chandler attack the previous spring. Thrapp, *Victorio*, 50–53. El Cautivo, an associate of Cochise, was one of the ringleaders.

24. JA, R37, Zuloaga to Padilla, February 25, 1857.

25. Steck Papers, Box 2, Envelope 4, Steck to Meriwether, March 15, 1857.

26. JA, R37, Padilla to Quintana, April 3, 1857.

27. AHSH, Folder 310, Zuloaga to Cruz, June 4, 1857; Norlega to Commander in Chief of Sonora, June 27, 1857.

28. SA, R19, Pesqueira to Municipal President of Huasabas, February 28, 1857.

29. Steck Papers, Box 2, Envelope 4, Steck to Bonneville, March 14, 1857.

30. SA, R19, García to Davila, July 6, 1857.

31. Ibid., Campuzano to Governor, July 26, 1857.

32. Ibid.

33. *Alta California*, December 24, 1857.

34. JA, R37, Rancherías at Peace, August 1, 1857.

35. SA, R19, Commanding General of Chihuahua to Governor of Sonora, July 15, 1857.

36. SA, R19, García to Governor, October 10, 1857.

37. Ibid.; Griffen, *Apaches at War and Peace*, 257.

38. SA, R50, Elías González to Governor, September 20, 1857.

39. SA, R19, Campuzano to Governor, September 29, 1857.

40. Acuna, *Sonoran Strongman*, 2.

41. *Alta California*, February 11, 1858.

42. SA, R19, Pesqueira to Corella, Instructions for Commander Rafael Corella regarding the Indians who have solicited peace at Fronteras, September 24, 1857. Almada, *sonorenses*, 76.

43. Ibid.
44. AHSH, Folder 304, Corella to Governor, October 15, 1857.
45. SA, R19, García to Prefect of Arispe, October 7, 1857.
46. Ibid., García to Governor, October 10, 1857.
47. Steck Papers, Box 2, Envelope 5, Steck to Collins, November 21, 1857.
48. *Conditions of the Indian Tribes,* 328.
49. SA, R19, Campuzano to Governor, November 16, 1857. Sylvester Mowry reported in early December that some six hundred Apaches had settled near Fronteras as a result of the Bonneville campaign. He heard they were under the control of Mangas Coloradas, but this seems improbable because no mention of Mangas can be found in Mexican documents. Furthermore, Mangas had returned to New Mexico by early December. National Archives and Records Center, RG75, Records of the Bureau of Indian Affairs, Letters Received, New Mexico Superintendency, M234, R548, Mowry to Mix, December 7, 1857.
50. SA, R19, Corella to Commander at Bavispe, November 5, 1857; García to Governor, November 30, 1857; García to Governor, December 16, 1857.
51. JA, R37, Padilla to Zuloaga, January 1, 1858.
52. *Alta California,* May 13, 1858.
53. AHSH, Folder 224, García to Governor, May 4, 1858.
54. *La Voz de Sonora,* June 18, 1858.
55. Ibid., May 28, 1858; June 18, 1858; July 2, 1858.
56. Edith Allen Millner, "Covered Wagon Experiences," unpublished manuscript in the Arizona Historical Society.
57. AHSH, Folder 224, García to Governor, July 13, 1858.
58. *La Voz de Sonora,* July 16, 1858; AHSH, Folder 224, García to Prefect of Arispe, July 25, 1858.
59. Ibid., July 23, 1858.
60. Opler, *Lifeway,* 349.
61. *San Diego Herald,* September 18, 1858; *Los Angeles Star,* October 2, 1858.
62. Thrapp, *Victorio,* 28.
63. RG75, LR,NMS, M234, R549, Mowry to Mix, September 14, 1858.
64. Opler, *Lifeway,* 336–39.
65. AHSH, Folder 322, Elías González to Governor, September 21, 1858. Manuel Sandomingo, *Historia de Sonora,* 373–74.
66. *Missouri Republican,* December 16, 1858.
67. SA, R50, Elías to Governor, October 22, 1858.
68. *La Voz de Sonora,* November 26, 1858.
69. Ibid., February 11, February 18, 1859. Note in Steck Papers (Feburary 1859?), Box 2, Folder 8.

*Chapter 7*

1. Dr. John B. White studied the Western Apaches in 1874 and found that the average Apache man was five feet six and a half inches tall and weighed 135 to 140 pounds. He described Cochise as follows: "This chief may be said to have been about the only one who really exercised control over any of the Apaches. He was a fine looking man, about five feet ten inches in height and well proportioned being about three and a half inches taller than the average Apache—of manly and martial appearance—not unlike our conceptions of the Roman soldier—possessing great

physical endurance, and one well calculated to command the respect of a band of savage warriors." White Manuscript No. 178.

2. Cozzens, *The Marvellous Country*, 86.

3. Tevis, *Arizona in the 50s*, 149.

4. Ewell was born in 1817 in the Georgetown section of Washington, D.C., graduated from the U.S. Military Academy in 1840, and earned a brevet for gallantry in the Mexican War of 1846. He served with distinction in both Arizona and New Mexico and was known affectionately as Old Baldy. Ewell resigned his commission at the outbreak of the Civil War and joined the Confederacy with the rank of lieutenant general. He died in Tennessee in 1872. Thrapp, *Encyclopedia*, 475–76; Heitman, *Historical Register* I, 410.

5. John Van Deusen Dubois, *Campaigns in the West, 1856–1861*, 20.

6. There is some uncertainty about where the attack took place, although I believe it occurred at Apache Pass on the basis on the following sources: The *Alta California* of November 7, 1857, reported that two men named Short and Irving were murdered at Doubtful Pass or Apache Springs, which could mean either Stein's Peak or Apache Pass. In a subsequent issue dated December 27, 1857, the *Alta California* reported that it occurred in a narrow pass near Dragoon Springs, about eighty miles from Fort Buchanan. If so, this would rule out Doubtful Canyon. The *San Diego Herald* published an account which stated that a party of immigrants had been attacked at Puerto del Dado (Apache Pass) by Apaches, who killed two men. *Alta California*, November 7, December 29, 1857. *San Diego Herald*, September 5, 1857.

7. *San Antonio Herald*, March 20, 1858; *The Butterfield Overland Mail Across Arizona*, 8–9. A four-year contract was awarded Birch on June 22, 1857, effective July 1, 1857, to carry two mails per month each way for $149,800 annually. The route was from San Antonio to San Diego, with stops in El Paso, Tucson, and Yuma Crossing. The trail followed known water holes through southern New Mexico and southern Arizona. The stations between Mesilla and Tucson were resting spots; no permanent structures were built until the Butterfield Overland Mail Company did so in 1858. Birch's operation lacked the necessary capital and was replaced by Butterfield. Wagoner, *Early Arizona*, 344–47.

8. *Alta California*, November 9, 1858; Diane M. T. North, *Samuel Peter Heintzelman and the Sonora Exploring and Mining Company*, 110. AHS, William H. Kirkland, Hayden File, contains Tom Jeffords's version. Contemporary accounts attributed this to the White Mountain Apaches, but, given Kirkland's and Jeffords's reminiscences, there is a good chance of Cochise's involvement.

9. Roscoe P. and Margaret B. Conkling, *The Butterfield Overland Mail, 1857–1869*, I, 128–31, 140–42; Leroy R. Hafen, *The Overland Mail, 1849–1869*, 86–89.

10. *Missouri Republican*, October 31, 1859.

11. Buckley employed six Americans to construct the Dragoon Springs station: Frank de Ruyther, William Brainard, James Laing, James Burr, Preston Cunningham, and Silas St. John. St. John, a native of New York, first worked for the Jackass Mail Route but severed his employment with Birch to accept a job with the Butterfield Overland Mail Company as construction foreman in Arizona and New Mexico. During the night of September 8, 1858, three Mexican laborers (Guadalupe Rameriz, Pablo Rameriz, and Bonifacio Miranda) brutally bludgeoned to

death Cunningham, Burr, and Laing while inflicting on St. John wounds which necessitated the amputation of his left arm by assistant surgeon B. J. D. Irwin of Fort Buchanan. Two stage stations were built in 1859: at San Simon, between Stein's Peak and Apache Pass, and at Ewell's Croxon Springs, between Apache Pass and Dragoon Springs. Conkling and Conkling, *Butterfield Overland Mail*, 142–45.

12. Tevis, *Arizona in the 50s*, 100.

13. *Weekly Missouri Democrat*, January 7, January 13, 1859.

14. Steck Papers, Box 2, Envelope 7, Steck to Collins, undated letter probably written in the fall of 1858.

15. Ibid., Steck to Collins, February 1, 1859. Abstract of Provisions, 1859. Steck's estimate of fifty warriors is far too low. At the time of his visit, two Chiricahua parties were raiding in Sonora. One returned about January 5 with fifty mules and two Mexican women; another party was reported to be out with Mangas Coloradas in Sonora. *Missouri Republican*, January 5, January 12, 1859. Geronimo might have been present. He recalled in his autobiography: "At Apache Pass I made a treaty with the post. This was done by shaking hands and promising to be brothers. Cochise and Mangas Coloradas did likewise. . . . This was the first regiment that ever came to Apache Pass. This treaty was made about one year before we were attacked in a tent [referring to the Bascom affair in February 1861]." Barrett, *Geronimo's Story*, 116–17.

16. Steck Papers, Box 2, Envelope 8, Steck to Collins, February 1, 1859.

17. *Weekly Arizonian*, March 31, 1859.

18. As mentioned before, this might have been Yaque. Tevis and Cozzens both referred to him as Old Jack, whose personality seems to fit Yaque's.

19. Tevis, *Arizona in the 50s*, 111–12.

20. Will C. Barnes, *Apaches and Longhorns: The Reminiscences of Will C. Barnes*, 51.

21. Francisco, a militant Eastern White Mountain Coyotero, was a Mexican captive who rose to prominence as a major war leader. Apparently he was a fine physical specimen, standing almost six feet tall. He once told Tevis that he would fight Mexicans "as long as he lived and had a warrior to follow him." Goodwin writes that the White Mountain bands living in the Eagle Creek and Graham Mountain area had some contact with the Chiricahua "up until 1870 or so." In Appendix I, Goodwin lists local groups and independent family clusters, with chiefs and subchiefs, from 1850 to 1875. A chief named Gotca-ha (Big One) was said to have been great friends with the Chiricahuas, and another chief, Na-ginit-a (He Scouts Ahead), also was said to have been close to the Chiricahuas. Na-ginit-a died in 1865 at the Goodwin Springs poisoning, which coincides with Francisco's death in 1865 from poisoning, although his was the lead variety. Another possibility is that Francisco was a Bedonkohe Apache, which Eugene St. John claimed in a letter to Frank C. Lockwood dated November 27, 1935. Mrs. Lori Davisson of the Arizona Historical Society has done extensive work on the Western Apaches and believes that Francisco was "most likely to have been an Eastern White Mountain Apache." (Letter to author February 27, 1980); *Weekly Arizonian*, July 14, 1859; Goodwin, *The Social Organization of the Western Apache*, 83–86, 661–62; AHS, Frank C. Lockwood Collection.

22. *Weekly Arizonian*, April 21, 1859.

23. Elías, a Chokonen leader, was a son of Matías. He should not be confused with Elías the Chihenne chief. A contemporary of Cochise, the Chokonen Elías

was involved in the Janos peace of 1842 and the bloody raids into Sonora in early 1844. He was with Cochise in 1861–62 near Fronteras and again in August 1865, at which time he was one of the leaders who were reportedly eager to make peace at Fronteras. He was killed near Janos by Mexican troops in August 1868. *La Estrella de Occidente,* December 4, 1868.

24. SA, R19, Military Commander at Fronteras to Prefect of Arispe, May 3, 1859.

25. Ibid. The Apaches told Tevis the Mexicans fired first. More likely, however, it was the Chiricahuas who instigated the combat; they were still smarting from the July 1858 massacre, and their revenge raid the previous September had been a bust. Furthermore, Cochise had the superior numbers and the whites hardly desired a fight. *Weekly Arizonian,* May 12, 1859.

26. *Weekly Arizonian,* June 9, 1859.

27. Ibid., July 14, 1859.

28. Bourke, *On the Border with Crook,* 119.

29. Farish, *History of Arizona,* II, 30.

30. Woodworth Clum, *Apache Agent: The Story of John P. Clum,* 33–34. Wellman, *Indian Wars,* 289; Ogle, *Federal Control of the Western Apaches,* 44; John Upton Terrell, *Apache Chronicle,* 216–19; Dan L. Thrapp, *Conquest of Apachería,* 14–17.

31. Clum, *Apache Agent,* 33–34.

32. *Missouri Republican,* September 16, 1859.

33. *Weekly Arizonian,* July 14, 1859.

34. RG 393, LR, DNM, R30, 1859, Reeve to Wilkins, July 20, 1859.

35. John Spring, *John Spring's Arizona,* 52.

36. RG 393, LR, DNM, R31, 1859, Reeve to Wilkins, July 21, 1859.

37. Spring, *Spring's Arizona,* 52; AHS, Fred Hughes Collection.

38. Higgins Manuscript 21–22.

39. *Missouri Republican,* August 29, 1859; *Weekly Arizonian,* August 18, 1859; Opler, *Lifeway,* 362–63; Basehart, "Chiricahua Apache Subsistence," 96–97.

40. Steck Papers, Steck to Collins, November 25, 1859.

41. RG393, LR, DNM, 57R, 1859, Reeve to Wilkins, November 27, 1859.

42. RG75, LR, 1824–61; Pima Agency SIA, 169M, 1860. Letter signed Yuma and sent by Sylvester Mowry, February 6, 1860.

43. Tevis, *Arizona in the 50s,* 168–69.

44. Rita Rush, "El Chivero, Merejildo Grijalva," *Arizoniana,* 1 (Fall 1960), 9.

45. *Missouri Republican,* December 23, 1859.

46. RG75, T21, R14, Walker to Collins, January 4, 1860.

47. Constance Wynn Altshuler, ed., *Latest from Arizona! The Hesperian Letters, 1859–1861,* 27–28.

48. Tevis, *Arizona in the 50s,* 137–40.

49. *Missouri Republican,* February 21, 1860.

50. Ibid.; RG393, LR, DNM, 4E, 1860, Ewell to Wilkins, February 1, 1860; Tevis, *Arizona in the 50s,* 170; Cremony, "Some Savages," 203–4. Apparently there was some uncertainty about whether the individual killed was an Apache or a Mexican captured by the Indians and raised as an Apache. Tevis, who was there, claimed José was a captive of Cochise.

51. RG393, LR, DNM, 4E, 1860, Ewell to Wilkins, February 1, 1860.

52. Ibid., 12E, 1860, Ewell to Wilkins, March 7, 1860.

53. *Missouri Republican,* May 8, 1860; *La Estrella de Occidente,* March 9, April 6, April 13, 1860.

54. *Missouri Republican,* May 2, 1860; Cozzens, *Marvellous Country,* 220–23.

55. *Missouri Republican,* June 3, 1860.

56. R6393, LR, DNM, 22E, 1860, Ewell to Maury, July 24, 1860.

57. Ibid.; Altshuler, *Latest from Arizona,* 102–5.

58. *Missouri Republican,* July 22, 1860; *Alta California,* July 4, 1860.

59. RG393, LR, DNM, 22E, 1860, Ewell to Maury, July 24, 1860.

60. *Alta California,* July 4, 1860.

61. *La Estrella de Occidente,* June 29, 1860. The *Alta California* of July 25, 1860, reported that Governor Pesqueira had "made a treaty with the Apaches and is to pay them 15,000 or 20,000 [in order] to abstain from further hostilities . . . also, that ten captains sued for peace at Corralitos." The Chokonen leaders who had left Apache Pass for Mexico included Chino, Yaque, and Miguel Yrigóllen. These leaders had their own followings distinct from Cochise's.

62. *La Estrella de Occidente,* June 29, July 6, 1860; *La Coalición,* September 4, 1860.

63. Ibid.

64. AHSH, Folder 354, Prefect of Arispe to Governor, September 2, 1860.

65. Ibid.

66. Ibid.; Prefect of Arispe to Governor, October 16, 1860.

67. RG75, M234, R550, Steck to Greenwood, May 11, May 15, 1860. The reservation would have included "the present communities of Gila, Cliff and Buckhorn, all northwest of Silver City, the boundary line going north almost to Shelly Peak, west to near Jackson on U.S. Highway 180 and its southern boundary would have touched Bald Knoll." Thrapp, *Victorio,* 65–66.

68. Altshuler, *Latest from Arizona,* 136, 147; RG393, LR, DNM, 46M, 1860, Morrison to Assistant Adjutant General, Department of New Mexico, October 27, November 10, 1860.

69. AHSH, Folder 354, Prefect of Arispe to Governor, December 23, 1860.

70. Higgins Manuscript, 20–21. Coyuntura (Kin-o-tero, Kin-o-tera), a younger brother of Cochise, was hanged at Apache Pass by Lieutenant Bascom in February 1861. Eve Ball identified him as Cochise's brother. This, the Higgins Manuscript, and Sonoran documents clearly identify Coyuntura as the Indian hanged at Apache Pass. Mrs. Ball said she "learned very little about him and that was from Ralph Chee, a grandson of Hugh Chee who was the son of Chie, a nephew of Cochise who would serve as a guide for General O. O. Howard." Based on this information, Chie (or Chisito) might have been the son of Coyuntura.

71. AHSH, Folder 354, Governor to Prefect of Arispe, December 28, 1860.

*Chapter 8*

1. Ball, *Indeh,* 22–30; Griswold, "Ft. Sill Apaches," biographies of Cochise, 24, Taza, 132, Naiche, 106, Dash-den-zhoos, 29, Naithlotonz, 110; AHS, Gatewood Collection, Box 1, Envelope 5.

2. Lockwood, *The Apache Indians,* 125.

3. Ball, *Indeh,* 25.

4. Opler, *Apache Lifeway,* 467.

5. Ball, *Indeh*, 25; Griswold, "Ft. Sill Apaches," 132; Katherine C. Turner, *Red Men Calling on the Great White Father*, 137–44.

6. Smithsonian Institution, Bureau of American Ethnology, George Wratten letter to W. Holmes, May 4, 1907.

7. Oury's account was published in the *Arizona Weekly Star* on June 28, July 5, and July 12, 1877. AHS, William Sanders Oury File. Policeman Oberly's recollections were published in an unidentified New York newspaper in 1886. A copy is in the files of the Arizona Historical Society. Captain Bernard J. D. Irwin's version was written in 1887 but published in 1928 in the *Infantry Journal*, 32 (April 1928); Daniel Robinson, "The Affair at Apache Pass," *Sports Afield*, 17 (August 1896), 79–84.

8. Driver A. B. Culver's account was published in *Arizonian* on February 9, 1861. A copy is in James Wallace's Hayden File in the AHS. William Buckley's version was reported in the *Alta California* issue of February 19, 1861. A copy is in Buckley's Hayden File in the AHS. The anonymous letter critical of Bascom was published in the *Missouri Republican*, December 27, 1861.

9. Benjamin H. Sacks, "New Evidence on the Bascom Affair," *Arizona and the West*, 4 (Autumn 1962), 261–78. Sacks cites Bascom's official reports, which can be found in NA, RG393, LR, Department of New Mexico, 1861.

10. Barrett, *Geronimo's Story*, 115–17; Betzinez, *I Fought with Geronimo*, 40–42; Ball, *Indeh*, 25; Ball, *In the Days of Victorio*, 155. Cochise's account, given to Arny at Cañada Alamosa, New Mexico, was reported in the *Santa Fe New Mexican* on November 1, 1870, and is in NA, RG75, M234, R557, Arny to Parker, October 24, 1870.

11. John Ward, born in Ireland about 1806, had come to Arizona from California in the late 1850s. By 1859 he had a ranch on Sonoita Creek and had taken in a widowed family: Jesúsa Martínez and two children, Félix and Teodora, ages twelve and ten, respectively. Ward and Jesúsa had five children before he died in 1867. Many accounts have vilified Ward, but he seems to have been an industrious farmer and family man who only wanted to rescue his stepson. Alan Radbourne, "Salvador or Martínez? The Parentage and Origins of Mickey Free," *English Westerners Society Brand Book*, 14 (January 1972), 2–26.

12. Ibid.; The Ward boy, known as Félix Ward and later in life as Mickey Free, spent the rest of his life with the Western Apaches. In the 1870s and 1880s he was a scout for the army against the Chiricahuas. He died on the Fort Apache Reservation in 1915.

13. George Nicholas Bascom, born in Kentucky about 1836, graduated from West Point in 1858 and reached Arizona in October 1860. He was killed by Confederates in the Battle of Valverde in February 1862. His courage was never questioned, but his judgment certainly could be. Heitman, *Historical Register*, I, 197.

14. *Los Angeles Star*, February 16, 1861, reprinted from the *Arizonian*. Copy in John Ward's Hayden File, AHS; Altshuler, *Latest from Arizona*, 165.

15. Altshuler, *Latest from Arizona*, 170.

16. Radbourne, "Salvador or Martínez?" 19.

17. National Archives and Record Center, M1072, Letters Sent, Department of New Mexico, R2, Wilkens to Reeve, September 11, 1859.

18. RG393, LR, DNM, E22, 1860, Ewell to Maury, July 24, 1860.

19. Irwin's account, 3–4; RG393, LR, DNM, Bascom to Maury, January [February] 14, 1861.

20. Irwin's account, 4.

21. Robinson was born in Ireland in 1830, immigrated to the United States in 1849, and enlisted in Company C, Seventh Infantry. He saw extensive duty in the post–Civil War campaigns in the West before retiring in 1889 with the rank of captain. He died in Iowa in 1911. Thrapp, *Encyclopedia*, 1230.

22. Robinson's account, 79–80.

23. Wallace, born in Massachusetts in 1828, was a stage driver for the Butterfield Overland Mail Company. He had married recently and owned a house in Tucson. *The Butterfield Overland Mail Across Arizona*, 19, 32; Altshuler, *Latest from Arizona*, 285.

24. Robinson's account, 80.

25. Both of Bascom's reports suggest that he met and captured Cochise's party on February 3. Benjamin Sacks, in his article "New Evidence on the Bascom Affair," uncovered the company returns for Company C for February 1861, which revealed that the prisoners were taken on February 4. Sacks, "New Evidence," 268. A. B. Culver, who arrived in Tucson on Friday, February 8, also dated the meeting February 4. James Wallace, Hayden File.

26. Robinson's account, 80; AHS, Nathan Benjamin Appel, Hayden File.

27. Robinson, who had a clear view of the participants, states that Ward shared Bascom's tent and acted as interpreter. If so, Ward probably was a Spanish interpreter because he knew no Apache. Robinson's account, 80; Oury recalled that Bascom's interpreter was Antonio, probably a Mexican who had been a captive of the Apaches. Antonio accompanied Bascom on other scouts, so it is conceivable that he was with the officer at Apache Pass, although I feel it more probable that Antonio, if present, arrived with one of the relief parties. Oury's account.

28. RG393, LR, DNM, Bascom to Maury, January 14 [February 14] and February 25, 1861 (cited hereafter as Bascom's reports).

29. Bascom's reports.

30. Culver's account in James Wallace's Hayden File.

31. RG393, LR, DNM, 65C, 1861, Chapin to AAG, Department of New Mexico, April 25, 1861.

32. Ball, *Indeh*, 25; Barrett, *Geronimo's Story*, 115; *Santa Fe New Mexican*, November 1, 1870. Turrill, "A Vanished Race," 14.

33. Robinson's account, 80–81.

34. Turrill, "A Vanished Race," 14–15.

35. Robinson's account, 80–81; Buckley's account; Oberly's account, 4; Oury's account.

36. Oberly's account, 4; *Missouri Republican*, December 27, 1861.

37. Robinson's account, 81.

38. Ibid. Irwin wrote that the parley was arranged by Bascom, who released one Indian woman. Irwin, however, was still 125 miles away when this took place. All other accounts agree that Cochise initiated the parley. Irwin's account.

39. Bascom's reports; Robinson's account, 81; Oury perpetuated the legend that Wallace was captured by Cochise immediately after his escape from Bascom on February 4. Actually, Wallace was captured the next day under different circumstance. Oury's account.

40. Oury's version was the only one which stated that Welch (or Walsh) was killed mistakenly by troops. One can infer from other accounts, however, that such was indeed the case. A. B. Culver stated that "Welch also escaped and got to the

corral of the station when he was shot dead." Buckley declared that the Indians "shot one and took one prisoner; the other man being shot at the station." This seems to suggest that the soldiers did the work. Bascom failed to mention who killed Welch; if his soldiers were responsible, it would hardly have been a credit to his record.

41. Bascom's reports; Robinson's account, 82. Mangas Coloradas may have been present, although Bascom's estimate of five hundred warriors is clearly too high. Probably they numbered one-third of that at best.

42. Robinson's account, 82.

43. Culver's account. A person speaking in normal tones in the canyon can be heard distinctly by anyone on Overlook Ridge.

44. Bascom's reports.

45. I don't believe Bernard marched with Bascom's command to Apache Pass. He probably arrived with one of the relief parties from either Fort Breckenridge or Fort Buchanan, probably the former. Benjamin Sacks concluded that Bernard, if indeed present, must have arrived with Lieutenant Moore on February 14 because Bernard was named on the muster rolls at Breckenridge before and after the affair. Sacks, "New Evidence," 273. It is unlikely that Bernard was with Robinson's detachment, as this command, like Bascom's, was stationed at Fort Buchanan.

46. Oury's account. He perpetuated the story that Bascom refused to trade because Cochise offered only Wallace for the Indians and would not include the other three white men taken on the late afternoon of the sixth. Oury's account (written in 1877 in response to Governor Safford's account, which was highly critical of Bascom) was easily the most confused of all those written some years after the incident. He defends Bascom's handling of Cochise. Interestingly enough, ten years earlier he was William A. Bell's source for the account published in *New Tracks in North America*. In it, if he is quoted correctly, he takes Bascom to task for the way he handled Cochise and inexplicably states that Bascom hanged the Indians before Cochise killed his white prisoners. William A. Bell, *New Tracks in North America*, 279–80.

47. Arizona Governor Anson Safford reported this version in the *Arizona Citizen* on December 7, 1872. In 1869 and 1870, Captain Reuben F. Bernard made reference to Wallace's fate. In one report, referring to Cochise, he claimed to know of fifteen whites killed by "putting lariats around their necks, tied their hands behind them and dragged to death." Don Russell, *One Hundred and Three Fights and Scrimmages: The Story of General Reuben F. Bernard*, 70–71. A similar version was furnished, possibly by Bernard, to Colonel George Stoneman's entourage in the fall of 1870. In this account, at a signal from Cochise, "the Indians started their horses on a run, the necks of the poor whites were broken, and their bodies dragged over sharp rocks." John H. Marion, *Notes of Travel Through the Territory of Arizona*, 35.

48. Culver's account.

49. The Chokonens captured this train after the Cochise-Bascom meeting of February 6, when Cochise offered to exchange Wallace for his family. Wallace returned later that evening with a note indicating that Cochise held three other prisoners. Buckley's stagecoach found the bodies in the early morning of the seventh. Buckley's account, Culver's account. The *Sacramento Daily Union* correspondent in Tucson wrote that the train was captured on February 6. *Sacramento Daily Union*, March 4, 1861.

50. Oury's account; *Mesilla Times,* February 21, 1861, quoted in *The Butterfield Overland Mail Across Arizona,* 24.

51. Buckley's account.

52. Robinson's account, 82; Barrett, *Geronimo's Story,* 117.

53. Dan Thrapp to author, March 28, 1985.

54. Bascom's reports; Robinson's account, 83; Culver's account; Buckley's account.

55. Robinson's account, 82.

56. Barrett, *Geronimo's Story,* 117.

57. Robinson's account, 82–83.

58. Ibid.

59. Bascom's reports; AHSH, Folder 364, Prefect of Arispe to Governor, March 9, 1861 Barrett, *Geronimo's Story,* 115–18.

60. Irwin's account.

61. Oury's account.

62. *Estrella de Occidente,* March 1, 1861.

63. Irwin's official report in Sacks, "New Evidence," 264–66.

64. AHSH, Folder 364, Corella to Governor, February 13, 1861.

65. Irwin's account.

66. Moore's report and Bascom's report, both cited in Sacks "New Evidence," 265–67.

67. Bascom's report; Moore's report. Irwin recalled incorrectly that there were six Americans, and Oury said there were three. Robinson remembered "Wallace and others." The official reports of Bascom and Moore seem to be correct. The *Mesilla Times* of February 21, 1861, also reported four victims.

68. In his report, Bascom clearly took responsibility for this decision. Oury, who was present, claimed that the men and soldiers voted unanimously to hang the prisoners. Bascom, however, objected, at which point Lieutenant Moore, the ranking officer, took command and assumed responsibility. Oury's account. Irwin suggests that he proposed the execution, claiming he would hang his three captives even if Bascom refused to execute his. Bascom then relented, probably under pressure from the other officers. The honest Robinson reported that "a council was held by the officers; and at this it was decided that the five [six] captive Apaches should die by hanging." It is interesting to note that the Apaches' version, as given by Betzinez and Mrs. Eve Ball's informants, insist that the whites killed their prisoners before the Apaches tortured theirs. This, of course, was wrong. Geronimo stated correctly that after Bascom refused to trade, "we killed our prisoners, disbanded, and went into hiding in the mountains." Barrett, *Geronimo's Story,* 117.

69. Bascom's reports.

70. Oberly's account.

71. Ibid.

72. *Mesilla Times,* February 21, 1861.

73. Robinson's account, 84; Oury's account.

74. Oberly's account. Cochise seems to have corroborated Oberly when he mentioned this to Arny in 1870. Oberly also claimed that the Indian prisoners' "fate . . . hung on a game of 7-up in which the side for mercy was beaten and the death sentence pronounced." Cochise's wife Dos-teh-seh was the only adult Indian to have witnessed the events and possibly leave behind an eyewitness account. *Santa Fe New Mexican,* November 1, 1870.

75. Moore's report, reprinted in Sacks, "New Evidence," 265.
76. Bascom's reports.
77. *Missouri Republican,* December 27, 1861.

*Chapter 9*

1. *Arizona Miner,* March 20, 1869.
2. *Alta California,* November 14, 1870.
3. RG75, LR, DNM, M234, R557, Arny to Parker, October 24, 1870.
4. Howard, *My Life and Experiences,* 208.
5. RG393, LR, DNM, 71C, 1861, Chapin to AAG, Department of New Mexico, May 18, 1861.
6. *Missouri Republican,* December 27, 1861.
7. Cremony, "Some Savages," 205.
8. Higgins Manuscript.
9. Bell, *New Tracks in North America,* 280.
10. RG393, Letters Sent, Subdistrict of Arizona, Devin to Sherburne, January 25, 1869.
11. Marion, *Notes of Travel,* 35.
12. Wellman, *Indian Wars,* 294.
13. Lockwood, *The Apache Indians,* 107.
14. Robert M. Utley, *A Clash of Cultures: Fort Bowie and the Chiricahua Apaches,* 23.
15. Clum, *Apache Agent,* 39.
16. See, for example, Barrett, *Geronimo's Story,* 118; Betzinez, *I Fought With Geronimo,* 41–42; Ball, *Indeh,* 25; Ball, *In the Days of Victorio,* 155.
17. James L. Collins, born in Kentucky in 1800, came to New Mexico in the mid-1820s and ran a mercantile business in Chihuahua until 1846. With the outbreak of the Mexican War, he relocated to Santa Fe, where he established the *Santa Fe Weekly Gazette,* which he published until 1858. He was appointed superintendent of Indian affairs for the Department of New Mexico by President James Buchanan, a position he held until early 1863. He was robbed and killed in Santa Fe on June 6, 1869. William A. Keleher, *Turmoil in New Mexico, 1846–1868,* 484.
18. RG75, LR, DNM, M234, R550, Collins to Greenwood, February 24, March 3, 1861.
19. RG393, Letters Sent, Department of New Mexico, AAG to Lynde, February 10, 1861.
20. Ibid., AAG to Lynde, February 25, 1861; *Mesilla Times,* March 16, 1861.
21. RG94, Records of the Adjutant General's Office, Loring to Townsend, May 19, 1861.
22. RG393, LR, DNM, 14L, 1861, Lynde to AAG, DNM, March 20, 1861; 18L, 1861, April 10, 1861.
23. Ibid.; RG393, LR, DNM, 7L, 1861, Buckley to Lane, February 16, 1861.
24. Barrett, *Geronimo's Story,* 118.
25. AHSH, Folder 364, Prefect of Arispe to Governor, March 19, 1861, Acuna, *Sonoran Strongman,* 70.
26. AHSH, Folder 364, Corella to Governor, February 13, 1861; Prefect of Arispe to Governor, March 19, 1861.
27. *Mesilla Times,* March 3, 1861.

28. Altshuler, *Latest from Arizona*, 182–83; *Missouri Republican*, December 27, 1861.

29. RG393, LR, DNM, 65C, 1861; Chapin to AAG, DNM, April 25, 1861; 22M, 1861, Morrison to AAG, DNM, February 28, 1861.

30. AHSH, Folder 364, Corella to Governor, May 6, 1861.

31. *Mesilla Times*, May 11, 1861.

32. Thrapp, *Conquest of Apachería*, 19. Hubert Howe Bancroft, *Scraps*, unidentified California newspaper item dated November 1863, copy in Arizona State University Library.

33. Emmie Giddings W. Mahon and Chester V. Kielman, "George H. Giddings and the San Antonio–San Diego Mail Line," *Southwestern Historical Quarterly*, 61 (Summer 1957), 238.

34. *Alta California*, June 22, 1861; *Sacramento Daily Union*, July 15, 1861; RG393, LR, DNM, 70C, 1861, Jones to Grant, May 4, 1861; Bennedict to Grant, May 4, 1861.

35. RG393, LR, DNM, 71C, 1861, Chapin to AAG, Department of New Mexico, May 18, June 3, 1861.

36. RG393, LR, DNM, 83C, 1861, Pesqueira to Chapin, June 5, 1861.

37. AHSH, Folder 364, List of Apaches at Peace, May 15, 1861; García to Governor, May 6, 1861.

38. Galindo, a contemporary of Cochise, was born about 1810. He was a member of the Janeros local group of the Nednhi band and was involved in the Janos peace of 1842–44. He succeeded Láceris as leader of the Janeros local group. Galindo was a major figure in the peace of 1860 at Janos and stayed at Fronteras through the summer of 1861. In late 1861 he and his brother Tonina began raiding in Sonora, primarily the districts of Sahuaripa and Alamos. He passed from the scene shortly thereafter.

39. AHSH, Folder 364, García to Governor, May 19, 1861; Prefect of Arispe to Governor, May 22, 1861.

40. Ibid., Prefect of Arispe to Governor, May 28, 1861.

41. *Missouri Republican*, July 6, 1861.

42. Raphael Pumpelly, *Travels and Adventures of Rafael Pumpelly*, 168.

43. NA, RG123. Pete Kitchen Indian Depredation Claim 6845.

44. RG393, LR, DNM, 81C, 1861, Bascom to Chapin, June 22, 1861; Chapin to AAG, DNM, June 23, 1861; AHS, W. M. Thompson manuscript, "The Fighting Doctor"; AHS, Frank C. Lockwood Collection; Constance Wynn Altshuler, "Arizona in 1861: A Contemporary Account by Samuel Robinson," *Journal of Arizona History*, 25 (Spring 1984), 62–63.

45. RG393, LR, DNM, 81C, 1861, Chapin to AAG, DNM, June 23, 1861.

46. Robert W. Frazer, *Forts of the West*, 4, 6.

47. *Alta California*, September 2, 1861.

48. As quoted in Wagoner, *Early Arizona*, 425.

49. James H. McClintock, *Arizona: Prehistoric, Aboriginal, Pioneer, Modern*, III, 182.

50. Turrill, "A Vanished Race," 20.

51. R. S. Allen, "Pinos Altos, New Mexico," *New Mexico Historical Review*, 23 (October 1948), 302–3.

52. Missouri Historical Society, Webb Collection.

53. Thrapp, *Victorio,* 68–71; RG393, LR, DNM, 35L, 1860, Lynde to AAG, December 18, 1860.

54. RG393, LS, DNM, M1072, R2, Frame 0287, Maury to Lynde, December 30, 1860; LR, DNM, 8L, 1861, Lynde to Maury, February 17, 1861.

55. Tully, born in 1824, was an important merchant in Arizona and New Mexico from the mid-1860s until 1880. Thrapp, *Encyclopedia,* 1445.

56. Steck Collection, Ochoa to Steck, March 26, 1861. Abstract of Provisions Issued.

57. *Missouri Republican,* December 27, 1861.

58. *Mesilla Times,* May 11, 1861.

59. RG75, M234, R550, Tully to Collins, June 2, 1861.

60. RG75, T21, R5, Labadie to Collins, June 2, 1861; *Missouri Republican,* July 6, 1861; *Santa Fe Gazette,* June 15, 1861.

61. *Mesilla Times,* June 15, June 30, 1861; *Missouri Republican,* July 6, 1861; *Estrella Occidente,* July 26, 1861.

62. RG75, M234, R550, Steck to Collins, July 15, 1861.

63. McClintock, *Arizona,* 180–81.

64. RG393, L5, DNM, Carleton to AAG, August 14, 1865.

65. *Santa Fe Gazette,* September 22, 1866; NA, RG393, E3161, Miscellaneous Letters Received, Department of New Mexico.

66. Arizona Historical Society, Diary of George Hand.

67. University of Arizona Library, Special Collections, AZ 300, Thomas Akers Diary.

68. As usual, accounts vary on the number of Indians involved. Billy Fourr estimated their number at 60, definitely too low, while Thomas Farish estimated them at 400 to 500, definitely too high. Mowry and Oury placed them at 200 and 300, respectively, the latter figure about the total number of warriors the two chiefs could have amassed. Two contemporary accounts provide insight. The white men who found the bodies estimated the number of Indians at 100 on the basis of their trail. An escaped Mexican captive claimed that Cochise had 180 fighting men at this time, which was too high for the Chokonens and must have included some Bedonkohes, Nednhis, and Chihennes. Arizona Historical Society, William Fourr manuscript. Farish, *History of Arizona,* II, 59–60. Mowry's account was in the *Arizona Miner,* November 7, 1868; Oury's account appeared in the *Arizona Daily Star,* July 27, 1879. The *San Francisco Evening Bulletin* of September 7, 1861, carried the account of the Americans who found the bodies. Bancroft, *Scraps,* contains the statement made by an escaped Mexican regarding Cochise's warrior strength. Unidentified California newspaper item dated November 1863.

69. *San Francisco Evening Bulletin,* September 7, 1861. *Arizona Daily Star,* July 27, 1879. W. W. Mills, *Forty Years at El Paso, 1848–1898,* 195–96.

70. *San Francisco Evening Bulletin,* September 7, 1861. Tevis, *Arizona in the 50s,* 229–30.

71. Fourr manuscript.

72. *Arizona Daily Star,* July 27, 1879.

73. New Mexico State University Library, Rio Grande Historical Collection, Keith Humphries File.

74. AHSH, Folder 364, Perez to Governor, November 4, 1861.

75. Moses Bradley Carson, born in 1792, was a successful trapper before he moved to New Mexico in 1826 and began a colorful forty-year career in the West. He died in 1868 at Eagle Flat, Texas, a mining camp northeast of El Paso. Thrapp, *Encyclopedia,* 235.

76. The primary source for the Ake party's retreat to New Mexico is *They Die But Once* by James B. O'Neil, in which one of Ake's sons relates his version. Although he claimed that "there were 47 men in the company all told when we pulled out from there (Tucson) seven women and sixteen children" he almost certainly meant forty-seven in all. This would put the number of men at twenty-four, which approximates the recollections of Tom Farrell (nineteen men); Robert Phillips, who recalled there were twenty-five to thirty men and boys; and Mariano Madrid, who said the Indians outnumbered the whites ten to one and he believed there were two hundred Indians in the fight, thereby putting the number of whites at twenty. In a later statement Ake indicated that only eight men escaped unharmed, which, if one takes into account the accepted casualties of four whites killed and five wounded, plus the seven men who bolted at the beginning of the fight, would mean that there were twenty-four men in the fight. James B. O'Neil, *They Die But Once: The Story of a Tejano,* 36–46; RG123, Indian Depredation File 3112, T. J. Cassner, Administrator.

77. O'Neil, *They Die But Once,* 41.

78. Ibid.; RG123, Indian Depredation File 3112.

79. University of Arizona Library, Special Collections, AZ 197, Palmer Manuscript.

80. O'Neil, *They Die But Once,* 41–43; NA, RG123, Indian Depredation File 3112.

81. George Wythe Baylor, *John Robert Baylor, Confederate Governor of Arizona,* 12.

82. W. Hubert Curry, *Sun Rising in the West,* 55.

83. Ibid.; Indian Depredation File 3112.

*Chapter 10*

1. *La Alianza de la Frontera,* October 10, 1861; AHSH, Folder 366, Sánchez to Governor, September 17, 1861.

2. AHSH, Folder 366, Sánchez to Governor, September 17, 1861.

3. Ibid., Folder 364, Perez to Governor, November 4, 1861.

4. Baylor was born in Kentucky on July 20, 1822, moved to Texas in 1840, and became an Indian fighter of some note, participating in several campaigns against the Comanches. In July 1861 he arrived in New Mexico with some four hundred Texas riflemen and by the end of the year was military governor of the territory. He died on February 8, 1894. Baylor, *John Robert Baylor.*

5. Ibid., 32.

6. Hurley is about ten miles southeast of Silver City. Pearce, *New Mexico Place Names,* 73.

7. Curry, *Sun Rising in the West,* 52–53.

8. As usual there is much disagreement about the number of Indians thought to be in the fight. The only contemporary account appeared in the *Mesilla Times* of October 3, 1861, which placed the Apaches at 250 to 300 warriors. One year later, Baylor reported the Indians at 400, while Carleton wrote in 1867 that some 500 Indians were involved. *Mesilla Times,* October 3, 1861; as quoted by James Collins

to W. P. Dole, October 8, 1861, 37 Cong., 2d sess., Pt. I. *Estrella de Occidente,* November 22, 1861, picked up the *Messila Times* account. Baylor's account can be found in *The War of the Rebellion,* 15, Pt. I, Baylor to Magruder, December 29, 1862, 916. *Santa Fe Gazette,* July 27, 1867. Mastin died on October 7, 1861, of blood poisoning. *Mesilla Times,* October 17, 1861.

9. Opler, *Lifeway,* 344-45.

10. Juárez Archives, UTEP, Roll 23, Ruiz to Ochoa, October 3, 1861; AHSH, Folder 364, Perez to Governor, November 4, 1861.

11. AHSH, Folder 364, Perez to Governor, November 4, 1861.

12. Ibid.

13. AHSH, Folder 366, Sánchez to Governor, December 3, 1861; December 16, 1861.

14. *Estrella de Occidente,* March 7, 1862.

15. *Missouri Republican,* November 29, 1861.

16. Charles Harkins, "A Scrap of Frontier History," *Overland Monthly,* 21 (March 1893), 266.

17. NA, RG94, Letters Received, Adjutant General's Office, M944, AGO, 1861, Mowry to Cameron, August 8, 1861.

18. *Santa Fe New Mexican,* June 15, 1866. Bancroft, *Scraps,* 48.

19. NA, RG94, LR, AGO, 1861, Mowry to Barlow, August 2, 1861: *Santa Fe New Mexican,* June 15, 1866.

20. Arizona State University, Tempe, Sylvester Mowry Files, Mowry to Sibley, December 14, 1861; NA, RG123, Indian Depredation File, 3358, Fritz Contzen Claim.

21. Lockwood Collection.

22. Bancroft, *Scraps,* 48.

23. Ibid.; *Estrella de Occidente,* March 7, 1862; J. Ross Browne, *Adventures in the Apache Country,* 201.

24. Hunter, born in Tennessee about 1824, had farmed along the Mimbres before the war. He joined Baylor's force in the summer of 1861 and was elected first lieutenant in Captain George Frazer's company of Arizona Guards. Boyd Finch, "Sherod Hunter and the Confederates in Arizona," *Journal of Arizona History,* 10 (Autumn 1969), 139-206.

25. NA, RG94, M619, R284, Mowry to West, June 28, 1862.

26. Mowry File, Hunter to Mowry, April 11, 1862.

27. Ibid.; Mowry to Editor, *San Francisco Call,* June 28, 1862.

28. Bancroft, *Scraps,* 48.

29. Mendibles, like most escaped prisoners, had an interesting story to tell. A band of White Mountain Apaches captured him in 1857 near San Xavier, Sonora. For the next seven years he lived in the White Mountain region until U.S. troops under Captain John S. Thayer recovered him from the Western Apaches in July 1864. *Alta California,* February 20, 1865; June 5, 1870.

30. Ibid.; *The War of the Rebellion,* (cited hereafter as *WOR Series*), 1, Pt. I, 1095. Edward Palmer, who was well acquainted with the Western Apaches, said Cochise led the Apaches. Palmer Manuscript.

31. Sibley, born in 1816 at Natchitoches, Louisiana, graduated from West Point in 1838 and was commissioned in the Second Dragoons. He fought with honor in the Mexican War and participated in the Mormon expedition of 1857-58 and the Navajo campaign of 1860. He resigned his commission when the Civil War started

and joined the Confederacy. In July 1861 he was appointed commander of the Department of New Mexico. He raised a regiment at San Antonio and marched to El Paso. After several battles with Union troops in New Mexico, Sibley withdrew to Texas in April 1862. He died at Fredericksburg, Virginia, in 1886. *Webster's American Military Biographies*, 388.

32. Baylor, *John R. Baylor,* 14–15; Baylor erred in writing that he followed the Indians to Carretas in Sonora. This hacienda was almost certainly deserted at the time. He meant Corralitos, Chihuahua, where the mines of José María Zuloaga were located. The Mexican account of Baylor's intrusion can be found in AHSH, Folder 378, Moreno to Governor, March 31, 1862.

33. *WOR Series,* 50, Pt. I, Baylor to Helms, March 20, 1862, 942.

34. West, born in New Orleans in 1822, was a captain of mounted volunteers in the Mexican War. He was named lieutenant colonel of the First California Infantry in August 1861 and became a colonel the following June. Like Carleton, he was a controversial figure in the Southwest. After the war he returned to his native state and in 1870 was elected to the U.S. Senate. He died in Washington in 1898. Thrapp, *Encyclopedia,* 1534–35.

35. Aurora Hunt, *Major General James Henry Carleton, 1814–1873, Western Frontier Dragoon,* 220–25.

36. Canby was born in Kentucky in 1817, graduated from West Point in 1839, and joined the Second Infantry. From 1839 to 1842 he fought the Seminoles in Florida. He was promoted to first lieutenant in 1846 and to captain in 1847. He saw extensive action in the Mexican War, receiving a brevet to lieutenant colonel. He participated in the Mormon expedition of 1857–58 and in 1861 was commissioned general of the Department of New Mexico. He was killed in 1873 during a peace conference with Captain Jack, a Modoc Indian leader. Thrapp, *Encyclopedia,* 218–19.

37. *WOR Series,* 50, Pt. I, 120.

38. Hunt, *Carleton,* 226.

39. Bancroft, *Scraps,* 193.

40. Ibid.

41. Ibid.; *WOR Series,* 9, Pt. I, 585–87; 50, Pt. I, 120–22.

42. Bancroft, *Scraps,* 193.

43. *WOR Series,* 50, Pt. I, 120–22.

44. Ibid.

45. Ibid., 128–31.

46. Accounts vary as to the number of Apaches involved. The *Sacramento Union* (August 14, 1862) and the *Santa Fe Gazette* (October 4, 1862) put the number at more than 100. Edward Palmer placed Cochise's strength between 200 and 300 warriors. Two participants, John C. Cremony and Albert J. Fountain, put Apache strength at 700 and 800, respectively, undoubtedly more than double the actual number of Indians involved. As was the case the previous summer, the allied Chiricahuas may have numbered 200 warriors. About a year after the battle at Apache Pass a captive who escaped from Cochise claimed he had mustered a following of 180 warriors, which must have included recruits from the Nednhis, Bedonkohes, and Chihennes. *Sacramento Union,* August 14, 1862; *Santa Fe Gazette,* October 4, 1862; Palmer Manuscript; Cremony, *Life Among the Apaches,* 161–67; Joseph Miller, ed., *Arizona Cavalcade: The Turbulent Times,* 30–35.

47. Ball, *Indeh*, 19–20; Eve Ball, "Cibicu: An Apache Interpretation," in Ray Brandes, ed., *Troopers West: Military and Indian Affairs on the American Frontier*, 123.

48. Miller, *Arizona Cavalcade*, 35.

49. Ball, "Cibicu," 123.

50. According to Lieutenant Fountain, Cochise told him that "you never would have whipped us if you had not shot wagons at us." Miller, *Arizona Cavalcade*, 35. Asa Daklugie told Eve Ball that "after they turned cannon loose on us at Apache Pass . . . my people knew that the Apaches were doomed." Ball, "Cibicu," 123. *Army and Navy Journal*, December 11, 1869, quoted a letter from Tucson which attributed the victory solely to the howitzers. It is interesting that Daklugie seemed to imply that the howitzers were some kind of secret weapon which they had never faced. Cochise had seen its awesome destructive capabilities at Fronteras on several occasions, and just nine months earlier these allied Chiricahuas had faced a cannon at Pinos Altos.

51. Asa Daklugie disputes this, having told Mrs. Ball that "most of the Indians were armed only with bows and arrows." Ball, *Indeh*, 20; Contemporary accounts are conflicting. Eyre, who had met with the Chiricahuas some three weeks before, reported they were well armed with six-shooters and single-barreled shotguns. *WOR Series*, 50, Pt. I, 120–22. The Indians probably had obtained many weapons from their victims and by trading in northern Mexico, but their most significant problem was keeping a dependable supply of ammunition. One year later an escaped captive declared that the Chokonens' ammunition was exhausted. Bancroft, *Scraps*, 48.

52. *WOR Series*, 50, Pt. I, 131; George Hand Diary. Ernest Marchand, ed., *News From Fort Craig, New Mexico, 1863*, 34. Henry P. Walker, "Soldier in the California Column: The Diary of John W. Teal," *Arizona and the West*, 13 (Spring 1971), 40. Konrad F. Schreier, Jr., "The California Column in the Civil War; Hazen's Civil War Diary," *Journal of San Diego History*, 22 (Spring 1976), 45.

53. *WOR Series*, 50, Pt. I, 128.

54. Cremony, *Life Among the Apaches*, 164.

55. Betzinez, *I Fought with Geronimo*, 42; Ball, *In the Days of Victorio*, 47.

56. Dan L. Thrapp, letters to author, December 5, 1975; December 16, 1981.

57. Walker, "Teal's Diary," 41.

58. Ball, *In the Days of Victorio*, 47; Cremony, *Life Among the Apaches*, 160; Ball, *Indeh*, 19–20.

59. Bancroft, *Scraps*, 196.

60. *WOR Series*, 50, Pt. I, 128–29, Pt. II, 40–41; 9, Pt. I, 565.

61. *WOR Series*, 50, Pt. II, 73–74, 146.

62. *Santa Fe Gazette*, October 4, 1862; *WOR Series*, 9, Pt. I, 565. The victims were Thomas Buchanon of Pennsylvania; William Allen of Illinois; Conrad Stark of Ohio; William Smith of Pennsylvania; David Berry of Iowa; James Burnes of Wisconsin; James Ferguson; and two Mexicans from Mesilla.

63. Ibid.; Cremony, *Life among the Apaches*, 174–75.

64. *WOR Series*, 15, 580.

65. Utley, *Frontiersmen in Blue*, 260.

66. AHSH, Folder 376, Prefect of Arispe to Governor, August 19, 1862.

67. Cremony, *Life Among the Apaches*, 176; Ball, *Indeh*, 20.

68. *WOR Series,* 15, 147–48.

69. For good accounts of Mangas's death, see Dan L. Thrapp, *Conquest of Apachería,* 21–23, and *Victorio and the Mimbres Apaches,* 82–84. West's duplistic report is in *WOR Series,* 50, Pt. II, 296–97. A reliable synthesis is Lee Myers, "The Enigma of Mangas Coloradas Death," *New Mexico Historical Review,* 41 (October 1966), 287–304. An eyewitness account can be found in Daniel Ellis Conner, *Joseph Reddeford Walker and the Arizona Adventure,* 34–42.

70. Thrapp, *Victorio,* 83.

71. Barrett, *Geronimo's Story,* 119–21.

*Chapter 11*

1. AHSH, Folder 376, Prefect of Arispe to Governor, August 19, 1862.

2. *La Alianza de la Frontera,* June 26, July 3, 1862. AHSH, Folder 372, García to Governor, July 6, 1862.

3. AHSH, Folder 372, García to Governor, July 31, 1862.

4. *Estrella de Occidente,* August 22, September 5, 1862.

5. Ibid.

6. Acuña, *Sonoran Strongman,* 75–79.

7. AHS, SA, R19, Pesqueira Circular dated January 2, 1863.

8. *Estrella de Occidente,* February 20, 1863.

9. *Uno de Tantos* (Ures), April 9, 1863.

10. *Estrella de Occidente,* April 3, April 10, 1863.

11. *WOR Series,* 50, Pt. II, 121. On September 15, 1862, Fergusson wrote Pesqueira: "I have been informed that several hundreds of Indians have been very lately in Fronteras, Sonora, making preparations for hostilities against the troops, citizens, residents, and travellers of Arizona, and that they even had the effrontery to send a deputation to Your Excellency [Remigio's party], with the hopes of obtaining a treaty of peace, in order that they might with more impunity commit their atrocities in this Territory."

12. RG393, LR, DNM, W120, 1863, Pesqueira to West, March 26, 1863.

13. Diary of John Bourke, entry dated February 3, 1873, copy in AHS.

14. RG393, Unregistered Letters Received, District of Arizona, Hinds to West, October 6, 1862.

15. *Estrella de Occidente,* April 3, April 10, 1863.

16. Seth-mood-a, born in the 1830s, was a son of Mangas Coloradas, hence probably a full brother of Dos-teh-seh. According to Griswold, he was killed in the Pinos Altos Mountains by Mexicans. I think it more probable that he was killed by U.S. troops. Griswold, "Ft. Sill Apaches," 123.

17. Debo, *Geronimo,* 71.

18. Barrett, *Geronimo's Story,* 121.

19. NA, Returns From Military Posts, Fort Bowie, M617, R129, February 1863.

20. NA, RG393, Letters Received, Fort Bowie, Fergusson to Qualey, March 12, 1863.

21. Barrett, *Geronimo's Story,* 123–24.

22. Fort West was established on February 24, 1863, by Captain William McCleave, First California Cavalry. It was on the east side of the Gila River in the Pinos Altos Mountains and was named for Brigadier General Joseph Rodman West.

It was abandoned January 8, 1864. Frazer, *Forts of the West*, 108.

23. RG393, LS, Fort West, Fritz to Bennett, March 26, 1863.

24. LR, DNM, B57, 1863, McCleave to Whitlock, April 8, 1863. *Santa Fe Weekly Gazette*, April 18, April 25, 1863.

25. *WOR Series*, 50, Pt. I, 213, Pt. II, 466.

26. *Estrella de Occidente*, June 12, 1863.

27. Ibid., April 10, April 17, 1863.

28. Ibid., April 17, 1863.

29. Ibid.

30. Bourke Diary, entry dated February 3, 1873.

31. *Estrella de Occidente*, June 12, 1863.

32. The volunteers killed Cojinillín and ten other men near Boca Grande in northwest Chihuahua in early May 1863. M619, R1410, Returns from Military Posts, Fort West, May 1863. *La Alianza de la Frontera*, May 29, June 6, 1863.

33. *La Alianza de la Frontera*, February 20, March 5, 1864.

34. Juh, born in the early 1820s, was undoubtedly one of the leading Nednhi warriors at this time. His Apache name, Tandinbilnojui (He Brings Many Things With Him), indicates his prowess and success as a warrior. According to Asa Daklugie, son of Juh, Cochise and his father were together during the 1860s and early 1870s. Physically, Juh was an atypical Apache, standing about six feet tall and weighing about 225 pounds. He headed the Nednhi band until his death in 1883. Grenville Goodwin, *Western Apache Raiding and Warfare*, 110; Ball, *Indeh*, 22–30. For a good biography of Juh, see Dan L. Thrapp, *Juh: An Incredible Indian*.

35. *Conditions of the Indian Tribes*, 105.

36. *WOR Series*, 50, Pt. II, 466.

37. *Alta California*, July 23, 1863. In late June a force from Fronteras scouted the Huachuca and Dragoon mountains without encountering recent signs of Apaches. *Estrella de Occidente*, July 17, 1863.

38. *Condition of the Indian Tribes*, 119. *Santa Fe New Mexican*, April 14, 1865. *WOR Series*, 50, Pt. II, 490. RG393, LR, DNM, Morrison to AAG, Department of New Mexico, June 24, 1863.

39. *WOR Series*, 50, Pt. II, 490.

40. Ray C. Colton, *The Civil War in the Western Territories*, 131.

41. RG393, District of Arizona, Unregistered Letters Received, Lambert to Captain ?, July 25, 1863.

42. Frazer, *Forts of the West*, 98.

43. *WOR Series*, 50, Pt. II, 571; RG393, LR, Department of New Mexico, West to McCleave, July 27, 1863; West to Whitlock, July 26, 1863.

44. Ibid., Pt. I, 233–34.

45. Ibid., 242; RG393, LR, DNM, S199, 1863, Shirland to West, September 9, 1863.

46. *Estrella de Occidente*, March 4, 1864.

47. Ibid., October 2, 1863; Bancroft, *Scraps*, 48.

48. Bancroft, *Scraps*, 48.

49. *Estrella de Occidente*, December 4, December 11, 1863.

50. Ibid., February 26, 1864.

51. *Santa Fe Gazette*, October 15, 1864.

52. *WOR Series,* 34, Pt. II, 593.

53. *Estrella de Occidente,* February 26, 1864.

54. *WOR Series,* 34, Pt. I, 122–23; University of Texas at El Paso, Carrizal Collection, Roll 8, document dated March 18, 1864.

55. See chapter 4, for an account of this raid.

56. *WOR Series,* 34, Pt. I., 123.

57. RG393, Letters Sent, Fort West, Whitlock to Smith, March 22, 1864.

58. *WOR Series,* 50, Pt. II, 826–29.

59. RG393, Unregistered Letters Received, District of Arizona, Stevens to Smith, May 5, 1864; Bancroft, *Scraps,* 209.

60. Bancroft, *Scraps,* 209. RG94, LR, AGO Main Series, Carleton to AAG, May 25, 1864.

61. *Estrella de Occidente,* June 24, 1864.

62. RG393, Unregistered Letters Received, District of Arizona, Carleton to Davis, April 1, 1864; *Condition of the Indian Tribes,* 172.

68.63. *Condition of the Indian Tribes,* 178.

64. Ibid., 177–78.

65. RG393, Letters Received, Fort Bowie, Carleton to Tidball, June 17, 1864.

66. *Condition of the Indian Tribes,* 178.

67. *Alta California,* March 1, 1864.

68. RG75, Records of Arizona Superintendency of Indian Affairs, M734, R1, McCormick to Poston, March 5, 1864.

69. *WOR Series,* 50, Pt. II, 869–72.

70. *Santa Fe Gazette,* October 15, 1864.

71. This was Caisca, a Chokonen who was on the Fronteras ration rolls of 1861 and 1862 as a member of Elías's and Miguel Yrigóllen's band.

72. *Santa Fe Gazette,* October 15, 1864.

73. RG393, LS, DNM, Carleton to Vickroy, July 3, 1864.

74. *WOR Series,* 41, Pt. I, 125–31.

75. *Estrella de Occidente,* August 19, 1864; January 20, 1865.

76. Ibid., January 13, 1865.

77. Nana, a Chihenne incorrigible from the word go, was born about 1800. His Apache name was Kas-tziden (Broken Foot). He had close ties with the Mescaleros throughout his lifetime, and was said to have been related to Delgadito, who had died recently, and he may have taken over the leadership of that small local group. Nana reportedly had five daughters, who were married to warriors of note, including Riñon, Horache, Vicente (a brother of Geronimo), and a Mescalero chief named Tomaso Palona. One of Nana's wives was a sister of Geronimo. Nana was a leading spirit in the wars of the 1880s. He died in 1896. Griswold, "Ft. Sill Apaches," 110–11; *Indian Raids as Reported in the Silver City Enterprise,* 38. For a good account of Nana's famous raid in 1881, see Stephen H. Lekson, *Nana's Raid: Apache Warfare in Southern New Mexico.*

78. Thrapp has a complete account of the Carleton-Steck fiasco, which eventually ended up being fought in the press by the two Santa Fe newspapers, the *Gazette,* and the *New Mexican.* Thrapp, *Victorio,* 87–91.

79. *Arizona Miner,* November 23, 1864.

80. RG393, LR, DNM, 42B, 1865, Houston to Burkett, March 22, 1865; italics mine.

*Chapter 12*

1. *WOR Series,* 48, Pt. I, 551.
2. John T. Smith came to Arizona with the California Volunteers. Discharged in November 1864, he went to the Santa Rita mines. He had several brisk encounters with Apaches in the late 1860s and early 1870s. Smith died on May 9, 1877, of heart disease. AHS, John T. Smith, Hayden File.
3. Bancroft, *Scraps,* 382.
4. *WOR Series,* 50, Pt. I, 402–3.
5. NA, RG393, E19, LR, District of Arizona, D48, 1865, Davidson to Carleton, February 22, 1865; *WOR Series,* 48, Pt. I, 552.
6. *El Republicano,* May 13, 1865.
7. Ibid.
8. RG393, LR, DNM, 98B, 1865, Davis to Cutler, May 3, 1865.
9. Opler, *Apache Lifeway,* 333–34.
10. *El Republicano,* May 13, June 3, 1865.
11. Ibid.
12. Irvin McDowell was born in Columbus, Ohio, in 1818, graduated from West Point in 1838, and was promoted to first lieutenant in 1842. Throughout the Mexican War he was an aide to General John E. Wool. In May 1861 he was promoted to brigadier general and in July of that year commanded Union troops in the First Battle of Bull Run, in which the North was soundly defeated. Charges were made against him but later were dropped. He also served in the Second Battle of Bull Run, though in a subordinate role. He was named commander of the Department of the Pacific in July 1864 and one year later became commander of the Department of California. He died in San Francisco in 1885. *Webster's Military Biographies,* 263.
13. Mason, born in Ohio in 1824, graduated from West Point in 1847. During the 1850s he served primarily in California, in 1862 becoming brigadier general of the California Volunteers. He died in Washington, D.C., on November 29, 1897. Constance Wynn Altshuler, *Chains of Command,* 258.
14. Altshuler, *Chains of Command,* 39–40; *Report of the Secretary of War,* 1866, 96–98.
15. RG75, M234, R3, Davidson to Dole, August 12, 1865; Altshuler, *Chains of Command,* 39–42; Hubert Howe Bancroft, *History of Arizona and New Mexico,* 555–56.
16. *WOR Series,* 50, Pt. II, 1247, 1263.
17. Ibid.
18. Miscellaneous Post Orders, Fort Bowie, 1865, in Fort Bowie files.
19. *WOR Series,* 50, Pt. I, 415–19.
20. Goodwin, *The Social Organization of the Western Apache,* 413.
21. *Alta California,* August 11, 1865; AHS, Hiram Storrs Washburn, Hayden File. Amelia Naiche, granddaughter of Cochise, told me a story in the presence of Mrs. Eve Ball that Cochise found a little white boy hidden under a wagon and put him on the back of his horse. Cochise then cared for the boy and reared him until, according to legend, he was released near Fort Apache. One wonders whether her story is connected with the July 1865 massacre at the Cienega. Interview with Eve Ball and Amelia Naiche, January 17, 1979.

22. RG393, LS, Fort Bowie, Merriam to Green, July 14, 1865.

23. RG393, E20, District of Arizona, 1862–70, Unregistered Letters and Orders Received, 1862–71, Higgins to Mason, August 1 [?], 1865.

24. This was Marcial Gallegos, who was captured by the Pinal band of the Western Apaches about 1843 and lived among them fourteen years, during which time he rose to prominence as a war leader. He left the Apaches in July 1857 after difficulty with a Pinal chief, returned to his family at San Ignacio, Sonora, and served as a scout for the United States Army against the Apaches. SA, R19, Aquilar to Governor, July 11, 1857.

25. RG393, E20, District of Arizona, Unregistered Letters, Higgins to Mason, July ?, 1865; Higgins Manuscript.

26. Born in Vermont in 1820, Washburn came to Arizona as a surveyor in 1857. After the volunteers were discharged, he moved to Washington, where he worked for the government for the rest of his life. Washburn, Hayden File.

27. Fort Mason, established August 21, 1865, at Calabasas on the Santa Cruz River, was named for Brigadier General John S. Mason. The Tubac post was abandoned and the garrison was relocated here. On September 6 it was renamed Camp McKee and abandoned on October 1, 1866, because of its unhealthy location. Frazer, *Forts of the West*, 11.

28. Arizona State Library, Territorial Records of Arizona, Military–Indian Affairs, voucher payable to Manuel Gallegos; Thrapp, *Apachería*, 34.

29. AHS, Washburn, Hayden File.

30. Palmer Manuscript, Pt. 2.

31. Washburn, Hayden File.

32. *Missouri Republican,* December 20, 1865.

33. Washburn, Hayden File.

34. Ibid.

35. Cornelius C. Smith, "Some Unpublished History of the Southwest," *Arizona Historical Review,* 5 (October 1932), 6 (January 1935), 45–64.

36. Territorial Records of Arizona, Washburn to Governor, October 5, October 9, 1865.

37. Smith, "Some Unpublished History of the Southwest" (6 January 1935), 49–53. M617, R129, Post Returns, Fort Bowie, October and November 1865.

38. Ibid.

39. RG393, LS, Fort Bowie, Gorman to Green, November 9, 1865; RG75, M234, R3, clipping from unidentified newspaper about Gorman's attack.

40. *Alta California,* December 31, 1865.

41. RG393, E29, Book of Scouts, District of Arizona, Codington to Lewis, February 11, 1866.

42. McDowell to Adjutant General, Washington, March 23, 1866, quoted in Pinckney Tully's Indian Depredation File 1515, RG123.

43. RG75, M234, R3, Pollock to Mason, November 11, 1865; RG393, E29, Book of Scouts, District of Arizona, Pollock to AAG, Subdistrict of the Gila, December 14, 1865.

44. *Missouri Republican,* February 24, 1866. AHS, Charles T. Connell manuscript titled "The Apaches Past and Present," chap. 14.

45. Frazer, *Forts of the West,* 102. RG393, Department of Missouri, Letters Received, 131W, 1866, Willis to De Forest, February 16, 1866; Brigadier General

Richard H. Orton, *Records of California Men in the War of the Rebellion, 1861 to 1867*, 78. In a letter to the author, Dan L. Thrapp suggests that "probably Juh led them, since Janos was largely [his] town, although Cochise was often there." Letter dated October 1, 1979.

46. Washburn's command in particular. See Thrapp, *Apachería*, 33–38; Altshuler, *Chains of Command*, 50–51, 53–55.

47. *Alta California*, May 6, 1866.

48. Ibid.

49. Halleck was born in New York State in 1815 and graduated from West Point in 1839. He resigned in 1854 and opened a law practice in San Francisco, becoming one of the most successful businessmen in California. In August 1861 he was commissioned a major general in the army and commanded the Department of Missouri in 1862. He displayed excellent administrative skills during the war, and these overshadowed his lack of military strategy. He commanded the Military Division of the Pacific from August 1865 to March 1869 before being transferred to the Division of the South. He died in Louisville, Kentucky, on January 9, 1872. *Webster American Military Biographies*, 158–59.

50. RG393, E19, LR, District of Arizona, Halleck to Scott, January 25, 1866.

51. RG393, E731, LR, Southern Subdistrict of the Gila, Pollock to Winchell, December 14, 1865.

52. Ogle, *Federal Control of the Western Apaches*, 60.

53. James M. Barney, *Forgotten Heroes of the Apache Wars*, 8–9. RG123, Indian Depredation File 9192, Thomas Yerkes File; AHS, Charles Shibell, Hayden File. Granger, *Arizona Place Names*, 317.

54. *Arizona Miner*, May 23, 1866; Report of the Secretary of the Interior, 39th Cong., 2d sess., House Ex. Doc. 1, Series II, 111–13.

55. AHS, Charles M. Wood Collection, interview with Henry I. Yohn, December 17, 1925; RG393, LS, Camp Wallen, Brown to Commander, Southern Subdistrict of the Gila, June 10, 1866; Spring, *Spring's Arizona*, 57–59; RG94, LR, AGO, R539, 1867, Report of Inspection by Major and Assistant Inspector General Roger Jones, May 18, 1867 (copy in AHS).

56. RG393, E29, Book of Scouts, District of Arizona, Dunkelberger to AAAG, Tucson, July 1, 1866.

57. Spring, *Spring's Arizona*, 55.

58. RG393, LS, Camp Wallen, Brown to Commander, Southern Subdistrict of the Gila, June 10, 1866.

59. Altshuler, *Chains of Command*, 61; Bancroft, *History of Arizona and New Mexico*, 556.

60. NA, RG59, M184, R2, Dispatches from U.S. Consulates in Ciudad Juárez, Pierson to U.S. Consulate, June 17, 1872.

61. AHSH, Folder 397, Toyos to Governor, October 13, 1867.

62. AHSH, Folder 390, Luna to Governor, September 12, 1866; Folder 391, Toyos to Governor, October 23, 1866. In February 1869, Cochise admitted that he had been wounded in the neck at Fronteras a few years earlier. This may have been the raid. *Arizona Miner*, March 20, 1869.

63. *El Boletin de Chihuahua*, September 15, 1866.

64. *La República*, February 22, 1867. The Apache prisoners told their captors this was the camp of Cusi, in all likelihood a corruption of the name *Cuchis*. Since

this Indian was later referred to as a *cabecilla* (big chief) instead of a *capitancillo* (little chief), plus the fact that he was known to have been in the area, I have concluded that this was probably Cochise's camp.

*Chapter 13*

1. *Army and Navy Journal,* December 11, 1869.
2. AHSH, Folder 397, Montana to Governor, February 12, 1867.
3. Ibid.; *Estrella de Occidente,* February 22, 1867.
4. RG393, LR, Fort Bowie, Eschenburg to AAAG, Tucson, February 28, 1867; *Santa Fe Gazette,* March 16, 1867.
5. RG393, LR, Subdistrict of Tucson, Brown to Toby, March 6, 1867; *Arizona Miner,* April 6, 1867; *Santa Fe New Mexican,* May 4, 1867; *Alta California,* October 22, 1873; RG123, Indian Depredation Files, Oscar Buckalew, File 8770, Thomas Yerkes File 9192.
6. *Estrella de Occidente,* March 8, 1867.
7. The son of U.S. Senator John J. Crittenden, Thomas Leonidas Crittenden was born in 1815 at Russellville, Kentucky, and fought in the Civil War on the Union side. On April 5, 1867, he succeeded Colonel Charles S. Lovell as commander of the Subdistrict of Tucson. Altshuler, *Chains of Command,* 73, 244.
8. AHS, Inspection Report of General Charles A. Whittier at Fort Bowie, February 27, 1866.
9. RG393, M617, R129, Post Returns, Fort Bowie, 1867–68.
10. *La República,* April 12, 1867; *Estrella de Occidente,* May 3, 1867.
11. *Estrella de Occidente,* June 21, 1867.
12. RG393, LR, Subdistrict of Tucson, Brown to AAAG, Subdistrict of Tucson, May 10, 1867.
13. RG393, LS, Subdistrict of Tucson, Crittenden to AAG, Department of California, May 8, 1867.
14. RG393, LR, Subdistrict of Tucson, McGarry to Ripley, June 16, 1867; 40th Cong., 2d sess., House Ex. Doc. 1324; Wood Collection; Spring, *Spring's Arizona,* 97–102; Floyd, *Chronological List of Actions,* 28. There is discrepancy as to the number of casualties. Spring did not recall any Indian fatalities. Floyd states that three Indians were killed and six captured. Opler may have heard the Chiricahua version, which admitted to two dead. Opler, *Lifeway,* 254.
15. 40th Cong., 2d sess., House Ex. Doc. 1324.
16. RG393, LS, Subdistrict of Tucson, Crittenden to McGarry, July 8, 1867; Crittenden to Ilges, July 11, 1867.
17. *Army and Navy Journal,* September 28, 1867.
18. *Estrella de Occidente,* July 19, 1867.
19. Ibid., August 16, August 30, 1867.
20. AHSH, Folder 397, Gallego to Governor, August 10, 1867; *Estrella de Occidente,* August 16, 23, 30, 1867; *Alta California,* October 28, 1867.
21. AHSH, Folder 397, Toyos to Governor, October 1, 1867.
22. Ibid.
23. RG393, LR, Department of Missouri, 15N, 1869, Russell to Post Adjutant, Fort Selden, December 10, 1868. Several complaints of this type were made by American officers. Brigadier General Edward Ord wrote Colonel George Washington Getty that at Janos, Apaches from Arizona traded powder, lead, and arms and

disposed of plunder obtained in Arizona. LR, DNM, M1088, R11, Ord to Getty, February 25, 1870.

24. RG393, LS, Fort Bowie, Hubbard to AAG, Department of California, November 8, 1867; Bell, *New Tracks in North America,* 282–85; Thomas Thompson Hunter, "Early Days in Arizona," *Arizona Historical Review,* 3 (April 1930), 105.

25. RG393, Fort Bowie, Pollock to Wright, December 17, 1867.

26. *La República,* April 17, 1868.

27. Ibid., March 13, 1868.

28. RG393, LS, Fort Bowie, Ripley to Wright, May 13, 1868.

29. Fort Bowie File, Shackleford Diary.

30. RG393, LS, Fort Bowie, Ripley to Commanding Officer, Ford Goodwin; May 28, 1868; Ripley to AAAG, District of Arizona, June 3, 1868; RG393, LR, Fort Bowie, Hubbard to Ripley, June 3, 1868; *Santa Fe Gazette,* June 20, August 1, 1868; *Alta California,* August 5, 1868; AHS, William Henry Larrabee File.

31. *El Republicano,* August 14, 1868; *Estrella de Occidente,* March 27, April 25, May 1, 1868.

32. RG393, LS, Fort McRae, Gilmore to AAAG, District of New Mexico, August 15, 1868.

33. RG393, LS, Fort Cummings, Moore to AAAG, District of New Mexico, September 4, 1868. These captured children were not Chihennes (Eastern Chiricahuas) because the following autumn (1869), Lieutenant Drew tried to return the prisoners to Victorio and Loco but no one knew who they were. One of them, later named Apache John, was adopted by William F. M. Arny, who claimed the Indian belonged to Cochise's band. Perhaps he discerned this after meeting Cochise in October 1870. Apache John died in December 1872 at Santa Fe. *Santa Fe New Mexican,* December 11, 1872.

34. Acuña, *Sonoran Strongman,* 100–101.

35. *Estrella de Occidente,* November 6, 1868.

36. Ibid., December 4, 1868.

37. *La República,* December 11, 1868.

38. *Arizona Miner,* March 20, 1869.

39. Devin, born in New York in 1822, served with distinction in the Civil War as a lieutenant colonel, Sixth New York Cavalry. He was appointed to the Eighth Cavalry on recommendation from Grant and Sheridan. He became involved with Cochise in New Mexico in 1872. Devin died in 1878. Thrapp, *Encyclopedia,* 400.

40. RG393, LS, Subdistrict of Tucson, Devin to Perry, December [?], 1868.

41. *Arizona Miner,* November 11, 1868.

42. AHS, Albert F. Banta File.

43. RG393, LS, Subdistrict of Tucson, Winters to Commanding Officer, Fort Goodwin, December 20, 1868.

44. RG393, LS, Subdistrict of Tucson, Devin to Perry, December ?, 1868.

45. *Arizona Miner,* January 30, 1869.

46. RG393, E13, LS, District of Arizona, Devin to Sherburne, January 25, 1869.

*Chapter 14*

1. LR, AGO, Main Series, M619, R737, 768P, 1869, Devin to Jones, August 26, 1869.

2. *Arizona Miner,* March 20, 1869. Many of Arizona's records from the days before it became a military department in 1870 were destroyed in the San Francisco earthquake of 1906.

3. Ibid.

4. This was probably a small patrol from Camp Wallen under Lieutenant William McK. Owen, who destroyed a deserted ranchería of twelve wickiups somewhere in the Dragoons about January 31, 1869. Post Returns, Camp Wallen, M617, R1348, January and February 1869.

5. *Arizona Miner,* March 20, 1869.

6. Ibid., March 6, 1869.

7. *San Francisco Daily Morning Call,* October 9, 1869.

8. Robert M. Utley, *Frontier Regulars: The United States Army and the Indians, 1866–1891,* 46–49.

9. RG393, LS, Camp Crittenden, Downey to Andrews, September 10, 1869; RG75, M734, R3, Downey to Andrews, September 10, 1869.

10. Samuel H. Drachman, "Arizona Pioneers and Apaches," *Arizona Graphics,* 1 (November 18, 1899), 7.

11. RG123, Thomas Yerkes Depredation File 9192.

12. Smith, Hayden File. *Weekly Arizonian,* April 24, 1869. Floyd, *Chronological List of Actions,* 39, places the fight on April 20, 1869, reporting one soldier killed.

13. RG75, M734, R8, Dent to Taylor, May 31, 1869.

14. RG393, LS, Camp Crittenden Whipple to Veil, June 11, 1869; *Weekly Arizonian,* June 19, July 17, 1869.

15. *Santa Fe New Mexican,* July 20, 1869.

16. *La Estrella de Occidente,* August 6 and 13, 1869.

17. Ibid.

18. *La República,* October 22, 1869.

19. Ibid.

20. *Estrella de Occidente,* October 1, 1869.

21. RG393, LS, Camp Grant, Green to AAG, District of Arizona, RG393, LR, Subdistrict of Tucson, Clendenin to Devin, February 24, 1870.

22. Stone, born in New York State in 1836, came to New Mexico in 1863 and served as a deputy U.S. marshal. In the late 1860s he developed the Apache Pass Mining Company. Thrapp, *Encyclopedia,* 1373–74. "Colonel John Finkle Stone and the Apache Pass Mining Company," *Arizona Historical Review,* 6 (July 1935), 74–80.

23. "Stone and the Apache Pass Mining Company," 77; LS, Subdistrict of the Gila, Devin to Sherburne, October 11, 1869.

24. *Army and Navy Journal,* December 11, 1869; LR, AGO, M619, R737, Winters to Devin, October 7, 1869; RG393, LS, Subdistrict of Southern Arizona, Devin to Sherburne, October 11, 1869; *San Francisco Daily Morning Call,* November 5, 1869; RG75, M234, R3, Andrew to Parker, November 9, 1869; RG123 Indian Depredation File Number 6875, William Eastwood File.

25. RG393, LS, Subdistrict of Tucson, Devin to Sherburne, October 11, 1869.

26. LR, AGO, M619, R737, Winters to Devin, 1 A.M. October 7, 1869.

27. Ibid., Winters to Bernard, 9 A.M., October 7, 1869.

28. Ibid., Winters to Devin, October 10, 1869; Grijalva, Hayden File.

29. LR, AGO, M619, R737, Winters to Devin, October 10, 1869; *Arizona Miner,* November 6, 1869.

30. *Arizona Miner,* November 20, 1869.

31. Frank D. Reeve, "Frederick E. Phelps: A Soldier's Memoirs," New Mexico Historical Review, 25 (April 1950), 118.

32. LR, AGO, M619, R737, Bernard to Devin, October 22, 1869.

33. RG393, LR, Fort Bowie, Putnam to Dunn, October 28, 1869.

34. LR, AGO, M619, R737, Bernard to Devin, November 2, 1869.

35. Ibid.; L. L. Dorr, "The Fight at Chiricahua Pass in 1869," *Arizona and the West,* 13 (Winter 1971), 377.

36. LR, AGO, M619, R737, Bernard to Devin, November 14, 1869.

37. Dan L. Thrapp, letter to author, March 28, 1985.

38. Dorr, "The Fight at Chiricahua Pass," 377; Sladen, "Making Peace," 34.

39. RG393, LS, Subdistrict of Southern Arizona, Devin to Putnam, October 22, 1869.

40. RG75, M234, R557, Shorkley to AAAG, District of New Mexico, December 25, 1869; Drew to Clinton, January 5, 1870. RG393, Green to AAAG, Department of California, December 6, 1869, copy in AHS.

41. RG393, LS, Fort Bowie, Bernard to Dunn, February 1, 1870.

42. RG393, LS, Fort Bowie, Dunn to Clendenin, January 4, 1870; RG393, LR, Subdistrict of Tucson, Clendenin to Devin, January 15, 1870; LS, Subdistrict of Southern Arizona, Devin to Clendenin, January 7, 1870.

43. Chackone, or Chacone, had been at Janos in 1843–44 and was with the hostile Chokonens under Miguel Narbona and Teboca in late 1850 and early 1851. He probably participated in the Pozo Hediondo fight. He died sometime in the 1870s.

44. RG363, LS, Fort Bowie, Bernard to Dunn, February 1, 1870.

45. RG123, Indian Depredation Files, Thomas Gardner File 8689.

46. *Alta California,* April 4, 1870.

47. *La República,* April 29, 1870.

48. *Estrella de Occidente,* May 13, June 18, 1870.

49. *Weekly Arizonian,* June 11, June 18, 1870; AHS, Thomas Gardner, Hayden File.

50. AHSH, File 434, Morales to Governor, July 15, 1870; *Weekly Arizonian,* July 23, 1870.

51. *Weekly Arizonian,* July 23, August 6, August 27, 1870.

52. Ibid., August 13, 1870.

53. RG75, M234, R4, Green to AAG, Department of Arizona, August 13, 1870.

*Chapter 15*

1. *Weekly Arizonian,* September 17, 1870.

2. *Alta California,* November 14, 1870.

3. Ibid.

4. Marion, *Notes of Travel,* 31–32.

5. *Arizona Citizen,* June 17, 1871.

6. Ibid., April 22, 1871.

7. George Stoneman was born on August 8, 1822, in Busti, New York. Graduating from West Point in 1846, he was commissioned in the First Dragoons and served as quartermaster with Cooke's Mormon Battalion. In 1855 he was promoted

to captain and in 1861 to major. During the Civil War, he earned several brevets and in July 1866 was promoted to colonel. He retired in August 1871 and served as governor of California from 1883 to 1887. He died in Buffalo, New York, on September 5, 1894. *Webster American Military Biographies,* 417–18. Heitman, *Historical Register,* I, 930.

8. RG94, LR, AGO, P734, 1870, filed with A551, Stoneman to AAG, Division of the Pacific, November 24, 1870.

9. Ibid.

10. RG94, LR, AGO, P801, 1871; Stoneman to AGO, Washington, February 17, 1871.

11. *Arizona Citizen,* May 6, 1871.

12. Ibid., May 13, 1871.

13. *Army and Navy Journal,* May 27, 1871.

14. *Alta California,* September 28, 1870.

15. Ibid., October 13, November 10, November 14, 1870.

16. Loco, born in the early 1820s, headed a local group of Chihennes. He was peacefully inclined, while his Chihenne contemporary Victorio was more militant. He lost an eye as a young man when he was attacked by a grizzly. I have not found any reference to Loco prior to 1868. He was considered to be a kind and friendly man respected by whites and Indians. He figured prominently in the affairs of the 1870s and 1880s and died in 1905 at Fort Sill, Oklahoma. See Thrapp, *Conquest of Apachería,* 231–50. Thrapp, *Victorio,* contains much information relative to Loco's life, and Ball, *Indeh,* 38–42, contains the Apache recollection of Loco. See also Griswold, "Ft. Sill Apaches," 87.

17. Salvadora was a son of Mangas Coloradas, hence a brother-in-law of Cochise. Born about 1830, he first came into the picture near Janos in 1854 when he and other Apaches attacked a wagon train in the Enmedio Mountains and afterward skirmished with Mexican troops. He was a voice in the ill-fated peace parleys in early 1865. The next year, he and Victorio led a war party of 125 Chihennes against Pinos Altos. By late 1868 he and Victorio were reported to be the leaders of the Chihennes. In the fall of 1870 he left Cañada Alamosa with Cochise and in early 1871 was killed in a battle with Americans in the rugged Mogollon mountain region. JA, R34, Padilla to Governor, February 23, 1854; *Santa Fe Gazette,* June 23, 1866; RG393, LR, DNM, 41S, 1865, Cook to Shaw, January 17, 1865, and 98D, 1865, Davis to Cutler, May 3, 1865; *Las Cruces Borderer,* April 13, 1871.

18. Thrapp, *Victorio,* 98.

19. Charles Edward Drew, a native of New Hampshire, was born in 1840. He enlisted in 1861 and became a lieutenant in the Twenty-sixth Massachusetts Infantry on September 23, 1861. In 1866 he transferred to the Regular Army and on July 20, 1869 was appointed agent for the Southern Apaches. Thrapp, *Victorio,* 342.

20. RG393, LS, Fort McRae, Gilmore to AAG, District of New Mexico, August 12, 1869.

21. RG75, M234, R556, Drew to Parker, September 3, 1869.

22. Thrapp, *Victorio,* 98.

23. RG75, M234, R557, Drew to Clinton, January 5, 1870.

24. Brevoort, born in Michigan in 1822, had been in New Mexico since the mid-1850s. He was at Fort Buchanan in 1857 as post sutler and was said to have been well acquainted with the Apaches. Thrapp, *Victorio,* 344; *Alta California,* October 15, 1857.

25. Thrapp, *Victorio*, 104–8.

26. RG75, M234, R557, "Traders with Gila Apache Indian License"; RG75, Miscellaneous Division, Traders' Licenses.

27. Thrapp, *Victorio*, 104–8.

28. Howard, *My Life and Experiences*, 187–88.

29. Farish, *History of Arizona*, II, 228; C. L. Sonnichsen, "Who Was Tom Jeffords?" *Journal of Arizona History*, 23 (Winter 1982), 388; RG123, Indian Depredation Files, Tom Jeffords File 9695. In testimony dated February 25, 1895, Jeffords said he came to Tucson in July 1862.

30. *Santa Fe New Mexican*, July 28, November 10, 1868. Alice Rollins Crane's article on Jeffords appeared in an unidentified Los Angeles newspaper. Copy in Huntington Library, San Marino, California.

31. RG75, M234, R557, Clinton to Parker, no date, probably April 1870.

32. Sonnichsen, "Who Was Tom Jeffords?" 382–83. AHS, "The Story of S. W. Grant."

33. Robert H. Forbes's account of his conversation with Jeffords was published in the *Journal of Arizona History*, 7 (Summer 1966), 87–88.

34. Farish, *History of Arizona*, II, 228–29. Actually Parker was the commissioner of Indian affairs, who reported to the secretary of the interior.

35. RG75, T21, R15, Piper to Pope, February 7, 1871.

36. *Arizona Citizen*, December 7, 1872.

37. Fred Hughes Collection.

38. Farish, *History of Arizona*, II, 228–29.

39. Forbes, letter to *Journal of Arizona History*, 87–88.

40. RG75, T21, R15, Piper to Pope, February 7, 1871.

41. Turrill, "A Vanished Race," 16–17; *Arizona Citizen*, December 7, 1872.

42. Lockwood, *The Apache Indians*, 112.

43. See chapter 13 for an account of this incident.

44. Ball, *Indeh*, 27–28.

45. Opler to author, August 29, 1979.

46. Henry Stuart Turrill, an assistant surgeon in the U.S. Army, claimed to have seen Jeffords trading contraband to the Apaches. According to Turrill, he "came upon Captain Jeffords with a half dozen of the most villainous-looking individuals. . . . They were arranging a lot of packs of powder and lead for transportation to the mountains." Turrill's account is unreliable at times and was written in 1907, thirty-five years after the alleged incident. "A Vanished Race," 16–17.

47. Major William Redwood Price, angry because the Chihennes from New Mexico were receiving shelter at Jeffords's Chiricahua reservation in Arizona, wrote that "I have witnesses here [Fort Tularosa] who will testify that Jeffords, the agent there, was a trader among them for several years before he was made their agent trading powder, lead and caps for their stolen stock." At district headquarters in Santa Fe, Colonel John Irvin Gregg endorsed Price's allegations, stating that information of a "similar character regarding Mr. Jeffords was received by Colonel Granger at the interview with Cochise in March, 1872." M666, R123, Price to AAG, District of New Mexico, August 1, 1873.

48. Dan L. Thrapp, letter to author, April 9, 1978.

49. Hennisee was born January 16, 1839, in Maryland. He fought in the Civil War for the First Eastern Shore, Maryland Infantry, and in 1867 joined the Regular Army. Thrapp, *Victorio*, 345.

50. RG75, T21, R11, Cady to Clinton, August 22, 1870; Hennisee to Clinton, August 31, 1870.

51. For a biography of Arny, see Lawrence R. Murphy, *Frontier Crusader— William F. M. Arny.*

52. RG75, T21, R12, Hennisee to Clinton, October 31, 1870.

53. RG75, M234, R557, Arny to Parker, October 24, 1870. Arny was clearly confused in making this statement, perhaps because Cochise had just been at Camp Thomas, the White Mountain Apaches' reservation. Cochise, of course, represented the Chiricahuas, whom Arny referred to as the Chillicorias.

54. Patterson, an able and conscientious interpreter, came to New Mexico in 1862 with the California Volunteers. At the end of his enlistment he settled at Cañada Alamosa, where he became acquainted with the Chiricahuas. Darlis M. Miller, *The California Column in New Mexico,* 64–65.

55. RG75, T21, R12, Hennisee to Clinton, October 31, 1870, Appendix A, Council held with Arny and Cochise.

56. Ibid.; RG75, M234, R557, Arny to Parker, October 24, 1870.

57. RG75, M234, R557, Arny to Parker, November 8, 1870.

58. Second Lieutenant Leverett Hull Walker was directed by Special Order No. 106, Headquarters Fort Craig, dated November 13, 1871, to "investigate the title" of two mules which were once in Jeffords's possession. By the time Walker reached Cañada Alamosa, he found the mules owned by a man named Arden, who had bought them from Jeffords. Walker investigated and concluded that Jeffords had traded whiskey to the Apaches for one mule in October 1870. He obtained the second from Apaches about March 1871. The Indians had stolen it in July 1870 from Mesilla. LR, District of New Mexico, M1088, R12, I82, 1871, Stafford to AAG District of New Mexico, November 17, 1871.

59. RG393, LS, Fort Bowie, Bernard to Stone, November 23, 1870.

60. Ibid., Bernard to Commanding Officer, Fort McRae, November 25, 1870.

61. RG393, LS, Fort McRae, Shorkley to Bernard, December 2, 1870.

62. RG75, T21, R12, Hennisee to Pope, November 30, 1870.

63. RG75, T21, R29, Pope to Parker, December 12, 1870.

64. RG75, T21, R12, Hennisee to Pope, December 8, 1870.

65. Piper hailed from Macomb, Illinois, and held a variety of civic positions throughout his life but was not suited to be an Indian agent. His appointment was sponsored by the Presbyterian Board of Foreign Missions. Thrapp, *Victorio,* 346.

66. Fred Hughes Collection.

67. RG75, T21, R12, Piper to Pope, December 31, 1870.

68. Ibid., December 16, 1870.

69. Ibid., December 31, 1870.

70. Ibid., January 26, 1871.

71. Ibid., January 31, 1871.

*Chapter 16*

1. *Las Cruces Borderer,* November 1, 1871.

2. RG393, LS, Fort Bowie, Russell to Stone, December 21, 1870.

3. *Alta California,* February 4, 1871.

4. RG393, LS, Fort Bowie, Bernard to Stone, January 24, 1871. Whether Cochise was present at this skirmish is not known. Bernard assumed that he was be-

cause he had no way of knowing that Juh's and Geronimo's Nednhis, who lived in the Chiricahuas at times, were distinct from Cochise's Chokonens.

5. *Alta California,* April 8, 1871; *Las Cruces Borderer,* April 27, 1871; RG393, LS, Department of Missouri, Kelly to Post Adjutant, Camp Bayard, February 19, 1871. Geronimo recalled that U.S. troops attacked his band, killing sixteen individuals and capturing his entire camp. Afterward he moved to New Mexico and joined Victorio's people before returning to Arizona and the Chiricahua Reservation. Barrett, *Geronimo's Story,* 124–26.

6. *Las Cruces Borderer,* March 16, 1871.

7. Ibid., *Alta California,* April 8, 1871.

8. RG75, T21, R15, Piper to Pope, March 31, 1871.

9. *Las Cruces Borderer,* April 13, 1871; RG393, Book of Scouts, 1869–94, Fort Bowie, Russell to Evans, March 25, 1871.

10. Thirty-five Chiricahua Apaches attacked an American group known as the Charles Keerle party on the morning of March 4, 1871, at Chocolate Pass, midway between Casas Grandes and Galeana. There were about eight Americans, including Keerle's wife. All were killed except one man, who managed to escape to Galeana and raise the alarm. Keerle was transporting a load of bacon from Chihuahua to Fort Bayard. The bodies "were horribly mutilated—the hands cut off and placed besides the bodies" and both Keerle and his wife were beheaded. Among the Americans murdered were Gus Hepner, Thomas Sunderland, and Charles Delard. *Las Cruces Borderer,* March 16, April 13, 1871; *Missouri Republican,* March 24, 1871.

11. *Las Cruces Borderer,* April 13, 1871; RG393, LR, Fort Bowie, 1862–71, Russell to Evans, April 4, 1871.

12. RG75, M234, R558, Pope to Parker, March 18, 1871; Piper to Pope, March 18, 1871.

13. RG75, T21, R13, Parker to Pope, March 18, 1871.

14. RG75, M234, R558, Pope to Parker, April 6, 1871.

15. RG75, T21, R15, Piper to Pope, February 7, 1871.

16. José María Trujillo was born in Carrizal, Chihuahua, in 1819 or 1820. He became a soldier at Janos, achieving a fine record, in the 1840s and 1850s before relocating in New Mexico. He became well acquainted with the hostile Chiricahuas while living at Janos. Trujillo was the justice of the peace at Cañada Alamosa in the early 1870s. JA, R30, R33, Record of Enlistments.

17. RG75, T21, R15, Piper to Pope, April 30, 1871; RG75, M234, R558, Pope to Parker, April 21(?), 1871.

18. *Las Cruces Borderer,* April 27, May 4, 1871; *Weekly Arizonian,* April 15, April 22, 1871.

19. RG393, LS, Fort Bowie, Evans to Russell, April 23, 1871; RG393, Book of Scouts, Fort Bowie, 1869–94, Russell to Evans, May 5, 1871. LS, Fort Bowie, Evans to Commissary General of Subsistence, August 14, 1871; *Las Cruces Borderer,* December 13, 1871.

20. Ibid.

21. *Estrella de Occidente,* May 19, 1871.

22. Ibid.

23. On April 30, 1871, an Anglo-Mexican-Papago party of 140 men led by William S. Oury attacked a band of Western Apaches ostensibly living at peace

near Camp Grant. Some of the raids into southern Arizona were blamed on these Apaches, many the work of other bands, of which the Chiricahuas were probably most accountable. Oury's party massacred over 100 Indians (mostly women and children), which prompted the government to send a peace commissioner (who turned out to be Vincent Colyer) to right the wrongs inflicted on both sides. See Thrapp, *Conquest of Apachería*, 79–94, for an unbiased account of the tragedy. See also Don Schellie, *Vast Domain of Blood: The Story of the Camp Grant Massacre.*

24. *San Diego Union,* copied from the *Arizona Citizen,* May 6, 1871.

25. Thrapp, *Conquest of Apachería,* 63.

26. *Army and Navy Journal,* May 27, 1871; Marion, *Notes of Travel,* 45.

27. Thrapp, *Conquest of Apachería,* 70–78; Ball, *Indeh,* 26–27.

28. *Estrella de Occidente,* May 5, May 12, 1871.

29. Ibid., May 19, 1871.

30. *Arizona Citizen,* May 27, 1871; *San Diego Union,* June 1, 1871; *Las Cruces Borderer,* June 8, 1871.

31. RG75, M234, R558, Pope to Parker, May 24, 1871; M234, R6, Piper to Hudson; RG393, LR, District of New Mexico, Pope to Granger, May 30, 1871; *Las Cruces Borderer,* June 8, 1871.

32. RG393, LR, District of New Mexico, Pope to Granger, May 31, 1871; RG75, M234, R558, Pope to Parker, May 24, 1871.

33. Cochise did not expect a troop evacuation. What he meant was that several patrols had remained active in southern Arizona since the Cushing fight. In fact, Captain Alexander Moore had twice attacked camps in the Huachuca Mountains, killing three Chiricahuas on June 2 and "scattering them in every direction through the mountains" on June 10. Afterward, Moore scouted the Whetstones and Dragoons and must have been in the vicinity when Jeffords found Cochise on June 16. Moore evidently reached the Dragoons on June 19 or 20, at which time Cochise either eluded detection or had moved south. RG94, Records of the Adjutant General, Muster Rolls, Third Cavalry, Company F, April 30–June 30, 1871.

34. RG75, M234, R558, Pope to Parker, June 28, 1871. RG75, T21, R15, Piper to Pope, July 23, 1871.

35. RG75, T21, R15, Jeffords to Pope, July 24, 1871.

36. RG75, Howard to Pope, October 11, 1872, copy in AHS.

37. Altshuler, *Chains of Command,* 196–97.

38. RG393, LS, District of New Mexico, M1072, R4, Granger to AAG, Department of Missouri, May 4, 1871.

39. *Army and Navy Journal,* May 20, 1871.

40. Ibid., May 27, 1871.

41. *Las Cruces Borderer,* April 13, 1871.

42. *Arizona Citizen,* January 14, 1871.

43. *Army and Navy Journal,* August 26, 1871.

44. *Arizona Citizen,* May 13, 1871.

45. *Army and Navy Journal,* July 15, 1871.

46. Ibid., August 26, 1871.

47. George Crook, *General George Crook: His Autobiography,* ed. by Martin F. Schmitt (cited hereafter as Schmitt, *Crook*), 160.

48. RG75, M234, R4, Crook to AGO, July 10, 1871.

49. RG75, M234, R558, Pope to Parker, August 26, 1871; Colyer to Pope, Au-

gust 21, 1871. *Peace with the Apaches of New Mexico and Arizona,* 44. RG75, M234, R4, Crook to AGO, September 1, 1871.

50. RG393, LS, District of Arizona, Crook to AGO, September 19, 1871.

51. Schmitt, *Crook,* 167.

*Chapter 17*

1. Thrapp, *Victorio,* 144.

2. Richard N. Ellis, *General Pope and U.S. Indian Policy,* 215. Lockwood, *The Apache Indians,* 185–86.

3. Colyer, *Peace with the Apaches,* 9.

4. Ibid., 44.

5. Ibid., 9–10.

6. Ibid.; AHSH, Folder 432, Tepeda to Governor, August 23, 1871; *Estrella de Occidente,* September 1, 1871.

7. RG393, LS, Fort Lowell, Mizner to AAG, October 8, 1871; Hunter, "Early Days in Arizona," 116–17.

8. *Arizona Citizen,* September 9, 1871.

9. RG75, T21, R15, Piper to Pope, September 26, 1871.

10. AHS, W. H. Harrison File, H3186.

11. Ibid.

12. RG75, T21, R15, Piper to Pope, September 30, 1871.

13. RG393, LR, District of New Mexico, Piper to Shorkley, September 27, 1871; Orlando F. Piper Collection at Presbyterian Historical Society, Philadelphia, Piper to Lowrie, October 9, 1871.

14. Chiva, Chivo, Cheever (ca. 1820–ca. 1887) was a friend of Cochise from the early 1840s, when both were at Janos. He was quite involved in Chiricahua affairs in the 1870s and 1880s and was one of the Apache leaders who did not go out with Geronimo in May 1885. He was removed to Florida in September 1886 and eventually died as a prisoner of war.

15. RG393, LR, District of New Mexico, Piper to Shorkley, October 19, 1871; RG75, M234, R558, Pope to Parker, October 19, 1871. Cochise is referring to members of his band who had not yet come in and who were, in all likelihood, going to remain at war. At least two Chokonen captains had refused to make peace, and then there were the Nednhis under Juh, Natiza, and Geronimo, who might depredate in southern Arizona, which Cochise realized would be charged to him.

16. Ibid., RG75, M234, R558, Davis to AAG, Department of Missouri, October 25, 1871. On several occasions Cochise refused this invitation to visit Washington, perhaps fearing he would never return. His son Taza had no such apprehensions, eventually journeying east in 1876, where he contracted pneumonia and died in the nation's capital.

17. Chise was a farming community about twelve miles southwest of Cañada Alamosa and twenty-four miles northwest of present-day Truth or Consequences, New Mexico. Pearce, *New Mexico Place Names,* 34.

18. Whitney, born in New York on January 9, 1840, had accompanied Captain Walker in his well-known mining expedition of 1863. After the Civil War he drifted back into New Mexico and was subcontractor for the mail between El Paso and Mesilla. He was described as standing six feet, four inches and was fluent in Spanish and some "Indian dialects." *Santa Fe Gazette,* January 2, 1869; *Alta California,* November 17, 1871; Thrapp, *Encyclopedia,* 1561.

19. RG98, Book of Scouts, Fort Bowie, 1869–94, Russell to Smith, October 27, 1871; James M. Barney, *Tales of Apache Warfare,* 22–24.

20. *Las Cruces Borderer,* December 13, 1871.

21. Historian Dan Thrapp points out that "Juh did a lot of the work that Cochise was blamed for, even in the Chiricahua Mountains, some of Russell's reports asserting that Cochise was the Indian he fought bear internal evidence suggesting that it was Juh, instead of Cochise." Juh never did come into Cañada Alamosa, at least as far as Mrs. Ball was told. Furthermore, the Nednhis and some Chokonens remained in the Chiricahua Mountains in the fall and winter of 1871–72. According to a captive who was freed near Fronteras in early January 1872, there was a large ranchería in the Chiricahuas. In February a Sonoran scout discovered a large camp near Batepito (probably Juh's) as northern Mexico exerted pressure on the Apache bands. In fact, one scout reported they had killed Cochise himself—one of the many times Cochise was killed by Sonoran troops. Thrapp to author, letter in author's file.

22. RG75, T21, R15, Colyer to Pope, November 6, 1871; Pope telegram reprinted in the *New York Times,* November 16, 1871. In January 1872, Jeffords told Captain George Shorkley that "Cochise had not left" the reservation. RG393, LS, Fort McRae, Shorkley to Devin, January 8, 1872.

23. *Las Cruces Borderer,* November 1, 1871.

24. Ibid.

25. Ibid.

26. RG75, Council with Mimbres Apaches at Fort Tularosa, September 11, 1872, copy in AHS.

27. RG75, M234, R558, Piper to Davis, September 30, 1871.

28. Ibid.

29. Piper Collection, Piper to Lowrie, October 9, 1871.

30. RG393, M1072, R4, LS, District of New Mexico, Granger to Pope, October 12, 1871.

31. RG75, M234, R558, Pope to Commissioner of Indian Affairs, October 17, 1871.

32. RG75, T21, R15, Piper to Pope, October 19, 20, 21, 1871.

33. RG75, M234, R558, Davis to AAG, Department of Missouri, October 25, 1871; RG94, M666, R24, Davis to AAG, Department of Missouri, October 25, 1871. Davis stated that Cochise refused to go to Washington but permitted his picture to be sent; whether a photograph was taken, however, is not known for sure.

34. RG393, LR, Department of Missouri, H300, 1871, Piper to Granger, October 30, 1871.

35. RG75, M234, R558, Pope to Commissioner of Indian Affairs, October 26, 1871.

36. RG348, Report Books of the Office of Indian Affairs, Clum to Delano, November 5, 1871.

37. RG75, M234, R558, Delano to Clum, November 7, 1871. *Army and Navy Journal,* December 9, 1871; RG75, T21, R15, Colyer to Pope, November 7, 1871.

38. RG393, M1088, R15, B1, 1872, Bennett to Granger, January 6, 1872.

39. *Las Cruces Borderer,* December 13, 1871.

40. LS, District of New Mexico, M1072, R4, Granger to AAG, Department of Missouri, December 11, 1871.

41. *Las Cruces Borderer,* December 13, 1871.

42. RG75, T21, R15, Piper to Pope, December 31, 1871.

43. Ibid., Piper to Pope, December 9, December 12, 1871; January 31, 1872.

44. RG, M234, R6, Crook to AAG, Military Division of the Pacific, December 7, 1871.

45. RG75, T21, R17, Moore to AAAG, Department of Arizona, November 29, 1871.

46. RG393, LR, District of New Mexico, Piper to Pope, March 11, 1872.

47. RG393, LR, District of New Mexico, Shorkley to AAG, April 6, 1872.

48. RG75, T21, R15, Editor of the *Borderer* to Piper, February 5, 1872; M234, R5, Smith to AAAG, Department of Arizona, January 25, 1872; *Arizona Miner,* February 10, 1872; RG393, LS, Fort Bowie, Smith to AAAG, Department of Arizona, January 25, 1872. This may have been the origin for the stories about Cochise's warriors' escorting the mail through hostile Apache country.

49. RG75, M234, R5, Piper to Colyer, January 27, 1872.

50. RG393, LS, Fort McRae, Shorkley to Devin, January 8, 1872.

51. Ibid.

52. RG393, LS, District of New Mexico, M1072, R4, AAAG, District of New Mexico to Jefferies [Jeffords], July 21, 1872.

53. RG393, LR, District of New Mexico, Piper to Shorkley, February 29, 1872.

54. Ibid.; RG75, T21, R17, Piper to Pope, February 29, 1872.

55. RG393, LS, District of New Mexico, Granger to Crook, January 27, 1872; Granger to AAG, Department of Missouri, March 16, 1872. RG75, M234, R559, Pope to Walker, March 18, March 20, March 28, 1872.

56. *Santa Fe New Mexican,* March 30, 1872; *Arizona Miner,* April 20, 1872.

57. Turrill, "A Vanished Race," 18.

58. Ellis, "Recollections," 391-92.

59. *Santa Fe New Mexican,* March 30, 1872. On March 28, 1872, Pope telegraphed Walker that "Cochise has renewed his promise made to me last fall to go in person and try to persuade roving Apaches to go to the reservation." RG75, M234, R559, Pope to Walker, March 28, 1872.

*Chapter 18*

1. Fred Hughes Collection.

2. RG75, M234, R559, Pope to Walker, April 29, 1872. RG75, T21, R17, Streeter to Pope, May 4, 1872; RG393, LR, District of New Mexico, Shorkley to AAG, April 6, 1872; Devin to AAG, District of New Mexico, April 13, 1872; Report of the Commissioner of Indian Affairs, 1872, 306.

3. RG393, LR, District of New Mexico, Devin to AAG, District of New Mexico, April 13, 1872.

4. RG393, LR, District of New Mexico, Shorkley to AAG, April 6, 1872.

5. RG75, M234, R559, Pope to Walker, April 29, 1872.

6. *Las Cruces Borderer,* May 1, 1872.

7. *Missouri Republican,* May 17, 1872.

8. RG75, T21, R17, Streeter to Pope, May 4, 1872.

9. There is a detailed account of the removal to Tularosa in Thrapp, *Victorio,* 144-54.

10. Born in New York State about 1838, Streeter led a fascinating and intriguing life. He was closely associated with the Chihennes and also was well acquainted with Jeffords as both assisted Piper in the move to Tularosa. Streeter accompanied

Jeffords and Howard on the historic visit to Cochise. In the late 1870s he allegedly turned renegade and was said to have participated in several raids against whites. He was killed in Sonora in 1889. Thrapp, *Encyclopedia,* 1378–79.

11. RG75, M234, R559, Pope to Walker, June 5, 1872.

12. Ponce, born about 1840, headed a small group of Chihennes in the 1870s. He was a heavy-set Indian with a tendency to stutter, and he and his followers spent much time in northern Chihuahua and southwestern New Mexico. He apparently married into Mangas Coloradas's family. His father also may have been named Ponce and perhaps was an influential chief, killed in the early 1850s, who was said to have been a literate, intelligent, and wealthy leader. The younger Ponce was one of the Indians captured with Geronimo by Clum in 1877. He passed from the scene shortly thereafter.

13. RG393, LS, Fort Stanton, Randlett to Devin, May 22, 1872; LR, District of New Mexico, Randlett to Devin, May 22, 1872.

14. RG393, M1088, R15, LR, District of New Mexico, Devin to AAG, District of New Mexico, May 9, 1872.

15. *Missouri Republican,* May 31, 1872.

16. RG75, T21, R17, Piper to Pope, May 31, 1872.

17. RG393, Returns from Military Posts, Fort Bowie, May 1872.

18. RG393, LS, Fort Bowie, Haskell to AAAG, Department of Arizona, May 10, 1872.

19. *Las Cruces Borderer,* June 5, July 10, 1872.

20. *Estrella de Occidente,* May 10, May 31, June 28, 1872; AHSH, Folder 443, Aragon to Governor, June 19, 1872.

21. Pionsenay, brother of Eskinya, "one of Cochise's war leaders," was a first-rate incorrigible in his own right. In April 1876 he led a small group of drunken warriors who attacked and killed Nick Rogers and O. O. Spence at Sulphur Springs. Two months later he was wounded by Taza and turned over to civil authorities by John P. Clum. Somehow he managed to escape and made his way into Mexico. For the next year and a half he was a hostile, raiding on both sides of the border before he was killed at or near Janos about December 1877. RG393, E204, Brief of Indian Affairs at San Carlos, 1878.

22. AHSH, Folder 443, Aragon to Governor, June 19, 1872; *Estrella de Occidente,* June 28, 1872; *La República,* May 24, 1872; RG393, LR, District of New Mexico, Devin to AAG, August 8, 1872. LR, Department of Missouri, Devin to AAG, District of New Mexico, July 29[?], 1872.

23. *Estrella de Occidente,* July 26, August 9, 1872.

24. *Arizona Miner,* July 13, July 27, 1872; Connell, "The Apaches Past and Present."

25. RG393, LR, District of New Mexico, Devin to AAG, August 8, 1872; LR, Department of Missouri, Stephenson to Granger, August 2, 1872; Reeve, "Frederick E. Phelps," 110–22; Floyd, *Chronological List of Actions,* 52.

26. Bowdoin College, Oliver Otis Howard Papers, Soule to Howard, September 11, 1872.

27. Connell, "The Apaches Past and Present." Reid T. Stewart graduated eighth in a class of forty-three from West Point in June 1871. Only twenty-two when he was killed, he was described as "genial and frank with a winning disposition." He grew up around Erie, Pennsylvania. His rifle was seen by Howard and Sladen in

Cochise's camp. Heitman, *Historical Register,* 925; *Army and Navy Journal,* September 21, 1872; Thrapp, *Encyclopedia,* 1368–69; Thrapp, *Apachería,* 115–16.

28. Thrapp, *Apachería,* 115–16; *Army and Navy Journal,* September 21, 1872; *San Diego Union,* September 7, 1872.

29. AHS, Petra Etchell File.

30. *Webster's American Military Biographies,* 185.

31. Howard Papers, Delano to Howard, February 29, 1872.

32. Howard, *My Life and Experiences,* 124.

33. Howard Papers, Howard to wife, April 15, 1872.

34. Schmitt, *Crook,* 169.

35. RG393, LR, District of New Mexico, Crook to Granger, April 20, 1872.

36. Howard, *My Life and Experiences,* 172–80.

37. Sladen, born in England in 1841, enlisted as a private in the Thirty-third Massachusetts Infantry in August 1862. He was awarded the Medal of Honor in 1895 for his actions in the Battle of Resaca, Georgia, on May 14, 1864. After the war he was commissioned a second lieutenant in the First Infantry. He became captain in 1888, retired in 1889, and went into insurance. He died in Oregon in 1911. Heitman, *Historical Register* 1, 890; Joseph Sladen Papers; Thrapp, *Encyclopedia,* 1319.

38. Howard, *My Life and Experiences,* 187.

39. Howard Papers, Howard to wife, August 12, 1872.

40. Stevens, a native of Massachusetts, was born about 1844 and came to Arizona in 1866. He married the daughter of a White Mountain Apache leader and later served as a scout for Crook and as sheriff of Graham County. Thrapp, *Encyclopedia,* 1366.

41. Sladen, "Making Peace," 2.

42. RG75, Howard to Crook, August 29, 1872, copy in AHS.

43. Farish, *History of Arizona,* II, 230; Howard Papers, Howard to wife, September 8, 1872.

44. Fred Hughes Collection; Howard Papers, Howard to wife, September 8, 1872.

45. Howard Papers, Howard to wife, September 8, 1872.

46. Ibid.

47. Farish, *History of Arizona,* II, 230–31.

48. Ibid.; Howard, *My Life and Experiences,* 188; Sladen, "Making Peace," 5.

49. RG75, Council of Mimbres Apaches at Fort Tularosa, September 11, 1872, copy in AHS.

50. RG75, T21, R17, Piper to Pope, September 13, 1872; Howard to Piper, September 16, 1872.

51. RG75, T21, R17, Howard to Pope, September 16, 1872.

52. Howard Papers, document originally dated September 16, 1872, and then changed to October 7, 1872.

53. Chie, Chee, or Chisito's identity is questionable. Jeffords, Howard, and Sladen all concurred that he was a nephew of Cochise. Mrs. Eve Ball's informants told her that Chie was a son of one of Cochise's sisters or brothers and also that Chie's father was believed to have been killed at Apache Pass, a fact corroborated by Howard. When he and Chie were in Apache Pass, the young Apache became distressed because this was where his father had been slain. Based on this, I believe

Chie was a Chokonen born about 1850, the son of Cochise's brother Coyuntura, who was hanged at Apache Pass in February 1861. After this, Cochise brought Chie up until the late 1860s, when Chie married a Chihenne, probably into Mangas Coloradas's family, and went to live with her people. It is also possible that Chie accompanied Cochise on one of his visits to Cañada Alamosa and remained there with the Chihennes. Chie remained at Tularosa and Cañada Alamosa even after the Chiricahua Reservation was established. He was killed in 1876 or 1877 by Apaches, probably in an incident involving alcohol. If Chie was Coyuntura's son, it is ironic that the death of his father ignited the war and the efforts of his son helped bring peace to Arizona.

54. RG75, T21, R17, Howard to Pope, September 19, 1872.

55. Howard Papers, Howard to Walker, September 15(?), 1872.

56. Howard, *My Life and Experiences*, 192–93; Sladen, "Making Peace," 13–15; RG94, General Howard correspondence relating to peace with Cochise, Howard to Commanding Officer, Fort Bowie, September 28, 1872; NA, RG217, Howard's accounts, 5911.

57. Ibid.

58. NA, RG94, Howard correspondence relating to peace with Cochise, Howard to Commanding Officer, Fort Bowie, September 28, 1872.

59. Unless specified, the sources for the Howard-Jeffords-Cochise treaty are Sladen's reminiscences at Carlisle Barracks; Howard's *My Life and Experiences* and "Account of His Mission to the Apaches and Navajos," published in the *Washington Daily Morning Chronicle* on November 10, 1872; and Tom Jeffords's account, which can be found in Farish, *History of Arizona*, II, 230–35, and in the AHS.

60. Cochise's sister was a widow about fifty years old and was described as "large and bony with strong marked features." The chief put much trust in her, placing her in charge of one of the outposts in the high Dragoons. Sladen, "Making Peace," 29.

61. Ibid., 27.

62. Ibid., 28.

63. Howard, *My Life and Experiences*, 207. Evidently, many of Cochise's band had no desire to live with the Chihennes in New Mexico, probably because of interband rivalries and disputes. Loco's and Cochise's bands had clashed the previous winter and the result was a couple of deaths. Cochise, with many relatives among the Chihennes, was more receptive than his other captains, who had no desire to leave their land in southeastern Arizona. Likewise, most of Victorio's and Loco's people had no wish to relocate to Cochise's reservation.

64. Ibid., 209.

65. RG393, LS, Fort Bowie, Sumner to AAAG, Department of Arizona, October 2, 1872.

66. RG75, M234, R560, Howard to Commanding Officer, Fort Lowell, October 2, 1872.

67. RG393, LS, Fort Bowie, Sumner to AAAG, Department of Arizona, October 2, 1872.

68. Farish, *History of Arizona*, II, 233. Sladen, "Making Peace," 42. This was probably the party which raided a ranch two miles from Camp Crittenden early on September 30, 1872, killed one Mexican, and ran off three horses. Second Lieutenant William Prebel Hall dispatched Sergeant George Stewart and five troopers to

warn Thomas Gardner, whose ranch was seven miles away. On their return trip the soldiers were attacked by "about 50 Indians who were lying in a little ravine." Stewart and three others were killed instantly. M234, R6, Hall to AAAG, Department of Arizona, October 1, 1872; *Arizona Citizen,* October 19, 1872.

69. Sladen, "Making Peace," 53–54.

70. Ibid., 40.

71. Howard continued to push for the Cañada Alamosa reservation as late as October 7, 1872, as is indicated by a document dated Dragoon Mountains, October 7, 1872, describing Cochise's reservation at Cañada Alamosa. Howard Papers.

72. Nahilzay (Ny-les-shizie) was considered by Fred Hughes and Charles T. Connell to be Cochise's war leader. He moved to San Carlos with Taza in 1876 and in late 1879 assisted in the delicate negotiatons to bring in Juh and Geronimo from Mexico to San Carlos Agency. He bolted with Naiche in the September 1881 exodus from San Carlos and was a leading man in the fight at Casas Grandes soon after that. He was captured at this time and sent to a Chihuahua prison, never to be heard from again. Fred Hughes Collection. Griswold, "Ft. Sill Apaches," 116.

73. Sladen, "Making Peace," 45–46.

74. AHS, Dan Williamson File.

75. Eve Ball to author, February 14, 1976.

76. Howard Papers, Alden to Howard, April 22, 1891.

77. Jeffords's account, copy in AHS.

78. NA, M666, R123, Howard to Commissioner of Indian Affairs, September 23, 1873.

79. Howard, *My Life and Experiences,* 220.

80. RG94, General Howard correspondence relating to peace with Cochise, Howard to Sumner, October 11, 1872.

81. RG75; AHS, Howard to Crook, October 11, 1872.

82. RG393, LS, Fort Bowie, Sumner to AAAG, District of Arizona, October 15, 1872.

83. *Boston Evening Transcript,* November 6, 1872.

84. Ibid.

85. Report of the Indian Commissioner to the Secretary of the Interior, 1872; Charles J. Kappler, *Indian Affairs, Laws and Treaties,* 802–3.

86. RG75, AHS, Howard to Sumner, October 13, 1872; Howard to Jeffords, October 13, 1872.

87. RG393, LS, Fort Bowie, Sumner to AAAG, October 15, 1872.

88. Report of the Commissioner of Indian Affairs, 1873, 292–93.

89. Bourke Diary, February 3, 1873.

*Chapter 19*

1. RG75, M234, R5, Orr to Howard, November 23, 1872; NA, RG217, Howard voucher for supplies purchased from Lord and Williams for Cochise, October 15, 1872; Report of the Commissioner of Indian Affairs, 1873, 291–92.

2. RG393, LS, Fort Bowie, Sumner to Nickerson, November 2, 1872.

3. Report of Commissioner of Indian Affairs, 1873, 291.

4. Chihuahua, born about 1822, succeeded his father as chief of a Chokonen local group which may have split from Cochise at this time. His Apache name was Kla-esch. Mrs. Ball was uncertain whether Chihuahua was present at the treaty signing but said he was on the reservation from time to time. In size, Chihuahua's

local group was "next in numbers to Cochise." He was one of the fighting leaders in the wars of the 1880s and was highly respected by both whites and Apaches. He died in 1901 at Fort Sill. Griswold, "Ft. Sill Apaches," 18; Opler to author, October 9, 1978; Ball to author, February 14, 1876.

5. Hughes was born in England in 1837 and came to Arizona with the California Volunteers in 1862. He provided much assistance to Jeffords and helped John Clum in the Indians' removal to the San Carlos Reservation in 1876. He was killed by lightning in 1911. Charles C. Colley, *Documents of Southwestern History,* 102. Miller, *The California Column,* 213. Fred Hughes Collection.

6. Fred Hughes collection.

7. Connell, "The Apaches Past and Present," 13.

8. Ibid., Fred Hughes Collection.

9. Hughes and Orr placed their number at 200. AHS, Fred Hughes Collection; Howard Papers, Orr to Howard, November 23, 1872. The *Arizona Citizen* of November 30, 1872, reported the Nednhis at 300; in his report for 1873, Jeffords wrote that they numbered 400. Report of Commissioner of Indian Affairs, 1873, 291.

10. Howard Papers, Orr to Howard, November 1, 1872.

11. Ibid., Thomas Hughes to Howard, November 23, 1872.

12. Ibid., Delong to Howard, December 20, 1872.

13. *Arizona Miner,* November 16, 1872.

14. *Arizona Citizen,* November 30, 1872.

15. Ibid., December 7, 1872.

16. Harry G. Cramer III, "Tom Jeffords, Indian Agent," *Journal of Arizona History,* 17 (Autumn 1976), 265–300. Cramer's excellent article documents the problems Jeffords faced.

17. RG75, T21, R17, Jeffords to Pope, November 26, 1872; T21, R17, Clum to Pope, November 14, 1872.

18. Ibid., Clum to Jeffords, November 14, 1872.

19. RG75, M734, R8, Bendell to Jeffords, December 7, 1872; January 2, 1873.

20. RG75, M734, R7, Jeffords to Bendell, December 20, 24, 1872.

21. RG75, M234, R7, Bendell to Commissioner of Indian Affairs, April 18, 1873.

22. RG75, M734, R8, Bendell to Jeffords, January 24, February 2, 1873.

23. RG75, M234, R8, Jeffords to Howard, February 11, 1873; M734, R7, Delano to Bendell, March 5, 1873.

24. RG75, M734, R8, Bendell to Commissioner of Indian Affairs, February 28, March 4, 1873; RG75, M234, R8, Delano to Acting Commission of Indian Affairs, March 24, 1873.

25. RG75, M234, R7, and M734, R8, Bendell to Delano, March 11, 1873.

26. RG75, M234, R7, Bendell to Commissioner of Indian Affairs, April 23, 1873.

27. *Estrella de Occidente,* March 14, 1873.

28. This was one opinion not shared by Crook's subordinate, John G. Bourke. Bourke believed that Howard's mission was completed at "great personal discomfort and no little risk." Bourke, *On the Border with Crook,* 235.

29. RG94, M666, R24, Delano to Belknap, December 10, 1872; Sherman to Belknap, December 17, 1872; Belknap to Delano, December 20, 1872.

30. Ibid. Crook to AAG, Military Division of the Pacific, February 11, 1873; *Estrella de Occidente,* July 4, 1873.

31. Fred Hughes Collection; *Alta California,* April 25, 1873.

32. RG159, Records of the Inspector General, D. B. Sacket Report on the Department of Arizona, June 30, 1873.

33. *Estrella de Occidente,* July 4, 1873.

34. RG393, E169, LS, Department of Arizona, Nickerson to Jeffords, January 29, 1873.

35. Bourke Diary, notation dated February 3, 1873.

36. *Estrella de Occidente,* July 4, 1873.

37. *Estrella de Occidente,* June 20, 1873; *Alta California,* April 25, 1873.

38. *Arizona Citizen,* November 29, 1873.

39. *Estrella de Occidente,* January 10, February 7, 1873; *Arizona Citizen,* February 15, 1873.

40. RG159, Sacket Report.

41. *Estrella de Occidente,* January 17, January 24, February 7, February 14, 1873.

42. *Arizona Citizen,* February 22, 1873.

43. M234, R8, Jeffords to Commissioner of Indian Affairs, March 21, 1873.

44. Luna, born about 1830, was in command of Sonora's National Guard. He was the only survivor of an Apache massacre near Fronteras in the fall of 1855. *Alta California,* May 13, 1873.

45. Delong, as did so many Arizona pioneers, came to Arizona with the California Volunteers in 1862. Born in New York State in 1828, he was a multitalented man. He was discharged from the volunteers in 1866 and went to work for Tully and Ochoa, noted merchants. He was appointed post trader at Fort Bowie on January 5, 1871. Four months later he participated in the Camp Grant massacre, which he later regretted. He died in 1914. For a biographical account of his life, see Randy Kane, "An Honorable and Upright Man: Sidney R. Delong as Post Trader at Fort Bowie," *Journal of Arizona History,* 19 (Autumn 1978), 297–314.

46. *Estrella de Occidente* June 20, 1873; Lockwood, *The Apache Indians,* 125–26; *Alta California,* May 13, 1873.

47. *Army and Navy Journal,* April 26, 1873.

48. Lockwood, *The Apache Indians,* 124–26.

49. RG393, LS, Fort Bowie, Sumner to Nickerson, April 22, 1873.

50. AHS, Al Williamson manuscript titled "Reminiscences of the Early Days of Arizona."

51. Ibid.; RG 393, LS, Fort Bowie, Sumner to Jeffords, May 14, 1873.

52. RG75, M734, R7, Jeffords to Smith, June 4, 1873.

53. RG393, LS, Fort Bowie, Sumner to Jeffords, July 12, 1873; *Arizona Citizen,* July 12, 1873.

54. RG393, LS, Fort Bowie, Sumner to Price, August 6, 1873.

55. RG75, M234, R9, Price to AAG, Department of Missouri, August 30, 1873; RG94, M666, R123, Price to Willard, August 1, 1873.

56. RG94, M666, R123, Howard to Commissioner of Indian Affairs, September 23, 1873.

57. Ibid., Crook to Adjutant General, Washington, December 8, 1873.

58. Ibid., Clum to Delano, September 26, 1873; Crook to Adjutant General, Washington, December 8, 1873.

59. LR, AGO, M689, R187, Bourke Report on the Apaches.
60. *Arizona Citizen,* October 11, 1873.
61. *Estrella de Occidente,* January 9, 1874.
62. Ibid., February 13, 1874.
63. RG75, M234, R8, Jeffords to Smith, September 25, 1873.
64. *Arizona Citizen,* August 23, 1873.
65. Ibid., October 4, 1873.
66. *Estrella de Occidente,* October 24, 1873.
67. *Arizona Citizen,* August 23, 1873.
68. RG75, M1070, R1, Vandever's Report, 1397, October 18, 1873.
69. *Estrella de Occidente,* November 21, 1873.
70. M666, R123, Smith to Jeffords, December 29, 1873.
71. M576, R16, Jeffords to Delano, January 1, 1874.
72. *Arizona Citizen,* February 28, 1874.

*Chapter 20*

1. RG75, M234, R563, Hughes to Editor, *Las Cruces Borderer,* February 11, 1874.
2. Report of the Commissioner of Indian Affairs, 1874, 300–2.
3. Ibid.
4. *Estrella de Occidente,* May 8, July 31, August 14, August 28, September 11, 1874; SA, R20, Ochoa to Governor of Sonora, August 26, 1874.
5. Report of the Commissioner of Indian Affairs, 1874, 300–2.
6. Ibid., 301.
7. Report of the Commissioner of Indian Affairs, 1874, 288; *Arizona Citizen,* May 16, 1874.
8. Sacket's Report.
9. Fort Bowie Files, Abstracts of an Inspection by Lieutenant Colonel Roger Jones of Fort Bowie, April 27, 1874.
10. *Arizona Citizen,* May 16, 1874.
11. Ibid., May 30, 1874.
12. Eskinya, born about 1820, appeared on the Janos ration rolls in 1843–44. He was also at Fronteras in the early 1860s and probably succeeded Taces as leader of a Chokonen local group in the mid-1860s. He and his brother Pionsenay sparked the uprising and ultimate closing of the Chiricahua Reservation in 1876. He was killed by Naiche in June 1876 during an interband fight. Fred Hughes Collection.
13. Sacket's Report.
14. RG75, M234, R10, Jeffords to Smith, June 10, 1874; Ball, *Indeh,* 25.
15. Fred Hughes Collection; Al Williamson, "Reminiscences."
16. Lockwood, *The Apache Indians,* 128–29.
17. Fred Hughes Collection.
18. Opler, *Apache Lifeway,* 472–78.
19. RG75, M234, R10, Jeffords to Smith, July 6, 1874.
20. Lockwood, *The Apache Indians,* 129–30. Other accounts of Cochise's death and burial are in *Army and Navy Journal,* July 11, 1874, which can also be found in Homer W. Wheeler, *Buffalo Days,* 349–50. Edward L. Keyes has a reliable account, reportedly obtained from Taza, which is similar to Williamson's. Keyes, "Some Recollections." See also Rockfellow, *Log of an Arizona Trail Blazer,* 84–85.

# BIBLIOGRAPHY

*Manuscript materials, Unpublished Documents, Collections*

Archivo Historico de Sonora, Hermosillo, Sonora.

Arizona Historical Society, Tucson. Hayden Files or collections: Nathan Benjamin Appel, Albert F. Banta, Diary of John Bourke, William Buckley, Charles T. Connell manuscript "The Apaches Past and Present," Petra Etchell, Robert Humphrey Forbes, William Fourr, Thomas Gardner, Charles Gatewood, Merejildo Grijalva, Diary of George Hand, W. H. Harrison, Fred Hughes, William H. Kirkland, William Henry Larrabee, Frank C. Lockwood, Edith Allen Milner unpublished manuscript "Covered Wagon Experiences," Policeman Oberly's account of the Bascom affair, William Sanders Oury, Charles Shibell, Joseph Sladen, John T. Smith, W. M. Thompson manuscript "The Fighting Doctor," James Wallace, John Ward, Hiram Storrs Washburn, Charles A. Whittier, Al Williamson manuscript "Reminiscences of the Early Days of Arizona," Dan Williamson, Charles M. Wood.

————. Film MC-6, Archivo General de Mexico, Roll 150.

————. Sonora State Archives, Rolls 12–20, 49–50.

Arizona State Library, Phoenix. Territorial Records of Arizona.

Arizona State University Library. Benjamin H. Sacks Collection; Sylvester Mowry File; Copy of Hubert Howe Bancroft, *Scraps,* a collection of Arizona items clipped from California newspapers.

Ball, Eve. Interviews, correspondence with author, 1975–83.

Basehart, Harry W. "Chiricahua Apache Subsistence and Socio-Political Organization." A report of the Mescalero-Chiricahua Land Claims Project. Contract Research No. 290–154. University of New Mexico, March 1959.

Basso, Keith. Correspondence with author, 1978.

Bowdoin College, Brunswick, Maine. Oliver Otis Howard Papers.

Davisson, Lori. Correspondence with author, 1980.

Goodwin, Grenville. Collection at Arizona State Museum, Tucson.

Griffen, William. Correspondence, 1983–89.

Griswold, Gillet M. "The Ft. Sill Apaches: Their Vital Statistics, Tribal Origins,

Antecedents." Unpublished manuscript, Field Artillery Museum, Fort Sill, Oklahoma, 1970.
Huntington Library, San Marino, California. Alice Rollins Crane article on Tom Jeffords which appeared in an unidentified Los Angeles newspaper.
Missouri Historical Society, St. Louis. Webb Collection.
National Park Service. Fort Bowie Collection.
New Mexico State University Library, Las Cruces. Rio Grande Historical Collection, Keith Humphries File.
Opler, Morris E. Correspondence with author, 1979–82.
Park, Joseph F. "The Assassination of Juan José Compá." Unpublished manuscript in author's files.
Pinart, Louis Alphonse. Microfilm Collection. Bancroft Library, University of California, Berkeley.
Piper, Orlando F. Collection at Presbyterian Historical Society, Philadelphia.
Sladen, Joseph Alton. Papers. United States Army Military History Institute, Carlisle Barracks, Pa.
Steck, Michael. Papers. Zimmerman Library, University of New Mexico, Albuquerque.
Sublette, Solomon. Papers. Missouri Historical Society, St. Louis.
Thrapp, Dan L. Interviews, correspondence with author, 1975–89.
United States Government, National Archives and Records Center. Record Group 94, Records of the Adjutant General's Office (AGO), 1780s–1917: AGO, Microcopy 619, Roll 737, Report of Bvt. Col. Reuben F. Bernard relating to the engagement at Chiricahua Pass, Arizona, on October 20, 1869; AGO, Microcopy 666, Roll 24, correspondence relating to Vincent Colyer's mission to the Apaches; AGO, Microcopy 666, Roll 123, correspondence relating to the agreement with Cochise negotiated by General Oliver Otis Howard; AGO, File titled "General Howard correspondence relating to peace with Cochise"; AGO, Letters Received, 1850–76, Miscellaneous Letters Received concerning Indian affairs in Arizona and New Mexico.
————. Record Group 75 (RG75), Records of the Bureau of Indian Affairs: Microcopy 234, Letters Received, 1824–80, Arizona Superintendency, 1863–80, Rolls 3-12; Microcopy 234, Letters Received, 1824–80, New Mexico Superintendency, 1849–80, Rolls 546–64; Microcopy 734, Records of the Arizona Superintendency of Indian Affairs, 1863–73, 8 rolls; Microcopy T21, Records of the New Mexico Superintendency of Indian Affairs, 1849–80, Rolls 1–18; Miscellaneous Division, Traders' Licenses; Report Books of the Office of Indian Affairs, 1838–85.
————. Record Group 123, Records of the United States Court of Claims, Indian Depredation Division.
————. Record Group 159, Records of the Office of the Inspector General.
————. Record Group 217, Records of the U.S. General Accounting Office.
————. Record Group 148, Records of the Office of the Secretary of the Interior; State Department Territorial Papers, Arizona and New Mexico.
————. Record Group 59, Microcopy 184, Roll 2, Dispatches from U.S. Consuls in Ciudad Juárez (Paso del Norte), Mexico, 1850–1906.
————. Record Group 393, Records of United States Army Continental Commands, 1821–1920. *Arizona:* Letters Received, Department of Arizona, 1871–74; Letters Sent, Department of Arizona, 1871–74; Letters Received,

District oif Arizona, 1862–71; Unregistered Letters and Orders Received, District of Arizona, 1862–71; Book of Scouts, District of Arizona; Brief of Affairs at San Carlos, 1878; Letters Sent, District of Arizona, 1862–71. Letters Received, Southern Subdistrict of the Gila; Letters Received, Subdistrict of Tucson; Letters Sent, Subdistrict of Tucson; Letters Sent, Subdistrict of Southern Arizona. *Missouri:* Letters Received, Department of Missouri, 1865–72. *New Mexico:* Letters Received, Department of New Mexico, 1849–65; Letters Received, District of New Mexico, 1866–74; Letters Sent, Department of New Mexico, 1849–65; Letters Sent, District of New Mexico, 1866–74; Records Relating to Indian Affairs, Department of New Mexico.

*Military Posts:* Returns from Fort Bowie, Fort West, Camp Wallen; Fort Bowie, Letter Received, Letters Sent; Camp Crittenden, Letters Sent; Fort Cummings, Letters Sent; Camp Grant, Letters Sent; Fort Lowell, Letters Sent; Fort McRae, Letters Sent; Fort Stanton, Letters Sent; Fort Tularosa, Letters Sent; Camp Wallen, Letters Sent; Fort West, Letters Sent.

United States Government, Smithsonian Institution. Copy of letter from George Wratten to Bureau of American Ethnology; J. B. White Manuscript Nos. 178, 179, and 188 on the Apache Indians; N. S. Higgins Manuscript No. 180, historical notes on the Apaches.

University of Arizona Library, Tucson. Special Collections. AZ 300, Thomas Akers Diary; AZ 197, Palmer Manuscript.

University of Texas at Austin. Janos Collection.

University of Texas at El Paso. Carrizal Collection; Janos Collection, 1700–1899. 37 rolls; Juárez Collection, 1619–1893, 12 rolls; Periodico Oficial de Chihuahua, Rolls 1–8.

Wilson, Benjamin. Reminiscences. Bancroft Library, University of California, Berkeley.

*United States Government Publications*

Abel, Annie Heloise, ed. *The Official Correspondence of James C. Calhoun While Indian Agent at Santa Fe and Superintendent of Indian Affairs in New Mexico.* Washington: Government Printing Office, 1916.

*Army and Navy Journal.* Various issues, 1867–74.

*Conditions of the Indian Tribes: Report of the Joint Special Commission.* Washington: Government Printing Office, 1867.

Heitman, Francis B. *Historical Register and Dictionary of the United States Army from its Organization, September 20, 1789, to March 2, 1903.* 2 vols. Urbana: University of Illinois Press, 1965.

Hodge, Frederick Webb. *Handbook of American Indians North of Mexico.* 2 vols. Washington: Government Printing Office, 1907.

Kappler, Charles J. *Indian Affairs, Laws and Treaties.* Washington: Government Printing Office, 1903.

Orton, Brigadier General Richard H. *Records of California Men in the War of the Rebellion, 1861–1867.* Sacramento: State Printing Office, 1890.

U.S. Congress: 39th Cong., House Ex. Doc. 1; 40th Cong., 2d sess., House Ex. Doc. 1324.

United States Department of the Interior. Annual Reports Commissioner of Indian Affairs, 1869–74.

United States Department of War. Reports of the Secretary of War, 1866–67.

*The War of the Rebellion: A Compilation of the Official Records of the Union and Confederate Armies.* Series I, 53 vols. Washington: Government Printing Office, 1880–1901.

*American Newspapers*

*Boston Evening Transcript*
*Las Cruces* (New Mexico) *Borderer*
*Los Angeles Star*
*Mesilla* (New Mexico) *Times*
(Prescott) *Arizona Miner*
*Sacramento Daily Union*
*San Antonio Herald*
*San Diego Herald*
*San Diego Union*
(San Francisco) *Alta California*
*San Francisco Daily Morning Call*
*San Francisco Evening Bulletin*
*Santa Fe Gazette*
*Santa Fe New Mexican*
*Silver City* (New Mexico) *Enterprise*
(St. Louis) *Missouri Republican*
(St. Louis) *Weekly Missouri Democrat*
(Tucson) *Arizona Citizen.*
(Tucson) *Arizona Daily Star*
(Tucson) *Arizona Weekly Star*

*Mexican Newspapers*

*Sonora (Bancroft Library, Berkeley)*

(Ures) *El Sonorense*
*La Estrella de Occidente*
*La Voz de Sonora*
(Ures) *Uno de Tantos*

*Chihuahua (University of Texas at El Paso Microfilm Collection, Oficial periodico de Chihuahua)*

(Chihuahua City) *El Antenor*
*El Boletin de Chihuahua*
*El Centinela*
*El Correo*
*El Eco de la Frontera*
*El Fanal de Chihuahua*
*El Faro*
*El Noticioso de Chihuahua*
*El Provisional*
*El Republicano*
*El Restaurador*
*La Alianza de la Frontera*
*La Coalición*
*La Luna*

*La República*
*La Voz del Pueblo*
*Revista Oficial*

Books: Primary Sources

Altshuler, Constance Wynn, ed. *Latest from Arizona! The Hesperian Letters, 1859–1861.* Tucson: Arizona Pioneer Historical Society, 1969.
Ball, Eve. *In the Days of Victorio: Recollections of a Warm Springs Apache.* Tucson: University of Arizona Press, 1970.
————. with Nora Henn and Lynda Sanchez. *Indeh: An Apache Odyssey.* Provo, Utah: Brigham Young University Press, 1980.
Barnes, Will C. *Apaches and Longhorns: The Reminiscences of Will C. Barnes.* Ed. by Frank C. Lockwood. Tucson: University of Arizona Press, 1982.
Barrett, Stephen M. *Geronimo's Story of His Life.* New York: Garrett Press, 1969.
Bartlett, John Russell. *Personal Narrative of Explorations and Incidents in Texas, New Mexico, California, Sonora and Chihuahua, Connected with the United States and Mexican Boundary Commission During the Years 1850, '51, '52, and '53.* 2 vols. Chicago: Rio Grande Press, 1965.
Bell, William A. *New Tracks in North America: A Journal of Travel and Adventure Whilst Engaged in the Survey for a Southern Railroad to the Pacific Ocean During 1867–68.* Albuquerque: Horn and Wallace, 1965.
Betzinez, Jason, with Wilbur Sturtevant Nye, *I Fought With Geronimo.* New York: Bonanza Books, 1959.
Bourke, John G. *On the Border with Crook.* New York: Time-Life Books, 1980.
Browne, J. Ross. *Adventures in the Apache Country: A Tour Through Arizona and Sonora, 1864.* Ed. by Donald M. Powell. Tucson: University of Arizona Press, 1974.
*The Butterfield Overland Mail Across Arizona.* Tucson: Arizona Pioneer Historical Society, 1958.
Calvin, Ross, ed. *Lieutenant Emory Reports: Notes of A Military Reconnaissance.* Albuquerque: University of New Mexico Press, 1968.
Clarke, Dwight L., ed. *The Original Journals of Henry Smith Turner with Stephen Watts Kearny to New Mexico and California, 1846–1847.* Norman: University of Oklahoma Press, 1966.
Clum, Woodworth. *Apache Agent: The Story of John P. Clum.* Lincoln: University of Nebraska Press, 1978.
Colyer, Vincent. *Peace with the Apaches of New Mexico and Arizona, Report of Vincent Colyer, Member of Board of Indian Commissioners, 1871.* Tucson: Territorial Press, 1964.
Conner, Daniel Ellis. *Joseph Reddeford Walker and the Arizona Adventure.* Ed. by Daniel J. Berthrong and Odessa Davenport. Norman: University of Oklahoma Press, 1956.
Cooke, Philip St. George. *Exploring Southwestern Trails, 1846–1854.* Ed. by Ralph P. Bieber. Philadelphia: Porcupine Press, 1974.
Cozzens, Samuel Woodworth. *The Marvellous Country, or Three Years in Arizona and New Mexico.* Boston: Lee and Shepard Publishers, 1876.
Cremony, John C. *Life Among the Apaches.* Tucson: Arizona Silhouettes, 1954.
Crook, George. *General George Crook: His Autobiography.* Ed. by Martin F. Schmitt. Norman: University of Oklahoma Press, 1946.

Curry, W. Hubert. *Sun Rising in the West: The Saga of Henry Clay and Elizabeth Smith*. Crosbyton, Texas: Crosby County Pioneer Memorial, 1979.

Dubois, John Van Deusen. *Campaigns in the West, 1856–1861*. Ed. by George F. Hammond. Tucson: Arizona Pioneer Historical Society, 1949.

Ellis, Richard N. *New Mexico Historical Documents*. Albuquerque: University of New Mexico Press, 1975.

Goodwin, Grenville. *Western Apache Raiding and Warfare*. Ed. by Keith H. Basso. Tucson: University of Arizona Press, 1973.

Gregg, Josiah. *Commerce of the Prairies*. Ed. by Max L. Moorhead. Norman: University of Oklahoma Press, 1958.

Hobbs, James. *Wild Life in the Far West*. Glorieta, New Mexico: Rio Grande Press, 1969.

Howard, Oliver Otis. *My Life and Experiences Among Our Hostile Indians*. New York: Da Capo Press, 1972.

*Indian Raids as Reported in the Silver City Enterprise*. Silver City, New Mexico: William H. Mullane, 1968.

Kendall, George W. *Across the Great Southwestern Prairies*. 2 vols. N.p.: Readex Microprint Corporation, 1966.

Lang, Walter B. *The First Overland Mail: Butterfield Trail, St. Louis to San Francisco, 1858–1861*. Washington: n.p. 1947.

McCarty, Kieran. *Desert Documentary: The Spanish Years, 1767–1821*. Tucson: Arizona Historical Society, 1976.

Marchand, Ernest, ed. *News from Fort Craig, New Mexico, 1863: Civil War Letters of Andrew Ryan with the First California Volunteers*. Santa Fe: Stagecoach Press, 1966.

Marion, John H. *Notes of Travel Through the Territory of Arizona, Being an Account of the Trip Made by General George Stoneman and Others in the Autumn of 1870*. Ed. by Donald M. Powell. Tucson: University of Arizona Press, 1965.

Miller, Joseph, ed. *Arizona Cavalcade: The Turbulent Times*. New York: Hastings House, 1962.

Mills, W. W. *Forty Years at El Paso, 1858–1898*. El Paso, Texas: Carl Hertzog, 1952.

Nentvig, Juan, S.J. *Rudo Ensayo: A Description of Sonora and Arizona in 1764*. Translated, clarified, and annotated by Alberto Francisco Pradeau and Robert R. Rasmussen. Tucson: University of Arizona Press, 1980.

North, Diane M. T. *Samuel Peter Heintzelman and the Sonora Exploring and Mining Company*. Tucson: University of Arizona Press, 1980.

O'Neil, James B. *They Die But Once: The Story of a Tejano*. New York: Knight Publications, 1936.

Pattie, James O. *Personal Narrative of James O. Pattie of Kentucky*. Ed. by Timothy Flint. Chicago: Donnelley and Sons, 1930.

Pumpelly, Raphael. *Travels and Adventures of Raphael Pumpelly*. New York: Henry Holt and Company, 1920.

Rockfellow, John A. *Log of an Arizona Trail Blazer*. Tucson: Arizona Silhouettes, 1955.

Ruxton, George Frederick. *Adventures in Mexico and the Rocky Mountains, 1846–1847*. Glorieta, New Mexico: Rio Grande Press, 1973.

Spring, John. *John Spring's Arizona*. Ed. by A. M. Gustafson. Tucson: University of Arizona Press, 1966.

Tevis, James Henry. *Arizona in the 50's*. Albuquerque: University of New Mexico Press, 1954.

Wheeler, Homer W. *Buffalo Days*. Indianapolis: Bobbs Merrill Co., 1926.

Wislizenus, Frederick A. *A Tour to Northern Mexico Connected With Col. Doniphan's Expedition in 1846–1847*. Glorieta, New Mexico: Rio Grande Press, 1969.

*Books: Secondary Sources*

Acuña, Rodolfo F. *Sonoran Strongman: Ignacio Pesqueira and His Times*. Tucson: University of Arizona Press, 1974.

Almada, Francisco R. *Diccionario de historia, geografía y biografía chihuahuenses*. Chihuahua: Talleres Graficos del Gobierno del Estado. 1927.

———. *Diccionario de historia, geografía y biografía sonorenses*. Chihuahua: n. p., 1952.

Altshuler, Constance Wynn. *Chains of Command: Arizona and the Army, 1856–1875*. Tucson: Arizona Historical Society, 1981.

Bancroft, Hubert Howe. *History of Arizona and New Mexico*. San Francisco: History Company, 1889.

———. *History of the North Mexican States and Texas*. San Francisco: History Company, 1889.

Barnes, Will C. *Arizona Place Names*. Revised and enlarged by Byrd H. Granger. Tucson: University of Arizona Press, 1979.

Barney, James M. *Tales of Apache Warfare*. Privately printed by James M. Barney, 1933.

———. *Forgotten Heroes of the Apache Wars*. Phoenix: n.p., 1951.

Barrick, Nona, and Mary Taylor. *The Mesilla Guard, 1851–1861*. El Paso: Texas Western Press, 1976.

Baylor, George Wythe. *John Robert Baylor, Confederate Governor of Arizona*. Ed. by Odie Faulk. Tucson: Arizona Pioneer Historical Society, 1966.

Brandes, Ray, ed. *Troopers West: Military and Indian Affairs on the American Frontier*. San Diego: Frontier Heritage Press, 1970.

Colley, Charles C. *Documents of Southwestern History*. Tucson: Arizona Historical Society, 1972.

Colton, Ray C. *The Civil War in the Western Territories*. Norman: University of Oklahoma Press, 1959.

Conkling, Roscoe P., and Margaret B. Conkling. *The Butterfield Overland Mail, 1857–1869*. 3 vols. Glendale: Arthur H. Clark Co., 1947.

Debo, Angie. *Geronimo: The Man, His Time, His Place*. Norman: University of Oklahoma Press, 1976.

Dunn, J. P. *Massacres of the Mountains*. New York: Archer House, n.d.

Ellis, Richard N. *General Pope and U.S. Indian Policy*. Albuquerque: University of New Mexico Press, 1970.

Farish, Thomas Edwin. *History of Arizona*. 8 vols. San Francisco: Filmer Brothers Electrotype Co., 1915–18.

Floyd, Dale E. *Chronological List of Actions etc. with Indians from January 15, 1837, to January, 1891*. Fort Collins, Colo.: Old Army Press, 1979.

Forbes, Jack Douglas. *Apache, Navaho and Spaniard*. Norman: University of Oklahoma Press, 1971.

Frazer, Robert W. *Forts of the West*. Norman: University of Oklahoma Press, 1977.

Gerald, Rex E. *Spanish Presidios of the Late Eighteenth Century in Northern New Spain*. Santa Fe: Museum of New Mexico Press, 1968.

Goodwin, Grenville. *The Social Organization of the Western Apache*. Tucson: University of Arizona Press, 1969.

Griffen, William B. *Apaches at War and Peace: The Janos Presidio, 1750–1858*. Albuquerque: University of New Mexico Press, 1988.

Hafen, Leroy R. *The Overland Mail, 1849–1869*. Cleveland: Arthur H. Clark Co., 1926.

Hunt, Aurora. *Major General James Henry Carleton, 1814–1873, Western Frontier Dragoon*. Glendale, California: Arthur H. Clark Company, 1958.

Keleher, William A. *Turmoil in New Mexico, 1846–1868*. Introduction by Lawrence R. Murphy. Albuquerque: University of New Mexico Press, 1982.

Lekson, Stephen H. *Nana's Raid: Apache Warfare in Southern New Mexico*. El Paso: University of Texas at El Paso, 1987.

Lockwood, Frank C. *Arizona Characters*. Los Angeles: Times Mirror Press, 1928.

———. *The Apache Indians*. New York: Macmillan Company, 1938.

Longstreet, Stephen. *War Cries on Horseback: The Story of the Indian Wars of the Great Plains*. Garden City, New York: Doubleday & Company, 1970.

McClintock, James H. *Arizona: Prehistoric, Aboriginal, Pioneer, Modern*. 3 vols. Chicago: S. J. Clarke Publishing Company, 1916.

McGaw, William Cochran. *Savage Scene: The Life and Times of James Kirker, Frontier King*. New York: Hastings House, 1972.

Miller, Darlis M. *The California Column in New Mexico*. Albuquerque: University of New Mexico Press, 1982.

Moorhead, Max L. *The Apache Frontier: Jacobo Ugarte and Spanish-Indian Relations in Northern New Spain, 1769–1791*. Norman: University of Oklahoma Press, 1968.

———. *The Presidio: Bastion of the Spanish Borderlands*. Norman: University of Oklahoma Press, 1975.

Murphy, Lawrence R. *Frontier Crusader—William F. M. Arny*. Tucson: University of Arizona Press, 1972.

Ogle, Ralph Hedrick. *Federal Control of the Western Apaches, 1848–1886*. Albuquerque: University of New Mexico Press, 1970.

Opler, Morris E. *An Apache Lifeway*. Chicago: University of Chicago Press, 1965.

Pearce, T. M. *New Mexico Place Names: A Geographical Dictionary*. Albuquerque: University of New Mexico Press, 1977.

Russell, Don. *One Hundred and Three Fights and Scrimmages: The Story of General Reuben F. Bernard*. Washington: U.S. Cavalry Association, 1936.

Sandomingo, Manuel. *Historia de Sonora*. Agua Prieta, Sonora: n.p., 1953.

Schellie, Don. *Vast Domain of Blood: The Story of the Camp Grant Massacre*. Los Angeles: Westernlore Press, 1968.

Terrell, John Upton. *Apache Chronicle*. New York: Thomas Y. Crowell Company, 1974.

Thrapp, Dan L. *Al Sieber: Chief of Scouts*. Norman: University of Oklahoma Press, 1964.

———. *Conquest of Apachería*. Norman: University of Oklahoma Press, 1967.

———. *Juh: An Incredible Indian*. El Paso: University of Texas at El Paso, 1973.

———. *Victorio and the Mimbres Apaches*. Norman: University of Oklahoma Press, 1974.

————. *Encyclopedia of Frontier Biography.* 3 vols. Glendale, Calif.: Arthur H. Clark Co., 1988.

Turner, Katherine C. *Red Men Calling on the Great White Father.* Norman: University of Oklahoma Press, 1951.

Utley, Robert M. *Frontier Regulars: The United States Army and the Indians, 1866–1891.* New York: Macmillan Co., 1973.

————. *A Clash of Cultures: Fort Bowie and the Chiricahua Apaches.* Washington: National Park Service, 1977.

————. *Frontiersmen in Blue: The United States Army and the Indians, 1848–1865.* Lincoln: University of Nebraska Press, 1981.

Villa, Eduardo W. *Compendia de Historia del Estado de Sonora.* Mexico: Patria Nueva, 1937.

Voss, Stuart F. *On the Periphery of Nineteenth Century Mexico: Sonora and Sinaloa 1810–1877.* Tucson: University of Arizona Press, 1982.

Wagoner, Jay J. *Early Arizona: Prehistory to Civil War.* Tucson: University of Arizona Press, 1975.

Weber, David J. *The Taos Trappers: The Fur Trade in the Far Southwest, 1540–1846.* Norman: University of Oklahoma Press, 1971.

*Webster's American Military Biographies.* Springfield, Mass.: G & C Merriam Company, 1978.

Wellman, Paul I. *The Indian Wars of the West.* Garden City, N.Y.: Doubleday & Company, 1947.

*Articles and Essays*

Allen, R. S. "Pinos Altos, New Mexico," *New Mexico Historical Review,* 23 (October 1948), 302–32.

Altshuler, Constance Wynn. "Arizona in 1861: A Contemporary Account by Samuel Robinson," *Journal of Arizona History,* 25 (Spring 1984), 21–76.

Brooks, Henry S. "A Scrap of Frontier History," *Californian,* 2 (October 1880), 344–48.

Cramer, Harry G. III. "Tom Jeffords, Indian Agent," *Journal of Arizona History,* 17 (Autumn 1976) 265–300.

Cremony, John C. "Some Savages," *Overland Monthly,* 8 (March 1872), 201–10.

Dorr, L. L. "The Fight at Chiricahua Pass in 1869," ed. by Marian E. Valputic and Harold W. Longfellow, *Arizona and the West,* 13 (Winter 1971), 369–78.

Drachman, Samuel H. "Arizona Pioneers and Apaches," *Arizona Graphics,* 1 (November 18, 1899), 3–7.

Dudley, Levi E. "Cochise, the Apache Chief, and Peace," *The Friend,* August 7, 1891.

Ellis, Anderson Nelson. "Recollections of an Interview with Cochise, Chief of the Apaches," *Kansas State Historical Society Collections,* 13 (1913–14), 387–92.

Finch, Boyd. "Sherod Hunter and the Confederates in Arizona," Journal of Arizona History, 10 (Autumn 1969), 139–206.

Forbes, Robert H. Letter in *Journal of Arizona History,* 7 (Summer 1966), 87–88.

Griffen, William B. "The Compás: A Chiricahua Apache Family," *American Indian Quarterly,* 7 (Spring 1983), 21–49.

————. "Apache Indians and the Northern Mexican Peace Establishments," in *Southwestern Culture History: Collected Papers in Honor of Albert Schroeder,* ed. Charles H. Lange. *Papers of the Archaeological Society of New Mexico,* Vol. 10 (1985), 183–95.

Harkins, Charles. "A Scrap of Frontier History," *Overland Monthly,* 21 (March 1893), 265–76.

Howard, Oliver Otis. "Account of His Mission to the Apaches and Navajos," *Washington Daily Morning Chronicle,* November 10, 1872. Copy in Arizona Historical Society, Tucson.

Hunter, Thomas Thompson. "Early Days in Arizona," *Arizona Historical Review,* 3 (April 1930), 105–20.

Irwin, Bernard John Dowling. "The Fight at Apache Pass," *Infantry Journal,* Vol. 32 (April 1928), 1–8.

Kane, Randy. "An Honorable and Upright Man: Sidney R. Delong as Post Trader at Fort Bowie," *Journal of Arizona History,* 19 (Autumn 1978), 297–314.

Keyes, Edward L. "Some Recollections of Arizona and Cochise," *The United Service,* July 1890, 98–101.

Lockwood, Frank C. "Cochise, the Noble Warrior," *Arizona Highways,* February 1939, 6–7, 24–27.

Mahon, Emmie Giddings W., and Chester V. Kielman. "George H. Giddings and the San Antonio–San Diego Mail Line," *Southwestern Historical Quarterly,* 61 (Summer 1957), 220–39.

Myers, Lee. "The Enigma of Mangas Coloradas' Death," *New Mexico Historical Review,* 41 (October 1966), 287–304.

Opler, Morris E., and Harry Hoijer. "The Raid and War-Path Language of the Chiricahua Apache," *American Anthropologist,* 42 (October–December 1942), 617–35.

Park, Joseph F. "The Apaches in Mexican-American Relations, 1848–1861," *Arizona and the West,* 3 (Summer 1961), 129–46.

———. "Spanish Indian Policy in Northern Mexico, 1765–1810," *Arizona and the West,* 4 (Winter 1962), 325–44.

Radbourne, Allan. "Ambush at Cocospera Canyon," *English Westerners Tally Sheet,* 25 (July 1979), 63–76.

———. "Salvador or Martínez? The Parentage and Origins of Mickey Free," *English Westerners Society Brand Book,* 14 (January 1972), 2–26.

Reeve, Frank D. "Frederick E. Phelps: A Soldiers' Memoirs," *New Mexico Historical Review,* 25 (April 1950), 109–35.

Rippy, J. Fred. "The Indians of the Southwest in the Diplomacy of the United States and Mexico, 1848–1853," *Hispanic-American Historical Review,* 2 (August 1919), 363–96.

Robinson, Daniel. "The Affair at Apache Pass," *Sports Afield,* 17 (August 1896), 79–84.

Rush, Rita. "El Chivero, Merejildo Grijalva," *Arizonian,* 1 (Fall 1960), 8–9.

Sacks, Benjamin H. "New Evidence on the Bascom Affair," *Arizona and the West,* 4 (Autumn 1962), 261–78.

Schreier, Konrad F., Jr. "The California Column in the Civil War: Hazen's Civil War Diary," *Journal of San Diego History,* 22 (Spring 1976), 31–47.

Smith, Cornelius C. "Some Unpublished History of the Southwest," *Arizona Historical Review,* 6 (January 1935), 45–64, 5 (October 1932), 333–40.

Smith, Ralph A. "Indians in American-Mexican Relations Before the War of 1846," *Hispanic American Historical Review,* 43 (February 1963), 34–64.

————. "The Scalp Hunt in Chihuahua—1849," *New Mexico Historical Review.* 40 (April 1965), 116–40.

Sonnichsen, C. L. "Who Was Tom Jeffords?" *Journal of Arizona History,* 23 (Winter 1982), 381–402.

Stevens, Robert C. "The Apache Menace in Sonora, 1821–1849," *Arizona and the West,* 6 (Autumn 1964), 211–22.

————. "Colonel John Finkle Stone and the Apache Pass Mining Company," *Arizona Historical Review,* 6 (July 1935), 74–80.

Strickland, Rex W. "The Birth and Death of a Legend: The Johnson Massacre of 1837," *Arizona and the West,* 18 (Autumn 1976), 257–86.

Sweeney, Edwin R. "I Had Lost All: Geronimo and the Carrasco Massacre of 1851," *Journal of Arizona History,* 27 (Spring 1986), 35–52.

Turrill, Henry Stuart. "A Vanished Race of Aboriginal Founders," *Publication Number 18 of the New York Society of the Order of the Founders and Patriots of America,* February 14, 1907.

Tyler, Barbara Ann. "Cochise, Apache War Leader, 1858–61," *Journal of Arizona History,* 6 (Spring 1965), 1–10.

Utley, Robert M. "The Bascom Affair: A Reconstruction," *Arizona and the West,* 3 (Spring 1961), 59–68.

Walker, Henry P. "Solider in the California Column: The Diary of John W. Teal," *Arizona and the West,* 13 (Spring 1971), 33–82.

# INDEX